Samuel G. Kling, one of the nation's leading divorce lawyers, has practiced law in Baltimore for more than thirty-six years and has gained wide recognition as an interpreter of the law for laymen.

Mr. Kling began his writing career in 1929 as a feature writer for the *Baltimore Sunday Sun.* From 1936 to 1942 he was book reviewer on criminology and penology for the late, lamented Sunday edition of the *New York Herald Tribune.* He was director of the "Crime Clinic" radio show over the Mutual Broadcasting System, 1937 to 1938, for which he received a national award. Mr. Kling has also been Consultant to the Federal Prison Industries Reorganization Administration under President Franklin D. Roosevelt and "special writer" with the United States Prison Bureau.

Beginning in 1948 and continuing until 1956, Mr. Kling wrote a daily nationally syndicated column, "Your Marriage," which appeared in fifty-five newspapers. He has contributed numerous articles to *Better Homes and Gardens, Look, Parade, McCall's, Cosmopolitan, This Week* and *Family Weekly.*

THE LEGAL ENCYCLOPEDIA AND DICTIONARY is essentially a new work but had its origin in two previous books by Mr. Kling, now both out of print—*The Popular Legal Encyclopedia for Home and Business,* originally published by Doubleday & Company, Inc., and *Your Legal Advisor.* Among his other books are *A Complete Guide to Divorce, Sexual Behavior and the Law* and *A Complete Guide to Everyday Law.* In addition, he has contributed legal articles to the *Encyclopedia Americana* and is legal editor of the *Jefferson Encyclopedia.*

SAMUEL G. KLING LL.B

Also by Samuel G. Kling:

The Complete Guide to Divorce
Sexual Behavior and the Law

Published by Pocket Books

THE
Legal
ENCYCLOPEDIA
and
DICTIONARY

SAMUEL G. KLING, LL.B.

PUBLISHED BY POCKET BOOKS NEW YORK

THE LEGAL ENCYCLOPEDIA AND DICTIONARY

A *Pocket Book* edition

1st printing............July, 1959
6th printing.........August, 1966

Revised Edition

1st printing..........March, 1970

The author gratefully acknowledges permission to include in this edition articles he originally wrote for the *Encyclopedia Americana*, published by Grolier Incorporated, New York, to wit, *Certificate of Title, Commitment, Commutation of Sentence, Days of Grace, Demand, Disclaimer, Foreclosure,* and *Indemnity.*

This *Pocket Book* edition is an enlarged, revised, and updated version of *The Legal Encyclopedia for Home and Business.* It is printed from brand-new plates made from completely reset, clear, easy-to-read type. *Pocket Book* editions are published by Pocket Books, a division of Simon & Schuster, Inc., 630 Fifth Avenue, New York, N.Y. 10020. Trademarks registered in the United States and other countries.

L

To Rena—with love and admiration

Note to the Reader

In the ten years since *The Legal Encyclopedia for Home and Business* has been in print, the book has enjoyed wide popularity among both lawyers and laymen, businessmen, secretaries and students. Indeed, the new Random House Dictionary includes *The Legal Encyclopedia* in its list of "major reference works."

At my publisher's suggestion, I have prepared a greatly expanded, revised and updated edition which should enhance the book's popularity and make it even more useful as a reference work for the layman, to whom it is primarily addressed. This new edition is also based on material in another of my earlier books, *Your Legal Advisor,* now out of print.

I have included nearly 1,000 new definitions of legal terms in common use, thus combining in one handy, compact volume both a legal encyclopedia and a legal dictionary.

In addition, I have updated sections dealing with divorce, social security, legal fees and civil rights and have completely rewritten and enlarged the section on contracts, which is basic to an understanding of business law.

Because of the fundamental importance of these subjects, I have also thought it worthwhile to describe our court system in some detail and to summarize some of the more important United States Supreme Court decisions in the field of civil liberties.

A final word of caution: just as no medical book can take the place of a physician, so no legal encyclopedia can take the place of a competent attorney. The primary purpose of my book is to provide basic legal information in order to aid the average man in understanding his legal rights. Without such an awareness there is little likelihood of justice. Law does not operate in a vacuum. Laws are drawn by human beings and interpreted by judges. Ignorance of the law, as many a man and woman have learned to their sorrow, is no excuse.

If my book enables the reader to cope more easily with his legal problems whenever and wherever they arise, it will have fulfilled the aim of its author.

SAMUEL G. KLING

Baltimore, Maryland

A

A FORTIORI Latin words meaning "by a stronger reason." The words are often used in judicial opinions to say that, since specific proven facts lead to a certain conclusion, there are, for this reason, other facts that logically follow which make stronger the argument for the conclusion.

A MENSA ET THORO A partial divorce or separation without the right of remarriage.

A PRIORI A generalization resting on presuppositions and not upon proven facts.

A VINCULO MATRIMONII An absolute divorce with a right to remarriage.

AB INITIO From the beginning.

ABANDONMENT The term applies to many situations. Abandonment of property is the giving up of the dominion and control over it with the intention to relinquish all claim to the same. Losing property is an involuntary act; abandonment is voluntary.

When used with duty, the word abandonment is synonymous with repudiation.

Abandonment of a child by its parents may be a criminal offense when such parents fail to perform their parental duty.

Abandonment in divorce law means the voluntary separation or desertion of one spouse from the other.

ABATEMENT A reduction or decrease. In contracts an abatement is the reduction made by a creditor for the prompt payment of a debt due by the debtor. An abatement of a legacy is a proportional reduction of the pecuniary legacies when the funds or assets out of which such legacies are payable are insufficient to pay them in full. The abatement of a nuisance is its removal.

ABDUCTION The forcible, unlawful taking or detention of a man's wife, child or maid. Though a criminal offense, a husband may claim damages in a civil suit for abduction of his wife. Unless provided by statute, one is not criminally indictable for marrying a woman under age without the consent of parents or guardian. However, the taking of a child from those having its care by violence, deceit, conspiracy, intoxication or other improper practices, for the purpose of marriage may be punished, even though both parties to the marriage themselves consent to the ceremony.

ABET To encourage, stir up or excite to commit a crime.

ABETTOR One who encourages the commission of a crime but is absent when the offense is actually committed. An accessory is either present promoting the crime or near enough to afford assistance if necessary, as where one stands watch outside when others perform the act. An abettor is equally guilty with the one who commits the crime.

ABEYANCE A state of suspension. An estate is in abeyance where there is no one alive in whom it is vested. Where an estate is to belong to one for life and to another yet unborn after his death, the latter estate is said to be in abeyance.

ABJURATION OF ALLEGIANCE In the United States, the necessary renouncing of one's former national allegiance upon naturalization.

ABORTION The expulsion of the foetus before it has acquired the power of sustaining an independent life. When it occurs from natural causes it is of course not criminal. But if performed by a drug, or by the application of external violence or the use of instruments with intent to cause such premature birth of the foetus, it is a misdemeanor at common law.

ABROGATE To annul a law by an act of the same authority which made or enacted it; to repeal.

ABSCOND To hide or conceal oneself. Applied to one who avoids legal process.

ABSENTEE One away from his usual domicile; one temporarily outside the jurisdiction of a court. Special definitions exist in various jurisdictions for such purposes as marriage.

ABSOLUTE CONVEYANCE A conveyance by which the right or property in a thing is transferred, free of any condition or qualification.

ABSOLUTE ESTATE An estate in lands not subject to any condition.

ABSQUE HOC Without this. Technical word of denial used in common law pleading by way of special traverse.

ABSQUE INJURIA Without violation of a legal right.

ABSTRACT OF TITLE A concise statement of the substance of documents or facts appearing on property records affecting title to real property.

ABUSE OF DISCRETION A denial of justice when discretion has not been justly and properly exercised.

ABUSE OF DISTRESS Excessive use of a distrained animal or chattel.

ABUSE OF PROCESS A malicious perversion of a regularly issued process whereby an opponent gains an unfair advantage.

ABUTTALS The buttings and boundings of lands, east, west, north and south, showing on what other lands, highways or places they abut, or are limited and bounded.

ACCELERATION The shortening of the time for the performance of a contract or the payment of a note by the operation of some provision in the contract or note itself.

ACCEPTANCE The receipt, or acknowledgment of receipt. Delivery and acceptance are usually necessary to complete an oral contract for the sale of goods.

The acceptance of a draft or bill of exchange by the person on whom it is drawn is usually effected by the acceptor writing the word "accepted" across the bill and signing his name, which means that he agrees to pay it when due. He may make this promise conditional. If he does, the holder is not bound to receive such an acceptance, but is bound by its terms if he does.

Where one on whom a draft or bill is drawn refuses to accept and this action is protested, another person may, before a notary, accept for the benefit or honor of the drawer or any endorser. If he does, he will be liable to such drawer or endorser (unless he accepts for his accommodation only) or to anyone to whom such drawer or endorser is liable. If upon further presentment of the bill to the drawee when due he still fails to pay, and it is further protested, this is an acceptance supra protest.

An acceptance may be made in writing before the bill is drawn. It is usually made after it is drawn and before it comes due, but may be made after it comes due or after a previous refusal to accept. A bill is dishonored if not accepted within 24 hours after presentment, or immediately upon actual refusal to accept. The acceptor is the principal debtor and the drawer stands in the position of a surety to the holder and endorser. By accepting, the acceptor admits the drawer's handwriting and is bound though he accepts simply for the accommodation of the drawer.

ACCEPTANCE SUPRA PROTEST An acceptance of a bill by a third person, after protest for nonaccept-

ance by the drawee, such acceptance being for the honor of the drawer, or some particular endorser.

ACCEPTILATION In civil law, either a creditor's cancellation of a debt without consideration, or the verbal release of a verbal contract regardless of payment.

ACCEPTOR The party accepting a bill of exchange who is the principal debtor, the drawer being the surety.

ACCESSORY An accessory before the fact procures, counsels or commands another to commit a crime. If the person whom he incites to commit the act, as in the case of a child, or insane person, is unaware of the consequences of his act, the inciter is in the position not of an accessory but of one who commits the actual crime.

An accessory after the fact is one who, knowing the felony to have been committed, receives, relieves, comforts or assists the felon.

In treason and in all offenses below the degree of felony, all concerned are considered principals whether present or absent. At common law an accessory to a felony could not be convicted before the principal, and if the principal were dead he could not be tried at all, but now under statutory provisions in most places he may be convicted irrespective of the principal.

ACCIDENT Something that happens by chance; a sudden and unexplained event; properly speaking an accident is something that happens without the fault, carelessness or negligence of the person involved. The word accident is particularly important in cases arising under the various Workmen's Compensation Acts. For a claim to be compensable under such acts an accident must have been sustained while arising out of and in the course of the employment. A person who lifts a heavy box and sustains a hernia has not met with such an accident as to be payable under Workmen's Compensation Acts. However, if that same person's foot slips or gives way while lifting a heavy weight, the resulting injury, to wit, the hernia, is said to have arisen as the result of an "accidental" injury.

Courts of equity will often relieve against injustice arising from accident if there is no negligence or misconduct on the party seeking relief. Thus, if a check is lost, recovery may be had upon giving proper indemnity to secure the person sued from a second payment to an innocent holder of the instrument, that is, one who bought it without knowing the instrument was lost or that it had been paid.

Where the law casts a duty on a person, performance will be excused if made impossible by a cause operating without intervention or aid of man—that is by nature or by act of God. However, one contracting expressly against natural contingencies cannot exempt himself from responsibility even though the result is accidental or beyond his control.

ACCOMMODATION PAPER A promissory note or bill of exchange made, accepted, or endorsed simply for the accommodation of another, and without benefit to such maker, acceptor or endorser. The paper is not binding between him and the person accommodated, but is binding to the holder of the note or other parties thereto.

ACCOMPLICE An accessory before or after the fact as well as an abettor is an accomplice and is himself guilty of the crime. One counseling another to commit suicide is guilty of murder if the suicide takes place. The testimony of an accomplice as to the guilt of a companion in crime is usually viewed with caution. If the statement of an accomplice who is allowed to testify is uncorroborated by any other evidence the jury is usually instructed to acquit. When testifying against his associates in guilt an accomplice is bound to make a full and fair confession of the whole truth respecting the subject matter of the prosecution. He is not bound to answer with respect to his share in other offenses in which he was not concerned with the prisoner.

ACCORD AND SATISFACTION A form of reparation. The payment of a part of a debt, even if it is accepted for the whole, will not defeat a suit for the balance except in the following cases: if the amount of the claim was in dispute when the part was so accepted; if the liability for payment was contingent upon some other event; if a new obligation of the debtor or a third person or other security is given for the part; or if in some other way the creditor is placed in a better position with respect to the part than he was previously with respect to the whole, or receives some additional benefit.

The performance of or the offer to perform a thing agreed to be done by way of satisfaction must be entire and not in part only. If the performance is to be in the future the time of performance must be agreed upon; otherwise the agreement of satisfaction will not be binding until it is consummated.

ACCOUNT STATED An account which has been rendered by one to another and which purports to state the true balance due and which balance is either expressly or impliedly admitted to be due by the debtor.

ACCRUAL BASIS An accounting method which shows expenses incurred and income earned for a given period even though they may not have been actually paid or received in cash.

ACCRUE In regard to a cause of action, to come into existence; to become a present and enforceable demand.

ACCUMULATIVE LEGACY A double or additional legacy; a legacy given in addition to another given by the same instrument or by another instrument.

ACCUMULATIVE JUDGMENT A second judgment to take effect after the expiration of the first.

ACKNOWLEDGMENT The certification of a declaration made in legal form. The object is to authorize the acknowledged deed or instrument and entitle it to be legally recorded. In some cases and in some states the acknowledgment is necessary to its validity. A certificate of acknowledgment where once made cannot be legally changed by the officer taking the acknowledgment or by anyone without a reacknowledgment.

A notary having any beneficial interest in a deed or mortgage should not take an acknowledgment.

Where the body of a certificate of acknowledgment recites the fact that the person taking it is a notary, the fact that the words "notary public" are not appended after his signature does not invalidate the certificate.

ACKNOWLEDGMENT

STATE OF MARYLAND, CITY OF BALTIMORE, to wit:

I HEREBY CERTIFY, that on this _____ day of _____ in the year 19___, before me, the subscriber, a Notary Public of the City of Baltimore, State of Maryland, personally appeared Samuel G. Kling and acknowledged the aforegoing deed to be his act.

_____
NOTARY PUBLIC

ACQUIT To free, clear or deliver from accusation, especially of a crime.

ACQUITTAL A deliverance or setting free from a criminal charge by the process of trial at law; also the verdict of a jury pronouncing the accused not guilty.

ACT IN PAIS A judicial or other act performed out of court.

ACT OF GOD Inevitable accident; any accident produced by any physical cause which is irresistible, such as lightning, tempests, perils of the sea, or earthquakes; also the sudden illness or death of persons.

ACTIO EX CONTRACTU An action arising out, or founded on, contract.

ACTIO EX DELICTO An action of tort, independent of contract, based on fault, negligence, misconduct or malfeasance.

ACTIONABLE That which can legally be made the ground for a lawsuit; the word actionable is chiefly applied to slanderous words uttered or published of another.

ACTIONABLE NUISANCE Something injurious to health or morals or so obstructing the free use of property as to interfere with its comfortable enjoyment.

AD DAMNUM In formal, legal pleading, the emphatic words of the clause at the end of the declaration in which a certain amount of damages is claimed.

AD HOC Latin words meaning, for this. An ad hoc refers to limited or particular situations. An ad hoc decision means "for this purpose only." An ad hoc committee is one limited to a special purpose. An ad hoc attorney is one appointed to do a special task in a particular case.

AD LITEM One appointed to prosecute or defend a suit on behalf of someone unable to do so by reason of infancy or other legal causes.

AD QUO DAMNUM To what loss. (1) A writ for an inquiry as to the damages likely to result from the opening of a highway or other public improvement. (2) The order paying damages when private property is taken for public use.

AD VALOREM According to value.

AD VALOREM TAXATION As typified by custom duties on imports, a system of taxation fixing the tax as a percentage of the value of the object taxed. It is opposed to specific taxation, which sets a fixed sum as the tax on each item of a class of objects.

ADEMPTION The disposal by a testator in his lifetime of specific property bequeathed in his will. Ademption of a legacy occurs where that which is left a child or one standing in the place of a child by a will, is advanced to him before the death of the testator. An advancement to such a person during the life of a testator is presumed to be an ademption, at least to the extent of the amount advanced, but the advancement to operate as an ademption must be of money or property of the same kind as the legacy. If the advancement is conditional only and the legacy or portion certain, the legacy will not be reduced by the advancement; so where the so-called advancement is given in consideration for something, or where the bequest is of uncertain amount or where the legacy is absolute and the advancement for life only or where the devise is of real estate, there is no ademption. But where the testator was not a parent of the legatee or *in loco parentis* the legacy is not considered a portion, and the rule as to ademption does not apply unless the bequest is for a particular purpose, and money has been advanced by the testator for that purpose.

A specific legacy is nullified by the extinction of the thing or fund bequeathed, unless it becomes extinct by act of law and a new thing takes its place, or unless a breach of trust has been committed or some trick or device practiced to defeat the specific legacy.

ADEQUATE REMEDY AT LAW A remedy at law which is complete and which is the substantial equivalent of the equitable relief.

ADJECTIVE LAW The rules of procedure used by and in courts for enforcing the duties and maintaining the rights defined by the substantive law. Adjective law primarily involves matters of evidence, procedure, and appeals. It is also called remedial law.

ADJOURNMENT SINE DIE A meeting that ends without setting a time for the next one.

ADMEASUREMENT OR ADMENSURATION An allotment by measure; the designation of one's portion of an estate.

ADMEASUREMENT OF DOWER Commonly, the fixing and granting of a dower; rarely, a remedy of an heir to correct an admeasurement of dower made during his minority.

ADMINISTER To manage, take charge and dispose of the property of an intestate, i.e., one dying without a will, or of a testator having no executor according to law.

ADMINISTRATION CUM TESTAMENTO ANNEXO Administration granted where a testator makes a will without naming any executors; or where the executors named in the will are incompetent to act, or refuse to act; or in the case of the death of the executors, or their survivors.

ADMINISTRATION DE BONIS NON Administration granted for the purpose of administering such goods of the deceased as were not administered by the former executor or administrator.

ADMINISTRATION DURANTE IN ABSENTIA Administration granted during the absence of an executor.

ADMINISTRATION DURANTE MINORE AETATE Administration granted during the minority of an executor.

ADMINISTRATION OF ESTATES The management of an estate by any executor, administrator, guardian, trustee or other person acting in a fiduciary capacity. It applies especially to one who has died without leaving a will, that is, intestate. In such case the administration is applicable primarily to personal estate only, which passes to the administrator. The real estate passes directly to the heirs and comes within the jurisdiction of the administrator only in case an Order of Court is obtained to sell and properly dispose of the proceeds.

Letters of administration are granted where the decedent resided at his death, but letters of administration (ancillary letters) will be granted in the state or county where the assets are situated, in case of a foreigner or one residing out of the state. The usual procedure in case of an ancillary administration is to collect the assets within the local jurisdiction and, subject to the direction of the local court, pay the expenses of administration and the local debts or claims against the fund and remit the balance to the principal administrator.

In general, letters of administration granted in one state confer no authority to act within another. To a limited extent this has been changed by various statutory enactments.

ADMINISTRATION PENDENTE LITE

One granted during the pendency of a suit touching the validity of a will.

ADMINISTRATORS An administrator is one appointed by a court authorized to manage and distribute the estate of one dying without leaving a will, or of a testator who has no executor. In the latter case he is called an administrator cum testamento annexo (with the will annexed). He is appointed where there is no executor, the one or ones named in the will having died or being incompetent or refusing to act. His authority with regard to the will is the same as that of the executor.

An administrator de bonis non (of goods not administered) is appointed where an administrator dies before completing his duties. In such a case an account of the administration of the first administrator must be made by his personal representative and the balance in his hands turned over to the administrator de bonis non. Similarly an *administrator de bonis non cum testamento annexo* is appointed where there is a vacancy in an administration under a will after the estate has been in part administered.

There are several kinds of temporary administration such as where an executor is overseas, or during the minority of the executor or while a controversy is pending respecting a will or right to letters thereunder.

Anyone who can contract is competent to act as an administrator. The surviving husband or wife is first entitled to letters, though in the case of a widow the court usually has the discretion of joining another person with her. The nearest relatives, after the surviving husband or wife, are entitled to preference, males having priority to females, and elder sons, other things being equal, being usually preferred to younger, though this is perhaps more often a matter of practice than of right.

Where appointments are made without notice to parties having prior rights, the letters of administration will be revoked upon proper application but acts done by one improperly appointed will not be void. Where relatives do not act, creditors, and after creditors, any suitable person may be appointed, and where there is no executor of a will the person having a residuary estate, if any, under the will is commonly entitled to letters in preference even to relatives.

Co-administrators in general must be joined in suing and being sued.

The act of each in the delivery, gift, sale, payment, possession or release of the intestate's goods is the act of all. If one dies or for other cause discontinues to act, the whole authority is vested in the survivors. Each is liable only for assets which have come into his possession, and is not liable for the torts of others unless guilty of negligence or fraud.

The duties of an administrator are usually set forth in his bond, and for their performance he must give security. He must publish a notice of his appointment and cause an inventory and appraisement of the personal estate to be filed in the proper office. He must collect outstanding claims and convert movable property into money. The personal estate vests in him and he is considered as having owned it from the time of the decedent's death, and he may maintain any necessary suit with respect thereto. Where the decedent was a partner, however, he has no power over the firm's assets until the debts are paid, it being the duty of the surviving partner to settle partnership affairs. If he himself owes the estate and denies it he may be removed.

An administrator may assign notes and bind the estate by arbitration. He may recover fraudulently conveyed real estate for the benefit of creditors. If it appears that the personal estate will not be sufficient to pay creditors he may sell the real estate for that purpose upon obtaining an order from the proper court, and for other purposes orders are issued to him to sell real estate, as for example, for purposes of distribution among heirs. But his authority extends to real estate only under an order of court.

Personal property in the hands of an administrator or executor cannot be seized for the debts of the decedent, though attachments are frequently issued against administrators as garnishees to secure the share of a distributee or a legatee in payment of a debt which he may owe to another. If there is any possibility of the estate being insolvent the administrator should not pay the general debts of the decedent until the decree of distribution is made by court fixing the amount to be paid to each creditor. If he pays in excess of the amount, he cannot usually recover it back if the party receiving the excess is financially responsible unless at the time of the payment there is an agreement made with the payee for the payment. In a suit against an administrator or executor for an alleged debt of the decedent he is not bound to plead the statute of limitations, that is, he is not bound to defend on the ground that the claim is "out of date," if he is satisfied the debt is just. To relieve an estate from sale by mortgage, he may lend money to the estate and charge interest. If he uses the funds of the estate he is liable for interest, and if he has large amounts of money of the estate which are likely to remain in his hands for a considerable length of time he is bound to make it earn some interest if practicable, especially if he can do so without risk.

The liability of an administrator is usually limited by the amount of assets of the estate. But to make himself personally liable for contracts relating to the estate he must undertake to pay personally, or guarantee payment or some consideration or advantage moving to him.

Like an executor, an administrator is liable for torts and gross negligence in managing the estate. He may be held liable for negligence in collecting notes or debts, for the unnecessary sale of property at a discount, or insufficient precautions in caring for it, as well as for paying excessive funeral expenses. If he uses the money of the estate he is liable not only for the money itself and interest, but for any profits he may make. He cannot buy the estate or any part of it when sold by an auctioneer, but when the auctioneer is a state officer and the sale is bona fide he may do so.

ADMINISTRATRIX A female who administers, or to whom the right of administration has been granted.

ADMIRALTY A Federal Court having extensive jurisdiction over maritime cases.

ADMISSION The term is applied in civil matters and to matters of fact in criminal cases not involving or including a criminal intent to the commission of a crime. An admission made by a party to a suit or one identified in interest with him may be used against him. Where, however, the party to the suit has no actual interest in it and is a nominal party only, his admission will not affect the real party in interest.

If two or more persons have a joint interest, the admission of one binds all, but this does not apply where there is mere community of interest as in case of co-executors, co-trustees and co-tenants. The declaration of a stranger to a suit sometimes binds the party to a suit, as where the issue concerns the right of such third party at a particular time, or where there are contractual relationships between the party to the suit and the third party as in case of ancestor and heir, assignor and assignee, intestate and administrator, grantor and grantee of land and others.

The admissions of an agent regarding matters within the scope of his authority from his principal binds the principal, but usually as to transactions completed at the time of the admission. The formal admissions of an attorney bind his client. Admissions may be not only expressed, but they may be implied from assumed conduct, character, acquiescence and from possession of documents.

In civil matters admissions, though made under compulsion, may be used in evidence if imposition or fraud is not practiced to secure them. They may not be used if made in an attempt to compromise. Admissions made in judicial proceedings, those which have been acted on by others, and those in deeds, are conclusive against those making them.

ADOPTION To adopt a child legally it is necessary for the adopting parents to obtain the formal consent, expressed in writing and in the form required by law, of the child's natural parents, or other persons having the legal control of the child. It is usually necessary to obtain the consent of both natural parents where they are living together. Where they are living separate and apart, the consent of one who has the legal custody of the child only is required. The same principle is applicable to the adopting parents. If the adopting parents are living together, the consent of both is usually required. Where they are living separate and apart, the consent of the adopting parent only is necessary. It is essential also that the adopting parents give evidence that they are of good character, are sober and industrious citizens of the community, and are financially and morally able to give the child the care and affection to which it is entitled. An additional requirement, applicable in cases where the infant child is fourteen years of age or over, is that the child give his formal consent to the adoption. All this is done in a court proceeding handled by attorneys for both sides.

ADULT One who is of full legal age, regulated by law in the various states. In the majority it is 21 for males and 18 for females.

ADULTERY The voluntary sexual intercourse of a married person with a person other than the offender's husband or wife. If one is not married that person is guilty of fornication only.

A husband may demand damages against one committing adultery with his wife, but he may not do so if he connives at or assents to the adultery. If the wife's character for chastity was bad before the plaintiff married her, or if he lived with her after knowing of her criminal intimacy with the defendant, or if he connived at her intimacy with other men, or if the

plaintiff has been unfaithful to his own wife, such facts will not defeat a suit for damages against the adulterer, but may be proven with a view to decreasing the damages.

ADVANCEMENT A gift during the lifetime of the parent to a child in anticipation of his portion or share of the estate, thus reducing the portion by the amount of the advancement.

In some places by statute the term applies also to a grandchild. Whether a gift is an advancement or not depends entirely upon the intent when it is made. Unless a contrary intent appears it is assumed to be an advancement. Money paid for the maintenance or education of a child or money advanced where security or a note is taken for re-payment is not an advancement. The amount of the advancement without interest is deducted from the child's share upon distribution of the estate. If the advancement exceeds the distributive share, the excess cannot be collected.

ADVERSE POSSESSION A conclusive presumption of title in the possessor from which he cannot be ousted. One does not hold land adversely to another where both claim under the same title, as in case of joint owners or tenants in common. This is also true where the possession of one is consistent with the title of the other or where two persons have been in possession, one rightfully and the other wrongfully. In this case the law assumes the possession of both to be the possession of the one who has the right; similarly where the occupier has acknowledged the claimant's title, as for example by paying rent and then holding possession for the period of limitation thereafter without paying rent.

The effect of a genuinely adverse possession for the period of limitation is to raise a conclusive presumption of title in the possessor from which he cannot be ousted.

ADVISEMENT When a court takes a case under advisement it delays its decision until it has examined and considered the questions involved.

ADVOCATE A person, usually a lawyer, who is called upon to assist or defend another.

ADVOWSON The right of a patron to present a clergyman to a church or vacant ecclesiastical benefice.

AFFIDAVIT A written statement or declaration sworn to or affirmed before an officer with authority to administer an oath or affirmation. Affidavits are usually taken by Notary Publics and Justices of the Peace.

An officer cannot take an affidavit outside of his jurisdiction. The affidavit therefore must show where it was taken. The deponent (the one making the affidavit) must sign it at the end, and the jurat or certificate of the officer that the affidavit was duly made must be signed by him with his official title added. Where a statute so requires the seal must be affixed. If the deponent is not acting for himself, the affidavit should state in which capacity he acts, whether as agent, attorney, etc.

AFFINITY The relationship which marriage creates between the husband and the blood relations of the wife, and between the wife and the blood relations of the husband.

AFFRAY The fighting of two or more persons in some public place.

AGE That time of life at which one becomes legally mature and is thus entitled to legal privileges. An adult is one who has reached the age of twenty-one years, which occurs on the day preceding the twenty-first anniversary of birth. Males at fourteen may consent to marriage, and females at twelve, though usually by statutory enactments minors under twenty-one

---

AFFIDAVIT

State of _____ County _____, ss:

Before me, the subscriber, a notary public for the City of Baltimore, State of Maryland, personally appeared John Jones, who being duly sworn, deposes and says, that (here set forth clearly the matter sworn to).

JOHN JONES

Sworn and subscribed this _____ day of _____, 19___

_____
NOTARY PUBLIC

years of age must have consent of parents or guardians. At fourteen males or females may choose a guardian. Males may hold office when twenty-one years of age un-less otherwise provided, but to be a Representative in Congress one must be twenty-five; a United States Senator, thirty; and President, thirty-five.

AGENT AND AGENCY An agent is one who acts with delegated authority. An agency may be created by writing either under seal or not, or verbally. It may be proved by showing the relations of the parties and the nature of the employment even though there is no express appointment.

Letter or Power of Attorney is the name of an instrument frequently used in formally constituting or appointing an agent. Written authority is not necessary to enable an agent to sign a written instrument or contract not required by law to be under seal. Where the law requires that the thing to be done by the agent shall be effected by writing under seal, the authority to him should be by writing under seal, but if the principal is actually present and verbally or impliedly authorizes the agent to affix his, the principal's name, this will be effective.

If the principal adopts or recognizes or acquiesces to the agent's act, he will be bound. A ratification may be presumed from the silence of the principal on being informed of the agent's act. The agency is void if it is to perform an illegal or immoral act. The agency may be revoked at any time by the principal, but not where the agent has an interest in the subject matter of the agency, nor so as to adversely affect persons dealing with the agent while he has authority. As to such persons, it would not be considered revoked until they have knowledge of it or at least until it is generally known. The revocation may take place even though there is an express agreement not to revoke. It may be ended by marriage of the principal, if a woman, by insanity or death of the principal or agent where the agency is not coupled with an interest, or by the destruction of the subject matter of the agency or of the principal's power over it.

The term agent is a broad one. It includes factors, brokers, attorneys, cashiers of banks, auctioneers, clerks, consignees, masters of ships, and the like. Anyone authorized by another to transact business for him is an agent.

Even persons who are legally disqualified from acting for themselves may act as agents, such as minors, aliens and others, but this does not include those lacking mental capacity. A married woman, even where unable to bind herself may, as agent for her husband, contract for him or contract with him for another. One cannot act as an agent for another against whom he has an adverse interest or employment with respect to the subject matter of the agency. An agent's contract with a principal with whom he holds a fiduciary relationship is subject to strict supervision.

The agent's express authority includes by implication all powers necessary and usual for executing it, but, with this exception: where the authority is by written instrument it will be strictly limited to the authority granted. When two or more are authorized in writing or otherwise to act jointly, all must concur to bind the principal, unless the authority is so worded as to show the principal intended that one or part of them might do so. This applies even though one dies or refuses to act. It does not apply to commercial transactions. In case of a public agency a majority will be sufficient. Where the agent's authority is special, and refers to the doing of a single definite thing, it must be strictly pursued, or it will be void, unless the variance is merely circumstantial. If the authority is to do a thing upon a given condition and the agent does it absolutely, his act is void as to his principal. If he does less than the authorized act it is also void, and if he does more it is good only for what he was warranted in doing, but void as to the rest.

The agent's obligations vary with the terms of his employment. He must confine himself within his instructions, though unforeseen circumstances may vary this rule. He is not bound to carry out instructions to do an illegal or immoral thing. If his instructions are not specific the implication is that he is to follow the customary course of the particular business, and if he is not limited to one course of action he may elect between different courses equally advantageous to the principal. He is bound to keep his principal informed of his transactions so that the principal may be the better judge of his interests in the premises and know how further to proceed. He must keep regular and correct accounts and render such to his principal.

If an agent is directed to sell goods at a given price but sells them for less without fraudulent intent the following holds true: The actual value of the goods sold or the highest value before suit was brought or before trial must be considered in estimating the damages occasioned to the owner by his failure to comply with instructions and not the price at which he was directed to sell.

Agents are liable to their principals for damages resulting from misconduct or negligence or omission in connection with the performance of the duties of their employment. The degree of neglect making an agent so responsible varies with the nature of the business and his relations with his principal. Where he represents himself as of a certain business, trade or profession and undertakes, gratuitously or otherwise, to perform an act relating to it, he must exercise the ordinary skill belonging to his art, business or profession. Where the employment does not necessarily imply skill and he acts gratuitously and to the best of his ability, he will not be liable. The general rule is that an agent is bound to exercise the skill, care and diligence usual with persons of common capacity similarly engaged or usual with persons of ordinary prudence in their own affairs.

Where an agent acts solely for a principal and the fact is known to the person with whom he is dealing no liability exists between him and such person. The relation is entirely between such person and the principal.

However, if the agent exceeds his authority or acts without authority unknown to such other person he will be responsible to him.

He will not be responsible in connection with an act done after his authority was revoked by the death of his principal, if he does not know of such revocation at the time.

The agent will be responsible to a person with whom he deals if he acts as if for himself, or if he personally gives a guaranty or makes an express warranty of title or, if though known to be an agent, he gives or accepts a check or note in his own name or if he acts for one who is himself legally incapacitated from acting. A public agent does not bind himself individually even though he exceeds his authority.

Shipmasters contracting for repairs and agents of residents of foreign countries though known to contract for others are nevertheless personally liable on their contracts, unless the liability is negatived in the contract or there is proof of a contract agreement. This follows a usage growing out of the necessities of trade because the principal is usually far away and comparatively inaccessible. If an agent is guilty of positive wrong, although authorized by his principal, he is liable to the third party. But if he is guilty of a mere omission of duty he is not liable to the third party but to his principal alone.

The agent's compensation if not expressly fixed by agreement is regulated by what is common in the trade, which is presumed to have been the intention of the parties. Before he can claim commission he must have completed the whole service agreed upon. His pay will be forfeited by gross negligence or gross misconduct in connection with his duties or for not keeping regular accounts or by acting contrary to his instructions, wilfully mingling his own goods with his principal's, fraudulent misapplication of funds or in any way betraying his trust.

He is entitled to have paid back to him any proper and reasonable disbursements made by him within the implied or expressed scope of his authority together with interest, where it can fairly be presumed that payment of interest was contemplated by the parties. In the absence of an agreement on the subject, usage in the trade will determine this. He cannot recover for advancements made in and about an illegal transaction even though requested by his principal to make them, nor where he has been guilty of gross negligence, fraud or misconduct nor after he is notified of the revocation of his authority.

If his principal sues him he may deduct his proper compensation and advancements if his claim is for a definite and certain amount, and in other respects a subject of set-off. Factors, insurance brokers, bankers, common carriers, lawyers, mechanics and others have a general lien upon the goods entrusted to them, or the proceeds, securities, or moneys coming to their hands in connection with their employment as the case may be, and may retain enough to meet their compensation and proper advancements.

Where a note is given to the agent in his own name or where the agent

AGENCY CONTRACT
WHEREBY A TRAVELING SALESMAN IS EMPLOYED

This agreement made this fifth day of June, 19___ by and between John Doe and Richard Roe, doing business under the name of The Mason Company, witnesseth:

1. The said salesman shall enter into the service of the said firm as a traveling salesman for them in their business of manufacturing boys' clothing for the period of one year from the 10th day of June, 19___, subject to the general control of said The Mason Company.

2. The said salesman shall devote the whole of his time, attention and energies to the performance of his duties as such salesman, and shall not, either directly or indirectly, alone or in partnership, be connected with or concerned in any other business or pursuit whatsoever during the said term of one year.

3. The said salesman shall, subject to the control of the said firm, keep proper books of account and make due and correct entries of the price of all goods sold, and of all transactions and dealings of and in relation to the said business, and shall serve the firm diligently and according to his best abilities in all respects.

4. The fixed salary of the said salesman shall be five thousand dollars per annum, payable in equal weekly installments.

5. The reasonable traveling expenses and hotel bills of the said salesman, incurred in connection with the business of the said firm, shall be paid by the said firm, and the said firm shall from week to week pay the said salesman the said traveling expenses and hotel bills in addition to the said fixed salary.

/s/   Richard Roe
THE MASON CO.

/s/   John Doe
SALESMAN

/s/   Robert Smith
WITNESS

---

sells the goods as though he were the owner, although he is not in fact the owner, or if he buys ostensibly for himself, he may maintain an action against the vendor or seller in his own name for damages for breach of the contract, even though the principal renounces the contract as to himself. An agent may sue in his own name when by the usage of trade he is authorized to act as owner or principal contracting party although his character as agent is known; also where he has made a contract in the subject matter of which he has an interest or property, he may enforce it whether his agency is known or not. Such is the case of an auctioneer who sells the goods of another. He may sue for the price because he has possession coupled with an interest to the extent of his commission. The right of the agent to sue, however, is inferior to that of the principal, except in special cases where the agent has a lien or other vested right.

An agent may sue to recover possession of his principal's goods and where a third party fraudulently induces him to sell or buy goods for his principal and he sustains a personal loss, he may sue for damages resulting to himself.

An agent cannot without authority appoint a sub-agent so as to create any responsibility between him and the principal unless it is in accordance with the usage of the particular business at hand. If the agent has authority to appoint sub-agents he will not usually be responsible for their acts to the principal, but the sub-agent will himself be directly responsible. On the other hand if his employment is without the knowledge and consent of the principal, he must look to his employer. Where sub-agents are ordinarily or necessarily employed both the agent and the principal will be liable to the sub-agents for compensation unless the agency is avowed and the sub-agent exclusively credits the principal. A sub-agency may be ratified, just as an agency may be, by the principal, the sub-agent then acquiring the position and rights of an agent with respect to the principal.

When an agent is authorized to make a contract for his principal in writing, it must, in general, be personally signed by him. An instrument which by law must be under seal and signed by an agent under a power of attorney should be signed in the name of the person giving the power thus: "J.S. by his attorney in fact J.D.," and not merely in the attorney's name, though the latter is described as attorney in the instrument.

AGENCY COUPLED WITH AN INTEREST When an agent has possession or control over the property of his principal and has a right of action against interference by third parties, an agency with an interest has been created. A, an agent, advances freight for goods sent him by his principal. He thus has an interest in the goods.

AGGRAVATED ASSAULT Assaults committed with a deadly weapon or with some ulterior and malicious motive not amounting to murder.

AGGREGATIO MENTIUM A meeting of the minds. It is a factor essential to the validity of a contract.

AGGRIEVED One whose legal rights have been invaded by the act of another. Also one whose pecuniary interest is directly affected by a judgment, or whose right of property may be divested.

AGREEMENT The term signifies the coming together of minds. It may be written or verbal, implied or express. Anyone undertaking an office, employment or duty agrees by implication to conduct it with integrity, diligence and skill and to do whatever is fairly within the scope of his employment. The agreement must be made by both parties and they must assent to the same thing in the same sense. There must be a request on one side and on the other an assent comprehending the whole of the proposition, and without qualification by any new matter, even a slight qualification destroying the assent. If there is a dispute as to the assent, where the evidence must be gathered from conversations, the question then becomes a fact for the jury to determine. An agreement without consideration is void, that is, there must be some benefit, even though it is small, moving from each party to the other.

An agreement to sell realty must be in writing and in some places must be under seal. In some cases by statutory enactments agreements as to personal property must also be in writing.

Where the meaning of an agreement is in doubt, a construction which will uphold the agreement will be preferred to one which will not. In interpreting, the aim is to give effect to the intention of the parties so far as the words and rules of law allow. Proven intent, however, cannot prevail against the plain meaning of the words, and rather than that the agreement become entirely inoperative it will be construed in proper cases somewhat at variance with the actual intention. The construction, if doubtful, will be more strongly against the party proposing or seeking the contract.

The remedy for failure to perform a contract is by suit for damages. If this is inadvisable a specific performance of the agreement may be compelled by a court of equity.

One may be discharged from his obligation under the agreement by a complete performance of what he is bound to do; also where the other party does or fails to do something which prevents such performance; by rescission of the agreement which may be by the act of both parties or by the act of one party accompanied by acquiescence on the part of the other; finally by acts of law, as where the subject matter of the agreement becomes extinct or where the time limited by law for performance has expired.

AIDERS AND ABETTORS Those who help others in the commission of some crime.

ALEATORY CONTRACT A contract is aleatory or hazardous when there is a risk on one side or both and when all risks appertaining to the contract and not excepted are assumed by the parties.

ALIAS Otherwise; also known as; at another time; as formerly.

ALIBI Evidence offered by one charged with a crime to support the statement that at the time of its commission he was at a place so remote or that the crime took place under such circumstances that he could not possibly have committed it.

ALIEN One born out of the United States who has not become a naturalized citizen. Formerly an alien could not acquire title to real estate by descent, and if he purchased land his title might be divested, if this were accomplished before its resale. These disabilities have been almost entirely removed and he stands on a like footing as to personal property. However, he cannot vote, fill an office, or serve as a juror. Alien friends may sue or be sued but alien enemies may not sue unless resident under a license, and the license will be presumed unless they are ordered away. Of husband and wife, one may be a citizen and the other an alien.

ALIENATE To convey or transfer land or property.

ALIENATION Transfer to another; the act of making a thing another's conveyance, especially of real estate, comprising any method by which estates are voluntarily resigned by one person and accepted by another.

ALIENATION OF AFFECTIONS Stealing the affections, society and fellowship of one of the spouses in marriage. Formerly suits for alienations of affections were common but they have recently been discouraged by statutes enacted in a number of states.

ALIMONY Alimony is the allowance a husband is compelled to pay, by order of court, for his wife's maintenance while she is living apart from him or after they are divorced. There are two kinds: alimony *pendente lite* (pending a suit for divorce) and permanent alimony which is fixed at the time the divorce is granted or subsequently, and which usually may be altered for proper cause by amendment of the decree. To secure alimony a legal and valid marriage must be proved.

Unless the wife has sufficient property to support herself and maintains her suit for divorce while in progress, she is entitled to alimony *pendente lite* and to an allowance to defray the expenses of the suit. Alimony, unless it is *pendente lite*, is a certain sum ordered by the court to be paid periodically. Title to any specific property cannot be decreed to the divorced wife as alimony nor can sale of property of the husband be ordered to pay it, but the husband is subject to punishment by the court for non-payment. Nor is alimony considered in itself as property which can be assigned or sold. Usually, if allowed to remain in arrears for a year it cannot be collected. If the wife saves anything from it, at her death it belongs to her husband, and arrears at her death cannot be recovered and further alimony will cease to accrue.

In fixing the amount of alimony courts consider the degree of necessity of the wife and particularly the ability of the husband to pay. His ability is judged from his income, both from property and from personal efforts. The wife's separate property and earnings, if there are any, are also considered. It is not uncommon to add the wife's to the husband's income, determine what proportion the wife should have of the aggregate (which is ordinarily one-half to one-third, and in case of alimony *pendente lite* usually not more than one-third), then deduct her separate income and allow the difference. The court also takes into consideration the sources from which the existing property came, whether through the wife or through the husband or whether it was accumulated by the exertions of both; whether children are to be supported and educated; the conduct or demeanor of the parties towards each other; the comparative needs of the two and any other circumstances affecting the justice and equity of the case.

ALIQUOT A subdivision or portion of the whole. An aliquot part.

ALL FOURS A case is said to rest on "all fours" when it is exactly similar to the case in support of which it is quoted; also when it is exactly to the point.

ALLEGATION Statement or pleading.

ALLONGE A paper attached to and made a part of a promissory note on which paper an endorsement is written.

ALONGSIDE A nautical term meaning that the charterer of a ship is to bring his cargo as near the ship as is practicable.

ALTERATION Change in an instrument. If it is made by a party thereto without the consent of the other party the change renders it void if it relates to a material matter. The question of materiality is one of law for the court to determine, not for the jury. The insertion of words which the law would supply is not material. The material alteration of a deed after delivery is said to destroy the deed as to the party altering it. But it does not defeat an estate or interest vested under the deed, though the party loses all remedy on the covenants contained therein.

Where there has been a manifestly material alteration of a check or negotiable promissory note, the party claiming under it is bound to explain the alteration. Before the holder can recover he must show that the change was made when the note was executed or that it was subsequently made fairly and without fraudulent intent and with the consent of the party sought to be held. To change the date in a promissory note from one day to the next or to insert a place of payment or the words "or bearer" or inserting another, has been held to be material, and the burden of explaining the alteration is on the holder. The maker is presumed to issue a note clear of alterations, and the purchaser, if it contains material alterations, takes it at his own risk. Inserting the words "or either of us" after "we" in a promissory note has been held to be not material where there was a statutory abolition of the distinction between notes joint and those joint and several. Whether an erasure of a place of payment is material or not is debatable. An unauthorized alteration by an agent will not be binding upon his principal.

Where an alteration is made in a written instrument before execution, the alteration and its nature should be noted and explained at the end prior to signing or at the place of attestation, that is, above the place where the witnesses are to sign, but under the clause or certificate of attestation.

AMBIDEXTERITY The act of a juror, and formerly of a lawyer, in taking money from both parties to a suit, promising to favor each of them.

AMBIGUITY Doubtfulness, uncertainty or obscurity of meaning.

AMBULANCE CHASER One who solicits accident cases for lawyers or a lawyer who actively solicits such cases on his own behalf. One to be avoided.

AMBULATORY Denoting that

which is not fixed, such as a will which may be changed.

AMEND To free from error or deficiency; to correct an error.

AMENDMENT The correction of an error committed in any process, pleading or proceeding at law or in equity. It is done either of course or by consent of the parties, or upon motion to the court in which the proceeding is pending.

AMERCEMENT A pecuniary penalty like a fine; technically, only a penalty imposed by a court on its own officers.

AMICABLE ACTION One begun and carried on according to a mutual understanding and arrangement.

AMICUS CURIAE A friend of the Court. It is usually someone who is allowed to introduce argument, authority or evidence upon some matter of law about which the Court is doubtful or mistaken.

AMORTIZATION The payment of the principal and accrued interest of an indebtedness at stated periods for a definite time, at the expiration of which the entire indebtedness is cancelled.

ANCESTOR In law, one who has preceded another in the possession of an inheritance, whether he be a progenitor or a collateral relative.

ANCIENT WRITINGS In the law of evidence, deeds, wills, leases and other instruments more than thirty years old.

ANCILLARY Attendant upon; sub-

servient to; auxiliary; subordinate; dependent; not original.

ANIMO REVOCANDI With the intention of revoking.

ANIMO TESTANDI With the intention of making a will.

ANNEXATION The fastening of chattels to the freehold which gives them the character of fixtures; they are therefore not removable.

ANNI NUBILES The marriageable age of women, which varies from state to state, the usual one being 18.

ANNUITY A yearly payment of a certain sum of money, granted to another in fee for life or years, charging the grantor only.

ANNULMENT A decree by a court declaring that a given marriage never existed from its very inception. Such a decree often has the effect of illegitimatizing the children; though in some states this is no longer the rule. Grounds for annulment often differ from grounds for divorce, the chief one being fraud. In all annulment proceedings suits should be instituted promptly; otherwise the action may be lost.

ANSWER Generally, any pleading (except a demurrer, by which the party claims he is not bound to answer) framed to meet a previous pleading.

ANTE Before.

ANTENUPTIAL SETTLEMENTS Contracts or agreements between a man

AN ANTENUPTIAL AGREEMENT OR MARRIAGE SETTLEMENT
WHERE ALL PROPERTY IS TO BE HELD JOINTLY

This agreement entered into this fourth day of August, 19____, by and between John Doe and Jane Roe, witnesseth:

1. That the parties hereby agree to enter into the marriage relation and hereafter live together as husband and wife.

2. That all moneys or property hereafter acquired or accumulated by them, or either of them, shall be held in joint or equal ownership.

3. That each of the parties hereby grants, bargains, sells and conveys to the other an undivided one-half interest in all the property, real and personal, which he or she now owns, for the purpose and with the intent of vesting in both parties the joint ownership of all property at this date owned in severalty by either of them.

4. In case of the death of one of the above-mentioned parties, all of said property shall, subject to the claims of creditors, vest absolutely in the survivor.

5. The consideration for this agreement is the marriage to be entered into pursuant to its terms and the mutual promises herein contained.

(Seal) Jane Roe
_____
JANE ROE

(Seal) John Doe
_____
JOHN DOE

/s/ Thomas Brown
_____
WITNESS

---

and woman before marriage, but in contemplation and generally in consideration of marriage, whereby the property rights and interests of either the prospective husband or wife, or both of them, are determined, or where property is secured to either or both of them, or to their children.

ANTICIPATORY BREACH The doctrine of the law of contracts that when the promisor has repudiated the contract before the time of performance has arrived the promisee may sue at once.

APPEAL The complaint to a superior court of an injustice done or an error committed by an inferior one, whose judgment or decision the court above is called upon to correct or reverse; the removal of a cause, or of some proceeding in a cause, from an inferior to a superior court, for the purpose of review.

APPEAL AND ERROR An appeal brings up questions of fact as well as of law, but upon a writ of error only questions of law apparent on the record can be considered, and there can be no inquiry whether there was error in dealing with questions of fact.

APPEARANCE The coming into court of either of the parties to an action. Where a suit has been filed the attorney must enter his appearance on behalf of his client in the manner prescribed by law before he can represent that client in the court proceeding. An attorney must also obtain the permission of the court, usually, before he can strike out his appearance in representing a client in court.

APPELLATE JURISDICTION Jurisdiction to retry and determine an issue which has already been tried in some other tribunal. Also the jurisdiction to review cases as law cases are reviewed at common law.

APPELLEE The party against whom an appeal is made.

APPELLOR One taking an appeal.

APPENDANT An appendage; something belonging to something greater and passing with it, such as a right to fish a stream that passes with a house. An appendant is created by personal use over a considerable time rather than by specific grant, which creates an appurtenance.

APPORTIONMENT The distribution of a claim or charge among persons having different interests or shares, in proportion to their interests or shares in the subject matter.

APPRAISEMENTS The act of setting a price upon property. Evaluation must be made of property of decedents, insolvents, etc. An inventory of the property with the appraisement or value must be filed in the proper court or office. The manner of making and filing is regulated by local laws. When private property is taken for the use of the public, as land for a highway or public building, or by a corporation having the right by law to do so, as a railroad company, it must be appraised by a legally constituted body to ascertain the amount to be paid to the owner.

APPROPRIATION The application of a sum of money paid by a debtor to his creditor, to one or more of several debts due from the former to the latter. This may be made by the debtor himself; or, in case of his neglect, by the creditor; or where neither has made it, by the law.

APPROVER In criminal law, one who confesses his part in a crime and gives evidence against his accomplice.

APPURTENANCES Things belonging to other principal things which pass as incident to or part of the principal. If land is conveyed, a right of way, water course or any right of privilege connected with the land and necessary to its enjoyment passes with it. Appurtenances of a ship include things on board necessary or designed to effect the objects of the voyage belonging to her owner, as a rudder, cordage, chronometer and, in case of a fishing vessel, fishing stores, but not, it seems, a small boat on the ship.

ARBITRATION The submission of a disputed matter for decision to private, unofficial persons, selected in a manner provided by law or agreement. There are two kinds, compulsory or voluntary. The former exists where the consent of one of the parties is enforceable by statutory enactment either in a court of law or before a justice of the peace; the latter where it is effected by mutual agreement of the parties by means of a rule of court or otherwise. Any matter may be voluntarily arbitrated which is capable of adjustment by agreement, or which can be the subject of a civil suit at law.

Any person capable of making a contract, disposing of his property or releasing his right of suing or being sued, may be a party to an arbitration on arriving at his majority, just as in the case of an agreement. Where the party beneficially interested is under legal incapacity to act (also in most cases of agency) the party having legal control of the property or rights to which the arbitration refers can make the submission, as a husband for his wife, a parent or guardian for a minor child, a trustee for the *cestui que trust* or one beneficially interested, and an agent, duly authorized, for his principal, and assignees for the benefit of creditors, but not a partner for a partnership.

The agreement to submit to arbitrators or a referee may be by parol (that is, oral or by written instrument not sealed), or by instrument under seal. An oral agreement is undesirable because of disputes that may arise as to the nature of the submission. The agreement should contain a mutual covenant to abide by the decision of the arbitrators. It may be in the form of a bond, each party executing an obligation to the other, conditioned to be void as to each party upon performance of the award by him. It may be and usually is couched in terms submitting both matters of law and fact relating to the issue, or it may be limited in some way, in which case the arbitrators cannot exceed their authority.

The destruction of a will or other instrument, damages for personal injury, indeed anything that would be a subject of a civil suit may be submitted. If a case already in court is voluntarily submitted to arbitration this works as a waiver of any defects in bringing the suit. If the action is to recover specific articles of personal property the sureties on the replevin bond to the sheriff to secure him against damage that might have been done to the owner in case the claimant should not prove title, are discharged from further responsibility. A replevin bond insures the person whose goods are removed under a court order so that he will not suffer any loss. Such a bond also protects the constable or sheriff executing the writ.

The revocation of a voluntary submission may take place any time prior to the award even though it is stated in the agreement that it is irrevocable. In such case, however, either party would have a right to sue for breach of agreement. If the submission is by deed (instrument under seal) it must be revoked by deed. A submission under rule at common law is generally irrevocable by the parties but will be revoked by the death of either party or of the arbitrator, or by his refusal to act or by the marriage of a single woman, if she is a party to the arbitration or if, under the law, by becoming married she places herself under disability to act for herself.

ARCHITECT'S CERTIFICATE A formal statement signed by an architect that a contractor has performed under his contract and is entitled to be paid. The construction contract provides when and how such certificates shall be issued.

ARRAIGNMENT The formal calling of a prisoner to the bar of a court to answer charges in the indictment, as to whether he is guilty or not guilty.

ARREARS Money remaining unpaid after it has become due, such as rent or interest due and unpaid.

ARREST The deprivation of a person's liberty by authority of the law. Arrest for debt having been quite generally abolished in civilized countries by statute, and arrest in a civil suit for damages in case of injury to the person and other torts being now extremely rare, arrest in criminal cases only will hereafter be referred to. In such cases any peace officer, as a justice of the peace, constable, policeman, watchman, sheriff or sheriff's officer may, even without a warrant, arrest any person committing a felony, or a breach of the peace in his presence during its continuance or immediately afterwards. If the offense amounts to a felony he may arrest where he reasonably suspects that it was committed, whether actually committed or not, and whether acting on his own knowledge or facts communicated by others.

A private person who is present when a felony is perpetrated or during the commission of a breach of the peace, should arrest the guilty party and may even arrest upon reasonable suspicion of the commission of a felony, but he will be liable for false arrest if he is unable to prove the offense or that he had reasonable grounds for suspicion. In case a warrant is issued for an arrest by a justice of the peace or other proper officer, the arrest should be made by the person to whom the warrant is issued whether he is described by name or not. If the warrant is irregular or informal or if it appears on its face to be issued without authority, the officer making an arrest will be liable as a trespasser.

An officer or private person may break open doors where he has the legal right to arrest. The arrest under a warrant must be within the jurisdiction of the court or magistrate under whose authority the officer acts. When a crime of a serious character is committed in one state and the criminal is in another, the arrest may be made by securing a requisition or request for arrest to be issued by the governor of the latter. The arrest of criminals escaped to foreign countries is regulated by treaties of extradition with the various countries.

An officer having lawful authority to arrest if he first notifies the supposed offender, may use necessary force even to the extent of killing a felon if he cannot otherwise be taken; so may a private person if asked by such officer to make arrest, and if either is killed in the attempt to do so by the supposed criminal, it will be murder. Any officer may command a bystander if necessary to assist in making arrest, and resisting the officer in the attempt to arrest is itself a crime. All persons are liable for arrest for crime except ambassadors and their servants.

What are the legal rights of a person who is arrested? After arrest, the accused is taken to a police station—normally one in the precinct in which the alleged crime has been committed—and "booked." By this is meant the recording of the arrest as well as the crime charged against the person. Under recent United States Supreme Court decisions, the accused must be informed of the charge before the police have the right to question him. If allowed by state law, the accused may also be fingerprinted and photographed.

The accused has the constitutional right to refuse to say anything that may be used against him later. In addition, he has the right to have the aid and advice of a lawyer at all times, including the time when he is being questioned by police. The accused has the right to refuse to sign any paper. If force is used or threats made to obtain information, he should promptly report the matter to his attorney and/or the court or district attorney. He should also report promptly any bruises or injuries suffered during or after arrest.

The accused also has the right to make one telephone call to notify his family, a friend, or an attorney of his predicament. He is entitled to an itemized receipt for all money and property taken from him when booked.

The accused has no right to resist an officer who arrests him legally. Nor should he talk back or otherwise act disorderly.

ARREST OF JUDGMENT The act of staying a judgment in an action at law, after verdict, for some matter appearing on the face of the record which would render the judgment, if given, erroneous or reversible.

ARSON The wilful and malicious burning of the dwelling of another. By statute the offense includes virtually all other buildings, and sometimes the burning of one's own house. The house or some part of it must be consumed by fire. It may be any outhouse which, though not contiguous to it or under the same roof, is still within the curtilage or same common fence as the mansion house itself and may be a barn, stable, cow house, sheep, cattle, dairy house or the like. It is even a felony at common law to burn a barn unconnected with the house, if it has corn or hay in it. The burning must be both wilful and malicious, but if wilful it is presumed to be malicious though the contrary may be proven. If homicide results in an attempt to commit arson, even though unintentionally, the crime is murder.

ARTIFICIAL PERSONS Persons created and devised by human laws, for the purposes of society and government, as distinguished from natural persons. Corporations are examples of artificial persons.

ASPORTATION The carrying away of goods; one of the ingredients constituting the crime of larceny.

ASSAULT AND BATTERY An unlawful offer or attempt with force or violence to do bodily harm to another. It is generally coupled with battery, which is the unlawful beating or other physical violence inflicted upon a person without his consent. It must be done wilfully or from want of due care. Any act causing a well-founded apprehension of immediate peril from a force already partially or fully put in motion is an assault. If the act is justifiable, however, it is neither assault nor battery, and if the evidence leaves doubt as to whether it was justifiable or not the party cannot be convicted.

The least touching of another person wilfully or in an angry, rude or insolent manner, is sufficient. Jostling him, spitting upon him, or striking him is a battery. A parent may reasonably correct his child, however.

Lawful acts in preserving peace or in the exercise of an office or making an arrest are not batteries. A battery may be committed lawfully in defense of one's self or wife, child or servant. The wife may defend her husband, the child a parent or the servant a master; and in such cases it is not necessary to wait until a blow has been given, which may be too late or disable one for self-defense. The attack, however, must be limited only to what is necessary for protection, to the violence to be resisted and to the danger to be warded off.

One may commit a battery in necessary defense of his property as well as his person. If one enters peaceably upon another's land, a request to depart is necessary before using force. If he refuses, the owner, or occupant, may use such force, and only such force, short of striking him, as is necessary to put or thrust him off, opposing force to force and doing whatever is necessary to self-defense if he resists. If the trespasser forcibly enters on the land or is discovered doing injury to it, a previous request is unnecessary. If one forcibly attempts to take away the personal property of another this will justify a battery on the part of the owner necessary to recover it.

If a physician unnecessarily strips a woman patient naked, under pretense that he is unable otherwise to judge her illness and helps remove her clothes, or if he has improper relations with a young girl under pretense that he is treating her medically for an ailment, and the girl does not resist because of a belief that such is the case, an assault is committed. An attempt to have carnal knowledge of a girl between ten and twelve years old, even though she consents, is an assault.

ASSENT Agreement to or approval of an act or thing done.

ASSIGN The transferring of some property or interest therein.

ASSIGNEE One to whom an assignment is made.

ASSIGNMENT A transfer by writing as distinguished from one by delivery. Any estate, interest or right in real estate, also any present and certain estate or interest in any incorporeal hereditaments may be assigned, and this includes any interest that is vested, though the enjoyment is not to take place until a future period. Rent to come due or the right to cut trees which one has purchased from the owner of land, for example, may be assigned, but a mere power or authority to do something, where the party having the power has no interest in the thing, cannot be assigned.

In order that the assignment may be valid at law the thing assigned must have an actual or potential existence of some kind at the time of the assignment. Courts of equity go further and will support an assignment, not only of interests which at the time of the assignment are contingent upon the happening or not happening of a future event, but also of things having no present actual or potential existence but resting in mere possibility only.

If one pays the debt of another on promise of the creditor to assign his claim to the one paying, the latter will be considered an equitable assignee of the debt, and may collect it from the party owing it even though no written assignment was executed. But one who merely pays the debt of another without request and without any agreement to assign cannot recover from the debtor unless the debtor subsequently ratifies his act, or promises payment.

A written assignment not under seal is usually sufficient to transfer a right granted by instrument under seal if the latter is delivered at the same time with the assignment. A formal transfer of personal chattels by a written instrument is called a bill of sale or chattel mortgage. In most cases, however, personal chattels are transferred by memorandum or by delivery only. In the case of negotiable paper it is done by mere endorsement, but it may be by delivery only. The words "assign, transfer and set over" are used in making an assignment or the words "give, grant, bargain and seal," but any words showing the intent to make a transfer will operate as an assignment. Under the statute of frauds an assignment of a lease must be by deed or note in writing, signed by the party assigning or his agent, and lawfully authorized by writing. If one holding the lease assigns his right under it for a portion of the time only during which the right is to last, it is considered a sublease rather than an assignment.

By the assignment of a right all its accessories pass with it. Thus in case of a bond assigned, any collateral security or lien on property which the assignor had to make it more secure will pass with it when assigned. The assignee of a chose in action (see also CHOSE IN ACTION) must bring the action in the name of the assignor for the use of the assignee, except in some states where there is statutory provision to the contrary allowing the assignee to sue in his own name, and whatever might have been shown by the party sued in defense against the assignor may be used against the assignee. Where the assignee sues in a court of equity, however, it may be in his own name, but there can be a suit in equity only where there would be no remedy in a court of law. Fraud will render an assignment void.

ASSIGNMENTS FOR THE BENEFIT OF CREDITORS

A transfer for the benefit of creditors. These are regulated mostly by statute. The one making the assignment may choose his own trustee or assignee and the title passes out of him to them. Preferences and priorities in assignments for part of one's creditors are allowed where not prohibited by statute but in most places under the statutes all creditors must be treated alike. The state laws relating to insolvency and assignments have been to a considerable extent superseded by the United States Bankruptcy Act.

ASSIGNOR One who assigns a right irrespective of whether or not he is the original owner.

ASSUMPSIT A civil action given by law to the party injured by the breach or non-performance of a parol contract (one not under seal).

ATHEISTS AND INFIDELS Those who do not believe in the existence of a God who will reward or punish in this world, or that which is supposed to come. At common law they are incompetent to testify as witnesses. To render one competent as a witness there must be a belief in punishment for false swearing, but the punishment may refer to punishment in this world as well as the next. The incompetency has been removed by the United States Supreme Court. A witness' belief is presumed until the contrary is proven and the witness himself may not be examined on the subject. His disbelief must be shown by others, and by evidence of declarations made by him previously.

ATTACHMENT The taking of the person or property into legal custody. An attachment of the person is usually made by the sheriff at the command of the court where the person has been guilty of contempt of court or refused to obey its orders. It is similar to an arrest. Attachments against property are sometimes made at the beginning of a suit, especially where the person against whom the suit is brought is a non-resident of the state and has property within the jurisdiction of the court where suit is brought (known as a foreign attachment), or where it is shown that a resident is about to remove property to escape creditors or for fraudulent purposes.

Domestic attachments may occur at the time suit is brought, but not usually unless fraud or intended removal of the property is alleged. It usually occurs after judgment is obtained, in which case it is termed an attachment in execution and is issued for the purpose of obtaining the debtor's legacy or distributive share in a decedent's estate, in the hands of his executor or administrator or to obtain a claim or debt owing to the debtor by another.

Attachments are regulated chiefly by statute laws, and of course the rights and proceedings vary with localities. In most places a debt, or legacy or distributive share, though not due or payable is attachable, though payment cannot be enforced until it becomes due. Usually the claim attached must be one arising on a contract wherein the specific amount due can be clearly established. In some states, however, damages arising in one's favor from a tort or injury even may be attached.

The person or corporation in whose hands the funds or property are attached is called the garnishee and the process of attachment is sometimes called garnishment. An attachment for a debt owing by a decedent or by one making an assignment for benefit of creditors, cannot be made against the heirs, executors, administrators, or assignees, as garnishees. The mere service of an attachment does not change the estate or title of a defendant in the property, nor does the attaching plaintiff acquire any property until it is delivered to him under a decree of the court directing it; nor can an attaching creditor acquire any rights to the property debt, legacy or distributive share attached superior to that of his debtor or the defendant in suit.

The levy of an attachment upon property creates a lien upon it so that the attaching creditor has a right against it in preference to other creditors who may afterwards attach or have it levied on under an execution. If the attaching creditor does not sustain the right claimed by him in his suit against the defendant the attachment will be of no effect. If two attachments are levied simultaneously or on the same date they will each be entitled to a pro rata portion of the proceeds. Where several are levied successively, the later attaching creditor may impeach the claim of the earlier for fraud, but not on account of informalities in the proceedings.

When an officer attaches personal effects he is responsible for their production at the proper time to satisfy the plaintiff's demand. If they are secretly removed from his possession, he has a sufficient right of property in them to maintain a suit to recover them. In some states the defendant or one having possession of the property may execute a bond with sureties to deliver it when the exigencies of the suit require and retain it in his possession meanwhile. Property thus bonded cannot be seized under another attachment or execution. Provisions exist in some places for dissolution of the attachment upon the defendant giving bond to secure payment of the judgment and costs if pronounced against him.

The plaintiff acquires no greater right against the garnishee than the defendant had, and in fact, practically stands in his shoes, and can enforce his claim against the garnishee only so long as he can enforce it against the defendant. No judgment can be rendered against the garnishee until there is a judgment against the defendant.

The garnishee's liability is based solely upon his indebtedness to the defendant or his having money in his possession coming to the defendant, or upon the possession by him of personal property belonging to the defendant, capable of being seized and sold under execution; the remedy against the garnishee is limited to such indebtedness or such property. A non-resident of the state where the attachment issues cannot be held as garnishee unless he has property of the defendant in the state, or is bound to pay him money or deliver him goods at some particular place in the state.

Money officially in the hands of a sheriff or constable or clerk or government disbursing officer cannot be attached.

The garnishee may be required to make a sworn answer as to property or money in his hands in response to interrogatories filed by the plaintiff. If he admits that he owes the defendant or that he has money or other attachable property of the defendant in his hands, this is sufficient to secure the entry of judgment against him. If he denies it the case may be tried before a jury.

The garnishee may set up any defense against the plaintiff that he could against the defendant if the defendant were suing. He may claim that the debt was paid or that it was barred by the statute of limitations, or that there was a failure of consideration between him and the defendant or that he has a set-off against the defendant's claim. A judgment against a garnishee and payment by him to the attaching creditor will release the garnishee of the defendant's claim against him, to the extent of the amount paid.

ATTAINDER That extinction of civil rights and capacities which takes place whenever a person who has committed treason or felony receives sentence of death for his crime.

ATTAINT A writ to inquire whether a jury of twelve men had given a false verdict, in order that the judgment might be reversed.

ATTEMPT An effort to commit a crime, carried beyond mere preparation, but falling short of actual commission.

ATTESTATION The witnessing of an instrument of writing at the request of the party executing the same and subscribing it as a witness. Statutory regulations as to attestation must be followed. The attesting witness need not actually see the party sign his name. If he signs in the presence of the party and at his request, this is sufficient.

ATTORNEY-AT-LAW An attorney-at-law is both an officer of the court and the agent of the client who employs him, and must be true to both, but the interest which he undertakes to protect should be just, or at least fairly disputable, and he is not required to assist his client in committing an obvious wrong. In general, any agreement by the attorney within the scope of his authority, and in particular any agreement respecting procedure or the conduct of the trial, binds the client. A reference of the suit to arbitrators by the attorney will bind the client even to the extent of agreeing not to carry the case to court. He may receive payment, but not less than the amount claimed in full in discharge of the debt, and that, too, in money only, unless specially authorized. He may bring a second suit if nonsuited in the first for want of formal proof, or may discontinue (stop) a suit—this does not prevent a new suit. He may waive objections to evidence and enter into agreements as to admission of facts on the conduct of the trial or may waive a required notice or the right of appeal. He cannot release sureties, nor can he enter a withdrawal of the suit amounting to relinquishment of the right of action, nor has he authority, when his client dies, to act for his legal representatives. He has no right to release a witness whose testimony is relevant to the issue. He may even agree to waive a judgment which might be obtained by default on the part of the opposing party to appear or file a plea or do any other act within the time allowed by law, but he cannot without special authority, purchase for his client at a sheriff's or other judicial sale.

An attorney by accepting employment undertakes to exercise ordinary care, skill and diligence. He must keep his client informed as to the state of his business and what is being done, and not reveal what is communicated to him in confidence even when called as a witness. He is privileged from testifying on such confidential communications received from the client. For violation of his duties or for injury resulting from lack of a reasonable degree of care, skill or diligence he is liable to suit in case damages occur therefrom.

ATTORNEY GENERAL The attorney of the government or state. The Attorney General of the United States is appointed by the President, and his office, besides special and incidental duties, is chiefly to prosecute and conduct all suits in the United States Supreme Court in which the United States has an interest. He is also required to give advice and opinion upon questions of law, when required by the President or heads of departments.

ATTORNEY IN FACT One who acts under special agency or letter of attorney authorizing him to do some specific thing or things. The instrument of writing giving him the authority is called a letter or power of attorney. An attorney in fact is simply an agent whose authority is strictly limited by the instrument appointing him, though he may do things not mentioned in

his appointment necessary to the performance of the duties specifically required of him by the power of attorney appointing him, such authority being necessarily implied.

If the authority delegated is to execute an instrument under seal, the power of attorney also must be sealed. The power to do other acts and to execute other instruments may be oral or in writing. Where, however, a grantor simply requests another in his presence to sign his, the grantor's name to a deed, and this is done accordingly without adding anything else, the signature it seems becomes the signature of the grantor and is valid. If he signs by virtue of a duly executed power of attorney he must sign the grantor's name and add "by A. B., his attorney." Where the power is in writing the extent of the power will be strictly limited thereby, such matters only being implied as are necessary to carry out the powers clearly expressed.

ATTORNEY'S LIEN The right of a lawyer to retain all papers, money or property belonging to his client as insurance that he will be paid a fee for his legal services.

AUCTION AND AUCTIONEER A public sale, usually conducted by an auctioneer—one who sells by taking bids. Those making a business of auctioneering must in most places be licensed. Where bidding at an auction is fictitious and arranged for, with the one bidding to mislead other bidders, it is a fraud upon them, and the purchaser may consider it fraudulent and void. The owner, however, may reserve bids, but this should be done openly and with good faith to prevent sacrifice of the property. Unfairness or trickery on the part of the purchaser as well as failure to comply with the conditions of sale will make the sale voidable.

If there is a material misdescription of real estate sold the sale can be set aside, and one bidding may withdraw his bid so long as it has not been accepted.

The auctioneer acts as the agent of the seller and also to some extent of the buyer. He may sue for the price of the goods sold, having a special property therein by virtue of his agency, and he has a lien upon the goods while in his possession for his commission as auctioneer. He is liable for damages arising from want of skill or from neglect and is bound to sell as advantageously as he can.

If an auctioneer does not disclose the name of the party for whom he is selling he is personally liable to the purchaser for carrying out the contract. If he sells the property of one as property of another and the buyer pays the other, the auctioneer cannot recover the price from the purchaser.

AUDITOR One appointed by a court to state an account between contending parties or to settle exceptions to an account of an administrator, executor, or one acting in a representative capacity, or to distribute a balance on an account among the persons legally entitled thereto, whether creditors, heirs, legatees or others.

When appointed to distribute, claims against the estate or fund to be distributed may be adjudicated before him, and testimony concerning the same may be taken before him under oath. His report both as to the law and facts of a case are subject to revision by the court appointing him, but the court will not reverse his findings of fact unless they are clearly wrong or unless impeached for fraud and misconduct.

AUTHENTICATION The act of giving legal authority to a statute, record or other written instrument, or a certified copy thereof, so as to make it legally admissible as evidence.

AUTREFOIS ACQUIT A plea by a criminal to an indictment that he has been formerly acquitted on an indictment for the same offense.

AVOWRY A pleading in an action of replevin, by which the defendant acknowledges the taking of the distress or property complained of, where he took it in his own right, and sets forth the reason for doing so.

AWARD The judgment or decision made and given by an arbitrator or arbitrators, or an umpire, respecting any matter in dispute submitted to them.

B

BAD FAITH The term means "actual intent" to mislead or deceive another. It does not mean misleading by an honest, inadvertent, or careless misstatement.

BAGGAGE Articles for the personal use, convenience, instruction or amusement of the passenger on the way, and usually carried by him on a trip.

BAIL The security given for release of a prisoner. Since the abolition of imprisonment for debt the giving of bail to keep out of prison in civil suits based upon contract is also abolished.

Where a case is carried from a lower to a higher jurisdiction on appeal of writ of error, bail for costs must be given, and not unfrequently it must be given to secure also the debt or damage recovered in the lower jurisdiction in case the judgment there should be sustained.

The defendant is usually entitled to be set at liberty on giving bail unless charged with committing an offense punishable by death and in some places and under some circumstances even in such cases. The amount of bail is fixed by the judge or magistrate having jurisdiction. The Constitution of the United States prohibits excessive bail, and if sufficient bail in a sufficient amount is offered in bailable cases it must be accepted.

BAILEE A person to whom goods are delivered or bailed for a certain purpose.

BAILIFF A sheriff, sheriff's officer or deputy.

BAILMENT A delivery of goods in trust upon a contract expressed or implied that the trust shall be duly executed, and the goods restored by the bailee as soon as the purposes of the bailment shall be answered. There are five kinds of bailments: 1. Deposit. 2. Mandate (where goods are committed to one to do something without payment). 3. Loan. 4. Pledge. 5. Hiring.

The bailee is in all cases bound to exercise a certain degree of care and diligence in performing what is committed to him, varying with the nature of the bailment. If the bailment is for the benefit of the bailor or someone whom he represents, the bailee is required to exercise slight care only and is responsible only for gross negligence.

If the bailment is for the benefit of the bailee or someone represented by him he must exercise a great care, and is liable for slight neglect. If, however, it is for the benefit of both parties, he must exercise ordinary care, and is liable for damages in case of ordinary neglect. Whether proper care under the circumstances has or has not been exercised is a question for a jury to determine after the court has given jurors proper instructions about the degree of care required in the case before them.

If one undertakes simply to care for another's goods without pay, acting in good faith and looking after them as his own, he cannot be held for their loss or injury and is responsible only for bad faith or gross negligence, though the degree of care in all cases of bailment may be varied by circumstances. Thus if one offers to keep the goods, his responsibility is greater than that of one who did it upon request. The case may be affected also by the character or value of the goods, whether or not they are such as require special care or might be easily lost or injured. One taking an article without pay from one place to another cannot usually be held responsible for loss or injury, if he carries it with the care and skill exercised with respect to his own property.

A borrower is liable in case of the slightest negligence resulting in injury or loss. If he uses the article borrowed for any other purpose than that for which it was borrowed or allows another to use it or keep it beyond the limit, then he is liable for anything that may happen to it. He cannot keep it as a pledge or set-off to a claim against the one he borrowed from.

Commission merchants, factors, carriers, pledgees and many other kinds of agents or bailees who are benefited by the bailment are bound to exercise ordinary care and diligence as is also an artisan who receives material of the bailor to work up into another form or an article to repair. Such an artisan may hold the articles committed to him until paid for his work.

A bailee has a right of possession of the article committed to his charge and may institute a suit to recover as against everybody but the owner, and can deliver it only to the owner or someone authorized by him to take it. If, however, he delivers it to the person who gave it to him, supposing him to be the true owner, he is not responsible to the owner.

BAILOR One who bails or delivers goods to another, in the contract of bailment.

BANC Bench; the place where a court permanently or regularly sits.

BANK NOTE A promissory note issued by a bank, payable to the bearer on demand and intended for circulation as money.

BANKRUPTCY The condition of one lacking sufficient assets to pay his debts. It is distinguished from insolvency, which is the inability to meet obligations as they mature.

The chief purposes of the United States Bankruptcy Act are to secure uniform administration of bankrupts' estates throughout the whole country, to prevent fraud upon and unfair and improper preferences to creditors, and to enable the bankrupt to become free and discharged of his debts upon honestly surrendering his property for the benefit of his creditors. Local bankruptcy and insolvency laws are still in force, insofar as they are not superseded or supplanted by the national bankruptcy act.

The act provides that "Any person who owes debts, except a municipal railroad, insurance or banking corporation, shall be entitled to the benefits of the act as a voluntary bankrupt;" also that "any natural person, except a wage earner or a person engaged chiefly in farming or the tillage of the soil, any unincorporated company, and any moneyed business or commercial corporation except a municipal railroad, insurance or banking corporation, owing debts to the amount of one thousand dollars or over, may be adjudged an involuntary bankrupt upon default or an impartial trial, and shall be subject to the provisions and entitled to the benefits of this act."

A corporation's bankruptcy will not release its officers, directors or stockholders, as such, from any existing liability.

A partnership may also be adjudged a bankrupt. Net proceeds of partnership property must be appropriated primarily to partnership debts, and net proceeds of the individual estate of each partner primarily to the payment of individual debts.

Acts of bankruptcy by a person consist of his having (1) conveyed, transferred, concealed, or removed, or permitted to be concealed or removed, any part of his property with intent to hinder, delay, or defraud his creditors, or any of them; or (2) transferred, while insolvent, any portion of his property to one or more of his creditors with intent to prefer such creditors over his other creditors; or (3) suffered or permitted, while insolvent, any creditor to obtain a preference through legal proceedings, and not having at least five days before a sale or final disposition of any property affected by such preference vacated or discharged such preference; or (4) made a general assignment for the benefit of his creditors; or, (5) admitted in writing his inability to pay his debts and his willingness to be adjudged a bankrupt on that ground.

"A petition may be filed to force one into bankruptcy who is insolvent and who has committed an act of bankruptcy, within four months after the commission of such act. Such time shall not expire until four months after the date of the recording or registering of the transfer or assignment when the act consists in having made a transfer of any of his property with intent to hinder, delay, or defraud his creditors or for the purpose of giving a preference as hereinbefore provided, or a general assignment for the benefit of his creditors, if by law such recording or registering is required or permitted, or, if it is not, from the date when the beneficiary takes notorious, exclusive, or continuous possession of the property unless the petitioning creditors have received actual notice of such transfer or assignment."

A complete defense exists if the party against whom adverse proceedings in bankruptcy have been instituted can show that he was not insolvent at the time of filing the petition.

"Any qualified person may file a petition to be adjudged a voluntary bankrupt.

"Three or more creditors who have provable claims against any person which amount in the aggregate, in excess of the value of securities held by them, if any, to five hundred dollars or over; or if all of the creditors of such person are less than twelve in number; then one of such creditors whose claim equals such amount may file a petition to have him adjudged a bankrupt.

"In computing the number of creditors of a bankrupt for the purpose of determining how many creditors must join in the petition, such creditors as were employed by him at the time of the filing of the petition or are related to him by consanguinity or affinity within the third degree, as determined by the common law, and have not joined in the petition, shall not be counted.

"Creditors other than original petitioners may at any time enter their appearance and join in the petition, or file an answer and be heard in opposition to the prayer of the petition.

"A voluntary or involuntary petition shall not be dismissed by the petitioner or petitioners or for want of prosecution or by consent of parties until after notice to the creditors."

The act requires the bankrupt to assist and facilitate the fair and honest administration of his estate, and give all information required relating to the same, or of attempts by creditors to evade the bankruptcy act and secure unlawful preferences, and he may be examined under oath by any creditor as to his estate and as to his own conduct in relation thereto.

"Any person may, after the expiration of one month and within the next twelve months subsequent to being adjudged a bankrupt, file an application for a discharge in court of bankruptcy in which the proceedings are pending; if it shall be made to appear to the judge that the bankrupt was unavoidably prevented from filing it within such time, it may be filed within but not after the expiration of the next six months."

The judge shall hear the application for a discharge, and the opposition thereto by the trustee (if authorized to object at a meeting of creditors called for the purpose) or other parties in interest, at such time as will give them a reasonable opportunity to be fully heard, and discharge the applicant unless he has (1) committed an offense punishable by imprisonment as herein provided; or (2) with intent to conceal his financial condition, destroyed or failed to keep books of account or records from which such condition might be determined; or (3) obtained money or property on credit upon a materially false statement in writing made by him to any person or his representative for the purpose of obtaining credit from such person; or (4) at any time subsequent to the first day of the four months immediately preceding the filing of the petition transferred, removed, destroyed or concealed, or permitted to be removed, destroyed, or concealed any of his property with intent to hinder, delay or defraud his creditors; or (5) in voluntary proceedings been granted a discharge in bankruptcy within six years; or (6) in the course of the proceedings in bankruptcy refused to obey any order or to answer any material question approved by the court.

"The confirmation of a composition shall discharge the bankrupt from his debts, other than those agreed to be paid by the terms of the composition and those not affected by a discharge.

"A discharge in bankruptcy shall release a bankrupt from all of his provable debts except such as (1) are due as a tax levied by the United States, the state, county, district, or municipality in which he resides; (2) are liabilities for obtaining property by false pretense or false representations, or for wilful and malicious injuries to the person or property of another, or for alimony due or to become due, or for maintenance or support of wife or child, or for seduction of an unmarried female, or for criminal conversation; (3) have not been duly scheduled in time for proof and allowance, with the name of the creditor if known to the bankrupt, unless such creditor had notice or actual knowledge of the proceedings in bankruptcy; or (4) were created by his fraud, embezzlement, misappropriation, or defalcation while acting as an officer or in a fiduciary capacity.

"A discharge may be revoked upon application made within one year after discharge, if upon trial it be made to appear that it was obtained through the fraud of the bankrupt and that the knowledge of the fraud came to the petitioner for the revocation since the granting of the discharge. One liable as a co-debtor, guarantor or surety will not be discharged by the discharge of the other or of the principal debtor.

"A bankrupt may offer, either before or after adjudication, terms of composition to his creditors after, but not before, he has been examined in open court or at a meeting of his creditors and filed in court the required schedule of his property and list of his creditors.

"An application for the confirmation of a composition may be filed in the court of bankruptcy after, but not before, it has been accepted in writing by a majority in number of all creditors whose claims have been allowed, which number must represent a majority in amount of such claims, and the consideration to be paid by the bankrupt to his creditors, and the money necessary to pay all debts which have priority and the cost of the proceedings have been deposited in such place as shall be designated by and subject to the order of the judge.

"A date and place, with reference to the convenience of the parties in interest, shall be fixed for the hearing upon each application for the confirmation of a composition, and such objections as may be made to its confirmation.

"The judge shall confirm a composition if satisfied that (1) it is for the best interests of the creditors; (2) the bankrupt has not been guilty of any acts or failed to perform any of the duties which would be a bar to his discharge; and (3) the offer and its acceptance are in good faith and have not been made or procured except as herein provided, or by any means, promises, or acts herein forbidden."

The confirmation will discharge the bankrupt from debts, except those agreed to be paid by the terms of the composition and those not affected by a discharge. The confirmation may be set aside for fraud in obtaining it on application within six months from confirmation by any party in interest who discovers the fraud after confirmation.

Taxes legally due and owing by the bankrupt to the United States, state, county, district or municipality are payable in advance of the payments of dividends to creditors. Wages due workmen, clerks or servants, earned within three months of the date of commencement of proceedings, not to exceed $300.00 to each claimant, have priority after payment of the costs of preserving, recovering, and administering the estate. After payment of wages, and aforementioned debts, any person, who by the laws of the state or the United States is entitled to priority, will have preference to those of general creditors. The bankruptcy act does not affect the allowance to bankrupts of the exemptions prescribed by the state laws in force at the time of the filing of the petition in bankruptcy in the state where they have had their domicile for six months or the greater portion thereof immediately preceding the filing of the petition.

"A person shall be deemed to have given a preference if being insolvent, he has, within four months before the filing of the petition, or after the filing of the petition and before the adjudication, procured or suffered a judgment to be entered against himself in favor of any person, or made a transfer of any of his property, and the effect of the enforcement of such judgment or transfer will be to enable any one of his creditors to obtain a greater percentage of his debt than any other of such creditors of the same class. Where the preference consists in a transfer, such period of four months shall not expire until four months after the date of the recording or registering of the transfer, if by law such recording or registering is required.

"If a bankrupt procure or suffer entry of judgment against him, or transfer property, and if, at time of entry or transfer (or, in case of transfer, at time of recording or registering, where required) and being four months before filing of petition in bankruptcy or after filing and before adjudication, the bankrupt be insolvent, and same then operates as a preference and the beneficiary or his agent then have reason to believe that it effects a preference it shall be voidable by the trustee.

"A lien created by or obtained in or pursuant to any suit or proceeding at law or in equity, including an attachment upon mesne process or a judgment by confession, which was begun against a person within four months before the filing of a petition in bankruptcy by or against such person shall be dissolved by the adjudication of such person to be a bankrupt if (1) it appears that said lien was obtained and permitted while the defendant was insolvent and that its existence and enforcement will work a preference, or (2) the party or parties to be benefited thereby had reasonable cause to believe the defendant was insolvent and in contemplation of bankruptcy, or (3) that such lien was sought and permitted in fraud of the provisions of this act; or if the dissolution of such lien would militate against the best interests of the estate of such person the same shall not be dissolved, but the trustee of the estate of such person, for the benefit of the estate, shall be subrogated to the rights of the holder of such lien and empowered to perfect and enforce the same in his name as trustee with like force and effect as such holder might have done had not bankruptcy proceedings intervened.

"Liens given or accepted in good faith and not in contemplation of or in fraud upon this act, and for a present consideration, which have been recorded according to law, if record thereof was necessary in order to impart notice, shall to the extent of such consideration only, not be affected by this act.

"All conveyances, transfers, assignments or encumbrances of his property, or any part thereof, made or given by a person adjudged a bankrupt under the provisions of this act within four months prior to the filing of the petition, with the intent and purpose on his part to hinder, delay, or defraud his creditors, or any of them, shall be null and void as against the creditors of such debtor, except as to purchasers in good faith and for a present fair consideration; and, all property of the debtor conveyed, transferred, assigned or encumbered as aforesaid, shall, if he be adjudged a bankrupt, and the same is not exempt from execution and liability for debts by the law of his domicile, be and remain a part of the assets and estate of the bankrupt and shall pass to his said trustee, whose duty it shall be to recover and reclaim the same by legal proceedings or otherwise for the benefit of the creditors. And all conveyances, transfers, or encumbrances of his property made by a debtor at any time within four months prior to the filing of the petition against him, and while insolvent, which are held null and void as against the creditors of such debtor by the laws of the State, Territory or District in which such property is situated, shall be deemed null and void under this Act against the creditors of such debtor if he be adjudged a bankrupt, and such property shall pass to the assignee and be by him reclaimed and recovered for the benefit of the creditors of the bankrupt." Persons to whom such conveyances, transfers, assignments or encumbrances have been made shall not participate in dividends as creditors unless the conveyances, etc., be surrendered.

"All levies, judgments, attachments or other liens, obtained through legal proceedings against a person who is insolvent, at any time within four months prior to the filing of a petition in bankruptcy against him, shall be deemed null and void in case he is adjudged a bankrupt, and the property affected by the levy, judgment, attachment, or other lien shall be deemed wholly discharged and released from the same, and shall pass to the trustee as a part of the estate of the bankrupt, unless the court shall, on due notice, order that the right under such levy, judgment, attachment, or other lien shall be preserved for the benefit of the estate. The court may also order such conveyances as are necessary to carry the purposes of this section into effect: PROVIDED, That nothing herein contained shall have the effect to destroy or impair the title obtained by such levy, judgment, attachment, or other lien, of a bona fide purchaser for value who shall have acquired the same without notice or reasonable cause for injury."

The courts of bankruptcy are the district courts of the United States, the Supreme Court of the District of Columbia and the district courts of the several territories. Appeals may be taken from these courts to higher United States courts.

Bankruptcy proceedings in large measure are conducted before referees appointed by the several courts of bankruptcy to act within the several counties or local districts. Their acts are subject to the supervision of the courts and their functions and their appointment seem to be for the convenience of parties interested, and to relieve the several courts of a large part of the many duties which would otherwise be imposed upon them. Trustees are also appointed in connection with bankruptcy estates.

Their duties in general are to handle and realize upon the bankrupt's assets and pay out dividends as declared by the referee. The creditors have the right to appoint the trustee; if they don't, the court will. A receiver is sometimes appointed to take charge temporarily until the trustee is appointed or until the court refuses to declare the party bankrupt. Courts may authorize businesses to be conducted for limited periods, by receivers, the marshal or trustees, if desirable. Referees, receivers and trustees must all give bond.

The act gives to creditors voting at meetings, of which due notice must be given them, a liberal voice in directing the management of a bankrupt's estate. All claims allowed must be proved under oath in writing signed by the creditor, and creditors of course may object to other creditors' claims.

"Claims shall not be proved against a bankrupt estate subsequent to one year after the adjudication; or if they are liquidated by litigation and the final judgment therein is rendered within thirty days before or after the expiration of such time, then within sixty days after the rendition of such judgment: PROVIDED, That the right of infants and insane persons without guardians, without notice of the proceedings, may continue six months longer."

Suits founded on claims from the obligation of which a discharge of the bankrupt would operate as a release, and which are pending against a person at the time of filing a petition in bankruptcy against him, may be stayed for times varying with the circumstances.

The bankruptcy act contains numerous other provisions relating to procedure and practice, designed to carry out the purpose of the law.

BANNS OF MATRIMONY A public notice that a couple intends to marry. Its purpose is to allow any person to object to the marriage because of any impediment or other just cause. Banns are usually published in church or chapel during service on three consecutive Sundays.

BAR The place in court which counselors or attorneys occupy while addressing the court or jury, and where prisoners are brought to be arraigned or sentenced; also, shorthand for bar association, either local, state or national, such as the American Bar Association.

BAR, BARR A special plea, constituting a sufficient answer to an action at law; so called because it barred or prevented the plaintiff from further prosecuting it with effect, and if established by proof, defeated and destroyed the action altogether. Now called a special plea in bar.

BARGAIN AND SALE An agreement to sell, followed and completed by an actual sale. The term is frequently applied to the transfer of property in goods. The word bargain means the arrangement of the terms upon which one party sells, and the other buys; the word sale expresses the completion of the contract, so as to pass the property from the seller to the buyer.

BARRATRY The crime of one who frequently excites and stirs up quarrels and suits at law. There must be proof of at least three instances of guilt.

BARRISTER A synonym for a lawyer in American law and a trial attorney in English law.

BASTARD An illegitimate child.

BASTARDY PROCEEDINGS Brought by the mother or a public welfare agency to establish the paternity of an illegitimate child.

BATTERY The unlawful beating of another. Any unlawful touching of the person of another, either by the aggressor himself, or any other substance put in motion by him, provided it is wilfully committed or proceeds from the lack of due care.

BEARER PAPER Any negotiable instrument which can be negotiated by delivery and does not require indorsement.

BENCH A seat of judgment, or tribunal for the administration of justice; the seat occupied by judges in courts; the judges themselves, as occupying the judgment seat in courts. The term is figuratively used in this last sense as a professional title, just as the bar is employed to denote the legal profession.

BENCH WARRANT Process issued by the court or "from the bench" for the arrest of the person named in the warrant.

BENEFICIARIES Those to whom the policy of insurance is payable. A beneficiary is also one for whose benefit a trust is created. He is, finally, one who receives benefits or advantages.

BENEFICIARIES, THIRD PARTY. A person who is not a party to a contract, agreement or instrument but is, by the terms of the contract, agreement, or written instrument, to receive the promised consideration or some portion of it.

BEQUEST A gift of personal property left by will.

BIGAMY When a man has two wives or a woman has two husbands living at the same time. The term is commonly used in legal proceedings even though there are more than two wives or husbands, which actually would be polygamy.

Even though a woman believes her husband dead, yet if he is actually alive and she marries another man within seven years after his disappearance she is guilty of bigamy. If after seven years she marries believing her first husband to be dead and he is alive, even though she could have discovered that he was living, she is not guilty of bigamy, because her act is not construed to be wilful, her husband being presumed to be dead after seven years of absence unaccounted for. If one is charged with bigamy where the first marriage occurred in a foreign country, this must be proven to be valid where made. Simple reputation in the neighborhood that two persons are man and wife is not sufficient proof of the first marriage to establish the charge of bigamy.

BILL A formal written statement of complaint to a court of justice; as a bill of privilege, a bill in equity and a bill of indictment. A record or written statement of proceedings is an action, as a bill of exceptions. A written statement of the terms of a contract, or specification of the items of a demand, or counter-demand, as a bill of exchange, a bill of lading, and a bill of particulars. A draft of an act of the legislature before it becomes a law; a proposed or projected law. A solemn and formal written declaration of popular rights and liberties, declared on certain extraordinary occasions, such as the Bill of Rights in English history.

BILL IN EQUITY The initial pleading in an equitable cause, resembling the complaint in a legal action. A divorce suit is a bill in equity.

BILL IN EQUITY or CHANCERY A complaint in writing, under oath, in the nature and style of a petition, addressed to the judge or judges of a court of equity, setting forth all the facts on which the complaint is founded, and requesting such equitable relief or for such a decree as the party may think he is entitled to, or the court thinks proper to grant.

BILL OF ATTAINDER An act of the legislature depriving a person of his property if found guilty of treason or felony. Such bills have been abolished by the United States Constitution as well as by the individual states.

BILL OF COSTS A statement in writing of the items composing the amount of costs awarded a plaintiff or defendant in a judicial proceeding.

BILL OF CREDIT Promissory notes or bills issued by a state government, exclusively on the credit of the state, and intended to circulate through the community for its ordinary purposes as money redeemable at a future day, and for the payment of which the faith of the state is pledged.

BILL OF EXCEPTIONS A formal statement in writing, of exceptions taken to the opinion, decision or direction of a judge delivered during the trial of a case, setting forth the proceedings on the trial, the opinion or decision given and the exception taken, and sealed by the judge as to its correctness. The bill is in the nature of an appeal; its object is to put the points decided on record, in order to bring them up before the court for review after trial.

BILL OF EXCHANGE A written order or request by one person to another, for the payment of money absolutely, and at all events.

BILL OF INDICTMENT A written accusation of one or more persons of some crime or misdemeanor, preferred to, and presented on oath by a grand jury.

BILL OF LADING A receipt from a carrier whether by land or water, such as railroad or steamship company, for goods to be shipped to some given destination, in which is incorporated the contract between the parties, such as the freight charge, destination, name of the consignee, description of goods, liabilities assumed by the carrier, etc. A bill of lading is assignable by endorsement, the assignee being entitled to the goods, subject, however, to the shipper's right of stoppage in transmission where such right exists, and to such liens as may exist against the property.

A contract made with the master

of a vessel for carrying merchandise binds the vessel to the performance of the contract irrespective of the ownership of the vessel, and whether the master acts for the owner or for one hiring the vessel. A contract for carrying goods in a vessel means carrying it under the deck unless otherwise stated.

BILL OF PARTICULARS A written statement or specification of the particulars of the demand for which an action at law is brought, or of a defendant's set-off against such demand (including dates, sums and items in detail), furnished by one of the parties to the other, either voluntarily or in compliance with a judge's order for that purpose.

BILL OF RIGHTS A formal and public declaration, in writing, of popular rights and liberties, usually expressed in the form of a statute, or promulgated on occasions of revolution, or the establishment of new forms of government or constitutions.

BILL OF SALE A deed of writing under seal, evidencing the sale of personal property, and conveying title to it.

BILLS OF EXCHANGE AND DRAFTS A bill of exchange is a written order from one person to another to pay a certain sum of money therein named at a given time. An inland or domestic bill of exchange is one in which the drawer and drawee are residents of the same country and usually called a draft, though the word "draft" is sometimes applied to orders for payment of money where the time of payment is not fixed.

In a foreign bill of exchange the drawer or drawee resides in different countries. These are commonly issued in duplicate or triplicate to secure greater certainty of prompt transmission, the duplicates or triplicates being sent by different mails. The one is to be paid only in the event that the other or others are not, and the two or three as the case may be are construed as constituting but one. The parties to a bill of exchange are a drawer, payee, endorser, and drawee. The one in whose favor the bill or draft is drawn is the payee. Where the bill is transferred the purchaser is called the holder and if he in turn transfers it he becomes an endorser.

The drawee (the one upon whom the bill is drawn) upon acknowledging the bill, that is, agreeing to pay it, is called the acceptor. His liabilities are the same as those of a drawer of a promissory note, and the drawer of the bill is in a position equivalent to that of a payee on a note. Even where the drawer and payee and endorser of a bill are fictitious persons, the holder will have the same rights as against the remaining parties to the bill as he would if all parties were real. The name of the same person may indeed appear in different capacities as, for example, drawer and payee.

A bill or draft must be written and should be dated at the time made. The correct place of making should be designated. If no time of payment is expressed it is payable on demand. The acceptor may designate the place of payment or it may be prescribed by the drawer. If there is no place designated it is considered payable and is to be presented at the acceptor's usual place of business, or if he has none, at his residence or to him personally anywhere. The order or request to pay contained in the bill or draft must be in such form as to be construed as a demand of a right and not as asking a favor, nor must it be conditional.

The bill should be presented to the drawee for acceptance during the usual business hours, and he may take until the next day to determine whether he will accept. A written promise to accept a bill is construed as acceptance of a bill drawn in strict accordance with the promise and within a reasonable time.

The wording must require payment, but one is not limited to the word

---

SIGHT DRAFT

$ __2,000.00__   *Baltimore, Md.*   __October 5,__ *19*____

                                    At Sight _____ *Pay to*

the order of ------------------Clementine Roberts------------------

----------------Two thousand and 00/100---------------- *Dollars*

Payable through the Planters Trust Company, Baltimore, Maryland

Value received and charge the same
to account of

                        Maryland Fertilizer Company, Inc.

*To*_____)
*No.*_____ } R. S. Thompson, Treasurer
U.S.   Bond.

pay. Anything amounting to that will be sufficient, such as the word "deliver." It must be for money and not merchandise and the amount must be fixed, and the bill or draft is usually not negotiable, if made payable in bank bills or any substitute for legal tender money. To be negotiable it must be payable to the order of the payee or to the bearer, or contain other equivalent and operative words permitting a transfer by delivery. The name of the payee should be designated. When it is not, the holder may fill up the blank with his own name. Negotiability, however, is not essential to the bill.

A statement of value received is not necessary in a negotiable bill or draft though often used, nor is a direction to charge or place to account of someone. "As per advice" inserted in a bill deprives the drawee of authority to pay until directed. The drawer's name should be subscribed to the bill, but if it appears in the body of the bill it is sufficient. It should be addressed to the drawee by his Christian name and surname, or by the full name of the firm or corporation if it be such.

BINDER A memorandum evidencing temporary insurance issued by the insurer to the insured to cover a period of time during which the insured is considering formal application for a policy. Although incomplete as to specific terms, it is understood to include the normal provisions found in regular policies of insurance.

BLACKLIST A document whereby, either voluntarily or in pursuance of a previous arrangement, one person communicates to another or other persons information about a third person which is likely to prevent them from entering into business relations with that third person.

BLACKMAIL Extortion by threats, either oral or written, with the intent to compel the person threatened to do some act against his will or which threatens that person with bodily harm, humiliation, ridicule or disgrace.

BLANK INDORSEMENT The indorsement of a bill of exchange or promissory note, by merely writing the name of the indorser, without mentioning any person to whom the bill or note is to be paid; called blank, because a blank or space is left for the insertion of the name of the indorser, or of any subsequent holder.

BLASPHEMY Blasphemy is a false reflection uttered with a malicious design of reviling God. It is speaking evil of the Deity with an injurious purpose to derogate the divine majesty and character, and to alienate the minds of others from the love and reverence of God. The offense is criminal both at common law and by statute in most states.

BLOOD Kindred; relation by natural descent from a common ancestor; consanguinity. A person is said to be of the blood of another when he is descended from or collaterally related to him.

BLUE RIBBON JURY A jury chosen for its outstanding qualifications, and used to consider cases of special importance.

BLUE SKY LAW Legislative acts intended to stop the sale of securities in fly-by-night concerns and other fraudulent exploitations.

BOARD OF DIRECTORS The governing body of a private corporation.

BODY CORPORATE OR INCORPORATE A corporation, so called because the persons composing it are made into a body.

BOGUS Spurious, fictitious or sham. A bogus check is a check given by a person upon a bank in which he has no funds.

BONA FIDE In good faith; honestly; without fraud, collusion or deceit; without knowledge or notice of prior transaction.

BONA FIDE PURCHASER A purchaser in good faith.

BOND An obligation in writing and under seal. A single (or simple) bond is one in which the obligation is to pay a certain sum of money to another on a day named. The bond is conditional where it states that if the obligor does some particular act the obligation shall be void, otherwise it shall remain in full force.

If the condition is to pay a certain amount of money at a given time, the bond is usually made for a sum double the amount to be so paid. This sum is called the penalty of the bond. No more can be ordinarily recovered in such a bond, however, than the amount owing, costs, interest and actual damages. But more than the penalty even against the surety may be recovered if this is necessary to obtain interest accruing after breach of the contract the performance of which the bond is given to secure. One cannot make a bond to himself even in connection with others. If a bond is given to several persons jointly they may all join in the suit thereon, though it is conditioned for the performance of different things for the benefit of each. A bond must be written to be sealed.

A seal sufficient where the bond is executed will be sufficient elsewhere even though it would be insufficient if executed in some other jurisdiction. The signature and seal may be in any part of the instrument. It must be delivered by the maker to the person in whose favor it is made, though others may act for each in the delivery. A date is not considered as part of the substance of a bond. If it lacks a date or contains an impossible one it will still be good provided the date of delivery can be proven.

If in a bond one binds himself without mentioning his heirs, executors or administrators, the executors and administrators will be bound in case of his death, but not his heirs. After twenty years a bond (which is under seal) is presumed to be paid, though this may be rebutted by proof to the contrary. At the end of twenty years the burden of proving payment, where the bond is still held by the person to whom it was given or his assignee, lies upon the holder. Before the end of twenty years the burden of proving payment is on the other party, the one holding the bond being required to prove its execution only.

If one signs and seals a bond as his own, and delivers it, he is bound by it, although his name is not mentioned in the bond. The execution of the bond by the obligor in blank, with verbal authority to fill it up, does not bind the obligor, though it is afterwards filled up, unless the bond is redelivered or acknowledged or adopted.

BOOKMAKING The recording or registering of bets or wagers.

BOTTOMRY In maritime law, a contract which pledges a ship to secure a loan. Unlike the case of an ordinary mortgage, the lender loses his interest if the security is lost.

BOUNDARY A line or object indicating the limit or farthest extent of a tract of land or territory. A separating or dividing line between countries, states, districts, cities or tracts of land.

Where a river or stream is named as a boundary the center of the stream is the line. Land bounded on a highway extends to the center, even though it is a private street, unless the description shows a contrary intention, or unless the grantor has no fee or estate in the land within the highway. The connecting lines between monuments fixed at angles of a property are always presumed to be straight unless otherwise described.

The most important matters in determining the limits of the property are: 1. Natural boundaries such as a river or stream, where they exist. 2. Lines actually run and corners marked at the time of the grant. 3. If a property is described as extending along the lines and courses of an adjoining tract which are more extensive than lines mentioned in the deed, the lines of the other tract, particularly if marked, will control and be considered the correct lines if no other departure from the description of the deed is required. Next, the courses and distances as taken from the deed will control. Established marks on the ground, such as old fences, monuments, etc., must prevail as against a strict following of courses and distances.

Parol (verbal) evidence is often allowed to identify and ascertain the locality of monuments called for by the description and in a deed where the description is ambiguous. Acts of the parties may be shown to indicate where the parties considered or admitted the line to be. Common reputation in the neighborhood may be admitted to identify monuments, especially if of a public or quasi-public nature.

BREACH The breaking or violating of a law, right or duty, either by commission or omission.

BREACH OF COVENANT The non-performance of any covenant agreed to be performed, or the doing of any act agreed not to be done.

BREACH OF PEACE One guilty of a violation of public order or disturbing the peace may be held to bail for good behavior. An act of public indecorum is a breach of the peace for which an indictment may be brought.

BREACH OF PRISON The act of breaking out of jail or prison with intent to escape or the escape from custody by a person lawfully arrested.

BREACH OF PROMISE *See* PROMISE OF MARRIAGE.

BREAKING In the law of burglary, a substantial and forcible irruption, as by breaking or taking out the glass of a window or otherwise opening it; picking a lock or opening it with a key; lifting up the latch of a door, or loosening any other fastening that the owner has provided.

BREAKING BULK The division or separation of the contents of a package or container.

BRIBERY The receiving or offering of any undue reward, by or to any person whose ordinary profession or business relates to the administration of public justice, in order to influence his behavior and incline him to act contrary to his duty and the known rules of honesty and integrity. It now applies to persons in almost all official positions, as well as to the giving or taking of a reward in connection with voting at public elections. To constitute the offense it is not necessary that the person sought to be bribed should even have a right to vote at all. Even an *attempt* to bribe is criminal.

A contract procured by bribery is of course void. Merely paying one in an official position for his time, and loss occasioned in his own business from attending a meeting in order to vote in favor of a contract with the one paying for such loss of time, etc., will vitiate the contract, unless, at least, such vote was not necessary to the passage of the resolution awarding the contract.

BRIEF A brief version of a plaintiff's or defendant's case, prepared by his attorney for the instruction of counsel on a trial at law. A brief generally consists of an abstract of the pleadings, a statement of the facts of the case as they will be proved and a list of the names of the witnesses, with a statement of what each will prove.

BROKER One who acts as agent for another and receives a commission for doing so.

BUILDING LINE The point past which the fronts of all buildings on the street are not allowed to project; building lines are usually drawn at a certain uniform distance from the curb or from the edge of the sidewalk.

BURDEN OF PROOF The duty to prove a fact or facts in dispute on an issue raised between the parties in a lawsuit. Generally speaking, the burden of proof in a civil suit falls on the plaintiff or the person suing; in a criminal case the burden is on the state to prove its case beyond a reasonable doubt.

BURGLARY The breaking and entering of the house of another in the nighttime with intent to commit a felony. It does not matter whether the felony is actually committed or not. It must in general be committed in a house actually occupied as a dwelling. However, if the owner is absent but intends to return, then, although no one resides in the house in his absence, it is still his mansion house and the crime is burglary. By dwelling house is meant the house usually occupied by the person there residing and his family. It must be a permanent structure, and it is sufficient if part of the structure only is used as an abode. A burglary may be committed in a church. One cannot commit burglary with respect to his own dwelling house.

The act must be done at night to constitute burglary, that is, when by the light of the sun the face or countenance of another cannot be clearly discerned, but the light referred to does not apply to moonlight which is reflected sunlight.

The breaking and entering may be done on different nights but both must be in the nighttime. There must be both breaking and entry, and both must be with felonious intent. The removal of any part of the house or fastenings provided to secure it is a breaking. It includes knocking out a pane of glass, taking out nails or other fasteners, or cutting and tearing down a netting at a window, or raising the latch or picking open the lock with a false key, or putting back the lock of a door or the fastening of a window by an instrument, turning the key when the door is locked on the inside, or picking a lock or lowering windows fastened only by a wedge or weight. But removing a loose plank in a partition wall has been held not to be breaking. So has been the further raising of a sash of a window already partly opened in order to admit the person. The breaking of an inner door only will be sufficient to constitute a burglarious breaking. There may be also constructive breaking as where entry is gained by fraud, conspiracy or threats, which will be as effectual in making out a charge of burglary as an actual breaking.

The least entry with all or any part of the body, hand, foot or with any instrument or weapon if for the purpose of committing a felony is sufficient to constitute the offense. The intent to commit a felony is a necessary part of the crime, and the jury must determine whether the intent existed or not.

If a felony is actually committed this will furnish prima facie evidence that the intent to commit a felony existed at the time of the breaking and entry. If breaking and entry is with intent to commit a trespass or a misdemeanor simply, and no felony is committed, the offense is not burglary.

Many states, by special law, have broadened burglary to include shops, stores, warehouses, etc. Burglary may now be committed during the daytime as well as at night.

BURIAL Interment of the dead. So far as practicable one's expressed wish as to place of burial must be carried out. The widow and the kin of one buried in the cemetery lot belonging to a daughter may all decorate his grave with flowers, and the widow may erect a monument on the lot where the body is allowed to remain, but may not place the daughter's name on the monument, or place a coping around the lot against her will.

BY-LAWS Rules adopted by an association or corporation for its own government. By-laws must be complied with strictly. In the case of a corporation, the powers of which are limited by law or by its charter, only such by-laws as are within the scope of those powers or are designed to regulate the exercise thereof may be adopted. If the power to make by-laws is not vested by law or by charter in any particular body, as the directors, for example, it resides in the members of the corporation at large and in them only.

Care should be taken to give all persons entitled to participate in the adoption of a constitution or by-laws ample notice of the time and place where they will be considered and voted upon. No by-law is valid if contrary to the law of the land. It is desirable that the fact of the adoption of by-laws by an organization appear in its minutes together with the by-laws themselves as adopted.

A majority vote is all that is necessary to repeal a by-law.

C

CALENDAR The list of cases established in each court to determine their orderly disposition and trial.

CALL A notice of a meeting to be held by the stockholders or board of directors of a corporation. Also a demand for payment.

CANCELLATION The crossing out, tearing or destroying of a written instrument. Cancelling a will with the intention of revoking it effects a revocation. The destruction or obliteration need not be complete. It must be done, however, by the testator or in his presence by his direction and consent. Evidence is admissible to show what the intent of the act was in order to determine whether or not there was a revocation.

The cancellation of a deed, conveying land after delivery to the purchaser and by mutual consent of the parties in interest, will not operate as a reconveyance or revocation of the conveyance, though the contrary is true as to incorporeal hereditaments, that is, rights issuing out of the land or concerning or annexed to, such as rights of way, rents and annuities.

A court of equity will decree the cancellation of a written instrument where it would otherwise operate as a fraud.

CANON LAW A collection of ecclesiastical statutes for the regulation of the polity and discipline of the Roman Catholic church. It consists, for the most part, of ordinances of general and provincial councils, and decrees promulgated by the popes.

CAPIAS A judicial writ in actions at common law commanding the sheriff to take or arrest the party named in it.

CAPIAS AD RESPONDENDUM A well-known writ (usually called a *capias*) which commands the sheriff to take the defendant, and him safely keep, so that he may have his body before the court on a certain day, to answer the plaintiff in the action.

CAPIAS AD SATISFACIENDUM A writ of execution, which a party may issue after having recovered judgment against another, in certain actions at law. It commands the sheriff to take the party named and keep him safely, so that he may have his body before the court on a certain day, to satisfy the party by whom it is issued. Its effect is to deprive the party taken of his liberty until he makes good the satisfaction awarded by the court.

CAPITAL The net assets of an individual enterprise, partnership, joint-stock company, corporation, or business institution, including not only the original investment, but also all gains and profits realized from the continued conduct of the business.

CAPITAL CRIME or OFFENSE One which is punishable by death.

CAPITAL STOCK The amount of stock fixed by a corporation charter to be subscribed and paid in by shareholders; it also frequently refers to the amount of stock that a corporation may issue.

CAPTION The title of a lawsuit containing the names of the plaintiff and defendant and the court in which it is being tried.

CARNAL KNOWLEDGE Sexual relations between a man and a woman. Even though the vagina isn't entered or the hymen ruptured, the entering of the vulva or labia is sufficient to sustain a conviction.

CARRY ON BUSINESS The phrase is used to define conduct or acts of persons, associations, or corporations which occupy their time and attention, wholly or in part, for the purpose of making a living or profit, or both. The acts or conduct must be continuous or successive. Doing a single act of a particular business is usually not considered as carrying on a business.

CARTE BLANCHE A signed blank instrument intended by the signer to be filled in and used by another person without restriction.

CASE The term used to name a cause of action in a court of law or equity. Any issue which is to be heard, tried, and decided by a judicial tribunal may be called a case.

CASE (ACTION ON) The term distinguishes between a common law action used as a remedy for damages resulting from the consequential results of a tort and a cause of action used to collect damages resulting from the direct result of a tort. Damages caused by a patent infringement would be a basis for "action on the case." The immediate damages caused by A striking B's car would give rise to a remedy in trespass, not case.

CASE LAW The law as found in cases decided by the courts. Through what is called "common law judicial process," the courts, by deciding cases, evolve legal principles that become law. This law is called "unwritten law" as distinguished from laws passed by Congress, state legislatures, and city councils.

CASH The word cash generally carries the idea of current coins—dollars, half-dollars, quarters, dimes, nickels, and pennies. It also includes paper money—United States silver certificates, and Federal Reserve bank notes. Legal tender as defined by the federal statute is cash. A check may be considered cash by the parties concerned, and if so tendered and accepted, will discharge a debt. Usually, however, a check is only conditional payment. The debt is not paid until the holder of the check receives the money at the drawee bank.

CASH ON DELIVERY (C.O.D.)

Transactions which require the buyer to pay for the merchandise in cash when it is delivered to him.

CASH SALE A present exchange of goods for money.

CASHIER'S CHECK A bill of exchange drawn by the cashier of a bank, for the bank, upon the bank. After the check is delivered or issued to the payee or holder, the drawer bank cannot put a "stop order" against itself. By delivery of the check, the drawer bank has accepted, and thus becomes the primary obligor. Note that an ordinary depositor after drawing a check, but before it is paid by the drawee bank, may countermand the same with a "stop order."

CAUSE OF ACTION A right of action at law arises from the existence of a primary right in the plaintiff, and an invasion of that right on the part of the defendant.

CAVEAT A notice from an interested party to an officer, ministerial or judicial, not to do a given act. It is a term applied to a notice to the proper officer not to probate a will or grant letters of administration to parties named.

It is of frequent occurrence in patent cases where it consists of a notice filed in the patent office not to issue a patent upon an article of a particular description (the description being intelligibly set forth in the notice), to any other person without allowing the caveator to be heard. Upon filing a caveat and paying a fee of $20.00, no patent will be issued answering the description of the article described in the caveat within one year after filing without giving the caveator an opportunity to show priority of in-

vention. This privilege will be renewed from year to year by paying $20.00 each year, and one such $20.00 fee and not more will be credited on the general patent fees. The chief object of the caveat is to allow the inventor further time to complete his invention without others getting ahead of him.

CAVEAT EMPTOR Let the buyer beware. The phrase means that when goods are sold without an express warranty by the seller as to their quality and capacity for a particular use and purpose, the buyer takes the risk of loss as to all defects in the goods. The rule applies at judicial sales, with the buyer obtaining no better title than that held by the debtor or defendant.

CERTIFICATE OF DEPOSIT A written receipt by a bank which indicates that there is a certain sum of money on deposit in the name of a designated person.

CERTIFICATE OF DOING BUSINESS Generally required when an individual or a partnership operates a business under an assumed or firm name.

CERTIFICATE OF INCORPORATION Also called a charter, the document which creates the corporation.

CERTIFICATE OF TITLE Written evidence of ownership or possession of property. A certificate of title may be bad, doubtful, good or marketable. It is bad when the certificate transfers property which legally does not belong to the owner. It is doubtful when something further remains to be done to clear up ownership of property. It is good when it entitles one to a property or estate, and to their lawful possession. It is marketable when the title is so clear that a court will enforce its acceptance by a buyer.

In insurance law, a certificate of title is a contract to indemnify or compensate the owner of property or the person who holds the mortgage on the property from loss because of defective title, liens or encumbrances. Without obtaining a marketable title, arranged usually by the attorney for the buyer, the purchaser runs the risk of loss. All titles should be properly recorded.

CERTIFICATION The return of a writ; a formal attestation of a matter of fact; the appropriate marking of a certified check.

CERTIFIED CHECK A check which has been "accepted" by the drawee bank and has been so marked or certified that it indicates such acceptance.

CERTIORARI A writ issued from a superior to an inferior court of record directing the latter to send to the former the record of a proceeding therein pending or terminated. Upon a *certiorari* there can be no revision of a decision insofar as it relates merely to matters of fact, nor to matters resting in the discretion of the judge of the inferior court, unless it is otherwise directed by special statute or unless obvious injustice has been done.

The purpose of a *certiorari* is ordinarily to correct errors in procedure or in the interpretation of the law of the case. Errors to be thus corrected must be substantial and not merely formal and if substantial justice has been done though the proceedings were informal, there will be no revision or reversal on a *certiorari*.

CESSER A neglect; a ceasing to do something or the termination of something, such as an estate or a lease.

CESSIO BONORUM Cession of goods. In civil law, the relinquishment of a debtor's assets to his creditors.

CESSION A yielding or ceding of property or of rights.

CESTUI QUE TRUST Beneficiary. One entitled in equity to take the rents and profits of land in which the legal estate is vested in some other person who is called the trustee.

CHALLENGE The right of a party to a lawsuit to object to a juror during the selection of the jury before the trial. A challenge to the array is an objection to all those arrayed or impanelled. It is usually founded on some error or obvious partiality committed in obtaining the panel, applying to all the jurors alike. The object is usually effected in the United States by a motion addressed to the court.

A challenge to the poll is an objection to a single juryman.

Peremptory challenges are those which a party at the trial may make without assigning any reason. The number of peremptory challenges allowed varies largely in the several states and jurisdictions.

Challenges for cause are those where some reason is assigned for the objection. These are always allowable if the reason is sufficient. The fact that a juror is a minor or foreigner or lacks some statutory requirement, bias or partiality either actually shown to exist or presumed from circumstances, as in case of relationship or interest in the result of the trial, conscientious scruples against conviction in a capital case are some of the grounds of challenge for cause. Disqualification may be shown by proving declarations or opinions of the juror as to the result of the trial, or opinions formed or expressed by him as to the guilt or innocence of the one accused.

One legally incompetent on the ground of infamy may not act as a juror.

Both parties to the suit in both civil and criminal cases may challenge for cause, and equal privileges are generally granted as to peremptory challenges. If a juror is challenged by one party and found satisfactory, he may be challenged by the other. The challenge must be made on the appearance and swearing of the jurors, and challenges to the array should precede those to the poll or individual juror and the making of the latter is a waiver of the former. A juror sucessfully challenged for cause may afterwards be challenged peremptorily. Challenges to the array must be in writing; those to the poll are made orally.

CHAMBERS The office or private rooms of a judge where parties are heard, and orders made in matters not required to be brought before a full court.

CHAMPERTY The unlawful maintenance of a suit, in consideration of some bargain to have some part of the thing in dispute, or some profit out of it.

CHANCELLOR A judge sitting in a court of equity.

CHANCERY A court of equity.

CHANGE OF VENUE The removal of a suit begun in one county or district to another county or district for trial. The purpose is to dissipate any charge of bias or prejudice on the part of the judge or potential jury.

CHARGE A burden, an incumbrance or lien on land; a duty or liability attached to or an obligation imposed on a person. In practice, an address by the presiding judge to a jury, after the case has been closed on both sides, summing up and commenting on the testimony produced by the respective parties and instructing the jury as to the law bearing on the facts.

CHARGE In criminal law, the accusation made against a person that he committed a crime. In a civil action, the instructions on the law which the court gives the jury at the end of the trial.

CHARGE OF THE COURT The address of instruction usually put to a jury. This consists of instructions to a grand jury or inquest of the county before entering upon their duties as to the nature of those duties, or it is the setting forth to a jury of the principles of law which bind them in arriving at a proper verdict in the case being tried under the facts proven. The jury is bound under the obligation of their oath to obey the instructions of the court as to the law of the case even though there is an error in the instructions. For such error, the remedy of the party injured is in securing a new trial or a review of the proceedings in a higher court.

A charge to a jury should be a clear and explicit statement of the law, applicable to the facts as proven, with such comments on the evidence as are necessary to explain its application. It may sometimes even include an opinion as to the weight of evidence, but it may not undertake to decide facts, as this is exclusively for the jury unless there is complete absence of opposing proof.

An omission to instruct a jury upon every point of law raised in the case does not constitute ground for reversing a judgment, provided no request was made by the party interested that the instructions be made. If erroneous or misleading instructions are given, which might have influenced the jury in arriving at a verdict, it constitutes a ground for a new trial, but not where the instruction could not prejudice the case. A court may instruct the jury upon the whole evidence to find for one or the other party, as where the evidence is undisputed or where the preponderance is so decided that a verdict against it would be set aside.

CHARTER The contract between the created corporation and the state, that is, the act creating the corporation. The word charter also includes the powers and privileges granted the corporation by the legislature. A city charter, on the other hand, is a delegation of powers by a state legislature to the governing body of the city.

CHARTER PARTY A contract by which an entire ship, or some principal part, is let to a businessman for the conveyance of goods on a determined voyage to one or more places.

CHATTEL A broad term that includes every kind of property that is not real property. An automobile or a stock certificate are chattels personal. Chattels real have to do with real property, such as a lease for a certain number of years, as is a building placed on land by a lessee.

CHATTEL MORTGAGE A written instrument by which the owner transfers conditional title to personal property to secure the payment of a debt or the performance of a contract or other obligation. It is a pledge that the debt will be paid. The mortgagor is one who conveys the property; the mortgagee is the person to whom the transfer is made. When the mortgagor fails to pay his debt, the mortgagee may usually seize and sell the property. In the absence of statute, no particular form is necessary to create a valid chattel mortgage. All such mortgages are required, by state law, to be recorded or filed and must usually be acknowledged or attested in the same way that a deed of real property is. Many states also require the affidavit of the mortgagor or mortgagee, or both.

CHEAT (1) To defraud; to swindle. (2) The wilful obtaining of another's property by deceitful practices and, in a narrower sense, by use of some device, such as false weights or symbols. Such action is punishable by law.

FORM OF CHATTEL MORTGAGE

This chattel mortgage, made this 17th day of August, 19——, John Doe to Richard Roe, witnesseth: that for and in consideration of the sum of Nine hundred dollars, the said John Doe doth hereby bargain and sell unto Richard Roe the following property: 19—— Chevrolet, coach, serial number 37167, engine number AA591679, provided, however, if the said John Doe shall pay the said Richard Roe the aforesaid sum of Nine hundred dollars, with interest, on or before the 17th day of August, 19——, then these presents shall be void. And it is also agreed that until default be made in the payment of the aforesaid sum of Nine hundred dollars, with interest, the said John Doe shall possess the property hereby mortgaged. But in case of default, then the said John Doe does hereby declare his assent to the passage of a decree for the sale of the property hereby mortgaged, in accordance with the Code provisions provided therefor.

(Seal) /s/ John Doe
MORTGAGOR

/s/ Richard Roe
WITNESS

CHECK An order drawn on a bank, payable on demand. A check is not due until presented, and is therefore negotiable at any time before presentment so that the holder can claim against the maker or prior endorsers, without regard to any equities or defenses that may exist as between them or any of them.

The drawer of a check is liable to the holder whether presented for payment promptly or not. To hold an endorser the check should be presented for payment or deposited for presentment or collection with all possible promptness. The drawer will be discharged only in case the neglect in presentment causes him actual damage and then only to the extent of the damage. If the holder of a check fails to present it within a reasonable time or for several days for payment, and in the meantime the bank on which it is drawn fails, the holder is the loser, if there were sufficient

funds to the credit of the drawer in the bank.

If the drawer of a check dies before the check is paid this operates as a revocation of the order to the banker to pay. A check is payable on demand without days of grace. If not paid when presented, the holder must have it protested in order to retain the claim against the endorsers. To be negotiable it must be made payable either to the bearer or to the order of the payee.

A banker is not bound for the payment of a check unless he has sufficient funds in his hands to meet it. Though a check is given, if the money against which it is drawn in a bank is subsequently otherwise lawfully appropriated before presentment of the check, the prior appropriation will be valid. If the depositor receives forged checks back from his bank and does not inform the bank of it, he cannot afterwards recover from

CHECK

Baltimore, Md. September 10, 19___ Account No. XY 721

THE EQUITABLE TRUST COMPANY $\frac{7\text{-}89}{520}$

Pay to the

Order of------------Claude Jones------------

DOLLARS	00
500	CENTS

----------------Five hundred----------------Dollars 00/100 Cts.

Check No. 185

Mary Jones

---

the bank for paying checks similarly forged.

If the bank certifies the check, that is, marks it on the face "Certified" or the like, it undertakes to pay it.

The mere giving of a check does not amount to a payment or settlement of a claim as to transfer of money. Giving the check is not payment and does not cancel the debt until the check itself is paid, unless there is an agreement to the contrary between the one giving and the one receiving the check, though it will operate as a tender if received and not objected to.

A check will not operate as a gift made by reason of impending death (*causa mortis*) unless it is presented and paid in the lifetime of the donor, the death, as before stated, revoking the order to the banker to pay; but such a check has been considered to be of a testamentary character.

CHECKING ACCOUNTS, JOINT

A checking account which entitles two people to draw from the same funds. Money deposited in a joint checking account may be removed, subject to the provisions of the bank by either or both parties signatory to the account. A person may make a deposit, however, in another person's name but cannot remove funds from such an account without the written authorization of such person. A joint checking account is usually so worded that upon the death of either person the balance goes to the survivor. Some checking accounts require signatures of both parties before money may be withdrawn. In determining the kind of checking account desired, it is always wise for the prospective depositors to find out from the bank the kind of checking account that will best fit their needs and requirements *before* making a deposit.

CHILD Legally the term implies a *legitimate* son or daughter. Children born in lawful wedlock or within a competent time thereafter are presumed to be the issue of the father. This presumption may be overthrown by such proofs as may satisfy juries to the contrary. Those born out of lawful wedlock follow the condition of the mother. The child is entitled to maintenance, education and protection from injuries from the father and usually, by statutory law, is required to maintain an indigent parent if able to do so. A child may commit assault in defense of his parent.

The father, generally, and the mother under some circumstances (that is, where parents have separated and the father is unfit or refuses or neglects to care for his children) will be entitled to custody of the child. Children may be subjected by their parents to reasonable correction.

The word "children," while usually limited to its strict meaning, may in case of necessity or where the will or other instrument containing it as a whole shows an intent to include grandchildren or issue generally, follow the intent. Also, unless a contrary intent appears, the word does not include illegitimate children. Posthumous children, or those born after the death of the parent, inherit as if they had been born at the time of the parent's death.

CHOSE IN ACTION A right to receive or recover a debt, money or damages for breach of contract, or for a wrong connected with a contract which cannot be enforced without suit. Debt on a book account or for anything sold by one person to another is an example.

Where this right to recover exists and is assigned by the owner to another, the one indebted or against whom the claim exists can set up any defense against the purchaser that he could against the original claimant. If the debtor makes a payment of the debt to the original holder after he has assigned it, but without knowing of the assignment he can defend as to this against the assignee. A negotiable instrument, as a promissory note or draft or bill of exchange is exceptional, and the holder or purchaser thereof can recover from the maker, payee or endorser whether there is any defense to the note as between them or not, provided he purchases the instrument before it matures or comes due and provided he has no knowledge of any such defense at the time of his purchase, or in other words provided he is an innocent holder.

Suit after assignment must be brought in the name of the assignor for the use of the assignee, unless there is a statute to the contrary or the debtor has made an express promise to the assignee to pay, in which case the assignee may sue in his own name.

To constitute an assignment no particular form of words or writing is absolutely necessary if a proper consideration for the assignment passes to the assignor and the meaning of the parties is apparent. A mere delivery of a written evidence of debt, or giving a power of attorney to collect it, is sufficient to effect an equitable transfer, if such is the intent of the parties.

Where an attorney agrees with a client that he shall receive a percentage of the amount recovered as his compensation, this operates as an equitable assignment of the sum mentioned and will belong to the attorney when the money is recovered, as against other assignments and attachments of the same thing.

There are some things that cannot be assigned, such as an officer's pay or commission, claims for bounty against the government or claims for damages on account of a fraud and claims for torts generally.

CHOSE IN POSSESSION A thing in possession, as distinguished from a thing in action. Taxes, if paid, are a chose in possession; if unpaid, a chose in action.

CIRCUIT A civil division of a county, state or kingdom, for the more convenient administration of justice; courts held in the different circuits at stated periods; in many states, circuit courts deal with equity matters, such as divorce cases.

CIRCUMSTANTIAL EVIDENCE Evidence derived from circumstances, as distinguished from direct and positive proof.

CITATION An official call or notice to appear in court; reference to a decision or statute.

CIVIL ACTION An action brought to recover some civil right or to obtain redress for some wrong, not a crime or misdemeanor. Actions for breach of contract or for damages arising from negligence are examples of civil actions.

CIVIL INJURY An infringement of some civil right which calls for redress or compensation, as distinguished from a crime which is punishable by fine and or imprisonment.

CIVIL LAW Civil law is a modern legal system based on ancient Roman law. In modern usage, however, civil law denotes the rules that govern private legal affairs, as distinguished from criminal law, which concerns acts against the state as such, rather than mere grievances between private citizens. The law of contracts, for example, is a part of the civil law, since it lays down the rules and regulations governing contractual obligations between individuals. In criminal law it is the state that is the aggrieved party, and in its name action must be taken. However, the distinction between criminal law and civil law is not always a clear one. An action may be both a public crime and a private wrong, as is the case with assault and battery. Thus a person who beats another may be prosecuted by the state for having committed the crime of assault and battery; and the victim may also institute a civil suit for damages resulting from the beating.

CIVIL LIBERTIES In a series of landmark decisions, the United States Supreme Court has drastically extended the area of civil liberties. Noteworthy decisions include the following: (1) There can be no officially prescribed prayers or Bible reading in the public schools. (2) Segregation in schools or in public accommodations is forbidden. (3) Restricting voting rights, such as using a poll tax, is now illegal. (4) Evidence taken in a search of a suspected person or of his immediate vicinity, without a search warrant, is inadmissible, if the arrest was not made according to law. (5) A confession is excluded as evidence if the police did not advise the person of his right to remain silent and of his right to have an attorney. (6) Neither the prosecution nor the judge can comment on the silence of an accused person who has taken advantage of the guarantee against self-incrimination. (7) A juvenile involved in a criminal matter has the same rights as an adult. (8) Interracial marriages are now legal. (9) Motion pictures are protected in the same way as are freedom of speech and of the press. (10) Anyone charged with a serious crime is entitled to counsel, even if he cannot afford one. The accused is entitled to the presence of counsel at every stage of the criminal proceeding.

CIVIL RIGHTS The basic, fundamental, and inalienable (non-transferrable) rights of man, especially as guaranteed by the first ten amendments to the United States Constitution, and by many of the state constitutions as well. They include freedom of religion, of speech, of the press, and the right of petition; included too are protection of persons and houses from unreasonable searches and seizures, the payment of just compensation for private property taken for public use, the guarantee of a jury trial in criminal and civil cases, as well as due process of law, and a ban against excessive bail, fines, and punishments.

On July 2, 1964, President Lyndon B. Johnson signed a bill designed to implement the constitutional rights of nearly 20 million Negroes many of whom had been deprived of their right to vote, their right to equal education, and their right to access to public accommodations. This piece of legislation is perhaps the most important of its kind ever passed by a United States Congress.

AN ACT

To enforce the constitutional right to vote, to confer jurisdiction upon the district courts of the United States to provide injunctive relief against discrimination in public accommodations, to authorize the Attorney General to institute suits to protect constitutional rights in public facilities and public education, to extend the Commission on Civil Rights, to prevent discrimination in federally assisted programs, to establish a Commission on Equal Employment Opportunity, and for other purposes.

Be it enacted by the Senate and House of Representatives of the United States of America in Congress assembled, That this Act may be cited as the "Civil Rights Act of 1964".

Title I—Voting Rights

SEC. 101. Section 2004 of the Revised Statutes (42 U.S.C. 1971), as amended by section 131 of the Civil Rights Act of 1957 (71 Stat. 637), and as further amended by section 601 of the Civil Rights Act of 1960 (74 Stat. 90), is further amended as follows:

(a) Insert "1" after "(a)" in subsection (a) and add at the end of subsection (a) the following new paragraphs:

"(2) No person acting under color of law shall—

"(A) in determining whether any individual is qualified under State law or laws to vote in any Federal election, apply any standard, practice, or procedure different from the standards, practices, or procedures applied under such law or laws to other individuals within the same county, parish, or similar political subdivision who have been found by State officials to be qualified to vote;

"(B) deny the right of any individual to vote in any Federal election because of an error or omission on any record or paper relating to any application, registration, or other act requisite to voting, if such error or omission is not material in determining whether such individual is qualified under State law to vote in such election; or

"(C) employ any literacy test as a qualification for voting in any Federal election unless (i) such test is administered to each individual and is conducted wholly in writing, and (ii) a certified copy of the test and of the answers given by the individual is furnished to him within twenty-five days of the submission of his request made within the period of time during which records and papers are required to be retained and preserved pursuant to title III of the Civil Rights Act of 1960 (42 U.S.C. 1974-74e; 74 Stat. 88): *Provided, however,* That the Attorney General may enter into agreements with appropriate State or local authorities that preparation, conduct, and maintenance of such tests in accordance with the provisions of applicable State or local law, including such special provisions as are necessary in the preparation, conduct, and maintenance of such tests for persons who are blind or otherwise physically handicapped, meet the purposes of this subparagraph and constitute compliance therewith.

"(3) For purposes of this subsection—

"(A) the term 'vote' shall have the same meaning as in subsection (e) of this section;

"(B) the phrase 'literacy test' includes any test of the ability to read, write, understand, or interpret any matter."

(b) Insert immediately following the period at the end of the first sentence of subsection (c) the following new sentence: "If in any such proceeding literacy is a relevant fact there shall be a rebuttable presumption that any person who has not been adjudged an incompetent and who has completed the sixth grade in a public school in, or a private school accredited by, any State or territory, the District of Columbia, or the Commonwealth of Puerto Rico where instruction is carried on predominantly in the English language, possesses sufficient literacy, comprehension, and intelligence to vote in any Federal election."

(c) Add the following subsection "(f)" and designate the present subsection "(f)" as subsection "(g)":

"(f) When used in subsection (a) or (c) of this section, the words 'Federal election' shall mean any general, special, or primary election held solely or in part for the purpose of electing or selecting any candidate for the office of President, Vice President, presidential elector, Member of the Senate, or Member of the House of Representatives."

(d) Add the following subsection "(h)":

"(h) In any proceeding instituted by the United States in any district court of the United States under this section in which the Attorney General requests a finding of a pattern or practice of discrimination pursuant to subsection (e) of this section the Attorney General, at the time he files the complaint, or any defendant in the proceeding, within twenty days after service upon him of the complaint, may file with the clerk of such court a request that a court of three judges be convened to hear and determine the entire case. A copy of the request for a three-judge court shall be immediately furnished by such clerk to the chief judge of the circuit (or in his absence, the presiding circuit judge of the circuit) in which the case is pending. Upon receipt of the copy of such request it shall be the duty of the chief judge of the circuit or the presiding circuit judge, as the case may be, to designate immediately three judges in such circuit, of whom at least one shall be a circuit judge and another of whom shall be a district judge of the court in which the proceeding was instituted, to hear and determine such case, and it shall be the duty of the judges so designated to assign the case for hearing at the earliest practicable date, to participate in the hearing and determination thereof, and to cause the case to be in every way expedited. An appeal from the final judgment of such court will lie to the Supreme Court.

"In any proceeding brought under subsection (c) of this section to enforce subsection (b) of this section, or in the event neither the Attorney General nor any defendant files a request for a three-judge court in any proceeding authorized by this subsection, it shall be the duty of the chief judge of the district (or in his absence, the acting chief judge) in which the case is pending immediately to designate a judge in such district to hear and determine the case. In the event that no judge in the district is available to hear and determine the case, the chief judge of the district, or the acting chief judge, as the case may be, shall certify this fact to the chief judge of the circuit (or, in his absence, the acting chief judge) who shall then designate a district or circuit judge of the circuit to hear and determine the case.

"It shall be the duty of the judge designated pursuant to this section to assign the case for hearing at the earliest practicable date and to cause the case to be in every way expedited."

Title II—Injunctive Relief Against Discrimination in Places of Public Accommodation

SEC. 201. (a) All persons shall be entitled to the full and equal enjoyment of the goods, services, facilities, privileges, advantages, and accommodations of any place of public accommodation, as defined in this section, without discrimination or segregation on the ground of race, color, religion, or national origin.

(b) Each of the following establishments which serves the public is a place of public accommodation within the meaning of this title if its operations affect commerce, or if discrimination or segregation by it is supported by State action:

(1) any inn, hotel, motel, or other establishment which provides lodging to transient guests, other than an establishment located within a building which contains not more than five rooms for rent or hire and which is actually occupied by the proprietor of such establishment as his residence;

(2) any restaurant, cafeteria, lunchroom, lunch counter, soda fountain, or other facility principally engaged in selling food for consumption on the premises, including, but not limited to, any such facility located on the premises of any retail establishment; or any gasoline station;

(3) any motion picture house, theater, concert hall, sports arena, stadium or other place of exhibition or entertainment; and

(4) any establishment (A) (i) which is physically located within the premises of any establishment otherwise covered by this subsection, or (ii) within the premises of which is physically located any such covered establishment, and (B) which holds itself out as serving patrons of such covered establishment.

(c) The operations of an establishment affect commerce within the meaning of this title if (1) it is one of the establishments described in paragraph (1) of subsection (b); (2) in the case of an establishment described in paragraph (2) of subsection (b), it serves or offers to serve interstate travelers or a substantial portion of the food which it serves, or gasoline or other products which it sells, has moved in commerce; (3) in the case of an establishment described in paragraph (3) of subsection (b), it customarily presents films, performances, athletic teams, exhibitions, or other sources of entertainment which move in commerce; and (4) in the case of an establishment described in paragraph (4) of subsection (b), it is physically located within the premises of, or there is physically located within its premises, an establishment the operations of which affect commerce within the meaning of this subsection. For purposes of this section, "commerce" means travel, trade, traffic, commerce, transportation, or communication among the several States, or between the District of Columbia and any State, or between any foreign country or any territory or possession and any State or the District of Columbia, or between points in the same State but through any other State or the District of Columbia or a foreign country.

(d) Discrimination or segregation by an establishment is supported by State action within the meaning of this title if such discrimination or segregation (1) is carried on under color of any law, statute, ordinance, or regulation; or (2) is carried on under color of any custom or usage required or enforced by officials of the State or political subdivision thereof; or (3) is required by action of the State or political subdivision thereof.

(e) The provisions of this title shall not apply to a private club or other establishment not in fact open to the public, except to the extent that the facilities of such establishment are made available to the customers or patrons of an establishment within the scope of subsection (b).

Sec. 202. All persons shall be entitled to be free, at any establishment or place, from discrimination or segregation of any kind on the ground of race, color, religion, or national origin, if such discrimination or segregation is or purports to be required by any law, statute, ordinance, regulation, rule, or order of a State or any agency or political subdivision thereof.

Sec. 203. No person shall (a) withhold, deny, or attempt to withhold or deny, or deprive or attempt to deprive, any person of any right or privilege secured by section 201 or 202, or (b) intimidate, threaten, or coerce, or attempt to intimidate, threaten, or coerce any person with the purpose of interfering with any right or privilege secured by section 201 or 202, or (c) punish or attempt to punish any person for exercising or attempting to exercise any right or privilege secured by section 201 or 202.

Sec. 204. (a) Whenever any person has engaged or there are reasonable grounds to believe that any person is about to engage in any act or practice prohibited by section 203, a civil action for preventive relief, including an application for a permanent or temporary injunction, restraining order, or other order, may be instituted by the person aggrieved and, upon timely application, the court may, in its discretion, permit the Attorney General to intervene in such civil action if he certifies that the case is of general public importance. Upon application by the complainant and in such circumstances as the court may deem just, the court may appoint an attorney for such complainant and may authorize the commencement of the civil action without the payment of fees, costs, or security.

(b) In any action commenced pursuant to this title, the court, in its discretion, may allow the prevailing party, other than the United States, a reasonable attorney's fee as part of the costs, and the United States shall be liable for costs the same as a private person.

(c) In the case of an alleged act or practice prohibited by this title which occurs in a State, or political subdivision of a State, which has a State or local law prohibiting such act or practice and establishing or authorizing a State or local authority to grant or seek relief from such practice or to institute criminal proceedings with respect thereto upon receiving notice thereof, no civil action may be brought under subsection (a) before the expiration of thirty days after written notice of such alleged act or practice has been given to the appropriate State or local authority by registered mail or in person, provided that the court may stay proceedings in such civil action pending the termination of State or local enforcement proceedings.

(d) In the case of an alleged act or practice prohibited by this title which occurs in a State, or political subdivision of a State, which has no State or local law prohibiting such act or practice, a civil action may be brought under subsection (a): *Provided,* That the court may refer the matter to the Community Relations Service established by title X of this Act for as long as the court believes there is a reasonable possibility of obtaining voluntary compliance, but for not more than sixty days: *Provided further,* That upon expiration of such sixty-day period, the court may extend such period for an additional period, not to exceed a cumulative total of one hundred and twenty days, if it believes there then exists a reasonable possibility of securing voluntary compliance.

SEC. 205. The Service is authorized to make a full investigation of any complaint referred to it by the court under section 204(d) and may hold such hearings with respect thereto as may be necessary. The Service shall conduct any hearings with respect to any such complaint in executive session, and shall not release any testimony given therein except by agreement of all parties involved in the complaint with the permission of the court, and the Service shall endeavor to bring about a voluntary settlement between the parties.

SEC. 206. (a) Whenever the Attorney General has reasonable cause to believe that any person or group of persons is engaged in a pattern or practice of resistance to the full enjoyment of any of the rights secured by this title, and that the pattern or practice is of such a nature and is intended to deny the full exercise of the rights herein described, the Attorney General may bring a civil action in the appropriate district court of the United States by filing with it a complaint (1) signed by him (or in his absence the Acting Attorney General), (2) setting forth facts pertaining to such pattern or practice, and (3) requesting such preventive relief, including an application for a permanent or temporary injunction, restraining order or other order against the person or persons responsible for such pattern or practice, as he deems necessary to insure the full enjoyment of the rights herein described.

(b) In any such proceeding the Attorney General may file with the clerk of such court a request that a court of three judges be convened to hear and determine the case. Such request by the Attorney General shall be accompanied by a certificate that, in his opinion, the case is of general public importance. A copy of the certificate and request for a three-judge court shall be immediately furnished by such clerk to the chief judge of the circuit (or in his absence, the presiding circuit judge of the circuit) in which the case is pending. Upon receipt of the copy of such request it shall be the duty of the chief judge of the circuit or the presiding circuit judge, as the case may be, to designate immediately three judges in such circuit, of whom at least one shall be a circuit judge and another of whom shall be a district judge of the court in which the proceeding was instituted, to hear and determine such case, and it shall be the duty of the judges so designated to assign the case for hearing at the earliest practicable date, to participate in the hearing and determination thereof, and to cause the case to be in every way expedited. An appeal from the final judgment of such court will lie to the Supreme Court.

In the event the Attorney General fails to file such a request in any such proceeding, it shall be the duty of the chief judge of the district (or in his absence, the acting chief judge) in which the case is pending immediately to designate a judge in such district to hear and determine the case. In the event that no judge in the district is available to hear and determine the case, the chief judge of the district, or the acting chief judge, as the case may be, shall certify this fact to the chief judge of the circuit (or in his absence, the acting chief judge) who shall then designate a district or circuit judge of the circuit to hear and determine the case.

It shall be the duty of the judge designated pursuant to this section to assign the case for hearing at the earliest practicable date and to cause the case to be in every way expedited.

SEC. 207. (a) The district courts of the United States shall have jurisdiction of proceedings instituted pursuant to this title and shall exercise the same without regard to whether the aggrieved party shall have exhausted any administrative or other remedies that may be provided by law.

(b) The remedies provided in this title shall be the exclusive means of enforcing the rights based on this title, but nothing in this title shall preclude any individual or any State or local agency from asserting any right based on any other Federal or State law not inconsistent with this title, including any statute or ordinance requiring nondiscrimination in public establishments or accommodations, or from pursuing any remedy, civil or criminal, which may be available for the vindication or enforcement of such right.

Title III—Desegregation of Public Facilities

SEC. 301. (a) Whenever the Attorney General receives a complaint in writing signed by an individual to the effect that he is being deprived of or threatened with the loss of his right to the equal protection of the laws, on account of his race, color, religion, or national origin, by being denied equal utilization of any public facility which is owned, operated, or managed by or on behalf of any State or subdivision thereof, other than a public school or public college as defined in section 401 of title IV hereof, and the Attorney General believes the complaint is meritorious and certifies that the signer or signers of such complaint are unable, in his judgment, to initiate and maintain appropriate legal proceedings for relief and that the institution of an action will materially further the orderly progress of desegregation in public facilities, the Attorney General is authorized to institute for or in the name of the United States a civil action in any appropriate district court of the United States against such parties and for such relief as may be appropriate, and such court shall have and shall exercise jurisdiction of proceedings instituted pursuant to this section. The Attorney General may implead as defendants such additional parties as are or become necessary to the grant of effective relief hereunder.

(b) The Attorney General may deem a person or persons unable to initiate and maintain appropriate legal proceedings within the meaning of subsection (a) of this section when such person or persons are unable, either directly or through other interested persons or organizations, to bear the expense of the litigation or to obtain effective legal representation; or whenever he is satisfied that the institution of such litigation would jeopardize the personal safety, employment, or economic standing of such person or persons, their familes, or their property.

SEC. 302. In any action or proceedings under this title the United States shall be liable for costs, including a reasonable attorney's fee, the same as a private person.

SEC. 303. Nothing in this title shall affect adversely the right of any person to sue for or obtain relief in any court against discrimination in any facility covered by this title.

SEC. 304. A complaint as used in this title is a writing or document within the meaning of section 1001, title 18, United States Code.

Title IV—Desegregation of Public Education
DEFINITIONS

SEC. 401. As used in this title—

(a) "Commissioner" means the Commissioner of Education.

(b) "Desegregation" means the assignment of students to public schools and within such schools without regard to their race, color, religion, or national origin, but "desegregation" shall not mean the assignment of students to public schools in order to overcome racial imbalance.

(c) "Public school" means any elementary or secondary educational institution, and "public college" means any institution of higher education or any technical or vocational school above the secondary school level, provided that such public school or public college is operated by a State, subdivision of a State, or governmental agency within a State, or operated wholly or predominantly from or through the use of governmental funds or property, or funds or property derived from a governmental source.

(d)   "School board" means any agency or agencies which administer a system of one or more public schools and any other agency which is responsible for the assignment of students to or within such system.

SURVEY AND REPORT OF EDUCATIONAL OPPORTUNITIES

SEC. 402.   The Commissioner shall conduct a survey and make a report to the President and the Congress, within two years of the enactment of this title, concerning the lack of availability of equal educational opportunities for individuals by reason of race, color, religion, or national origin in public educational institutions at all levels in the United States, its territories and possessions, and the District of Columbia.

TECHNICAL ASSISTANCE

SEC. 403.   The Commissioner is authorized, upon the application of any school board, State, municipality, school district, or other governmental unit legally responsible for operating a public school or schools, to render technical assistance to such applicant in the preparation, adoption, and implementation of plans for the desegregation of public schools. Such technical assistance may, among other activities, include making available to such agencies information regarding effective methods of coping with special educational problems occasioned by desegregation, and making available to such agencies personnel of the Office of Education or other persons specially equipped to advise and assist them in coping with such problems.

TRAINING INSTITUTES

SEC. 404.   The Commissioner is authorized to arrange, through grants or contracts, with institutions of higher education for the operation of short-term or regular session institutes for special training designed to improve the ability of teachers, supervisors, counselors, and other elementary or secondary school personnel to deal effectively with special educational problems occasioned by desegregation. Individuals who attend such an institute on a full-time basis may be paid stipends for the period of their attendance at such institute in amounts specified by the Commissioner in regulations, including allowances for travel to attend such institute.

GRANTS

SEC. 405. (a) The Commissioner is authorized, upon application of a school board, to make grants to such board to pay, in whole or in part, the cost of—

(1) giving to teachers and other school personnel inservice training in dealing with problems incident to desegregation, and

(2) employing specialists to advise in problems incident to desegregation.

(b) In determining whether to make a grant, and in fixing the amount thereof and the terms and conditions on which it will be made, the Commissioner shall take into consideration the amount available for grants under this section and the other applications which are pending before him; the financial condition of the applicant and the other resources available to it; the nature, extent, and gravity of its problems incident to desegregation; and such other factors as he finds relevant.

PAYMENTS

SEC. 406. Payments pursuant to a grant or contract under this title may be made (after necessary adjustments on account of previously made overpayments or underpayments) in advance or by way of reimbursement, and in such installments, as the Commissioner may determine.

SUITS BY THE ATTORNEY GENERAL

SEC. 407. (a) Whenever the Attorney General receives a complaint in writing—

(1) signed by a parent or group of parents to the effect that his or their minor children, as members of a class of persons similarly situated, are being deprived by a school board of the equal protection of the laws, or

(2) signed by an individual, or his parent, to the effect that he has been denied admission to or not permitted to continue in attendance at a public college by reason of race, color, religion, or national origin,

and the Attorney General believes the complaint is meritorious and certifies that the signer or signers of such complaint are unable, in his judgment, to initiate and maintain appropriate legal proceedings for relief and that the institution of an action will materially further the orderly achievement of desegregation in public education, the Attorney General is authorized, after giving notice of such complaint to the appropriate school board or college authority and after certifying that he is satisfied that such board or authority has had a reasonable time to adjust the conditions alleged in such complaint, to institute for or in the name of the United

States a civil action in any appropriate district court of the United States against such parties and for such relief as may be appropriate, and such court shall have and shall exercise jurisdiction of proceedings instituted pursuant to this section, provided that nothing herein shall empower any official or court of the United States to issue any order seeking to achieve a racial balance in any school by requiring the transportation of pupils or students from one school to another or one school district to another in order to achieve such racial balance, or otherwise enlarge the existing power of the court to insure compliance with constitutional standards. The Attorney General may implead as defendants such additional parties as are or become necessary to the grant of effective relief hereunder.

(b) The Attorney General may deem a person or persons unable to initiate and maintain appropriate legal proceedings within the meaning of subsection (a) of this section when such person or persons are unable, either directly or through other interested persons or organizations, to bear the expense of the litigation or to obtain effective legal representation; or whenever he is satisfied that the institution of such litigation would jeopardize the personal safety, employment, or economic standing of such person or persons, their families, or their property.

(c) The term "parent" as used in this section includes any person standing in loco parentis. A "complaint" as used in this section is a writing or document within the meaning of section 1001, title 18, United States Code.

SEC. 408. In any action or proceeding under this title the United States shall be liable for costs the same as a private person.

SEC. 409. Nothing in this title shall affect adversely the right of any person to sue for or obtain relief in any court against discrimination in public education.

SEC. 410. Nothing in this title shall prohibit classification and assignment for reasons other than race, color, religion, or national origin.

Title V—Commission on Civil Rights

SEC. 501. Section 102 of the Civil Rights Act of 1957 (42 U.S.C. 1975a; 71 Stat. 634) is amended to read as follows:

"RULES OF PROCEDURE OF THE COMMISSION HEARINGS

"SEC. 102. (a) At least thirty days prior to the commencement of any hearing, the Commission shall cause to be published in the Federal Register notice of the date on which such hearing is to commence, the place at which it is to be held and the subject of the hearing. The Chairman, or one designated by him to act as Chairman at a hearing of the Commission, shall announce in an opening statement the subject of the hearing.

"(b) A copy of the Commission's rules shall be made available to any

witness before the Commission, and a witness compelled to appear before
the Commission or required to produce written or other matter shall be
served with a copy of the Commission's rules at the time of service of the
subpena.

"(c) Any person compelled to appear in person before the Commission shall be accorded the right to be accompanied and advised by counsel, who shall have the right to subject his client to reasonable examination, and to make objections on the record and to argue briefly the basis
for such objections. The Commission shall proceed with reasonable dispatch to conclude any hearing in which it is engaged. Due regard shall be
had for the convenience and necessity of witnesses.

"(d) The Chairman or Acting Chairman may punish breaches of order
and decorum by censure and exclusion from the hearings.

"(e) If the Commission determines that evidence or testimony at any
hearing may tend to defame, degrade, or incriminate any person, it shall
receive such evidence or testimony or summary of such evidence or testimony in executive session. The Commission shall afford any person defamed, degraded, or incriminated by such evidence or testimony an opportunity to appear and be heard in executive session, with a reasonable
number of additional witnesses requested by him, before deciding to use
such evidence or testimony. In the event the Commission determines to
release or use such evidence or testimony in such manner as to reveal
publicly the identity of the person defamed, degraded, or incriminated,
such evidence or testimony, prior to such public release or use, shall be
given at a public session, and the Commission shall afford such person an
opportunity to appear as a voluntary witness or to file a sworn statement
in his behalf and to submit brief and pertinent sworn statements of others.
The Commission shall receive and dispose of requests from such person to
subpena additional witnesses.

"(f) Except as provided in sections 102 and 105(f) of this Act, the
Chairman shall receive and the Commission shall dispose of requests to
subpena additional witnesses.

"(g) No evidence or testimony or summary of evidence or testimony
taken in executive session may be released or used in public sessions
without the consent of the Commission. Whoever releases or uses in public without the consent of the Commission such evidence or testimony
taken in executive session shall be fined not more than $1,000, or impris-
oned for not more than one year.

"(h) In the discretion of the Commission, witnesses may submit brief
and pertinent sworn statements in writing for inclusion in the record. The
Commission shall determine the pertinency of testimony and evidence
adduced at its hearings.

"(i) Every person who submits data or evidence shall be entitled to
retain or, on payment of lawfully prescribed costs, procure a copy or
transcript thereof, except that a witness in a hearing held in executive

session may for good cause be limited to inspection of the official transcript of his testimony. Transcript copies of public sessions may be obtained by the public upon the payment of the cost thereof. An accurate transcript shall be made of the testimony of all witnesses at all hearings, either public or executive sessions, of the Commission or of any subcommittee thereof.

"(j) A witness attending any session of the Commission shall receive $6 for each day's attendance and for the time necessarily occupied in going to and returning from the same, and 10 cents per mile for going from and returning to his place of residence. Witnesses who attend at points so far removed from their respective residences as to prohibit return thereto from day to day shall be entitled to an additional allowance of $10 per day for expenses of subsistence, including the time necessarily occupied in going to and returning from the place of attendance. Mileage payments shall be tendered to the witness upon service of a subpena issued on behalf of the Commission or any subcommittee thereof.

"(k) The Commission shall not issue any subpena for the attendance and testimony of witnesses or for the production of written or other matter which would require the presence of the party subpenaed at a hearing to be held outside of the State wherein the witness is found or resides or is domiciled or transacts business, or has appointed an agent for receipt of service of process except that, in any event, the Commission may issue subpenas for the attendance and testimony of witnesses and the production of written or other matter at a hearing held within fifty miles of the place where the witness is found or resides or is domiciled or transacts business or has appointed an agent for receipt of service of process.

"(l) The Commission shall separately state and currently publish in the Federal Register (1) descriptions of its central and field organization including the established places at which, and methods whereby, the public may secure information or make requests; (2) statements of the general course and method by which its functions are channeled and determined, and (3) rules adopted as authorized by law. No person shall in any manner be subject to or required to resort to rules, organization, or procedure not so published."

SEC. 502. Section 103(a) of the Civil Rights Act of 1957 (42 U.S.C. 1975b(a); 71 Stat. 634) is amended to read as follows:

"SEC. 103. (a) Each member of the Commission who is not otherwise in the service of the Government of the United States shall receive the sum of $75 per day for each day spent in the work of the Commission, shall be paid actual travel expenses, and per diem in lieu of subsistence expenses when away from his usual place of residence, in accordance with section 5 of the Administrative Expenses Act of 1946, as amended (5 U.S.C. 73b-2; 60 Stat. 808)."

SEC. 503. Section 103(b) of the Civil Rights Act of 1957 (42 U.S.C. 1975b(b); 71 Stat. 634) is amended to read as follows:

"(b) Each member of the Commission who is otherwise in the service of the Government of the United States shall serve without compensation in addition to that received for such other services, but while engaged in the work of the Commission shall be paid actual travel expenses, and per diem in lieu of subsistence expenses when away from his usual place of residence, in accordance with the provisions of the Travel Expenses Act of 1949, as amended (5 U.S.C. 835-42; 63 Stat. 166)."

SEC. 504. (a) Section 104(a) of the Civil Rights Act of 1957 (42 U.S.C. 1975c(a); 71 Stat. 635), as amended, is further amended to read as follows:

"DUTIES OF THE COMMISSION

"SEC. 104. (a) The Commission shall—

"(1) investigate allegations in writing under oath or affirmation that certain citizens of the United States are being deprived of their right to vote and have that vote counted by reason of their color, race, religion, or national origin; which writing, under oath or affirmation, shall set forth the facts upon which such belief or beliefs are based;

"(2) study and collect information concerning legal developments constituting a denial of equal protection of the laws under the Constitution because of race, color, religion, or national origin or in the administration of justice;

"(3) appraise the laws and policies of the Federal Government with respect to denials of equal protection of the laws under the Constitution because of race, color, religion, or national origin or in the administration of justice;

"(4) serve as a national clearinghouse for information in respect to denials of equal protection of the laws because of race, color, religion, or national origin, including but not limited to the fields of voting, education, housing, employment, the use of public facilities, and transportation, or in the administration of justice;

"(5) investigate allegations, made in writing and under oath or affirmation, that citizens of the United States are unlawfully being accorded or denied the right to vote, or to have their votes properly counted, in any election of presidential electors, Members of the United States Senate, or of the House of Representatives, as a result of any patterns or practice of fraud or discrimination in the conduct of such election; and

"(6) Nothing in this or any other Act shall be construed as authorizing the Commission, its Advisory Committees, or any person under its supervision or control to inquire into or investigate any membership practices or internal operations of any fraternal organization, any college or university fraternity or sorority, any private club or any religious organization."

(b)   Section 104(b) of the Civil Rights Act of 1957 (42 U.S.C. 1975c(b); 71 Stat. 635), as amended, is further amended by striking out the present subsection "(b)" and by substituting therefor:

"(b)   The Commission shall submit interim reports to the President and to the Congress at such times as the Commission, the Congress or the President shall deem desirable, and shall submit to the President and to the Congress a final report of its activities, findings, and recommendations not later than January 31, 1968."

SEC. 505.   Section 105(a) of the Civil Rights Act of 1957 (42 U.S.C. 1975d(a); 71 Stat. 636) is amended by striking out in the last sentence thereof "$50 per diem" and inserting in lieu thereof "$75 per diem."

SEC. 506.   Section 105(f) and section 105(g) of the Civil Rights Act of 1957 (42 U.S.C. 1975d (f) and (g); 71 Stat. 636) are amended to read as follows:

"(f)   The Commission, or on the authorization of the Commission any subcommittee of two or more members, at least one of whom shall be of each major political party, may, for the purpose of carrying out the provisions of this Act, hold such hearings and act at such times and places as the Commission or such authorized subcommittee may deem advisable. Subpenas for the attendance and testimony of witnesses or the production of written or other matter may be issued in accordance with the rules of the Commission as contained in section 102 (j) and (k) of this Act, over the signature of the Chairman of the Commission or of such subcommittee, and may be served by any person designated by such Chairman. The holding of hearings by the Commission, or the appointment of a subcommittee to hold hearings pursuant to this subparagraph, must be approved by a majority of the Commission, or by a majority of the members present at a meeting at which at least a quorum of four members is present.

"(g)   In case of contumacy or refusal to obey a subpena, any district court of the United States or the United States court of any territory or possession, or the District Court of the United States for the District of Columbia, within the jurisdiction of which the inquiry is carried on or within the jurisdiction of which said person guilty of contumacy or refusal to obey is found or resides or is domiciled or transacts business, or has appointed an agent for receipt of service of process, upon application by the Attorney General of the United States shall have jurisdiction to issue to such person an order requiring such person to appear before the Commission or a subcommittee thereof, there to produce pertinent, relevant and nonprivileged evidence if so ordered, or there to give testimony touching the matter under investigation; and any failure to obey such order of the court may be punished by said court as a contempt thereof."

SEC. 507.   Section 105 of the Civil Rights Act of 1957 (42 U.S.C. 1975d; 71 Stat. 636), as amended by section 401 of the Civil Rights Act of

1960 (42 U.S.C. 1975d (h); 74 Stat. 89), is further amended by adding a new subsection at the end to read as follows:

"(i) The Commission shall have the power to make such rules and regulations as are necessary to carry out the purposes of this Act."

Title VI—Nondiscrimination in Federally Assisted Programs

SEC. 601. No person in the United States shall, on the ground of race, color, or national origin, be excluded from participation in, be denied the benefits of, or be subjected to discrimination under any program or activity receiving Federal financial assistance.

SEC. 602. Each Federal department and agency which is empowered to extend Federal financial assistance to any program or activity, by way of grant, loan, or contract other than a contract of insurance or guaranty, is authorized and directed to effectuate the provisions of section 601 with respect to such program or activity by issuing rules, regulations, or orders of general applicability which shall be consistent with achievement of the objectives of the statute authorizing the financial assistance in connection with which the action is taken. No such rule, regulation, or order shall become effective unless and until approved by the President. Compliance with any requirement adopted pursuant to this section may be effected (1) by the termination of or refusal to grant or to continue assistance under such program or activity to any recipient as to whom there has been an express finding on the record, after opportunity for hearing, of a failure to comply with such requirement, but such termination or refusal shall be limited to the particular political entity, or part thereof, or other recipient as to whom such a finding has been made and, shall be limited in its effect to the particular program, or part thereof, in which such noncompliance has been so found, or (2) by any other means authorized by law: *Provided, however,* That no such action shall be taken until the department or agency concerned has advised the appropriate person or persons of the failure to comply with the requirement and has determined that compliance cannot be secured by voluntary means. In the case of any action terminating, or refusing to grant or continue, assistance because of failure to comply with a requirement imposed pursuant to this section, the head of the Federal department or agency shall file with the committees of the House and Senate having legislative jurisdiction over the program or activity involved a full written report of the circumstances and the grounds for such action. No such action shall become effective until thirty days have elapsed after the filing of such report.

SEC. 603. Any department or agency action taken pursuant to section 602 shall be subject to such judicial review as may otherwise be provided by law for similar action taken by such department or agency on other grounds. In the case of action, not otherwise subject to judicial review, terminating or refusing to grant or to continue financial assistance upon a inding of failure to comply with any requirement imposed pursuant to ection 602, any person aggrieved (including any State or political subdivision thereof and any agency of either) may obtain judicial review of such ction in accordance with section 10 of the Administration Procedure Act, nd such action shall not be deemed committed to unreviewable agency iscretion within the meaning of that section.

SEC. 604. Nothing contained in this title shall be construed to authorize action under this title by any department or agency with respect o any employment practice of any employer, employment agency, or abor organization except where a primary objective of the Federal financial assistance is to provide employment.

SEC. 605. Nothing in this title shall add to or detract from any existing authority with respect to any program or activity under which Federal inancial assistance is extended by way of a contract of insurance or guaranty.

Title VII—Equal Employment Opportunity

DEFINITIONS

SEC. 701. For the purposes of this title—

(a) The term "person" includes one or more individuals, labor unions, partnerships, associations, corporations, legal representatives, mutual companies, joint-stock companies, trusts, unincorporated organizations, rustees, trustees in bankruptcy, or receivers.

(b) The term "employer" means a person engaged in an industry affecting commerce who has twenty-five or more employees for each working day in each of twenty or more calendar weeks in the current or preceding calendar year, and any agent of such a person, but such term does not include (1) the United States, a corporation wholly owned by the Government of the United States, an Indian tribe, or a State or political subdivision thereof, (2) a bona fide private membership club (other than a labor organization) which is exempt from taxation under section 501(c) of the Internal Revenue Code of 1954: *Provided,* That during the first year after the effective date prescribed in subsection (a) of section 716, persons having fewer than one hundred employees (and their agents) shall not be considered employers, and, during the second year after such date, persons having fewer than seventy-five employees (and their agents) shall not be considered employers, and, during the third year after such date, persons having fewer than fifty employees (and their agents) shall not be considered employers: *Provided further,* That it shall be the policy of the United States to insure equal employment opportunities for Federal employees without discrimination because of race, color, religion, sex, or national origin and the President shall utilize his existing authority to effectuate this policy.

(c) The term "employment agency" means any person regularly under taking with or without compensation to procure employees for an employer or to procure for employees opportunities to work for an employer and includes an agent of such a person; but shall not include an agency of the United States, or an agency of a State or political subdivision of a State, except that such term shall include the United States Employment Service and the system of State and local employment services receiving Federal assistance.

(d) The term "labor organization" means a labor organization engaged in an industry affecting commerce, and any agent of such an organization and includes any organization of any kind, any agency, or employee representation committee, group, association, or plan so engaged in which employees participate and which exists for the purpose, in whole or in part of dealing with employers concerning grievances, labor disputes, wages rates of pay, hours, or other terms or conditions of employment, and any conference, general committee, joint or system board, or joint council so engaged which is subordinate to a national or international labor organization.

(e) A labor organization shall be deemed to be engaged in an industry affecting commerce if (1) it maintains or operates a hiring hall or hiring office which procures employees for an employer or procures for employees opportunities to work for an employer, or (2) the number of its members (or, where it is a labor organization composed of other labor organizations or their representatives, if the aggregate number of the members of such other labor organization) is (A) one hundred or more during the first year after the effective date prescribed in subsection (a) of section 716, (B) seventy-five or more during the second year after such date or fifty or more during the third year, or (C) twenty-five or more thereafter, and such labor organization—

(1) is the certified representative of employees under the provisions of the National Labor Relations Act, as amended, or the Railway Labor Act, as amended;

(2) although not certified, is a national or international labor organization or a local labor organization recognized or acting as the representative of employees of an employer or employers engaged in an industry affecting commerce; or

(3) has chartered a local labor organization or subsidiary body which is representing or actively seeking to represent employees of employers within the meaning of paragraph (1) or (2); or

(4) has been chartered by a labor organization representing or actively seeking to represent employees within the meaning of paragraph (1) or (2) as the local or subordinate body through which such employees may enjoy membership or become affiliated with such labor organization; or

(5) is a conference, general committee, joint or system board, or

joint council subordinate to a national or international labor organization, which includes a labor organization engaged in an industry affecting commerce within the meaning of any of the preceding paragraphs of this subsection.

(f) The term "employee" means an individual employed by an employer.

(g) The term "commerce" means trade, traffic, commerce, transportation, transmission, or communication among the several States; or between a State and any place outside thereof; or within the District of Columbia, or a possession of the United States; or between points in the same State but through a point outside thereof.

(h) The term "industry affecting commerce" means any activity, business, or industry in commerce or in which a labor dispute would hinder or obstruct commerce or the free flow of commerce and includes any activity or industry "affecting commerce" within the meaning of the Labor-Management Reporting and Disclosure Act of 1959.

(i) The term "State" includes a State of the United States, the District of Columbia, Puerto Rico, the Virgin Islands, American Samoa, Guam, Wake Island, the Canal Zone, and Outer Continental Shelf lands defined in the Outer Continental Shelf Lands Act.

EXEMPTION

SEC. 702. This title shall not apply to an employer with respect to the employment of aliens outside any State, or to a religious corporation, association, or society with respect to the employment of individuals of a particular religion to perform work connected with the carrying on by such corporation, association, or society of its religious activities or to an educational institution with respect to the employment of individuals to perform work connected with the educational activities of such institution.

DISCRIMINATION BECAUSE OF RACE, COLOR, RELIGION, SEX, OR NATIONAL ORIGIN

SEC. 703. (a) It shall be an unlawful employment practice for an employer—

(1) to fail or refuse to hire or to discharge any individual, or otherwise to discriminate against any individual with respect to his compensation, terms, conditions, or privileges of employment, because of such individual's race, color, religion, sex, or national origin; or

(2) to limit, segregate, or classify his employees in any way which would deprive or tend to deprive any individual of employment opportunities or otherwise adversely affect his status as an employee,

because of such individual's race, color, religion, sex, or national origin.

(b) It shall be an unlawful employment practice for an employment agency to fail or refuse to refer for employment, or otherwise to discriminate against, any individual because of his race, color, religion, sex, or national origin, or to classify or refer for employment any individual on the basis of his race, color, religion, sex, or national origin.

(c) It shall be an unlawful employment practice for a labor organization—

(1) to exclude or to expel from its membership, or otherwise to discriminate against, any individual because of his race, color, religion, sex, or national origin;

(2) to limit, segregate, or classify its membership, or to classify or fail or refuse to refer for employment any individual, in any way which would deprive or tend to deprive any individual of employment opportunities, or would limit such employment opportunities or otherwise adversely affect his status as an employee or as an applicant for employment, because of such individual's race, color, religion, sex, or national origin; or

(3) to cause or attempt to cause an employer to discriminate against an individual in violation of this section.

(d) It shall be an unlawful employment practice for any employer, labor organization, or joint labor-management committee controlling apprenticeship or other training or retraining, including on-the-job training programs to discriminate against any individual because of his race, color, religion, sex, or national origin in admission to, or employment in, any program established to provide apprenticeship or other training.

(e) Notwithstanding any other provision of this title, (1) it shall not be an unlawful employment practice for an employer to hire and employ employees, for an employment agency to classify, or refer for employment any individual, for a labor organization to classify its membership or to classify or refer for employment any individual, or for an employer, labor organization, or joint labor-management committee controlling apprenticeship or other training or retraining programs to admit or employ any individual in any such program, on the basis of his religion, sex, or national origin in those certain instances where religion, sex, or national origin is a bona fide occupational qualification reasonably necessary to the normal operation of that particular business or enterprise, and (2) it shall not be an unlawful employment practice for a school, college, university, or other educational institution or institution of learning to hire and employ employees of a particular religion if such school, college, university, or other educational institution or institution of learning is, in whole or in substantial part, owned, supported, controlled, or managed by a particular religion or by a particular religious corporation, association, or society, or if the curriculum of such school, college, university, or other educational institution or institution of learning is directed toward the propagation of a particular religion.

(f) As used in this title, the phrase "unlawful employment practice" shall not be deemed to include any action or measure taken by an employer, labor organization, joint labor-management committee, or employment agency with respect to an individual who is a member of the Communist Party of the United States or of any other organization required to register as a Communist-action or Communist-front organization by final order of the Subversive Activities Control Board pursuant to the Subversive Activities Control Act of 1950.

(g) Notwithstanding any other provision of this title, it shall not be an unlawful employment practice for an employer to fail or refuse to hire and employ an individual for any position, for an employer to discharge any individual from any position, or for an employment agency to fail or refuse to refer any individual for employment in any position, or for a labor organization to fail or refuse to refer an individual for employment in any position, if—

(1) the occupancy of such position, or access to the premises in or upon which any part of the duties of such position is performed or is to be performed, is subject to any requirement imposed in the interest of the national security of the United States under any security program in effect pursuant to or administered under any statute of the United States or any Executive order of the President; and

(2) such individual has not fulfilled or has ceased to fulfill that requirement.

(h) Notwithstanding any other provision of this title, it shall not be an unlawful employment practice for an employer to apply different standards of compensation, or different terms, conditions, or privileges of employment pursuant to a bona fide seniority or merit system, or a system which measures earnings by quantity or quality of production or to employees who work in different locations, provided that such differences are not the result of an intention to discriminate because of race, color, religion, sex, or national origin, nor shall it be an unlawful employment practice for an employer to give and to act upon the results of any professionally developed ability test provided that such test, its administration or action upon the results is not designed, intended or used to discriminate because of race, color, religion, sex, or national origin. It shall not be an unlawful employment practice under this title for any employer to differentiate upon the basis of sex in determining the amount of the wages or compensation paid or to be paid to employees of such employer if such differentiation is authorized by the provisions of section 6(d) of the Fair Labor Standards Act of 1938, as amended (29 U.S.C. 206(d)).

(i) Nothing contained in this title shall apply to any business or enterprise on or near an Indian reservation with respect to any publicly announced employment practice of such business or enterprise under which a

preferential treatment is given to any individual because he is an India
living on or near a reservation.

(j) Nothing contained in this title shall be interpreted to require any
employer, employment agency, labor organization, or joint labor-manage
ment committee subject to this title to grant preferential treatment to any
individual or to any group because of the race, color, religion, sex, o
national origin of such individual or group on account of an imbalance
which may exist with respect to the total number or percentage of per
sons of any race, color, religion, sex, or national origin employed by any
employer, referred or classified for employment by any employment agen
cy or labor organization, admitted to membership or classified by any
labor organization, or admitted to, or employed in, any apprenticeship o
other training program, in comparison with the total number or percent
age of persons of such race, color, religion, sex, or national origin in any
community, State, section, or other area, or in the available work force i
any community, State, section, or other area.

OTHER UNLAWFUL EMPLOYMENT PRACTICES

SEC. 704. (a) It shall be an unlawful employment practice for ar
employer to discriminate against any of his employees or applicants fo
employment, for an employment agency to discriminate against any individ-
ual, or for a labor organization to discriminate against any member there
of or applicant for membership, because he has opposed any practice
made an unlawful employment practice by this title, or because he has
made a charge, testified, assisted, or participated in any manner in ar
investigation, proceeding, or hearing under this title.

(b) It shall be an unlawful employment practice for an employer, la
bor organization, or employment agency to print or publish or cause to be
printed or published any notice or advertisement relating to employment
by such an employer or membership in or any classification or referral fo
employment by such a labor organization, or relating to any classificatior
or referral for employment by such an employment agency, indicating any
preference, limitation, specification, or discrimination, based on race, col-
or, religion, sex, or national origin, except that such a notice or advertise
ment may indicate a preference, limitation, specification, or discriminatior
based on religion, sex, or national origin is a bona fide occupational qualifi
cation for employment.

EQUAL EMPLOYMENT OPPORTUNITY COMMISSION

SEC. 705. (a) There is hereby created a Commission to be known a
the Equal Employment Opportunity Commission, which shall be com
posed of five members, not more than three of whom shall be member
of the same political party, who shall be appointed by the President by

nd with the advice and consent of the Senate. One of the original members shall be appointed for a term of one year, one for a term of two ears, one for a term of three years, one for a term of four years, and one or a term of five years, beginning from the date of enactment of this title, ut their successors shall be appointed for terms of five years each, except hat any individual chosen to fill a vacancy shall be appointed only for the nexpired term of the member whom he shall succeed. The President hall designate one member to serve as Chairman of the Commission, and ne member to serve as Vice Chairman. The Chairman shall be responsible on behalf of the Commission for the administrative operations of the Commission, and shall appoint, in accordance with the civil service laws, uch officers, agents, attorneys, and employees as it deems necessary to ssist it in the performance of its functions and to fix their compensation n accordance with the Classification Act of 1949, as amended. The Vice Chairman shall act as Chairman in the absence or disability of the Chairman or in the event of a vacancy in that office.

(b) A vacancy in the Commission shall not impair the right of the emaining members to exercise all the powers of the Commission and hree members thereof shall constitute a quorum.

(c) The Commission shall have an official seal which shall be judicially oticed.

(d) The Commission shall at the close of each fiscal year report to the Congress and to the President concerning the action it has taken; the ames, salaries, and duties of all individuals in its employ and the moneys t has disbursed; and shall make such further reports on the cause of and neans of eliminating discrimination and such recommendations for further egislation as may appear desirable.

(e) The Federal Executive Pay Act of 1956, as amended (5 U.S.C. 2201-2209), is further amended—

    (1) by adding to section 105 thereof (5 U.S.C. 2204) the following clause:

    "(32) Chairman, Equal Employment Opportunity Commission"; and

    (2) by adding to clause (45) of section 106(a) thereof (5 U.S.C. 2205(a)) the following: "Equal Employment Opportunity Commission (4)."

(f) The principal office of the Commission shall be in or near the District of Columbia, but it may meet or exercise any or all its powers at any other place. The Commission may establish such regional or State offices as it deems necessary to accomplish the purpose of this title.

(g) The Commission shall have power—

    (1) to cooperate with and, with their consent, utilize regional, State, local, and other agencies, both public and private, and individuals;

    (2) to pay to witnesses whose depositions are taken or who are

summoned before the Commission or any of its agents the same wit
ness and mileage fees as are paid to witnesses in the courts of the
United States;

(3) to furnish to persons subject to this title such technical assis
tance as they may request to further their compliance with this title
or an order issued thereunder;

(4) upon the request of (i) any employer, whose employees or
some of them, or (ii) any labor organization, whose members or some
of them, refuse or threaten to refuse to cooperate in effectuating the
provisions of this title, to assist in such effectuation by conciliation or
such other remedial action as is provided by this title;

(5) to make such technical studies as are appropriate to effectuate
the purposes and policies of this title and to make the results of such
studies available to the public;

(6) to refer matters to the Attorney General with recommendations for intervention in a civil action brought by an aggrieved party
under section 706, or for the institution of a civil action by the Attorney General under section 707, and to advise, consult, and assist the
Attorney General on such matters.

(h) Attorneys appointed under this section may, at the direction of the
Commission, appear for and represent the Commission in any case in
court.

(i) The Commission shall, in any of its educational or promotional
activities, cooperate with other departments and agencies in the performance of such educational and promotional activities.

(j) All officers, agents, attorneys, and employees of the Commission
shall be subject to the provisions of section 9 of the Act of August 2, 1939,
as amended (the Hatch Act), notwithstanding any exemption contained in
such section.

PREVENTION OF UNLAWFUL EMPLOYMENT PRACTICES

SEC. 706 (a) Whenever it is charged in writing under oath by a person claiming to be aggrieved, or a written charge has been filed by a
member of the Commission where he has reasonable cause to believe a
violation of this title has occurred (and such charge sets forth the facts
upon which it is based) that an employer, employment agency, or labor
organization has engaged in an unlawful employment practice, the Commission shall furnish such employer, employment agency, or labor organization (hereinafter referred to as the "respondent") with a copy of such
charge and shall make an investigation of such charge, provided that such
charge shall not be made public by the Commission. If the Commission
shall determine, after such investigation, that there is reasonable cause to
believe that the charge is true, the Commission shall endeavor to elimi-
nate any such alleged unlawful employment practice by informal methods

f conference, conciliation, and persuasion. Nothing said or done during
and as a part of such endeavors may be made public by the Commission
without the written consent of the parties, or used as evidence in a subsequent proceeding. Any officer or employee of the Commission, who shall
make public in any manner whatever any information in violation of this
subsection shall be deemed guilty of a misdemeanor and upon conviction
hereof shall be fined not more than $1,000 or imprisoned not more than
one year.

(b) In the case of an alleged unlawful employment practice occurring
in a State, or political subdivision of a State, which has a State or local
law prohibiting the unlawful employment practice alleged and establishing
or authorizing a State or local authority to grant or seek relief from such
practice or to institute criminal proceedings with respect thereto upon
receiving notice thereof, no charge may be filed under subsection (a) by
the person aggrieved before the expiration of sixty days after proceedings
have been commenced under the State or local law, unless such proceedings have been earlier terminated, provided that such sixty-day period
shall be extended to one hundred and twenty days during the first year
after the effective date of such State or local law. If any requirement for
the commencement of such proceedings is imposed by a State or local
authority other than a requirement of the filing of a written and signed
statement of the facts upon which the proceeding is based, the proceeding
shall be deemed to have been commenced for the purposes of this subsection at the time such statement is sent by registered mail to the appropriate State or local authority.

(c) In the case of any charge filed by a member of the Commission
alleging an unlawful employment practice occurring in a State or political
subdivision of a State, which has a State or local law prohibiting the
practice alleged and establishing or authorizing a State or local authority
to grant or seek relief from such practice or to institute criminal proceedings with respect thereto upon receiving notice thereof, the Commission
shall, before taking any action with respect to such charge, notify the
appropriate State or local officials and, upon request, afford them a reasonable time, but not less than sixty days (provided that such sixty-day
period shall be extended to one hundred and twenty days during the first
year after the effective day of such State or local law), unless a shorter
period is requested, to act under such State or local law to remedy the
practice alleged.

(d) A charge under subsection (a) shall be filed within ninety days
after the alleged unlawful employment practice occurred, except that in
the case of an unlawful employment practice with respect to which the
person aggrieved has followed the procedure set out in subsection (b),
such charge shall be filed by the person aggrieved within two hundred
and ten days after the alleged unlawful employment practice occurred, or
within thirty days after receiving notice that the State or local agency has

terminated the proceedings under the State or local law, whichever is earlier, and a copy of such charge shall be filed by the Commission with the State or local agency.

(e) If within thirty days after a charge is filed with the Commission or within thirty days after expiration of any period of reference under subsection (c) (except that in either case such period may be extended to not more than sixty days upon a determination by the Commission that further efforts to secure voluntary compliance are warranted), the Commission has been unable to obtain voluntary compliance with this title, the Commission shall so notify the person aggrieved and a civil action may, within thirty days thereafter, be brought against the respondent named in the charge (1) by the person claiming to be aggrieved, or (2) if such charge was filed by a member of the Commission, by any person whom the charge alleges was aggrieved by the alleged unlawful employment practice. Upon application by the complainant and in such circumstances as the court may deem just, the court may appoint an attorney for such complainant and may authorize the commencement of the action without the payment of fees, costs, or security. Upon timely application, the court may, in its discretion, permit the Attorney General to intervene in such civil action if he certifies that the case is of general public importance. Upon request, the court may, in its discretion, stay further proceedings for not more than sixty days pending the termination of State or local proceedings described in subsection (b) or the efforts of the Commission to obtain voluntary compliance.

(f) Each United States district court and each United States court of a place subject to the jurisdiction of the United States shall have jurisdiction of actions brought under this title. Such an action may be brought in any judicial district in the State in which the unlawful employment practice is alleged to have been committed, in the judicial district in which the employment records relevant to such practice are maintained and administered, or in the judicial district in which the plaintiff would have worked but for the alleged unlawful employment practice, but if the respondent is not found within any such district, such an action may be brought within the judicial district in which the respondent has his principal office. For purposes of sections 1404 and 1406 of title 28 of the United States Code, the judicial district in which the respondent has his principal office shall in all cases be considered a district in which the action might have been brought.

(g) If the court finds that the respondent has intentionally engaged in or is intentionally engaging in an unlawful employment practice charged in the complaint, the court may enjoin the respondent from engaging in such unlawful employment practice, and order such affirmative action as may be appropriate, which may include reinstatement or hiring of employees, with or without back pay (payable by the employer, employment agency, or labor organization, as the case may be, responsible for the unlawful employment practice). Interim earnings or amounts earnable with reasonable diligence by the person or persons discriminated against shall operate to reduce the back pay otherwise allowable. No order of the court shall require the admission or reinstatement of an individual as a member of a union or the hiring, reinstatement, or promotion of an individual as an employee, or the payment to him of any back pay, if such individual was refused admission, suspended, or expelled or was refused employment or advancement or was suspended or discharged for any reason other than discrimination on account of race, color, religion, sex, or national origin or in violation of section 704(a).

(h) The provisions of the Act entitled "An Act to amend the Judicial Code and to define and limit the jurisdiction of courts sitting in equity, and for other purposes," approved March 23, 1932 (29 U.S.C. 101–115), shall not apply with respect to civil actions brought under this section.

(i) In any case in which an employer, employment agency, or labor organization fails to comply with an order of a court issued in a civil action brought under subsection (e), the Commission may commence proceedings to compel compliance with such order.

(j) Any civil action brought under subsection (e) and any proceedings brought under subsection (i) shall be subject to appeal as provided in sections 1291 and 1292, title 28, United States Code.

(k) In any action or proceeding under this title the court, in its discretion, may allow the prevailing party, other than the Commission or the United States, a reasonable attorney's fee as part of the costs, and the Commission and the United States shall be liable for costs the same as a private person.

SEC. 707. (a) Whenever the Attorney General has reasonable cause to believe that any person or group of persons is engaged in a pattern or practice of resistance to the full enjoyment of any of the rights secured by this title, and that the pattern or practice is of such a nature and is intended to deny the full exercise of the rights herein described, the Attorney General may bring a civil action in the appropriate district court of the United States by filing with it a complaint (1) signed by him (or in his absence the Acting Attorney General), (2) setting forth facts pertaining to such pattern or practice, and (3) requesting such relief, including an application for a permanent or temporary injunction, restraining order or other order against the person or persons responsible for such pattern or practice, as he deems necessary to insure the full enjoyment of the rights herein described.

(b) The district courts of the United States shall have and shall exercise jurisdiction of proceedings instituted pursuant to this section, and in any such proceeding the Attorney General may file with the clerk of such court a request that a court of three judges be convened to hear and determine the case. Such request by the Attorney General shall be accompanied by a certificate that, in his opinion, the case is of general public importance. A copy of the certificate and request for a three-judge cour shall be immediately furnished by such clerk to the chief judge of th circuit (or in his absence, the presiding circuit judge of the circuit) i which the case is pending. Upon receipt of such request it shall be th duty of the chief judge of the circuit or the presiding circuit judge, as th case may be, to designate immediately three judges in such circuit, o whom at least one shall be a circuit judge and another of whom shall be district judge of the court in which the proceeding was instituted, to hea and determine such case, and it shall be the duty of the judges so desig nated to assign the case for hearing at the earliest practicable date, t participate in the hearing and determination thereof, and to cause th case to be in every way expedited. An appeal from the final judgment o such court will lie to the Supreme Court.

In the event the Attorney General fails to file such a request in an such proceeding, it shall be the duty of the chief judge of the district (o in his absence, the acting chief judge) in which the case is pending imme diately to designate a judge in such district to hear and determine th case. In the event that no judge in the district is available to hear an determine the case, the chief judge of the district, or the acting chie judge, as the case may be, shall certify this fact to the chief judge of th circuit (or in his absence, the acting chief judge) who shall then designat a district or circuit judge of the circuit to hear and determine the case.

It shall be the duty of the judge designated pursuant to this section t assign the case for hearing at the earliest practicable date and to cause th case to be in every way expedited.

EFFECT ON STATE LAWS

SEC. 708. Nothing in this title shall be deemed to exempt or relieve any person from any liability, duty, penalty, or punishment provided by any present or future law of any State or political subdivision of a State other than any such law which purports to require or permit the doing o any act which would be an unlawful employment practice under this title.

INVESTIGATIONS, INSPECTIONS, RECORDS, STATE AGENCIES

SEC. 709. (a) In connection with any investigation of a charge filed under section 706, the Commission or its designated representative shall at all reasonable times have access to, for the purposes of examination and the right to copy any evidence of any person being investigated o proceeded against that relates to unlawful employment practices covered by this title and is relevant to the charge under investigation.

(b) The Commission may cooperate with State and local agencies charged with the administration of State fair employment practices laws and, with the consent of such agencies, may for the purpose of carrying out its functions and duties under this title and within the limitation of funds appropriated specifically for such purpose, utilize the services of such agencies and their employees and, notwithstanding any other provision of law, may reimburse such agencies and their employees for services rendered to assist the Commission in carrying out this title. In furtherance of such cooperative efforts, the Commission may enter into written agreements with such State or local agencies and such agreements may include provisions under which the Commission shall refrain from processing a charge in any cases or class of cases specified in such agreements and under which no person may bring a civil action under section 706 in any cases or class of cases so specified, or under which the Commission shall relieve any person or class of persons in such State or locality from requirements imposed under this section. The Commission shall rescind any such agreement whenever it determines that the agreement no longer serves the interest of effective enforcement of this title.

(c) Except as provided in subsection (d), every employer, employment agency, and labor organization subject to this title shall (1) make and keep such records relevant to the determinations of whether unlawful employment practices have been or are being committed, (2) preserve such records for such periods, and (3) make such reports therefrom, as the Commission shall prescribe by regulation or order, after public hearing, as reasonable, necessary, or appropriate for the enforcement of this title or the regulations or orders thereunder. The Commission shall, by regulation, require each employer, labor organization, and joint labor-management committee subject to this title which controls an apprenticeship or other training program to maintain such records as are reasonably necessary to carry out the purpose of this title, including, but not limited to, a list of applicants who wish to participate in such program, including the chronological order in which such applications were received, and shall furnish to the Commission, upon request, a detailed description of the manner in which persons are selected to participate in the apprenticeship or other training program. Any employer, employment agency, labor organization, or joint labor-management committee which believes that the application to it of any regulation or order issued under this section would result in undue hardship may (1) apply to the Commission for an exemption from the application of such regulation or order, or (2) bring a civil action in the United States district court for the district where such records are kept. If the Commission or the court, as the case may be, finds that the application of the regulation or order to the employer, employment agency, or labor organization in question would impose an undue hardship, the Commission or the court, as the case may be, may grant appropriate relief.

(d) The provisions of subsection (c) shall not apply to any employer, employment agency, labor organization, or joint labor-management committee with respect to matters occurring in any State or political subdivision thereof which has a fair employment practice law during any period in which such employer, employment agency, labor organization, or joint labor-management committee is subject to such law, except that the Commission may require such notations on records which such employer, employment agency, labor organization, or joint labor-management committee keeps or is required to keep as are necessary because of differences in coverage or methods of enforcement between the State or local law and the provisions of this title. Where an employer is required by Executive Order 10925, issued March 6, 1961, or by an other Executive order prescribing fair employment practices for Government contractors and subcontractors, or by rules or regulations issued thereunder, to file reports relating to his employment practices with any Federal agency or committee, and he is substantially in compliance with such requirements, the Commission shall not require him to file additional reports pursuant to subsection (c) of this section.

(e) It shall be unlawful for any officer or employee of the Commission to make public in any manner whatever any information obtained by the Commission pursuant to its authority under this section prior to the institution of any proceeding under this title involving such information. Any officer or employee of the Commission who shall make public in any manner whatever any information in violation of this subsection shall be guilty of a misdemeanor and upon conviction thereof, shall be fined not more than $1,000, or imprisoned not more than one year.

INVESTIGATORY POWERS

Sec. 710. (a) For the purposes of any investigation of a charge filed under the authority contained in section 706, the Commission shall have authority to examine witnesses under oath and to require the production of documentary evidence relevant or material to the charge under investigation.

(b) If the respondent named in a charge filed under section 706 fails or refuses to comply with a demand of the Commission for permission to examine or to copy evidence in conformity with the provisions of section 709(a), or if any person required to comply with the provisions of section 709 (c) or (d) fails or refuses to do so, or if any person fails or refuses to comply with a demand by the Commission to give testimony under oath, the United States district court for the district in which such person is found, resides, or transacts business, shall, upon application of the Commission, have jurisdiction to issue to such person an order requiring him to comply with the provisions of section 709 (c) or (d) or to comply with the demand of the Commission, but the attendance of a witness may not be required outside the State where he is found, resides, or transacts business and the production of evidence may not be required outside the State where such evidence is kept.

(c) Within twenty days after the service upon any person charged under section 706 of a demand by the Commission for the production of documentary evidence or for permission to examine or to copy evidence in conformity with the provisions of section 709(a), such person may file in the district court of the United States for the judicial district in which he resides, is found, or transacts business, and serve upon the Commission a petition for an order of such court modifiying or setting aside such demand. The time allowed for compliance with the demand in whole or in part as deemed proper and ordered by the court shall not run during the pendency of such petition in the court. Such petition shall specify each ground upon which the petitioner relies in seeking such relief, and may be based upon any failure of such demand to comply with the provisions of this title or with the limitations generally applicable to compulsory process or upon any constitutional or other legal right or privilege of such person. No objection which is not raised by such a petition may be urged in the defense to a proceeding initiated by the Commission under subsection (b) for enforcement of such a demand unless such proceeding is commenced by the Commission prior to the expiration of the twenty-day period, or unless the court determines that the defendant could not reasonably have been aware of the availability of such ground of objection.

(d) In any proceeding brought by the Commission under subsection (b), except as provided in subsection (c) of this section, the defendant may petition the court for an order modifying or setting aside the demand of the Commission.

NOTICES TO BE POSTED

SEC. 711. (a) Every employer, employment agency, and labor organization, as the case may be, shall post and keep posted in conspicuous places upon its premises where notices to employees, applicants for employment, and members are customarily posted a notice to be prepared or approved by the Commission setting forth excerpts from, or summaries of, the pertinent provisions of this title and information pertinent to the filing of a complaint.

(b) A willful violation of this section shall be punishable by a fine of not more than $100 for each separate offense.

VETERANS' PREFERENCE

SEC. 712. Nothing contained in this title shall be construed to repeal or modify any Federal, State, territorial, or local law creating special rights or preference for veterans.

RULES AND REGULATIONS

SEC. 713 (a) The Commission shall have authority from time to time to issue, amend, or rescind suitable procedural regulations to carry out the provisions of this title. Regulations issued under this section shall be in conformity with the standards and limitations of the Administrative Procedure Act.

(b) In any action or proceeding based on any alleged unlawful employment practice, no person shall be subject to any liability or punishment for or on account of (1) the commission by such person of an unlawful employment practice if he pleads and proves that the act or omission complained of was in good faith, in conformity with, and in reliance on any written interpretation or opinion of the Commission, or (2) the failure of such person to publish and file any information required by any provision of this title if he pleads and proves that he failed to publish and file such information in good faith, in conformity with the instructions of the Commission issued under this title regarding the filing of such information. Such a defense, if established, shall be a bar to the action or proceeding, notwithstanding that (A) after such act or omission, such interpretation or opinion is modified or rescinded or is determined by judicial authority to be invalid or of no legal effect, or (B) after publishing or filing the description and annual reports, such publication or filing is determined by judicial authority not to be in conformity with the requirements of this title.

FORCIBLY RESISTING THE COMMISSION OR ITS REPRESENTATIVES

SEC. 714. The provisions of section 111, title 18, United States Code, shall apply to officers, agents, and employees of the Commission in the performance of their official duties.

SPECIAL STUDY BY SECRETARY OF LABOR

SEC. 715. The Secretary of Labor shall make a full and complete study of the factors which might tend to result in discrimination in employment because of age and of the consequences of such discrimination on the economy and individuals affected. The Secretary of Labor shall make a report to the Congress not later than June 30, 1965, containing the results of such study and shall include in such report such recommendations for legislation to prevent arbitrary discrimination in employment because of age as he determines advisable.

EFFECTIVE DATE

SEC. 716. (a) This title shall become effective one year after the date of its enactment.

(b) Notwithstanding subsection (a), sections of this title other than sections 703, 704, 706, and 707 shall become effective immediately.

(c) The President shall, as soon as feasible after the enactment of this title, convene one or more conferences for the purpose of enabling the leaders of groups whose members will be affected by this title to become familiar with the rights afforded and obligations imposed by its provisions, and for the purpose of making plans which will result in the fair and effective administration of this title when all of its provisions become effective. The President shall invite the participation in such conference or conferences of (1) the members of the President's Committee on Equal Employment Opportunity, (2) the members of the Commission on Civil Rights, (3) representatives of State and local agencies engaged in furthering equal employment opportunity, (4) representatives of private agencies engaged in furthering equal employment opportunity, and (5) representatives of employers, labor organizations, and employment agencies who will be subject to this title.

Title VIII—Registration and Voting Statistics

SEC. 801. The Secretary of Commerce shall promptly conduct a survey to compile registration and voting statistics in such geographic areas as may be recommended by the Commission on Civil Rights. Such a survey and compilation shall, to the extent recommended by the Commission on Civil Rights, only include a count of persons of voting age by race, color, and national origin, and determination of the extent to which such persons are registered to vote, and have voted in any statewide primary or general election in which the Members of the United States House of Representatives are nominated or elected, since January 1, 1960. Such information shall also be collected and compiled in connection with the Nineteenth Decennial Census, and at such other times as the Congress may prescribe. The provisions of section 9 and chapter 7 of title 13, United States Code, shall apply to any survey, collection, or compilation of registration and voting statistics carried out under this title: *Provided, however,* That no person shall be compelled to disclose his race, color, national origin, or questioned about his political party affiliation, how he voted, or the reasons therefore, nor shall any penalty be imposed for his failure or refusal to make such disclosure. Every person interrogated orally, by written survey or questionnaire or by any other means with respect to such information shall be fully advised with respect to his right to fail or refuse to furnish such information.

Title IX—Intervention and Procedure After Removal in Civil Rights Cases

SEC. 901. Title 28 of the United States Code, section 1447(d), is amended to read as follows:

"An order remanding a case to the State court from which it was removed is not reviewable on appeal or otherwise, except that an order remanding a case to the State court from which it was removed pursuant to section 1443 of this title shall be reviewable by appeal or otherwise."

SEC. 902. Whenever an action has been commenced in any court of the United States seeking relief from the denial of equal protection of the laws under the fourteenth amendment to the Constitution on account of race, color, religion, or national origin, the Attorney General for or in the name of the United States may intervene in such action upon timely application if the Attorney General certifies that the case is of general public importance. In such action the United States shall be entitled to the same relief as if it had instituted the action.

Title X—Establishment of Community Relations Service

SEC. 1001. (a) There is hereby established in and as a part of the Department of Commerce a Community Relations Service (hereinafter referred to as the "Service"), which shall be headed by a Director who shall be appointed by the President with the advice and consent of the Senate for a term of four years. The Director is authorized to appoint, subject to the civil service laws and regulations, such other personnel as may be necessary to enable the Service to carry out its functions and duties, and to fix their compensation in accordance with the Classification Act of 1949, as amended. The Director is further authorized to procure services as authorized by section 15 of the Act of August 2, 1946 (60 Stat. 810; 5 U.S.C. 55(a)), but at rates for individuals not in excess of $75 per diem.

(b) Section 106(a) of the Federal Executive Pay Act of 1956, as amended (5 U.S.C. 2205(a)), is further amended by adding the following clause thereto:

"(52) Director, Community Relations Service."

SEC. 1002. It shall be the function of the Service to provide assistance to communities and persons therein in resolving disputes, disagreements, or difficulties relating to discriminatory practices based on race, color, or national origin which impair the rights of persons in such communities under the Constitution or laws of the United States or which affect or may affect interstate commerce. The Service may offer its services in cases of such disputes, disagreements, or difficulties, whenever, in its judgment, peaceful relations among the citizens of the community involved are threatened thereby, and it may offer its services either upon its own motion or upon the request of an appropriate State or local official or other interested person.

SEC. 1003. (a) The Service shall, whenever possible, in performing its functions, seek and utilize the cooperation of appropriate State or local, public, or private agencies.

(b) The activities of all officers and employees of the Service in providing conciliation assistance shall be conducted in confidence and without publicity, and the Service shall hold confidentially any information acquired in the regular performance of its duties upon the understanding that it would be so held. No officer or employee of the Service shall engage in the performance of investigative or prosecuting functions of any department or agency in any litigation arising out of a dispute in which he acted on behalf of the Service. Any officer or other employee of the Service, who shall make public in any manner whatever any information in violation of this subsection, shall be deemed guilty of a misdemeanor and, upon conviction thereof, shall be fined not more that $1,000 or imprisoned not more than one year.

SEC. 1004. Subject to the provisions of sections 205 and 1003(b), the Director shall, on or before January 31 of each year, submit to the Congress a report of the activities of the Service during the preceding fiscal year.

Title XI—Miscellaneous

SEC. 1101. In any proceeding for criminal contempt arising under title II, III, IV, V, VI, or VII of this Act, the accused, upon demand therefor, shall be entitled to a trial by jury, which shall conform as near as may be to the practice in criminal cases. Upon conviction, the accused shall not be fined more than $1,000 or imprisoned for more than six months.

This section shall not apply to contempts committed in the presence of the court, or so near thereto as to obstruct the administration of justice, nor to the misbehavior, misconduct, or disobedience of any officer of the court in respect to writs, orders, or process of the court. No person shall be convicted of criminal contempt hereunder unless the act or omission constituting such contempt shall have been intentional, as required in other cases of criminal contempt.

Nor shall anything herein be construed to deprive courts of their power, by civil contempt proceedings, without a jury, to secure compliance with or to prevent obstruction of, as distinguished from punishment for violations of, any lawful writ, process, order, rule, decree, or command of the court in accordance with the prevailing usages of law and equity, including the power of detention.

SEC. 1102. No person should be put twice in jeopardy under the laws of the United States for the same act or omission. For this reason, an acquittal or conviction in a prosecution for a specific crime under the laws of the United States shall bar a proceeding for criminal contempt, which is based upon the same act or omission and which arises under the provisions of this Act; and an acquittal or conviction in a proceeding for criminal contempt, which arises under the provisions of this Act, shall bar a prosecution for a specific crime under the laws of the United States based upon the same act or omission.

SEC. 1103. Nothing in this Act shall be construed to deny, impair, or otherwise affect any right or authority of the Attorney General or of the United States or any agency or officer thereof under existing law to institute or intervene in any action or proceeding.

SEC. 1104. Nothing contained in any title of this Act shall be construed as indicating an intent on the part of Congress to occupy the field in which any such title operates to the exclusion of State laws on the same subject matter, nor shall any provision of this Act be construed as invalidating any provision of State law unless such provision is inconsistent with any of the purposes of this Act, or any provision thereof.

SEC. 1105. There are hereby authorized to be appropriated such sums as are necessary to carry out the provisions of this Act.

SEC. 1106. If any provision of this Act or the application thereof to any person or circumstances is held invalid, the remainder of the Act and the application of the provision to other persons not similarly situated or to other circumstances shall not be affected thereby.

Approved July 2, 1964.

Supplementing the Civil Rights Act of 1964 is Public Law 90-284 passed by Congress in 1968. Among other things, the federal statute prohibits discrimination in sale or rental of 80 percent of all housing. Most housing built with federal assistance, such as public housing and urban renewal projects, were covered immediately on enactment of the bill in April 1968.

On January 1, 1969, coverage was extended to all multiple units except for owner-occupied dwellings with no more than four units. Also covered were single-family houses, such as real estate developments that were not owned by private individuals. Privately owned single-family homes sold or rented by real estate agents or brokers were covered as of January 1, 1970.

Private owners selling or renting their houses without the services of a real estate agent or broker are exempt. The ban against discrimination also applies to financing and brokerage services.

Criminal penalties for injuring or interfering with a person because he is exercising specific rights, including rights to vote, to serve on a jury, to participate in government or government-aided programs, to work, to attend school or college, and to enjoy public accommodation are also provided.

Penalties are also included for the manufacturing of or teaching the use of firearms or explosives for use in a civil disorder.

CLEAN HANDS The doctrine that relief may be denied in equity because of the injurious and unfair conduct of the one seeking relief.

CLIENT One who employs or retains an attorney, solicitor, proctor or counselor to appear for him in court, to advise, assist and defend him in legal proceedings and to act for him in any legal business.

CLOSE CORPORATION A corporation wherein a major part of the persons to whom the corporate powers have been granted have the right to fill vacancies occurring in their ranks.

CLOSING OF TITLE In real property, the time when the buyer of a piece of real estate pays the money due under the contract in exchange for a deed to the property.

CLOUD ON TITLE Some claim or encumbrance which affects or impairs the title of the owner of a particular estate, but which can be shown by proof to be invalid or inapplicable to the property in question.

CODE A collection or compilation of laws by public authority. A code may be either a mere compilation of existing laws, or a new system of laws founded on new fundamental principles.

CODE CIVIL A code of law prepared under the direction of Napoleon, and promulgated in 1804, as the civil law of France.

CODICIL An addition to a will explaining, adding to, or subtracting from it. It must be executed with the same solemnity as a will.

COGNIZANCE Acknowledgment or recognition of right. Acknowledgment, confession or admission. The name of an answer made by a defendant in an action of replevin, where he has acted as bailiff to another in making a distress, by which he acknowledges the taking, but insists that such taking was legal, as he acted by the command of one who had a right to distrain. Judicial notice or examination; the hearing of a matter judicially; as, "to take cognizance of a cause."

COIF In English practice, a covering for the head, formerly worn as a distinctive badge by sergeants-at-law.

CO-INSURER A term in a fire insurance policy that requires the insured to bear a certain portion of the loss when he fails to carry complete coverage. For example, unless the insured carries insurance which totals 80 percent of the value of the property, the insurer shall be liable for only that portion of the loss that the total insurance carried bears to 80 percent of the value of the property.

COLLATERAL Connected by, or on the side. Coming in, or adhering to the side of any thing. Heirs coming in, on, or from the side; collateral heirs.

COLLATERAL With reference to debts or other obligations, the term "collateral" means security placed with a creditor to secure the performance of the obligor. If the obligor performs, the collateral is returned by the creditor. A owes B $1,000. To secure the payments, A places with B a $500 certificate of stock in X Company. The $500 certificate is called collateral security.

COLLATERAL ANCESTORS Relatives, including uncles and aunts, who are predecessors but not actually ancestors.

COLLATERAL ATTACK An attempt to impeach a decree, a judgment or other official act in a proceeding which has not been instituted for the express purpose of correcting or annulling or modifying the decree, judgment or official act.

COLLATERAL FACTS Facts foreign to the matter at issue.

COLLATERAL INHERITANCE TAX A tax levied on property after the death of the testator, collateral ancestors being usually used to designate uncles, aunts and others who are not strictly ancestors of the deceased. (*See also* INHERITANCE TAX.)

COLLATERAL ISSUE An issue not pertinent to the merits of a case.

COLLATERAL PROCEEDINGS Proceedings which are not direct impeachments of a prior cause but may call it into question.

COLLATERAL SECURITY In banking practice, any security required in addition to the borrower's promise or security given for a loan or a debt.

COLLATION In civil law, the return to an estate of property received in advance by an heir for the purpose of equal distribution.

COLLOQUIUM In pleading. Conversation; discourse. A term applied to that part of the declaration in actions of slander, where it is alleged that the defendant spoke the words in a certain discourse or conversation which he had with others, or with the plaintiff in the presence of others, concerning the plaintiff.

COLLUSION A secret combination or conspiracy between two or more persons having a fraudulent or deceitful purpose.

COLOR OF OFFICE The claim or assumption of the right to do an act by virtue of an office.

CO-MAKER A person who with another or others signs a negotiable instrument on its face and thereby becomes primarily liable for its payment.

COMITY AMONG NATIONS The friendly relations existing between them so that the laws and institutions of each are recognized by the other.

COMMERCIAL LAW That branch of the law used to designate the rules that determine the rights and duties of persons engaged in trade and commerce. The Law of Negotiable Instruments, the Law of Partnership, and the Law of Sales are examples of commercial law.

COMMINATORY Threatening, coercive. Denoting a penalty in a business agreement so heavy as to be unenforceable.

COMMISSION The sum of money, interest, brokerage, compensation, or allowance given to a factor or broker for carrying on the business of his principal.

COMMISSION MERCHANT One who sells goods in his own name at his own store, and on commission, from sample. Also one who buys and sells goods for a principal in his own name and without disclosing his principal.

COMMITMENT The order of a court which directs a person to be kept in custody either in a penal or a mental institution. The warrant, order or process by which a court or magistrate directs a lawful officer to take a person to prison, either to await trial or to serve a sentence imposed by law. A person may be committed to await trial either when he is unable to put up bail, or when he is charged with a crime which may not be bailable, such as first degree murder or high treason. Commitments for whatever reason should be in writing. They should plainly state the name and address of the person committed, the name of the committing magistrate or judge, the offense charged, and the amount of bail for lack of which the prisoner is committed. If, after commitment, the prisoner is able to arrange for his bail, he will be released, upon proper application, to await trial.

COMMON A profit which a man has in the land of another; as to feed his beasts, to catch fish, to dig turf, to cut wood or the like. A right or privilege which one or more persons claim, to take or use some part of that which another man's lands, waters, woods, etc., naturally produce, without having an absolute property in such lands, waters, woods, etc. A privilege which a man may enjoy, of taking a profit in common with many, in the land of another, as to feed his beasts, etc. A right of taking a profit in the land of another, in common either with the owner or with other persons. The radical meaning of the term common, in all its applications is—something enjoyed by more than one person; properly, by many together.

COMMON CARRIER One whose business or calling is to carry chattels or portable personal property for all persons who may choose to employ and remunerate him. It may be by railroad, bus, boat, etc., etc., and the undertaking may be to carry goods from one part of a town to another or between different places at a distance from each other or from one country to another, or across the sea and without respect to the motive power used.

Common carriers are responsible for loss and damages during transportation from whatever cause or agency, except a public enemy or act of God, by which latter is meant inevitable accidents that occur without the intervention of man's agency. For loss occurring from ordinary natural causes such as frost, fermentation, evaporation, natural decay or necessary wear in transportation, the carrier is not responsible, provided he exercise all reasonable care to prevent such loss or deterioration. Railroads in operating their trains are bound to exercise diligence in the use of the most effective means to prevent sparks from flying from engines and setting property on fire.

Common carriers have public duties to perform, and for their usual or a reasonable compensation, are bound to carry, so far as their ability and capacity allow, all things coming within their particular lines of business, and unless the goods would endanger them or they would themselves incur extraordinary danger. If they do not they are liable to suit, but they are not bound to accept goods of a character and description not commonly carried by them, or in other words which it is not their regular business to carry.

The carrier may require freight charges to be paid in advance, but, in a suit for refusing to carry, it is only necessary to show a readiness to pay and not an actual tender of money, where the carrier refuses to accept the goods. A carrier has a lien on the goods themselves for freight and for advances made to other carriers and may hold them until this is paid. Generally the shipper or consignor is liable for the freight.

The responsibility of the carrier may be varied by a special contract, also by simple notice on his part to the shipper qualifying his responsibility, such notice or qualification being assented to by the shipper, but no such notice will excuse gross negligence on the part of the carrier. The contract between the shipper and the carrier is a bill of lading which is also a receipt for the goods, and this is expected to contain any exemption from responsibility which the carrier can or does claim.

This contract cannot be avoided by verbal evidence, yet the bill of lading is not conclusive in its statement of the quantity or condition of the goods receipted for, especially if there is no opportunity to inspect them when receipted. Carriers on whose trains or boats express companies transmit goods are themselves liable to the owner for loss or damage to the same notwithstanding the contract with the express company.

The liability for loss or injury to baggage of passengers is the same as that for other goods carried as freight, and this responsibility exists until the baggage is delivered to the passenger or to someone on his order. If baggage is checked over a succession of lines owned by different companies, each company is responsible for the whole route. The baggage check is prima facie evidence of the liability of the company. It stands in the place of a receipt or bill of lading.

The responsibility of common carriers begins with the delivery of the goods to them for transportation either at the usual place of receiving freight or to an employee of the company in the usual place of business. If goods delivered at a warehouse are not to be forwarded until some future event occurs, the carrier in the meantime is only responsible as a depositary, or if goods are received by the parties merely as/wharfingers, or warehousemen for the time being and not as carriers, there will be liability only in case of lack of ordinary care until the functions of carriers begin. Where goods are to pass over successive lines having no partnership connection, the respective carriers are liable only from the time of receiving the goods, but if there is such a business connection between the carriers composing the route that each one may give bills of lading for the entire route, the rule is to the contrary.

The liability terminates after a sufficient time has elapsed from the arrival of the goods at their destination for the owner to receive them at the proper station or wharf in business hours. After that the carrier may put them in the warehouse and will be responsible as a warehouseman for ordinary care. As to goods arriving by water, however, the carrier is bound to give notice to the consignee of the arrival of the goods in order to relieve himself from a carrier's responsibility, and carriers by truck are supposed to deliver the goods at the proper parties' place of business or residence or where directed. Agents of corporations which are common carriers will bind their principals to the full extent of the business entrusted to them whether they follow instructions or not, and even if they wilfully disregard their instructions.

Known usage and custom in the course of the business of carriers will be read into contracts, and will control and qualify them unless the contracts stipulate to the contrary. Those who do business with them are considered to do so in accordance with uniform usages and customs of long standing, and generally known and understood by those familiar with the business.

The carrier having so great a degree of responsibility may have goods in his charge insured against fire or marine disasters, but not against matters for which he is not responsible, the so-called acts of God. He is bound only to deliver goods within a reasonable time under all the circumstances unless he absolutely contracts to deliver at a particular time, in which case he must pay damages.

Whether the time is reasonable or not under the circumstances, in case of dispute it must be determined by a jury. For failure to deliver goods through default of his the damages will be measured by the value of the goods at the point of destination which includes the profits thereon. If the goods are delivered in a damaged condition or not delivered in time, the recovery will be in accordance with the amount of damages actually incurred. The owner cannot refuse the goods and claim a total loss.

COMMON CARRIERS OF PASSENGERS Common carriers of passengers are those who carry persons for hire, such as automobiles, airplanes, steamships, etc. They are bound to carry all desiring passage over their whole route or part of it, in accord with their general usage and the customs of their business, but are not bound to carry persons who are guilty of offensive, indecent and disorderly conduct or so offensive in character, health or habits as to be unsuitable companions for other passengers. They are not required to do what is impossible, as when travel is unexpectedly large and their means are exhausted.

Non-payment of fare is sufficient cause of ejection from a train. If parent and child are on a train together, the latter being of such age that he is required to pay under the company's rules, and the former pays and no payment is made for the latter, an ejectment of the child will operate as an ejectment also of the parent who follows the child though voluntarily. Such an ejection is unlawful unless the unearned portion of the parent's fare is returned.

Passenger carriers are bound to exercise the very highest degree of care and watchfulness to secure the safety of their passengers, who have an unquestionable right to demand of them all that human foresight can accomplish in securing their safety, but if injury results from a cause which no degree of watchfulness in the carrier would enable him to discover, he is not liable.

Carriers of passengers, however, are not insurers of the safety of their passengers as are carriers of goods, but as to baggage, the responsibilities are those of a common carrier. (*See also* COMMON CARRIER.) If an employee of a passenger carrier, as a captain of a steamboat or conductor of a train, is allowed to carry parcels, the carrier is responsible for their safe delivery though the employee is not required to pay over what he receives as compensation.

The mere fact that a passenger has not paid his fare will not excuse the carrier's negligence or failure to exercise the required care. The passenger, however, must be willing and ready to pay the fare in accordance with the established regulations of the carrier, but an actual tender of the passage money is not necessary in order to hold the carrier responsible for damages for refusal to carry and much less for an injury sustained. Owing to the custom of paying fare in advance, the implication will be that one already on a train has paid his fare, but this may be rebutted by proof.

If an injury results in any degree from the negligence of the passenger, the carrier will not be responsible even though he himself is negligent unless there is intentional wrong on his, the carrier's part, or unless the passenger's negligence contribute to the injury and the carrier's lack of care or culpability is the immediate cause; or unless, though there is want of prudence on the part of the passenger, the defendant is guilty of such a degree of negligence that the plaintiff could not hope to escape the consequences whether prudent or not. A passenger leaping from a car from a just sense of peril for which the carrier is responsible may yet recover.

A railroad company is liable for damages to a passenger whom the conductor permits a drunken and disorderly fellow passenger to insult and abuse, or for injuries inflicted upon the passenger by an attack from an employee in the course of his employment. A railroad company owes to a sick passenger the best care practicable under the circumstances, and without unduly retarding the train and interfering with its duties to other passengers. A conductor knowing a passenger on the platform to be intoxicated as to be incapable of taking care of himself, should see that he does not remain on the platform.

The sale of a through ticket over several lines owned by companies having no partnership relation will not render any of the companies liable excepting the one in default or guilty of the negligence. By statute the right to recover for an injury survives the death of the injured. A passenger injured through negligence of the carrier is entitled to recover damages to the time of trial, and all prospective damages likely to accrue. (*See also* DAMAGES.)

The over-turning of a bus or injury of a passenger on a railway raises a presumption of negligence on the part of the carrier which of course may be rebutted. An injury to a passenger on a railway is prima facie evidence of negligence on the part of the company. A pilot is considered the agent of the owner of the vessel he is piloting, and his direction of the vessel will not ordinarily exonerate the owner from responsibility.

COMMON COUNTS In pleading. Counts of invariable form, framed upon certain general principles of statement, and therefore common in their application to a great variety of actions. It is distinguished from special counts, which are adapted to the special circumstances of each particular case, and are peculiar to the individual actions in which they are employed.

COMMON LAW Those principles, usages and rules of action applicable to the government and security of persons and property which do not rest for their authority on any express and positive declaration of the will of the legislature. The common law of England is the common law of the United States except as it has been altered by statute or judicial decision. This does not apply, however, to Louisiana, the law of which is based upon the civil law or Roman jurisprudence because Louisiana was formerly a French possession and in France the civil law prevails.

COMMON LAW MARRIAGE One which lacks a wedding ceremony but is created by the couple holding themselves out as man and wife and actually living as such. A number of states fail to recognize the validity of such marriages.

COMMON NUISANCE A nuisance affecting the public, being an annoyance to the whole community in general; it is distinguished from a private nuisance, which is confined in its effects to particular individuals.

COMMON SCOLD One who by frequent scolding disturbs the neighborhood. This was punishable at one time by the ducking stool at common law, for which fine and imprisonment are now substituted.

COMMUNITY PROPERTY Property acquired during marriage by husband and wife, or either, which was not acquired as the separate property of either. Community property states include Arizona, California, Idaho, Louisiana, Nevada, New Mexico, Texas and Washington. In these states, property owned before marriage remains separate, except in Texas, Louisiana and Idaho, where it becomes community property.

Even in community property states, the parties, by contract, before or after the marriage, may hold their property separately. After separation or divorce, the court may dispose of all property, whether separate or community, as it sees fit, regardless of the wishes of the party who actually accumulated the property.

At death, most of the community property states allow a surviving spouse to retain only half of the community property. Finally, it should be noted that in the eight community property states, a wife has a vested interest in her husband's earnings and assets acquired during the marriage.

COMMUTATION The change of a punishment from a greater to a lesser; as from hanging to imprisonment.

COMMUTATION OF SENTENCE The reduction of punishment or sentence after conviction for a crime. Such power is generally vested in either the pardoning board of a state or by the governor. A reduction in sentence, after conviction, is not a matter of right, but one of grace, privilege or favor. The power to commute or reduce a sentence after imprisonment is broad. A death sentence may be commuted to life imprisonment or for a term of years. A ten-year sentence may be reduced to one year. One commutation of sentence does not necessarily preclude further reduction. A man originally sentenced to death may have his sentence reduced to life imprisonment. He may, upon further application, have his sentence further reduced. A commutation does not remove the stigma of guilt or restore civil privileges, such as the right to vote or hold public office, except by operation of a specific statute. Commuted sentences may be revoked where they have been obtained by fraud. A commutation

of sentence may be conditional. It may be conditioned on the prisoner's future behavior; or that he abide by the rules imposed by the commuting authority. The commission of a new crime, after commutation, ordinarily revokes the commutation, so that the prisoner may be compelled to serve not only the full original sentence, but another sentence for the new crime. A sentence can be commuted to the point where the prisoner is completely discharged from serving any future time. A prisoner applying for commutation is usually allowed to state his reasons for requesting a reduction in sentence, either in person or through counsel.

COMPARATIVE NEGLIGENCE A principle of law which takes into account the negligence of both sides in an accident.

COMPENSATORY DAMAGES A sum of money awarded to a plaintiff by a court or jury as a fair and just recompense for injury sustained to person, property or reputation.

COMPETENCY In the law of evidence, the presence of facts that legally qualify a witness as fit to testify.

COMPLAINANT *In equity,* the petitioner; *at law,* the plaintiff; *in criminal law,* one who files a formal accusation of crime.

COMPOSITION WITH CREDITORS A settlement with creditors for a reduced amount by one unable to pay his debts in full, the creditors relinquishing all further claim against him.

COMPOUNDING CRIMES Compounding a felony is the act of a party immediately aggrieved in agreeing with a thief or other felon, not to prosecute. Merely taking back the goods stolen is no offense unless the owner agrees not to prosecute. A mere failure to prosecute is not compounding a felony but the accepting of a promissory note signed by the thief as a consideration for not prosecuting is sufficient to constitute the offense and to render one guilty. Compounding felonies is criminal. So is compounding misdemeanors where the injury is particularly to an individual who would have a right to recover in a civil suit, as in case of embezzlement. Where the offense is serious in character or of a notably public nature no agreement to stifle a prosecution is valid. Generally it may be said that where a prosecution has been instituted and there is evidence to support the charge, there should be no settlement of the case except by express permission of the court. No recovery can be had in any agreement or obligation given for compounding felonies or misdemeanors where the compounding of such misdemeanors is illegal.

COMPREHENSIVE AUTOMOBILE INSURANCE COVERAGE A policy of insurance which covers the owner of an automobile for damage to his car resulting from certain stated risks.

COMPROMISE Any adjustment by mutual concession of matters in dispute, without resort to the law.

CONCEALMENT The improper suppression of a fact or circumstance by a party to a contract which in justice ought to be known to the other party to enable him to form a correct judgment regarding the matter. Thus one applying for insurance who suppresses facts material to the risk and known to him at the time or who makes a false statement of facts in answer to questions propounded to him whether material or not, will void the insurance. Any concealment when fraudulent voids a contract or renders the party offending liable for damages that may arise therefrom. The concealment must be regarding facts which the party is bound to communicate. Where the other party has full opportunity to observe for himself but does not do so, there is no fraudulent concealment.

Latent defects in the subject of the contract which cannot be observed by examination should be made known. The act of concealment is more fraudulent or rather the rule as to fraud is more stringent where the party practicing it stands in a fiduciary or confidential relation to the person against whom it is practiced.

CONCLUSIVE EVIDENCE Evidence, which, in its nature, does not admit of explanation or contradiction. Evidence which, of itself, whether contradicted or uncontradicted, explained or unexplained, is sufficient to determine the matter at issue.

CONCLUSIVE PRESUMPTION A species of presumption of law, which cannot be disputed or rebutted.

CONCUBINE A woman with whom a man cohabits without marriage, as distinguished from a lawful wife.

CONCURRENT Running with, simultaneous with. The word is used in different senses. In contracts, concurrent conditions are conditions which must be performed simultaneously by the mutual acts required by each of the parties.

CONCURSU A proceeding in Louisiana law allowing conflicting claims among creditors to be resolved in a suit against the debtor.

CONCUSSION In civil law, extortion, the taking of property by threats of violence.

CONDEMNATION The sentence of a court of competent jurisdiction that a ship or vessel taken on the high seas was liable to capture, and was legally captured; the taking of private property for public, or quasi-public use, by legal proceedings.

CONDITION A provision or clause in a contract which operates to suspend or rescind the principal obligation. A qualification or restriction annexed to a conveyance of lands, whereby it is provided that in the case a particular event does or does not happen, or in case the grantor or grantees do or omit to do a particular act, an estate shall begin, be enlarged or be defeated. Conditions are of frequent occurrence in deeds and wills. A condition annexed to a bond whereby in a certain event it is to be void is termed a defeasance. A mortgage is a conveyance of land with a condition that it be defeated upon the happening of a given event, to wit, the payment of a given amount of money.

The conditions which require the performance of acts forbidden by law or which require the omission of some act commanded by law or which encourage such unlawful acts and omissions are unlawful and void. A condition must be made at the same time as the original conveyance or contract, and may be in any part of the instrument, and may even be by a separate instrument, the whole being considered as one transaction.

Conditions in restraint of marriage generally are held void. Therefore a grant, bequest or devise to one with such a condition annexed will remain good even though the condition is violated, but conditions in restraint of a particular marriage, that is, to a particular person or restraining a widow from a second marriage are not void. A condition in general restraint of alienation or conveyance is void, but not with one in restraint of alienation for a limited time.

Where land is devised upon condition there need be no statement in the devise as to what is to become of the land upon violation of the condition in order that the condition may be valid, though the contrary is true in case of a bequest of personal property. If there is a direction as to the subsequent disposition of the personalty in the event of non-compliance with the condition the bequest is divested upon such non-compliances.

Conditions which go to defeat an estate or destroy an act are strictly construed, that is, the estate or act will be sustained if possible, while those which go to vest an estate are liberally construed, that is, so as to establish the estate if possible. The condition of an obligation is presumably construed to suit the obligee or one to whom it is given, and for that reason will be construed liberally in favor of the obligor or one executing it. However, where an obligation is imposed by a condition it will be liberally construed in favor of the obligee.

For a condition to be effective, performance must be complete and effectual, though an inconsiderable casual failure to perform will be construed as performance, since it would not be equitable that an inconsequential failure should defeat the intention. Anyone in interest may perform a condition and obtain the benefit, but a stranger or outsider can derive no benefit from performing it. Conditions to be fulfilled precedent to the vesting of land must be strictly performed even if relating to marriage. But in cases of conditions subsequent, as where the property vests and the vesting is to continue upon the condition that a certain thing shall or shall not be performed, a court of equity will relieve where there is only a delay of performance or where there has been part performance only, if performance is possible and the parties are ready and willing to perform. An example is in a mortgage, for though the condition is not fulfilled at the time indicated, to wit, when the mortgage comes due, yet the condition may be subsequently complied with and the mortgage still becomes void.

Generally where there is a gift over to someone else in case of nonperformance, the parties will be held more strictly to a performance than where the estate or gift is to go back to the grantor or his heirs. If no time of performance is mentioned the one who has the benefit of the contract or conveyance or devise may perform any time during his life, and is not required to do so merely upon request unless a prompt performance would be necessary to carry out the general intent of the grantor or testator. If the place of performance is designated or agreed upon neither party can change it without the consent of the other.

Non-performance will be excused if rendered impossible by act of God, or by act of the law, even though performance were possible at the time the condition was made. If it is made impossible by the act of the party imposing the condition or if such party accepts another thing in lieu of the performance of the condition and it seems that if performance of only part of the condition becomes impossible by the act of God, the whole will be generally excused.

CONDITION PRECEDENT A condition preceding an estate; a condition which must happen, or be performed, before the estate to which it is annexed can vest or be enlarged. A condition preceding the accruing of a right or liability. An act essential to be performed by one party, prior to any obligation attaching upon another party, to do or perform another given act.

CONDITION RESTRICTIVE A condition for not doing a thing; as, for example, that a tenant shall not remove or destroy the fixtures in an apartment.

CONDITION SUBSEQUENT A condition following an estate. A condition annexed to an estate already vested, by the performance of which such estate is kept and continued, and by the failure or non-performance of which it is defeated.

CONDITIONAL ACCEPTANCE An acceptance of a bill of exchange containing some qualification limiting or altering the acceptor's liability on the bill.

CONDITIONAL FEE A fee restrained in its form of donation to some particular heirs, exclusive of others, as the heirs of a man's body, by which only his lineal descendants were admitted, in exclusion of collateral heirs.

CONDONATION The conditional forgiveness by a husband or wife of a matrimonial offense which is a ground for divorce, the condition being that the offense should not be repeated. However, should the offense be repeated, the party aggrieved has a right to proceed with the original ground for divorce.

CONFESSED JUDGMENT NOTE A note which allows the holder or the person to whom it is payable to appear before a Justice of the Peace and obtain judgment simply by making affidavit before him that the note is bona fide. This precludes the holder from filing formal proceedings in court and enables him to obtain judgment more or less automatically.

CONFESSED JUDGMENT NOTE

$_____ 19____

_____ after date _____ promise to

pay to the order of _____

_____ Dollars

Payable at _____

Without defalcation, value received, with interest

    And further, _____ do hereby empower any Attorney of any Court of Record within the United States or elsewhere to appear for _____ and after one or more declarations filed, confess judgment against _____ as of any term for the above sum with Costs of suit and Attorney's commission of _____ per cent for collection and release of all errors, and without stay of execution and inquisition and extension upon any levy on real estate is hereby waived, and condemnation agreed to and the exemption of personal property from levy and sale on any execution hereon, is also hereby expressly waived, and no benefit of exemption be claimed under and by virtue of any exemption law now in force or which may be hereafter passed.

Witness _____ hand and seal   _____(SEAL)

No. _____ Date _____   _____(SEAL)

CONFESSION The voluntary declaration by a person who has committed a crime or misdemeanor to another. The word "confession" also applies where a prisoner, when arraigned for an offense, acknowledges that he committed the crime with which he is charged. Confessions, if voluntary, are admissible as against the party making them, but not if obtained by inducement, threats, promises or hope of favor held out to him by a person in authority; nor is such confession admissible where there is reason to presume that a person in authority was understood by the party confessing to sanction such threat or inducement or promise. A confession is admissible if the inducement was from a person not in authority over the prisoner, or if the inducement is merely spiritual. The temporal inducement to prevent the use of the confession as evidence must usually have been held out by the person to whom the confession was made.

A confession where no threats or inducements are made or offered as above indicated is admissible even if made in response to questions put to the prisoner by a constable, magistrate or other person. This holds true even though the question assumes the prisoner's guilt or the confession is obtained by trick or artifice, or whether or not the prisoner is warned that his statement will be used against him. Any statement not compulsory, made by one not a prisoner, is admissible against him whether made under oath or not. This would not be true, however, if he were compelled to answer. A confession may be inferred from the demeanor of the prisoner when a statement is made in his presence affecting himself, but not where the statement is made in the form of a deposition of a witness or the examination of another prisoner before a magistrate.

Where a confession is inadmissible because of improper inducement, a later confession made where nothing is said about inducements will be inadmissible unless from length of time intervening or from proper warning of the consequences or from other circumstances there is reason to presume that the hope or fear which brought forth the first confession is dispelled. But it must be proved affirmatively that such hope or fear has been dispelled before the latter confession can be used as evidence. Even though a defendant may have made a confession which in itself is inadmissible, yet, if such confession results in any act of his which reveals a fact relevant to the issue, so much of the confession as relates to the act will be admissible.

Verbal evidence, precise and distinct, of a statement made by a prisoner before a magistrate during the examination, is admissible though such statement neither appears in the written examination or is vouched for by the magistrate. This holds true provided it is not of a character which the official duty of the magistrate required him to note, for in the latter case, being official and supposed to be prepared with special care, it would be relied on. But where a magistrate is required to take down a written examination and if he fails to do so, or if it is inadmissible through informality, verbal evidence of the confession would be admissible. The whole of what the prisoner said must be taken together in order to determine its complete effect. The fact that a crime was actually committed must be proved by other evidence than the prisoner's confession before he can be convicted.

CONFESSION AND AVOIDANCE The admission of the truth of a statement of fact contained in the pleading of the opposite party, coupled with the allegation of a new fact, which obviates or repels its legal effect, and thus avoids it. A pleading framed upon this principle is called a pleading in confession and avoidance, or by way of confession and avoidance.

CONFIDENTIAL COMMUNICATIONS Statements with regard to any legal transaction made by one person to another during the continuance of some relation between them which calls for or warrants private or confidential communications. Some classes of such communications are of such character that their disclosure in a court of justice will not be permitted upon grounds of public policy.

Communications between husband and wife may not be proved by one where the interests of the other are involved, irrespective of the time when the marriage relation began or when it terminated. The confidential counselor, solicitor or attorney of a party cannot be compelled to discuss papers delivered to him or communications made to him or letters written or entries made by him as such, nor will he be permitted to do so against his client's will. It does not matter whether legal proceedings were in progress at the time of the communication or not. Nor can the attorney be required to reveal matters discovered by him as such attorney and in consequence of his relation. An interpreter or agent or lawyer's clerk is in the same position as an attorney, but not one who is simply a student at law in an attorney's office.

If the communication was made before the attorney was employed as such or after the employment ceased; or if he was spoken to because he was an attorney but did not act in that capacity for a client; or if there was nothing in the circumstance amounting to a communication when the fact took place, despite his presence and status as a lawyer; or if the matter communicated was not private or confidential in its character and had no reference to professional employment though the attorney was employed at the time of the disclosure, the communication cannot be excluded on the ground that it is privileged.

An attorney also cannot be excluded from testifying as a subscribing witness on such ground when he was a party to the transaction, even though, at the same time, he acted as attorney for another party. The rule as to privileged communications does not apply to physicians except where otherwise regulated by statute nor to confidential friends or clerks.

CONFINEMENT Restraint or restriction of a person's freedom of movement.

CONFISCATION The act of taking private property as a penalty and a forfeit for public use.

CONFLICT OF LAWS The conflict between the municipal laws of different countries or states.

CONFRONTATION The right of a person to face witnesses who charge him with a crime.

CONFUSION The mingling of goods of different owners into a common mass.

CONJUNCTA Things joined. In civil law, things joined together, as opposed to *disjuncta*, things separated.

CONNIVANCE A secret and usually criminal understanding with another, or secret permission given to another to commit a crime.

CONSANGUINITY Relationship by blood from the same stock or common ancestor.

CONSENT A concurrence of wills. An agreement as to something to be done or proposed to be done. Consent is an act of reason accompanied with deliberation,. the mind weighing, as in a balance, the good or evil on each side.

CONSERVATOR (OF AN INSANE PERSON) A person appointed by a competent court to take care of and oversee the person and estate of an idiot or other incompetent person.

CONSIDERATION The material cause of a contract, without which no contract is binding. The reason which moves the contracting party to enter into the contract. The thing given in exchange for the benefit which is to be derived from a contract; the compensation. The price or motive of the contract. The natural love and affection existing among those bound together by close family ties alone are considered by law a good, as distinguished from a valuable, consideration upon which to base a contract or a transfer of property valid as between the parties thereto. Such a transfer, however, will not be effective or good against existing rights, if any, of third parties, such as creditors of the one making the transfer. In other words one cannot give his property away even to one bound by close ties of blood and so defeat the rights of his creditors.

Valuable considerations on the other hand are those where some actual benefit is conferred upon the party by whom the agreement or promise is made, or upon a third party at his instance or request, or some detriment is sustained at the instance of the party in whose favor the promise is made. A valuable consideration usually, but by no means always, is money or something convertible into money, and though small, it will make a contract binding if free from fraud. If there is no consideration the contract cannot be enforced. Consideration is the very essence of a contract.

Where a consideration is expressed in the contract this is presumed to be the actual consideration though this may be rebutted by proof. As a defense it may be shown that there was actually no consideration unless the contract is an instrument under seal, commonly termed a specialty.

An instrument under seal is at law considered of specially binding character and although no consideration is mentioned therein, the seal imports a consideration. When under seal the instrument is supposed to be so solemnly executed and of such a binding character that the parties would not have entered into it if there were no consideration. This presumption is conclusive in most jurisdictions and cannot be rebutted by parol testimony unless by proof of fraud or mistake in the execution of the instrument. By statute in some places, specialties do not have this special binding effect.

Negotiable instruments, as checks, bills of exchange and promissory notes, are presumed to have been given for valuable consideration even though this is not expressed. In most cases of parol contracts, that is, those which are oral or written but not under seal, if the consideration is not expressed it must be proved in order to show that the contract is binding. Where the consideration is merely a good (not valuable) consideration and the contract remains unexecuted it is not binding. If executed, that is, if a transfer has been made in pursuance of the agreement, the transfer will be binding between the parties.

A moral obligation is said to be a sufficient consideration to support a promise. If one promises to do what he morally ought to do, though he is not legally bound to do it, the promise will bind him. This is really true, however, only where a legal obligation actually once existed; thus where one owed a debt which became barred by limitation or "out of date," the moral obligation to pay exists though not legal. The debt is not extinguished though the power to enforce payment is, and the new promise merely revives that power. There is a moral obligation to be charitable. However, a naked promise to contribute something to a charitable institution—since no legal obligation to pay existed previously—will not be binding without other circumstances, such as to pay if others pay a given amount or like.

Work, service, and money are the most common considerations, but the things which will constitute valuable considerations are practically limitless. The waiver of a legal or equitable right at another's request is a sufficient consideration. An extension of time for paying a note or fulfilling a contract is consideration for a new promise, either by the original debtor or contractor or by one who in consideration of the extension becomes surety for the debtor or guarantees performance of the contract.

Where a claim in dispute is either valid or doubtful (but not if it is utterly unfounded), an agreement to compromise in a given manner or at a given figure is supported by a sufficient consideration to make it binding. So is an agreement to submit to arbitrators a matter in dispute. The one submits upon consideration that the other do so. Compromises are highly favored by law, and parties will be held to their agreements.

Where one deposited something with another simply for safekeeping, there is an implied contract on the part of the bailee to return the thing to the owner and to exercise some degree of care in keeping it. It requires some effort to see what the consideration for such a contract is, yet certainly there does exist an obligation or a contract under the law, and the only consideration that can be suggested is simply the fact that the party depositing trusts the bailee, the latter undertaking to do a certain thing in consideration of the confidence reposed in him. Mutual promises made at the same time are consideration for each other and if one party complies, the other will be bound to do so also. This of course does not apply where one is under legal disability to make a promise or contract as in case of a minor. Marriage or promise of marriage is a valuable consideration.

As a general rule, if the consideration is valuable it need not be adequate, that is, the courts will not inquire as to whether a consideration is sufficient or not. They leave that to the judgment of the parties. If the contract is fairly made the courts will not undertake to set it aside or vary its terms; they will not undertake to do the contracting or to relieve people from the effects of unwise transactions.

If one performs services for another gratuitously or without the request of another, he cannot recover compensation. This does not apply where the services are rendered under such circumstances as to raise an implication that the party intends to pay. One may not stand by without objection, knowing that services are being rendered for him where payment might be fairly expected, and afterwards allege that he had made no request for the services. Liability for services or for merchandise delivered depends upon the circumstances of the case and the conduct of the parties.

A promise is a sufficient consideration for a promise. Where one undertakes to do a given thing in consideration that another do another given thing, the performance or a tender of performance on the part of one is sufficient to bind the other. If one tendering performance is prevented or unable to perform on account of the other's act or failure to do some necessary preliminary act, he may recover damages from the party failing in his agreement. If one offers to sell goods or to perform services, he may withdraw his offer at any time before acceptance, but if acceptance is made within a reasonable time, while the offer is still pending, he is bound. All of this, of course, must be qualified by the assumption that the party contracting is not a minor or a person otherwise incapable of contracting.

Illegal considerations will not make a binding contract. A contract containing an agreement to do anything immoral, indecent or contrary to law or against the policy of the law is void, as for example contracts to commit, conceal or compound a crime or to perpetrate a fraud upon a third party. If only part of the consideration is contrary to law the entire contract is void. A contract founded on a consideration naturally or physically impossible is also void. So is one based on a consideration which at the time appeared to be valuable, but afterwards turns out to be a mere nullity and totally fails, as for example, where one agrees to do what he was already obliged to do. It sometimes happens that a consideration partially fails; if the portion which does not fail can be set off against a corresponding portion of what the other party agrees to do or not to do such remaining portion of the contract will stand and the other portion will be void. This is true, however, only in case the contract is severable or divisible into parts.

CONSIGN To send or transmit goods to a merchant or factor for sale.

CONSIGNATION The payment of money into the hands of a third party when the creditor refuses to accept it.

CONSORTIUM The right which a person has to the affections, services and society of his spouse.

CONSPIRACY Conspiracy is a combination of two or more persons by some concerted action to accomplish a criminal or unlawful purpose or to accomplish a purpose not unlawful by criminal or unlawful means.

The conspiracy or unlawful combination is itself a criminal offense and is punishable whether the object of the conspiracy is accomplished or not. It is not necessary that any person be actually injured by the conspiracy or that any act at all be done towards carrying out the intended plan. It is not necessary that the thing proposed to be done be itself criminal.

A combination to destroy one's reputation by a verbal report is indictable though the verbal report itself would not be; so is a combination between two or more whereby the goods of one may be disposed of to the other or to a third person for the purpose of defeating creditors; so is a combination to go to a theatre and hiss an actor or to prosecute one for the purpose of extorting money from him.

A combination by two or more to falsely charge one with poisoning another or with being the father of a bastard child, or to induce a girl by false statement to leave her parents' home with a view of facilitating her prostitution, or to affect the price of public stocks by false rumors, or to prevent competition at an auction, or to coerce workmen to quit work, or to injure one in his trade or business or profession, or with the object of benefiting themselves to the prejudice of the public or the oppression of individuals, such prejudice or oppression being the natural or necessary consequence of the proposed acts, is a conspiracy.

The declaration or statement of one conspirator made while acting in the common design is evidence against all. But if it is made after the accomplishment of the intended purpose and after the concert of action is ended, it is evidence only against the one making it.

If retail dealers combine and refuse to purchase from wholesalers unless they discontinue to sell to brokers, this is unlawful, and those injuring the business of the broker by so doing may be held for damages resulting from the destruction of his business.

CONSTABLE A public civil officer whose duty is to keep the peace within his district, though he is frequently charged with additional duties.

CONSTITUTION OF THE UNITED STATES OF AMERICA

PREAMBLE

We, the people of the United States, in order to form a more perfect union, establish justice, insure domestic tranquility, provide for the common defense, promote the general welfare, and secure the blessings of liberty to ourselves and our posterity, do ordain and establish this Constitution of the United States of America.

ARTICLE I.

Legislative Powers Vested in Congress.

Section 1.

All legislative powers herein granted shall be vested in a Congress of the United States, which shall consist of a Senate and House of Representatives.

Section 2.

1. The House of Representatives shall be composed of members chosen every second year by the people of the several states, and the electors in each state shall have the qualifications requisite for electors of the most numerous branch of the state legislature.

2. No person shall be a Representative who shall not have attained the age of twenty-five years, and been seven years a citizen of the United States, and who shall not, when elected, be an inhabitant of that state in which he shall be chosen.

3. Representatives and direct taxes shall be apportioned among the several states which may be included within this union, according to their respective numbers, which shall be determined by adding to the whole number of free persons, including those bound to service for a term of years, and excluding Indians not taxed, three-fifths of all other persons. The actual enumeration shall be made within three years after the first meeting of the Congress of the United States, and within every subsequent term of ten years, in such manner as they shall by law direct. The number of Representatives shall not exceed one for every thirty thousand, but each state shall have at least one Representative; and until such enumeration shall be made, the state of New Hampshire shall be entitled to choose three, Massachusetts, eight, Rhode Island and Providence Plantations, one, Connecticut, five, New York, six, New Jersey, four, Pennsylvania, eight, Delaware, one, Maryland, six, Virginia, ten, North Carolina, five, South Carolina, five, and Georgia, three.

4. When vacancies happen in the representation from any state, the executive authority thereof shall issue writs of elections to fill such vacancies.

5.   The House of Representatives shall choose their speaker and other officers: and shall have the sole power of impeachment.

Section 3.

1.   The Senate of the United States shall be composed of two Senators from each state, chosen by the legislators thereof, for six years; and each Senator shall have one vote.

2.   Immediately after they shall be assembled in consequence of the first election, they shall be divided as equally as may be into three classes. The seats of the Senators of the first class shall be vacated at the expiration of the second year, of the second class at the expiration of the fourth year, and of the third class at the expiration of the sixth year, so that one-third may be chosen every second year; and if vacancies happen by resignation, or otherwise, during the recess of the legislature of any state, the executive thereof may make temporary appointments until the next meeting of the legislature, which shall then fill such vacancies.

3.   No person shall be a Senator who shall not have attained to the age of thirty years, and been nine years a citizen of the United States, and who shall not, when elected, be an inhabitant of that state for which he shall be chosen.

4.   The Vice-President of the United States shall be president of the Senate, but shall have no vote, unless they be equally divided.

5.   The Senate shall choose their other officers, and also a president pro tempore, in the absence of the Vice-President, or when he shall exercise the office of the President of the United States.

6.   The Senate shall have the sole power to try all impeachments. When sitting for that purpose, they shall be on oath or affirmation. When the President of the United States is tried, the Chief Justice shall preside; and no person shall be convicted without the concurrence of two-thirds of the members present.

7.   Judgment in cases of impeachment shall not extend further than to removal from office, and disqualification to hold and enjoy any office of honor, trust or profit under the United States: but the party convicted shall nevertheless be liable and subject to indictment, trial, judgment and punishment, according to law.

Section 4.

1.   The times, places and manner of holding elections for Senators and Representatives, shall be prescribed in each state by the legislature thereof; but the Congress may at any time by law make or alter such regulations, except as to the places of choosing Senators.

2.   The Congress shall assemble at least once in every year, and such meeting shall be on the first Monday in December, unless they shall by law appoint a different day.

Section 5.

1. Each House shall be the judge of the elections, returns and qualifications of its own members, and a majority of each shall constitute a quorum to do business; but a smaller number may adjourn from day to day, and may be authorized to compel the attendance of absent members, in such manner, and under such penalties as each House may provide.

2. Each House may determine the rules of its proceedings, punish its members for disorderly behavior, and, with the concurrence of two-thirds expel a member.

3. Each House shall keep a journal of its proceedings, and from time to time publish the same, excepting such parts as may in their judgment require secrecy; and the yeas and nays of the members of either House on any question shall, at the desire of one-fifth of those present, be entered on the journal.

4. Neither House, during the session of Congress, shall, without the consent of the other, adjourn for more than three days, nor to any other place than that in which the two Houses shall be sitting.

Section 6.

1. The Senators and Representatives shall receive a compensation for their services, to be ascertained by law, and paid out of the treasury of the United States. They shall in all cases, except treason, felony and breach of the peace, be privileged from arrest during their attendance at the session of their respective Houses, and in going to and returning from the same; and for any speech or debate in either House, they shall not be questioned in any other place.

2. No Senator or Representative shall, during the time for which he was elected, be appointed to any civil office under the authority of the United States, which shall have been created, or the emoluments whereof shall have been increased during such time; and no person holding any office under the United States, shall be a member of either House during his continuance in office.

Section 7.

1. All bills for raising revenue shall originate in the House of Representatives; but the Senate may propose or concur with amendments as on other bills.

2. Every bill which shall have passed the House of Representatives and the Senate, shall, before it becomes a law, be presented to the President of the United States; if he approve he shall sign it, but if not he shall return it, with his objections to that House in which it shall have originated, who shall enter the objections at large on their journal, and proceed to consider it. If after such reconsideration two-thirds of that House shall approve to pass the bill, it shall be sent, together with the objections, to the other House, by which it shall likewise be reconsidered,

and if approved by two-thirds of that House, it shall become a law. But in all such cases the votes of both Houses shall be determined by yeas and nays, and the names of the persons voting for and against the bill shall be entered on the journal of each House respectively. If any bill shall not be returned by the President within ten days (Sundays excepted) after it shall have been presented to him, the same shall be a law, in like manner as if he had signed it, unless the Congress by their adjournment prevent its return, in which case it shall not be a law.

3. Every order, resolution, or vote to which the concurrence of the Senate and House of Representatives may be necessary (except on a question of adjournment) shall be presented to the President of the United States; and before the same shall take effect, shall be approved by him, or being disapproved by him, shall be repassed by two-thirds of the Senate and House of Representatives, according to the rules and limitations prescribed in the case of a bill.

Section 8.

1. The Congress shall have power to lay and collect taxes, duties, imposts and excises, to pay the debts and provide for the common defense and general welfare of the United States; but all duties, imposts and excises shall be uniform throughout the United States.

2. To borrow money on the credit of the United States.

3. To regulate commerce with foreign nations, and among the several states, and with the Indian tribes.

4. To establish an uniform rule of naturalization, and uniform laws on the subject of bankruptcies throughout the United States.

5. To coin money, regulate the value thereof, and of foreign coin, and fix the standard of weights and measures.

6. To provide for the punishment of counterfeiting the securities and current coin of the United States.

7. To establish postoffices and postroads.

8. To promote the progress of science and useful arts, by securing for limited times to authors and inventors the exclusive right to their respective writings and discoveries.

9. To constitute tribunals inferior to the Supreme Court.

10. To define and punish piracies and felonies committed on the high seas, and offenses against the law of nations.

11. To declare war, grant letters of marque and reprisal, and make rules concerning captures on land and water.

12. To raise and support armies, but no appropriation of money to that use shall be for a longer term than two years.

13. To provide and maintain a navy.

14. To make rules for the government and regulation of the land and naval forces.

15. To provide for calling forth the militia to execute the laws of the

Union, suppress insurrections and repel invasions.

16.   To provide for organizing, arming, and disciplining the militia, and for governing such part of them as may be employed in the service of the United States, reserving to the states respectively, the appointment of the officers, and the authority of training the militia according to the discipline prescribed by Congress.

17.   To exercise exclusive legislation in all cases whatsoever, over such district (not exceeding ten miles square) as may, by cession of particular states, and the acceptance of Congress, become the seat of the government of the United States, and to exercise like authority over all places purchased by the consent of the legislature of the state in which the same shall be, for the erection of forts, magazines, arsenals, dock yards, and other needful buildings; and

18.   To make all laws which shall be necessary and proper for carrying into execution the foregoing powers, and all other powers vested by this constitution in the government of the United States, or in any department or officer thereof.

Section 9.

1.   The migration or importation of such persons as any of the states now existing shall think proper to admit, shall not be prohibited by the Congress prior to the year one thousand eight hundred and eight, but a tax or duty may be imposed on such importation, not exceeding ten dollars for each person.

2.   The privilege of the writ of habeas corpus shall not be suspended unless when in cases of rebellion or invasion the public safety may require it.

3.   No bill of attainder or ex post facto law shall be passed.

4.   No capitation, or other direct tax shall be laid, unless in proportion to the census or enumeration herein before directed to be taken.

5.   No tax or duty shall be laid on articles exported from any state.

6.   No preference shall be given by any regulation of commerce or revenue to the ports of one state over those of another; nor shall vessels bound to or from one state, be obliged to enter, clear, or pay duties in another.

7.   No money shall be drawn from the treasury, but in consequence of appropriations made by law; and a regular statement and account of the receipts and expenditures of all public money shall be published from time to time.

8.   No title of nobility shall be granted by the United States; and no person holding any office of profit or trust under them, shall, without the consent of the Congress, accept of any present, emolument, office, or title, of any kind whatever, from any king, prince, or foreign state.

Section 10.

1.   No state shall enter into any treaty, alliance, or confederation; grant letters of marque and reprisal; coin money, emit bills of credit; make

anything but gold and silver coin tender in payment of debts; pass any bill of attainder, ex post facto law, or law impairing the obligation of contracts, or grant any title of nobility.

2. No state shall, without the consent of the Congress, lay any imposts or duties on imports or exports, except what may be absolutely necessary for executing its inspection laws; and the net produce of all duties and imposts, laid by any state on imports or exports, shall be for the use of the treasury of the United States; and all such laws shall be subject to the revision and control of the Congress.

3. No state shall, without the consent of Congress, lay any duty of tonnage, keep troops, or ships of war in time of peace, enter into any agreement or compact with another state, or with a foreign power, or engage in war, unless actually invaded, or in such imminent danger as will not admit of delay.

ARTICLE II.

Of the President—The Executive Power.

Section 1.

1. The executive power shall be vested in a President of the United States of America. He shall hold his office during the term of four years, and, together with the Vice-President, chosen for the same term, be elected, as follows:

2. Each state shall appoint, in such manner as the legislature thereof may direct, a number of electors, equal to the whole number of Senators and Representatives to which the state may be entitled in the Congress; but no Senator or Representative, or person holding an office of trust or profit under the United States, shall be appointed an elector.

3. The electors shall meet in their respective states and vote by ballot for two persons, of whom one at least shall not be an inhabitant of the same state with themselves. And they shall make a list of all the persons voted for, and of the number of votes for each; which list they shall sign and certify, and transmit sealed to the seat of the government of the United States, directed to the President of the Senate. The President of the Senate shall in the presence of the Senate and House of Representatives, open all the certificates, and the votes shall then be counted. The person having the greatest number of votes shall be the President, if such number be a majority of the whole number of electors appointed; and if there be more than one who have such majority, and have an equal number of votes then the House of Representatives shall immediately choose by ballot one of them for President; and if no person have a majority, then from the five highest on the list the said House shall in like manner choose the President. But in choosing the President, the votes shall be taken by states, the representation from each state having one vote; a quorum for this purpose shall consist of a member or members

from two-thirds of the states and a majority of all the states shall be necessary to a choice. In every case, after the choice of the President, the person having the greatest number of votes of the electors shall be the Vice-President. But if there should remain two or more who have equal votes, the Senate shall choose from them by ballot the Vice-President.

4. The Congress may determine the time of choosing the electors, and the day on which they shall give their votes; which day shall be the same throughout the United States.

5. No person except a natural-born citizen or a citizen of the United States, at the time of the adoption of this Constitution, shall be eligible to the office of President; neither shall any person be eligible to that office who shall not have attained to the age of thirty-five years, and been fourteen years a resident within the United States.

6. In case of the removal of the President from office, or his death, resignation, or inability to discharge the powers and duties of the said office, the same shall devolve on the Vice-President, and the Congress may by law provide for the case of removal, death, resignation or inability, both of the President and Vice-President, declaring what officer shall then act as President, and such officer shall act accordingly, until the disability be removed, or a President shall be elected.

7. The President shall, at stated times, receive for his services, a compensation, which shall neither be increased nor diminished during the period for which he shall have been elected, and he shall not receive within that period any other emolument from the United States, or any of them.

8. Before he enter on the execution of his office, he shall take the following oath or affirmation: "I do solemnly swear (or affirm) that I will faithfully execute the office of the President of the United States, and will to the best of my ability, preserve, protect and defend the Constitution of the United States."

Section 2.

1. The President shall be Commander-in-Chief of the Army and Navy of the United States, and of the militia of the several states, when called into the actual service of the United States, he may require the opinion, in writing, of the principal officer in each of the executive departments, upon any subject relating to the duties of their respective offices, and he shall have power to grant reprieves and pardons for offenses against the United States, except in cases of impeachment.

2. He shall have power, by and with the advice and consent of the Senate, to make treaties, provided two-thirds of the Senators concur; and he shall nominate, and by and with the advice and consent of the Senate, shall appoint ambassadors, other public ministers and consuls, judges of the Supreme Court, and all other officers of the United States, whose appointments are not herein otherwise provided for, and which shall be

established by law: but the Congress may by law vest the appointment of such inferior officers, as they think proper, in the President alone, in the courts of law, or in the heads of departments.

3.   The President shall have power to fill up all vacancies that may happen during the recess of the Senate, by granting commissions which shall expire at the end of their next session.

Section 3.

He shall, from time to time give to the Congress information of the state of the Union, and recommend to their consideration such measures as he shall judge necessary and expedient; he may, on extraordinary occasions, convene both Houses, or either of them, and in case of disagreement between them, with respect to the time of adjournment, he may adjourn them to such time as he shall think proper; he shall receive ambassadors and other public ministers; he shall take care that the laws be faithfully executed, and shall commission all the officers of the United States.

Section 4.

The President, Vice-President and all civil officers of the United States shall be removed from office on impeachment for, and conviction of treason, bribery, or other high crimes and misdemeanors.

ARTICLE III.

Judicial Power—How Vested—Term of Office and Compensation of Judges.

Section 1.

The judicial power of the United States, shall be vested in one Supreme Court, and in such inferior courts as the Congress may from time to time ordain and establish. The judges, both of the Supreme and inferior courts, shall hold their offices during good behavior, and shall, at stated times, receive for their services a compensation which shall not be diminished during their continuance in office.

Section 2.

1.   The judicial power shall extend to all cases, in law and equity, arising under this Constitution, the laws of the United States, and treaties made, or which shall be made, under their authority; to all cases affecting ambassadors, other public ministers and consuls; to all cases of admiralty and maritime jurisdiction; to controversies to which the United States shall be a party; to controversies between two or more states; between a state and citizens of another state; between citizens of different states; between citizens of the same state claiming lands under grants of different

states, and between a state, or citizens thereof, and foreign states, citizens or subjects.

2. In all cases affecting ambassadors, other public ministers and consuls, and those in which a state shall be party, the Supreme Court shall have original jurisdiction. In all the other cases before mentioned, the Supreme Court shall have appellate jurisdiction, both as to law and fact, with such exceptions, and under such regulations as the Congress shall make.

3. The trial of all crimes, except in cases of impeachment, shall be by jury; and such trial shall be held in the state where the said crimes shall have been committed; but when crimes be not committed within any state the trial shall be at such place or places as the Congress may by law have directed.

Section 3.

1. Treason against the United States, shall consist only in levying war against them, or in adhering to their enemies, giving them aid and comfort. No person shall be convicted of treason unless the testimony of two witnesses be had to the same overt act, or on open confession in court.

2. The Congress shall have power to declare the punishment of treason, but no attainder of treason shall work corruption of blood or forfeiture except during the life of the person attained.

ARTICLE IV.

Each State to Give Full Faith and Credit to the Public Acts and Records of Other States.

Section 1.

Full faith and credit shall be given in each state to the public acts, records, and judicial proceedings of every other state. And the Congress may by general laws prescribe the manner in which such acts, records and proceedings shall be proved, and the effect thereof.

Section 2.

1. The citizens of each state shall be entitled to all privileges and immunities of citizens in the several states.

2. A person charged in any state with treason, felony or other crime, who shall flee from justice, and be found in another state, shall on demand of the executive authority of the state from which he fled, be delivered up, to be removed to the state having jurisdiction of the crime.

3. No person held to service or labor in one state, under the laws thereof, escaping into another, shall in consequence of any law or regulation therein, be discharged from such service or labor, but shall be delivered up on the claim of the party to whom such service or labor may be due.

Section 3.

1. New states may be admitted by the Congress into this Union; but no new state shall be formed or erected within the jurisdiction of any other state; nor any state be formed by the junction of two or more states, or parts of states, without the consent of the legislatures of the states concerned as well as the Congress.

2. The Congress shall have power to dispose of and make all needful rules and regulations respecting the territory or other property belonging to the United States; and nothing in this Constitution shall be so construed as to prejudice any claims of the United States, or of any particular state.

Section 4.

The United States shall guarantee to every state in this Union a republican form of government, and shall protect each of them against invasion; and on application of the legislature, or of the Executive (when the legislature cannot be convened) against domestic violence.

ARTICLE V.

Ways in Which the Constitution Can be Amended.

The Congress, whenever two-thirds of both Houses shall deem it necessary, shall propose amendments to this Constitution, or, on the application of the legislatures of two-thirds of the several states, shall call a convention for proposing amendments, which, in either case, shall be valid to all intents and purposes, as part of this Constitution, when ratified by the legislatures of three-fourths of the several states, or by conventions in three-fourths thereof, as the one or the other mode of ratification may be proposed by the Congress; provided that no amendment which may be made prior to the year one thousand eight hundred and eight shall in any mannner affect the first and fourth clauses in the ninth section of the first article; and that no state, without its consent, shall be deprived of its equal suffrage in the Senate.

ARTICLE VI.

Debts Contracted under the Confederation Secured.

1. All debts contracted and engagements entered into, before the adoption of this Constitution, shall be as valid against the United States under this Constitution, as under the confederation.

2. This Constitution and the laws of the United States which shall be made in pursuance thereof; and all treaties made, or which shall be made, under the authority of the United States, shall be the supreme law of the land; and the judges in every state shall be bound thereby, anything in the Constitution or laws of any state to the contrary notwithstanding.

3. The Senators and Representatives before mentioned, and the members of the several state legislatures, and all executive and judicial officers,

both of the United States and of the several states, shall be bound by oath or affirmation, to support this Constitution; but no religious test shall ever be required as qualification to any office or public trust under the United States.

ARTICLE VII.

Constitution to be Considered Adopted When Ratified by Nine States.

The ratification of the conventions of nine states shall be sufficient for the establishment of this Constitution between the states so ratifying the same.

Done in convention by the unanimous consent of the states present the seventeenth day of September in the year of our Lord one thousand seven hundred and eighty-seven and of the independence of the United States of America the twelfth. In witness whereof we have hereunto subscribed our names.

AMENDMENTS TO THE CONSTITUTION.

ARTICLE I.

Freedom of Religion, of Speech, of the Press and Right of Petition.

Congress shall make no law respecting an establishment of religion, or prohibiting the free exercise thereof; or abridging the freedom of speech, or of the press; or of the right of the people peaceably to assemble, and to petition the government for a redress of grievances.

ARTICLE II.

Right of People to Bear Arms Not to be Infringed.

A well-regulated militia, being necessary to the security of a free state, the right of the people to keep and bear arms, shall not be infringed.

ARTICLE III.

Quartering of troops.

No soldier shall, in time of peace be quartered in any house, without the consent of the owner, nor in time of war, but in a manner to be prescribed by law.

ARTICLE IV.

Persons and Houses to be Secure from Unreasonable Searches and Seizures.

The right of the people to be secure in their persons, houses, papers, and effects, against unreasonable searches and seizures, shall not be violated, and no warrants shall issue, but upon probable cause, supported by oath or affirmation, and particularly describing the place to be searched, and the persons or things to be seized.

ARTICLE V.

Trials for Crimes—Just Compensation for Private Property Taken for Public Use.

No person shall be held to answer for a capital, or otherwise infamous crime, unless on a presentment or indictment of a grand jury, except in cases arising in the land or naval forces, or in the militia, when in actual service in time of war or public danger; nor shall any person be subject for the same offense to be twice put in jeopardy of life or limb; nor shall be compelled in any criminal case to be a witness against himself, nor be deprived of life, liberty or property without due process of law; nor shall private property be taken for public use, without just compensation.

ARTICLE VI.

Civil Rights in Trials for Crimes Enumerated.

In all criminal prosecutions, the accused shall enjoy the right to a speedy and public trial, by an impartial jury of the state and district wherein the crime shall have been committed, which district shall have been previously ascertained by law, and to be informed of the nature and cause of the accusation; to be confronted with the witnesses against him; to have compulsory process for obtaining witnesses in his favor, and to have the assistance of counsel for his defense.

ARTICLE VII.

Civil Rights in Civil Suits.

In suits at common law, where the value in controversy shall exceed twenty dollars, the right of trial by jury shall be preserved, and no fact tried by jury shall be otherwise re-examined in any court of the United States, than according to the rules of the common law.

ARTICLE VIII.

Excessive Bail, Fines and Punishments Prohibited.

Excessive bail shall not be required, nor excessive fines imposed, nor cruel and unusual punishments inflicted.

ARTICLE IX.

Reserved Rights of the People.

The enumeration in the Constitution, of certain rights, shall not be construed to deny or disparage others retained by the people.

ARTICLE X.

Powers not Delegated, Reserved to States and People Respectively.

The powers not delegated to the United States by the Constitution, nor prohibited by it to the states, are reserved to the states respectively, or to the people.

ARTICLE XI.

Judicial Power of United States not to Extend to Suits Against a State.

The judicial power of the United States shall not be construed to extend to any suit in law or equity, commenced or prosecuted against one of the United States by citizens of another state, or by citizens or subjects of any foreign state.

ARTICLE XII.

Mode of Electing President and Vice-President by Electors.

The electors shall meet in their respective states and vote by ballot for President and Vice-President, one of whom, at least, shall not be an inhabitant of the same state with themselves; they shall name in their ballots the person voted for as President, and in distinct ballots the person voted for as Vice-President, and they shall make distinct lists of all persons voted for as President, and of all persons voted for as Vice-President, and of the number of votes for each, which lists they shall sign and certify and transmit sealed to the seat of the Government of the United States, directed to the President of the Senate;—the President of the Senate shall, in the presence of the Senate and House of Representatives, open all the certificates and the votes shall then be counted;—The person having the greatest number of votes for President shall be the President, if such number be a majority of the whole number of electors appointed; and if no person have such majority, then from the persons having the highest numbers not exceeding three on the list of those voted for as President, the House of Representatives shall choose immediately, by ballot, the President. But in choosing the President, the votes shall be taken by states, the representation from each state having one vote; a quorum for this purpose shall consist of a member or members from two-thirds of the states, and a majority of all the states shall be necessary to a choice. And if the House of Representatives shall not choose a President whenever the right of choice shall devolve upon them, before the fourth day of March next following, then the Vice-President shall act as President, as in the case of death or other constitutional disability of the President. The person having the greatest number of votes as Vice-President, shall be the Vice-President, if such number be a majority of the whole number of electors appointed, and if no person have a majority, then from the two highest numbers on the list, the Senate shall choose the Vice-President; a quorum for the purpose shall consist of two-thirds of the whole number of Senators, and a majority of the whole number shall be necessary to a choice. But no person constitutionally ineligible to the office of President shall be eligible to that of Vice-President of the United States.

ARTICLE XIII.

Slavery Prohibited.

Section 1.

Neither slavery nor involuntary servitude, except as a punishment for crime whereof the party shall have been duly convicted, shall exist within the United States, or any place subject to their jurisdiction.

Section 2.

Congress shall have power to enforce this article by appropriate legislation.

ARTICLE XIV.

Citizenship Defined—Privileges of Citizens.

Section 1.

All persons born or naturalized in the United States, and subject to the jurisdiction thereof, are citizens of the United States and of the state wherein they reside. No state shall make or enforce any law which shall abridge the privileges or immunities of citizens of the United States; nor shall any state deprive any person of life, liberty, or property, without due process of law; nor deny to any person within its jurisdiction the equal protection of the laws.

Section 2.

Representatives shall be apportioned among the several states according to their respective numbers, counting the whole number of persons in each state, excluding Indians not taxed. But when the right to vote at any election for the choice of electors for President and Vice-President of the United States, representatives in Congress, the executive and judicial officers of a state, or the members of the legislature thereof, is denied to any of the male inhabitants of such state, being twenty-one years of age, and citizens of the United States, or in any way abridged, except for participation in rebellion, or other crime, the basis of representation therein shall be reduced in proportion which the number of such male citizens shall bear to the whole number of male citizens twenty-one years of age in such state.

Section 3.

No person shall be a Senator or Representative in Congress, or elector of President and Vice-President, or hold any office civil or military, under the United States, or under any state, who, having previously taken an oath, as a member of Congress, or as an officer of the United States, or as a member of any state legislature, or as an executive or judicial officer of any state, to support the Constitution of the United States, shall have engaged in insurrection or rebellion against the same, or given aid or comfort to the enemies thereof. But Congress may by a vote of two-thirds of each House, remove such disability.

Section 4.

The validity of the public debt of the United States, authorized by law, including debts incurred for payment of pensions and bounties for services in suppressing insurrection or rebellion, shall not be questioned. But neither the United States nor any state shall assume or pay any debt or obligation incurred in aid of insurrection or rebellion against the United States, or any claim for the loss or emancipation of any slave; but all such debts, obligations and claims shall be held illegal and void.

Section 5.

The Congress shall have power to enforce, by appropriate legislation, the provisions of this article.

ARTICLE XV.

Right of Certain Citizens to Vote Established.

Section 1.

The right of citizens of the United States to vote shall not be denied or abridged by the United States or by any state, on account of race, color, or previous condition of servitude.

Section 2.

The Congress shall have power to enforce this article by appropriate legislation.

ARTICLE XVI.

The Congress shall have power to lay and collect taxes on incomes, from whatever sources derived, without apportionment among the several states, and without regard to any census of enumeration.

ARTICLE XVII.

1. The Senate of the United States shall be composed of two Senators from each state, elected by the people thereof, for six years and each Senator shall have one vote. The electors in each state shall have the qualifications requisite for electors of the most numerous branch of the State Legislatures.

2. When vacancies happen in the representation of any state in the

Senate, the executive authority of such state shall issue writs of election to fill such vacancies: Provided, that the Legislature of any state may empower the Executive thereof to make temporary appointment until the people fill the vacancies by election as the Legislature may direct.

3.   This amendment shall not be so construed as to affect the election or term of any Senator chosen before it becomes valid as part of the Constitution.

ARTICLE XVIII.

1.   After one year from the ratification of this article the manufacture, sale, or transportation of intoxicating liquors within, the importation thereof into, or the exportation thereof from the United States and all territory subject to the jurisdiction thereof for beverage purposes is hereby prohibited.

2.   The Congress and the several states shall have concurrent power to enforce this article by appropriate legislation.

3.   This article shall be inoperative unless it shall have been ratified as an amendment to the Constitution by the Legislature of the several states, as provided in the Constitution, within seven years from the date of the submission hereof to the states by the Congress.

Repealed by Article XXI effective Dec. 5, 1933.

ARTICLE XIX.

1.   The right of citizens of the United States to vote shall not be denied or abridged by the United States or by any state on account of sex.

2.   Congress shall have power to enforce this article by appropriate legislation.

ARTICLE XX.

Section 1.

The terms of the President and Vice-President shall end at noon on the 20th day of January, and the terms of Senators and Representatives at noon on the 3rd day of January, of the years in which such terms would have ended if this article had not been ratified; and the terms of their successors shall begin.

Section 2.

The Congress shall assemble at least once in every year, and such meeting shall begin at noon on the 3rd day of January, unless they shall by law appoint a different day.

Section 3.

If, at the time fixed for the beginning of the term of the President, the President elect shall have died, the Vice-President elect shall become

President. If a President shall not have been chosen before the time fixed for the beginning of his term, or if the President elect shall have failed to qualify, then the Vice-President elect shall act as President until a President shall have qualified, declaring who shall then act as President, or the manner in which one who is to act shall be selected, and such person shall act accordingly until a President or Vice-President shall have qualified.

Section 4.

The Congress may by law provide for the case of the death of any of the persons from whom the House of Representatives must choose a President whenever the right of choice shall have devolved upon them, and for the case of the death of any of the persons from whom the Senate may choose a Vice-President whenever the right of choice shall have devolved upon them.

Section 5.

Sections 1 and 2 shall take effect on the 15th day of October following the ratification of this article (Oct., 1933).

Section 6.

This article shall be inoperative unless it shall have been ratified as an amendment to the Constitution by the Legislatures of three-fourths of the several states within seven years from the date of its submission.

ARTICLE XXI.

Section 1.

The eighteenth article of amendment to the Constitution of the United States is hereby repealed.

Section 2.

The transportation or importation into any state, territory, or possession of the United States for delivery or use therein of intoxicating liquors, in violation of the laws thereof, is hereby prohibited.

Section 3.

This article shall be inoperative unless it shall have been ratified as an amendment to the Constitution by convention in the several states, as provided in the Constitution, within seven years from the date of the submission hereof to the states by the Congress.

ARTICLE XXII.

No person shall be elected to the office of the President more than twice, and no person who has held the office of President, or acted as

President, for more than two years of a term to which some other person was elected President shall be elected to the office of the President more than once. But this Article shall not apply to any person holding the office of President when this Article was proposed by the Congress, and shall not prevent any person who may be holding the office of President, or acting as President, during the term within which this Article becomes operative from holding the office of President or acting as President during the remainder of such term.

ARTICLE XXIII.

1.   The District constituting the seat of Government of the United States shall appoint in such manner as the Congress may direct:

A number of electors of President and Vice President equal to the whole number of Senators and Representatives in Congress to which the District would be entitled if it were a State, but in no event more than the least populous State: they shall be in addition to those appointed by the States, but they shall be considered, for the purposes of the election of President, and Vice-President, to be electors appointed by a State; and they shall meet in the District and perform such duties as provided by the twelfth article of amendment.

2.   The Congress shall have power to enforce this article by appropriate legislation.

ARTICLE XXIV.

1.   The right of citizens of the United States to vote in any primary or other election for President or Vice-President, for electors for President, or Vice-President, or for Senator or Representative in Congress, shall not be denied or abridged by the United States or any State by reason of failure to pay any poll tax or other tax.

2.   The Congress shall have the power to enforce this article by appropriate legislation.

ARTICLE XXV.

1.   In case of the removal of the President from office or his death or resignation, the Vice-President shall become President.

2.   Whenever there is a vacancy in the office of the Vice-President, the President shall nominate a Vice-President who shall take the office upon confirmation by a majority vote of both houses of Congress.

3.   Whenever the President transmits to the President pro tempore of the Senate and the Speaker of the House of Representatives his written declaration that he is unable to discharge the powers and duties of his office, and until he transmits to them a written declaration to the contrary, such powers and duties shall be discharged by the Vice-President as Acting President.

4. Whenever the Vice-President and a majority of either the principal officers of the executive departments or of such other body as Congress may by law provide, transmit to the President pro tempore of the Senate and the Speaker of the House of Representatives their written declaration that the President is unable to discharge the powers and duties of his office, the Vice-President shall immediately assume the powers and duties of the office as Acting President.

Thereafter, when the President transmits to the President pro tempore of the Senate and the Speaker of the House of Representatives his written declaration that no inability exists, he shall resume the powers and duties of his office unless the Vice-President and a majority of either the principal officers of the executive department or of such other body as Congress may by law provide, transmit within four days to the President pro tempore of the Senate and the Speaker of the House of Representatives their written declaration that the President is unable to discharge the powers and duties of his office. Thereupon Congress shall decide the issue, assembling within 48 hours for that purpose if not in session. If the Congress, within 21 days after receipt of the latter written declaration, or, if Congress is not in session within 21 days after Congress is required to assemble, determines by two-thirds vote of both houses that the President is unable to discharge the powers and duties of his office, the Vice-President shall continue to discharge the same as Acting President; otherwise, the President shall resume the powers and duties of his office.

CONSTRUCTION A putting together of the words of an instrument; an arrangement or marshaling of words or clauses so as to extract, by a process of inference, the meaning or intent; exposition; interpretation.

CONSTRUCTIVE FRAUD Fraud inferred by law, as distinguished from positive, actual or intentional fraud; fraud in law, as distinguished from fraud in fact.

CONSTRUCTIVE LARCENY Larceny made out by construction, or inferred from the acts of a party, where the taking itself was not apparently felonious.

CONSTRUCTIVE NOTICE Notice inferred by law, as distinguished from actual or formal notice; no-

tice in law; that which is held by law to amount to notice. Actual notice to a party's attorney is constructive notice to the party himself.

CONSTRUCTIVE TRUST A trust raised by construction of law, or arising by operation of law, as distinguished from an express trust. A trust implied or inferred from circumstances; otherwise called an implied trust, and sometimes a resulting trust.

CONTEMPT Wilful disobedience to a judicial court or legislature. Any legislative body may punish its members in contempt for disorderly conduct or disobeying its rules, but the power does not extend beyond the session of the legislature. The term contempt is most commonly applied in connection with contempt of court. All courts have power to punish persons for contempt or violations of their rules and orders or for disorderly conduct or disobeyance of their commands, and may punish by fine or imprisonment or both. Generally, statements which would constitute contempt if made in the presence of the court, are, if made either orally or by publication not in the presence of the court, not contempt.

The court itself, against which the contempt is committed, can alone judge as to its commission, subject to review by a court of superior jurisdiction, but in case of such review where the party has been imprisoned for contempt, he must remain in prison pending the decision of the higher court.

Preventing a witness from attending court where he had been duly subpenaed is contempt of court; so is locking a courthouse door during adjournment of court and preventing the entry of the judge, officers and parties to a suit; so is attaching or unlawfully interfering with property known to be in the hands of a receiver who is the agent of the court.

CONTINGENT REMAINDER A remainder limited to take effect either to a dubious and uncertain person, or upon a dubious and uncertain event (and by which no present interest passes), so that the particular estate may chance to be determined and the remainder never take effect.

CONTINUANCE The adjournment of the proceedings in a cause from one day or one term to another.

CONTINUING GUARANTY An undertaking by one person to another person to answer from time to time for moneys to be loaned or goods to be sold to a third person. The term refers to the future liability of the principal for a series of future transactions. It is usually revocable upon actual notice as to all future transactions.

CONTRA A term constantly used in law reports to denote the opposition of counsel in a cause; the disallowance by the court of a point in argument; the opposition of cases cited as establishing opposite doctrines.

CONTRABAND Any article which has been declared illegal for export or import.

CONTRACT OF SALE A contract by which one of the contracting parties, called the seller, enters into an obligation to the other, called the buyer, to cause him to have something for the price of a certain sum of money, which the buyer obliges himself to pay.

CONTRACTS A contract is a definite agreement between two or more competent parties, based upon a lawful consideration, to do or not to do some lawful thing. For a contract to be binding and enforceable, it must fulfill four legal requirements: there must be mutual assent or consent, competent parties, lawful consideration, and valid subject matter.

A contract may be valid, unenforceable, voidable, or void.

A valid contract is one that fulfills all four legal requirements.

An unenforceable contract is a contract that cannot be enforced by court action.

A voidable contract is a contract in which one of the parties has the option not to perform. For example, a contract made by an infant (that is, a person under twenty-one years of age) or by a person induced through fraud or misrepresentation is a voidable contract. An infant may, as we shall see, accept or reject the contract at his option. A person whose consent has been obtained by fraud may either elect to stand on the contract or to repudiate it at his option.

A void contract is a contract that is a nullity and has no legal effect. A contract to murder someone is void as against public policy.

Contracts are also classified as formal or informal (or simple).

Formal contracts are those under seal. They must be in writing, sealed by the promisor, and delivered. Negotiable instruments, such as checks and promissory notes, are also considered formal contracts.

Contracts are executory or executed. Contracts are executed when nothing more remains to be done.

Contracts are also called express or implied. If all the terms of the agreement are stated, either verbally or in writing, the contract is expressed. A contract may be implied from the conduct or behavior of the parties. An implied contract exists, for example, when a passenger boards a train without a ticket: he will have to pay the fare.

To establish a valid contract there must be a meeting of the minds. The parties must be in complete agreement as to what is being offered and what is being accepted. If you offer your 1963 Chevrolet for sale to a friend who believes it is a 1964 model, there is obviously no meeting of the minds as to the thing being sold, and no contract is consummated. The elements of mutual consent, therefore, are offer and acceptance.

An offer is a promise intended to create a legal obligation. A promise to attend a dance, a dinner or a social gathering is not legally binding, and is not a legal offer. Nor is a promise to do something in the future an offer. An offer to sell your house "one of these days" at a certain price is not binding. Neither an offer made in jest, nor a vague, ambiguous offer, such as a promise to pay a salesman "a fair share of the profits," or a promise to pay more "if I can afford it," is binding. However, an offer to sell merchandise or goods at a future date, at the prevailing market price, is neither vague nor indefinite, since the future market price can be readily ascertained on the date of delivery.

Price lists, catalogs, circular letters and advertisements of sales are merely invitations to trade, like a government's invitation to receive bids.

An offer becomes effective when the offerer (the person making the offer) communicates the proposal to the offeree (the person to whom the offer is made). An offer may be communicated orally, in writing, or by conduct. An offer is communicated orally or verbally when you attend an auction and make a bid. It is communicated in writing when you send in a written bid to construct a school or other public building. It is communicated by conduct when you pay the taxicab driver the amount indicated on the meter.

A failure to read a written offer is not a valid defense. A person is bound by what he signs. An exception is when the person signing a written offer is induced to do so by fraud or trickery.

Printed notices on receipts and documents are considered part of the communicated offer. For example, you sign an order for merchandise. At the bottom of the order blank is the notation, in red ink, that "no claims will be accepted for defective merchandise unless made within twenty-four hours after receipt." You fail to read the notation, but forty-eight hours after delivery you notice that the merchandise is defective and attempt to return the goods. In this case you will be liable for the goods. However, if the written offer contained terms so inconspicuous that the average person would not take notice of them, you would not be bound, especially if no reference to them is made in the body of the writing.

An offer may be accepted, rejected, revoked or allowed to lapse. An offer may be accepted only by the person to whom it is made, the offeree, or by his duly authorized agent. The act of an agent is considered the act of the principal; knowledge by the agent is considered knowledge by the principal; and delivery to the agent is considered delivery to the principal. An offer made by mail is accepted when the letter of acceptance, properly addressed and posted, is dropped into the letter box. It need not be actually received by the person who made the offer. In this instance the post office becomes the agent of the offerer, the dropping of the letter into the mail box constituting acceptance on the part of the offerer's agent, the post office department. The same principle holds true of telegrams. For example, you wire Smith an offer. Smith receives the telegram at 10 A.M. and wires his acceptance a half hour later. Through some error the wire is not received by you until the following morning. In this case the offer was accepted by Smith at 10:30 A.M., and you will be legally bound.

If no time for acceptance is stated in an offer, the offer terminates on the lapse of a reasonable time, which depends on the circumstances of each case. An offer to sell real estate at a certain price must be accepted within a matter of days. An offer of a reward for the capture of a criminal may be open for acceptance for a very long time.

An offer, unless under seal or given for a consideration, may be revoked at any time before acceptance. However, if the offerer wishes to revoke his offer, he must communicate his revocation to the offeree. In all but four states—California, Montana, North Dakota, and South Dakota—a letter, telegram, or message of revocation is not effective until received by the offeree. In these four states, the revocation is effective when dispatched.

An offer to the general public is made by making a general announce-
ment of the offer. This may be made by radio, television, newspaper, or
by other means suitable to the purpose. Once made, the offer may only
be revoked in substantially the same way as that used to announce the
offer. If the offer is made by newspaper, it should be revoked by that
medium; if by television, then by that medium. An attempt to accept after
the publication of the withdrawal is ineffective.

An offer may be rejected. If it is, any later attempt to accept it is
inoperative. A counteroffer is a rejection of the original offer. So is a
conditional acceptance of an offer. An offer to sell an automobile for
$2,500 is rejected when the buyer says he will pay only $2,300, the counteroffer. It is also rejected when he demands additional equipment for the
car.

An inquiry by the prospective purchaser regarding the terms of the
offer is neither a counteroffer nor a conditional acceptance, and will not
terminate the offer.

An offer is terminated by the death or insanity of either party. This is
true even though the offeree has no notice of the actual death or insanity.
An offer is also terminated with the destruction of the subject matter,
provided the offer has not previously been accepted and the subject matter has been destroyed without the knowledge or fault of either party.

An offer may be kept open by obtaining an option. An option is a
promise, for a consideration, to keep an offer open for a certain length of
time. If the offer is not accepted within the time allowed, the offerer may
keep the consideration—the money given for the option.

Silence does not generally imply acceptance of an offer. The fact that
one writes to another, "If I do not hear from you within ten days, I shall
assume that you accept my offer," does not mean that the offeree has to
do anything about the offer. Silence indicates rejection. To this general
rule there is an important exception, as when the offeree accepts benefits
though it is clear they are not conferred as gifts. If, for example, a tie
company sends you a half dozen ties through the mail without your having
ordered them, you are under no obligation to return them. But if you use
the ties, you become obligated to pay the sale price.

Though minors—or those under twenty-one—have the right to enter
into contracts, the businessman who deals with those under the age set as
the majority in the various states does so at his peril, for the law considers
that the young are too immature to be held fully responsible for their
contracts and provides them with special safeguards for their protection.

The contracts of an infant, therefore, are not void, but merely voidable
at his option; that is, the infant has the right to affirm or disaffirm his
contracts, either during his minority or within a reasonable time after he
reaches his majority, except for those contracts involving necessaries, and
for these he must pay, not the contract price, but merely their fair value.

The right to affirm or repudiate the contract belongs to the infant only.

The adult contracting party is bound by the terms of the agreement and cannot defend on the basis that the other party was an infant. After a minor reaches his majority he can repudiate contracts he made as a minor within a reasonable time, depending upon the circumstances of the individual case.

Minors are liable for what the law considers necessaries. These include food, clothing, shelter, medicine, and an elementary or vocational education. For the minor to be held responsible for payment, the articles furnished must be suitable to his station in life. But even for necessaries the minor is only liable for the reasonable value of goods or services furnished, not for the actual contract price. To recover payment for a minor's necessaries, the seller must prove that the goods were suitable to the condition in life of the infant and that he did not at the time have an adequate supply from other sources.

A minor, therefore, cannot bind himself even for necessaries if he lives with a parent or guardian, unless it can be proved that the parent or guardian is unable or unwilling to furnish him with necessaries.

Generally excluded from the term "necessaries" are liquor, expensive foods for parties, diamonds, violins, guns, saddles, horses (except where riding is necessary to the health of the minor), automobiles and motorcycles.

Cars and motorcycles are not considered necessaries even though they are used by a minor to carry on a business operated by him. This follows the theory that the law views with disfavor any minor who engages in a business involving a variety of contracts, since he doesn't normally have sufficient discretion to engage in a business or trade.

A minor may disaffirm or avoid any contract at any time during his minority or within a reasonable time after reaching his majority. He may not, however, repudiate contracts involving real estate until after he reaches his majority. The repudiation may be either verbal or written, and it must be of the entire contract, not of a part only. Repudiation is an action, express or implied, showing the minor's intention not to abide by the contract.

If the minor does not repudiate an executed contract (an agreement in which nothing further remains to be done), he is assumed to have ratified the contract and decided to elect to claim its privileges. Since repudiation requires some positive action, silence constitutes affirmation of an executed contract after a lapse of a reasonable time. A longer time is allowed to repudiate a real estate transaction than for one involving personal property.

All courts agree that if the minor can restore what he has received, or any part of it, he must do so before he can recover the amount paid by him. Most courts hold that even if the goods are injured, depleted or entirely lost, the minor may repudiate the contract and recover his consideration, on the theory that he would not otherwise be protected by the

ws which were specifically designed for the purpose, since any other
le would limit his repudiation to his foresight in keeping the goods.

Nor does a minor lose all his rights even if he fraudulently misrepre-
ents his age; though if he does, the adult may have a claim against him in
amages for deceit. A minority of states provide that when an infant
eturns property in a depreciated state, he may be charged with the value
f its use and its depreciation for the time he had it.

Intoxication, on the other hand, is a defense regardless whether it was
oluntary intoxication or intoxication produced by the intervention of an-
ther. The important question concerns the capacity of the contracting
arty; namely, was he in such a condition that he was unable to understand
he nature and effect of the instrument? If he was, his contracts are
oidable and may be repudiated within a reasonable time after he be-
omes sober. Promptly upon recovering his judgment, the individual must
lect either to affirm or repudiate the agreement.

The general rule is that notes, contracts and conveyances of an insane
erson, even though he has not been adjudged insane, are voidable like
hose of minors and may be ratified or repudiated when the infirmity is
emoved. Similarly, if the contract is for necessaries or for the benefit of
he insane person, the contract may be enforced against him.

If the contract is an executory one (one in which something remains to
e done), it will not be enforced.

The weight of authority is to the effect that, when a contract with an
nsane person has been entered into in good faith, without fraud or impo-
ition, for a fair consideration, without notice of insanity, and has been
xecuted in whole or in part, it will not be set aside unless the parties can
e restored to their original position. However, if the sane party to the
ontract knew of the other's insanity, or if the circumstances were such
hat a reasonable and prudent person should have known of it, the con-
ract may be repudiated at the option of the lunatic or his representative
vithout regard to the fairness of the contract.

After a person has been adjudged insane by a court, any acts, contracts
r conveyances entered into thereafter are void.

An inmate in a jail or prison or a person convicted of a crime does not
ose his right to make a valid will, contract or deed. However, he cannot
nforce any contract on his own behalf, because his civil rights are sus-
ended; hence, mistakes cannot sue for breach of contract, though his
reditors may reach any property that belongs to him.

Certain mistakes make contracts defective: mistakes as to the identity of the
ubject matter; mistakes as to the nature of the agreement; and mistakes as to
he identity of the parties.

For example, a mutual mistake concerning the identity of the subject
natter may arise when one party agrees to sell to another a lot on a street
vith a certain name in Baltimore, Maryland. Unknown to both parties is
he fact that there are two streets with that name in Baltimore. The seller

has in mind a lot on one street and the prospective buyer has in mind
lot on the other. The agreement is defective because of the mutual mi
take about which lot is the subject matter of the contract.

A mutual mistake as to the existence of the subject matter may aris
when the one party agrees to buy a specific pair of racing dogs from th
prospective seller. Unknown to both parties, both dogs have died fro
poisoning the day before. The agreement is defective because of the m
tual mistake as to the existence of a particular pair of animals.

A mistake as to the nature of the agreement may arise when one part
is handed a document which in reality is a deed. Instead of reading th
document himself, Jones asks that it be read to him. It is read in a wa
that indicates that the paper is a lease rather than a deed. The agreemer
to sell the property rather than to lease it is defective because Jones doe
not know the nature of the paper he has signed. If, however, Jones read
the paper himself and then signs it, he can be charged with negligenc
and will not be able to disaffirm the contract.

A mutual mistake as to the identity of the parties may arise whe
contracts are negotiated by mail, telegram or telephone, as when eac
party believes the other to be someone else.

Certain agreements are considered illegal and therefore unenforceabl
Gambling and wagering contracts are both illegal and void. So are agree
ments that charge interest at usurious rates, that is, at rates the law co
siders excessive. These rates vary from state to state. (See accompanyin
chart.)

All agreements that the law considers to be against public policy a
invalid and unenforceable. Such contracts include those which unreason
ably restrain trade, those which interfere with public service, and thos
which obstruct the administration of justice.

Agreements in unreasonable restraint of trade are void. An agreement
considered unreasonable when it is not reasonably limited in time an
space. You agree, for example, to sell your drugstore for $25,000 and als
agree, at the insistence of the purchaser, not to open another drugstore i
the United States for a period of ten years. Within six months you decid
to open a store within three blocks of your competitor. You would b
within your legal rights, since the agreement would be considered a
unreasonable restraint of trade. Had the buyer merely insisted that yo
not open a drugstore within a specified area of the city for a certai
period of time, the contract would have been enforced in the courts.

Agreements are invalid when they interfere with public service, suc
as: (1) An agreement to pay money to legislators in order to influenc
legislation; (2) an agreement to pay money to a public official for a
appointment to public office; (3) an agreement to pay money for publi
employment.

Agreements also are illegal when they obstruct the administration o
justice: contracts which encourage lawsuits and those which provide fo

e concealment of a crime, for the false swearing of witnesses, and for
e bribing of jurors are all illegal and unenforceable. In addition they
ay subject both parties to criminal penalties.

Consideration, in the law of contracts, is that which binds the parties to
contract. It is the price, motive or inducement that leads one party to
 something he is not otherwise bound to do, or to forbear or refrain
om doing something he is otherwise free to do.

Whenever possible, *all* contracts should be in writing in order to pro-
de written proof of what the parties actually agreed to in case of a
spute.

Certain contracts, by law, are required to be in writing. If they are not,
ey are unenforceable. The Statute of Frauds, which has been adopted
 every state of the Union, provides that the following contracts must be
 writing:

1. A contract which by its terms cannot be performed within one year
om the date it is made. If, for example, you enter into a contract of
ployment for more than one year, such contract must be reduced to
riting. If the contract is merely a verbal one, you can be fired without
y legal redress. If the contract is in writing, you may have a claim for
amages as a result of the contract's breach.

2. A contract for the sale of real property, or of any interest in real
roperty, or for the lease of real property for more than a year. Suppose,
r example, you agree to buy one hundred acres of land. Before the
ntract can be reduced to writing, the land is sold to someone else. Do
u have a claim? No. The fact that the agreement was not in writing
akes it unenforceable.

3. A contract to answer for the debt or default of another person. A
iend of yours owes money to a third person. You tell that person that if
ur friend does not pay the debt, you will. When your friend defaults,
u are sued. Can there be a recovery against you? No, since the agree-
ent was merely a verbal one. Had you signed a written promise, you
uld have been held.

4. Agreements made in consideration of marriage. A verbal promise
ade before marriage to make a settlement after marriage is unenforce-
ble. The promise must be in writing.

5. A contract for the sale of goods, wares and merchandise for a stated
alue, or over, unless the buyer accepts part of the goods and actually
ceives the same or gives something in part payment, or unless some note
 memorandum is made in writing and signed by the party to be charged
 such contract or his authorized agent. The Statute of Frauds in most
ates specifies the minimum amount for which a sale of goods must be
ade in writing, the amount varying from $50 to $2,500 (in Ohio).

In general, all contracts involving money or property may be trans-
rred or assigned to third persons. The person who assigns a contract
 known as the assignor. The person to whom the contract is assigned is

known as the assignee. Unless prohibited by some statute or by the original contract itself, assignments may be either oral or written. If the person to whom the contract has been assigned fails to live up to the agreement liability then falls on the assignor.

Contracts involving a special skill, knowledge, or judgment cannot be assigned or transferred without the consent of both parties to the contract.

An assignee legally stands in the shoes of the assignor, having no better title or rights than had the assignor. He can enforce whatever rights the assignor had, and would be subject to whatever defenses the assignee could raise had he been sued.

All contracts, not of a personal nature, are performed by the deceased executor or administrator. This is known as assignment by operation of law. A similar disposition is also made when a person becomes bankrupt, in which case a trustee takes over the bankrupt's contracts and enforces them for the benefit of creditors.

Contracts may be terminated by (1) performance, or the rendering of services; (2) a subsequent impossibility of performance, for example, by strike, a change of law, or the death or serious illness of the contracting party when the contract is for personal services, as in the serious illness of a lecturer or star performer in a show; (3) the agreement of both parties to end the contract.

A breach of contract is the failure of one party to perform his part of the contract. There are remedies for a breach of contract: (1) The injured party may sue for damages, provided he can show loss. But he must also minimize damages. Thus an employee wrongfully discharged is entitled to recover as damages the salary fixed by the agreement, less whatever money he has been able to earn in other employment. If the contract breached is for the payment of money, the injured party is entitled to recover interest at the legal rate from the time the debt is due in addition to the full amount of the debt. (2) The injured party may have a right to sue for the reasonable value of the services actually performed by him. (3) The injured party may have a right to sue for specific performance. If, for example, you contract to sell your house for $20,000 and later change your mind, the buyer may petition the court to compel you to go through with the sale, instead of seeking money damages. Specific performance is a special remedy and is granted only in cases involving real property and such personal property as valuable paintings and jewels unobtainable elsewhere. (4) There may also be a right to enjoin another person. While it is true that contracts for personal services will not be enforced, an injunction will prevent the performer's accepting employment elsewhere during the term of the contract if his services are rare and unique. (5) A contract may also be dissolved by proper arbitration proceedings. Arbitrators are usually businessmen experienced in the kind of work in which the contracting parties are engaged. The decision of the arbitrators is binding and

hay not be disturbed except on the ground of fraud or obvious errors in
omputation. The decision of the arbitrators is final, and from it no award
hay be taken to the courts, except in the case of fraud or error.

Where one of the parties refuses to comply with the award in an arbi-
ration proceeding, the aggrieved party may then apply to the appropriate
ourt to make the award into a judgment of the court, so that the award
hay be judicially enforced.

CONTRACT—SIMPLE FORM

This agreement entered into between _____ party of the
first part, and _____ party of the second part.

The party of the first part, in consideration of _____
agrees to _____

The party of the second part, in consideration of (can be the undertaking) _____ agrees to (Pay the sum of _____ dollars) as follows:, etc. _____

In witness whereof, the parties hereto have set their hands and seals the
_____ day of _____ 19___ at Baltimore, Md.

_____(SEAL)

_____(SEAL)

CONTRACT FOR THE SALE OF A HOUSE

*Note: The following agreement is merely a contract whereby one party
agrees to buy and the other to sell a house. It is not a deed, which represents
the completed transaction.*

This agreement, made this first day of June, 19___, between John Doe,
hereinafter called the vendor or seller, of the one part, and Thomas Brown,
hereinafter called the purchaser, of the other part, witnesseth:

That the said John Doe, vendor, hereby agrees to sell to the purchaser,
who agrees to purchase, for the sum of Ten thousand dollars, the fee simple,
in possession, free from all encumbrances, of and in all that dwelling house
and land belonging thereto situate on 10 Bayley Avenue, Yonkers, New
York, heretofore in the occupation of said vendor, all which said premises
are delineated on a plan here to be annexed and signed by the parties
hereto; together with all the rights, easements and appurtenances thereto
belonging; which said premises are sold and purchased upon and subject to
the following terms and conditions:

1. That the purchaser shall take, and on the completion of the purchase
pay for, the fixtures and fittings in the said dwelling house and buildings,
and specified in the schedule hereto annexed, at the valuation therein
mentioned.

2. That on payment of the purchase money, and the value of said fixtures and fittings, the vendor shall execute a proper conveyance of the
property according to the stipulations herein contained, which conveyance
shall be prepared by and at the expense of the vendor, and sent to the said
purchaser for approval fifteen days prior to August 30, 19___.

3. That the purchaser shall pay to the said vendor, upon the execution
of these presents, a deposit of five hundred dollars on and in part of his

purchase-money, and pay him the residue thereof on the 30th day of August, 19___, when the purchase shall be completed.

4. That if from any cause whatever, the purchase shall be delayed beyond September 15, 19___, the purchaser shall thenceforth be entitled to the rents and profits of the property and shall pay interest at the rate of 6 per cent per annum on the purchase-money till the completion of the purchase.

5. That if any obstacle or difficulty shall arise in respect to the title, the completion of the purchase, or otherwise, the vendor shall be at full liberty, at any time, to abandon this contract on returning the deposit money only to the purchaser.

6. That if the purchaser shall refuse or neglect to complete his purchase at the time hereby appointed, his deposit money shall be absolutely forfeited to the vendor, who shall be at full liberty, at any time afterward, to resell the property, either by public auction or private contract; and the deficiency, if any, occasioned thereby, together with all losses, damages and expenses of and attending the same, shall be borne and paid by the purchaser, but any increase in the price obtained at such sale shall belong to the vendor.

7. That time in all respects shall be of the essence of this contract.

In witness whereof we have hereunder set our hands and seals.

/s/ Thomas Brown	(Seal)
PURCHASER	
/s/ John Doe	(Seal)
VENDOR OR SELLER	

/s/ Robert Smith

WITNESS

CONTRAVENTION The act of breaking through any restraint imposed by deed, by covenant or by a court.

CONTRIBUTION The making-up of a loss sustained to one of their number, by several parties jointly interested or indebted, or payment made by one for the benefit of all. Thus, when one of several sureties has been compelled to pay the whole of the money for which they all became bound, he is entitled to receive contribution from all the others for what he has done in relieving them from a common burden.

CONTUMACY Disobedience to the rules or orders of a court, especially a refusal to appear in court when legally summoned.

CONVERSION An appropriation of property; one of the grounds of the actions of *trover*. "Conversion" and "carrying away" are not synonymous or convertible terms; there may be a conversion without any carrying away.

CONVEY To pass or transmit from one to another; to transfer property, or the title to property, by an instrument in writing. In a stricter sense, to transfer by deed or instrument under seal.

CONVEYANCE A transfer of legal title to land, usually in an instrument in writing under seal, such as a deed or mortgage.

CONVEYANCING The business or practice of preparing conveyances, especially of real estate, including the investigation of titles, the preparation of abstracts, etc.

CONVICT To condemn; to find guilty of an offense, usually by the verdict of a jury.

CONVICTION The finding a person guilty of an offense with which he has been charged, either by the

verdict of a jury or on his own confession.

CO-PARTNERSHIP *See* PARTNERSHIP.

COPYRIGHT The sole right granted the applicant to print, publish, or sell one's literary, musical, or artistic compositions. The law provides that the application for copyright shall specify to which of the following classes the work belongs: (a) books, including composite or other cyclopedic works, directories, gazetteers, and other

---

ASSIGNMENT OF A COPYRIGHT OF A BOOK

Note: The person or firm receiving such an assignment should have it recorded with the Register of Copyrights within three months after the date thereof.

This agreement made this 15th day of July 19——, between John Doe, called the vendor, and the Blank Publishing Company, called the vendee, or purchaser, to wit:

Whereas the said vendor is the author and absolute proprietor of the copyright of a book entitled "YOUR LEGAL RIGHTS," and has agreed with the said purchaser for the absolute sale to him of the said copyright, free from encumbrances, at the price of ——————— dollars;

Now this agreement witnesseth, that in pursuance of the said agreement, and in consideration of the sum of ——————————— dollars by the said purchaser to the said vendor now paid, the receipt of which is hereby acknowledged, the said vendor hereby assigns, and, as absolute owner, conveys unto the said purchaser, his executors, administrators and assigns, the unencumbered copyright of and the sole privilege of printing all the said book or work entitled YOUR LEGAL RIGHTS, and all future impressions of said work. To have, hold, exercise and enjoy the said copyright and premises unto the said purchaser, his executors, administrators, and assigns, henceforth during the residue of the term of the said copyright now unexpired, for his and their own use and benefit, but subject always to such right as may now be subsisting in the publisher or proprietor of the last edition of the said book or work to prevent the publication of any future edition of the same until such last edition shall be out of print.

Witness our hands and seals.

(Seal) Blank Publishing Co.
—————————————————————————————
                              PURCHASER
(Seal) John Doe
—————————————————————————————
                              VENDOR

compilations; (b) periodicals, including newspapers; (c) lectures, sermons, addresses prepared for oral delivery; (d) dramatic or dramatic-musical compositions; (e) musical compositions; (f) maps; (g) works of art; (h) reproductions of works of art; (i) drawings of plastic works of a scientific or technical character; (j) photographs; (k) prints and pictorial illustrations; (l) motion picture plays; (m) motion pictures other than motion picture plays.

To obtain a copyright, first, print the work with the copyright notice on it—for example, "Copyright, 1965 by John Smith"; or, in the case of works specified, from (f) to (k), the notice may consist of the letter C enclosed in a circle, thus ©, accompanied by the initials, monogram or symbol of the owner—provided his name appears on some accessible part of the copies.

Second, send to the Register of Copyrights, Library of Congress, Washington, D.C., two copies of the work, together with an application for registration. The copies deposited must be accompanied by an affidavit, stating that the typesetting, printing and binding of the book, etc., have been performed within the United States.

Application blanks and affidavit forms may be had from the Copyright Office, Library of Congress, Washington, D.C.

A copyright protects the author or owner for twenty-eight years.

However, within one year prior to the expiration of the twenty-eight years, the owner, or his next of kin, may secure a renewal for another twenty-eight years.

The fee for a copyright is four dollars. This includes the certificate from the Register of Copyrights under seal. Provided the assignment is in writing, a copyright may be assigned to another.

CORAM NON JUDICE In the presence of a person not a judge. Applied to a suit before a court not having jurisdiction.

CO-RESPONDENT The person charged with adultery and made a party to a suit for divorce.

CORONER A county officer whose principal duty is to investigate the causes of any death suspected of not having been brought about by natural causes. His principal duty is to hold an inquisition with the assistance of a jury, over the body of a person who has come to a violent death or who has died in prison. Where there is a vacancy in the office of sheriff or where the sheriff is a party interested in a proceeding it is the coroner's duty to serve all writs which the sheriff is usually required to serve.

CORPORAL OATH An oath taken by laying hand on the Bible.

CORPORATION A body consisting of one or more natural persons, established by law, usually for some specific purpose, continued by a succession of members. Corporations are created by the legislatures of each state with power to create corporations.

A corporation may be perpetual or its duration may be fixed by the terms of the charter. It was formerly said to speak or become bound only by its corporate seal, much as an individual binds himself by his signature. It is a good practice to include the adoption of a corporate seal in the by-laws, an impression from the seal itself being made on the record of the by-law adopting it and as a part thereof. To bind a corporation now, however, a seal is required only in the execution of instruments of a solemn and formal character, such as a conveyance. It becomes bound now in about the same manner as an individual, through the medium of its agents and officers.

The powers of all corporations are limited to those mentioned in their charters or in the general acts under which they are created. With these are those necessarily implied from what are expressly mentioned, both as to what they may do and the manner of doing it.

In general a corporation has the power of perpetual succession, the right to admit new members and, except in case of stock corporations, the right to remove old members for cause; it also has the power to sue and be sued, grant and receive grants, and do all acts within the limit prescribed, in its corporate name; purchase and hold lands and lease or transmit them in succession, have a common seal and break, alter or renew it at pleasure and to make by-laws for its government not inconsistent with law; and in general it may do all acts, not inconsistent with its charter or the law which are either appropriate or necessary to the purposes of its creation.

A corporation exceeding its power is liable to forfeiture of its charter. Where certain powers are designated this implies an exclusion of all others which are not necessary to carry into effect those expressly granted.

In contracting with corporate officers and agents it is well to determine whether or not they are acting within the charter powers of the corporation and in accordance with the by-laws and are duly authorized by the Board of Directors. In those cases involving matters of great moment to the corporation, it is also wise to inquire whether or not the authority to act is vested in the directors by the stockholders.

Generally speaking, so long as the officer acts within the powers usual to such officer, one dealing or contracting with him without knowing or having reason to think that he is exceeding his authority in the particular case may hold the corporation responsible. That a corporation has entered into a contract may be implied from its acts or the acts of its officers or agents.

Another general rule is that though the corporate powers are exceeded, yet if the corporation has actually received and accepted the benefit of a contract it cannot afterwards repudiate it without at least reinstating the party contracted with. Authority to convey real estate, in particular, should be granted to a proper person, as the President, by resolution entered on the corporate minutes.

Corporations have authority to borrow money for purposes within their corporate powers, and to execute and endorse notes in the prosecution of their legitimate business. This does not include the power of endorsing or acting as surety for others except where specially granted by law. The power to own and dispose of real estate, unless there is statutory provision to the contrary, includes the power to mortgage it, though the authority to acquire realty is generally limited to that required for corporate purposes and that which it becomes necessary to purchase in collecting debts.

The charter may be forfeited and the corporation dissolved if it neglects the duties required of it or abuses the privileges granted to it, upon proper suit being brought for that purpose. Where a duty clearly rests upon a corporation or corporate officers which it or they refuse to perform, or where a right of a member or stockholder is denied to him, a writ of mandamus may be obtained to compel performance, or the restoration of the right.

A corporation may be dissolved voluntarily or by surrender of its franchise and acceptance of the same by the state or authority granting it; also, in case of a corporation without shares of stock, through loss of all its members; similarly, where its duration is limited by its charter or by general law, or the happening of some contingent event, it will be dissolved by the expiration of the term designated, or the happening of the contingency.

A charter of a private corporation is an executed contract between the government and the corporation, and if the corporation is not in default the legislature cannot repeal, revoke or alter the charter against the consent of the corporation. This does not apply as against a provision, if there is one, in the charter or act of incorporation providing for a revocation or amendment upon conditions mentioned.

The right of eminent domain, however, that is, the power of the state to take private property for public use, will at all times prevail, even against a corporate franchise, if just compensation is paid for the taking. Thus a corporate franchise to build and maintain a toll bridge may be taken by legislative enactment for the purpose of erecting a bridge free to the public.

A corporation is not bound by the agreement of its promoters, unless it has accepted and received the benefit of the contract; it may become bound by the agreement by ratifying it or entering into it anew after incorporation. Grants of corporate rights, privileges and franchises are always considered to be subject to police powers of the state, and the state may enact such laws as come within its police powers even though corporate rights seem to be interfered with. Where there is reasonable doubt about the meaning of a charter provision or the extent of the corporate powers, the doubt is resolved in favor of the public interest.

Besides being liable on contracts, a corporation may be liable in damages like individuals for torts committed by it or by its agents or employees in the course of their employment, such as trespass, libel and slander, nuisance, conspiracy, malicious prosecution, false imprisonment and even assault and battery, as well as for frauds committed by them. A corporation is not, however, liable for the wilful act of its agent or employee done otherwise than in connection with the business in which it is engaged.

Joint-stock companies and limited partnerships are in effect similar to corporations, are sometimes called quasi-corporations and are governed by much the same rules. They are formed by the execution of requisite papers showing membership, capital subscribed, etc., recorded in a proper public office open to the public inspection in accordance with a statute authorizing their organization. When duly formed by a strict compliance with the law, the liability of the individual members or stockholders for the debts of the concern is limited to the amount subscribed by them to be capital stock or otherwise as the particular statute may provide.

A distinction is made between strictly private and quasi-public corporations, the latter being those which make it a business to supply general public needs, such as railroad, water and gas companies and the like. These must perform their duties to the public, and cannot refuse to render their usual services to anyone applying to the extent of their capacity, subject, however, to their reasonable rules and regulations.

PROMOTER'S AGREEMENT

This agreement by and between John Doe, Richard Roe, and Thomas Brown, parties of the first part, and Ralph Powers, party of the second part, witnesseth, that whereas the said parties of the first part have arranged and agreed among themselves to organize a corporation to be known as the Pioneer Automobile Company, with a capital stock of $75,000, divided into 15,000 shares of the par value of $5.00 each, the same to be located at the City of Baltimore, Md. for the purpose of engaging in the manufacture and sale of automobile sundries and supplies; and

Whereas, the said parties of the first part have agreed among themselves to take and pay for 10,000 shares of the said capital stock on the complete organization of said company; and,

Whereas, the said party of the second part, having had experience as a promoter, has signified a willingness to secure subscriptions for 400 additional shares of the capital stock of said company.

Now, therefore, it is hereby agreed that the said party of the second part shall within ninety days from the date hereof secure bona fide solvent subscriptions to the capital stock of said proposed corporation, the same to be paid on such terms as the Board of Directors of said corporation after its incorporation may determine, consistent with the governing statute of the state.

In consideration of the services so to be rendered by the said party of the second part, the said parties of the first part hereby undertake that the said company, on complete organization by its proper officers, shall issue to said party of the second part 3,000 shares of the capital stock of said corporation as full paid, and for which the said party of the second part shall pay no other consideration whatever. On failure or refusal of the said corporation to so issue said shares of stock to said second party, the said parties of the first part hereby agree and bind themselves to pay to said second party the sum of $15,000 in cash.

On failure of said second party to secure said solvent and bona fide subscriptions within said time this agreement shall be of no force and effect. In case said second party shall procure said subscriptions in said time, then the said parties of the first part agree to sign any proper papers, instruments, articles or certificate necessary to complete the incorporation of said proposed company, and to pay the necessary fees, expenses and charges for the incorporation thereof.

In Witness Whereof, the parties have hereunto set their hands this 10 day of November, 19___.

(Signed)   _____

PARTY OF FIRST PART

_____

PARTY OF SECOND PART

AGREEMENT TO ORGANIZE A CORPORATION

Whereas, the party of the first part has made certain discoveries relating to the manufacture of synthetic rubber, apparently of material commercial value, and has associated the party of the second part with him to further the marketing thereof, and the party of the third part is willing to form and finance a company to manufacture and market the same, if he finds to his satisfaction, after investigation, that said discoveries are valuable commercially: Now, therefore, this agreement witnesseth that in consideration of these presents and of one dollar paid by each of the parties hereto to each of the others, receipt of which is hereby acknowledged, the parties hereto jointly and severally covenant and agree as follows:

1. The party of the third part within 30 days from date is to investigate the commercial value of said discoveries, without expense to the other parties hereto, and if satisfactory is so to notify said other parties within 90 days, and to forthwith incorporate a company to manufacture and sell the products made pursuant to said discoveries, with which company the parties hereto shall be associated as herein indicated.

2. The capital stock of said company is to be issued for said discoveries, and shall be $1,000,000, of 100,000 shares of the par value of $10.00 each, of which the party of the first part is to receive 50,000 shares, the party of the second part 45,000 shares, and the party of the third part 5,000 shares for which he is to pay the company $50,000 as it is needed by it for capital and in installing its plant to supply its business.

3. The said company shall have 6 directors.

4. The said company shall, immediately on its organization, pay said first party $50,000 for his said discoveries which shall be written out in detail and placed in a safety deposit box in the name of the company.

5. The said company shall engage the said party of the first part as consulting engineer and chemist at a salary of $10,000 for the first year,

payable in monthly installments, which salary shall be annually increased, if the business warrants, at the rate of $5,000 a year, until same amounts to $35,000 yearly.

6. The said party of the second part shall be the president of the company at a salary of $10,000 yearly, to be increased as the business of the company warrants.

7. The said party of the third part shall be treasurer of the company at a salary of $7,500 per year.

8. The said parties of the first, second and third parts hereby accept said positions respectively on the basis herein expressed.

9. All obligations hereunder shall terminate 60 days from date, unless favorable action be taken as above indicated.

_____
PARTY OF THE FIRST PART

_____
PARTY OF THE SECOND PART

_____
PARTY OF THE THIRD PART

ARTICLES OF INCORPORATION

Note: When organizing a corporation, particular attention should be paid to the statutes in which the proposed corporation is to be organized. The following form is merely suggestive.

We, the undersigned, hereby mutually agree to unite and associate ourselves as a corporation and for such purpose we hereby make, execute and adopt the following Articles of Incorporation:

Art. 1. The name of this corporation shall be The Outlet Co., Inc.

Art. 2. The period of the existence and the duration of the life of this corporation shall be perpetual.

Art. 3. The principal office and place of business of this corporation shall be at the city of Baltimore, in the state of Maryland.

Art. 4. The objects and purposes of this corporation shall be of manufacture and sale of men's shoes.

Art. 5. The business and affairs of this corporation shall be managed and controlled by a board of three directors, to be elected annually at the annual meeting of the stockholders.

Art. 6. The names and residences of the persons who have been selected as the board of directors to manage the business and affairs of this corporation for the first year are as follows:

Names	Residences
John Doe	Baltimore, Md.
Jane Doe	Baltimore, Md.
Thomas Doe	Baltimore, Md.

Art. 7. The annual meeting of the stockholders for the election of directors and for the transaction of other business shall be held at the office of the corporation on the first Saturday in January, 19____, and on the first Saturday in January in each year thereafter. The vote in the election for directors shall be by ballot, and the election may be conducted in such manner and form as may be provided by the by-laws. The three directors receiving the highest number of votes shall hold their office for three years and until their successors are elected; the next three directors receiving the next highest number of votes shall hold their office for two years and until their successors are elected; the three directors receiving the lowest number

of votes shall hold their office for one year and until their successors are elected. At the first annual meeting thereafter, three directors shall be elected for the term of three years and at each annual election thereafter, three directors shall be elected for the term of three years, the intention being that one-third of such board of directors shall be elected annually.

Art. 8. In all elections for directors each stockholder shall be entitled to one vote for each share of stock owned by him for each director.

(Where the statute permits, the following may be added): In all elections for directors each stockholder shall have the right to vote the number of shares of stock held by him for as many persons as there are directors to be elected; and in casting such vote, he may cumulate his votes and give one candidate as many votes as the number of directors multiplied by the whole number of his shares of stock shall equal; or he may distribute his votes on the same principle among two or more of the candidates for directors. On all matters involving corporate acts transacted in stockholders' meeting, any stockholder may demand a vote according to the ownership of stock.

Art. 9. The capital stock of this corporation shall be $10,000, which shall be divided into common and preferred stock. Of the common stock there shall be 1,000 shares, of the par value of $5.00 each. The said dollars of preferred stock shall be entitled to receive dividends at the rate of 7 per cent per annum, payable semi-annually on the first Monday of January and the first Monday of July in each year, out of the earnings of said corporation before any dividends shall be paid upon the said common stock, and such dividends shall be cumulative so that any deficiency in the dividends to be paid on said preferred stock in any year shall be made good out of the earnings of subsequent years before any dividend shall be paid upon the said common stock. And in case the earnings of the corporation shall permit a dividend in excess of said 7 per cent so to be paid semi-annually, then and in any such event the preferred stockholders, after receiving such preferred dividend, shall be entitled to share equally with the holders of the common stock as to any dividend over and above the said preference dividend. And on the final liquidation of this corporation and the distribution of its assets, all arrears of dividends shall be paid to the holders of such preferred stock and the shares of preferred stock shall be paid in full before any payment shall be made to the holders of the common stock; but when such arrears of dividends and the face value of such preferred stock shall have been paid, the holders thereof shall receive no other or additional payments whatever. The amount of such preferred stock shall not be changed or altered by any increase or reduction in the capital stock of said corporation without the consent in writing of the holders of a majority thereof. The holders of the common stock shall have the management and control of this corporation so long as the business of said corporation is able to pay from its earnings the said preference dividends on such preferred stock and during such time the holders of such preferred stock shall have no voting power. But in case said dividends on said preferred stock shall not be earned and paid for a period of two years, then and in that event the holders of preferred stock shall have the same voting power in the elections and in the management and control of said corporation as the common stockholders.

Art. 10. Immediately, upon the election of directors and the adjournment of the stockholders' meetings, or as soon thereafter as convenient, the directors so elected shall meet and organize by electing one of their number president and one of their number vice-president, and by electing from their number or from the stockholders (or same persons if desired) a secretary and treasurer, each of whom shall perform such duties and powers as generally appertain to such offices and as may be stated or required of them by the by-laws or by the board of directors.

Art. 11. All stockholders must vote in person and cannot vote by proxy. And all persons holding stock in a fiduciary capacity shall be entitled to vote the shares so held by them; and all persons whose stock has been pledged shall be entitled to vote the same, unless the transfer of the stock on the books of the corporation shall show that the pledgee is entitled to vote the same, and in all such cases the pledgee only shall have the right to vote such stock. And the holders of any bond or debenture issued or to be issued by this corporation, whether secured by mortgage or otherwise, shall have the same power to vote in respect to the corporate affairs and management to the same extent and in the same manner as stockholders; that is, in determining the number of votes to be cast by each bond or debenture holder, the amount of his bond or bonds shall be divided by the par value of a share of the capital stock and the result will be the number of votes to which he is entitled. In case of default in the payment of either principal or interest of any bond or debenture, any such bond or debenture holder may have the same right of inspection of the corporate books, accounts and records as any stockholder.

Art. 12. This corporation shall have and hold a lien on all stock subscribed to secure the payment of such subscriptions, and no sale or transfer of stock or shares shall avoid such lien; and as against this corporation, no sale or transfer of stock shall be valid and convey title to the shares unless entered upon the books of the corporation as required by the by-laws.

Art. 13. No single person or corporation shall subscribe for, own or hold at any time more than 1,000 shares of the capital stock of this corporation.

Art. 14. The subscriptions for and the ownership of all stock in this corporation are made and taken upon the condition that any holder of stock desiring to sell the same shall first offer his stock to the corporation at his lowest price and the corporation shall have 30 days in which to exercise its option to purchase the same. On its refusal to purchase, the stockholders shall have 60 days to exercise their option to purchase said stock at said price. After the expiration of such time, the stockholder shall be free to make any other sale of this stock.

Art. 15. The greatest amount of indebtedness to which this corporation may at any time subject itself shall not exceed $15,000.00; or shall not exceed two-thirds of the capital stock actually subscribed.

Art. 16. The private property of the stockholders of this corporation shall not be subject to the corporate debts in any amount or to any extent whatever.

Art. 17. The stock of this corporation shall be non-assessable.

Art. 18. These articles may be changed, altered or amended at any authorized meeting of the stockholders by a vote of the stockholders representing a majority of the stock.

Art. 19. The names and places of residence of the incorporating members, the subscribers hereto, and the number of shares subscribed by each of them and which each agrees to take and pay for, are as follows:

Names	Places of Residence	No. of Shares
John Doe	Baltimore, Md.	500
Jane Doe	Baltimore, Md.	500
Thomas Doe	Baltimore, Md.	1,000

In witness whereof we have set down our signatures this 6th day of April, 19____.

_____
JOHN DOE

_____
JANE DOE

_____
THOMAS DOE

MINUTES OF FIRST MEETING OF INCORPORATORS

The first meeting of the incorporators and subscribers to the capital stock of the Rex Company held at the office of John Brown in the city of Baltimore, upon the 2 day of August, 19____, at the hour of 10 o'clock A.M., pursuant to the agreement and waiver of notice in the articles of incorporation (or pursuant to notice).

And the meeting was called to order by Richard Roe, and upon his motion and nomination Mr. Smith was duly elected chairman of the meeting. On assuming the chair and stating the purpose of the meeting, he called for nominations for secretary, whereupon Mr. Brown was selected for that position and immediately assumed the duties thereof.

At the request of the president the roll of the subscribers and corporators was called and the following persons representing the number of shares of stock were reported as present in person:

Names	No. of Shares
John Redding	500
William Walker	500
Chester Lawrence	500
Ralph Black	20
Hugo Small	60

And the following names and number of shares were present by proxy:

Names	Name of Proxy	No. of Shares
Stanley Taub	Betty Taub	300
George Bank	Joseph Ellisson	450

The proxies were ordered placed on file.

The chairman then stated that since the execution of the articles of incorporation the following named persons had subscribed to the capital stock of the corporation and that the same were present and entitled to vote as follows:

Names	No. of Shares
William Johnson	75
Henry Louis	125
George Stone	100

Thereupon Mr. White (a promoter) reported that the articles of incorporation had been filed in the office of the secretary of state and duplicate certificates had been issued by that officer, one of which had been duly recorded in the office of the clerk (or reporter of deeds), and the other was presented to the meeting, which was thereupon ordered spread.

On motion of Messrs. Redding, Walker, Black, and Lawrence, the directors named in the articles of incorporation were recognized as the directors of the company for the first year of its existence, and those named as such were directed to be entered upon the minutes of the meeting.

On motion it was ordered that the meeting proceed to the election of directors; and thereupon the chair appointed Mr. Black and Mr. Small inspectors of election and they were sworn to discharge their duties as such.

The chair then called for nominations of directors and the following-named gentlemen were placed in nomination, to hold their office for the ensuing year, to wit: Mr. Redding, Mr. Walker and Mr. Lawrence. No further nominations being made, the polls were duly opened and all stockholders present and proxies were permitted to vote. After all had voted, the chair declared the polls closed, and after a count of the ballots, the inspectors reported and presented their certificates showing that the following-named persons had received the number of votes as follows: Mr. Redding, 1,080; Mr. Walker, 1,080; Mr. Lawrence, 1,080; and thereupon the said named persons were declared duly elected directors of the corporation.

It was suggested to the chair that a committee on by-laws had been appointed, and the chair called upon the committee for a report. Thereupon the committee, by its chairman, Mr. Black, asked to submit the following report. The by-laws prepared by the committee were thus read, section by section, and after full discussion, the following by-laws were unanimously adopted for the government of the affairs of the company: (Here insert by-laws adopted.)

On motion of Mr. Small, the board of directors was authorized to make calls upon the stock subscribed for up to the limit of the par value thereof, payable at such times and place as the board of directors should determine.

On motion of Mr. Black, the directors were also authorized to issue stock to all subscribers therefor upon full payment of the same.

Upon motion, the board of directors was also authorized from time to time, in its discretion, to accept in full or in part-payment for stock such property as the board may from time to time determine to be necessary in carrying on the business of this company.

On motion it was ordered:

(1) That in compliance with the laws of the state, the regular registered office of the company in this state shall be established and continuously maintained at No. 100 Doe Street, in the city of Baltimore, state of Maryland.

(2) that Mr. Small be and is hereby appointed the agent of this com-

pany in charge of said office, upon whom process against this corporation may be served, and that he be directed and authorized to keep in said office the stock-transfer books, to register transfers therein, and to keep all other books and records of this company which the laws of this state require to keep therein, during the usual office hours of business, and open to the examination of all stockholders and other persons entitled to inspect the same.

(3) That any stockholder shall be entitled to a list of the names and addresses of the stockholders, with a statement of the number of shares held by each, upon payment of such reasonable fee as the board of directors may determine.

(4) That the name of this corporation shall be at all times conspicuously displayed in plain letters on a sign at the entrance of said office.

(5) That the secretary send a copy of the foregoing resolution, duly certified by him under the seal of the corporation, to the said Mr. Small, and to file such copies thereof with such officials as the law requires.

_____

SECRETARY

GENERAL BY-LAWS OF CORPORATION
ANNUAL MEETING

Section 1. The annual meeting of the stockholders of this company shall be held at the office of the corporation, in the city of Denver, on the first Monday in January of each and every year, at 10 o'clock A.M. for the election of directors and such other business as may properly come before said meeting. Notice of the time, place and object of such meeting shall be given by publication thereof, at least once in each week for two successive weeks immediately preceding such meeting, in the manner required by the laws of the state, and by serving personally or by mailing at least 10 days previous to such meeting, postage prepaid, a copy of such notice, addressed to each stockholder at his residence or place of business, as the same shall appear on the books of the corporation. No business other than that stated in such notice shall be transacted at such meeting without the unanimous consent of all the stockholders present thereat, in person or by proxy.

SPECIAL MEETINGS

Section 2. Special meetings of stockholders, other than those regulated by statute, may be called at any time by a majority of the directors. It shall also be the duty of the president to call such meetings whenever requested in writing so to do, by stockholders owning 51% of the capital stock. A notice of every special meeting, stating the time, place and object thereof, shall be given by mailing, postage prepaid, at least 10 days before such meeting, a copy of such notice addressed to each stockholder at his postoffice address as the same appears on the books of the corporation.

QUORUM

Section 3. At all meetings of stockholders, there shall be present, either in person or by proxy, stockholders owning 51% of the capital stock of the corporation, in order to constitute a quorum, except at special elections of directors pursuant to the laws of the state governing corporations.

VOTING CAPACITY

Section 4. At all annual meetings of stockholders the right of any stockholder to vote shall be governed and determined as prescribed in the laws of the state governing corporations.

POSTPONED ANNUAL MEETING

Section 5. If, for any reason, the annual meeting of stockholders shall not be held as hereinbefore provided, such annual meeting shall be called and conducted as prescribed in the laws of the state governing corporations.

REGISTERED STOCKHOLDERS ONLY MAY VOTE

Section 6. At all meetings of stockholders, only such persons shall be entitled to vote in person and by proxy who appear as stockholders upon the transfer books of the corporation for 30 days immediately preceding such meeting.

ORDER OF BUSINESS

Section 7. At the annual meetings of stockholders the following shall be the order of business, viz:

1. Calling the roll.
2. Reading, notice and proof.
3. Report of officers.
4. Report of committees.
5. Unfinished business.
6. New business.
7. Election of directors.
8. Miscellaneous business.

MANNER OF VOTING

Section 8. At all meetings of stockholders all questions, except the question of an amendment to the by-laws, and the election of directors and inspectors of election, and all such other questions, the manner deciding which is specially regulated by statute, shall be determined by a majority vote of the stockholders present in person or by proxy; provided, however, that any qualified voter may demand a stock vote, and in that case, such stock vote shall immediately be taken, and each stockholder present, in person or by proxy, shall be entitled to one vote for each share of stock owned by him. All voting shall be viva voce, except that a stock vote shall be by ballot, each of which shall state the name of the stockholder voting and the number of shares owned by him, and in addition, if such ballot be cast by proxy, it shall also state the name of such proxy.

SAME

Section 9. At special meetings of stockholders, the provisions of the laws of the state governing corporations shall apply to the casting of all votes.

DIRECTORS
ELECTION

Section 1. The directors of this corporation shall be elected by ballot, for the term of one year, at the annual meeting of stockholders, except as hereinafter otherwise provided for filling vacancies. The directors shall be chosen by a plurality of the votes of the stockholders, voting either in person or by proxy, at such annual election as provided by the laws of the state governing corporations.

VACANCIES

Section 2. Vacancies in the board of directors, occurring during the year, shall be filled for the unexpired term by a majority vote of the remaining directors at any special meeting called for that purpose, or at any regular meeting of the board.

DEATH OR RESIGNATION OF ENTIRE BOARD

Section 3. In case the entire board of directors shall die or resign, any stockholder may call a special meeting in the same manner that the president may call such meetings, and directors for the unexpired term may be elected at such special meeting in the manner provided for their election at annual meetings.

RULES AND REGULATIONS

Section 4. The board of directors may adopt such rules and regulations for the conduct of their meetings and management of the affairs of the corporation as they may deem proper, not inconsistent with the laws of the state of _____ , or these by-laws.

TIME OF MEETING

Section 5. The board of directors shall meet on the first Monday of every month, and whenever called together by the president upon due notice given to each director. On the written request of any director, the secretary shall call a special meeting of the board.

COMMITTEES

Section 6. All committees shall be appointed by the board of directors.

OFFICERS
APPOINTMENT TERM

Section 1. The board of directors, immediately after the annual meeting, shall choose one of their number by a majority vote to be president, and they shall also appoint a vice-president, secretary and treasurer. Each of such officers shall serve for the term of one year, or until the next annual election.

DUTIES OF PRESIDENT

Section 2. The president shall preside at all meetings of the board of directors, and shall act as temporary chairman at, and call to order all meetings of the stockholders. He shall sign certificates of stock, sign and execute all contracts in the name of the company, when authorized so to do by the board of directors; countersign all checks drawn by the treasurer; appoint and discharge agents and employees, subject to the approval of the board of directors; and he shall have the general management of the affairs of the corporation and perform all the duties incidental to his office.

DUTIES OF VICE-PRESIDENT

Section 3. The vice-president shall, in the absence or incapacity of the president, perform the duties of that officer.

DUTIES OF TREASURER

Section 4. The treasurer shall have the care and custody of all the funds and securities of the corporation, and deposit the same, in the name of the corporation, in such bank or banks as the directors may elect; he shall sign all checks, drafts, notes and orders for the payment of money, which shall be countersigned by the president, and he shall pay out and dispose of the same under the direction of the president; he shall at all reasonable times exhibit his books and accounts to any director or stockholder of the company upon application at the office of the company during business hours; he shall sign all certificates of stock signed by the president; he shall give such bonds for the faithful performance of his duties as the board of directors may determine.

DUTIES OF SECRETARY

Section 5. The secretary shall keep the minutes of the board of directors, and also the minutes of the meetings of stockholders; he shall attend to the giving and serving of all notices of the company, and shall affix the seal of the company to all certificates of stock, when signed by the president and treasurer; he shall have charge of the certificate-book and such other books and papers as the board may direct; he shall attend to such correspondence as may be assigned to him, and perform all the duties incidental to his office. He shall also keep a stock-book, containing the names, alphabetically arranged, of all persons who are stockholders of the corporation, showing their places of residence, the number of shares of stock held by them respectively, the time when they respectively became the owners thereof, and the amount paid thereon, and such book shall be open for inspection as prescribed by the laws of the state governing corporations.

CAPITAL STOCK
SUBSCRIPTIONS—PAYMENT

Section 1. Subscriptions to the capital stock must be paid to the treasurer at such time or times, and in such installments, as the board of directors may by resolution require. Any failure to pay an installment when required to be paid by the board of directors shall work a forfeiture of such shares of stock in arrears, pursuant to the laws of the state governing corporations.

CERTIFICATES OF STOCK

Section 2. Certificates of stock shall be numbered and registered in the order they are issued, and shall be signed by the president or vice-president and by the secretary and treasurer, and the seal of the corporation shall be affixed thereto. All certificates shall be bound in a book, and shall be issued in consecutive order therefrom, and in the margin thereof shall be entered the name of the person owning the shares therein represented, the number of shares and the date thereof. All certificates exchanged or returned to the corporation shall be marked canceled, with the date of cancellation, by the secretary, and shall be immediately pasted in the certificate-book opposite the memorandum of its issue.

TRANSFERS OF STOCK

Section 3. Transfers of shares shall only be made upon the books of the corporation by the holder in person, or by power of attorney duly executed and acknowledged and filed with the secretary of the corporation, and on the surrender of the certificate or certificates of such shares.

INCREASE—SUBSCRIPTIONS

Section 4. Whenever the capital stock of the corporation is increased, each bona fide owner of its stock shall be entitled to purchase at par value thereof, an amount of stock in proportion to the number of shares of stock he owns in the corporation at the time of such increase.

DIVIDENDS

Section 1. Dividends shall be declared and paid out of the surplus profits of the corporation as often and at such times as the board of directors may determine, and in accordance with the laws of the state governing corporations.

INSPECTORS

Section 1. Two inspectors of election shall be elected at each annual meeting of stockholders to serve for one year, and if any inspector shall refuse to serve or shall not be present, the meeting may appoint an inspector in his place.

SEAL

Section 1. The seal of the corporation shall be in the form of a circle, and shall bear the name of the corporation and the year of its incorporation.

AMENDMENTS

Section 1. These by-laws may be amended at any stockholders' meeting by a vote of the stockholders owning a majority of the stock, represented either in person or by proxy, provided the proposed amendment is inserted in the notice of such meeting. A copy of such amended by-law shall be sent to each stockholder within ten days after the adoption of the same.

By-laws are not required to be filed in any public office. After adoption they should be entered in the book of minutes of the corporation.

WAIVER OF NOTICE

Section 1. Whenever, under the provisions of these by-laws or of any of the corporate laws, the stockholders or directors are authorized to hold any meeting after notice or after the lapse of any prescribed period of time, such meeting may be held without notice and without such lapse of time by a written waiver of such notice signed by every person entitled to notice.

NOTICE OF FIRST MEETING

State of Maryland } SS.
City of Baltimore }

You are hereby notified that the first meeting of the subscribers and corporators to the articles of incorporation and an agreement to associate themselves for the purpose of forming a corporation to be known by the name of Johnson, Inc., dated on the 1 day of October, 19___, for the purpose of organizing said corporation by the election of directors, the adoption of by-laws, and the transaction of such other business as may properly come before the meeting, will be held at the office of John Doe in the city of Baltimore, state of Maryland, on the 15 day of June, 19___, at 10 o'clock A.M. of said day.

_____

SECRETARY

NOTICE OF DIRECTORS' MEETING

June 1, 19___.

Dear Sir: Your are hereby notified that the regular monthly meeting of the board of directors of the Rex Company will be held at the office of the company, Room 101, Randall Building, No. 100 Doe Street, city of Baltimore, at 10 o'clock A.M. on the 15 day of June, 19___.

_____

SECRETARY

NOTICE OF ELECTION AND MEETING OF DIRECTORS

June 10, 19___.

Mr. John Doe, 1410 U Street.

Dear Sir: At a meeting of the directors of this company held this 2 day of June, 19___, you were duly elected a member of the board to fill the vacancy caused by the death of Mr. Joseph Brown.

The next regular meeting of the board will be held at the office of the company on the 15 day of July, 19___.

Will you kindly indicate your acceptance of the election at your earliest convenience?

Respectfully,

_____

SECRETARY

DECLARATION OF DIVIDENDS

Resolved, that a dividend of 6 per cent on the capital stock of this company be, and the same is hereby declared payable out of the surplus earnings of the company to the stockholders according to their respective holdings; the same to be paid on the 15 day of December, 19___.

STOCKHOLDERS' REQUEST FOR CALLING SPECIAL MEETING

To John Doe, President of the Rex Company:

We, the undersigned, owners of not less than two-thirds of the entire voting stock of the said Rex Company, do hereby request you to call a special meeting of its stockholders, to be held in the office of the company, at No. 100 Doe Street, city of Baltimore, at 2 o'clock in the afternoon on the 2 day of July, 19___, for the purpose of considering the action of the directors of this company in purchasing, in opposition to the expressed wishes of a majority of its stockholders, the real estate and manufacturing plant of the

Matson Company, located at 200 East Street, and to take such action in regard thereto as may seem necessary or desirable to the stockholders.

We further request that you have due and timely notice of said meeting sent to each stockholder of this company.

Names	No. of Shares
William Brown	225
Harriet Scott	301
Timothy O'Neal	450
Jonathan Wild	610
Russell Jones	790

NOTICE TO STOCKHOLDER OF ANNUAL MEETING

Jan. 2, 19____.

Dear Sir: You are hereby notified that the annual meeting of the stockholders of the Rex Company will be held at the office of the Company, Room 101, Randall Building, 100 Doe Street, city of Baltimore, at 10 o'clock A.M. on Tuesday, 2 day of Feb., 19____, for the election of directors and for the transaction of such other business as may come before the meeting.

The stock-transfer book of the company will be closed at 5 o'clock P.M. of the 1 day of March, 19____, for the purpose of transfers for qualification of stockholders for said meeting.

(Signed)_____
SECRETARY

CALL FOR SPECIAL MEETING BY STOCKHOLDERS

We, the undersigned, being all the stockholders of the Rex Company, of Baltimore, hereby call a special meeting of the stockholders of the said company, to be held at its office, No. 100 Doe Street, city of Baltimore, on the 2 day of June, 19____, at 1 o'clock P.M. of said day, for the purpose of electing a director and we hereby waive all statutory and by-law requirements as to notice of time, place and object of said meeting, and hereby agree to the transaction thereat of any and all business pertaining to the affairs of said company.

(Signed)_____

CERTIFICATE OF CHANGE OF PRINCIPAL OFFICE VOTE
OF STOCKHOLDERS

We, the undersigned, John Doe, president, and Richard Roe, secretary, and a majority of the board of directors of The Long Company, a corporation organized under the laws of the state of New York, do hereby certify as follows, to wit:

That a duly called special meeting of the stockholders of this corporation was held at its principal office in the city of New York, state of New York, on the 2 day of June, 19____, at which meeting stockholders owning 900 shares of the stock were present in person and by proxy.

That the meeting was organized by the selection of John Doe as chairman and Richard Roe as secretary.

Thereupon the following resolution was offered for adoption:

"Resolved, That the principal office and place of business of this corporation be changed from the city of New York, state of New York, to the city of Baltimore, state of Maryland.

"And Be It Further Resolved, That the president, secretary and directors be authorized, and they are hereby directed and authorized to effect such changes pursuant to law."

And thereupon on motion the said resolution was adopted by a majority of all the votes cast on such motion to adopt.

1. The name of this corporation is The Long Company.

2. That its principal office and place of business as fixed by the original articles of incorporation was and still is in the city of New York, state of New York.

3. That it is desired to change its principal office and place of business of the corporation to the city of Baltimore, state of Maryland, and that it is the purpose of said corporation to actually transact and carry on its regular business from day to day at such last-named place.

4. That said change has been authorized by a vote of the stockholders of said corporation, at a special meeting of the stockholders called for that purpose as above shown.

5. That the names of the directors and their respective places of residence are as follows, to wit:

Names	Residences
John Doe	New York
Richard Roe	Philadelphia
Samuel Black	Baltimore
William Brown	Washington, D.C.

In Witness Whereof, we have hereunto set our hands this 10 day of June, 19____.

Subscribed and sworn to this 10 day of January, 19____.

_____
NOTARY PUBLIC

GENERAL FORM OF PROXY TO VOTE STOCK

Know all Men by These Presents:

That John Doe _____ does hereby constitute and appoint Richard Brown attorney and agent for John Doe, and in his name, place and stead to vote as _____ proxy at the next election of Directors of the Rex Co., Inc., and for inspectors of election, according to the number of votes and upon the shares of stock he should be entitled to vote, if then personally present, and authorize him to act for me and in my name and stead, at the next meeting for the election of directors as fully as I could act if I were present, giving to said Richard Brown, agent and attorney, full power of substitution and revocation.

This proxy is to continue in force until the 10 day of Nov., 19____, unless sooner revoked.

_____
                                                        JOHN DOE

_____
          WITNESS

WAIVER OF NOTICE OF MEETING

State of Maryland } SS.
City of Baltimore }

We, the undersigned, incorporators of the Rex Company, a corporation of the state of Maryland, do hereby severally waive notice of the time, place and purpose of the first meeting of incorporators of said company, and hereby consent that the same be held at the office of John Doe in the city of Baltimore, state of Maryland, on the 10 day of November, 19____, at 10 o'clock A.M.; and we do further hereby consent to the transaction of any and all business that may come before the meeting, including the election of directors and the adoption of by-laws.

Dated this 16 day of October, 19____.

                    _____
                                     INCORPORATOR

                    _____
                                     INCORPORATOR

                    _____
                                     INCORPORATOR

                    _____
                                     INCORPORATOR

DISSOLUTION BY INCORPORATORS

We, John Doe, Richard Brown, and Thomas Smith, being all the incorporators named in the articles and certificate of incorporation of the Ogden Manufacturing Company, and which said articles and certificate of incorporation were filed for the purpose of creating a domestic corporation, other than a moneyed or transportation corporation, do hereby, pursuant to the governing statute, certify as follows:

1. That the above are the names of all the incorporators of the said Manufacturing Company.

2. That no part of the capital stock of said corporation has been paid.

3. That said corporation has no liabilities whatever.

4. That the business for which said corporation was created has not been begun and that the said incorporators have not undertaken or conducted any business whatever under said organization or as a corporation.

5. That we, the above named incorporators, do hereby surrender to the state and its proper officers all the rights and franchises obtained for and in behalf of said corporation, and that we hereby, on our part, disaffirm and revoke the said articles of incorporation and hereby declare our intention not to undertake, conduct or carry on the objects of said corporation and hereby declare that we will no longer act as a corporation.

In Witness Whereof, we have executed this certificate in duplicate.

Dated this 10 day of October, 19____.

State of California   } SS.
County of Los Angeles }

John Doe, Richard Brown, and Thomas Smith, being severally duly sworn, each for himself, deposes and says, that he is one of the incorporators named in the foregoing certificate; that he has read the foregoing certificate subscribed by him and knows the contents thereof, and that such certificate is true in substance and in fact.

_____

NOTARY PUBLIC

CORPORATION DE FACTO If persons have attempted in good faith to organize a corporation under a valid law (statute) and have failed in some minor particular, but have thereafter exercised corporate powers, such is a corporation de facto. Failure to have incorporators' signatures on applications for charter notarized is an illustration of non-compliance with statutory requirements.

CORPORATION DE JURE A corporation that has been formed by complying with the mandatory requirements of the law authorizing such a corporation.

CORPOREAL That which can be touched and seen; material.

CORPOREAL HEREDITAMENTS Such hereditaments as are of a material and tangible nature and may be perceived by the senses, consisting wholly of substantial and permanent objects, all of which may be comprehended under the general denomination of land only.

CORPUS A body; a human body.

CORPUS DELICTI The legal term for the actual tangible evidence to prove that the crime was committed.

CORPUS JURIS A body of law. A term introduced in the Middle Ages, to signify a book comprehending several collections of law. There are two principal collections to which that appellation is given: the Corpus Juris Civilis and the Corpus Juris Canonici. A third is Corpus Juris Secundum, an encyclopedia of law for lawyers and judges.

COST, INSURANCE AND FREIGHT (C.I.F.) Terms in a contract for the sale of merchandise which requires the seller to pay the insurance, cost and freight of the goods to the point of destination.

COSTS The expenses which are incurred either in the prosecution or defense of an action, or in any other proceeding at law, or in equity; consisting of the fees of attorneys, solicitors and other officers of court, and such disbursements as are allowed by law.

COUNSELOR, COUNSELLOR AT LAW A person whose occupation and office it is to give counsel or advice as to the management of suits and other legal business, to conduct the trial or argument of cases in court (in which sense the word is synonymous with advocate) and to do any other acts requiring a personal presence there.

COUNTER-CLAIM A term embracing both set-off and recoupment.

COUNTERFEITING The unlawful forging, copying or imitating in order to deceive or defraud by passing the copy or thing forged for that which is original or genuine. Counterfeiting is usually applied to the unlawful printing or imitation of money.

COUNTERMAND To revoke an order previously given.

COUNTER-OFFER A cross-offer made by the offeree to the offeror.

COUNTY WARRANT A non-negotiable instrument in the form of a bill of exchange drawn by the proper officer of the county, upon the county treasurer, directing the treasurer to pay out of a particular fund a sum of money to the order of the payee or bearer. School warrants, city warrants, and state warrants are of the same character.

COUPON Usually interest certificates attached to term bonds. When the interest is due, these coupons are cut off the original bond and cashed or sold. Such coupons may or may not be negotiable. The bonds to which such certificates are attached are called coupon bonds.

COURT A tribunal established for the public administration of justice. It is composed of one or more judges, who sit for that purpose at certain fixed times and places, attended by proper officers.

COURT MARTIAL A court held in the military and naval service for the trial and punishment of offenses against the regulations of the service.

COURT OF CHANCERY *See* CHANCERY.

COURT OF CLAIMS A federal tribunal established to hear and investigate claims against the United States. Its opinion is merely advisory.

COURT OF RECORD A court where the acts and judicial proceedings are enrolled in parchment (or paper) for a perpetual memorial and testimony, and which has power to fine and imprison for contempt of its authority.

COURTS The function of a court is to provide a governmental intermediary whereby the law of a particular state may be applied to controversies or disputes coming before it. State and federal courts may be divided, generally, into courts of original jurisdiction and courts of appeal.

A court of original jurisdiction is one in which a case is tried for the first time, witnesses heard, evidence introduced, and a verdict handed down, either in favor of the plaintiff (the party suing) or in favor of the defendant (the party sued). The losing party has the opportunity to appeal his case to a higher court.

In a court of appellate jurisdiction, the original case is argued, but not retried, on the written record of the trial in the court having original jurisdiction. No witnesses are heard, and no additional evidence is presented. Briefs containing a transcript of the original testimony, together with citations from appropriate and pertinent legal authorities, are included in the record and turned over to the clerk of the court of appeals. The clerk in turn sees that the copies of the record are submitted to each of the judges of the court of appeals. In such a court, counsel for both sides may, if they wish, submit oral arguments based on the written records already submitted. After reading the transcript of the record and applying what each judge believes to be the applicable law, the appeal is either sustained or denied. If denied, that is usually the end of the matter. If the appeal is sustained, the court may reverse the decision of the court of original jurisdiction by granting a new trial, cutting down the amount of any award, or doing whatever else it deems necessary in order that justice be done.

Inferior courts of limited jurisdiction are variously known as courts of justices of the peace, municipal courts, small claims courts and traffic courts.

The jurisdiction of these courts is limited usually by amount or by subject matter. For example, a traffic court judge, usually a justice of the peace, will hear only infractions of the traffic rules; and being in a sense a criminal court, the traffic court has no jurisdiction to impose damages for either personal injuries or property damage. The fact that the defendant is found guilty or not guilty of a traffic violation, such as a failure to yield the right of way, is not even admissible as evidence in a civil suit for damages. A municipal court, or people's court, is usually limited both by amount and by the kind of cases it can hear. Such a court cannot try a person accused of a crime or dissolve a marriage by either annulment or divorce. Cases usually tried in a municipal court range in amounts from $300 to $1,000. They may involve damages as a result of injuries sustained in an automobile accident, suits between landlords and tenants, breaches of contract, and other civil suits. The decisions of these inferior courts may be appealed to courts of general jurisdiction.

State courts of general jurisdiction are known as courts of common pleas, circuit courts, superior courts, or, in New York State, supreme courts.

With the exception of criminal cases, all kinds of suits involving any amount of money are heard before the judges of such courts, including suits for damages, breach of contract, divorce, and every other sort of legal matter. Appeals from the verdicts of courts of general jurisdiction may be taken to the state's highest court, usually known as the Court of Appeals or Supreme Court. Criminal cases are heard in criminal courts, which are a distinct part of courts of general jurisdiction. The verdicts of criminal courts may also be appealed to the state's highest appellate court.

Courts handling probate and estate matters are called probate courts, orphan's courts, or surrogate courts.

Equity courts, sometimes known as circuit courts, are courts of general jurisdiction that evolved originally to correct a too technical system of law. When legal remedies for wrongs would not otherwise exist, equity courts supply suitable remedies.

As a general rule, if an adequate remedy can be had in a law court, courts of equity will not assume jurisdiction. But to this rule there are a number of exceptions. The cases most frequently heard in equity courts concern divorce, fraud, accident or mistake, imperfect consideration, and the cancellation or reformation of legal documents such as contracts or deeds. Such courts also have the power to grant injunctions to force or restrain an individual or corporation to do or not to do a specific act. Relief will also be granted if mischief would result if the court did not interfere, as when contracts are made in restraint of trade, public offices are bought and sold, and agreements are founded on corrupt considerations.

When, from a relation of trust and confidence, the parties do not stand on equal ground in dealing with each other, as in the case of parent and child, guardian and ward, attorney and client, principal and agent, executor and legatee, equity courts will assume jurisdiction. They will also hear cases involving trusts, account, partition, dower, and land boundary disputes.

The federal courts are those established under Article III, Section I, of the United States Constitution, which provides that "the judicial Power of the United States, shall be vested in one supreme Court, and in such inferior Courts as the Congress may from time to time ordain and establish." Under this authority Congress has created the Supreme Court of the United States, comprising the Chief Justice of the United States and (at present) eight Associate Justices, and a system of inferior courts. The trial courts with general federal jurisdiction are the district courts. Coming between the district courts and the Supreme Court are the various courts of appeal, one for each of the eleven judicial circuits in the United States. In addition to these courts Congress has from time to time created certain special courts: the Court of Claims, the Customs Court, the Court of Customs and Patent Appeals, the Court of Military Appeals, and various territorial courts comparable in jurisdiction to the district courts. Congress has also established a Tax Court, which, however, is an executive agency and not a direct part of the federal judicial system.

The judicial power of the Supreme Court extends to all cases arising under the Constitution, laws, and treaties of the United States; to cases involving foreign diplomats and admiralty practice; to diversity cases (those between citizens of different states); and to cases to which the United States or a state is a party. The Supreme Court has original jurisdiction in cases to which foreign diplomats or a state of the Union is a party. In all other federal cases the Supreme Court hears cases only on appeal from the lower federal courts. The Supreme Court determines the constitutionality not only of state laws thought to be in conflict with the Federal Constitution, but of acts of Congress as well. When the Supreme Court rules against the constitutionality of a statute or an executive action, its decision can only be reversed by an amendment to the Constitution or by the Court itself—if it later overrules or modifies its previous opinion.

The Supreme Court thus potentially wields the highest power in the federal government, since it can veto the acts of both the legislative and the executive branches.

A district court is the court of original jurisdiction under the federal system. Such courts have exclusive jurisdiction over admiralty, maritime, and prize cases. They may try cases relating to patents, copyrights, and trademarks, as well as all matters pertaining to bankruptcy. District courts also have original jurisdiction to try all civil cases in which the matter in controversy exceeds $10,000 and the dispute arises under the Constitution or treaties of the United States. They also have original jurisdiction over all civil cases in which the matter in controversy exceeds $10,000 and the action is between citizens of different states, between citizens of a state and a foreign state or citizen or subject thereof, and between citizens of different states and to which foreign states or citizens are additional parties. District courts also have jurisdiction over criminal matters in which a federal statute is alleged to have been violated, as, for example, over violations of the income tax laws.

Appeals from the decisions of the judge in a district court are taken, generally, to the court of appeals having jurisdiction over the circuit in which the district court is located. In certain instances the decisions of the district court may be appealed directly to the Supreme Court.

Federal courts of appeals are intermediate appellate courts in the federal judicial system. They review all decisions of the district courts (with certain exceptions), and are empowered to review and enforce the orders of many federal administrative bodies. The decisions of the courts of appeals are final except as they are subject to discretionary review or appeal in the Supreme Court.

The Court of Claims allows individuals an opportunity to sue the federal government for certain designated claims. Appeals from the decisions of the court are heard by the Supreme Court.

The Customs Court reviews appraisals of imported merchandise and all decisions of collectors of customs, including orders on rate of duty, exclusion of merchandise, and liquidation of entries.

Cases heard by the Court of Customs and Patent Appeals include appeals from the decisions of the Customs Court and of the Board of Patent Appeals, the Board of Patent Interferences, and of the examiners of the Patent Office. It has jurisdiction to review decisions of the Commissioner of Patents on trademark applications. It may also review questions of law of the United States Tariff Commission on unfair practices in import trade. The Supreme Court may hear appeals taken from the Court of Customs and Patent Appeals.

The Court of Military Appeals is the final appellate court for convictions by military courts.

The Tax Court reviews the decisions of the Bureau of Internal Revenue on income tax matters.

The steps in a civil lawsuit are:

1. Every person sued is entitled to notice of the nature of the suit so that he can properly defend himself. The first step, usually, is the issuing of a summons to the party being sued. The summons, issued by the sheriff, briefly states the nature of the suit and when the defendant must enter his appearance, or the date and time when he is to appear in court. Upon receiving the summons, the defendant should immediately get in touch with his counsel or take steps to engage counsel if he has none. While state rules vary widely, the usual practice is to have the summons served personally on the defendant by the sheriff or one of his deputies at the place where the defendant resides or is employed. (In some states, especially in suits arising in municipal, people's, or small claims courts, service may be had by registered mail.) The defendant is usually handed, with the summons, a copy of the declaration drawn by the plaintiff's attorney. The declaration states the plaintiff's complaint and sets forth his demand for damages if damages are involved. (Damages may be requested in a variety of legal matters.) If the defendant wishes to contest the suit, he engages counsel who, after one or more conferences with his client, draws up an answer to the declaration. In this answer the defendant may specifically deny or admit each of the individual points raised by the plaintiff's attorney. In addition, there may be a further exchange of what are known as legal pleadings, or documents that narrow down the issues of the case so that they may be properly tried.

2. On the other hand, if the defendant's counsel believes that the declaration of the plaintiff (the party suing) has failed to set forth a valid legal action, he will file what is known as a demurrer, which will then be heard by the trial judge merely on the legal merits of the case. If the demurrer is sustained, the plaintiff either loses his case completely or is allowed to amend his declaration to conform with the rulings of the judge.

3. The third step in a civil suit is the actual trial. The trial may be held with or without a jury, usually at the option of the plaintiff. A jury is chosen from a list of prospective jurors handed both attorneys at the trial table. Once a jury has been selected, counsel for the plaintiff has the right to make an opening statement in which he outlines, as briefly and as clearly as possible, the basis for his client's claim and states the amount of damages he seeks. The attorney for the defendant then proceeds to make his opening statement, in which he generally denies the plaintiff's claim. Witnesses are then called by the plaintiff to substantiate the claim set forth in the declaration. These witnesses are cross-examined by defendant's counsel in order to discredit their testimony and weaken the plaintiff's case. The witnesses for the defendant are next called to further destroy the plaintiff's case or minimize the amount of damages or both. Such witnesses, of course, are also subject to cross-examination by counsel for the plaintiff.

4. After all the testimony has been heard by the court and jury, or by the court sitting as a jury, counsel for the defendant or for the plaintiff

may ask for a "directed verdict," which means that the case will be taken away from the jury and decided solely by the judge. The granting of a directed verdict on behalf of counsel for the defendant indicates that the plaintiff has failed to make out a legal case sufficient even to be considered by the jury or by the judge sitting as a jury. An additional point must be made: when a case is heard by a jury, it is the latter that is exclusive judge of the facts, while the judge merely instructs the jury on the law applicable in the particular case.

5. If the trial judge dismisses the motion for a directed verdict, the counsel for the plaintiff sums up his case in an oral argument before the court and jury. Counsel for the defense then has the opportunity of rebutting the defendant's allegations in his closing argument. In many states the attorney for the plaintiff closes the case by attempting to rebut the arguments brought forth by the defendant's counsel.

6. After the jury returns its verdict for plaintiff or defendant, either counsel may request the court for a judgment "notwithstanding the verdict." If, for example, a jury brings in a verdict of $10,000 in a negligence suit, defendant's counsel may request the trial judge to set the verdict aside on the ground that there was no legal evidence to support such a verdict.

7. If the motion to set aside the jury's verdict fails, judgment is entered for $10,000 against the defendant. However, the defeated party still has the opportunity to move for a new trial. If this motion is granted, a special day is set aside for the hearing before the same judge who heard the original trial, with only the counsel for both sides present to argue the legal merits of the case. If the request for a new trial is denied, the defeated party has the further right of appeal to a court of appellate jurisdiction.

If a defendant refuses to pay the amount of a judgment, the plaintiff—the party suing—may, through his counsel, direct the sheriff or marshal to execute upon the judgment; the latter makes a seizure or levy upon the judgment debtor's property, sells it at public auction, and applies the proceeds in payment of the judgment. If any money is left over from the proceeds of the sale, the balance is turned over to the defendant or judgment debtor, less costs of the sale.

COURTS OF ASSIZE AND NISI PRIUS Courts in England composed of two or more commissioners, called judges of assize, who are twice in every year sent by the Queen's special commission, on circuits all around the kingdom to try, by a jury of the respective counties, the truth of such matters of fact as are then under dispute in the courts of Westminster Hall. In American law, trial courts.

COVENANT An agreement entered into by deed, that is, by instrument of writing under seal, whereby one of the parties promises the performance or non-performance of a certain act or acts, or that a given state of things does or shall or does not or shall not exist. It is frequently and indeed usually but part of an entire contract or conveyance and is collateral to it.

Where one party to such a contract is ready and offers to perform his part and the other refuses or neglects to perform his, the former has a right of action against the latter although it is not expressed who shall do the first act in the performance. This will not be true if in the very nature of the case or by implication in the contract itself one must or is required to perform before the other or before performance on the party of the other can become effective. In determining whether or not the performance of one covenant depends upon or is to follow the performance of another, the intention of the parties will control, rather than the mere structure of the instrumentor, the arrangement of the covenants in the instrument.

Covenants are void if expressly forbidden by law or if they are immoral or against public policy or in general restraint of trade, or if fraudulent between the parties. Even if valid between the parties they will be void as to third parties if fraudulent as to them.

In some states, the words "grant, bargain and sell" in conveyances in fee contain an implied covenant that the grantor is the owner in fee and that the grantee shall be kept free from injuries done or suffered by him (the grantor) and for quiet enjoyment against his acts.

The word "give" implies a covenant of warranty during the life of the grantor and in a lease the words "grant" and "demise" raise an implied covenant on the part of a lessor. The word "covenant" is not necessary to create a covenant and the words "I oblige," "I agree" or "I bind myself" or any words showing the intent of the parties to do or not to do a certain thing is sufficient.

In case of a transfer of land in parcels subject to a covenant, the several purchasers may recover pro rata on the covenant thus running or attached to the land, the original covenantee recovering according to his share of the original estate remaining.

There are certain covenants called real covenants which are said to "run with the land." They are so connected with the realty that he who owns it is entitled to the benefit of them or is bound to perform them as the case may be, even though the land may have passed out of the hands of the original parties to the covenant.

Covenants concerning title to the property usually run with the land. Whether a covenant is to be considered as running with the land or not, is determined from the apparent intent of the parties gathered from the language of the covenant read in the light of the surrounding circumstances. Such covenants enter into the consideration for which land, or some interest therein to which the covenant is annexed, passes between the covenantor and covenantee whether in case of a lease, mortgage, or a conveyance in fee simple. They are in some cases to preserve the property such as to keep in repair or to keep buildings insured or reinstate them if burned, or for renewal of a lease or given condition, or to protect the tenant in the enjoyment of the premises, or to make further assurances of title, or for quiet enjoyment, or never to claim or assert title, or to warrant and defend the title, or to remove encumbrances, or to supply water to the premises, or not to establish another mill in the same stream, or not to erect buildings on adjoining lands, or to use the land in a specified manner or to create, provide and preserve rights of way and the like for the benefit of the land granted, etc., etc.

One who covenants for further assurance, that is, for the completion of a transfer already made and intended to be made at the requirement of the covenantee, must remove a judgment or other encumbrance. A failure to comply with such a covenant may be enforced by bill in equity for specific performance, or an action to recover damages may be brought.

When there is a covenant against encumbrances the mere existence of one constitutes a breach of the covenant and will furnish ground for a suit whether the grantee or purchaser know of its existence or not. Such covenants do not, however, run with the land though it is otherwise if the encumbrance is a mortgage and there is a covenant of warranty *(see below)*. In case of a covenant against encumbrances, the injured party may sue either before he pays it off or after at his option.

A covenant not to sue is equivalent to a release, that is, if it is general and not limited to a particular time. Such a covenant with one of several jointly and severally bound will not protect the others so bound.

A covenant for quiet enjoyment is an assurance of guarantee against the consequences of a defective title to the land coveyed and of any disturbances thereon. By it the covenantor stipulates to indemnify the covenantee against all acts committed by virtue of a paramount title, but this does not include the acts of a mob or even a mere trespass by the lessor.

The guaranty may be for quiet enjoyment against the acts of a particular person or it may be limited in any other way but is usually general. It most frequently occurs in leases where it is said to be implied by such words as grant, demise, lease, yielding and paying, give, etc. Such an agreement exists impliedly in a parol lease. The covenant required for quiet enjoyment in deeds frequently takes the form of what is termed a covenant of warranty.

The covenant of warranty is an assurance by the grantor to the grantee that he shall enjoy the premises without interruption by virtue of any paramount title. It runs with the land and applies to it without respect to who may become the owner by subsequent conveyance and is good against the covenantor, and at his death, against his executors and administrators to the extent of the estate of the covenantor coming into their hands at his death.

Warranties are of two kinds, general and special. The former is a covenant against adverse claims of all persons whatever. The latter only against those of particular persons or claims set forth, usually those of the grantor and his heirs and those claiming by, from or under him, them or any of them.

A covenant of warranty gives the covenantee the benefit of any title that may be acquired by the grantor subsequent to the conveyance, even though such title is paid for or obtained for value by the covenantor. An action for breach of the covenant may be brought by the owner of the land against the covenantor, but where the original covenantee, having sold the land, satisfied the owner, he may bring the suit against the covenantor.

To constitute a breach of the covenant there must be an eviction or deprivation of possession by one holding paramount title. This eviction may, however, be constructive as where a tenant recognizes and pays rent to the true owner by paramount title, or where, the premises being vacant, such owner takes possession. The damage for failure of warranty is measured in most states by the value of the land at the time of conveyance with warranty with interest added. In some places it is the value at the time of the eviction.

COVENANT IN LAW A covenant implied by law from certain words in a deed which do not express it.

COVERTURE The condition of being a married woman.

COVIN A conspiracy to defraud another.

CRAFT UNION A labor organization limited to members who have special skills, such as typesetters, die workers, carpenters, plumbers, bricklayers, and so forth.

CREDIBLE WITNESS A witness competent and worthy of belief.

CREDIBILITY Worthiness of belief; that quality in a witness which renders his evidence worthy of belief. After the competence of a witness is allowed, the consideration of his credibility arises, and not before.

CREDITOR One to whom money is owed. Where one creditor has a lawful claim against two funds and another against one fund only, courts of equity exercise the right to marshal the assets, and will compel the creditor who has the right against both funds first to exhaust that against which the other creditor has no right. This gives both an opportunity if possible to recover, or if the one having the claim against both funds has been satisfied without the observance of this rule, the other creditor may be substituted or subrogated to his right against both.

If a creditor has a judgment lien against a tract of land which is subsequently subdivided and portions sold off therefrom still subject to the lien of a judgment, the creditor may be compelled to first exhaust his rights against the property remaining in the hands of the debtor, if any, and with respect to portions sold, to resort to the same in the reverse order of their sale.

CREDITOR BENEFICIARY A person who is not a party to a contract yet is to receive the consideration contracted for by the promisee in discharge of a debt owed by the promisee to the creditor beneficiary.

CREDITOR'S BILL A bill in equity filed by creditors for an account of the assets and a settlement of the estate of a decedent.

CRIME An offense against the state, punishable in its name.

CRIMINAL ACTION Prosecutions for crimes brought in the name of the state or the supreme ruling power, and which are based upon the assumption that the injury done is to the public generally. An injury to a private person is compensated by a civil suit for damages even where the injury involves a crime. Thus the state prosecutes for the crime of assault and battery. The individual injured in order to be compensated for the injury done him would have to bring a civil suit against the offender to recover damages. It is true that the person injured is usually the prosecutor in a criminal suit, but this is not necessarily so. Anyone might start the machinery of the law in motion to punish a criminal offense by making a formal information as to the commission of the crime under oath before a magistrate. This is not infrequently done by peace officers with respect to crimes as to which they were in no way parties and were not even present at their commission, though generally speaking such officers cannot be compelled to make formal information before a magistrate. Giving formal information is open to anyone, but no one should do so unless he has personal knowledge of the commission of the offense or unless from information obtained by him, he has just grounds for believing the accusation true.

If an innocent person is prosecuted maliciously and without probable cause the prosecutor will be liable in a civil suit for damages to the person injured. The Constitution of the United States provides the "the accused shall enjoy the right to be confronted with witnesses against him." Hence, testimony, obtained under a commission or rule of court, of one residing out of the state, or sick or infirm and unable to attend court cannot be used against him.

A crime is said to be *malum in se,* that is, bad in itself, when it is against the moral sense of the community. Some crimes are such simply because they are made so by statute and are not essentially bad from a moral point of view.

The law places a number of safeguards around those accused of crime. Every man is presumed to be innocent until the contrary is shown, and if there is reasonable doubt as to his guilt he is entitled to the benefit of it. Statutory laws creating crimes and offenses are strictly construed; if there is doubt as to their meaning it will be resolved in favor of the accused. The proof as to what was done by the alleged offender must come strictly within the definition of the offense charged.

No one can be brought to trial until a grand jury on examination has found reason to subject him to trial, and the prisoner is then entitled to a trial by a jury of his peers chosen by the body of the people with a view to their impartiality, and whose decision as to the facts of a case are final. The prisoner's former conduct or general habits of life cannot be inquired into unless he first attempts to show good reputation among people who know him, in which case this evidence may be rebutted by contrary testimony.

The prisoner cannot be compelled to testify against himself but he may if he choose testify in his own defense. He cannot be twice put in jeopardy for the same offense or punished under a law passed after the offense was committed.

There must be a criminal intent to constitute a crime as well as actual commission of the offense, but criminal willfulness and malicious intent are to be presumed from the very commission of the offense, which may, however, be rebutted by circumstances. It is presumed that the natural and even probable results flowing from a wrong act were intended. Thus if one takes and carries away another's property in the belief that he himself is the owner of it, that is, under claim of right, there will be no larceny even if he is not the owner of it in fact. Where one fails to accomplish an intended wrong, but at the same time accidentally commits another, he will, unless the particualr intent is a substantive part of the crime, be held to have intended the act he did commit.

Notwithstanding this, one is not excused by ignorance of what constitutes a crime. Ignorance is not a defense to a crime but mental incapacity to comprehend the nature of the crime is a defense. A foreigner committing a crime which he does not know to be such and which is not a crime in his country is still liable to prosecution where the offense was committed.

CRIMINAL CONVERSATION Adultery in its civil aspect, allowing the husband to sue for damages.

CRIMINAL LAW That branch or division of law which treats of crimes and their punishments.

CRIMINATE To expose a person to a criminal charge. A witness cannot be compelled to answer any question which has a tendency to incriminate him.

CROSS ACTION An action upon the same subject matter (as upon the same contract) brought by a party sued against the party who has sued him.

CROSS BILL Suit brought by a defendant against the party suing on a cause of action arising out of the same transaction; often applicable to divorce cases where the defendant files counter-charges against the complainant.

CROSS-EXAMINATION The examination of the plaintiff or his witnesses by his own counsel is known as direct examination. The examination by the opposing counsel to test the truth, veracity or credibility of the plaintiff and his witnesses is known as cross-examination. Cross-examination, of course, applies equally to the defen-

ant and his witnesses by plain-
ff's counsel.

In some jurisdictions this must
e limited to facts and circum-
ances testified to by the witness-
-chief though in some places he
ay be cross-examined, even
ough, after being called and
worn, nothing is asked him on di-
ct examination. Collateral facts,
owever, in any case, may be elic-
ed to some extent, as for the
urpose of testing the recollection
f the witness and determining the
liability of his testimony. How-
ver, such questioning is largely in
e control of the court. Leading
uestions, that is, questions which
uggest the answer desired, may be
ked on cross-examination but not
a direct examination.

RUELTY Such conduct on the
art of a husband towards his wife
s affords a reasonable apprehen-
ion of bodily hurt. It is usually
onsidered ground for divorce.

**UJUS EST SOLUM, EJUS EST
SQUE AD COELUM ET AD IN-
EROS** The owner of the soil
wns to the heavens and also to
e lowest depth.

ULPABLE Censurable, also some-
mes used to mean criminal.

UMULATIVE VOTING A method
f voting by which an elector en-
tled to vote for several candidates
or the same office may cast more
han one vote for the same candi-
ate, distributing among the candi-
ates as he chooses a number of

votes equal to the number of candidates to be elected.

A stockholder in voting for a director may cast as many votes for
one candidate for given office as
there are offices to be filled multiplied by the number of shares of
his stock, or he may distribute this
same number of votes among the
other candidates as he sees fit.

CURIA ADVISARI VULT The
court will advise. Postponement of
a decision after argument to allow
the court to consider the matter.

CUSTODIA LEGIS The custody of
the law. When property is lawfully
taken, by virtue of legal process, it
is in the custody of the law.

CUSTODY The bare control or
care of a thing as distinguished
from the possession of it.

CUSTOM Something which has
by its universality and antiquity acquired the force and effect of law,
in a particular place or country, in
respect to the subject matter to
which it relates; generally practiced, judicially noticed without
proof.

CY PRES, DOCTRINE OF The
doctrine of construing written instruments as near to the intention
of the parties as possible. It is most
commonly applied to the construction of wills, and is only another
name for the general principle of
carrying into effect the testator's
intention as nearly as possible in
conformity to the rules of law.

D

DAMAGE FEASANT OR FAISANT
Doing damage. A term applied to a person's cattle or beasts found on another's land, doing damage by treading down the grass, grain, etc

DAMAGES Indemnity to the person who suffers loss or harm from a injury; a sum recoverable as amends for a wrong. An adequate compensa tion for the loss suffered or the injury sustained. A distinction is mad between general and special damages, the former being those which ne essarily and by implication of law result from an act or default con plained of, and the latter being such as arise from actual injury incurre through the peculiar circumstances of the individual case, above an beyond those presumed by law from the general nature of the wrong.

Thus in an action for libel, where the law presumes an injury to b necessarily involved in the loss of reputation, general damages will b awarded. But if the injured person can show particular loss suffered in th individual case, as for example that his marriage was prevented or h business diminished through the libel, he may recover special damages i addition. To recover special damages he must allege the special injury i his suit, that is, in the statement of his cause of action or ground c complaint which must be filed under the rules of pleading at some perio before the trial.

To recover general damages he need not allege or prove any specifi injury. The law in such case presumes the injury to have resulted an leaves it to the jury to determine the amount, the jury being limited onl by the amount demanded, that is, they cannot award more than is de manded in the declaration or statement filed.

Damages can be recovered only where it is shown that the loss c injury is the natural and proximate consequence of the wrong committe By proximate cause is meant the direct and not the remote cause of th injury. Difficult questions arise sometimes as to what is and what is not proximate cause. Remote causes are not permitted to furnish the basis c claim for damages because there must be more or less speculation as t whether such remote causes are in truth and in fact responsible for th injury or loss.

Damages will be awarded not merely for a loss in money or goods bu for injured feelings, bodily pain, injury to reputation and other suffering where it would be impossible to make exact proof and computation i respect to the amount of loss sustained.

No damages can be awarded where there is no wrong committed b another and no default on his part. But it is not necessary that the wron

e wilful or that it involve moral guilt. It may result from mere neglect or
ailure to discharge a duty with the skill or fidelity which one has a right
o expect under the circumstances, as where a surgeon is held liable for
malpractice or a sheriff for the escape of his prisoner or a carrier for
neglect to deliver goods, or it may be from a breach of contract, such as a
refusal to deliver goods sold or to perform services agreed upon, or it may
be for a wrong committed by a third person for whose act or default the
defendant is legally liable as in the case of a railroad company responsible
or an accident due to the negligence of an employee. But one may suffer
injury and no one be responsible in damages, for the injury may be from
accident without negligence or it may result from the rightful action of
nother.

There are cases in which damages awarded may exceed actual loss or
injury as where gross fraud or actual malice or deliberate violence or
ppression appears. The jury may in such cases in assessing damages fix an
mount adequate to compensate for the loss or injury sustained and add a
um by way of punishment for the wrong committed. Such additional
amages are called punitive, exemplary or vindictive damages. They are
ot fixed in the verdict as a separate sum but the whole of the damages
indictive and otherwise are as one sum. Such damages are of frequent
ccurrence in actions for libel, assault and battery, seduction, false im-
risonment and the like.

In a suit for damages resulting from negligence the plaintiff must ap-
ear free from fault of his own, for if his own negligence in any degree
ontribute directly to produce the injury he cannot recover, whatever
nay have been the negligence of the defendant. This is termed contribu-
ory negligence. The law will not as a rule attempt to apportion the loss
ccording to the different degrees of negligence of the plaintiff and the
defendant.

Formerly damages could not be recovered where the injured person
lied. This is now generally changed by statute. Necessarily, jurors have a
vide discretion in fixing the amount of damages though the court may set
side the verdict if the damages seem grossly excessive or unreasonably
nadequate. But the rule is that courts will not interfere unless the verdict
s such as to satisfy it that the jury was misled by passion, prejudice,
gnorance or partiality. The power is sparingly used and frequently,
hough dissatisfied with the verdict, the courts have refused to interfere.
t is seldom that a new trial is granted because damages are too small. In
ny case where there is a legal rule fixing the measure of damages it must
e stated to the jury by the judge and his failure to do so is ground for
eversal. If the jury disregard the instructions, the verdict may be set
side.

Where a vendor of real estate fails to convey according to his contract
nd has acted in good faith and supposed he had good title and could
onvey, the purchaser's damages have been limited to the amount of his

advance, if any, with interest and expenses of examining the title. But in case of a willful or fraudulent refusal to convey, the purchaser has been held entitled to the value of the land with interest though not uncommonly the damages are considered to be the difference between the price fixed in the contract and the value of the land at the time fixed for the delivery of the deed.

Where land is conveyed with a covenant of seisin or warranty in the deed and the purchaser is evicted, the consideration money, interest and costs of defending the eviction may be recovered from the seller. In some states, however, the amount to be recovered is the value of the land at the time of eviction together with the expenses of the suit.

If there is a breach of a covenant in a deed against encumbrances the purchaser is entitled to recover what it costs him to extinguish the encumbrance.

If the seller of goods fails to perform his agreement the damages consist ordinarily in the difference between the contract price and the market price of the article at the time and place fixed for delivery.

DAMNATUS Condemned; prohibited by law; unlawful.

DAMNUM Damage; the loss or diminution of what is a man's own, either by fraud, carelessness or accident.

DAMNUM ABSQUE INJURIA Loss without injury. A loss for which no action will lie.

DAMNUM FATALE Fatal damage; loss happening from a cause beyond human control, and for which bailees are not liable, such as shipwreck, lightning and the like.

DATE OF ISSUE As the term is applied to notes, bonds, etc., of a series, it usually means the arbitrary date fixed as the beginning of the term for which they run, without reference to the precise time when convenience or the state of the market may permit of their sale or delivery.

DAYS OF GRACE Additional days allowed, beyond the time originally contracted, for the payment of a debt, such as a promissory note, mortgage, or check. The Uniform Commercial Code adopted by 46 states, as well as the District of Columbia and the Virgin Islands, has abolished days of grace.

However, by specific agreement of the parties an extension of time beyond the original period contemplated may be agreed upon whether in a note, check, or mortgage.

In insurance law the grace period, usually thirty days, is the time beyond the due date of the premium during which insurance is continued in force and during which payment may be made to keep the policy in good standing. Whether or not a policy contains a grace period depends on the individual policy which all holders are cautioned to read. Payment of a claim on a policy is usually allowed during the grace period.

When the last day of grace falls on a Sunday or general holiday, ayment is usually due on the next ucceeding business day. Failure to uake such payment allows the hold-r of a note, check, or mortgage, tc., to institute immediate suit, nd an insurance policy to lapse or erminate.

E BENE ESSE Of being good. A hrase, denoting temporary or pro-isional validity, which implies that thing now good may later be hanged—for example, testimony iat may be suppressed depending n later events.

E BONIS ASPORTATIS The ac-ion of trespass for taking personal roperty.

E BONIS NON ADMINISTRATIS Vhen the administration of the es-ate of an intestate is left unfin-hed, in consequence of the death r removal of the administrator, nd a new administrator is ap-ointed, the latter is termed an *ad-ministrator de bonis non*, i.e., of the oods of the deceased not adminis-ered by the former administrator.

E NOVO, TRIAL Anew; over gain; a second time. A trial de ovo is a new trial in which the ntire case is retried in all its de-ail.

DEAD FREIGHT In maritime law, kind of freight payable by the harterer of a vessel, when the argo in respect of which it, or ome part of it, is payable has, rom some cause on the part of the harterer, not been conveyed as rovided.

EBENTURE A written acknowl-dgment of a debt; specifically an nstrument under seal for the re-ayment of money lent.

DEBT A sum of money due by certain and express agreement; as by bond for a definite sum, a bill or note, a special bargain or a rent reserved on a lease, where the amount is fixed and specific, and does not depend upon any subse-quent valuation, to settle it.

DEBT OF RECORD A debt which appears to be due by the evidence of a court of records, as by a judg-ment or recognizance.

DECEDENTS' DEBTS The debts of deceased persons. All of a de-ceased person's real and personal estate is liable for payment of his debts, and, ordinarily and unless otherwise regulated by statute, is liable in the following order. First, personal estate not specifically be-queathed; second, real estate de-vised or ordered to be sold for the payment of debts; third, real estate descended (that is not devised by a will) but not charged with debts; fourth, real estate devised and charged generally with the pay-ment of debts by the will; fifth, gen-eral pecuniary legacies; sixth, real estate devised and not charged with debts.

Growing crops are included with the personal property with respect to payment of debts. An administra-tor or executor selling real es-tate under order of court must spe-cially reserve growing crops, other-wise they will pass with the land to the purchaser. Nurseries likewise are personal property though not trees in general. So are bricks in a kiln, also buildings intended not to be a part of the real estate on which they are erected, estates or leases for years and mortgages and rent which has come due before the decedent died. Fixtures are usually part of the real estate. The wearing apparel of minor children and widows is to be retained by them and is not assets for payment of debts. There is reserved also to the widow forty days of food and clothing.

Services rendered by one to his parent or child, or to another living in the same family relations with him, are not usually to be paid for unless there is an express agreement for payment, the presumption being that the services are given freely or in view of other benefits received, and that no payment is intended between the parties. Where the relations between the parties are not so close, but a near kinship nevertheless exists, the presumption that there is an implied contract for payment for services rendered is more easily overcome by evidence than in the case of persons not related.

So-called "stale claims" against decedents' estates, that is, claims for indebtedness owing for a considerable length of time before the death of a decedent, but not presented or demanded until after his death, are regarded with close scrutiny by the courts and must be accompanied by strong proof. This is especially true with respect to wages which are ordinarily paid for by the week or by the month.

DECEIT A subtle trick or device.

DECISION (JUDICIAL) The word "decision" may mean a final judgment of a court of last resort, a conclusion of law or facts, the opinion of the court, or the report of the court. Generally speaking, a decision means the judgment of the court as to the disposition of the case—for the plaintiff, for the defendant, or for neither. Decision

must be distinguished from opinion. An opinion of the court constitutes the reasons given for its decision or judgment. The report of the case is a printing of the opinion and decision.

DECLARATION A plaintiff's statement in writing of the circumstances which constitute his cause of action. It is the first of the pleadings in an action at law, and is usually divided into several sections or paragraphs, termed counts. It consists of the following formal parts: the title, the venue, the commencement, the statement of the causes of action, the several counts, and the conclusion.

DECLARATION OF INTENTION The act by which an alien declares before a court of record, that he intends to become a citizen of the United States.

DECLARATION OF TRUST A declaration by a party who has made a conveyance to another that the subject conveyed is to be held in trust. An admission by an individual that a property, the title of which he holds, is held by him as trustee for another. If it is a declaration in relation to real estate, it should be executed and acknowledged with the same formality as a conveyance of land.

DECLARATORY JUDGMENT A court's declaration or opinion of the rights of contesting parties on some matter of law without ordering anything to be done.

DECLARATORY STATUTE A statute which, instead of introducing a new law, only declares what is the existing law, and the object of which is to remove doubts which have arisen on the subject.

DECREE A sentence or order of a court of equity or admiralty after trial which determines the rights of parties to the suit.

DEDICATION An appropriation of land by the owner to some public use which is accepted for such use by or on behalf of the public as a public road or highway, square, cemetery, school or monument. The dedication may be express, that is, where it is effected by deed or specific declaration, or it may be implied, that is, presumed from simple acquiescence on the public use by the owner. A dedication to public use to be valid must not be in favor of part of the public only within given territory.

No particular formality is required to effect a dedication. Any act or declaration written or oral which clearly expresses an intent to dedicate will effect the result if the thing is accepted by the public, and will prevent the donor from asserting any right incompatible with the public use. If the public uses the land with the knowledge of the owner for twenty years, dedication will be presumed from this use without proof of an express appropriation by the owner; or the presumption may arise from a use for even a shorter period accompanied by other circumstances favoring the presumption. It is for the jury to determine whether the dedication was intended or not, but where the use has been for less than twenty years any presumption of dedication arising from such use may be rebutted by evidence showing that no intent to dedicate existed.

An acceptance by or in behalf of the public is necessary to complete a dedication. The weight of authority seems to show that in order to constitute an acceptance of a road or highway there must not only be a use by the public, but also an acceptance by the officer having charge of highways either formally or by indirectly recognizing it, as by repairing or setting up guide posts or the like. This question of acceptance is important in determining the liabilities of the municipality, in case of a road or highway, in the matter of repair or in the event of accident resulting from failure to keep it in repair.

DEED A deed is a writing, sealed and delivered by the parties. The word has a very broad meaning but is most commonly applied to the instrument used to convey a freehold estate in land. To be effective the parties to it must be competent to contract and there must be a proper subject matter and a good and sufficient consideration.

The deed must be written or printed. It must be read, if desired, and signed, sealed and delivered, also attested or executed in the presence of subscribing witnesses, though requirements in many states as to attestation and sealing have been abolished. Where sealing is still required a scroll purporting to be a seal is sufficient. In a conveyance by a corporation, however, its seal should always be attached. A delivery of the deed by the grantor to the grantee either directly or through others, as well as an acceptance by the grantee are essential to effect a conveyance.

DEED

This indenture made on the _____ day of _____
A.D. One Thousand Nine Hundred _____ by and between
_____ of _____ party (or parties) of the first
part, and _____ of the County of _____
in the State of _____ party (or parties) of the second part:

Witnesseth, that the said party _____ of the first part, in consideration of the sum of _____ dollars, to _____
_____ paid by the said party _____ of the second part, the receipt
of which is hereby acknowledged do (or does) by these presents, grant,
bargain and sell, convey and confirm, unto the said party _____ of
the second part _____ heirs and assigns, the following described lots,
tracts or parcels of land, lying between and situate in the County of
_____ and State of _____ to wit: All
(describe property).

To have and to hold the premises aforesaid, with all and singular the
rights, privileges, appurtenances and immunities thereto belonging or in anywise appertaining unto the said party _____ of the second part,
and unto _____ heirs and assigns, forever, the said
_____ hereby covenanting that they are (or he or she is)
lawfully seized of an indefeasible Estate in Fee in the premises herein conveyed; that _____ have (or has) good right to convey the
same; that the said premises are free and clear of any encumbrances done or
suffered by them (or him or her) or those under whom _____
claim _____ and that _____ will warrant and
defend the title to the said premises unto the said party _____ of the
second part, and unto _____ heirs and assigns, forever, against
the lawful claims and demands of all persons whomsoever.

In Witness Whereof, the said party _____ of the first part has
_____ hereunto set _____ hand _____ the day and year
first above written.

_____

_____

Signed and delivered in the presence of us,

_____

_____
ADD ACKNOWLEDGMENT.

(For forms of acknowledgment to be added to deeds *see also*
ACKNOWLEDGMENT.)

The formal parts of the deed are: 1. The premises, where the names of
the parties, the consideration, the recitals inserted for explanation and the
description of the property with intended exceptions appear. 2. The habendum, that is, the part beginning with the words "to have and to hold,"
which limits and defines the estate which the grantee is to receive. 3. The
reddendum, consisting of any reservation which the grantor may make in
his own favor, such as rent or a right to a living for himself, etc. 4.
Conditions or clauses of contingencies on the happening or not happening

of which the estate granted may be defeated. 5. Covenants, consisting of some guarantees with respect to the estate granted. 6. The conclusion mentioning simply the fact of execution and the date of the deed, etc.

Where the construction of a deed is doubtful and one meaning would sustain the deed and the other defeat or invalidate it, the former will prevail. Punctuation is not regarded in construing a deed and in case of doubt, that construction will prevail which is favorable to the party to whom the conveyance is made. The habendum will be rejected if repugnant to the rest of the deed. An error in the description of the property will not affect the deed so long as the intent can be arrived at. As to the conveyance of lands and contracts relating thereto, the law of the place where the land is situated controls, even though the contracts are made out of the state or jurisdiction.

Real estate once duly conveyed cannot be returned to the grantor simply by return or destruction of the deed. There must be a reconveyance by another deed.

DEED OF TRUST An instrument by which title to real property is conveyed to a trustee to hold as security for the holders of notes or bonds. It is like a mortgage except the security title is held by a person other than the mortgagee-creditor. Most corporate bonds are secured by a deed of trust.

DEED POLL A deed of one part, or executed by one party only (instead of between parties, and in two or more parts), and distinguished from an indenture by having the edge of the parchment or paper on which it is written cut even (or polled, as it was anciently termed), that is, without being indented.

DE FACTO and DE JURE A de facto officer is one who acts with apparent right and under claim and color and pretense of appointment or election, but without being actually qualified in law so to act. The one who is actually so qualified is termed an officer de jure even though in fact he may

not be acting. The acts of an officer de facto are usually valid. This is necessary as a matter of convenience and of protection to the people who act upon the faith of the official and binding character of the acts of the officer, whether he has the legal right to hold the office or not.

DEFALCATION A person occupying a trust or fiduciary relation who, by reason of his own fault, is unable to account for funds left in his hands, has committed a defalcation. The word often means to embezzle or misappropriate funds.

DEFAMATION The offense of injuring a person's character, fame or reputation, either by writing or by words. Written defamation is otherwise termed libel, and oral defamation, slander.

DEFAULT Fault, neglect; omission; the failure of a party to an action to appear when properly served with process; the failure to perform a duty or obligation; the failure of a person to pay money when due or when lawfully demanded.

DEFEASANCE A condition annexed to a deed, bond or collateral instrument by the performance of which the principal deed is rendered void.

DEFEASIBLE (OF TITLE TO PROPERTY) Capable of being defeated. A title to property which is open to attack or which may be defeated by the performance of some act.

DEFENDANT The party against whom an action at law or in equity is brought; the party denying, opposing, resisting or contesting the action.

DEFENSE The act of protection. A man may defend himself, his wife, children and servants even to killing the assailant where necessary, but he must be careful to use only such force as is necessary to the occasion and to act in defense only and not in revenge. He may repel force by force in defense of his personal property, and justify homicide against one manifestly endeavoring by violence or surprise to commit a known felony such as robbery. One will be justified even in killing another in defense of his possession of real property where necessary to prevent burglary or arson, but in such case the one in possession must be wholly without fault. It is generally lawful for an occupant to resist by force an illegal attack upon his dwelling where the intention is merely to commit a trespass only.

DEFICIENCY That part of a debt which a mortgage was made to secure, not realized by the liquidation of the mortgaged property. Something which is lacking.

DEFICIENCY JUDGMENT If, upon the foreclosure of a mortgage, the mortgaged property does not sell for a sufficient amount to pay the mortgage indebtedness, such difference is called a "deficiency" and is chargeable to the mortgagor or to any person who has purchased the property and assumed and agreed to pay the mortgage.

DEFORCEMENT The withholding of real property from one who has title but not possession.

DEFRAUD To deprive one of some right by deceitful means. To cheat or withhold wrongfully that which belongs to another. Conveying one's property for the purpose of avoiding payment of debts is a transfer to "hinder, delay, or defraud creditors."

DE JURE By right; complying with the law in all respects.

DEL CREDERE AGENT An agent who guarantees his principal against the default of those with whom contracts are made.

DELIVERY One of the essential requisites to the validity of a deed. This may be either absolute, that is, to the party or grantee himself or to a third person, to hold till some condition is performed on the part of the grantee, in which case it is not delivered as a deed but as an escrow, that is, as a writing which is not to take effect as a deed till the condition is per

formed, at which time it becomes
a deed.

DELUSION A false belief for
which there is no reasonable foundation, and which would be incred-
ible, under the given circumstances, to the same person, if of
sound mind.

DEMAND Before a party can assert his rights and bring a legal action, it is frequently necessary that
he make a "demand" on the party
bound to perform the contract or
discharge the obligation. The demand should be in writing or,
where made verbally, should be
witnessed. A demand for rent is
necessary before a landlord can exercise his right to re-enter the premises for non-payment of rent. A
demand is a prerequisite where a
nuisance has been erected or
created, the demand being equivalent to written notice that action
will be taken unless the nuisance is
eliminated. Basically, a legal demand differs from a right in that
the former presupposes that there
is no defense or doubt about the
matter in question. A demand note,
for example, is a note that is due at
once, on which suit may be
brought without additional notice.

DE MINIMIS NON CURAT LEX
The law is not concerned with
trifles. The maxim has been applied to exclude the recovery of
nominal damages where no unlawful intent or disturbance of a right
of possession is shown, and where
all possible damage is expressly
disproved. For example, it will disregard an error of a fraction of a
cent. (This applies, of course, under those circumstances in which a
fraction is a trifle.)

DEMISE A conveyance of an estate to another for life, for years,
or at will. It is synonymous with a
lease.

DEMUR To raise an objection in
point of law, and rest or pause
upon it, referring its decision to the
court; to object to the pleading of
the opposite party as insufficient to
sustain his action or defense, and
refer it to the judgment of the
court whether it ought to be answered.

DEMURRAGE The detention of a
vessel beyond the time allowed by
the charter party for loading or unloading, or for sailing. The allowance or payment made for such
detention or delay.

DEMURRER An allegation of a defendant which, admitting the matters of fact alleged by the bill to
be true, shows that, as they are set
forth, they are insufficient for the
plaintiff to proceed upon, or to
oblige the defendant to answer; or
that, for some reason apparent on
the face of the bill, or because of
the omission of some matter which
ought to be contained therein, or
for want of some circumstance
which ought to be attendant thereon, the defendant ought not to
be compelled to answer. It therefore demands the judgment of the
court, whether the defendant shall
be compelled to make answer to
the plaintiff's bill or to some certain part thereof.

DEPENDENT COVENANTS Covenants made by two parties to a
deed or agreement which are such
that the thing covenanted or promised to be done on each part enters into the whole consideration

for the covenant or promise on the part of the other, or such covenants as are concurrent, and to be performed at the same time. Neither party to such a covenant can maintain an action against the other without averring and proving performance on his part.

DEPONENT One who deposes (that is, testifies or makes oath in writing) to the truth of certain facts; one who gives, under oath, testimony which is reduced to writing; one who makes oath to a written statement. The party making an affidavit is generally so called.

DEPOSE To state or testify under oath, in writing; to make a statement or give testimony under oath, which is reduced to writing; to make a statement which is reduced to writing and sworn to; to put down in writing what is afterwards sworn to. A word constantly used in affidavits, as "A. B. of—, being duly sworn, deposes and says that," etc.

DEPOSIT A deposit in its strict sense is when one gives a thing to another to keep and he undertakes to do so gratuitously, obliging himself to return it when requested. The person receiving the article is bound only to ordinary care, varying generally, however, with the character of the article and other circumstances. He has in general no right to make use of it unless permission is granted or unless permission is implied from the nature of the case. He must return the thing itself, not a substitute, in the condition in which he receives it. If lost, injured or spoiled by his fraud or gross negligence he is responsible for the loss or injury. He must restore also any increase or profits accrued from it.

If a depositary delivers to the rightful owner a thing placed in his care by another, he is not responsible to the latter. If the thing deposited belongs to two or more and is capable of division, he may on demand divide it and restore to each his portion. In general the depositary discharges his duties by delivering or offering to deliver the thing deposited where it is, or at his own residence or place of business. One to whom goods are pawned or pledged as security becomes a depositary upon payment of the debt. So is one who takes charge of property on finding it, and he may charge the owner with the necessary expense and labor required in caring for it.

A deposit with a banker is different. The relation of banker and customer being that of debtor and creditor, it does not partake of a fiduciary character. No trust is created. The money when deposited becomes the money of the banker. The banker is not liable for interest unless specially contracted for and the deposit is subject to the bar of the statute of limitations.

If one is indebted to a bank as on a promissory note, and the debt is due and the debtor has a deposit to his credit on the books of the bank, the bank may charge the debt up against him on his account, and refuse thereafter to honor any check drawn against the deposit unless there is sufficient money to pay the check in excess of the debt so charged up. A depositor is bound to promptly notify the bank of a forgery of checks returned to him, and must suffer any loss occasioned by failure to do so.

DEPOSIT (IN GENERAL) A bailment by which a person receives property of another to be redelivered on demand.

DEPOSITION The testimony of a witness reduced to writing in due form of law taken by virtue of a commission or rule issued from a court or other competent tribunal. A deposition is often used on the trial of some question of fact in a court of justice. Its use at the trial is allowed only in cases of necessity as where a witness resides out of the state or is sick, aged, about to leave the state, or where for any cause it is or may be impossible for him to attend in person. Testimony of witnesses residing out of the state is more commonly taken by commission issued from the court to someone at a distance accompanied by interrogatories for the witness to answer.

DEPOSITOR Any person who deposits money or commercial paper in any bank, either on open account subject to check, or to be withdrawn otherwise than by check, whether interest is allowed or not, including holders of demand or time certificates of deposit lawfully issued.

DEPUTY A person subordinate to a public officer whose business and object is to perform the duties of the principal.

DESCENT AND DISTRIBUTION Descent applies to real estate, distribution to personal estate. Title to real estate by descent is that which one, upon the death of another, acquires as his heir at law. The legal title to personal estate upon one's death vests in his executor or administrator, through whom it may be transferred or distributed to the persons beneficially interested after payment of debts and charges of administration.

The term distribution is frequently also applied to proceeds of the sale of real estate. The law of the domicil of the decedent governs the distribution of his personal estate unless otherwise provided by statute.

The rules of descent apply only to estates or interests in land that can be inherited. They do not apply to an estate for the life of the decedent for this terminates at his death. Estates for life of another are governed by rules peculiar to themselves. An estate for a term of years is regarded as personalty and passes to the executor or administrator upon the death of the owner, and does not descend to the heirs.

DESERTION Abandonment of public service in the army or navy without official leave is desertion. It is a criminal offense which subjects the offender to such punishment as a court martial may impose. One deserting to an enemy may be punished by death.

One who deserts his wife and children may be compelled by the court to pay a certain amount for their support and maintenance in default of which he will be imprisoned. A continued, wrongful desertion by either husband or wife furnishes grounds for divorce in most places.

DESTINATION The "destination of goods" is the place of delivery as provided for in the shipping contract. The carrier is under a duty to deliver the goods at such a place unless ordered otherwise by the consignee.

DESTITUTE The term applied to persons who do not have the necessaries of life and have no means of obtaining them.

DETAINER The keeping another out of possession of lands or tenements. Withholding possession of another's goods.

DETINUE A common law action to recover property. It is to be distinguished from trover which is an action to recover damages for taking property, not the recovery of the actual property.

DETRIMENT Any act or forbearance by a promisee. A loss or harm suffered in person or property.

DEVISE A gift or disposition of lands or other real property by a last will and testament. It is contingent where the vesting is made to depend upon some future event, and if the event does not occur or until it does occur no estate vests under the devise. If, however, the future event is referred to simply for the purpose of determining or fixing a time when the devise shall come into use, then the estate or devise will vest and belongs to the devisee immediately upon the death of the testator.

Where the language of a will renders it doubtful whether the in-

tent was to make a devise vest upon the death of the testator or not, the law favors the construction favorable to the immediate vesting but if the intent of the testator is plain from the whole will this intent must prevail. If the estate is given absolutely, thus vesting in the devisee, the time of possession only being referred, the devisee (or legatee in case of a legacy), though he should never arrive at the age to take possession, will, however, have acquired an estate which he may transmit to his heirs or others according to law.

A general devise of all the testator's real estate will include a reversion in fee even though the testator has other lands which will satisfy the words of the devise and even though it may seem that he did not have such reversion in mind. A general devise will pass a lease for a term of years if the testator has no other real estate upon which the will may operate. But if he has other lands in fee, a devise of all his real estate will commonly pass only the lands held in fee simple unless a contrary intention appear from the will as a whole. Where one has been invested with the power to devise land which he does not own or to name the person or persons to whom it shall pass, a devise in a will will never be considered as an execution of the power unless that intention is manifest. Such intention would be manifest where there was no other estate that the words of the will could operate upon, and a devise in order to be execution of the power need not necessarily refer to the power in express terms.

Though a mortgage is in form a conveyance of land yet a devise of all one's land will not usually in-

clude that against which one holds
a mortgage; yet if the mortgagee
(the one holding the mortgage), is
in possession of the land by virtue
of the mortgage this may alter the
rule. A mortgage is commonly considered personal estate.

DICTUM A saying or remark; an
opinion expressed by a judge in deciding a cause or question, either
aside from the point to be decided
(hence said to be extra-judicial), or
obiter (by the way).

DIRECTORS The members of the governing board of a corporation. They
are elected by the stockholders subject to the by-laws of the corporation.
In some cases, especially where the corporation exists for non-profitable
purposes, directors may be appointed by the president of the corporation
depending upon the by-laws of the organization.

The actual conduct of a business of a corporation is almost always
entrusted to the directors, and the acts of the board evidenced by a legal
vote are ordinarily as completely binding upon the corporation, and as
complete authority to its agents, as the most solemn acts done under the
corporate seal.

The acts of the corporation should be noted in the minutes though even
this is not absolutely necessary to bind the corporation. In order that the
binding character of the acts of the board may be beyond question, they
should be done either at a regular stated meeting at the regular place of
meeting, or if at a special meeting, all the members of the board should
have notice of the purpose for which it is called, and thus have an opportunity to attend, consult and be consulted with. There must be a sufficient
number present to constitute a quorum.

The number that constitutes a quorum may be fixed by the by-laws. If
not fixed by the by-laws, or by statute law, a majority will be necessary
and, except when otherwise directed by statute or the by-laws, a majority
of the quorum will be sufficient to pass any order of resolution at the time
and place of holding special meetings and of matters to be acted on there.
Every director should have reasonable notice. They should also have notice of matters of great and vital concern to be considered even at regular
meetings. Necessary notice is presumed to have been given, and he who
alleges the contrary must prove it.

Directors of a corporation are in a measure trustees, and as such are
required to use due diligence and care in managing its affairs and are
bound to a faithful discharge of their duties.

They must not use their positions to promote their personal interests,
nor must they permit themselves to become interested against the corporation, for this would conflict with a fair and proper discharge of their
duties. They cannot bind the company by a contract with themselves if
pernicious or if tending to work a fraud on the corporation, or if there is
the slightest unfairness, in the transaction. They cannot speculate with the
funds of the company, and if they do, they may be required to desist and
to yield up their profits to the company.

They are not liable for mere errors of judgment, though they are bound to bring to the performance of their duties a degree of ability and competence adequate to the performance of the duties undertaken. They are liable to stockholders when there has been fraud perpetrated upon them or where the directors have been guilty of gross negligence or have transcended or abused their powers.

The by-laws should as far as practicable define the duties and the extent of the powers of directors and officers generally, and the directors and officers are bound to conform thereto. If one who is not eligible receives a majority of the votes of the stockholders, his ineligibility will not result in the election of another person. Another vote should be taken. But if one who is ineligible, is permitted to serve, his acts will bind the corporation as if he had been eligible. In voting for directors, the stockholders as they appear in the books of the association, are the ones entitled to vote, yet even where the law requires that directors shall be stockholders one is eligible even though the stock which he owns is not yet transferred on the books.

The directors for most purposes are substitutes, so to speak, for the body of the stockholders, and one dealing with them deals with the corporation. They may delegate powers to do given things to others but all their acts to be legal must be done at a duly convened meeting where all have an opportunity to be present, and to discuss and consider matters to be acted upon. The assent of the majority of directors or even all of them is insufficient if given or obtained when not assembled unless the act is subsequently ratified at a meeting. Notice of meeting and the manner of giving it should be regulated by the by-laws. In this connection it may be noted that acts irregular in themselves may for the most part be made binding by proper approval or ratification.

Though the powers of directors are quite complete with respect to the matters in the general range of the corporation's usual business they are not unlimited. They cannot divert the organization from the purposes for which it was formed or fundamentally alter its character. The whole property of a railroad company, for example, cannot be sold or leased without the consent of the stockholders given at a stockholders meeting. They may, however, pledge personal property as security, or contract debts or authorize the execution and sealing of instruments with the corporate seal by the president or other person, subject, however, to any limitations that may be imposed by legislative enactment, their charter or the by-laws. Directors must not act where their interests conflict with those of the corporation.

Corporations will be affected by knowledge of the existence of a given state of things, the same as an individual. Such knowledge by the directors is knowledge by the corporation. The notice, however, should be to the board or to an officer through whom such communications are usually transmitted, as the secretary, for private information given to a director and not communicated to the board and mere rumors or reports do not constitute notice.

Directors rendering services without any provision in the by-laws for pay and without a vote of the stockholders providing for compensation, are not entitled to receive any, and they are not allowed to favor or give any preference to any shareholder or to themselves as against other shareholders.

DISABILITY Disqualification in law for lack of necessary legal requirements.

Incapacity to do a legal act, as to enter upon lands, to inherit or convey, to sue or be sued, etc., arising from the peculiar condition of a person, as from infancy, coverture, lunacy, alienage, imprisonment or absence.

DISAFFIRM To renege or to refuse to go through with an agreed transaction.

DISBAR To expel a barrister from the bar, so as to forbid him from practicing law.

DISCHARGE A setting free; a clearing, acquitance, release or delivery. The instrument by which a person is discharged from a debt or obligation, or an encumbrance is cancelled; as the discharge of an insolvent, the discharge of a mortgage, etc. In maritime law: The unloading of a cargo from a vessel. In equity practice: A statement of disbursements and an ofrset of counter-claims, brought in and filed before a master in chancery, and which follows the charge in the order of the proceedings, though not properly a defense to it.

DISCLAIMER A disavowal or renunciation, especially the refusal or rejection of an estate or right offered to a person. A disclaimer may also be the declaration, or the instrument, by which such disclaimer is published. In estates, a disclaimer is the act by which a person refuses to accept an estate which has been offered him. Thus, a trustee is said to disclaim when he releases his estate to his fellow trustees, and relieves himself of his trust.

In the law of landlord and tenants, a disclaimer is the act of one who denies holding the estate of the person who claims to be the owner. At common law a disclaimer works a forfeiture of the lease.

In patent law, a disclaimer is a declaration in writing, filed under the patent laws, by an inventor whose claim as filed covers more than that of which he was the original inventor, renouncing such parts as he does not claim to hold.

In formal, legal pleading, a disclaimer is a renunciation by the defendant of all claim to the subject of the demand made by the plaintiff.

DISCONTINUANCE The termination of a suit by the plaintiff's failure to prosecute it.

DISCOUNT If a seller reduces the price of his goods to a buyer, upon payment of cash, he has sold the goods at a discount. For example: "Cash 20 days 10 percent." In banking, the term is applied to the purchase of negotiable instruments.

DISCOVERY A bill used chiefly to obtain a discovery of facts which are material in a case. Such bills of discovery were much more common in earlier practice than at present owing to changes in the law of evidence permitting the compelling of parties in interest to testify and produce books and papers in their possession or control in courts of law.

Where necessary for the securing of evidence, bills of discovery are greatly favored in equity, and are sustained in all cases where some well-founded objection does not exist for exercising the jurisdiction. Courts of equity, once having obtained jurisdiction for purposes of discovery will dispose of a case finally, if it is proper that it be considered in a court of equity even though an adequate remedy might be obtained in a court of law. Such a bill in equity will not, however, lie in aid of a criminal prosecution or a mandamus or a suit for a penalty.

One can in this manner have a discovery only of what is necessary to sustain his own suit, or show his own title if the suit relates to real estate, as for example, to bring to light deeds in the chain of his title under which he claims. The purpose or the effect of the bill, however, cannot simply be to pry into the title of the defendant.

DISMISS To send away; to send out of court; to dispose of finally.

DISORDERLY CONDUCT Any behavior contrary to law, but, more particularly, conduct that tends to disturb the peace or shock the public sense of morality.

DISPOSSESS The term used when a tenant of real estate is ousted from possession by an order of a court at the request of the landlord.

DISSOLUTION *Of a corporation*— The termination of a corporation at the expiration of its charter, by the Attorney General of the state under proper statutory authority, by consolidation, or by the action of the stockholders, is dissolution.

Of a partnership—The termination of a partnership by the express will of the partners at a fixed or indefinite time, or by operation of law due to the incapacity, death, or bankruptcy of one of the partners, is dissolution.

DISTRAIN To take possession of goods as a pledge for the performance of an obligation or until replevied by the sheriff.

DISTRESS The taking of a personal chattel out of the possession of a wrongdoer into the custody of the party injured, in order to procure a satisfaction for a wrong committed, as for non-payment of rent.

DISTRIBUTION Commonly used to express the division of the personal effects of an intestate among his widow and children or next of kin.

DIVERSE CITIZENSHIP A term of frequent use in the interpretation of the federal constitutional provision for the jurisdiction of the federal courts which extends it to controversies between citizens of different states.

DIVIDED COURT A court so described when there has been a division of opinion between its members on a matter submitted to it for decision.

DIVIDEND A dividend is a stockholder's pro rata share in the profits of a corporation. Dividends are declared by the board of directors of a corporation. Dividends are cash, script, property, and stock.

DIVORCE By divorce is meant either the absolute dissolution or the partial suspension by law of the marriage relation. The former is termed *divorce a vinculo matrimonii* (from the bond of marriage), and puts an end to the marriage. The latter is called a *divorce a mensa et thoro* (from bed and board), and is more in the nature of a legal separation leaving the marriage still in force for the most part.

A decree of divorce from bed and board, made as a result of an agreement between the parties or otherwise, may be revoked, the parties thereby being restored to their former status. Strictly and logically speaking, a divorce from the bonds of matrimony could only work a dissolution of a valid marriage. Where a marriage was illegal and void from the beginning there would be no marital relation to dissolve, yet the term divorce is in some states applied to a decree of nullity which merely establishes the fact that there was never a legal marriage.

The marriage contract is peculiar in that when once established it cannot be dissolved by agreement of the parties but only by legal authority, and then only for certain causes designated by law. Marriage is more than a contract. It is a legal relation which must last until the death of one of the parties unless ended sooner by law.

Embarrassing questions have sometimes arisen as to the effect in one jurisdiction of a divorce granted in another. Any state, of course, may pass laws upon the subject which will be binding within its limits, but under proper conditions a divorce granted in one jurisdiction will be valid everywhere. It will not be valid out of the state if neither of the parties has an actual bona fide domicil within the state where the divorce is granted, though it is sufficient if one of the parties is domiciled therein.

It may be stated as a general rule that a divorce granted in a state where both parties have their actual domicil and where the marriage took place, is valid everywhere. As a general rule, too, every state recognizes the validity of a divorce obtained where both parties at the time have their actual domicil, if granted according to the law of that place, the place of marriage being immaterial.

The place where the offense furnishing the ground for divorce was committed also is generally immaterial. It may be where the divorce is granted or not.

If one party consents to conduct of another which would ordinarily furnish grounds for divorce he cannot afterwards complain and obtain a divorce, for he cannot allege that he was injured thereby.

If the husband and wife enter into an agreement or have an understanding that one shall commit or appear to commit a breach of matrimonial obligations for the purpose of enabling the other to sue for a divorce, that is, where collusion exists between the parties, no divorce will be allowed if it is known, and the decree of divorce may be revoked if it is afterwards shown that there actually was such breach of matrimonial duty so perpetrated by agreement, for this would be a fraud upon the court.

If there is a condonation of an offense committed by either of the parties, that is, a forgiveness or remission of the offense on condition, either expressed or implied, that it will not occur again, while this condition is unbroken no divorce can be obtained for the injury condoned. Condonation may take place either by word or act. Thus if one of the parties is guilty of adultery and the other knowing it, afterwards exercises the marital functions with the guilty party this will be a condonation.

Recrimination is also a defense in a suit for divorce. This exists where the one complaining is as guilty as the one complained against. One asking the benefit of divorce laws must come into court with clean hands.

After a divorce from the bonds of matrimony the parties are single to all intents and purposes, though in some places disabilities as to remarriage are imposed. As to property of the respective parties, divorce leaves them practically as it finds them, and divests each of his or her rights in property of the other, after the other's death.

Alimony is an incident of *divorce a mensa et thoro,* and of divorce from the bonds of matrimony.

In case of divorce the court has authority to make orders as to the custody of children and may make direction as to their maintenance out of the husband's estate. As to such custody and maintenance the court has a great deal of discretion. It will be guided primarily in its action by what seems to be the child's welfare rather than by any supposed rights of the parent, and as between the parents, the innocent will be preferred to the guilty. In the absence of a controlling necessity or a good reason to the contrary arising from the circumstances of the case, the claim of the father will be preferred after the child has passed the tender age during which it requires the special administrations and care of a mother. Prior to this time the same preference is accorded to the mother. Upon being divorced the woman retains the name of her former husband unless the decree of divorce directs otherwise or unless there is statutory law to the contrary. Anyone, however, has a common law right to assume any name he likes. Following are the divorce laws of the various states.

Alabama Adultery, physical violence, abandonment for one year, imprisonment in penitentiary for two years where sentence is seven years or more, sodomy before or after marriage, habitual drunkenness or drug addiction contracted after marriage, five successive years in insane asylum after marriage, spouse being hopelessly and incurably insane when divorce bill is filed, or final decree of divorce from bed and board or final decree of separate maintenance in effect for more than two years. Husband may obtain divorce on ground of wife's pregnancy at time of marriage without his knowledge or agency. Wife may obtain divorce for non-support for two years.

RESIDENCE: Plaintiff must have lived in state one year if defendant is a non-resident, except that no particular or specific period of residence is required where court has jurisdiction of both parties, and one party is domiciled in Alabama.

REMARRIAGE: Neither party may remarry (except each other) within sixty days of decree or pending appeal unless decree expressly forbids right of guilty party, in which case guilty party may not rewed without permission of the court.

Alaska Impotency at time of marriage, continuing until commencement of action; adultery; conviction of felony; wilful desertion for one year; cruelty impairing health, life or personal indignities making life burdensome; incompatibility; drunkenness, habitual and gross, contracted after marriage and continuing for one year before filing of bill; husband's failure to provide necessaries for twelve months when he is able to do so; incurable mental illness when spouse confined to an institution for at least eighteen months preceding commencement of action; habitual drug addiction after marriage.

RESIDENCE: One year when marriage not solemnized in Alaska.
REMARRIAGE: No restrictions.

Arizona Adultery, impotency at time of marriage, continuing until time of suit; conviction of felony and sentence of imprisonment; wilful desertion for one year, habitual intemperance, extreme cruelty, non-support for one year, conviction of felony before marriage unknown to other party, wife's pregnancy by another man at time of marriage and unknown to husband, separation for five years or more for any reason.

RESIDENCE: One year.
REMARRIAGE: No restrictions.

Arkansas Adultery, impotency at time of marriage continuing to filing of suit, desertion for one year without reasonable cause, husband or wife by former undissolved marriage living at time of marriage, felony conviction, habitual drunkenness for one year, cruelty, intolerable indignities, separation for three consecutive years, whether or not by mutual consent, wilful non-support.

RESIDENCE: 60 days.
REMARRIAGE: No restrictions.

California Incurable insanity, irreconcilable differences between husband and wife.

RESIDENCE: Six months.

REMARRIAGE: Six months between interlocutory and final decree.

Colorado Impotency, adultery, desertion for one year, failure to support for one year, habitual drunkenness or drug addiction for one year, felony conviction, cruelty, insanity for three years, separation of parties for three or more years.

RESIDENCE: One year, except in cases of adultery and extreme cruelty, provided offenses were committed in the state, in which case year's residence is waived.

REMARRIAGE: No restrictions.

Connecticut Adultery, fraudulent contract, wilful desertion for three years, seven years' absence unheard from, habitual intemperance, intolerable cruelty, life imprisonment, any infamous crime involving a violation of conjugal duties by confinement in state prison, or legal confinement because of mental illness for a total period of five years within the six-year period next preceding the complaint.

RESIDENCE: Three years unless cause of divorce arose after removal to state; plaintiff was domiciled in state at time of marriage and has returned with intention of remaining permanently; or defendant has resided in state for three years and has actually been served.

REMARRIAGE: No restrictions.

Delaware Adultery, bigamy, imprisonment for two years, extreme cruelty, desertion for one year, non-support, habitual drunkenness for two years, complaining party under age of consent at time of marriage and marriage not confirmed after reaching such consent, mental illness for five years, incompatibility for two years.

RESIDENCE: Two years, except for adultery or bigamy in which case suit may be instituted promptly provided either party was a bona fide resident at time cause of action arose.

REMARRIAGE: No restrictions.

District of Columbia Adultery, desertion for one year, voluntary separation for one year, felony conviction for not less than two years. When decree of legal separation has been granted and separation has continued for one year it may be enlarged on application of innocent spouse.

RESIDENCE: One year.

REMARRIAGE: No restrictions.

Florida Parties within degree prohibited by law, natural impotence, adultery, extreme cruelty, habitual indulgence in violent and ungovern able temper, desertion for one year, divorce in any other state or country, either party had a husband or wife living at time of marriage.

RESIDENCE: Six months.

REMARRIAGE: No restrictions.

Georgia Relationship between parties such that marriage prohibited, mental incapacity at time of marriage, impotency at time of marriage, force, menaces or fraud in obtaining marriage, pregnancy at time of marriage unknown to husband, adultery, desertion for one year, conviction of offense involving moral turpitude (depravity) where penalty is two years or more, habitual intoxication, cruelty, physical or mental, incurable insanity accompanied by confinement for two years in a mental institution immediately preceding filing of suit.

RESIDENCE: Six months.

REMARRIAGE: Judge or jury may impose certain restrictions.

Hawaii Adultery, desertion for six months, imprisonment for life or seven years or more, habitual drunkenness or habitual excessive use of drugs for more than one year, mental cruelty for not less than sixty days making life intolerable, non-support, living separate and apart for two years without reconciliation having been effected, voluntary separation for three years.

RESIDENCE: One year.

REMARRIAGE: No restrictions.

Idaho Adultery, extreme cruelty, wilful desertion, wilful neglect, habitual intemperance, felony conviction, permanent insanity with three years confinement, separation for five years without cohabitation.

RESIDENCE: Six weeks.

REMARRIAGE: No restrictions.

Illinois Impotency, another husband or wife living at time of marriage, adultery, desertion for one year, habitual drunkenness for two years, attempt on life of spouse, extreme and repeated mental or physical cruelty, conviction of felony or infamous crime, venereal disease, excessive use of addictive drugs for two years.

RESIDENCE: One year, unless offense committed in Illinois in which case residence of only six months required.

REMARRIAGE: No restrictions.

Indiana Adultery, impotency existing at time of marriage, abandonment for two years, cruelty, habitual drunkenness, non-support for two years, conviction after marriage of infamous crime, incurable insanity in a hospital for five years.

RESIDENCE: One year.

REMARRIAGE: No restrictions, unless divorce obtained by default, in which case plaintiff may not rewed for two years.

Iowa Adultery, desertion for two years, felony conviction after marriage, chronic alcoholism, extreme cruelty, pregnancy of wife by another man.
RESIDENCE: One year, with certain exceptions.
REMARRIAGE: One-year restriction, unless court grants permission.

Kansas Abandonment for one year, adultery, extreme cruelty, habitual drunkenness, gross neglect of duty, felony conviction, mental illness with confinement in an institution for three years.
RESIDENCE: One year.
REMARRIAGE: Sixty days after decree becomes final.

Kentucky Impotency, living apart without cohabitation for five consecutive years, abandonment for one year, adultery, conviction of felony, concealing or contracting a loathsome disease, habitual drunkenness, non-support, cruelty, pregnancy of wife by another man.
RESIDENCE: One year.
REMARRIAGE: No restrictions.

Louisiana Adultery, felony conviction, extreme cruelty, public defamation, abandonment, non-support, voluntary separation for one year.
RESIDENCE: None, where either party is domiciled in state.
REMARRIAGE: A wife may not rewed until ten months after dissolution of prior marriage.

Maine Adultery, impotency, extreme cruelty, desertion for three years, habitual intoxication or use of drugs, non-support.
RESIDENCE: Six months.
REMARRIAGE: No restrictions.

Maryland Impotence at time of marriage; any cause rendering marriage null and void *ab initio* under Maryland laws; adultery; abandonment for at least eighteen months; voluntary separation for at least eighteen months; felony or misdemeanor conviction involving sentence of at least three years, eighteen months of which have been served; permanent and incurable insanity, provided insane spouse has been confined in institution for not less than three years prior to filing of bill.
RESIDENCE: One year, where grounds for divorce occurred outside Maryland.
REMARRIAGE: No restrictions.

Massachusetts Adultery, impotency, desertion for two years, habitual drunkenness or drug addiction, cruelty, non-support, sentence to confinement for life or for five years or more in prison.

RESIDENCE: None if parties domiciled in state; five years if plaintiff is resident; three years if both parties were residents at time of marriage.
REMARRIAGE: No restrictions.

Michigan Adultery, impotency at time of marriage, desertion for two years, habitual drunkenness, extreme cruelty, non-support, sentence to imprisonment for three years or more.
RESIDENCE: One year, with exceptions.
REMARRIAGE: No restrictions, unless provided in divorce decree.

Minnesota Adultery, impotency, cruelty, sentence to prison, desertion for one year, habitual drunkenness for one year, incurable insanity, continuous separation under a decree of limited divorce for more than five years, continuous separation under order or decree of separate maintenance for two years.
RESIDENCE: One year.
REMARRIAGE: Six months.

Mississippi Adultery, impotency, prison sentence, desertion for one year, habitual drunkenness, habitual excessive use of drugs, cruelty, insanity, prior undissolved marriage, pregnancy by person other than husband at time of marriage.
RESIDENCE: One year.
REMARRIAGE: Court may prohibit remarriage of guilty party in cases of adultery.

Missouri Impotency at time of marriage, prior undissolved marriage, adultery, desertion for one year, conviction of felony or infamous crime, habitual drunkenness for one year, cruelty, vagrancy of husband, pregnancy of wife by another man other than husband at time of marriage without knowledge of husband.
RESIDENCE: One year, with exceptions.
REMARRIAGE: No restrictions.

Montana Adultery, extreme cruelty, wilful desertion, wilful neglect, habitual intemperance, felony conviction, incurable insanity.
RESIDENCE: One year.
REMARRIAGE: No restrictions.

Nebraska Adultery, impotency, sentence to prison for three years or more, desertion for two years, habitual drunkenness, incurable insanity.
RESIDENCE: One year, with exceptions.
REMARRIAGE: No restrictions.

Nevada Impotency, adultery, felony conviction or infamous crime, habitual gross drunkenness, extreme cruelty, non-support for one year, insanity for two years, incompatibility.

RESIDENCE: Six weeks.

REMARRIAGE: No restrictions.

New Hampshire Impotency, extreme cruelty, sentence and imprisonment for more than one year, absence and unheard of for two years, adultery, habitual drunkenness for two years, joining any religious sect or society which believes the relation of husband and wife unlawful, refusal to cohabit for six months, desertion for two years.

RESIDENCE: One year, with exceptions.

REMARRIAGE: No restrictions.

New Jersey Adultery, desertion for two years, extreme cruelty.

RESIDENCE: Two years, with exceptions.

REMARRIAGE: No restrictions.

New Mexico Adultery, impotency, cruelty, pregnancy of wife by another man at time of marriage without husband's knowledge, abandonment, felony conviction, habitual drunkenness, incurable insanity for five years, incompatibility, non-support by husband according to his ability, means or station in life.

RESIDENCE: One year.

REMARRIAGE: No restrictions.

New York Cruel and inhuman treatment, abandonment for two or more years, imprisonment of defendant for three or more years after marriage, adultery, living apart for two years pursuant to separation decree, living apart for two years pursuant to written separation agreement.

RESIDENCE: One year, with exceptions.

REMARRIAGE: No restrictions.

North Carolina Adultery, impotency, pregnancy of wife by another at time of marriage without knowledge of husband, one-year separation, separation for five years by reason of incurable insanity, crime against nature, bestiality.

RESIDENCE: Six months.

REMARRIAGE: No restrictions.

North Dakota Adultery, extreme cruelty, wilful desertion, wilful neglect, habitual intemperance, felony conviction, insanity for five years.

RESIDENCE: One year.

REMARRIAGE: Permission to rewed may be restricted by divorce decree.

Ohio Prior existing marriage, desertion for one year, adultery, impo tency, extreme cruelty, fraudulent contract, gross neglect of duty, habitual drunkenness, imprisonment.

RESIDENCE: One year.
REMARRIAGE: No restrictions.

Oklahoma Abandonment for one year, adultery, impotency, pregnancy of wife at time of marriage by another man, extreme cruelty, fraudulent contract, incompatibility, habitual drunkenness, gross neglect, insanity for five years.

RESIDENCE: Six months.
REMARRIAGE: Six months' restriction while other party lives. Remarriage forbidden for thirty days after final judgment on appeal.

Oregon Impotency, adultery, felony conviction, drunkenness for one year, desertion for one year, cruelty, permanent mental illness.

RESIDENCE: One year.
REMARRIAGE: Neither party may rewed for sixty days or if an appeal has been taken, until it has been heard and disposed of.

Pennsylvania Incapability of procreation, subsisting prior marriage, adultery, desertion for two years, cruelty, indignities, uncondoned force, fraud or coercion, conviction of certain crimes.

RESIDENCE: One year.
REMARRIAGE: Either party may remarry except that defendant guilty of adultery may not marry other party to adultery during life of plaintiff.

Puerto Rico Adultery, felony conviction, habitual drunkenness or drug addiction, cruelty or grave injury, abandonment for one year, impotency, attempt of husband or wife to corrupt sons or prostitute daughters, husband's proposal to prostitute wife, separation for three years, incurable insanity.

RESIDENCE: One year, unless grounds for divorce arose in Puerto Rico or while one of the spouses lived there.
REMARRIAGE: Remarriage of divorced woman within 310 days after divorce is forbidden.

Rhode Island Impotency, adultery, extreme cruelty, wilful desertion for five years or at discretion of court, habitual drunkenness or drug addiction, non-support for one year, any other gross misbehavior or, at the discretion of the court, when the parties have lived apart for ten years.

RESIDENCE: Two years.
REMARRIAGE: No restrictions.

South Carolina Adultery, desertion for one year, physical cruelty, habitual drunkenness or drug addiction.

RESIDENCE: One year.
REMARRIAGE: No restrictions.

South Dakota Adultery, extreme cruelty, wilful desertion, wilful neglect, habitual intemperance, felony conviction, and insanity for five years. Neglect, desertion and intemperance must have continued for at least one year.
RESIDENCE: One year, with exceptions.
REMARRIAGE: Provision against remarriage of guilty party during lifetime of innocent party.

Tennessee Impotency, prior existing marriage, adultery, desertion for one year, conviction of infamous crime, felony conviction, attempts on life of other party, non-support, separation for more than two years.
RESIDENCE: One year.
REMARRIAGE: None, except that defendant guilty of adultery may not marry person with whom act was committed during lifetime of former spouse.

Texas Cruelty, desertion for three years, adultery, parties have lived separate and apart for three years, conviction of felony, confinement to mental hospital for five years.
RESIDENCE: One year.
REMARRIAGE: Neither party may rewed (except each other) within twelve months for cruelty.

Utah Impotency, desertion for one year, wilful neglect, habitual drunkenness, felony conviction, extreme cruelty, permanent insanity, separation for three years.
RESIDENCE: Three months.
REMARRIAGE: Forbidden pending appeal.

Vermont Adultery, imprisonment for three years, intolerable severity, desertion for three years, failure of husband to provide suitable maintenance, insanity, separation for three years.
RESIDENCE: Six months.
REMARRIAGE: County court may permit remarriage in shorter period than usual one or two years.

Virginia Adultery, sodomy, buggery, impotency at time of marriage, prison sentence, desertion for one year, pregnancy of wife by another man other than husband, prostitution of wife before marriage and unknown to husband, separation for two years.
RESIDENCE: One year.
REMARRIAGE: If ground was adultery, final decree may forbid remar-

BILL FOR TOTAL DIVORCE ON THE GROUND OF ADULTERY

JOHN DOE	:	
Complainant	:	CIRCUIT COURT
vs.	:	OF
JANE DOE	:	BALTIMORE CITY
Defendant	:	

To the Honorable, the Judge of said Court:

Your Orator, complaining, says:

1. That he and the defendant were married July 15, 1965, in Baltimore, Maryland, in a religious ceremony.

2. That both your Orator and the defendant have resided in the City of Baltimore, State of Maryland, for more than one year prior to the filing of this Bill of Complaint.

3. That one child was born of said marriage, namely, John Doe, Jr., whose age is six months.

4. That ever since their said marriage your Orator has behaved himself as a faithful, affectionate and kindly husband toward the said defendant.

5. That the said defendant did on September 15, 1965 commit the crime of adultery with a person whose name will be revealed at the hearing of the above mentioned cause and that said adultery took place in the City of Baltimore, State of Maryland.

6. That your Orator has not lived nor cohabited with the said defendant since he has discovered the said adultery, nor has he condoned, connived, nor forgiven such adultery.

TO THE END THEREFORE:

(1) That your Orator may be divorced *a vinculo matrimonii* from the defendant.

(2) That your Orator may be permitted to have the custody of the said infant child.

(3) That your Orator may have such other and further relief as his case may require.

And as in duty bound, etc.

/s/   Samuel G. Kling
_____
SOLICITOR FOR COMPLAINANT

/s/   John Doe
_____
COMPLAINANT

---

riage of guilty person but for good cause, after six months, such part of decree may be revoked.

Virgin Islands   Impotency, adultery, felony conviction, desertion for one year, cruelty, insanity, habitual drunkenness for one year, incompatibility.

RESIDENCE: Six weeks.

REMARRIAGE: Thirty days, or until expiration of appeal time.

Washington Fraudulent consent, adultery, impotency, abandonment for one year, cruelty, habitual drunkenness, husband's non-support.

RESIDENCE: One year.

REMARRIAGE: No restrictions.

West Virginia Adultery, felony conviction, desertion for one year, cruelty, habitual drunkenness or habitual addiction to drugs.

RESIDENCE: None required in cases of adultery, if personal service can be obtained. For other grounds, one year's residence required.

REMARRIAGE: Neither party may rewed for sixty days from date of decree and guilty party may be prohibited from remarrying for not over one year.

Wisconsin Adultery, imprisonment for three years, desertion for one year, cruelty, habitual drunkenness for one year, voluntary separation of five year's duration, husband's refusal or neglect to provide for wife.

RESIDENCE: Two years.

REMARRIAGE: Either party forbidden to remarry for one year.

Wyoming Adultery, impotency, felony conviction, desertion for one year, habitual drunkenness, extreme cruelty, husband's non-support of wife, personal indignities, vagrancy of husband, felony conviction prior to marriage unknown to other party at time of marriage, pregnancy of wife at time of marriage by person other than husband, incurable insanity, separation of parties for two or more years.

RESIDENCE: Sixty days.

REMARRIAGE: No restrictions.

Canada Adultery, sodomy, bestiality, rape, homosexual act, extreme cruelty, that husband and wife are living separate and apart and that there has been a permanent breakdown in the marriage.

DOCKET A brief or abstract in writing. An abridged entry of an instrument or proceeding in an action; a list or register of such abridged entries. The list or calendar of causes ready for hearing or trial, prepared by clerks for the use of courts, is, in some states, called a docket.

DOCTOR *See* MALPRACTICE.

DOLI CAPAX Capable of criminal intent or malice; able to know right from wrong.

DOLI INCAPAX Incapable of criminal intent or malice. Thus a young child may be considered *doli incapax*.

DOMICIL The place where a man has his true, fixed and permanent home and establishment and to which he has the intention of returning when away. The word is used both in a national sense having reference to the country in which he lives, and in a local sense having reference to some subdivision or district of a country.

The question of domicil is frequently important in determining the rights relating to personal property, the right to vote, and in other respects. One's domicil is where he has his home and where he exercises his political rights. Two facts must combine to fix a domicil, one actual residence, and the other permanency of residence or intention of remaining. Once established a mere temporary absence with intent to return will not destroy it, however long continued, and the presumption is in favor of the continuance of domicil. It continues until changed for another.

Where a foreign domicil has been acquired the former one revives with an intention to return; not so however where both domicils are domestic. A mere taking up of residence elsewhere is not sufficient to effect a change of domicil unless there is an intention to abandon the former one, nor is a mere intention to adopt a new domicil unless accompanied by some action in furtherance of the intention. A temporary residence may, however, be transformed into one's domicil by a subsequent intent to make it permanent. If one goes to a place for an indefinite period with a purpose of making a fixed present domicil this will constitute a domicil though there is a floating intention to return.

Both habitation and intention may be shown by slight indications, and the place where one lives is presumed to be his domicil unless the contrary is shown. The place of birth will be the domicil of the child if it is that of the parents, and the child's domicil will change with that of the parents, or parent, if there is but one. It will not, however, if the one parent is a widow who acquires the new domicil of a husband by a remarriage. Children of ambassadors and children born at sea and usually those born on a journey take the domicil of their parents. The domicil of an illegitimate child is that of its mother, of a legitimate child that of a father.

Children of citizens of the United States born in foreign lands have their domicil of birth in the United States. The husband's domicil is also the wife's. A widow's domicil remains that of her deceased husband until changed, and the domicil of the ward will be that of the guardian, but it is doubtful whether a guardian by changing his national domicil can change the national domicil of his ward. Ambassadors and foreign ministers retain the domicil of their own country, but this is not necessarily true of consuls and commercial agents. Commercial establishments in another country may acquire a domicil there in relation to their transactions.

Neither a husband nor a wife can make a change of domicil after committing an offense entitling the other to a divorce so as to deprive the other of the right to sue for a divorce. A wife divorced from bed and board or deserted may acquire a separate domicil so as to sue her husband. A divorce valid under the law of the domicil of both parties is good everywhere, but there must be an actual domicil of one party at least to obtain a divorce.

The succession to personal property, wherever situated, of a decedent and the ascertainment of the persons who are to take it, and the question whether debts are to be paid from personalty or realty, the interpretation of a will and the capacity of the testator to make it as well as its validity and effect in relation to transfer of personal property, are all determined in accordance with the law of the decedent's domicil at the time of his death. This is chiefly on the theory that personal property, being movable, accompanies the party wherever he goes together with the law relating thereto, to wit, the law of his place of residence. Real estate and its transfer being immovable is governed by the law of the place where it is situated.

Whether a thing is real or personal property must be determined by the law where it is located. As to transactions relating to personalty or to its transfer, the forms and solemnity required in the place of domicil must be observed. In the matter of interpreting or ascertaining the intent of a will, the law of the domicil prevails unless in case of real estate it can be clearly gathered from the will that the testator had in mind the law of the place where the real estate was situated when he made it.

An assignment for the benefit of creditors valid by the law of the domicil is generally recognized as valid everywhere, but not to the injury of citizens of another state or country in which property is situated. A compulsory assignment brought about by creditors by force of a statute, has no extraterritorial operation. One going into another country and engaging in trade is considered a merchant of that country, and subject to its laws as such and acts done, rights acquired and contracts made in another state or country are done, acquired or made with respect to the law thereof and are interpreted and controlled thereby.

In the distribution of a decedent's or an insolvent's or bankrupt's estate located in a jurisdiction out of such person's domicil, resident creditors will usually be preferred.

All this, it must be remembered, is subject to the right of any state or country to make laws absolutely controlling the disposition of property, personal or real, within its limits without regard to the domicil of the owner.

DOMICILE OF ORIGIN The home of the parents. That which arises from a man's birth and connections. The domicile of the parents at the time of birth, or what is termed the domicile of origin, constitutes the domicile of an infant and continues until abandoned, or until the acquisition of a new domicile in a different place.

DOMINION (PROPERTY) Those rights which a man may acquire in and to such external things as are unconnected with his body.

DONATIO A gift of lands or chattels.

DONEE One who receives a gift or bequest.

DONOR One who makes a gift or bequest.

DORMANT PARTNER A partner

who is not known to third persons, but is entitled to share in the profits and is subject to the losses. Credit is not extended upon the strength of such partner's name, thus he may withdraw without notice and is not subject to debts contracted after his withdrawal.

DOUBLE INDEMNITY The provision in an insurance policy that under certain conditions the insurance company will pay to the beneficiary under the policy twice the face amount of the policy.

DOWER A woman's life share in her dead husband's estate. Under the common law the widow is entitled to one-third of all the land of which her husband may have been seized, during the marriage, in fee simple or fee tail. Her rights in the real estate, however, have been considerably altered by statute. In some states she has dower only in the real estate that her husband owns at his death. In others, she may claim common law dower after his death in any real estate he may have conveyed during life, unless she herself has done some act to preclude her from making the claim.

The widow has no endowable right in land to be held for a term of years only (leased land). Where several hold an estate in common the share of each is subject to dower in favor of the widow of each. A widow is entitled to dower in mines belonging to her husband if opened by him in his lifetime on his own or another's land. Where rents are estates of inheritance she is entitled to dower in them, but not in a pre-emption claim, nor in realty mortgage to her husband unless after due process of law the

mortgage becomes irredeemable in which case it becomes in fact the conveyance which it was before in form. Where a husband has entered into a contract to purchase land and dies before the deed is delivered, if after his death by direction of a proper court there is a specific performance of the contract, the widow is entitled to her dower.

Divorce extinguishes the right of dower as does also eloping with another man than the husband and living in adultery with him. The most common method of divesting the wife's dower interest in lands conveyed by her husband is for her to join in the conveyance, and usually the husband should join in her act of conveyance to defeat the dower, that is, the wife should not attempt to execute a paper alone for that purpose. She should be of age, and the instrument must be acknowledged in accordance with the form provided by statute. She cannot release dower by parol. She may, however, preclude herself from claiming dower by acts on her part negativing the right of dower, in consequence of which acts another is led to do something with respect to the property which he otherwise would not have done.

The widow is entitled to have her dower assigned, that is, to have a specific part of the estate set aside to her exclusive use for life, or proceedings may be had whereby the land will be charged with a specific sum during her life, the interest thereof to be paid to her by the owner, or the real estate may be sold for payment of debts of the decedent clear of the dower, and the proper portion of the fund remaining after payment of the debts invested, she receiving the income therefrom during her life. Where the husband conveys land in his lifetime without the extinguishment of the dower right and the land has enhanced in value at the time of the husband's death the widow is not entitled to share in this enhancement if it is the result of the purchaser's labor and improvements. But if due to extraneous circumstances, as from general rise in the value of the property in the neighborhood, she is so entitled. If the land deteriorates from any cause she must take her interest in it as she finds it at the death of her husband.

Dower is a species of property which may be transferred or assigned by the widow and is liable for debts and she may release it in favor of the owner of the land. It is a continuation of the husband's estate by appointment of law, but until his death is not an interest of which value can be predicated.

DOWRY The portion or property which the wife brings her husband in marriage.

DRAFT *See* BILLS OF EXCHANGE.

DRAWEE The person to whom a bill of exchange is addressed, or on whom it is drawn.

DRUNKENNESS Intoxication. Drunkenness does not excuse crime. But one cannot be held guilty where there is no criminal intent provided the intent is an essential part of the criminal offense. Courts, however, afford no relief either in civil or criminal cases merely because of drunkenness, and will not do so unless it appears that the drunkenness was such that

the power of comprehension was absent.

In actions for torts drunkenness may not be shown for the purpose of lessening the damages, and in fact it rather tends to aggravate the injury than otherwise. Where one induces another to drink to excess and causes him to be intoxicated for the purpose of procuring him to do an act which he would not do if sober, this partakes of the nature of fraud and the act will be subject to a different rule from the prevailing in an ordinary case of voluntary drunkenness.

Obtaining property of one who is intoxicated and incapable of protecting his interests is fraudulent and may be set aside or proper damages may be recovered. One who is so drunk that he is not capable of comprehending what he is doing cannot make a binding contract. But he must not use intoxication as a cloak with the intention of entering into a contract and afterwards declaring it void. If he purchases goods when drunk and keeps them when sober he must pay for them, and a failure to promptly return them when sober would no doubt be construed as a ratification of the purchase; but if the purchase is of necessaries he will be bound although intoxicated at the time.

DUCES TECUM A term applied to certain writs, in which a party summoned to appear in court is required to bring with him some paper or piece of evidence, or other thing requested by the court.

DUE BILL A brief written acknowledgment of a debt, usually in the following words: "Due A. B.—dollars (payable on demand). Dated, etc. C. D." It is not made payable to order like a promissory note.

DUE PROCESS OF LAW Law in its regular course of administration through courts of justice; such a process is guaranteed by the United States Constitution.

DUMMY One posing or represented as acting for himself, but in reality acting for another. A tool or straw man for the real parties in interest.

DUPLICITY The technical fault of having two counts in a plea or two subjects in a statute.

DURESS A contract entered into under coercion of mind or will, which, when proved, makes the contract void. Duress to avoid a contract must be either actual violence or a threat which negatives consent on the part of the party under duress, and excites in him a fear of some grievous wrong, death, great bodily injury or unlawful imprisonment; or loss of good name. It must be such as to overcome the will of the party imposed upon and lead him to do what he otherwise would not do. Imprisonment is duress where there are any circumstances of unnecessary pain, privation or danger which induces the party to make the contract. A contract made under duress is voidable and not void, and may be ratified and adhered to by the party who was wrongfully compelled to execute it.

The foregoing applies rather to cases where there may be a motive for executing the contract in addition to the desire to escape from injury or personal restraint. If there is no other cause than duress operating to induce one to execute a paper or enter into a contract, any threat, even the slightest, will invalidate it. If one is illegally deprived of his liberty or placed under personal restraint until he does an act desirable to another he may avoid the act by proving the duress. But if he was legally imprisoned and does the act to secure his discharge in a fair and legal manner it is otherwise.

Acts done as the result of threat of loss of life or limb or from fear of imprisonment where there is a sufficient reason to believe that the threat may be carried out may be avoided. It is also duress if the violence or threat is directed against one's wife, husband, descendants, parents or grandparents, but it must be of such character as would inspire fear of great injury to person, reputation or fortune. The degree or character of the duress which will have such effect will, of course, vary with the age, sex and disposition of the party threatened. Restraint of goods even under circumstances of hardship will sometimes avoid a contract. There will be no avoidance, however, where the threat is to do something which one has a right to do.

DYING DECLARATIONS Declarations made when the party is at the point of death, when every hope of survival is gone and every motive to falsehood is silenced, and the mind is induced by the most powerful consideration to speak the truth.

"DYING WITHOUT ISSUE" or "DIE WITHOUT ISSUE" In common law, an indefinite failure of issue or children.

E

EARNEST The payment of part of the price of goods sold, or delivery of part of the goods to bind the contract. The effect of this seems to be to furnish more satisfactory and definite evidence of the fact that a contract of sale was made. It renders the existence of the contract more definite and certain. A sale good and binding between the parties may take place, however, without such earnest and without delivery of the goods.

Even though earnest is given, however, the purchaser cannot take away the goods until he pays the price, unless there is an agreement to the contrary. The vendor, if he has received earnest, cannot resell without a default on the part of the vendee and should make a demand upon him for payment before such resale, and then only after giving him reasonable time to take the goods away and pay the money.

EASEMENT The right of the owner of a given piece of land to use land belonging to another for a special purpose not inconsistent with the general property right in the owner. The land to which the privilege is attached is said to be the dominant tenement, that upon which it is imposed, the servient. Among such easements are the right of way over another's lands or of obtaining water from a well or ,wood, minerals, pasture, or other produce of the soil, the right of fishing, or the right of receiving or discharging water over another's land or of having support for buildings or of receiving light or air from another's land, or of burying in a cemetery or particular vault, etc., etc.

Easements confer no right to any profits arising from the servient tenement, and impose no duty upon the owner of the same except that he shall do nothing to interfere with the use or right.

Easements may be either permanent or temporary. All easements are supposed to be acquired by grant, but actual and uninterrupted enjoyment of the easement immemorially or for twenty years or whatever period is required locally to acquire title to real estate by possession (from which a grant is presumed), will give title to the easement.

No immemorial usage, however, will give rise to what is termed a negative easement, that is, one forbidding an owner of land from building and causing obstruction of light to a house on an adjoining property. The mere use of windows for twenty years or more will not usually create a right to continue them as against an adjoining owner. Easement may be extinguished by a formal release, or by merger (that is, where the servient and dominant tenements come to be owned by the same person) by a non-user for twenty years or more where the right was acquired by prescription, also by a license to the servient owner to do something inconsistent with the existence of the easement.

EDICT A command or prohibition promulgated by a sovereign and having the effect of law.

EJECTMENT The name of the action brought to regain possession of real property with damages for its unlawful detention. The plaintiff in such a suit cannot recover by showing lack of title in his opponent, but must depend upon the strength of his own title. Ejectment may be brought to enforce a right to possession of the land whether based on an estate in the claimant in fee simple, fee tail, for life, or for years, and it may be maintained by one joint owner or tenant in common against another who dispossesses him.

Formerly nominal damages could be recovered in an action of ejectment, party being compelled to have recourse to a second suit, an action of trespass, to recover mesne profits, that is, profits which the one dispossessed has lost. However, now it is common to recover the land and mesne profits in the same suit.

ELEEMOSYNARY CORPORATION A corporation created for a charitable purpose or purposes.

ELEGIT He has chosen. A writ of execution to satisfy a judgment; a title to goods or land held under such a writ.

EMANCIPATE To release; to set free. Where a father expressly or impliedly, by his conduct waives his right generally to the services of his minor child, the child is said to be emancipated and he may sue on contracts made by him for his services.

EMBEZZLEMENT The appropriating to one's own use that which is entrusted to one for another. Embezzlement is closely allied to larceny, the chief difference being that in embezzlement the property comes lawfully into the possession of the offender, and in larceny it does not. In one respect it is even more odious than larceny, since it involves a breach of confidence reposed in the offender. Larceny is an offense at common law. The crime of embezzlement is for the most part the creature of the statute laws, which must be consulted to determine what particular classes of embezzlement are made criminal in any particular jurisdiction. The appropriation by a bailee to his own use of property in his possession as such is sometimes called larceny by bailee, and may be said to be a species of embezzlement.

EMBLEMENTS Annual products of the land which have resulted from the care and labor of a tenant and which he has a right to take and carry away after his tenancy has ended. The right to emblements arises from necessity, as where good husbandry requires that a crop shall be sown before the termination of a tenancy, but necessarily cannot be reaped until after its termination.

The principle applies also when the tenancy is ended through some unforeseen event. Thus if a lease is made to a husband and wife as long as they continue married, and they are divorced or the wife dies, the husband will be entitled to the emblements; so also, if the landlord, having the power, terminates the tenancy by notice to quit; but if the termination of the tenancy is by the act of the tenant there is a forfeiture of emblements and the landlord takes them.

Grass cut from the soil after a sale on an execution, but before confirmation of the sale by the court, will not belong to the purchaser of the real estate. If one, mistakenly believing the grass belongs to him, cuts and cures it, with the knowledge and without the objection of the owner, he may retain it, but will be liable to the real owner for the value of it uncut.

The term emblements applies to all the crops which are the result of labor and expense bestowed upon them by the tenant within the current year, such as grains, peas, beans, hemp, flax, potatoes and even artificial grasses which are usually annually renewed like other crops. It does not apply to roots and trees which are not annual in character or the fruit thereon though ripe, nor to ordinary grass growing even if ready to cut or to a second crop of clover although the first was cut before the end of the term.

It must be said, however, that where contracts of lease and contracts for cropping are not explicit, they are understood to be made with reference to the custom in the vicinity of the land with respect to which they are made, and such custom will be referred to to explain the contracts and to supply what is not expressed therein, both as to emblements and other matters. The rights of tenants will vary as to the way-going crop with different sections. In some places the outgoing tenant by custom may be entitled to the privilege of retaining possession of the land on which his way-going crops are sown, with the use of barns and stables for

housing and carrying them away the incoming tenant having the privilege of plowing and manuring the land during the continuance of the old tenancy. But independent of any custom the one entitled to emblements may have all necessary ingress or egress to cut and carry away.

EMBRACERY An attempt to corrupt or influence a jury or in any way incline them to be more favorable to one side than the other by money, promises, threats or persuasion, whether the juror on whom such an attempt is made renders any verdict or not, or whether the verdict is true or false. The offense is criminal.

EMINENT DOMAIN The power to take private property for public use. The owner of the land, however, must be compensated and there is in most all cases statutory provision made for appointment of viewers to assess damages in such cases, provided the party taking and the one from whom the property is taken cannot themselves agree upon the damages. The right to appeal from the finding of the viewers and a trial by jury exists in favor of one dissatisfied with their findings.

The right of eminent domain exists upon the theory that private ownership of land is subordinate to the public necessities. Land may be taken by the state itself or the right to take it for public use may be granted to a municipality, such as a city, county, borough, school district and the like or even to a private corporation whose duties are to the public at large, as a railroad. A corporation having the right is usually required to either pay or give security for damages before actually taking the property. If the use for which the land was taken at any time ceases, it reverts to the owner of the soil, his heirs, and assigns, his title to the land never having in reality passed from him but only its use. The right of eminent domain extends not to land merely but to things incorporeal, such as a franchise. Franchises granted a corporation as well as to individuals may be taken by the state when public necessities require provided due compensation is made.

EMPLOYER AND EMPLOYEE The employer is one who hires another, the employee, who works for wages, salary or other consideration. Where one is hired for a definite term the employer may recover damages against the person who entices away or harbors the employee or servant knowing him to be in the employ of another. The employer may dismiss the employee before the expiration of the term for immoral conduct, wilful disobedience or habitual neglect, and the one hired will not in such case be entitled to wages that would otherwise have subsequently accrued. If the dismissal is without just reasons the employee may recover damages to indemnify him for the loss of wages during the time necessarily spent in obtaining another situation, and for the loss of excess, if any, of the wages he had contracted for above the rate he has been able after due diligence to obtain.

If the employee quits work without reasonable cause before the end of the term of employment, the employer it seems is required to pay him either the contract price for the time he worked, or, if there is no contract price, the rate that is usually paid in the vicinity for the same kind of work, but he will be entitled to offset against the claim for wages, such loss as he may suffer from deprivation of the employee's assistance until he can with reasonable diligence secure other assistance.

A master may justify an assault in defense of his servant and a servant in defense of his master. The master or employer is liable for injuries occasioned by the neglect or unskillfulness or by the tortious acts of his servants and employees committed while in the course of their employment, even though done contrary to express orders, provided they are not done in wilful disregard thereof. He is not liable for acts committed out of the course of their employment or for wilful trespasses of his employees, and he is not criminally liable for their acts unless committed by his command or with his assent. The employer's responsibility is measured by and begins and ends with his right of control over his employee. One is not therefore liable for the act of one with whom he contracts otherwise than as a master or employer, or for the act of the employee of the contractor, unless the thing contracted for be in itself unlawful or a public nuisance. All contracts made by an employee within the scope of his authority bind the master.

One who does work agreeing to do so without pay cannot recover for it, but if there is a contract to render services without an express agreement as to compensation, an implied undertaking exists to pay for the services, the amount common in such cases in the vicinity. If the one employed agrees to leave the compensation to the employer a jury may award what the employer ought to pay acting bona fide.

One is bound to take all reasonable precautions to secure the safety of his employees acting in the course of their duties. He must caution them against risks or dangers that are not in themselves apparent to them. If an employer or master uses due diligence in the selection of competent and trusted employees and furnishes them with proper means to perform the service in which he employs them, he is not liable to one of them for an injury resulting from the carelessness of another while they are both engaged in the same service, but if the injury results from failure to provide suitable means to perform the service or to use reasonable care in the selection of the fellow employee or servant, the employer will be liable.

If the employee works with defective appliances for a considerable length of time, knowing them to be such, he assumes the risk, and his employer will not be liable for accidents resulting therefrom. In general it may be said the employee assumes and takes upon himself such risks as he knows about, or which with reasonable care he should have known about, and injury resulting from disobeying rules which the employee has opportunity of being acquainted with, provided for the safety of the employees, will not be a ground for recovering damages.

ENCUMBRANCE Any right to or interest in or burden upon land which may subsist in third persons to the diminution of the value, of the estate of the holder but which does not interfere with an estate in fee in the holder, such as an easement or lien. A public highway is an encumbrance for one may be the owner in fee of the land over which a highway passes. So is a private right of way, a claim of dower even though inchoate (that is, even though the husband is still living), and a mortgage. All these and also liens under tax laws have been held to be encumbrances within the meaning of the covenant against encumbrances contained in conveyances. A condition on which an estate may be held is not an encumbrance.

One selling real estate is bound to disclose to the purchaser the existing encumbrances and to deliver to him the instruments by which they were created or on which the defects arise. A failure to do this is fraud. It is the duty of the tenant for life (if there is one), of the real estate to pay interest on encumbrances to the extent of the rents or profits yielded. For any sum paid beyond that he becomes a creditor of the estate. If the principal of an encumbrance is paid off, the portion to be paid to the owner of the life estate is the present worth of an annuity in his favor for life equal to the annual interest or income which he would receive, and this rule applies to estates in dower and courtesy as well as other life estates.

ENDORSE To write one's name on the back of a bill, note or check.

ENDORSEMENT   A sanction or approval. An endorsement on a negotiable instrument may either be in blank, in which case the name of the endorser only is written upon the instrument (usually on the back though the same purpose may be answered by writing the name across the face), or it may be in full in which case the endorsement in full is commonly in one of the following forms: "Pay to the order of John Smith" or "Pay to John Smith or order" with the endorser's name signed thereunder. Where there is a blank endorsement, the instrument may be transferred by delivery only, though there is a new endorsement with each transfer.

Each person endorsing the negotiable instrument renders himself liable to all subsequent endorsers and holders for the amount therof, if the drawer, in the case of a promissory note, or the acceptor, in the case of a bill of exchange, fails to pay upon proper and prompt demand made, and upon proper and prompt notice of such failure given to him by the endorser. The endorser may in any way qualify his endorsement so that he shall not be responsible on non-payment by the drawer or acceptor, his endorsements in such case only evidencing a transfer of the instrument. The words "without recourse" are commonly used to effect this result.

One endorsing a check warrants the genuineness of all endorsements preceding his own. An endorsement may also be conditional, to operate as a transfer only in case a given condition is performed. It may also be so expressed as to a particular person or for a particular purpose. The payee in a promissory note or the drawee in a bill of exchange becomes, of course, also the first endorser when it is transferred unless it is made payable to "bearer" or to the party "or bearer," in which case the endorsement is unnecessary to a transfer. The endorsement of a blank note binds the endorser to any terms as to amount and time of payment which the party to whom he entrusts the paper may insert.

The drawer of a note may set up any proper defense to it as against the payee. Any person having possession of a negotiable instrument is presumed to be the legal bona fide owner for value until the contrary is shown. If the endorsement and transfer of a note is made before it becomes due, the endorsee and all subsequent holders are entitled to recover the face of the note against the maker without deduction or offset of claims which the drawer may have against the payee, and without defense on his part even for fraud or want of consideration if the note is genuine, provided, however, the holder has no notice or direct and sufficient means of knowing of the fraud, want of consideration or right of offset against the payee prior to his purchase of the note.

If one having knowledge that the note is uncollectible by the payee takes it from the payee with his endorsement thereon and sells it and endorses it in favor of an innocent purchaser for value before maturity of the note, and such innocent purchaser in turn endorses it to still another who knows the character of the note, the last-mentioned may recover on the note. This is because the right of an innocent purchaser having attached he is enabled to pass that right to anyone unimpaired. A defense may be set up against anyone in case of instruments not negotiable.

The mere writing of one's name on the back of an instrument not negotiable creates no liability. This was formerly construed to be a contract to guarantee payment to the payee of a note. However, under the statutes of fraud in force in most places requiring a written memorandum or instrument of writing signed by the party to make him liable on a promise to stand good for the debt of another, it has been decided that a mere signature is not such a memorandum or instrument of writing as the act requires, and that it creates no liability on such an instrument.

Each endorsement is in the nature of a new obligation to subsequent holders, and even though collection cannot be enforced against the pretended maker of a note or drawer of a bill of exchange because his name is forged, yet the endorser is liable. The law of the state where each endorsement is made controls it.

If one partner draws a note in his own name, payable to the order of his firm, and discounts it at a bank with the firm endorsement on it, all in his own handwriting and has the proceeds credited to his individual account, the other partner will not be held if he did not authorize the transaction. It is the bank's duty under the circumstances to inquire into the partner's authority, because the firm endorsement, not being followed by the individual endorsement of the endorsing partner, raises the presumption that the proceeds of the note are to belong to the firm and not to the individual.

ENDOWMENT In life insurance provides for the payment of the face amount of the policy if the insured survives the agreed term of the policy or dies while it is in effect.

ENOCH ARDEN The name given to a proceeding which permits the dissolution of a marriage when one of the parties disappears and is absent for a designated period of time, usually seven years, creating the legal presumption that he is dead.

ENTAIL To create an estate in tail; to settle an estate according to a certain rule of descent; to limit to certain heirs.

ENTRAPMENT An official's in-ducement of a person to commit a crime in order to prosecute him.

ENTRY *In real property law,* taking land possessed by another but claimed by oneself; *in criminal law,* going into a house for an illegal purpose; *in practice,* formally putting into an official record some act or document.

EQUITABLE DEFENSE Any matter which would authorize an application to a court of chancery for relief against a legal liability, but which at law could not be pleaded in bar.

EQUITABLE ESTATE An estate acquired by operation of equity, or cognizable in a court of equity; such as the estate or title of a person for whose use or benefit lands are held in trust by another, the latter having the legal estate; also the estate of a mortgagor, after the mortgage has become forfeited by non-payment, and before foreclosure.

EQUITABLE MORTGAGE A mortgage arising in equity, out of the transactions of the parties, without any deed or express contract for that special purpose.

EQUITY A system or code of laws compiled as corrective to a too technical system. Remedies in courts of law are so limited and precise in their application and so rigid as to procedure that they are in many instances inadequate to mete out justice. This accounts for courts of equity which supply suitable remedies for wrongs committed when such remedies would otherwise not exist, and in many cases stopping and even preventing the commission of wrongs. The procedure is more pliable than in the law courts, and the judgment or decree may be moulded into such form as suits the exigencies of the case.

It is a general rule that where an adequate remedy can be had at law one cannot resort to a court of equity. But even if the remedy at law is sufficient, equity will entertain jurisdiction where a multiplicity of suits at law will be avoided, for frequently the rights of all may be adjudicated in a suit in equity where they could not do so in a suit at law, as where the rights of the parties plaintiff or defendant vary, or where different rights of the same parties are to be adjudicated.

There are certain classes of cases which are peculiarly within the jurisdiction of a court of equity, such as fraud, accident or mistake, imperfect consideration, cancellation and reformation of instruments, etc. Courts of Equity with regard to all such matters will entertain jurisdiction and afford relief in proper cases, as well as in restraining the commission or continuing of harmful acts by injunction. Relief will also be granted because of mischief which would result if the court did not interfere, as in case of contracts in restraint of trade, buying and selling public offices, and agreements founded on corrupt considerations.

Where from a relation of trust and confidence or from consanguinity the parties do not stand on equal ground in dealing with each other, as in case of a parent and child, guardian and ward, attorney and client, principal and agent, executor and legatee, administrator and distributee, trustee and *cestui que trust*, or where the party is incapable of taking care of his own rights, as in case of idiots and lunatics, or where the forms of procedure in law courts are inadequate to the due investigation of the particulars and details of the case, as in matters of account, partition, dower, and ascertainment of boundaries, or where the relations are impediments to a legal remedy, as in cases between partners or joint tenants or in the marshalling of assets, in these and other proper cases courts of equity have jurisdiction.

EQUITY OF REDEMPTION The right which equity gives to a mortgagor of redeeming his mortgaged estate after the appointed period has gone by, for repayment of the sum of money which was due on the mortgage.

ESCHEAT The right to an estate left vacant when no one is otherwise legally entitled to make claim thereto.

ESCROW A deed delivered to a third person to be by him delivered to the grantee upon the happening of a certain condition. The transmission of title is complete and the deed takes effect only from the second delivery and after performance of the condition. There must be a condition to be performed precedent to the second delivery, not a mere postponement. The intent of the first delivery should be clearly expressed at the time and it should be to one not interested in the conveyance. If the deed is delivered into the possession of the grantee merely to enable him to carry it to the third person to hold as an escrow, this will not effect an absolute delivery to the grantee and will operate as if the deed were originally put into the hands of the third party. It is not advisable in practice to deliver the deed to the third party through the agency of the grantee.

ESQUIRE A name or title of dignity in English law, above the rank of gentleman, and below knight. Also, a title of office given to sheriffs, sergeants and barristers at law, justices of the peace, and others.

ESTATE This word is frequently applied to all of one's possessions and more particularly to the property which one owns at death. It is sometimes applied to a portion of such property only as this, that or the other estate. Under this title, however, the word is used in a different sense, and refers to the quantity, nature and extent of interest which one may have in real property.

What is known as an estate for life may be during one's own life, or for the life or lives of one or more other persons, or for an indefinite period which may endure for the life or lives of persons in being, but not beyond the period of one or another of them. Life estates may be created by deed or by operation of law. An example of the latter occurs where there is an estate in fee tail (*see below*), and there is no longer possibility of issue surviving to take the property at the death of the tenant in fee tail.

Another instance of an estate for life is that of a tenant by the curtesy. This exists where a wife dies leaving the lands of which she was seized in possession in fee simple or fee tail during the marriage, provided they have had lawful issue, born alive which might have been capable of inheriting the estate. The requirement as to having had issue is abolished in some places. The surviving husband is entitled to his wife's land during his life.

The largest estate which one can have in land is an estate in fee simple, where one holds lands to himself, his heirs and assigns absolutely without any end or limit to his estate. It is distinguished from an estate in fee tail in that in the latter the estate is limited to descent to certain classes of heirs, as for example, "heirs of the body," etc., and not to heirs generally whatever their degree of relationship. Both are said to be estates of inheritance because either may descend to heirs. The term freehold applies both to estates in fee and estates for life.

If one takes an estate of freehold by will or deed, providing that it shall go to him and his heirs in fee simple or fee tail or to him during his life and at his death to the heirs, the word "heirs" in either case is a word of limitation of the estate and not a word of purchase; it simply describes the estate and determines that the first taker acquires an estate in fee simple or fee tail, not an estate for life only. This is in accord with what is known as the rule in Shelley's case. It has frequently defeated the real intention of a testator where he has desired the first taker to have a life estate only without power over the property after his death. The rule has been abolished in many jurisdictions.

An estate for years is the interest which one has in lands by virtue of a contract for the possession of them for a definite and limited period of time. The length of time it is to endure does not matter, even though it extends far beyond the life of persons in being or for a thousand years. Such estates are regarded as personal and subject to the rules thereof. If the tenant or holder dies they pass as part of his personal estate.

An estate at will is one held during the joint wills of the parties. They are usually construed to exist for years, or from year to year.

An estate at sufferance exists where one has come rightfully into possession of lands by permission of the owner, but continues to occupy it after the period for which he is entitled to hold. If the tenant has personally left the house the landlord may break open doors or use force to regain possession provided a breach of the public peace is not committed.

An estate in common exists where land is held in joint possession by two or more at the same time by several and distinct titles. They are accountable to each other for the profits of the estate, and if one turns another out of possession an action of ejection will lie against him to recover the possession. They may hold each other responsible also for waste.

An estate at sufferance exists where lands or tenements have been granted or devised to more than one to hold in fee simple for life for years or at will. Joint tenants must have the same interest arising from the same conveyance or will at the same time and held by one and the same undivided possession. The essential practical difference between this estate and that in common is that there is a survivorship between joint tenants, that is, upon the death of one his interest goes to the survivor or survivors, the last survivor taking the entire estate. Today joint tenancy is to all intents and purposes equivalent to tenancy in common. It may be said, however, that where the land is conveyed to a husband and wife, there will be survivorship as between them arising from the theory that husband and wife are but one. An estate in coparcenary exists where

several persons hold by descent (not by will) as one heir, though the
interest of the coparceners may be unequal as where they are of different
degrees of relationship to the decedent.

ESTATE IN COMMON An estate
in lands held by two or more persons, with interest accruing under
different titles; or accruing under
the same title, but at different periods; or conferred by words of limitation importing that the grantees
are to take in distinct shares.

ESTOPPEL Where a fact has been
admitted or asserted for the purpose of influencing the conduct of
another or deriving personal benefit so that it cannot be denied
without a breach of good faith, or
where one, by words or conduct,
wilfully or designedly causes another to believe in the existence of
a certain state of things and induces him to act on that belief or
to alter his own previous position,
the law enforces the rule of good
morals and precludes or estops the
party from repudiating his representations or denying the truth of
his admissions.

It is a general rule that a party
to a deed is estopped to deny
anything stated in it which
operated upon another party as an
inducement to accept and act under the deed. Where the deed contains a covenant warranting the
title even this estops the one giving
the deed from claiming under title
acquired after the deed is given.
To create an estoppel the deed
must be good and valid in its form
and executed. Estoppels affect the
party to the transaction and also
those in privity with him, that is,
those having mutual or successive
relationships with him to the same
rights of property.

One is estopped from alleging

anything contrary to the final adjudication of a court. If one says or
does things designed to induce another to act in a particular way he
cannot repudiate his conduct to
the injury of the other, as where
one dedicates land to public use
and the public has accepted it and
expended money or labor upon it
and used it. One cannot even stand
by and see his land improved by
another without objecting and then
escape paying for it, for his silence
is an implied assent, and he is estopped from alleging that he did
not order or contract for the improvement.

ET AL. Literally translated means
"and other persons." Words used
in pleading and cases to indicate
that persons other than those specifically named are parties to a lawsuit.

ET UX. The abbreviation of *et
uxor,* meaning "and wife."

EVICTION Eviction is depriving a
person of possession of his lands or
tenements. Actual physical expulsion is not necessary to constitute
an eviction. Any act of a landlord
tending to diminish the enjoyment
of the premises amounts to an eviction in law. Thus if he erects a nuisance so near the premises as to
deprive the tenant of the use of
them, or if he otherwise intentionally disturbs the tenant's enjoyment
so as to injure his business or destroy the comfort of himself and
family it will amount to an eviction.
If there is an eviction of a pur-

chaser in whose deed there is a covenant of seisin or for quiet enjoyment, he may recover from the grantor the consideration money paid for the land, with interest. In most places, in case of an eviction of a lessee, the rent ceases and he can recover the expenses he is put to in defending his possession and damages caused by the evictor.

Of course, an action for ejectment will lie for recovery of the land itself if one is wrongfully kept out of possession. In case crops to which a tenant is entitled are taken from him he may recover proper damages for it. To effect a suspension of rent, however, there must be something equivalent to an expulsion from the premises and not a mere trespass or disturbance in the enjoyment of them. If the eviction is only partial, that is, of a portion of the premises, whether in case of a purchaser or lessee, the injured person is entitled to recover in proportion to the value of the premises to which the eviction applies. The whole consideration money cannot be recovered.

EVIDENCE   Testimony, or that which furnishes proof or gives ground for belief. The existence or non-existence of a fact may be shown by the testimony of witnesses; by public records such as judgments and proceedings of courts, etc.; by judicial writings such as inquisitions, depositions and the like; by public documents having an official or semi-official character, such as statute books published by authority of the government and documents printed by authority of Congress; by private writings such as deeds, contracts and wills; and by personal inspection by the jury or other tribunal whose duty it is to determine the matter in dispute, as by viewing the premises to which the controversy relates or examining the machine or weapon produced in the case. Of certain things courts will take judicial notice without proof, such as the laws of their own state or country, the extent of their own jurisdiction, etc.

Evidence is said to be direct and positive when the very facts in dispute are communicated by those having actual knowledge of them by means of their senses.

Circumstantial evidence is that which tends to prove a disputed fact by proof of other facts which have a legitimate and natural tendency to lead the mind to a conclusion that the fact exists which is sought to be established.

What are termed presumptions of fact may be said to be those things which are established by circumstantial evidence. They are conclusions drawn from common experience and a knowledge of human character and motives to arise from given circumstances. Besides such presumptions of fact there are also presumptions of law, which exist where from motives of public policy the law requires and directs that a given inference be drawn from proof of the existence of a particular fact or facts.

In presumptions of fact the jury or other tribunal having the determination of the fact, uses its own judgment as to the inference to be drawn from proof of the existence of a particular fact or facts. In case of presumptions of law such tribunal would be bound to adhere to the inferences prescribed by law, the court instructing them as to their duty in this respect.

Presumptions of law are of two kinds. First, there are conclusive presumptions of law as in the case of the record of a judgment, which except in some proceeding to amend or reverse it, is conclusively presumed to be rightly entered. In such a case evidence will not be admitted in a collateral proceeding or suit to impeach a judgment. Second, there are no presumptions of law which may not be rebutted by counter testimony. Thus a man is presumed in law to be sane, or not to have committed a crime, or to be still living where once shown to be alive, until some fact is shown to repel the presumption, as in the last case, for example, that he was killed or died or has been absent from his place of residence unheard of for seven years or more.

Primary evidence, or, as it is often called, the best evidence, is that which with most certainty exhibits the true state of facts. Secondary evidence is admissible only where it is shown that primary evidence cannot be produced. If a contract has been entered into and it is necessary to prove what the contract was, the original writing must be produced if it is possible to do so, that is, if it is not lost, stolen, or destroyed. Proof that diligent search has been made for it without success, or that it has been lost or destroyed, must be adduced before other evidence can be admitted of its contents.

The person who possesses the primary evidence must be applied to whether a stranger or the opposite party. If a stranger, he should be subpoenaed to appear as a witness and bring the written instrument with him. If it is in possession of the opposite party notice to produce it must be given to him before the secondary evidence will be admitted. If the original cannot be obtained a counterpart should be used if there is one, or if not a counterpart, a copy may be proven by any witness who knows it to be a copy by having compared it with the original, and if there is neither counterpart nor copy the party may produce an abstract if such exists or produce verbal evidence of the contents.

Statements by the witness as to the facts concerning which he does not himself have knowledge or recollection, his information being secondhand and from other sources, are in most all cases inadmissible because the party who was heard to say the thing was not under oath at the time and there is no opportunity of cross-examining him, and statements not made under oath are frequently at random, inaccurate and unreliable and based more or less upon supposition.

The rule excluding hearsay evidence does not apply to confessions, declarations or admissions which a party or one in privity with him may make. Nor does it apply to declarations or accusations of third persons made in the presence and hearing of the party relating to matters af-

ecting his interest. These may be proven in connection with his reply or
is silence to show an admission on his part. Silence, where one may
easonably be expected to deny, if innocent, will be evidence against him.
or does the rule against hearsay apply to dying declarations in cases of
omicide nor to opinions of experts relating to matters of skill and ex-
erience concerning which a jury or persons in general are ignorant and
nable properly to form opinion of their own, in which case they must as
matter of necessity be aided by the opinions of others shown to be
apable of instructing them.

Communications between husband and wife, between attorney and
lients, secrets of state and proceedings of grand jurors are not usually
ermitted to be given in evidence.

Evidence must be given only of matters relating to the point in issue,
at is, it must be relevant. The substance of the issue between the parties
ust be proved, otherwise the suit will fail. It will not do to allege one
ing in the pleadings and prove another. Thus it is a fatal variance if the
roofs offered show that someone who has been omitted in the suit is a
arty to a contract and ought to have been joined as a plaintiff. The
onsideration of a contract including the time, manner and other circum-
ances of its performance must be proven, that is, it must appear that the
arty claiming has performed his part of the contract. A negotiable instru-
ent is exceptional, for in order to recover on it, it is not necessary to
rove that consideration was given for it.

If one is charged with a crime he may be convicted of a lesser crime
hich is included in the greater, if the evidence does not reach so far as
then support the greater. Thus one indicted for robbery may be found
uilty of larceny and one indicted for assault and battery might be con-
icted of simple assault. In case of theft the thing stolen must be proved
have been identical with the thing alleged to have been taken. The one
ho asserts the affirmative of an issue must prove it before the opposing
arty can be required to produce any proofs. Where there is a presump-
on of law, however, in favor of an affirmative proposition it need not be
roven. The burden is then upon the opposing party to disprove it. Thus
e legitimacy of a child need not be proven for this is presumed, and it
evelops upon him who asserts the illegitimacy to prove it.

Where the existence of records is the question in issue an exemplifica-
on, that is, a perfect copy duly authenticated or certified, may be used
proving its existence. Where it is merely desired to prove something by
e record a copy duly proven to be such by one who has compared it
ith the original, will in general be sufficient. Private papers are proved
y attesting witnesses or by proving their handwriting in case of death,
osence or any legal inability to testify. If there is no witness to the
strument its execution may be proven by evidence of the handwriting of
e party signing from a person who has seen him write, or in course of
orrespondence has become acquainted with his handwriting.

EX AEQUO ET BONO In equity and good conscience.

EX CONTRACTU Arising out of, or founded on contract.

EX DEBITO JUSTITIAE From a debt of justice; from that which is owing; from one's right; as of right.

EX DELICTO Arising out of, or founded upon misconduct, malfeasance or tort, such as negligence, libel and slander, etc.

EX PARTE A case heard on application by one party to a proceeding in the absence of the other.

EX POST FACTO LAW Any law which makes an innocent act a crime after the act was committed. This term applies only to criminal laws. The Constitution of the United States and of the individual states forbids the passing of any law that makes criminal an act done before the passing of the law and which was innocent when done, or any law that aggravates a crime or makes it greater than it was when committed. It also forbids laws inflicting a greater punishment than that annexed to the crime when committed, or which changes the punishment without mitigating it, also any law that alerts the rules of evidence and permits the receiving of less or different testimony than that which was required to establish the crime at the time of its commission.

Ex post facto laws are retrospective, but all retrospective laws are not ex post facto, because most of them apply to matters not criminal. Retrospective laws may be passed if they do not apply to crimes, and if they do not violate the obligation of contracts contrary to the Constitution of the United States or any other constitutional provision, and in fact such laws frequently are enacted. No law should, however, be considered as applying to cases which arose previous to their passage, where such an intent does not clearly appear.

EXACTION The wrongful taking of a fee by an official when none is due him.

EXAMINATION BEFORE TRIAL A part of legal procedure which permits one litigant to make the other answer questions under oath before the actual trial of the case.

EXAMINER IN CHANCERY An officer of the court of chancery before whom witnesses are examined and their testimony reduced to writing, for the purpose of being read on the hearing of the cause.

EXCEPTION (1) *In trial practice*, notice that a judge's ruling, such as his overruling of an objection, not acquiesced in but will be specific matter of appeal. (2) A clause in a deed excluding some specific portion from a general grant. (3) *In equity practice*, a pleading that an adversary's pleading is insufficient.

EXECUTED CONTRACT A contract which transfers the possession of a thing, together with the title; a contract which conveys a chose in possession, as distinguished from a chose in action.

EXECUTED ESTATE An estate in possession by which a present interest passes to, and resides in the tenant, not depending on any sub sequent circumstance or contingency.

EXECUTED REMAINDER A remainder by which a present interest passes to the party, though to be enjoyed in the future.

EXECUTION A writ or order issued from a court or other proper tribunal, to the sheriff, constable or other proper officer directing him to carry into effect a judgment previously obtained. Most frequently it is an authority to sell, first personal property and then real estate to raise money to pay the judgment, including costs of suit. In an action of replevin, which is a suit to recover specific personal property, the execution will include an order for the delivery of the property itself, and a collection of damages awarded by the jury by the sale of other property or otherwise.

Formerly where the party had no means he was imprisoned in default of payment. This is now eliminated. In an action of ejectment, which is a suit to recover possession of lands, if the judgment is for the plaintiff, the writ of execution will be an order to deliver the possession to the plaintiff. In some cases it will include an order to collect an award by a jury of damages for loss of profits while the plaintiff was deprived of possession. Debts due to the defendant in the judgment and other interests belonging to him, such as distribu-

tive shares or legacies from a decedent's estate may be taken by process called attachment execution.

In levying upon goods and chattels in general, a seizure of a part of the goods in the name of the whole on the premises is a good seizure of the whole. It may be executed at any time before or on the return day of the writ, that is, the day on which the officer is directed to make his report to the tribunal from which the writ issues, but not on Sunday where it is forbidden by statute. The officer cannot break open or, it seems, even unlatch an outer door of a house in the execution of a writ, nor break a window. He may, however, having once lawfully entered, break open inner doors or chests to seize the goods even without a request to open them. The officer cannot enter the house of one who is not the defendant in the execution to search for the defendant's goods without being guilty of a trespass, unless the defendant's goods are actually in the house.

When a writ of execution known as a writ of *fieri facias* is issued to a sheriff for the seizure of goods and chattels it creates a lien on such goods and chattels immediately on its reaching the sheriff's hands. In order to determine the time when the lien begins the sheriff is required to endorse on the writ the precise time when he receives it. If the defendant in the execution sells it after that time it will still be subject to seizure.

EXECUTORS AND ADMINISTRATORS An executor is the one named in a will to carry out its provisions. All persons capable of making wills and some others may act as executors. Children may be appointed executors but cannot act as such until attaining sufficient age which at common law is seventeen years. Foreigners may also act if not belonging to a hostile country. Executors are generally required to give security. Idiots and lunatics cannot act and one becoming a lunatic may be removed. In the appointment of an executor in a will the word "executor" need not be used. It is only necessary that from the words of the will an intent exist on the part of the testator to designate someone and clothe him with authority to carry out the provisions of the will.

An appointment may be absolute and unconditional. It may also limit the powers of the executor to the time during which or the place in which he is to act or the particular subject matters of his action. Thus his authority may end when another person reaches the age of 21 years or it may be limited to a particular estate, or one person may be appointed as executor, of one portion of the estate, and another of another portion. Nevertheless, as to creditors of the testator, the executor will be considered as one and may be used as one. Two executors may be appointed at the same time with the condition that one shall act only in case the other shall refuse, or shall die before the death of the testator, or shall resign.

The one appointed may accept or refuse, but his acceptance will be implied from acts exercising authority over the property and evincing a purpose to accept. His refusal may also be inferred from his keeping aloof from the management of the estate. If one or two or more executors accept and others decline, those accepting will act alone.

Even before the will is probated an executor may do nearly all the acts he is authorized by the will to do or to perform. He can receive payments, discharge debts, collect and recover assets, sell bank stock, give or receive notice of dishonor of a check or draft; sell personal property in some states, pay legacies and where he has acted before proving the will, he may also be sued before proving it.

He may commence suits before probate of the will, but cannot maintain them except such suits as are founded on actual possession. It has been said, however, that he cannot sell land without letters testamentary (at least in some states), nor transfer a mortgage or remain in his own state and sue by attorney elsewhere, nor endorse notes so that he can be sued thereon as executor. No executor, however, can proceed to a general administration of the estate until the will has been proven and letters testamentary giving him full authority have been issued. Titles both to real and personal estate frequently depend upon wills, and for this reason also they should be properly and promptly probated.

An executor may do in general whatever an administrator can. His authority begins with the testator's death and the source of authority is the will, the probate of the will and the letters testamentary issued thereon being simply the evidence of the authority. In most places he has power over the real estate only where expressly granted by the will, or where he obtains authority under an order of court, as in case of an administrator to sell to pay debts or for distribution or otherwise. All the executors or administrators, should join in bringing suit. It is not advisable for him to sign or endorse a renewal of a note on which the name of the testator appears.

Co-executors are regarded as one, and in general the act of one is the act of all. The sale of one is the sale of all, and a payment by or to one is a payment by or to all. The assent of one to delivery or payment of a legacy is effective as to all, but each is liable only for the assets which have come into his own hands and if one only is guilty of negligence or a tort, his co-executor is not liable, unless he connived at it or aided in its commission. A power to sell land conferred on several executors should be executed by all who have undertaken to act as such, and if one only undertakes to act as executor his conveyance will be effective without the joinder of the others. If one joint executor dies the rights and powers of all are vested in the survivor or survivors.

An executor must prove the will before the proper officer and take out letters testamentary. He must bury the deceased in a manner suitable to his estate. Unreasonable expenses will not be allowed, nor if the estate is insolvent will unnecessary expenses be permitted, and the same is true in case of an administration. He must collect the goods and outstanding claims of the decedent, peaceably if he can, by process of law if he must, as must also an administrator, though neither is warranted in making costs in connection with a claim which is clearly uncollectible by process of law. Gross delay in collecting where the debtor becomes insolvent resulting in failure to make collection where collection could otherwise have been made, will make him liable for the loss.

Notice of the appointment together with a request for payment of debts owing to the decedent and presentment of claims against him should be advertised as provided by law. Usually one of the first duties of an executor or administrator is to file with the proper officer an inventory and appraisement of the personal estate.

Debts are the first charge against the estate and personal estate not specifically bequeathed in kind should first be made use of in their payment. Personal property generally is liable for the payment of debts before real estate, a testator, however, having a right to direct otherwise. An administrator must as promptly as is expedient collect outstanding claims and sell the whole of the movable personal estate. The safe method of sale for the executor or administrator is at public auction, after due advertisement as required by law. If a private sale is effected care should be exercised to realize full value.

The executor or administrator should keep the money of the estate safely. He should not mix it with own, and if he does, he may be charged with interest on it. If he uses the funds in any way he is liable for interest and in case the funds must necessarily lie idle for a considerable length of time he is bound to exercise reasonable effort to make them earn some interest if he can do so without risk to the fund. He must at all times be ready to account to the proper authorities if proper cause is shown for requiring it, and in most places at the end of a year after taking out letters, parties in interest may require the filing of an account unless cause is shown to the contrary. Debts and legacies must be paid in the order required by law. Executors and administrators are trustees.

An executor or administrator is always allowed reasonable expenses necessarily incurred in the administration of the estate. He is also allowed such commission as will fairly compensate him for his trouble and responsibility. The amount of commission commonly allowed varies.

An executor *de son tort* is one who attempts to act as executor without lawful authority. An executor *de son tort* is liable only for such assets as come into his hands and is not liable for not reducing assets to possession. His liability is to the rightful executor or administrator with the will annexed or to the heir at law. Interfering thus wrongfully in the estate, he puts himself in such position that he may be sued by creditors of the decedent but he cannot sue. If he takes out letters of administration his previous acts are legalized, and he is regarded as having been the rightful administrator with the will annexed from the beginning.

A note given by an executor or administrator will bind him personally, but not the estate, unless he expressly limits his promise by adding such words as "out of the assets of my testator" or "if the assets are sufficient" or the like. Executors and administrators if they voluntarily pay claims in full against insolvent estates may not recover back the excess paid over and above the dividend the creditors would have been entitled to. If an agent sells goods after his principal's death, the executor may, if he choose, ratify the sale and sue for the price.

EXECUTORY CONTRACT A contract which is to be executed at some future time, and which conveys only a chose in action.

EXECUTORY DEVISE By what is termed an executory devise no estate vests under the will at the death of the devisor or testator, but simply on the happening of a future contingency. The rule of law to prevent perpetuities is applicable to executory devises. This rule requires that the contingency on which the executory devise depends must take effect, if at all, during the time of a life or lives in being at the testator's death, or within twenty-one years after with

the months allowed for gestation added, making about twenty-one years and nine months. An example of an executory devise is land devised to such unborn son of a married woman as shall first reach the age of twenty-one years.

It is plain that if an executory devise or bequest is made to take effect after a general or indefinite failure of issue of someone in life no matter when this failure may occur, and not after a definite failure of issue (that is, a failure of issue within the period referred to in the preceding paragraph), this would be a violation of the rule against perpetuities and the devise or bequest would therefore be void.

EXEMPLARY DAMAGES A sum assessed by the jury in a tort action (over and above the compensatory damages) as punishment in order to make an example of the wrongdoer and to deter like conduct by others. Injuries caused by wilful, malicious, wanton, and reckless conduct will subject the wrongdoers to exemplary damages.

EXEMPTION A release from some burden, duty or obligation; a grace; a favor; an immunity; taken out from under the general rule, not to be like others who are not exempt.

EXEMPTION AND HOMESTEAD LAWS This is a right given by law to a debtor to retain a portion of his property as against an execution at the suit of a creditor or a distress for rent.

EXHIBITS Documents or other tangible evidence used at a trial to prove certain facts to the court and jury.

EXPATRIATION The voluntary act of abandoning one's country.

EXPROMISOR One who assumes another's debt rather than merely guarantees it.

EXTENDED COVERAGE An agreement of insurance which covers damage resulting from windstorm, hail, riot, explosion and similar stated risks.

EXTENDI FACIAS You may cause to be extended. A writ of execution against a debtor's property.

EXTORTION By criminal extortion is meant the unlawful taking by any officer, by reason of or through his office, of any money or thing of value, that is not due him or more than is due or before it is due. To constitute the crime there must be a receipt of money or something of actual value. The taking of a promissory note which is void is not sufficient to constitute an extortion, for this has no value. The note will not be enforceable, at least any part of it which was for an extortionate fee or compensation. An officer may not take money other than regular fees for the performance of his duty, even though it is in the exercise of a discretionary power.

The word extortion has a more extended popular meaning than that indicated above. If money or some other valuable thing is extorted by one not an officer by way of blackmail or other species of coercion, the injured person has a right of action to recover it from the offender.

EXTRADITION The surrender by one sovereign country or state to another, on its demand, of persons charged with the commission of crime within its jurisdiction. As between countries extradition is practiced chiefly in accordance with treaty stipulations as to what crimes shall be considered extraditable, the party making the requisition paying the expense of the apprehension and delivery of the prisoner. The higher grades of crimes are made so extraditable as between all the civilized nations, including murder, attempts to commit murder, piracy, arson, robbery, forgery, the utterance of forged papers, embezzlement by public officers, etc.

Extradition as between states of

the United States is practiced with respect to all the important crimes, but not with respect to the lesser offenses or to prosecutions, one purpose of which is the collection of a debt. A governor may revoke his warrant for the surrender of a fugitive any time before he has been transmitted from the state. The surrender of criminals from one country to another is not nec-

essarily limited to offenses in treaty regulations. As a matter of comity foreign nations may and sometimes do, grant the request for the surrender of a criminal for other offenses.

EXTRALATERAL RIGHT In mining law, the right to follow a vein or lode beyond the limits of the claim.

F

F.A.S. An abbreviation for the expression "free alongside steamer."

F.O.B. Goods, wares or merchandise to be loaded for shipment "Free on Board" without expense to the buyer.

FACE VALUE The nominal or par value of an instrument as expressed on its face; which in the case of a bond is the amount really due including interest.

FACTOR An agent who not only negotiates a contract of sale or purchase, but is in duty bound to carry it through to performance in behalf of his principal. Hence, he is given either actual or constructive possession of his principal's goods; and it is customary for him to advance money on them. He has implied authority to contract either in his own name without disclosing that of his principal, or in the name of his principal; and a payment to the factor is a complete discharge of his principal's debtor.

He differs from a broker principally in the fact that he takes the possession, management and control of goods, whereas a broker does not. He has a special property and lien on them for his labor and trouble about them, which a broker does not, and he may buy or sell as the case may be for his principal in his own name or in the name of the principal (for the term factor applies to an agent who buys as well as to an agent who sells), whereas a broker should buy and sell in the name of his principal only.

As regards a domestic factor, that is, one within the same country where the principal resides, he as well as his principal is liable for the debt in case of a purchase by him for his principal. In case of a sale the buyer is liable for the purchase money both to the factor and principal, unless the agreement is to the contrary at the time of the sale.

Foreign factors are personally liable on all contracts made by them for their employers whether they are described as agents in the contract or not, the presumption being that the credit is given exclusively to the factor, though this presumption may be rebutted by a proof of a contrary agreement. Though generally the third party may not sue the principal, yet the principal may sue the third party with whom the foreign factor deals.

A factor is required to use reasonable skill and ordinary diligence in his vocation and to obey his instructions if he has any, and if not, he should act according to the general usages of the trade, selling for cash if that is usual and giving credit where that is customary. He may sell the goods in his own name and, if not otherwise instructed, may sell them at such times, and for such prices as, in the exercise of a just discretion, he may think best for his employer.

For most purposes as between himself and third parties he is considered the owner and may sell and buy, recover the price of the goods sold, receive payment and give receipts in his own name and discharge the debt, unless the debtor has had notice from the principal not to pay him. Here he differs from an attorney-in-fact, who must act in the name of his principal. (*See also* ATTORNEY-IN-FACT.) He has a lien on the goods for advances made by him such as freight charges and other necessary expenses, and for his commission. He has no right to pledge the goods to raise money for himself or to secure a debt he may owe, but he may pledge them for advances made for his principal or to raise money for him or to reimburse himself to the extent of his lien or to pay duties or anything charged, allowed or justified by the usages of the trade.

The factor must obey positive instructions precisely (but not mere wishes or inclinations) unless in case of unforeseen emergency he disobey in good faith for the obvious and certain advantages of his principal. Where express instructions are not given he must conform to the usages of the business. He has discretion as to time and mode of sale if he acts in good faith, but if he expedites a sale improperly it is void, or he may be held for resulting damages.

If the factor fails and the goods of the principal in his possession still retain their identity or can be pointed out or distinguished from other like property in his possession, the creditors of the factor will have no right to the property, and the principal may take it back on payment of proper charges against the same. Where, however, the factor has dealt in his own name and neither the principal nor his rights with respect to the property have appeared in the transaction, the rights of the third parties with reference thereto in their dealings with the factor will be protected.

Neither a broker nor a factor is entitled to his commission until the whole service is performed, unless an irresistible obstacle intervenes, in which case he is entitled to proportionate compensation, if he is himself without fault. For injurious default, from lack of care, skill or fidelity, he not only loses his commission but is liable to his principal for damages. If he contracts to give his whole time to his employer, he may not lawfully receive pay elsewhere. He cannot recover for services in themselves illegal, immoral or against public policy.

If a factor having goods for sale at a given or limited price makes advances to the owner upon the goods in his possession, and in good faith, after reasonable delay and effort to obtain the price named by the principal and after proper precautions, sells them at a fair market price though less than the limited price, he is entitled to the amount he advanced without deduction.

FAIR MARKET VALUE Words used to express "that price which a seller would be willing to take for goods but who is not obliged to sell, and that price which a buyer would be willing to pay but who is not obligated to buy."

FALSE ARREST The unlawful physical restraint by one of another's liberty.

FALSE IMPRISONMENT The unlawful restraint of a man's liberty whether in a place made use of for imprisonment generally or in one used only on a particular occasion, or even if it is by words and an array of force without bolts or bars in any locality whatever. The remedy to obtain relief from the imprisonment is by writ of habeas corpus. An action to recover damages for the injury to the individual will also lie. The injury is considered a public wrong and the offender may be indicted.

FALSE PRETENSES A false statement or misrepresentation with fraudulent intent. Not every false representation or statement is a false pretense in a criminal sense. To be so it must have been with fraudulent design to obtain money, goods, wares or merchandise with intent to cheat. It must relate either to past events or existing facts. Representations as to future transactions may amount to a promise or covenant or warranty but not to a false pretense. It must be such as to impose upon a person of ordinary strength of mind.

The pretense must be such as leads one to give credit upon a false assumption that there is a basis for credit. And it is only necessary that one of several pretenses be false if without that one the credit would not have been given or the property delivered. The false pretense, however, must have occurred before the contract was completed and the goods delivered. An intent to cheat or defraud must exist and this may be inferred from a false representation. To constitute the crime it is not necessary that the party defrauded should sustain loss, unless by statute, obtaining goods is made part of the crime.

FAMILY PURPOSE The doctrine that the owner of an automobile is liable for damages resulting from the negligent operation of his automobile by members of his family whom he has permitted to use it.

FATHER The male parent. The husband is presumed to be the father of the wife's children born during the marriage or within a competent time thereafter, even if begotten before marriage, but this presumption may be rebutted by showing circumstances which render his parentage impossible. The mere declaration of either spouse, however, cannot affect the condition of a child born during marriage.

FEATHERBEDDING A term used in labor relations to describe the situation in which demand is made for the payment of wages when the particular service is not rendered.

FEE SIMPLE The highest estate

which can be conveyed. It entitles the owner to the entire property so that he can dispose of it unconditionally during his lifetime. A fee simple estate descends to the owner's heirs and legal representatives when he dies without leaving a will.

FEE TAIL An estate given to a man and the heirs of his body or limited to certain classes of particular heirs.

FEES Charges for professional services. The following list of fees is merely suggestive of minimum fees the average lawyer charges an average client. Where the work to be done is complicated or unusual, the charges are likely to be higher than the range indicated. In every case, the prospective client will save himself much anxiety if he ascertains at the first interview what the fee is likely to be.

1. **Administrative practice**
   A. Administrative Agency appearance. . . . . $ 50.00
   B. Administrative Board hearings $150.00
   C. Tax Court
      Retainer of $250.00 to be credited against one-third of any amount saved, if any.

2. **Adoption**
   A. Open court hearings:
      1. Compassionate cases involving relatives, welfare, etc.. . $150.00
      2. Uncontested cases $250.00
      3. Contested cases $350.00
   B. Open court hearing not required. $150.00

3. **Advice, consultation and hourly rate.**
   Minimum hourly rate, based on experience of attorney, in accordance with following schedule:
      0 to 2 years experience. $ 15.00
      2 to 5 years experience. $ 20.00
      Over 5 years experience . . . . $ 50.00

4. **Appeals**
   A. From Administrative Agency $250.00
   B. To the Court of Appeals $750.00

   C. To U.S. Court of Appeals. $750.00
   D. From a People's, Magistrate's or Municipal Court
       to a Circuit Court. $150.00

5. **Assignments for benefit of creditors** $350.00
   This fee may be grossly inadequate, if the case involves a
   complex business structure with many creditors and en-
   tangled accounts. In that event the attorney should negotiate
   a more realistic flat fee or else predicate the value of his
   services on an hourly basis.

6. **Bankruptcy**
   A. Simple (no substantial assets). $350.00
      In complex cases where there are substantial assets, great-
      ly involved accounts and contested claims of creditors
      requiring numerous court appearances, the fee of neces-
      sity would have to be substantially more.

7. **Change of name**
   A. Unopposed. . . . . $ 75.00
   B. If opposed, an additional charge should be made.

8. **Chattel mortgages** (financing statement and security agreement)
   A. Prepare and record . . . . $ 35.00
   B. Foreclosure $150.00

9. **Civil cases**
   A. Circuit Court—per diem $150.00
   B. Small Claims Court . . . . $ 50.00

10. **Collections** (Fees contingent upon collection)
   A. Commercial claims
      1. The following rates are net to the receiving lawyer
        and are to apply where there is no suit involved or
        extraordinary work:
          15% on the first $1,000.00
          10% on the excess over $1,000.00
          Minimum commission $18.00
          On collections of $54.00 or less—33⅓%
        The above rate is to apply where a claim is re-
        ceived from another lawyer or commercial agency.
      2. The following is a schedule of commissions recom-
        mended as compensation for a lawyer receiving a
        commercial claim from a client:
          21% on the first $1,000.00

15% on the excess over $1,000.00
Minimum commission—$25.00

3. Suit fees

A minimum suit fee is to be charged of $7.50;
however, a suit fee is not contingent. It is payable in
addition to commissions. It belongs exclusively to the
attorney receiving the claim, unless there is a division
of services or responsibility between receiving and
forwarding attorneys. Where there is such a division,
it is based on and commensurate with the service and
responsibility of each, but in no event shall the suit
fee of the receiving attorney be less than $7.50. Be-
fore commencing suit it is advisable to arrange for a
suitable suit fee in line with the services to be performed, the amount involved, and possibly the results
to be accomplished.

B. Retail claims

1. A retail claim is one where merchandise is sold and
delivered, services are rendered or money loaned to
an individual for his personal use and benefit. Generally it is against people not in business.

33⅓% of the amount collected whether or not suit
is filed.

If a non-contingent suit fee is required it is to be
paid in advance, and by arrangement can be deducted
from the total commissions so that the total compensation will not exceed 33⅓%. This rate is based on receiving a claim from another lawyer or commercial
agency.

2. If a claim is received direct from a client and is a
retail claim, the following rate is recommended:

50% of the amount collected whether or not suit is
actually filed.

11. **Committee or conservator.** $300.00

12. **Conditional sales contracts**
Prepare and record . . . . $ 35.00

13. **Confessed judgment suit.** . . . . $ 35.00
The above fee does not include collection of the judgment
or execution on the same.

14. **Corporations**
A. Organizing corporation including charter, by-laws and
minutes of first meeting of corporation involving less

than $10,000 capital investment $250.00

B. In the event that numerous conferences with client, accountant and others are held in discussing structure of business for tax and other purposes, or if more than one class of stock is issued, then an additional fee commensurate with the time spent should be charged.

15. Criminal cases
A. People's, Magistrate's or Municipal Court
1. All motor vehicle and traffic cases other than those involving automatic revocation or suspension of permit. . . . . $ 50.00
2. All motor vehicle cases involving automatic revocation or suspension of permit. $200.00
3. Minor criminal cases . . . . $ 75.00
4. All other criminal cases. $200.00

B. Circuit or Criminal Court
1. Other than capital cases $250.00
2. Capital cases $750.00

C. Juvenile matter. $100.00

16. Domestic relations
A. Custody
1. Uncontested. $250.00
2. Contested . . . . .Hourly Basis

B. Divorce or annulment
1. Uncontested . . . . $250.00 and up
2. Contested . . . . .Hourly basis
An uncontested divorce is one in which there is no dispute concerning grounds for divorce, nor necessity to negotiate concerning alimony, custody, support and maintenance of children, or time spent in the division of personal or real property.

C. Guardianship. $150.00

D. Separation, custody, maintenance and property settlement agreements
1. Preparation without negotiations. . . . . $ 75.00
2. Where negotiated . . . . .Hourly basis or to be negotiated with client

E. Pre-nuptial agreement $200.00

18. Injunction or mandamus
A. Uncontested $250.00
B. Contested. $500.00

19. Negligence
A. Representation of defendant
1. Review of file and preparation and filing of
General Issue Plea to Declaration . . . . $ 75.00
2. Taking of deposition of plaintiff or witness . . . . $ 50.00
3. Settlement negotiation and office work . . Hourly Rate
4. Demurrer, motions—including preparation and
arguments $100.00
5. Trial rate
a. Circuit Court—per diem $150.00
b. People's or Magistrate's Court . . . . $ 50.00
6. Friendly suit. . . . . $ 50.00

B. Representation of plaintiff
1. Contingency basis.
25% if settled before suit; 33⅓% after suit.
2. Other than contingency basis . . . . .Hourly rate

20. Power of attorney . . . . $ 25.00

21. Partnership
A. General Agreement $150.00
B. Limited Agreement $250.00
C. Dissolution
1. Voluntary $150.00
2. Involuntary (by decree of court). $350.00

22. Real estate transactions
A. There are wide discrepancies throughout the states as to fees charged for title work. In certain areas, the charge is broken down into the component parts of the service rendered, i.e., so much for abstracting and examining, so much for conveyancing, so much for settlement services, so much for title insurance premium. In other areas, an all-inclusive charge is made, and, to complicate matters, it is the practice in some areas to include some of the components in the charge and make additional charges for the other components.

Certain titles require more time to abstract and examine than others, the degree of difficulty varies from title to title, and search time required varies from county to county. In general, the easiest titles to search are in cities where a block-large index system enables one to make his search geographically. The hardest titles to search are in the heavily populated metropolitan counties where voluminous grantor-grantee indices make the location of conveyances out of a common-name quite a burdensome task.

Title insurance companies are regulated by the State Insurance

Department. The rates of title insurers are filed with and approved by the Insurance Commissioner. The rates are based upon the consideration involved in a real estate transaction and, under the law, the insurer cannot deviate from its filed rates.

The so-called "all-inclusive" rate filed by title insurers covers the title search and examination, and the title insurance policy. It is recommended that lawyers charge not less than this "all-inclusive" rate applicable to the particular county wherein the land lies after deducting therefrom that portion of the rate which is attributable to risk premium only.

Many lawyers who are primarily engaged in title work have arrangements with other lawyers and with title insurance companies to certify titles on a cooperative basis under which the fee or charge of the originating lawyer or title company is shared by the certifying lawyer in accordance with a negotiated formula. It is not anticipated that the recommended fee should affect this type of arrangement, and lawyers should be free to cooperate with other lawyers and title insurers under any arrangements which are mutually agreeable.

B. Condemnation—minimum retainer. $250.00

This sum to be offset against a percentage contingent fee of 25% of the difference between the offer made to condemnee by the condemnor and the final settlement price if made before trial. If settlement is made after trial begins or case proceeds to judgment, the above percent should be 33⅓%.

C. Conveyancing
   1. Preparation of Sales Contract . . . . $ 25.00
   2. Preparation of Deed—Simple . . . . $ 15.00
                      Metes & Bounds . . . . $ 25.00
   3. Preparation of Deed of Trust or
      Mortgage and Note—Simple. . . . . $ 20.00
                      Metes & Bounds . . . . $ 30.00
   4. Prepare release and pay-off of existing
      encumbrance . . . . $ 25.00
   5. Preparation of Subordination Agreement . . . . $ 50.00
   6. Recording (Deed, Deed of Trust, Mortgage, etc.) . . . $ 10.00
   7. Release of Dower and Statutory Interests. . . . . $ 50.00
   8. Set-up and recording of restrictive covenants—
      (Hourly rate) with a minimum charge of . . . . $ 50.00
   9. Attendance at Settlement . . . . $ 35.00

D. Foreclose Mortgage of Deed of Trust where
   Attorney is not Trustee $250.00

E. Lease Agreement. . . . . $ 50.00

F. Mechanic's Lien
   1. Give notice, prepare and record lien $100.00

    2. Enforcement of Mechanic's Lien:

      a. One-third of the amount recovered if
        case goes to trial or

      b. Cash retainer $250.00
        The retainer to be offset against a contingent per-
        centage fee of 25% if the case is settled before
        actual trial. In the event that the case goes to trial
        or ends by way of a judgment, the contingency
        should be 33⅓%.

G. Partition

    1. Uncontested. $350.00
    2. Contested $500.00

H. Quieting Title to Real Estate $300.00

I. Right of Way or Easement Agreement . . . . $ 75.00

J. Specific performance:

    1. Uncontested $250.00
    2. Contested $500.00

23. Replevin

A. People's or Magistrate's Court:

    1. Uncontested. . . . . $ 75.00
    2. Contested $100.00

B. Circuit Court:

    1. Uncontested. $150.00
    2. Contested $300.00

24. Sale of Business

A. Conferring with client, drawing of sales contract and dis-
bursement of funds in compliance with Bulk Sales Act in
connection with a small business $350.00

B. Where the business is of substantial size the fee should
probably be predicated upon a per diem or hourly rate.

25. Specific performance of contract

A. Uncontested $250.00

B. Contested. $500.00

26. Tax matters

A. Income Tax Returns. . . . . . . .Hourly rate—Minimum $ 25.00

B. Estate Gift and Fiduciary Returns . . . . . . .Hourly rate

27. Wills

    In drawing wills, the counsel fee should, except in the
very simplest of cases, be based primarily on the time spent.
A so-called "simple" will may require many hours of legal

time, because the testator insists on many conferences and many changes. On the other hand, a "complicated" will may be largely standard "boiler plate," although taking up many pages.

Wills containing trust provisions will normally take more time than those that do not, and so the fee should be higher for them. The more complex the provisions, and the greater the tax involvement, the greater the time required.

A minimum fee of $35.00 might be set for the simpler sort of will. Above that, the fee may range upward to a very substantial figure. The lawyer's time, and responsibility, should be the principal guidelines; an arbitrary dollar figure cannot properly reflect the correct charge in every case.

28. Workmen's compensation

Although the Workmen's Compensation Commission must approve all legal fees, it should be borne in mind that the Commission will normally approve of a fee equal to 20% of the amount recovered.

29. Writ of Scire Facias . . . . $ 35.00

FELLOW SERVANTS Persons working together at a common task and controlled by the same master or employer.

FELONY A word used to distinguish higher crimes, such as murder, manslaughter, arson, burglary, robbery, rape, sodomy, mayhem and larceny, etc. (*which see*), from misdemeanors. At common law all crimes were divided into treason, felonies and misdemeanors.

FEME COVERT A married woman.

FEME SOLE A single woman. One having no husband living.

FEOFFEE A person to whom a fee is conveyed; a person to whom a feoffment is made.

FEOFFMENT The transfer of a fee, a freehold or a corporeal hereditament, by livery of seisin. It operated on the possession, and effected the transmutation thereof.

FEOFFOR A person who conveys a fee; a person who makes a feoffment.

FEUDAL LAW The system of tenures of real property which prevailed in western Europe during the Middle Ages, whereby all land was held primarily from the king by his military chieftains, they in turn granting the right to hold it to their subordinates and the subordinates again to their immediate retainers. The right of those holding lands was on condition of performing services and rendering allegiance to the superior lord.

Military service and mutual protection furnished the basis of the feudal system. There were certain incidents and obligations attending the holding of land under this system, but as they never obtained a hold in America and have long since been extinguished in the greater part of Europe it seems pointless to pursue the subject further.

FICTION OF LAW An assumption, or supposition, that something is true and exists, that in actual fact does not exist. "It is used as a rule of convenience, but cannot be used to work a wrong." To say a corporation is a person is a fiction at law. It is of great public convenience to use the idea that a corporation may act as a person. If the corporation wrongfully uses this artificial or fictitious person, the courts will "look behind the corporate veil or person," to the natural persons using the fiction and hold them personally liable.

FIDUCIARY CAPACITY The position of one receiving money or handling property not in his own interest, such as an attorney, a guardian, a banker, a broker, or a public official. Under such circumstances, the business which he transacts is not an express trust, but a technical one, holding him to special standards of high conduct.

FILIATION (1) Determination of the paternity of a child, fixing the obligation for its maintenance. (2) In French law, a form of adoption.

FINDER One who finds or acquires by chance. A finder of personal property is governed by the same general rules as in case of a deposit and must exercise the same reasonable care and diligence in preserving it and will be responsible for gross negligence. He is not bound, however, to take the goods he finds. He is entitled to recover all expenses necessarily incurred in preserving it, and in case of an animal or other thing would be entitled to reimbursement for its keeping and for advertising the finding of it in a reasonable manner, and to any reward that might be offered for the recovery thereof.

If the lost goods are not reclaimed they belong to the finder. Where one finds an article which has been lost or which he reasonably supposes to have been lost, and appropriates it with intent to take entire dominion over it, really believing that the owner cannot be found, this is not larceny; but if he takes it with the intent though lost or reasonably supposed to be lost, but reasonably believing that the owner can be found, it is larceny.

FINE A sum of money collected by a court from a person guilty of some criminal offense. The amount may be fixed by statute or left to the discretion of the court. The term "fine" is to be distinguished from penalty which means a sum of money exacted for the doing or failure to perform some act. Payment of a penalty of $5 for failure to secure a license to sell tobacco is different from paying a $5 fine for committing the offense of larceny.

FIT FOR HUMAN CONSUMPTION A promise implied by the seller of food.

FIXTURES Personal chattels affixed to real estate which may be severed and removed by the party who has affixed them, or by his personal representative against the will of the owner of the freehold. Difficult questions frequently arise as to what are fixtures and what are not,—what is to be considered as a part of the real estate, and what as personal property only. As a general rule fixtures once annexed to the freehold become part of the realty. The article must not merely be laid upon the ground but must be fastened, fixed or set into the land, or fastened to some erection on the land which is unquestionably a part of the realty, as a house. Otherwise it can in no sense be regarded as part of the real estate. Exceptions to this, however, are deeds or any instrument relating to the title of the real estate. Also deer in the park, fish in a pond, doves in a dovehouse are heirlooms which are constructively annexed to the inheritance and go with the land. Loose movable machinery used in prosecuting any business upon the property cannot be considered as part of the real estate or in any way appurtenant to it.

To the rule that annexed fixtures become part of the realty there are many exceptions, as where the manifest intention is to use the fixture in some employment distinct from that of the occupant of the real estate, also where it has been annexed merely for the purposes of carrying on a trade, such a purpose indicating that the fixtures should remain only so long as the trade continue at the particular place.

The controlling question in determining whether fixtures are part of realty or not is whether they were intended to be permanently fixed or not, and this intention may either be arrived at from the declarations or statements of the parties or it may be inferred from circumstances. It has been said that there where a tenant erects fixtures on the premises, and at the expiration of his lease, leases for another year without reserving or claiming the fixtures, they will remain as part of the real estate and cannot be removed by the tenant at the end of the term. And particularly would this be true if there is a covenant in the second lease to surrender the premises at the end of the second term of lease in as good condition as when entered upon.

As between vendor and vendee all fixtures belonging to the premises at the time of sale or which were erected by the vendor for any purpose pass to the vendee unless expressly reserved, and the same holds between a mortgagor and a mortgagee, between an administrator on the one hand who is entitled to personalty of a decedent, and a devisee or heir who is entitled to the land on the other, the doubt, if any existing, being resolved in favor of the last-mentioned party in each case.

Between the landlord and his tenant the general rule that fixtures are part of the real estate is much relaxed, and the tenant whether for life, for years or at will may at any time before the expiration of his tenancy sever and carry away such fixtures of a chattel nature as he may have erected for ornament, domestic convenience or to carry on trade, if this is done without material injury to the freehold. This is true in the case of bakers' ovens, salt pans, carding machines, cider mills, furnaces, steam engines, vats, copper stills, mill stones, shelves, cupboards, bells, electric fixtures, chimney pieces, grates, window blinds and curtains. This has been determined to extend even to a dutch barn standing on a foundation of brickwork set in the ground and a varnish house similarly built with a chimney, and to a ballroom erected by the lessee of an inn resting upon stone posts slightly imbedded in the soil. The law, however, is adverse to the removal of hearth stones, doors, windows, locks and keys because peculiarly adapted to the house, also to the removal of substantial additions to the premises such as conservatories, or greenhouses (unless erected by a professional gardener), stables, pig pens and other outhouses and shrubberies, flowers planted in the garden and erections for agricultural purposes.

A lessee for years should remove fixtures before surrendering possession of the premises, but as the duration of the term of a tenant for life or at will is uncertain, fixtures in such cases may be removed within a reasonable time after the termination of the estate. If a tenant for a definite period, however, surrenders possession without removing his fixtures they immediately vest in the landlord and even if afterwards dissevered the tenant acquires no right to them, so that if he wishes to sell them to an incoming tenant without removing them he should obtain the assent of the landlord before quitting the premises.

Sometimes the custom of a neighborhood will determine whether or not a fixture shall be considered a part of the real estate, particularly where there are outgoing and incoming tenants.

FLOATING POLICY A fire insurance policy that covers a class of goods located in a particular place that the insured has on hand at the time the policy was issued, but which goods at the time of fire may not be the identical items that were on hand at the time the policy was issued. A fire policy covering the inventory of a grocery store is an example.

FORBEARANCE An act of delay or indulgence in not proceeding against a delinquent debtor.

FORCE AND ARMS A phrase denoting that an act was done violently.

FORCED SALE A sale of a debtor's property by public officials to secure money to pay the debtor's creditors is a forced sale. Sales by sheriff after judgment, foreclosure, and so forth, are illustrations.

FORCIBLE ENTRY Originally, an entrance into real property, such as land or a building, with actual violence. Now, in most jurisdictions, any entry without consent is considered forcible.

FORCIBLE ENTRY AND DETAINER A remedy given to a landowner to evict persons unlawfully in possession of his land. A landlord may use such remedy to evict a tenant in default.

FORECLOSURE The legal means

by which the mortgagor (the one making a mortgage to borrow money) loses his right to redeem the mortgaged estate. For example, a person borrows money and gives as security a mortgage on his home. If the borrower fails to keep up his payments, the mortgagee (the lender of the money) has the right to bring foreclosure proceedings and sell the property at auction. If the property fails to bring enough to pay the claim, the mortgagee can hold the borrower responsible for the difference between what the property brought at a sale and the balance due on the mortgage. Should the property sell for more than the amount of the mortgage (plus interest, legal fees and court costs) the surplus is turned over to the borrower or mortgagor.

Where the amount is due in installments a tender of the installment due, with interests and costs, will prevent sale of the mortgaged premises, provided the mortgage does not contain an acceleration clause, which allows the entire mortgage to become due on failure to comply with conditions contained in the mortgage. All foreclosure proceedings, whether a party is suing or being sued, should be handled by competent counsel.

FOREIGN ATTACHMENT The process involved in starting a suit against one who is outside the jurisdiction of the complaining party. Suit cannot ordinarily be brought against one outside of the state because service of a summons upon him cannot be obtained. But if he has property within the state, suit may be begun by a process called a foreign attachment—that is, by a seizure of the property by the sheriff in lieu of the service of a summons upon him.

The property seized will be held to satisfy the claim of the plaintiff if judgment is obtained by him, and the plaintiff will have a lien thereon from the time of seizure unless the defendant gives bond for the payment of what may be recovered in the suit in which event the bond will stand as a substitute for the property.

FOREIGN BILL OF EXCHANGE A bill of exchange drawn in one state or country, upon a foreign state or country.

FOREIGN CORPORATION A corporation created by or under the laws of another state, government or country.

FOREIGN JUDGMENT A judgment obtained in a foreign court, or in the court of a foreign country.

FOREIGN LAWS Laws of foreign countries. The courts do not judicially take notice of foreign laws and they must therefore be proven as facts. In the case of written foreign laws, they are usually proven by an exemplification or perfect copy of the lawful record of the original under the great seal of the foreign country or state or by copy proven by oath to be a true copy, or by the certificate of an officer authorized by law to make the certificate, which certificate must itself be duly authenticated.

Foreign unwritten laws, customs and usages may be proven by witnesses learned in the law and competent to state it correctly under oath. A printed volume purporting on its face to contain the laws of any state of the United States is admissible in another state as prima facie evidence to prove the statute law of that state.

FOREMAN The spokesman and presiding member of a jury who is usually elected to that position by the jury itself, but sometimes is appointed by the court.

FORFEITURE A forfeiture implies a penalty and the word forfeit is often used synonymously with penalty, but in its strict sense a forfeiture implies a divestiture of property without compensation, as a result of a default or offense.

Deprivation of something by way of penalty; especially, in old law, the loss of one's lands as a penalty for crime either to the person injured or to the state.

FORGERY The fraudulent making or alteration of a writing to the prejudice of another man's right. Fraudulently securing a true signature to a false instrument, or one not intended by the signer, is forgery. For example, if one is requested to draw a will for a sick person in a particular way and instead of doing so inserts legacies other than those directed and procures the signature of the sick person to the will so made without revealing to him the insertion of the additional legacies, he is guilty of forgery.

Making an instrument in a fictitious name or in the name of a person not existing is a forgery; so is the making of an instrument in one's own name and representing it to be the instrument of another of the same name when there is no such other person would seem to be a forgery. In the drawing of a will the fraudulent omission of a legacy which one is directed to insert, causing material alteration in a bequest to another (as where omission of a devise of an estate for life to one causes a devise of the same lands to another to pass a present estate which otherwise would have passed as a remainder only), will be a forgery.

Signing the name of another to a note with an addition over the signer's name stating that it was done by the other's authority, will not constitute forgery though no authority was given. Forgery may be committed by simply changing the second initial of a name.

Forgery may be complete without a publication or circulation of the forged instrument. It is forgery to falsify or falsely make records and other matters of a public nature, as a parish register or a letter in the name of a magistrate or of the warden of a prison directing the discharge of a prisoner.

A letter of recommendation of a person as a man of property and pecuniary responsibility, a guarantee of payment for goods delivered, a testimony of character, or a railway pass or ticket may all be forged. Fraudulently attesting or falsely making a deed or will and of course falsely signing or endorsing one's own name on a promissory note, check or bill of exchange are forgeries. There may be forgery of a printed or engraved instrument as well as a written one, but it must be of some document or writing. Printing an artist's name in the corner of a picture to falsely represent it as an original picture by the artist is said not to be forgery.

There must be an intent to defraud another to constitute forgery, but it is not necessary that one should have been actually injured and it is sufficient if the instrument forged might have proved prejudicial. By statute in most states, some acts are made forgery which would not be so at common law.

To utter or publish a forged instrument is to assert and declare directly or indirectly by words or actions that the instrument is good. It is not necessary that it should be passed in order to complete the uttering. Merely showing it with intent to gain a credit without an intention or attempt to pass it would not, it seems, amount to an uttering, but offering or using a forged instrument in some way in order to get money or credit is sufficient to constitute an uttering. The uttering, that is, knowing, offering or publishing or making use of an instrument which is forged is a crime in itself and may be committed by one not implicated in the original forgery.

FORNICATION Unlawful carnal or sexual knowledge by an unmarried person (male or female) of another, whether the latter is married or unmarried. In some states by statute, though the woman only is married, the offense is made adultery in both. Where the charge in an indictment is adultery, if there is a failure to prove the marriage and hence a failure to prove adultery, there may yet be a conviction of fornication.

FORWARDER A person who, having no interest in the freight of goods and no ownership or interest in the means of their carriage, undertakes, for hire, to forward them by a safe carrier to their destination.

FRANCHISE A right to be and exercise the powers of a corporation; they are usually granted by legislatures and are held subject to the right of eminent domain. Franchises cannot be sold or assigned without the consent of the legislature.

FRAUD Such intentional perversion of the truth which prejudices the rights of another; it is such deception that its practice induces another to surrender some legal right or property. Fraud implies deceit, deception, artifice and trickery.

Fraud is said to vitiate everything it touches. It contaminates and renders void all contracts and transactions so far as concerns the party against whom the fraud is committed. Covin and collusion are combinations among two or more to work a fraud upon another, and deceit, another means of perpetrating fraud, exist where there is a misrepresentation or contrivance by words or acts to deceive a third person who, relying thereupon without carelessness or neglect on his own part, sustains damage. If the party misrepresenting, however, was himself mistaken no blame can attach to him. Such fraud may occur by a deliberate assertion of a falsehood to the injury of another or by failure to disclose a latent defect or by concealing an apparent defect, but the party deceived must have been in such a situation as to have no means of detecting the deceit. Where there is a combination of two or more to practice fraud upon another they may be indicted for conspiracy. If two enter into a fraudulent scheme and one secures all the profits, the other cannot recover a share from him.

There are actual or positive frauds and legal or constructive frauds. The former exists where there is intentional and successful employment of any cunning deception or artifice used to circumvent or deceive another; the latter where the injury does not originate in any actual or evil design or contrivance to perpetrate a fraud, but where nevertheless the contract or act has a tendency to deceive or mislead others or to violate public or private confidence, and is consequently prohibited by law as a matter of policy.

Among constructive frauds may be noted cases arising from some particular confidential or fiduciary relation between the parties where advantage is taken of that relation by the person in whom the trust or confidence is reposed. An example is conveyances without valuable consideration, as affecting the title and rights of subsequent purchasers and of creditors of the grantor.

There may even be an unintentional misrepresentation as to a state of facts which if acted upon would amount to a legal or constructive fraud, and in which the evil result of the misrepresentation must fall upon the party responsible for them.

As to actual or positive frauds they include suppressions of material facts which one party is legally or equitably bound to disclose to another; all cases of unconscionable advantage in bargains obtained by imposition, circumvention and undue influence over persons in general and especially over those who are by reason of age, infirmity, idiocy, lunacy, drunkenness or other incapacity unable to take care of and protect their own rights and interests; bargains of such an unconscionable nature and of such gross inequality as naturally lead to the presumption of fraud, imposition or undue influence; cases of surprise and sudden action without due deliberation of which one party improperly takes advantage; cases of fraudulent suppression or destruction of deeds and other instruments to the injury of others and in violation of their rights; fraudulent prevention of acts to be done for the benefit of others through false statements or false promises; frauds in relation to trusts of a secret or special nature; frauds in verdicts, judgments and other judicial proceedings; frauds in the confusion of boundaries of estates and matters of partition and dower; frauds in the administration of charities, upon creditors and other third parties having equitable rights; and misrepresentations of material facts by word or deed by which one exercising reasonable discretion and confidence is misled to his injury, whether the misrepresentation is known to be false or only not known to be true. In all such and other cases of fraud, courts of equity will grant relief if there is no remedy in a court of law.

Fraud in its ordinary application to cases of contract includes any trick or artifice employed by one to induce another to fall into or keep him in error so that he may make an agreement contrary to his interest. It may consist in either misrepresenting or concealing material facts and may be effected by words or by actions but neither law nor equity will relieve one who has not himself exercised a due degree of caution. While cunning and circumvention are frowned upon, vigilance is exacted commensurate somewhat with the party's ability. But if a person misrepresents or conceals a material fact which is particularly within his own knowledge, even if it is within the reach of the other party, yet in such way as to induce him to refrain from inquiry and from informing himself regarding the transaction, such transaction would be void on the ground of fraud, and concealment of a matter which may disable another party from performing the contract is a fraud if injurious to the other party.

There is more latitude of proof in equity with respect to fraud than in law. Ordinarily, misrepresentation as to a fact, the truth or falsehood of which the other party has an opportunity of ascertaining, or the concealment of a matter which a person of ordinary skill or vigilance might discover, does not constitute fraud. Also, misrepresentation as to the legal effect of an agreement, every man of mature discretion being presumed to know the legal effect of an instrument which he signs or of an act which he performs, does not constitute fraud. It is deception as to facts which operates as fraud.

Frauds are almost infinite in kind and are scarcely limited by any rule or definition. Fraud may be shown from actual facts and circumstances of imposition, from the intrinsic nature and subject matter of the bargain itself, that is, if it is of such character as no man in his senses and not under delusion or imposition would make on the one hand and no honest or fair man would accept on the other. It may also be shown from circumstances and conditions of the parties, for it is as much against conscience to take advantage of a man's weakness or necessity as of his ignorance. Fraud may be shown also from the nature and circumstances of the transaction with respect to third parties and its being an imposition upon them, as for example, creditors of one of the original parties to the contract, or to the transfer of property, as the case may be.

Though a fraudulent contract is void from the beginning as against any party intended to be defrauded or against the public if it is interested, the party committing the fraud cannot avoid the contract and may be held to it or be held accountable for damages for the breach by any party in interest desiring to so hold him.

Some frauds, usually under some statute, are punishable criminally such as issuing a fictitious bank bill, selling unwholesome provisions, rendering false accounts and other wrongful acts by persons in official positions, cheating by false weights and measures and in general fraudulently obtaining the property of another by deceitful or illegal practice, where one falsely pretends that he owns property and obtains credit on purchases.

The celebrated statute of frauds, passed in the reign of Charles II, King of England, which has in large measure been re-enacted in all or nearly all of the states of the Union, provides among other things that conveyances, leases, surrenders of interests in lands, declarations of trusts respecting interests in land, special promises of executors and administrators to pay debts or damages out of their own estates, promises by one to answer for the debt or default of another, agreements made upon consideration of marriage contracts for the sale of lands or any interests therein, agreements not to be performed within the space of one year from the making thereof, and contracts for the sale of goods, wares, and merchandise to the amount of ten pounds sterling or upwards, must be put in writing and signed by the party to be held responsible or his attorney, otherwise they will be void. As to goods, wares and merchandise, the payment of money on account or acceptance and receipt of part of the goods dispenses with the written memorandum.

FRAUDULENT CONVERSION The unauthorized assumption of the possession of goods to the exclusion of the owner.

FRAUDULENT CONVEYANCE A conveyance, the object, tendency or effect of which is to defraud another, or the intent of which is to avoid some debt or duty due by, or incumbent on, the party making it.

FREE ALONGSIDE SHIP (F.A.S.) A provision in a contract of sale which requires the seller to deliver the merchandise at a designated place for loading aboard ship.

FREE ON BOARD (F.O.B.) A provision in a contract of sale which requires the seller to deliver the merchandise at a designated place, usually to a carrier.

FREEHOLD Any estate of inheritance or for life in either a corporeal or incorporeal hereditament existing in or arising from real property of free tenure.

FRUCTUS INDUSTRIALES Those products of the earth which are annual, and which are raised by yearly planting, and which essen-

tially own their annual existence to the cultivation of man.

FRUCTUS NATURALES Natural fruits—the fruit of trees, perennial bushes and grasses growing from perennial roots.

FUGITIVE FROM JUSTICE One who flees the law. Article IV, Section 2, of the Constitution of the United States provides that "a person charged in any state with treason, felony or other crime who shall flee from justice and be found in another state, shall on demand of the executive authority of the state from which he fled be delivered up, to be removed to the state having jurisdiction of the crime." The method of procedure under this section of the Constitution is prescribed by statute. To secure action on the part of the executive authority of the state from which the alleged offender has fled it must be shown to him that an indictment has been found, or at least an affidavit or affidavits must be presented to him explicitly setting forth just cause for arrest and commitment.

In general, requisitions to governors of other states are not in practice granted in case of offenses of a minor character and particularly, where the main purpose seems to be to enforce the collection of a debt by criminal prosecution, though the power to issue requisitions under the Constitution applies to all crimes. The accused must have fled from the state where the crime was committed and the executive authority to which the requisition is addressed should have evidence of this fact. But in the absence of such direct evidence if the crime is atrocious and recently committed and the prosecution promptly instituted, the unexplained presence of the accused in another state immediately after the commission of a crime, itself furnishes prima facie evidence of a flight sufficient to warrent an order of arrest.

The order of arrest may be issued by the governor of the state to which the flight is alleged to have taken place, and the arrest itself may be made before an order of surrender is granted to the agent of the demanding state, appointed by the governor to receive the fugitive, thus allowing an opportunity for a writ of habeas corpus and a hearing to be had as to the propriety of the arrest before the surrender is made.

FUNDED DEBT The term applies to a debt where provision is made for a method of paying off the debt and its interest at fixed periods. A funded debt of a municipality is one where provision is made for the annual raising by tax of the sum necessary to pay the interest and principal as they respectively mature.

FUNERAL EXPENSES The costs accrued from the rites and ceremonies preceding and accompanying a burial. The person who orders the things necessary for a burial is responsible personally for the expenses and, if the estate is insolvent, must suffer the loss. If there are sufficient assets of the estate the executor or administrator is bound to pay them, if reasonable in amount under the circumstances.

As to what is reasonable, this is controlled by the decedent's financial condition in life, by the distance to be traveled in burying, particularly if the decedent directs by will where he shall be buried, and whether or not the estate is sufficient in amount to pay creditors. The amount to be thus expended may generally be regulated by what is usual in the neighborhood with respect to one dying whose circumstance in life is similar to those of the decedent, always observing what is equitable to creditors. A husband is liable for the maintainance of his wife and must pay her funeral expenses even though she has a separate estate of her own.

FUNGIBLE GOODS Goods any unit of which is from its nature or by mercantile custom, treated as the equivalent of any other unit.

FUTURES Contracts for the sale and future delivery of stocks or commodities, wherein either party may waive delivery, and receive or pay, as the case may be, the difference in market price at the time set for delivery.

G

GAGE A pawn or pledge to be forfeited if an act is not done or money is not paid.

GAMBLING Playing at games for stakes. In the United States playing at games of chance is forbidden almost everywhere by criminal statutes and money lost at such games cannot be recovered, and keeping houses or booths for purposes of gambling is criminal and a nuisance in that it promotes cheating and other corrupt practice.

GARNISHEE A party in whose hands money or property is attached by the creditor of another, and who has had warning or garnishment not to pay or deliver it to the defendant.

GARNISHMENT A warning to a person in whose hands the effects of another are attached, not to pay the money or deliver the property of the defendant in his hands to him, but to appear and answer the plaintiff's suit.

GENERAL ISSUE A plea of the defendant amounting to a denial of every material allegation of fact in the plaintiff's complaint or declaration.

GIFT NOTE A donor's promissory note payable to the donee. Such a note is invalid according to the weight of authority.

GIFTS Presents, or things given free of cost. Gifts are of two kinds,

those *causa mortis*, made in prospect of death, and those *inter vivos*, made between persons living and without any prospect of immediate death. The latter have no reference to the future and go into immediate and absolute effect upon delivery of the thing donated.

An actual delivery is essential to a gift *inter vivos*, and without possession in the donee the title does not pass to him. A mere intention or promise to give amounts to nothing if not followed up by a delivery. What constitutes delivery, however, will depend upon the nature of the thing. If the subject of the gift is incapable of physical delivery there must be some act equivalent to it, and the donor must part with his control over the thing.

It has been held that where one had stock issued in the names of his sons, and left it with a third person, subject, however, to the donor's control, there was no gift.

To complete a gift there must be mutual consent and the concurrent will of both the donor and donee as well as a delivery. Upon delivery and acceptance a gift becomes irrevocable if not prejudicial to creditors and if the donor was not under legal incapacity to make a gift or circumvented by fraud. A gift to an employee actually made cannot be revoked on the ground that the donor at the time overlooked the fact that he had previously increased the salary of the employee to whom the gift was made. That the note of a donor to

253

a donee is not the subject of the gift is well-settled law and it will not be binding. The gift cannot be completed until the money is paid.

A *donatio causa mortis* is a gift made by a person in mortal sickness, who, apprehending his death, delivers or causes to be delivered to another the possession of any personal goods to keep as his own in case of the donor's death. It differs from a legacy since it does not require proof like a will in the court of probate, and no assent is required from the executor to perfect the donee's title, but the debts of the person making the gift if he dies must be paid before it can become effective, and if he lives, the gift is revocable.

The thing given must be personal property. It may be a bond or bank note or it may be a check if the money is collected on it during the life of the donor from the bank on which it is drawn but not a promissory note of the sick person given in his last illness without consideration. It would seem that a gift *causa mortis* of bank stock may be made by delivery. To constitute a gift of this description (*causa mortis*) the giver must be in peril of death and it must be expressed to take effect only in case he die. A delivery to or for the donee is as essential as in the case of an absolute gift by one not anticipating death, but it may be made to a third person for the use of the donee. Though such a gift is revocable by the donor during his life, it is not revocable by subsequent will.

GIVE TIME To allow a debtor an extension beyond the time originally stipulated. If this is done without the consent of sureties or guarantors, they are released.

GO WITHOUT DAY A phrase meaning that a case has been dismissed—that is, no date has been set for a return.

GOING BUSINESS An establishment which is still continuing to transact its ordinary business, though it may be insolvent.

GOOD FAITH The simple honesty which precludes a man from taking an unconscionable advantage of another.

GOOD WILL The advantage or benefit acquired by an established business or profession beyond the mere value of the capital, stocks, funds or property employed therein.

With respect to professional partnerships, when one partner dies the good will passes to the survivor or survivors unless the benefit is previously excluded from them by agreement. Good will in a trade or business is frequently bought or sold in which case the vendor must not afterwards engage in business so as to interfere therewith.

Contracts in general restraint of trade, that is, not to engage at all or at any place in a particular pursuit, are void; but if the contract is limited in its application as to time or place or persons it is regarded as valid. The extent of this limit is not clearly defined. If one agrees upon proper consideration not to engage in a trade or profession in given neighborhood or even over more extended territory, so as not to interfere with the business of his successor with whom the agreement is made, he is generally bound.

GOODS AND CHATTELS The meaning of the word "chattels" and the term "goods and chattels" seems to be the same. They include not only movable personal property in possession but choses in action (see also CHOSE IN ACTION) and chattels real or interests in real estate less than a freehold, that is, less than a life estate or a fee, such as a lease for years of land. The duration of the lease is immaterial even if it is for a thousand years.

All chattels whether real or personal are treated as personal property, and at the death of the owner belong to the executor or administrator as personal assets and do not go to the heirs at law like real estate. To this there are a few exceptions of movable things which are necessarily or naturally attached to the freehold such as deeds and other papers constituting muniments of title to the real estate, shelves and family pictures in a house and fences. Deer in a park and fish in an artificial pond go with the real estate to the heir at law. Fixtures, that is, movable things attached to the realty sometimes are part of the realty and sometimes not.

By "personal chattels" is commonly meant things movable and in criminal law the term "goods" and "chattels" will not include choses in action, but in wills, unless a contrary intent appears, these words will pass all personal property.

GRAND JURY A body of not less or more than twenty-four men returned by the sheriff of every county to every criminal court and to whom indictments are preferred. Although twenty-four men are called, not more than twenty-three are sworn. The number that may sit as a grand jury varies somewhat in different states.

The foreman acts as president, the jury usually appointing someone as a secretary, but no record of the proceedings is kept except for their own use and the proceedings are secret, and must remain secret. Grand jurors giving information to a defendant that a bill has been found against him thus enabling him to escape or otherwise disclosing the proceedings unless under sanction of law, will be liable to punishment. If a witness in open court swears directly the opposite of what he swore before the grand jury, the law sanctions a revelation of the fact by a juror, and the latter may be sworn to testify as to what was stated by the witness in the grand jury room in order that the witness may be prosecuted for perjury.

The prosecuting officer presents the grand jury with the bills of indictment and they must hear under oath all the witnesses offered against the defendant unless a part only are sufficient to satisfy them that the case should be tried by a petit jury. This is called finding the bill a true bill. At least twelve must concur in the finding of a true bill in which case the foreman writes on the back of the indictment, "a true bill," and signs his name and date of finding. If they make a contrary finding the endorsement on the bill is "ignoramus" or "not a true bill" or similar words. If a witness refuses to be sworn or to answer questions propounded by members of the grand jury or acts disrespectfully, the officer in attendance upon them may be required to take the witness before the court to be properly dealt with.

Grand jurors, besides considering indictments supplied to them by the proper prosecuting officer, should themselves make presentments to the court of all criminal offenses that have come to their knowledge, naming the offenders with a view to indictment. A bill of indictment will then be framed by the prosecuting officer and sent to the grand jury for furthur action. Members of the grand jury themselves may testify before the jury regarding matters within their knowledge.

GRAND LARCENY In English criminal law, a stealing of property above the value of twelve pence. So distinguished from petit larceny, which was theft of property to the value of twelve pence or under. The distinction between these two kinds of larceny is of great antiquity, and was only recently abolished in England. In the United States it is generally retained, although the sum adopted as its basis is much above the old English standard.

GRANDFATHER CLAUSE Discriminatory legislation of some Southern states of the United States which had the effect of limiting suffrage to those whose ancestors were qualified— that is, whites.

GRANT In a general sense, the passing of a thing from one person to another. In this sense it comprehends feoffments, bargains and sales, gifts, leases, etc., for a person who gives or sells also grants.

GRANTEE The person to whom a grant is made.

GRANTOR The person by whom a grant is made.

GRAVAMEN Gist, essence; substance. The grievance complained of; the substantial cause of the action.

GROSS EARNINGS Gross earnings are the total "receipts," "proceeds," or "income" derived from the pursuit of a trade, business or profession.

GROSS NEGLIGENCE (1) *In bailment*, such behavior as indicates that the ordinary care which even a thoughtless man would give to his own property has been omitted. (2) *In torts*, wanton recklessness.

GROUND RENT A rent reserved by one who conveys land to another in fee simple, that is, land conveyed as an absolute inheritance free and clear of any condition, limitation or restriction to particular heirs, thus making it the highest estate known to the law.

Rent paid for the privilege of building on another man's land is in fee simple to himself and his heirs out of the land conveyed. In case of death of the owner, if there is no will, it goes to the heir and not the administrator. The owner of the rent and the one to whom the land is conveyed subject to the rent, is each the owner of a fee simple estate, the former being an incorporeal and the latter a corporeal interest.

The owner of the ground and

not the owner of the ground rent is liable for taxes. Ground rent being real estate may be bound by judgment or mortgage. If the owner purchases the land the two estates will ordinarily be merged and the ground rent estate ceases or if he purchases part it will cease *pro tanto*. This merger is not favored in equity and as a general rule the intention of the person owning both estates will govern as to the matter of merger, and that the intent is against the merger will be presumed where his interest is against it even though the intent is not expressed.

Arrearages of rent are a lien upon the land, but if they are due for twenty years before commencement of suit to recover them they are presumed to have been paid. Arrearages are discharged as a claim against the land by judicial sale of the land and attach to the fund raised by the sale. The owner of the rent may recover for arrearages by ordinary suit or by distress or if there is not sufficient personal property to distrain, he may peaceably or by process of law re-enter and hold the land as if by his original title, the estate of the owner being forfeited by non-payment of rent.

In Maryland prior to 1884, leases for ninety-nine years, renewable forever, were commonly made and the rent payable under such leases is termed ground rent, but the incidents of such ground rent and the rights and interests of the lessor and lessee are essentially the same as in case of an ordinary lease.

All leases and sub-leases made after April 5th, 1888, for longer than fifteen years may be redeemed by the tenant at any time after ten years from the date thereof, after six months' notice to the landlord, for a sum of money equal to the capitalization of the rent reserved at a rate not to exceed six percent. On application for renewal of one of the ninety-nine-year leases, if rent is in arrears, no more than three years' back rent can be collected before execution of the renewal lease, and if no demand or payment of any specific rent has been made for twenty consecutive years the rent is conclusively presumed to have been extinguished.

GROWING CROPS Crops that are still being raised and cultivated. All annual crops raised by cultivation are sometimes personal property and sometimes part of real property. While growing and owned by the owner of the soil they are usually regarded as part of the real property, and if the land is sold without reservation of the crops they will pass with it; but they may be seized in execution and sold separately from the land as personal property, and the owner may himself sell them while growing, thus practically severing them in contemplation of the law from the realty and making them personalty. Upon the death of the owner they are appraised as part of his personal estate, but if the real estate is sold under an order of court, it is necessary to expressly reserve them or they will pass with the land by the sale. Annual crops and even trees in a nursery planted by a tenant are personal chattels when fit for harvest or ready for transplanting.

The right of a tenant to take and carry away, after his tenancy has ended, such annual products of the land as have resulted from his own care and labor is what is known as the right to emblements.

GUARANTOR The party assuming legal responsibility for debt or default of another.

GUARANTY This is an undertaking to do something or pay a debt in case another does not. It differs from suretyship in being a secondary liability, a surety being primarily liable as well as his principal. An offer to guarantee is binding only in case it is accepted and until then it is revocable.

A guarantor may be discharged by the creditor's neglect to pursue the principal debtor though the same strictness as to demand at the precise time when the obligation becomes due is not necessary as is required to hold an endorser. In the case of a guaranteed note, a demand on the maker must be made within a reasonable time and if he is solvent at the time of the maturity of the note and remains so for such reasonable time afterwards, the guarantor does not become liable if the principal later becomes insolvent. Notice of non-payment must also be given to the guarantor before suit is brought against him, but if a guaranty of payment of a promissory note does not appear on the note itself and notice of non-payment when due is not given to the guarantor, this will in itself be a defense in a suit against the guarantor. It will discharge the guarantor only to the extent that he may have been damaged, if any, from lack of notice.

It is not necessary to sue the principal debtor before suing the guarantor if only demand has been made upon the principal debtor as above stated. This is true when the guaranty is of payment. When the guaranty is, however, that the note is collectible, the guarantor cannot be sued until the principal has been sued and all available means to collect have failed.

A guarantor is discharged by material alteration in the contract without his consent. There may be a guaranty with respect to the tort of another as well as his contract, and it may be for a single act or a continuous succession of acts. Any guaranty needs a consideration to support it, that is, it must be made upon consideration that the person in whose favor the guaranty is made shall do something or forego something and in a written guaranty the consideration should be expressed. Forbearance to sue or an extension of time or giving credit to the obliger is a good consideration. If the guaranty is made at the same time with the principal obligation the consideration for the latter will operate as the consideration for the former.

It has been held that where a guaranty was made to two and acted on by one only, the guarantor was not bound; where the guaranty was so made to two persons and one died, the survivor could not enforce it with respect to matters occurring after death.

The statute of frauds passed in the reign of Charles II and re-enacted generally in the United States provided that "no action shall be brought whereby to charge the defendant upon any special promise to answer for the debt, default or miscarriage of another person, ... unless the agreement upon which such action shall be brought or some memorandum or note thereof, shall be in writing, signed by the party to be charged therewith or by some person thereunto by him lawfully authorized." Commonly, guaranties for small amounts are by statute excepted from this provision.

Certain kinds of promises relating to obligations of others have been held not to be embraced within the provisions of this law. This is true where the obligation has already been in existence and a new promise with respect thereto is made by a stranger to the original promise, the original obligation of the original debtor being at the same time extinguished. Such a new promise therefore will be good even if not in writing. It will also be good if the new promise is in consideration of property passed by the original debtor to the new promissor's hands, or where the new promise does not relate to the promissor's property but to that of the debtor in the hands of the new promissor or guarantor, where the promise is made to the debtor and not to the creditor upon lawful consideration, and where the creditor surrenders a lien on the debtor or his property for the benefit in some way of the new promissor. In all cases, it will be observed, the guaranty is made after the contraction of the original debt and, strictly speaking, a new promise is made upon a consideration moving to a new promissor and he is entering into a new and original contract rather than a contract for guaranty simply.

If a debt is incurred for the benefit of one, but the credit is given exclusively to another who undertakes to pay, it is not a guaranty but an original obligation of the party to whom the credit is given and need not be in writing to bind the latter. In case of dispute it is a question of fact for a jury to determine whether such exclusive credit was given or not, and a mere charge on a book account may be rebutted by evidence that such was the intention.

GUARDIAN AND WARD   A guardian is one who legally has the care and management of the person or estate or both, of a child during its minority, the child being the ward. The father, and on his death, the mother is guardian by nature of the person of the minor but not of its property, and the father being of sufficient ability must support the child, even though it has an estate of its own. However, if the father's means are limited the court will grant an allowance out of the child's estate. A mother, however, is not obligated to support her child if it has sufficient means of its own, and she is not entitled to be paid for its services where she is not bound to maintain it. The father, even though himself a minor, may by last will appoint a guardian for his minor child to have control of his person and estate but this does not apply to grandchildren.

Guardians are mostly appointed by court in conformity with statutes. If more than fourteen years old, the child may name the person it desires to have appointed, but the court may reject the choice for good reason, and the child will be entitled to choose again. If the guardian is appointed when the child is less than fourteen years of age he may, in most places on reaching that age, select another if he so desire, the one first appointed, however, continuing to act if no change is made. The appointment is made in the county where the minor resides, but anyone residing within the state may be appointed. A married woman may act as guardian.

A guardian is a trustee—an agent of the court appointing him—and to avoid personal liability, important steps should be taken by him only with permission of the court. He will not be allowed to make profit from his ward's estate, but must account to the ward for all profits made, and the ward may elect either to take the profits or to charge interest on any capital of his that the guardian may have used. The guardian, indeed, has no right to use his ward's money and should securely invest it so that it may earn interest, and this should be done under order of court if the rate of interest obtained is to be less than the legal rate. If he wishes to convert the real estate of his minor into money or convert his money into real estate, it should be done only under order of court, but he may sell his ward's personal property without such order. He may lease the land of his ward, but not beyond the ward's minority. He is bound to earn interest on his ward's money so far as he is able, but will be allowed a reasonable time to find investment. Use of any portion of the ward's estate, and particularly the principal for maintenance and education of the minor should be by permission obtained from court.

If the guardian erects buildings on the ward's estate out of his own money without permission of court he will not be reimbursed. He is not chargeable with the services of his wards if, for their own benefit, he requires them to work for him. If a married woman is a guardian it is not necessary that her husband join in the deed to convey her ward's real estate.

Contracts made between guardian and ward immediately after the latter has attained his majority are regarded with scrutiny by the courts, and will be set aside where the guardian obtains an unfair advantage. It is considered that the ward is not yet free from the influence of his guardian and is liable to act to his own disadvantage.

The guardian is not allowed to purchase at the sale of his ward's property. If he does, the sale may be set aside or he may be personally charged with the difference between the real value and the price at which he purchased. Ordinarily he must not remove his ward's property from the state. He cannot release a debt due his ward without payment, though he may submit a disputed claim to arbitration, and he cannot, by a contract made for his own benefit, bind his ward or his ward's estate, nor can he set aside a beneficial contract made by his ward, for a minor's contract is voidable only, not void. That is, it may be repudiated by him on arriving at full age or not, as he chooses.

A guardian is entitled to the care and custody of the person of his ward if the ward has no parent living, or unless, being a female, she is married. He is entitled to the ward's property until the latter arrives at full age. A guardian may change the residence of the ward from one county to another but it seems the proper court in the other county may appoint another guardian, for by the common law a guardian's authority, both as to the person and property of his ward, is strictly local. In this country, except for limited purposes, this authority does not extend beyond the state, and a guardian in one state cannot bring suit in another. He cannot waive the rights of his ward, not even as a result of neglect or omission as the ward might himself do if at full age. He is not bound to maintain the ward at his own expense. The court will aid a guardian in enforcing obedience of the ward where he has custody of the ward's person.

As above stated a ward's contracts generally are voidable as to him and may be set aside if he so desires on his arriving at full age, though they are good as to the party contracting with him, if such party is himself competent to make a contract. Some contracts of a ward, however, are so clearly prejudicial that they are held to be absolutely void, such as contracts of suretyship.

Anyone marrying or aiding in the marrying of a ward without the consent of the guardian is guilty of a contempt of court, and in most states is punishable under statute law. The ward is in reality the ward of or under the protection of the court, the guardian being substantially the court's agent with respect to the ward.

Minors are liable for torts which they commit in the same manner as a person of full age. A ward is entitled to his own earnings, that is, if there are no parents who are entitled to them. He attains his majority the day before the 21st anniversary of his birthday. He can only sue by his guardian or by a next friend, that is, someone who will stand good for costs that may be adjudged against him. He may not sue a guardian at law, but may have a citation issued from court or file a bill in equity calling him to account. The statute of limitations will not run or apply against him during the guardianship.

Statutory authority exists quite generally for the sale or mortgaging of real estate of a ward by the guardian under an order obtained from court, where this is necessary for the minor's education and maintenance or where the estate is becoming dissipated or unproductive and generally where it will be to the interest of the minor that the real estate be sold.

Under statute laws there are provisions for the appointment of guardians or committees to take charge of the estates of persons insane or unable to take care of their estates, and of drunkards and in some cases of spendthrifts.

A guardian *ad litem* is one appointed for the purposes of a particular suit where no guardian has been previously appointed in the usual way. The power to appoint such a guardian rests in every court before which a case is to be tried. His duty is to manage the interests of the minor in the suit. He cannot in writing or otherwise waive service of any process in the suit. The process must be served on him in the regular manner. In criminal cases no guardian *ad litem* is appointed, the court itself acting as such.

H

HABEAS CORPUS A writ directed to a sheriff or other person detaining another, commanding him to produce the body of the prisoner at a certain time and place and to report the day and cause of his taking and detention to the judge awarding the writ. Upon proper hearing the court will remit the party to, or discharge him from custody as seems just and legal. Habeas corpus is the remedy against illegal restraint upon personal liberty and has been frequently called the great writ of liberty.

By the Constitution of the United States the privilege of this writ "shall not be suspended unless when in cases of rebellion or invasion, the public safety may require it." United States courts will not issue such a writ and inquire into the cause of commitment if the prisoner is imprisoned under process issued from the state. The state courts will only entertain jurisdiction in such a case. Where one is under arrest, however, as a fugitive from justice, at the instance of the authorities in one state and is in custody of the authorities of another state to which he fled, a writ of habeas corpus may issue from the United States courts. Such an arrest is really made under a provision of the Constitution of the United States.

The purpose of the writ of habeas corpus is to inquire into the cause of imprisonment and detention and to procure the release of a prisoner where that is found to be illegal. If the imprisonment is alleged to have been made by virtue of illegal process, the validity and present force of such process and not the guilt or innocence of the party is the subject of investigation and as to this proceeding, the process will not be invalidated by errors which merely render it irregular. The defects to entitle the prisoner to discharge must be such as to render the process under which he was arrested void. The writ cannot be used by one court simply to oust the jurisdiction of another or to divert or defeat the course of justice.

This writ may be also employed on behalf of one entitled to the custody of the person where such person is detained in the custody of another. It may be used by a parent to recover the custody of his child or by a guardian to secure his ward, a husband, his wife.

The application for the writ may be made by the prisoner or person detained or by anyone in his behalf if for any reason he is unable to make it. If the prisoner is under sentence for crime after conviction or is committed for treason or felony plainly expressed on the warrant for his

PETITION FOR WRIT OF HABEAS CORPUS

To the Judge of the Baltimore City Court:

The petition of John Doe respectfully shows that he was illegally restrained of his liberty by the warden of the Baltimore City Jail. Your petitioner, therefore, prays that the writ of habeas corpus issue, commanding said Warden to produce before this Honorable Court, the body of your petitioner, to abide such directions as may be given in the premises.

_____

PETITIONER

WRIT OF HABEAS CORPUS

State of Maryland:

To Warden, Baltimore City Jail:

You are commanded to have the body of John Doe, detained under your custody, as it is said, together with the cause of his detention, by whatsoever name he be called, before the Baltimore City Court, immediately after receipt of this writ to submit to and receive what shall be considered and determined in that behalf; and have you there this writ.

Issued this 11 day of June, 19____.   _____

CLERK

(Seal of Court)

---

arrest, he is not usually entitled to the writ. The body of the prisoner must be produced by the person to whom the writ is addressed if in his custody or power, unless this cannot be done without serious injury to his life, and any evasion is summarily dealt with by the court. The questions arising are determined by the court or judge and not by a jury. Evidence may be adduced on the hearing by witnesses or otherwise, and sometimes even affidavits are admitted, this being in the sound discretion of the court. A discharge because the process of arrest is void will not prevent another arrest for the same criminal act.

HABEAS CORPUS AD TESTIFICANDUM A writ commanding the sheriff to bring a witness into court, when he is in custody at the time of a trial, to testify in the cause.

HABENDUM In conveyancing. One of the eight formal and orderly parts of a deed, following immediately after the premises; so called from the Latin word *habendum*, with which it commenced, and literally translated and retained in modern deeds in the clause beginning with the words "To have and to hold."

HABITUAL CRIMINAL In some jurisdictions, a person who has been convicted a specified number of times will receive in the future heavier sentences than are provided in ordinary cases.

HANDWRITING The writing peculiar to an individual. Proof of handwriting is made by the testimony of a witness who saw the paper or signature actually written, or by one who has by sufficient means acquired such a knowledge of the general character of the handwriting of the party as will enable him to state his belief that the handwriting in question is that of the person alleged.

HEARSAY EVIDENCE Evidence which derives its value not solely from the credit to be given to the witness himself, but in part on the veracity and competency of some other person. As a general rule hearsay, that is, matters not within the knowledge of the witness himself but derived from the statements of others, are not admissible as evidence. This is true whether the statements referred to are oral or written. Such evidence is objectional because the party making the statement usually is not under oath at the time. and is not present to be cross-examined.

To the rule, however, against the admission of hearsay evidence there are exceptions, such as declarations, confessions or admissions made by the party to a suit, expressions of feeling of one whose physical condition at the time is the subject of inquiry or the conversation of one suspected of insanity, and general repute in the family concerning questions of pedigree. One's general reputation among people who know him may sometimes be proven to show the probability or improbability of the commission of an act by him. Entries made by a third person in the discharge of official duties will be admitted to prove the facts therein set forth, and entries in a party's shop book and sometimes in other books kept in the regular course o business are admissible.

HEDGING CONTRACT A con tract of purchase or sale of a equal amount of commodities i the future by which brokers, deal ers, or manufacturers protec themselves against the fluctuation of the market. It is a type of insur ance against changing prices. A grain dealer, to protect himself may contract to sell for future de livery the same amount of grain he has purchased in the present mar ket.

HEIR One upon whom the law casts an estate in lands, tenements or hereditaments immediately upon the death of the owner. No person can be heir of a living person. One having an indefeasible right to the inheritance, provided he outlives the owner, is termed, however, an heir apparent. An heir presumptive is one who, under present circumstances, would be entitled to the inheritance, but whose rights may be defeated by the birth of a nearer heir.

The word "heirs" properly includes heirs or heirs without end, but in wills it is sometimes construed to mean next of kin or children in order to effectuate the intention of the testator as gathered from the whole will. As between the heir to real estate and an administrator of the decedent, the latter may claim the growing crops and nurseries (though not trees in general), bricks in a kiln and a building held as personal property by consent of the owner of the land on which it is built, and leases and mortgages held by the decedent and rent accrued at the time of the decedent's death on the property descending to the heirs. Whether fixtures go to the heir or administrator depends upon circumstances.

HEIRLOOMS Certain chattels which, contrary to the usual course, descend to the heir as appendages of the real estate, and do not go to the administrator of the owner upon his death. They include deeds and other evidences of title of land and the box or chest containing them, also the keys of a house, fish in a pond, doves in a dovecote, and deer in a park.

HEREDITAMENTS That which may be inherited; everything which passes to the heir by hereditary right.

HERITAGE In civil law, every kind of immovable property regardless of whether it was obtained by descent or by purchase.

HIGH SEAS Waters open to all nations and not within the jurisdiction of any one nation. International law has not decided whether the high seas commence at the low-water mark or three miles or farther offshore.

HIGHWAYS Public thoroughfares. Highways are usually created and laid out under statute laws. Compensation to the owner of the land taken for the use as highway must be made. The constitutions of the various states in the United States contain provisions against the taking of private property for public use without compensation. The amount of compensation is usually fixed by a jury or commissioner as provided by statute, and if there is no such statutory provision suit may be brought in the ordinary way for damages resulting from the taking.

Not unfrequently highways are created by dedication, that is, an appropriation of land by the owner to the use of the public followed by an acceptance of the same by the public for the public use. In some places the acceptance may be shown by the mere fact of use. In others it appears there is no acceptance unless it is done by official action, evinced either by resolution of the officers having charge of highways or by an actual taking possession on their part by doing repairs on the highways or the like.

As against the owner of the land a dedication may be proved by his express declaration, verbal or written, that he had appropriated it to the use of the public, or by an act unequivocally showing his intent to dedicate as where he himself opens the way for the public over the land. The dedication may be implied from his acquiescence in the use of the land as a public way for twenty years (or whatever the statutory period may be within which suit must be brought to recover the land in the state where the highway is located), though a shorter period will suffice if such acquiescence cannot reasonably be accounted for except by supposing an intent to dedicate. Anything showing an intent to dedicate is sufficient to establish the dedication.

The dedication may be for a limited purpose, as for a footway, and the use cannot be extended beyond such purposes, but to be effective against the owner of the land the dedication must be to the use of the whole public. If limited to part of the public it will not be a public highway.

If a highway is impassable from being out of repair or for other cause, the public has the right to pass in another line, even to going over adjoining property whether sown with grain or not, but doing as little injury as possible. However, the municipal authorities are bound to be diligent in re-opening the obstructed roadway.

The highway is an easement. In cities it may be used for purposes of sewage, distribution of light and water, and for the furtherance of public health, trade and convenience as well as an avenue for passage for persons and vehicles. The owner of the land on which it is located retains the fee and all rights of property not incompatible with the public enjoyment such as the right to the herbage, trees and fruit growing thereon or minerals below. He may work a mine or set a draw in or have a cellar or carry water in pipes beneath it, not interfering of course with the public use. He may stop encroachments not connected with the public use as a highway. He may bring suit against one building on it, or digging up and removing the soil or cutting down trees for use as a highway, or stopping upon it and using abusive or insulting language.

A grant of land bounded "by" or "on" or "along" a highway means to the middle thereof if the grantor owns so far, but if the language of the deed shows a contrary intent as in using the words "by the side of," "by the margin of" or "by the line of" this contrary intent will prevail. If the highway is abandoned the original owner of the soil or his heirs or assigns recovers dominion thereof.

By statute, the city, town or township in which the highway is located and in some cases the county, is responsible for repairs. The municipality upon which is imposed the duty of repair is liable for injuries resulting to individuals from neglect to keep it in safe condition or to provide sufficient guard rails or other protection at points of danger. The amount of protection required of the municipality depends upon the location of the road. The officers having the duty of repairs in charge are indictable for not keeping roads in reasonably good and passable condition. Where individuals or corporations own or have in charge a highway, their duties and responsibilities are similar.

Any act or obstruction necessarily interfering with the lawful use of the highway by the public is a common law nuisance, and may be abated by anyone whose passage is obstructed and the person causing and maintaining it may be indicted, or may be sued for damages by one specially injured. Railroad companies must not unnecessarily obstruct public highways with their trains. Water accumulating in a road may be turned onto adjoining private property where necessary to keep the road in proper condition.

HINDER AND DELAY CREDITORS
To impede or retard creditors in their lawful effort to subject the property of their debtor to the payment of their claims, whether done innocently or with intent to hinder and delay them. A debtor's sale of his property for less than its fair value may be such a hindrance and delay, although innocently made.

HOLDER IN DUE COURSE A holder who has taken a negotiable instrument under the following conditions: (1) that is complete and regular on its face; (2) that he became the holder of it before it was overdue, and without notice that it had been previously dishonored, if such was the fact; (3) that he took it in good faith and for value; (4) that at the time it was negotiated to him he had no notice of any infirmity in the instrument or defect in the title of the person negotiating it.

HOLDING COMPANY A corporation organized for the purpose of owning and holding the stock of other corporations. Shareholders of underlying corporations receive in exchange for their stock, upon an agreed value, the shares in the holding corporation.

HOLD OVER To retain possession as tenant of leased property after the expiration of the lease.

HOLIDAYS, BUSINESS OR LEGAL A day appointed by law on which general business and judicial proceedings are suspended. The laws of the several states regarding holidays follow.

Alabama Bank may do business on any legal holiday except Sunday. Contracts, including conveyances, made on Sunday are void, except in cases of necessity, or of contracts of a religious or charitable character; but contracts and conveyances made on other legal *holidays* are valid.

Alaska When a holiday falls on Sunday, the following Monday is a holiday. When money or notes fall due on a legal holiday, they are payable on the following Monday.

Arizona Public offices may not be opened on holidays, nor may any judicial business be transacted, except that courts of justice may be opened to give, upon request, instructions to the jury when deliberating, to receive a verdict or discharge a jury, and for exercise of powers of magistrates in criminal proceedings. Injunctions, attachments, claim and delivery and writs of prohibition may be issued and served on any day.

Arkansas Transactions on legal holidays are valid, except that contract made on Sunday is void unless ratified on a subsequent weekday.

California When holiday falls on Sunday, following Monday is a holiday. Saturday from noon until midnight is a holiday as regards transaction of business in public offices of state, and also in political divisions where laws, ordinances or charters provide that public offices shall be closed on holidays; provided, this shall not be construed to prevent or invalidate the issuance, filing, service, execution or recording of any legal process or written instrument during said 12 hours. Special or limited holidays of limited effect may be appointed by Governor. Saturday is a holiday for acts performed at or by a bank. When a secular act shall be performed, or when the last day for performance of any act falls on a holiday, it may be performed on next business day.

If any city, county, state or other public office (other than a branch) is closed for the whole of any day, as to its business the day shall be considered as a holiday in computing time when an act is legally required to be performed within a specified period. Every Saturday from noon to midnight is a half holiday as regards business of state offices and offices or cities or districts so providing, except for essential public services.

When date of maturity of commercial paper falls on a holiday, instrument is payable on next business day not a Saturday. Specified days are designated optional bank holidays, on which the holder of a negotiable instrument payable at a bank may present it (if bank is open thereon), with option of presentation on next business day not a Saturday.

Colorado Feb. 12, Aug. 1, and Oct. 12 are legal holidays for courts, but any type of banking institution may close or remain open. When holiday falls on Sunday, following Monday is a holiday. Saturday afternoon is a holiday during June, July and Aug. in cities of over 25,000 population. Sunday is *dies non*, that is, not a day. Banking institutions may close on Saturdays and in such event Saturday is a legal holiday with respect to such banks for all purposes. A note maturing on holiday or Sunday is payable on next business day. Process may be issued and served on holiday. Commercial paper, conveyances and other legal documents dated or delivered on Sunday are valid.

Connecticut When a holiday falls on Sunday, next Monday is a holiday. Saturday is a legal holiday for purposes of the negotiable instruments law. A contract made on Sunday is voidable on return of consideration.

Delaware A holiday is not considered *dies non*, that is, a day in which courts are not open for business. Transactions on holidays are therefore binding.

District of Columbia There is no statute declaring illegal or void transactions made on a legal holiday.

Florida When a legal holiday falls on Sunday, the following Monday is a holiday. Service or execution on Sunday of any writ, process, warrant, order, judgment or decree, is void, unless the person liable to have any such service or execution upon him intends to withdraw himself from the state, in which case such service may be obtained upon the information under oath of two respectable persons furnished to any judge, justice of the peace, or magistrate.

Hawaii Notes or money due on Sunday or a legal holiday are due the following day or Monday.

Idaho Where day fixed by law or contract for doing an act falls on a holiday, performance on the next business day is sufficient.

Illinois When last day on which an act must be performed is a holiday or Sunday, such act may be performed on the next business day. Banks may select one day a week to remain closed. Contracts may be made or performed on holidays or Sundays.

Indiana All notes, drafts, checks, or commercial paper falling due on any of such holidays shall be payable on the next succeeding business day. When legal holiday comes on Sunday, the day following is a holiday.

Iowa Contracts executed on holidays are voidable but may be later ratified. Banking transactions on holidays are valid.

Kansas It is lawful for banks to pay checks, drafts or other bills of exchange on a holiday if such payment is otherwise lawful.

Kentucky No objections may be taken to any process, writ, summons, affidavit, order for provisional remedy or bond in any action because issued, made or dated on a holiday but a distinction has been taken between a holiday and a Sunday. Summons, subpoena, notice or order for provisional remedy may be issued, given or executed on a holiday or Sunday on affidavit of belief that it cannot be given or executed thereafter.

Louisiana Negotiable paper falling due on Sunday, holiday or Saturday payable on next business day other than Saturday, except that demand papers may be presented before noon on a Saturday which is not a whole holiday.

Maine Every negotiable instrument falling due on Saturday, Sunday or holiday is payable on next business day.

Maryland Acts done on a holiday are not void.

Massachusetts Transactions between the hours of 7:00 A.M. and 1:00 P.M. on May 30, Nov. 11 and Oct. 12 are subject to the Sunday laws and are therefore void unless they constitute works of charity or necessity.

Michigan Sunday contracts are void except as to works of necessity or charity. Otherwise contracts are not effected, except that time for performance of acts is extended to next business day, including acts with respect to negotiable instruments. If bank elects to close Saturdays, such Saturdays are deemed holidays as regards presentment, protest and giving notice of dishonor.

Minnesota Civil process may not be served on holiday. Acknowledgment or publication of summons on holiday is valid, but no civil process may be served thereon.

Mississippi Notes and money due on Sunday or a legal holiday are due the following day or Monday.

Missouri In general, contracts or other transactions on holidays or Sundays are valid.

Montana An act performed or contract made on holiday is valid.

Nebraska In general, contracts or other transactions on holidays or Sundays are valid.

Nevada Additional nonjudicial days include Sundays and the day when a state primary or general election is held. On such days, with certain exceptions, no judicial business may be done. When performance of any act fixed by law or contract falls upon holiday or nonjudicial day it may be performed on the next business day.

New Hampshire Notes and money due on Sunday or a legal holiday are due the following day or Monday.

New Jersey Business may be transacted on holidays except Sundays, with some exceptions.

New Mexico When maturity of instrument for payment of money falls on a holiday or on a Saturday or Sunday, it is payable on the next succeeding business day, except that a demand instrument may be presented before noon on Saturday where that entire day is not a holiday.

New York Banking organizations may, on proper resolution of governing bodies, remain closed on Saturdays throughout the year.

North Dakota Business done on a holiday (excepting Sunday and proceedings in court) is valid.

Ohio Written contracts entered into Saturday afternoon, Sundays, and on other holidays, are valid if not prohibited by statute. Any financial institution may, at its option, outside of regular banking hours or on a day which is in whole or in part a holiday, pay, certify, or accept negotiable or non-negotiable instruments including a demand instrument dated on the holiday on which it is presented for payment, certification, or acceptance, and transact any other business which would be valid if done on a business day during regular banking hours.

Oklahoma If holidays fall on Sunday, the succeeding Monday is a holiday. Any act authorized, required or permitted to be performed on above days may be performed on next succeeding business day. Additional days designated as holidays on which any act authorized, required or permitted to be performed on said days may and shall be performed on said days the same as on any business day. A commercial paper falling due on Sunday or holiday is payable on the next business day. Same applies to instruments falling due on Saturday, except that instrument payable on demand may be presented before noon.

Oregon Transactions on holidays are as valid as on any other day.

Pennsylvania Worldly employment and business (works of necessity and charity only excepted) are prohibited on Sunday. The Act has been liberally construed. Executory contracts made on Sunday are voidable. Contracts made on Sunday and executed by one party are enforceable against the other.

Puerto Rico In civil causes orders of arrest may be made and served; proceedings to recover possession of personal property may be had; and suits for obtaining any such writs and proceedings may be instituted, on any day.

Rhode Island No commercial or industrial work is permitted except that which is absolutely necessary and can lawfully be performed on Sundays or legal holidays. There are criminal penalties for violations. Director of Labor is authorized to grant permits for work on such days upon showing of economic hardship provided overtime rate is paid.

South Dakota Service of process may be made on any holiday except Sunday, and may be made on Sunday if, for good cause shown, a judge in whose court an action has been, or is about to be brought, endorses on the process, permission for service on Sunday. Negotiable instruments falling due on Sunday or holiday are due the next succeeding business day.

Tennessee Bank transactions on holiday or after noon on Saturday are valid. Business activities may be suspended on Wednesdays, Thursdays, or Saturdays.

Texas Contracts made on Sunday or a holiday are valid, unless made in respect to matters prohibited to be done on such a day. Judicial acts performed on a Sunday are of doubtful validity, but are probably valid when performed on a holiday.

Utah Whenever an act of secular nature, other than work of necessity or mercy is appointed by law or contract to be performed on a particular day, and that day falls on a holiday, such act may be performed upon the next business day, with the same effect as if performed on the day appointed.

Vermont Contracts made on Sunday are void.

Virginia No transaction of contract, or in administration of justice, or relating to banking is invalid because done on such a holiday or half holiday.

Virgin Islands Negotiable instruments falling due on Sunday or holiday are due the next succeeding business day.

Washington Business transactions on holidays are not void by the laws of this state.

West Virginia Banking transactions are not invalid because done on Sunday or legal holiday.

Wisconsin As to negotiable instruments, where the last day for doing any act required or permitted falls on a Saturday, Sunday or a legal holiday, the act may be done on the succeeding secular or business day.

Wyoming Where the day, or last day, for doing an act, or filing a pleading, or permitted by the Negotiable Instruments Law falls on a Sunday or holiday, the act may be done on the next succeeding secular or business day.

HOLOGRAPHIC WILL A holographic will is one written *entirely* by the hand of the testator. It may be written in pencil or ink, or partly in both. It may take the form of a letter or notation or a note. It must be entirely written, signed and dated by the testator. Not all states recognize such wills, nor are witnesses required in all jurisdictions allowing holographic wills. (*See also* WILL.)

Holographic wills are recognized in the following states:

Alaska: no witnesses.

Arizona: no witnesses.

Arkansas: three disinterested witnesses.

California: no witnesses.

Idaho: no witnesses.

Kentucky: no witnesses.

Louisiana: no witnesses.

Mississippi: no witnesses.

Montana: no witnesses.

Nevada: no witnesses.

New York: holographic wills by soldiers or sailors while in actual military service, or by a mariner while at sea, were valid during the war. Such wills are unenforceable and invalid upon the expiration of one year following discharge from military service, provided testator still retains capacity to execute a valid will. Where, after his discharge from service, a testator still lacks such capacity, the holographic will is valid and enforceable until the expiration of one year from the time capacity is regained.

North Carolina: must appear that the will was found among the valuable papers of the testator. Testator's handwriting must be proved by three witnesses.

North Dakota: no witnesses.

Oklahoma: no witnesses.

Puerto Rico: no witnesses.

South Dakota: no witnesses.

Tennessee: substantially the same provisions are in force as in North Carolina.

Texas: no witnesses.

Utah: no witnesses.

Virginia: no witnesses.

West Virginia: no witnesses.

Wyoming: no witnesses.

HOMESTEAD In a legal sense the word means the real estate occupied as a home and also the right to have it exempt from levy and forced sale. It is the land, not exceeding the prescribed amount, upon which the dwelling house, or residence, or habitation or abode of the owner thereof and his family reside; and includes the dwelling house as an indispensable part.

HOMESTEAD LAWS See EXEMPTION AND HOMESTEAD LAWS.

HOMICIDE The killing of any person. Homicide is not necessarily a crime. If a homicide is committed with malice or premeditation, it may be murder in the first or second degree; some homicides are excusable as when one kills in self-defense. Some homicides are justifiable as where a sheriff lawfully executes a prisoner convicted by due process of law. (*See also* MURDER.)

HOSTILE WITNESS A witness who, when examined in the first instance by the party who called him, is so evidently hostile and prejudiced that he may be subjected to cross-examination as if he had been called by the opposing party.

HOTEL An establishment that provides lodging for pay. A hotel is bound to receive all travelers and wayfaring persons and entertain them, if they can be accommodated, for a reasonable compensation.

The hotel-keeper must furnish reasonable accommodations and is entitled to just compensation for his care and trouble and expense, and has some special privileges in securing the same. He has a lien upon the goods and property brought into the hotel or placed in his custody by the guest, such as baggage and the like, and may detain them as security for payment of his bill, even though the goods belong to a third person if he was ignorant of the fact in extending credit to the guest. This lien applies only to transient guests, not to boarders. One who entertains strangers occasionally, although he may receive compensation for it, is not an inn-keeper.

An inn-keeper is practically in the position of an insurer of the safety of property committed to his care against everything but the "act of God," or the public enemy or fraud of the owner of the property or his servant or companion. He is responsible for loss occasioned by his own servants, by guests, or by rioters or mobs. Sickness will not excuse him, for he is bound to have competent servants and agents. Unless the guest fails to observe reasonable precautions and directions of the inn-keeper in disposing of his goods, the fact that the guest merely leaves his door unlocked will not ordinarily relieve the inn-keeper from responsibility.

If the guest is disorderly the inn-keeper may refuse to receive him or require him to leave, but ordinarily he must make no distinction as to applications for accommodation. With respect to boarders at a hotel, the responsibility peculiar to a hotel-keeper with respect to transient guests, does not exist. The liability of the inn-keeper to his guests applies only to things brought within the hotel, or otherwise distinctly placed in his custody in a customary and reasonable way.

With respect, however, to any injury in the nature of a tort done by the landlord's servants or others to the person of his guest without his own cooperation or consent, he is not responsible, nor is he responsible if the loss occurs through the fault of the guest.

HOUSE OF ILL FAME A house kept for the resort and unlawful commerce of lewd people of both sexes. A brothel or common habitation of prostitutes is a bawdy-house. The keeper of such a house may be indicted for maintaining a nuisance. If the proprietor is a married woman, she may be indicted either alone or with her husband. Even one who assists in establishing the house is guilty. So is the lessor of the house if he knows the use to which it is put.

To be a bawdy-house the house must be of ill fame or have a bad reputation, and more than one woman must live or resort there, but it may contain but one room, and it need not be kept for gain.

If it is falsely alleged that one keeps a bawdy-house an action will lie to recover damages for slander or libel as the case may be. A landlord cannot recover rent for a house let for the purpose of prostitution. If a lodger lets her room for the purpose of prostitution, she is guilty of keeping a house of ill fame as much as if she were proprietor of the whole house.

HUSBAND AND WIFE A man and woman who have joined their lives together and have complied with the requirements to make their union legal. The husband is bound to furnish his wife with necessaries and conveniences in accord with his ability and situation in life.

The husband as well as the wife may be punished for keeping a disorderly home to the annoyance of the neighborhood even though the wife is the principal actor, and he is liable for torts committed by her, such as slander or trespass. He has the right to determine where their home shall be located and need not be controlled as to this by his wife provided he furnishes her a fit place to live under the circumstances. He is not under her control as to acquiring property, but cannot sell real estate discharged of her dower without her consent expressed in a manner provided by law unless otherwise provided by statute.

Where a husband and wife live together, a presumption arises that the husband assents to contracts made by the wife to supply articles for family consumption suitable to their station and means of life. Where they live apart this presumption does not exist, but her authority may be shown from the nature and circumstances of the separation or conduct of the husband, or the condition of the wife and nature of the articles supplied by her. If the wife leaves the husband without just cause she loses the right to be maintained and supported by him.

The husband and wife may enter into a contract of separation which will be obligatory so long as the separation continues. However, the obligation of the marriage contract is peculiar and cannot be annulled simply at the pleasure of one or both. (*See also* SEPARATION.)

Where there is a separation and reasonable allowance made to his wife for necessaries, the husband will not in general be liable for necessaries supplied to her, and the rule is that he is liable only where she has no means of obtaining the necessaries from other sources. If one holds a woman out to the public as his wife, or lives with her as his wife, he is liable for necessaries for her support as if she were really his wife.

If the wife elopes with another man or deserts her husband without cause he is not bound to support her, is not liable for alimony and he is not bound to pay her debts, contracted when the separation is notorious. Whoever gives her credit under such circumstances does so at his peril.

If a letter of credit is purchased with the husband's money, payable to husband and wife, and one of them dies, the unpaid portion will belong to the survivor; in general property owned by husband and wife jointly at the death of one becomes the other's in its entirety.

HYPOTHECATE To pledge a thing without delivering the possession of it to the pledgee.

HYPOTHECATION A pledge without possession by the pledgee.

HYPOTHETICAL QUESTION A set of assumed facts asked of an expert who gives evidence at a trial.

I

IDEM SONANS Absolute accuracy in spelling names is not required in legal documents. If a name spelled in a document is different from the correct name, it is still legally effective as sufficient name of a person, if, when pronounced, it sounds to the ear the same as the correct name. This is called the doctrine of *idem sonans*. For example: Smythe and Smith; Mackey and Macky.

INDEMNITY In the law of contracts indemnity is the obligation on one person to make good any loss or damage another has incurred or may incur by acting at his request or for his benefit.

The right to indemnity and the obligation to indemnify or compensate arises from contract, express or implied. The promise is an original and not a collateral undertaking and the liability assumed is primary, not secondary. An insurance policy is a contract of indemnity, as when the company agrees to make good any loss sustained by the policyholder as a result of fire, theft, etc.

An indemnity differs from a guaranty in that the latter is an undertaking to do something or pay a debt in case another doesn't. A guaranty is a secondary liability, as when a building contractor may be required to obtain a "completion bond," that is, the promise of the bonding company that if the building contractor fails to complete the building, the institution will do so. Indemnity differs from sure-tyship in that the latter is an undertaking to answer for the debt, default, or miscarriage of another. Thus, an employee may be required to be bonded before being hired. The surety company will issue a "fidelity bond" (the contract) in which it agrees to make good any losses suffered by the employer as a result of the employee's theft.

IGNORANCE OF THE LAW The state of being or claiming unfamiliarity with the law. It is said that mere ignorance of the law will not excuse or protect one. (*See also* CRIMINAL ACTION.) One is bound by the law though ignorant of it; thus, if one marries a woman knowing her to have a husband living even though he may think he has a legal right to marry her, he will be guilty of adultery. It would be different if the ignorance were of a matter of fact. Thus if one believes a woman to be unmarried at the time he married her, though in fact she is married, he will not be criminally responsible.

IGNORANTIA LEGIS NEMINEM EXCUSAT Ignorance of the law excuses no one.

ILLEGAL Conduct that is contrary to public policy and the fundamental principles of law is illegal. Such conduct includes not only violations of criminal statutes, but also the creation of agreements that are prohibited by statute and the common law.

275

ILLEGITIMATE CHILDREN Those born out of lawful wedlock. If begotten before but born after the marriage they are legitimate, and quite generally by statute, a marriage of the parents after the birth of the child will legitimate it. One is a bastard if born under such circumstances as to make it impossible that the husband of the mother can be the father and this impossibility may be only a strong moral impossibility or such improbability as to be beyond a reasonable doubt. He is also a bastard who is born beyond a competent time after the coverture is determined by the death of the husband or otherwise. If the marriage is void from the beginning, as where one party has a wife or husband living at the time of the marriage, the issue will be illegitimate. So also are offspring of a marriage later annulled.

The putative or reputed father is bound to support his bastard child, and this may be enforced by the courts. The father is entitled to the natural guardianship and care of the person of the child in preference to all persons unless it is the mother. The child was formerly unable to inherit from anyone, but this has been for the most part changed by statute so as to at least enable the child to inherit from his mother, but he may take a demise or bequest under a will.

ILLUSORY Deceiving or intending to deceive, as by false appearances; fallacious. An illusory promise is a promise which appears to be binding but which in fact does not bind the promisor.

IMMATERIAL AVERMENT A pleading which contains unnecessary particulars in the description of what is pleaded as material.

IMMORAL CONSIDERATION An inducement to contract which is contrary to good morals. Such contracts are generally void.

IMMOVABLES Property which, because of its nature or its attachment to something else, cannot be moved.

IMMUNITY Freedom from the legal duties and penalties imposed upon others. The "privileges and immunities" clause of the United States Constitution means no state can deny to the citizens of another state the same rights granted to its own citizens. This does not apply to office holding.

IMPAIRING THE OBLIGATION OF CONTRACTS The Constitution of the United States prohibits any state from passing a law impairing the obligation of contracts. This provision is one of the chief supports of the right of private property. Strange to say the Constitution has not imposed this limitation upon Congress. The prohibition extends to the essence or obligation of the contract only, and therefore mere remedies or methods of enforcing rights under the contract or for a breach may be altered after the contract is made. All executory contracts, that is, those to be executed in the future, express or implied, are within the provisions of this clause. No state law can revoke a corporate franchise (which is regarded as a contract with the state) unless the grant is coupled with a condition of right to revoke, or unless under the law or constitution of the state such right of revocation was reserved before the franchise was granted. Nor can a private conveyance (for this is a contract) be annulled by a law passed after it is made.

The prohibition as to impairing the obligation of contracts was not intended to apply to public property or to discharge of public duties or to the exercise of possession of public rights nor to any change or qualifications in these which the legislature or state may at any time deem expedient. Thus, the term of office of a public officer may be abbreviated by a legislative enactment, and the legislature has full authority to exercise unlimited power in the matter of eminent domain (*see also* EMINENT DOMAIN), and may delegate this power to municipal corporations and even to corporations of a quasi-public character, whose duties are to the public generally, as railroads, electric light and power companies, etc. but may not grant such right to private individuals for simply private purposes.

The provision applies to marriage and divorce, and laws permitting divorce must be limited to marriages taking place after the law is enacted or to transactions occurring after its passage, but no law creating new grounds or new facilities for divorce can apply to a marriage already made. However, this is not generally held to apply where there is an absolute breach of the contract of marriage, for in this case no obligation remains to be impaired.

The discharge of a bankrupt from his debt under a state bankruptcy law would operate as an impairment of the obligation of his contracts, but this is permissible even as to contracts made before the passage of a national bankruptcy law because the United States Constitution expressly authorizes the passage of such laws by Congress. Where a law exempts property from attachment or from being taken in execution it can apply only with reference to contracts or debts created after the passage of the law, for otherwise the value of the contract or right already existing of the creditor seeking to enforce his claim would be lessened.

IMPANELING The process of selecting those who will or may be jurors. In United States practice, it extends through the actual selection of a jury for a particular case.

IMPARLANCE A continuance granted to a party to respond to a pleading. Originally, it allowed time for an amicable settlement, but in modern usage the term refers merely to time granted to a defendant to plead.

IMPEACH To deny or contradict or to question the veracity of a witness.

IMPEACHMENT Synonymous with an indictment in a criminal proceeding. It is usually instituted against a public officer. Under the Federal Constitution a President is impeached by the House of Representatives of the United States, with the United States Senate sitting as a jury. To convict, two-thirds of the Senate must vote for the impeachment.

IMPEDIMENT The absence of an essential qualification for capacity to contract, such as infancy, lunacy, or marriage.

IMPERTINENT (1) Denoting any matter of pleading which is irrelevant and cannot be received by the court. (2) In evidence, it is a question or answer which has no logical bearing on the matters at issue.

IMPLEAD To sue, or prosecute by due course of law.

IMPLIED Contained in substance or essence or by fair inference but not actually expressed; deductible by inference or implication.

IMPLIED ASSUMPSIT An undertaking or promise not formally made, but presumed or implied from the conduct of a party.

IMPLIED CONTRACT A contract implied by reason and justice, and which therefore the law presumes that every man undertakes to perform.

IMPLIED COVENANT A covenant implied or inferred from certain words in deeds, leases, etc.; as "give," "grant, bargain and sell," "demise," and the like.

IMPLIED TRUST A trust raised or created by implication of law; a trust implied or presumed from circumstances.

IMPLIED WARRANTY An implied warranty arises by operation of law and exists without any intention of the seller to create it. It is a conclusion or inference of law, pronounced by the court, on facts admitted or proved before the jury.

IMPOTENCE The inability to have sexual intercourse, largely psychological in origin. It is often a ground for divorce or for the annulment of a marriage.

IMPOUNDED To shut up stray animals or distrain goods in a pound; to seize and hold a fund of money or goods by legal process.

IMPRISONMENT Forcible confinement by the law. Imprisonment may be in a place used for that purpose generally or for the particular occasion only, or it may be by words, threats, and an array of force without bolts or bars in any locality whatever. A forcible detention in the street or a touching of a person by a peace officer by way of arrest is imprisonment.

IMPROVEMENT A capital addition which permanently enhances the value of real property beyond mere repairs or the replacement of waste.

IN CAMERA In chambers. In the judge's private room; when the public is excluded.

IN EXTENSO In full length. Omitting nothing.

IN FRAUDEM LEGIS In fraud of the law. Done with a view of evading the law.

IN FULL LIFE Alive both civilly and physically.

IN LOCO PARENTIS In the place of a parent.

IN MORA In delay. In default, as when one does not pay on time.

IN PARI CAUSA POSSESSOR POTIOR HABERI DEBET In equal cause he who has possession should be preferred. Where both parties to a cause have an equal right, the party in possession is supposed to be preferred.

IN PARI DELICTO In equal fault. Where both parties are equally at fault, the court will grant relief to neither.

IN PERSONAM Against the person.

IN PROPRIA PERSONA In one's own person. Where a litigant conducts his case by himself rather than by an attorney.

IN REM An action brought against an object (or even a status, such as marriage) rather than directly against an individual.

IN SOLIDO or IN SOLIDUM In the whole or for the whole. In civil law, a term for jointly and severally, meaning that any one of a group is liable to discharge the entire obligation.

IN STATUS QUO In the same condition in which a person or a thing was.

IN TERROREM In terror. Said of a threat or a warning in a will that legacies are given on condition that if the legatee disputes the will, the legacy is void.

IN TRANSITU On the journey. Goods are as a rule considered as *in transitu* while they are in the possession of a carrier, whether by land or water, until they arrive at the ultimate place of their destination and are delivered into the actual possession of the buyer, whether or not the carrier has been named or designated by the buyer.

INADEQUATE REMEDY AT LAW Law damages consist of money only. Equity will not take jurisdiction except where money damages are considered insufficient in view of the injury or the relief sought.

INADMISSIBLE Denoting a statement not receivable as evidence under one or another of the rules of law—for example, oral evidence to contradict a written contract.

INALIENABLE Incapable of being aliened, transferred, or conveyed; non-transferable.

INCEPTION Initial stage. The word does not refer to a state of actual existence, but to a condition of things or circumstances from which the thing may develop; as the beginning of work on a building.

INCEST The sexual intercourse of a man and woman related to each other in any of the degrees within which marriage is prohibited by law. The offense is, of course, punishable criminally.

INCHOATE Begun; commenced; incipient; incomplete. A term applied to dower.

INCOME TAX A tax on the

yearly profits from property, professions, trades or offices over a certain amount which is called the exemption. Income taxes are levied by both Federal and State governments.

INCONTESTABLE As applied to insurance, a clause in an insurance policy which states that after a certain period of time the policy may not be contested except for nonpayment of the premiums.

INCORPOREAL HEREDITAMENTS Inheritable rights issuing out of and annexed to some corporeal inheritance, as the right of way over another's land.

INDEBITATUS ASSUMPSIT Being indebted he undertook. That form of assumpsit which is available for the recovery of any simple common law debt without regard to any express promise to pay the debt. The remedy is also available upon an express contract, when nothing remains to be done but the payment of money. In some states the common law forms of action are no longer in use.

INDECENCY Vulgarity or immorality in action, printed word, pictures, etc. The law in general will repress indecency as contrary to good morals, but if the public good requires it, the mere indecency of disclosures will not prevent their being given in evidence.

Public indecency, such as exposure of the naked person on a balcony to public view, or nude bathing in public, or exhibiting bawdy pictures, is punishable by indictment.

INDEMNITY A duty resting on

one person to make good a loss or damage another has suffered. A contracts to build a house for B. B contracts with C for a premium to answer for any loss B may suffer by reason of A's default. If A defaults and B suffers loss, C will indemnify B.

INDEPENDENT CONTRACTOR One independently employed who contracts to do a piece of work according to his own methods without being subject to the control of his employer except as to the result of the work.

INDETERMINATE SENTENCE A sentence to imprisonment for the maximum term defined by law subject to termination by the Parole Board or any other agency after the prisoner has served the minimum term.

INDICT To accuse by the finding or presentment of a grand jury; to find an indictment against.

INDICTMENT The written accusation at the suit of the commonwealth found to be true by a grand jury. The accusation is called a bill of indictment before the grand jury acts upon it and finds it to be a true bill.

INDISPENSABLE PARTIES Parties having not merely an interest in an action, but such a vital interest that to decide the question without their presence would be unjust and not final.

INDORSEE The party in whose favor a bill of exchange, promissory note or check is indorsed.

INDORSEMENT The writing of

one's name on the back of a bill of exchange, promissory note or check; the writing of the name of the payee, or holder of a bill, note or check on the back of it, by which the property in it is assigned and transferred.

INDORSEMENT IN BLANK An indorsement consisting merely of the signature of the party making it.

INDORSEMENT IN FULL An indorsement which mentions the name of the person in whose favor it is made, thus: "Pay A. B., on order, C. D."

INDORSER The party by whom a bill of exchange, promissory note or check is indorsed.

INDUCEMENT The consideration or benefit which, as received or promised, forms the basis on which a party enters into a contract.

INFAMY The condition of one who has been convicted of an infamous crime, involving the lessening of his civil rights. If one is convicted of an offense inconsistent with the common principles of honesty and humanity, the law considers his oath of no weight, and excludes his testimony as of too doubtful and suspicious a nature to be admitted in a court of justice to deprive one either of life, liberty or property.

The crimes which render one thus incompetent to testify are treason, felonies, receiving stolen goods, swindling, cheating, perjury, forgery, barratry, conspiracy, bribing a witness to absent himself from a trial and such crimes as involve the charge of falsehood and fraud. Conviction of obtaining goods by false pretenses does not seem to render the party incompetent as a witness. In order to incapacitate, the judgment must be shown to have been pronounced by a court having competent jurisdiction but it seems that a conviction of an infamous crime in another country or in another state of the United States does not render the witness incompetent.

Evidence of pardon or of reversal of the judgment by writ of error by production of the record or showing want of jurisdiction or right to entertain the case on the part of the court pronouncing the judgment, will rebut the allegation of infamy, and a defendant may be heard on his own oath in relation to the irregularity of a judgment against himself for an infamous crime. However, he cannot be so heard as complainant. One rendered incompetent as above stated cannot testify as attesting witness even to prove the execution of an instrument before his conviction, and in such case evidence must be adduced of his handwriting.

INFANT A person under the age of twenty-one years; a minor.

INFANTICIDE The murder of a newborn infant. It is distinguishable from abortion and foeticide which are limited to the destruction of the life of the foetus *in utero*.

The crime of infanticide can be committed only after the child is wholly born. This question involves an inquiry, first, into the signs of maturity, the data for which are— the length and weight of the foetus, the relative position of the center of its body, the proportional development of its several parts as compared with each other, especially of the head as compared with the rest of the body, the degree of growth of the hair and nails, the condition of the skin, the presence or absence of the *membrana pupillaris*, and in the male, the descent or non-descent of the testicles.

Second, was it born alive? The second point presents an inquiry of great interest both to the legal and medical professions and to the community at large. In the absence of all direct proof, what organic facts proclaim the existence of life subsequent to the birth? These facts are derived principally from the circulatory and respiratory systems.

The fact of life at birth being established, the next inquiry is, how long did the child survive? The proofs here are derived from three sources. The foetal openings, their partial or complete closure. The more perfect the closure, the longer the time. The series of changes in the umbilical cord. These are: 1. The withering of the cord. 2. Its desiccation or drying and, 3. Its separation or dropping off,—occurring usually four or five days after birth. 4. Cicatrization of the umbilicus,—occurring usually from ten to twelve days after birth. The changes in the skin, consisting in the process of exfoliation of the epidermis, which commences on the abdomen and extends thence successively to the chest, groin, axillae, interscapular space, limbs, and finally, to the hands and feet.

As to the means by which the life of the child may have been destroyed, the criminal means most commonly resorted to are—1. suffocation; 2. drowning; 3. cold and exposure; 4. starvation; 5. wounds, fractures, and injuries of various kinds; a means not infrequently resorted to is the introduction of sharp-pointed instruments in different parts of the body; also, luxation and fracture of the neck, accomplished by forcibly twisting the head of the child, or pulling it backwards; 6. strangulation; 7. poisoning; 8. intentional neglect to tie the umbilical cord; 9. causing the child to inhale air deprived of its oxygen, or poisonous gases.

INFORMATION A written accusation of crime preferred by a public prosecuting officer without the intervention of a grand jury.

INFRINGEMENT Infringement of a patent on a machine is the manufacturing of a machine that produces the same result by the same means and operation as the patented machine. Infringement of a trademark consists in the reproduction of a registered trademark and its use upon goods in order to mislead the public to believe that the goods are the genuine, original product.

INHERITANCE An estate or property which one has by descent or which may be transmitted to another as an heir.

INHERITANCE TAX A tax on the right to acquire property occasioned by death.

INJUNCTION A legal writ issued on application from a court of equity to restrain the party enjoined from doing or continuing to do something wrong complained of, either temporarily or during the continuance of the suit in which such injunction is granted and until the rights of the parties have been finally determined by the court. This final determination, if favorable to the complaint, will result in a final or perpetual injunction though this may be granted at the end of the suit whether a preliminary injunction was issued or not.

The remedy by injunction is used in a great variety of cases: to stay improper preceedings at law, to restrain the transfer of stocks, promissory notes, bills of exchange and other evidences of debt to the injury of the party applying for the injunction; to restrain the transfer of the title to property, to restrain one from setting up an inequitable defense in a suit at law, to prevent infringement of a patent or the pirating of trademarks, to prevent the removal of property or of evidences of indebtedness or of title to property out of the jurisdiction of the court, to restrain the committing of waste or to prevent the creation or continuation of a private nuisance or of a public nuisance particularly noxious to the party asking for injunction or to prevent illegal acts of municipal officers, etc.

Before an injunction or other equitable remedy can be obtained there must be no plain, adequate and complete remedy by a suit at law. An injunction will not be granted while the rights between the parties are undetermined except in cases where material and irreparable injury will otherwise be done. If the injury will be of a nature which cannot be compensated or irreparable and there is no adequate remedy at law an injunction will be granted which may be perpetual. The party disobeying an injunction may be punished for disobeying its process.

INJURY Any wrong, damage or mischief done or suffered. Injury may arise from nonfeasance or not fulfilling a legal obligation or duty or contract. It may arise also from misfeasance or the performance in an improper manner of an act which it was either the party's duty or his contract to perform, and by malfeasance or the unjust performance of some act which he had no right to do or which he had contracted not to do. The remedies for injuries are either preventive such as defense, resistance, recaption, abatement of nuisance, surety of peace, injunction, etc.; or for compensation, as by arbitration suit, action or summary proceedings before a magistrate; or by way of punishment, as by indictment or summary proceedings.

There are many injuries for which the law really affords no remedy, including many cases of malignant mental injury and sufferings, presumably involving no pecuniary loss. A parent for example cannot recover for an injury inflicted upon his child not involving a loss of its services even though it ruin its domestic happiness and cause him or her great mental suffering. One cannot recover for suffering occasioned by verbal slander where the facts stated are true and there can be no punishment criminally for verbal slander imputing the most infamous crimes unless done with intent to extort. Compensation is not allowed for such mental suffering it would seem, because of the uncertain character of the injury inflicted, the impossibility of properly measuring the compensation, and the danger of improper compensation being allowed.

INQUEST A judicial inquiry or examination; most commonly applied

to the inquiry made by a coroner's jury to determine the cause of death.

INQUISITION The finding of a jury; especially, the finding of a jury under a writ of inquiry.

INSANITY In law, such an impairment of the mind as prevents a person from distinguishing between right and wrong.

Of late, this word has been used to designate all mental impairments and deficiencies formerly embraced in the terms lunacy, idiocy and unsoundness of mind. Even to the middle of the eighteenth century the law recognized only two classes of persons requiring its protection on the score of mental disorder: lunatics and idiots. The former were supposed to embrace all who had lost the reason which they once possessed, and their disorder was called *dementia accidentalis;* the latter, those who had never possessed any reason, and this deficiency was called *dementia naturalis.* Lunatics were supposed to be much influenced by the moon; and another prevalent notion respecting them was that in a very large proportion there occurred lucid intervals, when the reason shone out, for a while, from behind the cloud that obscured it, with its natural brightness. It may be remembered, in passing, that lucid intervals are far less common than they were once supposed to be, and that the restoration is not so complete as the descriptions of the old writers would lead us to infer. In modern practice, the term lucid interval signifies merely a remission of the disease, an abatement of the violence of the morbid action, a period of comparative calm, and the proof of its occurrence is generally drawn from the character of the act in question. It is hardly necessary to say that this is an unjustifiable use of the term, which should be confined to the genuine lucid interval that does occasionally occur.

It began to be found at last that a large class of persons required the protection of the law, who were not idiots, because they had reason once, nor lunatics in the ordinary meaning of the term, because they were violent, exhibited no very notable derangement of reason, were independent of lunar influences, and had no lucid intervals. Their mental impairment consisted in a loss of intellectual powers, of interest in their usual pursuits and of the ability to comprehend their relations to persons and things. A new term—unsoundness of mind—was, therefore, introduced to meet this exigency; but it has never been clearly defined.

The law has never held that all lunatics and idiots are absolved from all responsibility for their civil or criminal acts. This consequence was attributed only to the severest grades of these affections,—to lunatics who have no more understanding than a brute, and to idiots who cannot number twenty pence nor tell how old they are. Theoretically the law has changed but little, even to the present day; but practically it exhibits considerable improvement; that is, while the general doctrine remains unchanged, it is qualified, in one way or another by the courts, so as to produce less practical injustice.

Insanity implies the presence of disease or congenital defect in the brain, and though it may be accompanied by disease in other organs, yet the cerebral affection is always supposed to be primary and predominant. It is to be borne in mind, however, that bodily disease may be accompanied, in some stage of its progress, by mental disorder which may affect the legal relations of the patient.

Most of the attempts to define insanity are sententious descriptions of the disease, rather than proper definitions. For all practical purposes, however, a definition is unnecessary, because the real question at issue always is, not what constitutes insanity in general, but what constitutes the insanity of a particular individual. Neither sanity nor insanity can be regarded as an entity to be handled and described but rather as a condition to be considered in reference to other conditions. Men vary in the character of their mental manifestations so much that conduct and conversation perfectly proper and natural in one might in another, differently constituted, be indicative of insanity. In determining the mental condition of a person, he must not be judged by any arbitrary standard of insanity or sanity, nor compared with other persons unquestionably sane or insane. He can properly be compared only with himself. When a person, without any adequate cause, adopts notions he once regarded as absurd, or indulges in conduct opposed to all his former habits and principles, or changes completely his ordinary temper, manners and dispositions,—the man of plain practical sense indulging in speculative theories and projects, the miser becoming a spendthrift and the spendthrift a miser, the staid, quiet, joyous citizen becoming noisy, restless, and boisterous, the gay and joyous becoming dull and disconsolate even to the verge of despair, the careful and cautious man of business plunging into hazardous schemes of speculation, the discreet and pious becoming shamefully reckless and profligate,—no stronger proof of insanity can be had. And yet not one of these traits, in and by itself alone, disconnected from the natural traits of character, could be regarded as conclusive proof of insanity. In accordance with this fact, the principle has been laid down that it is the prolonged departure, without any adequate cause, from the states of feeling and means of thinking usual to the individual when in health, which is the essential feature of insanity.

That insanity, in some of its forms, annuls all criminal responsibility, and, in the same or other forms, disqualifies its subject from the performance of certain civil acts, is a well-established doctrine of the common law. In the application of this principle there has prevailed, for many years, the utmost diversity of opinion. The law as expounded by Hale, Pleas of the Crown, 30, was received without question until the beginning of the last century. In the trial of Madfield, Mr. Erskine contended that the true test of such insanity as annulled responsibility for crime was delusion; and accordingly the prisoner was acquitted with the approbation of the court. Subsequently, in Bellingham's case, 5, Carr. and P. 168, the court declared that the prisoner was responsible if he knew right from wrong, or knew that murder was a crime against the law of God and nature. Similar language was used in other cases. This test has sometimes been modified so as to make the knowledge of right and wrong refer solely to the act in question. This was formerly pronounced to be the law of the land by the English judges, in their reply to the questions propounded by the House of Lords on the occasion of the McNaughton trial. 10 Clark & F. Hou. L. 200. A disposition to multiply the tests, so as to recognize essential facts in the nature of insanity, has been occasionally manifested in this country. In Com. vs. Rogers, 7 Metc., Mass. 500, the jury was directed to consider, in addition to the above test, whether the prisoner in committing the homicide, acted from an irresistible and uncontrollable impulse; and this case has been much relied on in American courts. Occasionally, the court has thought it sufficient for the jury to consider whether the prisoner was sane or insane—of sound memory and discretion or otherwise.

To this remarkable diversity of views may be attributed the actual diversity of results. To anyone who has followed with some attention the course of criminal justice in trials where insanity has been pleaded in defense, it is obvious that if some have been properly convicted, others have just as improperly been acquitted. It must be admitted, however, that the verdict in such cases is often determined less by the instructions of the court than by the views and feelings of the jury and the testimony of experts.

Side by side with this doctrine of the criminal law which makes the insane responsible for their criminal acts is another equally well-authorized view: that a kind and degree of insanity which would not excuse a person for a criminal act may make him legally incompetent to manage himself or his affairs. This implies that the mind of an insane person acts more clearly and deliberately, and with a sounder view of its relations to others, when about to commit a great crime than when buying or selling a piece of property. It is scarcely necessary to add that no ground for this distinction can be found in our knowledge of mental disease. On the contrary, we know that the same person who destroys his neighbor, under the delusion that he had been disturbing his peace or defaming his character, may, at the very time, dispose of his property with as correct an estimate of its value and as clear an insight into the consequences of the act as he ever had. If a person is incompetent to manage property, it is because he has lost some portion of his mental power; and this fact cannot be justly ignored in deciding upon his responsibility for criminal acts.

Insanity once admitted, it is virtually impossible to know exactly how far it may have affected the quality of his acts. To say that, possibly, it may have had no effect at all, is not enough; it should be proved by the party who affirms it.

The effect of the plea of insanity has sometimes been controlled by the instructions of the court in regard to the burden of proof and the requisite amount. The older doctrine was that the person is to be considered sane until proved beyond a doubt to be insane. Thus, in State vs. Spencer, 1 Sabr., N.J., 196, the court (S. J. Hornblower) said, "Where it is admitted, or clearly proved, that he (the prisoner) committed the act, but it is insisted that he was insane at the time,—and the evidence leaves the question of insanity in doubt,—there the jury ought to find against him." In a later case in New York it was held, all the judges concurring, "that it was an error in the judge to charge the jury that, sanity being the normal state, there is no presumption of insanity; that the burden of proving it is upon the prisoner; that a failure to prove it, like a failure to prove any other fact, is the misfortune of the party attempting the proof, and thus they must be satisfied of his insanity beyond a reasonable doubt, or otherwise must convict." So, too, in Com. vs. Rogers, 7 Metc., Mass. 500, the court (C. J. Shaw) told the jury "that if the preponderance of the evidence were in favor of his insanity,—if its bearing and leaning, as a whole, inclined that way,—they would be authorized to find him insane."

INSOLVENCY One is said to be insolvent when he is unable to pay his debts as they fall due in the usual course of trade or business. Insolvent laws are to be distinguished from bankrupt laws. The latter apply usually to traders or merchants only, the former to all classes of people. Under bankrupt laws the debts of honest debtors are discharged though not paid in full. Under insolvency laws they are not discharged except insofar as they are paid. Both contemplate a fair division of the debtor's effects among his creditors pro rata.

The Constitution of the United States gives Congress authority "to establish a uniform system of bankruptcy throughout the United States," and so long as a United States bankruptcy law may be in force it will supersede state insolvency or bankruptcy laws insofar as they conflict. Where state bankruptcy laws are in force and undertake to discharge a debtor from the obligation of his debts upon surrender of his property, this discharge will be valid in respect to creditors residing in the state, but not with respect to contracts made, or debts existing before the passage of the law, nor will it be binding in another state as against a citizen thereof.

By statute laws, insolvency is frequently of two kinds; voluntary where one of his own will turns over his property for the benefit of his creditors, and involuntary where he is driven into doing so by creditors by reason of his having fraudulently concealed his property or conveyed it away or allowed it to be attached or seized by creditors either fraudulently or for the purpose of giving them a preference. Proceedings under such statutes vary, but are similar in character to those under the United States Bankrupt Law.

INSTALLMENT BUYING AGREEMENT *See* RETAIL INSTALLMENT SALES AGREEMENT.

INSURANCE A system by which individuals pay premiums to build up funds from which themselves or their beneficiaries are compensated when death, loss or disability occurs. When the parties to a contract of insurance have reached an agreement, and all has been done which is required by the terms thereof, such as payment of premium or the like, the contract is complete even before the execution or signing and delivery of the policy, for a contract of insurance may be verbal as well as written. The usual written and printed contract merely furnishes evidence as to what the contract consists of.

If the policy, however, provides that it shall not become effective until the payment of the required premium, or that it shall cease to be effective upon non-payment of a premium at the time and in the manner designated in the policy, the insurer may treat it as inoperative until payment is made. Yet this right may be waived by the insurer by any act reasonably indicating that it will not be insisted upon, and that waiver may be either expressed or implied, orally or in writing, and it may be by the company or by its agent, and indeed the powers of the agents to bind an insurance company in dealing with the general public, are quite extensive. But, of course, if the contract itself expressly limits the power of an agent to bind the company with respect thereto, the limitation will be effective. The insured will, however, be excused from payment at the requisite time if any act of the company causes the delay or renders it impracticable for the party to make payment.

If the company is a foreign one and war breaks out between the countries of the insured and insurer, the policy will become inoperative if not entirely void during the progress of the war and premiums need not meantime be paid. A policy of insurance will be construed as favorably as possible for the party against whom it was made. If a special clause conflicts with a general one, the former will prevail; and if the printed and written portions of the policy conflict the latter will prevail. If the description of the property insured is in part incorrect, but the property can be identified from the portion of the description which is correct, the insurance will still be effective.

A policy of insurance is void unless the insured has an interest in the subject matter of the insurance, and anyone who would suffer from a destruction or loss of the subject matter has an interest such as the owner of real estate, or one who has contracted for its purchase or mortgagee or a lessee. In fact anyone having an interest may contract for the insurance of that interest. Anyone may contract for the insurance of the life of another upon whom he is dependent for support, since he has an interest in that life. Parents and children have insurable interests in the lives of each other, as have also husbands and wives. A sister and brother may or may not according to circumstances. A creditor has an interest in the life of his debtor; an employee in the life of his employer and vice versa, if the employment is of a permanent character, and a partner in that of his co-partner.

If an insurance or other contract expressly states that it is made with reference to the laws of another state or country, those laws will control it, and an application for insurance which states that it is subject to the laws of New York, though signed elsewhere, is to be interpreted and enforced in accordance with those laws.

Frequently by the terms of a policy the written application commonly made by the insured is made a part of the contract or policy. If the insured in the application guarantees or warrants the existence of a given state of facts with reference to the subject matter of the insurance, the policy is void if the statements or any portion thereof are untrue.

It may be noted, however, that a warranty that the applicant's habits are correct or temperate will not be construed as having reference to occasional transgressions. If there is a mere statement or allegation as to the fact or facts without any warranty connected with it, upon the faith of which, however, the insurance is made, the policy will not be avoided so long as the allegations are substantially true. To make void the policy they must not only be either partly or totally false at the time the contract is made but must materially affect the risk.

If questions in an application are not answered and the application is accepted in that form, the effect is the same as if the questions were not there.

The fact that application questions are not answered does not amount to an allegation that there was no answer to make. The application when in writing, is presumed to contain all the allegations of fact made by the insured, and usually evidence of oral statements will not be admitted. An error in stating the value of the property will not render the policy void unless it is shown that the misstatement was with fraudulent intent. The insurer is entitled to be informed of matters material to the risk, and if such matters are concealed and the insurer does not know of them, or does not have fair opportunity to know of them, the policy is void. Thus attempts to set fire to the property insured or adjoining property, or any matter materially affecting the risk, if it is not easily ascertainable by the insurer, should be revealed to him. Where, however, an agent of an insurance company, knowing of the existence of a fact material to the risk, fills up a blank application for the insured to sign, containing a question to which that fact is pertinent, and omits to state or misstates the fact in answer to the question, and the applicant then signs without knowing of the omission or misstatement, the company will not be released.

A notice to a general agent has the effect of a notice to the company. Unless expressly forbidden by the policy, an agent may waive conditions therein contained, and in some cases notwithstanding such prohibition, may prevent fraud upon the insured. Thus an agent may waive a requirement as to prepayment of premium, or that there shall be no other insurance, or that the premises shall not remain vacant.

One employed as a clerk by an insurance agent cannot make the agent liable to the company for loss accruing on a policy which the company forbade the agent to issue, but which the clerk issued forging the agent's name thereon.

Upon sale of real estate with insured buildings thereon, care should be taken to have the insurance transferred to the buyer with the written consent of the insurer.

INTENT The design, resolve or determination with which a person acts. Since the intent with which a person acts is a state of mind, such intent must be inferred from the facts.

INTER ALIA Among other things or matters.

INTER VIVOS Between living persons. Said of a trust created by a living person rather than by will.

INTEREST Compensation for the use of money which is due. Tenants for life must pay interest on encumbrances on the estate. Executors, administrators, assignees for the benefit of creditors, guardians and trustees who have kept money an unreasonable length of time or who have made or might have made it productive in their hands are chargeable with interest. Where money is loaned there is either an express or implied contract to pay interest, but interest will not accrue on a note until the note becomes due unless there is an express agreement to pay interest before due, and if the note is to pay a given sum "with interest" this means with interest from the date thereof.

Where for the interest and advantage of an estate an executor or administrator or trustee advances money he will be allowed interest out of the estate. If one accepts the principal in settlement of a debt where there has been no express promise to pay interest he cannot afterwards recover interest. A promise to pay interest may be implied from the previous practice of the parties. Interest may be collected on an account or other liquidated sum (that is, a sum computed or capable of definite computation), when the debtor knows previously what he is to pay and when he is to pay it, but interest is not due for unliquidated damages or ordinarily on a running account. It may be collected on arrears of an annuity secured by a specialty or given in lieu of dower.

Notes payable on demand bear interest after demand is made. If a note is payable in installments at given periods, with the provision that the whole will become due upon the failure of payment of any installment when due, interest on the whole will be collectible from the first default. Where interest is payable annually and the principal at a distant day, the interest may be recovered by separate suit as it becomes due without awaiting the recovery of the principal.

Interest will accrue on a deposit on account made by a purchaser which he is entitled to recover back, also on the price of goods sold and delivered after the customary or stipulated term of credit has expired. Judgment debts bear interest from entry of judgment or, in case of judgment entered on a judgment note, from the time provided in the note.

Interest will accrue on money obtained by fraud or wrongfully detained or paid by mistake or recovered on a void execution, or lent or laid out for another's use, also on purchase money of real estate which has lain dead because the vendor cannot or does not make a title at the time agreed upon, and on purchase money remaining in the purchaser's hands to pay off encumbrances. Rent in arrears due by covenant ordinarily bears interest which may be recovered by suit for which no distraint can be had.

On specific legacies, interest is to be calculated from the death of the testator, but on general legacies, when the time of payment is not named by the testator, it does not begin to accrue until the end of a year after his death. If only interest is bequeathed, no payment will be due until the end of the second year after the death, but where the time of payment of a general legacy is named by the testator, interest will accrue from that time. If a vested legacy is made payable at a future date with interest previously accrued and the legatee dies before it is payable, the arrears of interest to his death as well as the principal must be paid to his personal representatives. If the legatee is the legitimate child of the testator or one with respect to whom he has placed himself in *loco parentis*, though illegitimate, the legacy bears interest from the testator's death whether it is specific or residuary, vested but payable at a future time, or contingent, provided the child has no maintenance. Courts in such case do what the father may reasonably be supposed to have intended to do, that is, provide necessaries for the child. But in case of an after-born child, interest will be allowed only from its birth. If a will provides for payment of less than a legal rate of interest on legacies, this, of course, will be allowed.

Interest will not be allowed for maintenance, though there is a bequest made for that purpose, if the father of the legatee is still living under legal obligation to support him and of sufficient ability to do so. In such cases interest will accumulate until the principal becomes payable or until the legatee reaches an age when the father is not bound to support him though this rule is not without exceptions. In general it may be said that where interest has accrued in one's favor whether yet payable or not and he dies, it will go to his executors or administrators irrespective of what is to become of the principal fund. Where no time of payment is made by a testator, annuities bequeathed by him are considered as commencing from his death, the first payment to be made at the end of the one year thereafter.

In general, where debts are payable on demand, interest accrues only from the time of demand. In case of money had and received (that is, money which one by some means obtained which in justice and equity he ought to refund or pay over to another and which he cannot with a good conscience retain, as for example, where one cuts down another's timber, sells it and obtains the money), interest would accrue only from the time of the service of the writ on bringing suit. If a debt barred by a statute of limitations (commonly said to be "out of date") is revived by acknowledgment or promise to pay, it will bear interest for the whole time it is not paid.

Compound interest is not allowed except in very special cases, though in some places where executors, administrators or trustees apply trust money to their own use or employ it in business or trade, and do not invest it to earn interest, they are chargeable with compound interest. Generally the penalty of a bond limits the amount to be recovered thereon but where a plaintiff is kept out of his money for a long time by legal proceedings or if the recovery of a debt is delayed by the obligor, or if extraordinary profits are derived from withholding the money or if the bond is taken as collateral security, interest may be recovered beyond the amount of the penalty. If an agreement is made to add interest to the principal and consider it part of the principal for the future, interest thereon may, of course, be collected, or if accounts bearing interest are settled between the parties and a balance is shown to be due, interest may be collected upon it, though a portion of it is made up of interest. Compound interest actually paid, though not by law collectible, cannot be recovered. In general an agreement to pay compound interest in the future is not binding, and the collection of simple interest only can be enforced.

The law of the place where the contract is to be performed or the money is to be paid, if such place is specified, fixes the rate of interest where the rate is not fixed by the contract itself, though this cannot be more than the legal rate. If no place of performance or payment is designated the law of the place of making the contract prevails. The contract may legally provide for the lawful rate of either the place of making the contract or the place of payment. (See also CONTRACT.) A payment on a debt will be first applied to interest unless otherwise agreed upon, and when partial payments exceed the interest due when made, it is correct to compute the interest to the time of first payment, add it to the principal, subtract the payment, count interest on the remainder to time of second payment, subtract the second payment and continue in like manner. A part payment of principal before interest is due will stop accumulation of interest on the amount paid thereafter.

When money due is tendered to the person entitled to it, interest ceases. If the one claiming interest was absent in foreign parts beyond seas, this may be proven in order to extinguish interest accruing after the debt becomes due. If payment of principal is at any time prohibited by law or legal process, interest is not demandable after the prohibition. If a plaintiff has accepted the principal he cannot afterwards recover the interest by suit. Where a husband uses his wife's money, although an indebtedness may exist as to the principal, yet no interest will accrue thereon unless there be an express agreement to that effect.

The legal rate of interest that may be charged where no specific rate is mentioned varies in different places.

Interest Laws and Consumer Finance Loan Rates

Most states have laws regulating interest rates. These laws fix a legal or conventional rate which applies when there is no contract for interest. They also fix a general maximum contract rate, but there are exceptions for particular purposes including consumer finance loan laws. In many states there are so many exceptions that the general contract maximum actually applies only to exceptional cases.

The legal or conventional rate of interest applies to money obligations when no interest rate is contracted for and also to judgments. The rate is usually 6% a year, but in some states it is 5% or 7%.

All states, except Colorado, Massachusetts, and New Hampshire have general laws fixing the maximum rate of interest which may be contracted for, unless another law authorizes a higher rate. The general maximum is fixed by the state constitution in Arkansas, California, Oklahoma, Tennessee and Texas. The most common maximum rates are 6% and 8% a year, but some states permit 10% or 12%. Rhode Island permits 21%. Penalties for infraction range from forfeiture of interest to loss of the entire principal and even imprisonment. Loans to corporations are frequently exempted or subject to a higher maximum. Courts generally hold that installment sale charges are not interest, but installment sale charges are limited by laws in many states.

In many states special statutes permit industrial loan companies and banks to charge interest and fees without regard to installment payments which yield $1\frac{1}{2}$% a month or more. Credit unions may generally charge 1% a month. Pawnbrokers' rates vary widely. Building and loan associations, loans insured by the Federal Housing Administration, and frequently retail charge account credit are also specially regulated.

Under the Truth-In-Lending Act passed by Congress in 1968, consumers must be informed of the complete cost of credit. The Act also requires disclosure of interest rates in department store and catalog house revolving charge accounts, of annual interest rates in credit advertising, and of true annual interest rates of first mortgages on housing. Loan-sharking is banned. Those who feel their legal rights have been violated in this area should consult the U.S. District Attorney's office, usually located in the Federal Post Office Building in the city or county concerned.

Consumer finance loan statutes are based on early models drafted by the Russell Sage Foundation (1916–1942) to provide small loans to wage earners under license and other protective regulations. In general, licensed lenders may charge 2½% or 3% a month for $300 or less and reduced rates for additional amounts up to $1,000, $1,500 or more. A number of states permit add-on rates of 17% to 20% ($17 to $20 per $100) a year of the original principal for $300 and lower rates for additional amounts. An add-on of 17% ($17 per $100) per year yields about 2½% per month when the loan is paid in equal monthly installments. In the table following unless otherwise stated, monthly rates are based on reducing principal balances, annual add-on rates are based on the original principal for the full term, and two or more rates apply to different portions of balance or original principal.

The states with consumer finance loan laws and the rates of charge as of October 1, 1968, are as follows:

State	Maximum Rate
	(Monthly unless otherwise stated)
Alabama	3% to $200, 2% to $300. Special rate up to $75.
Alaska	4% to $300, 2½% to $600, 2% to $1,000; 5% for loans up to $50.
Arizona	3% to $300, 2% to $600, 1% to $1,000.
California	2½% to $200, 2% to $500, 1½% to $700, 1% to $5,000.
Colorado	3% to $300, 1½% to $500, 1% to $1,500.
Connecticut	Annual Add-on: 17% to $300, 9% to $1,000.
Dist. of Columbia	1% to $200.
Florida	3% to $300, 2% to $600.
Hawaii	3½% to $100, 2½% to $300.
Idaho	3% to $300, 2% to $500, 1% to $1,000.
Illinois	3% to $150, 2% to $300, 1% to $800.
Indiana	3% to $150, 2% to $300, 1½% to $1,000.
Iowa	3% to $150, 2% to $300, 1½% to $700, 1% to $1,000.
Kansas	3% to $300, ⅚% to $2,100.
Kentucky	3% to $150, 2% to $600, 1% to $800; or annual add-on of 20% to $150; 15% to $600, 11% to $800.
Louisiana	3½% to $150, 2½% to $300.
Maine	2½% to $300, 1½% to $2,000; 25c minimum.
Maryland	3% to $300, 2% to $500.
Massachusetts	2½% to $200, 2% to $600; 1¾% to $1,000, ¾% to $3,000.
Michigan	2½% to $300, 1¼% to $1,000.
Minnesota	2¾% to $300, 1½% to $600, 1¼% to $900.
Mississippi	Interest and service charges combined exceed 3% per month.
Missouri	2.218% to $500, 8% per annum on any remainder.
Montana	Annual Add-on: 20% to $300, 16% to $500, 12% to $1,000. Special rate to $90.
Nebraska	30% per annum to $300, 24% to $500, 18% to $1,000, 12% to $3,000.

Nevada	Annual Add-on: 9% to $1,000, 8% to $2,500; monthly fee of 1% on first $200, and ½% on next $200.
New Hampshire	2% to $600, 1½% to $1,500, 1½% on larger loans to $5,000.
New Jersey	24% per annum to $500, 22% to $1,000.
New Mexico	3% to $150, 2½% to $300, 1% to $1,000.
New York	2½% to $100, 2% to $300, ¾% to $800.
North Carolina	Annual Add-on: 20% to $100, 18% to $200, 15% to $300, 6% to $600. Special rates up to $75.
North Dakota	2½% to $250, 2% to $500, 1¾% to $750, 1½% to $1,000.
Ohio	Annual Add-on: 16% to $500, 9% to $1,000, 7% to $2,000; or equivalent simple interest rate.
Oklahoma	10% per annum plus various fees to $300.
Oregon	3% to $300, 2% to $500, 1% to $1,500.
Pennsylvania	3% to $150, 2% to $300, 1% to $600.
Puerto Rico	Annual Add-on: 20% to $300, 7% to $600.
Rhode Island	3% to $300; 2½% for loans between $300 and $800; 2% for larger loans to $2,500.
South Carolina	Annual Add-on: 20% to $100, 18% to $300, 9% to $1,000; 7% for larger loans to $7,500, plus service fee. Special rate to $150.
South Dakota	3% to $300, ¾% to $2,500; $2 minimum.
Tennessee	6% per annum plus 4% fee; no size limit.
Texas	Annual Add-on: 18% to $300, 8% to $2,500. Special rates to $100.
Utah	3% to $300, 1% to $600.
Vermont	2½% to $125, 2¼% to $300, 1% to $600.
Virginia	2½% to $300, 1½% to $1,000; or annual add-on of 17% to $300, 12% to $1,000.
Washington	3% to $300, 1½% to $500, 1% to $1,000; $1 minimum.
West Virginia	3% to $200, 2% to $600, 1½% to $800; or annual add-on of 19% to $200, 16% to $600, 12% to $800.
Wisconsin	2½% to $100, 2% to $200, 1% to $300.
Wyoming	3½% to $150, 2½% to $300, 1% to $1,000; plus $1. for loans up to $50.

INTERLOCUTORY DECREE A preliminary or intermediate decree; a decree which does not determine the suit, but directs some further proceedings before a final decree can be had. A decree pronounced for the purpose of ascertaining matter of law or fact preparatory to a final decree.

INTERNATIONAL LAW Rules of action recognized by enlightened nations in their relations with each other. These rules are established either by common consent, practice or by treaty.

When two nations are at war other nations are bound to observe neutrality between them. Territory of the neutral may not be occupied by either belligerent for war purposes. The rule of neutrality is extended so far as to impose upon each nation the duty of restraining its own subjects or citizens in lending aid to either of the belligerents, and such violations of neutrality as preparing expeditions or vessels or "privateering" against a belligerent are made crimes against the neutral country. Yet an individual citizen may leave his country with the intention of enlisting without offending against the neutrality laws.

When nations are at war contracts between citizens of the respective parties, as well as their allies, are suspended and become unenforceable and further valid contracts are made impossible. Where debts already exist when war begins they are not usually considered forfeited. Citizens or subjects of nations at war are all treated as enemies, and property of an enemy seized at sea is liable to confiscation. Property seized on land is not usually confiscated unless a necessity therefor exists, either for the purpose of weakening and exhausting the enemy or for other cause. When hostilities commence it is usual to allow vessels and cargoes of the enemy a reasonable time to depart before seizure.

Intercourse between belligerents under truce is recognized under the law of nations for mutual necessary convenience, and a violation of good faith in this connection gives the injured party a right to impose punishments upon the other not ordinarily considered proper. An armistice usually involves an agreement by both parties to remain temporarily as if in a state of peace, and for violation each belligerent will punish offenders within its own ranks. Unless so expressly agreed, however, supplies may be increased and fortifications not under siege may be repaired or erected. A passport gives the individual to whom it is issued safe passage in the enemy's territory.

Implements and munitions of war and things in general much used in the conduct of war are contraband and liable to confiscation if captured, and if found in a vessel which by treaty is prohibited from carrying contraband goods, the vessel itself is liable to confiscation. Materials used in making gunpowder or in constructing vessels, wagons, harness, coal, money and iron in a form suitable for war purposes are some of the things which are considered contraband. Articles used simply for food are not commonly included in this category, though what is contraband may vary somewhat with the circumstances.

Neutral vessels which are not ships of war may be stopped and searched by a belligerent to determine whether or not they carry contraband goods, and such a vessel has no right to resist, but may not be subjected to more detention than is necessary to make the required examination. If neutral goods, not contraband in their character, are found on a belligerent ship they are ordinarily not liable to confiscation, but the burden is upon the owner to prove that they are neutral, and any ship carrying a hostile flag is treated as a belligerent.

A belligerent has the right to blockade an enemy's port as against neutrals, but in order to keep neutral vessels from passing to and fro there must be a genuine and actual blockade which the belligerent is capable of maintaining, and the port must be in a closed state with respect to the enemy's vessels. If the blockading fleet is driven away temporarily by a storm a neutral vessel has no right to take advantage of it, but if driven away by the enemy they will have the right to enter until the blockade is re-established and the neutral is notified. A breach of a blockade or sailing with intent to make such a breach renders the vessel and cargo liable to confiscation if captured. A neutral vessel in an enemy's port when blockaded may come out in ballast, but may not carry a cargo from the hostile country.

A neutral vessel carrying enemies belonging to the military, or carrying dispatches for the enemy, or one chartered or loaned to and in use by a belligerent or the belligerent's subjects or citizens may be confiscated by the opposing belligerent. Prizes captured must be brought to port and subjected to condemnation proceedings, parties interested having an opportunity to contest the condemnation. Where a capture is made by a vessel belonging to a fleet, the capture is considered to be by the whole fleet and the prize money must be divided accordingly.

INTERPLEADER A mode of obtaining the settlement of a question of right to certain property or money adversely claimed by compelling the parties claiming it to interplead, that is, to litigate the title between themselves, for the benefit and relief of a third person of whom they claim.

INTERPRETATION All sound interpretation of contracts, statutes, wills, etc., is based upon good faith and good sense. The purpose in all interpretation or construction is to learn the intention of the party or parties. Words must be taken to mean what those who used them intended, that is, they must actually have their proper and ordinary significance, but technical terms are mostly intended to have their technical meaning. If words have two senses one of which is agreeable to law and the other not, the former must prevail, and if one is inconsistent with the apparent intention it will be rejected. If words are inadvertently omitted and the meaning is obvious they will be supplied.

An intent to do or require an impossible, illegal, immoral, or fraudulent thing or things against public policy will not be presumed where the words will permit of any other possible construction. The subject matter, nature of the context or the situation of the parties and the laws or customs of the place or in a particular trade where, or in connection with which a contract is made must sometimes be consulted in order to arrive at the meaning intended to be conveyed. The meaning to be gathered from the instrument as a whole will control rather than that to be obtained from a particular part, and effect must be given to every part of the instrument if possible. If one part is totally repugnant to all the rest, it will be stricken out, but not if it is merely explanatory or is intended to limit the operation of the whole.

Words spoken cannot vary the terms of a written instrument for the written instrument is supposed to contain the final agreement of the parties, though in cases where its enforcement would operate as a fraud, verbal statements made at the time may be proven to overthrow the agreement or even to amend it, and where there is a latent ambiguity in the contract, that is, one which does not appear in the instrument itself but would only be shown by a revelation of the circumstances to which the language applies, such explanation may be furnished by verbal proof.

Where there is doubt as to the meaning, an agreement will be construed most strongly against the party benefited. Penal and criminal statutes will be construed most strictly and not beyond their plain meaning. Generally the construction given to statutes in the country or state where enacted will be adopted elsewhere.

General expressions used in a contract will be controlled somewhat and limited by the special provisions therein. Agreements relating to real property are made with reference to the law existing where the property is situated, and their meaning is supposed to be in consonance with such law. Agreements on personal property are made and interpreted in consonance with the law where the contract is to be performed, or, if the place of performance is not fixed, in consonance with the law of the place where the contract is made, which is in such case presumed to be the place of intended performance.

If there are two clauses in a deed which cannot stand together the first prevails. In a will the rule is directly to the contrary. In all instruments the written part controls the printed. A grant of a thing carries with it whatever is essential to its use and enjoyment.

Parties binding themselves are presumed to bind their personal representatives, that is, executors and administrators, in case of death. When no time is mentioned a reasonable time is meant and in general it may be said that reasonable things are presumed to be intended. It devolves upon the court to interpret the meaning of written instruments, written evidence and foreign laws, and to instruct the jury as to such meaning.

INTERROGATORIES A series of formal written questions to be answered by a party to a suit.

INTERSTATE COMMERCE Traffic, trade or transportation of persons or property between the states of the United States.

INTESTACY The state of an intestate; the condition of a party who dies without having made a will.

INTESTATE One dying without leaving a will.

INVENTORY A detailed account of the property of a deceased person. When one dies or makes a surrender of his property for creditors an inventory of the personal estate and sometimes of real estate also, together with an appraisement must be filed in the proper office. Where one dies without a will the inventory generally includes the personal property only. Claims due the estate should be classified, those which are desperate or bad being so returned, or, better still, both movable personal property and claims, including book accounts, notes, bonds, stocks, mortgages, judgments, and . the like, should be set forth severally and separately and valued separately at whatever sum the appraisers think they are worth or would sell for.

Legatees or next of kin should be notified of the appraisement and have an opportunity to attend. The appraisers are sworn to perform their duties with fidelity and to the best of their judgment.

INVOLUNTARY MANSLAUGHTER

Unlawfully killing a human being in the commission of an illegal act not amounting to felony; or the commission of a legal act which might produce death illegally or without due care and caution. (*See also* MANSLAUGHTER.) The unintentional killing of a trespasser is involuntary manslaughter, sometimes called manslaughter in the second degree.

IPSO FACTO
By the fact itself; by the very fact; by the act itself.

IRREPARABLE DAMAGE OR INJURY
Irreparable does not mean such injury as is beyond the possibility of repair, but it does mean that it is so constant and frequent in occurrence that no fair or reasonable redress can be had in a court of law. Thus, the plaintiff must seek a remedy in equity by way of an injunction.

IRRIGATION
The artificial watering of land. Riparian owners have a right to what is termed a reasonable use of flowing water for the purposes of irrigation. Regard, however, must be had to the rights and needs of all other proprietors on the same stream. What the extent of the use may be, that is, what is reasonable in each particular case, depends upon the circumstances connected with the case, and where a dispute arises, is a matter of fact to be determined by a proper tribunal. Generally speaking it would seem that one in using the water for purposes of irrigation may not deprive another of the use of the same for domestic purposes and for watering stock, such uses being superior to all others. One riparian owner may not take all or too great a portion of the water for irrigation to the detriment of the established rights of others, and no one may waste water that others having common rights with himself need. (*See also* RIPARIAN OWNERS.)

A prior right to the waters of a stream for irrigation purposes may be acquired by prior appropriation which under various statutory enactments must usually be evidenced by certain acts or proceedings. The right once vesting, will be maintained and upheld, but it would appear that the right from prior appropriation will not be exclusive or superior to the rights of other riparian owners with respect to the quantity of water to be consumed except where there is statutory authority therefor.

ISSUE (IN PLEADING)
The purpose of pleading in a court proceeding is to find the "issue": that is, a point which is affirmed on one side and denied on the other.

JEOPARDY The danger to which a prisoner is exposed when he is legally charged with a crime before a court competent to try him.

JETTISON Casting cargo overboard from a ship in order to lighten a vessel in extreme danger.

JOINDER OF ACTIONS The uniting of several causes of action in one suit.

JOINDER OF ISSUE In pleading, the arrival of the parties at a material disputed fact.

JOINDER OF PARTIES The joining of several litigants as co-plaintiffs or co-defendants in a single suit.

JOINT ADVENTURE When two persons enter into a single enterprise for their mutual benefit without the intention of continuous pursuit, they have entered a joint adventure. They are essentially partners.

JOINT AND SEVERAL A phrase used when a number of persons are so obligated that any one of them or all of them may be sued at the creditor's option.

JOINT BANK ACCOUNT A bank account of two persons so fixed that they are joint owners during their mutual lives, and the survivor takes the whole on the death of the other.

JOINT TENANCY A joint holding; a union or conjunction of interest in land or other property.

JOINT TENANTS Joint holders; persons who hold an estate or property jointly.

JOINT TORT-FEASORS When two persons commit an injury with a common intent, they are joint tort-feasors.

JOINT WILL A joint will is a single will of two or more persons. A mutual will is one by which each testator makes a testamentary disposition in favor of the other.

JOINTLY Acting together or in concert or cooperating; holding in common or interdependently, not separately. Persons are "jointly bound" in a bond or note when both or all must be sued in one action for its enforcement, not either one at the election of the creditor.

JOINTLY AND SEVERALLY Persons who find themselves "jointly and severally" in a bond or note may all be sued together for its enforcement, or the creditor may select any one or more as the object of his suit.

JOINTURE An estate in land secured to a wife, to start at her husband's death and to continue for at least her life.

JUDGE One who presides at the

300

rial of cases involving matters in which the public is interested. Judges are either appointed by the government of a state or elected by the people. Impartiality is the first duty of a judge. If he has the slightest interest in a cause he is disqualified from sitting as judge, and if aware of the interest he should himself refuse to sit. It seems to be discretionary with him whether he will sit in a cause in which he has formerly been counsel though he will generally in such cases refuse to sit, delicacy if not the law forbidding.

It is the duty of a judge to expound the law, not to make it, while acting within the bounds of his jurisdiction. He is not responsible for any error of judgment or mistake he may make as judge though if he acts wrongfully or is guilty of misconduct in office he may be impeached. He cannot act as witness in a case being tried before him.

JUDGMENT The decision or sentence of the law given by a court of justice or other competent tribunal as the result of proceedings instituted therein. Final judgments are said to be conclusive as to the rights of the parties so that no other suit can be brought for the same subject matter either in the same or another court. This does not apply in case of a judgment of non-suit against a plaintiff, which occurs where a plaintiff has failed to adduce evidence to support his allegations, or where he voluntarily suffers such a judgment to be entered against him.

A judgment which concludes a party will conclude those also in privity with him, such as his heirs or his executors or administrators, his grantee or lessee or any person substituted in place of himself with respect to the subject matter of the suit. A judgment of a court of competent jurisdiction cannot be impeached or set aside in any collateral proceeding, that is, any proceeding other than the one in which the judgment is obtained, except on the ground of fraud. If attacked on other grounds than fraud it must be done by a party to the suit in which it was rendered or by one in privity with him, and this must be done by carrying the case to a higher court or by an attempt to open or strike off the judgment, in which cases the attack will be a part of or an addition to the original proceeding and not in another suit. As to matters of defense, however, arising after judgment has been rendered and working a discharge of the judgment, such as payment, proceedings may be had either to secure the entry of satisfaction on the record thereof or to prevent execution from issuing thereon.

All judgments must be regularly docketed and an index must be kept, and such docketing and index operate as notice to all purchasers and encumbrancers of land upon which the judgment is a lien, and to all subsequent judgment creditors, of the existence and amount of the judgment. If the one upon whom devolves the duty of entering and indexing the judgments makes an error, therein causing injury or loss to such purchaser or encumbrancer or subsequent judgment creditor, he is liable in damages.

The status of judgments as liens varies in the different states. A judgment in a civil suit for the recovery of money is made in many states a lien upon the land from time of entry.

JUDGMENT IN PERSONAM A judgment against a person directing the defendant to do or not to do something, is a judgment *in personam*.

JUDGMENT IN REM A judgment against a thing, as distinguished from a judgment against a person.

JUDGMENT LIEN The statutory lien upon the real property of a judgment debtor created by the judgment itself. At common law a judgment imposes no lien upon the real property of the judgment debtor and to subject the property of the debtor to the judgment it was necessary to take out an elegit.

JUDGMENT NOTES AND AMICABLE CONFESSION OF JUDGMENT In some jurisdictions promissory notes are made use of to each of which is appended a confession of judgment for the sum therein named or a power of warrant of attorney to another to appear and confess judgment without the commencement of a suit. It not infrequently contains a number of stipulations to be annexed to the judgment, such as the waiver of the benefit of laws exempting property from attachment or sale on execution and of laws granting stay of execution and the right of appeal and the like. In other places it is common to file an amicable confession of judgment not associated with a promissory note.

JUDGMENT N.O.V. Judgment notwithstanding the verdict. Under certain circumstances the judge has the power to enter a judgment which is contrary to the verdict of the jury.

JUDICIAL SALE A judicial sale is a sale authorized by a court that has jurisdiction to grant such authority. Such sales are conducted by an officer of the court.

JUDICIAL WRIT A writ issuing under the private seal of a court, and tested in the name of the chief or senior justice.

JURY A group of persons, usually twelve, sworn to listen to the evidence at a trial and pronounce a true verdict. Trial by jury is guaranteed by the Constitution of the United States in all criminal cases except upon impeachments, and in all suits at common law where the subject matter of controversy exceeds $20.00 in value, but some state constitutions fix the limit at less than $20.00. Jurors must be possessed with such qualifications as may be prescribed by statute, must be free from any bias caused by relationship to the parties or interest in the matter in dispute, and in criminal cases must not have formed any opinion as to the guilt or innocence of the accused.

Jurors must be selected impartially. Their duties are limited to determining the facts in civil cases and the guilt or innocence of the party in criminal cases and if they exceed those duties their verdict may be set aside.

JUSTICE OF THE PEACE A judicial officer of inferior rank having limited jurisdiction in civil and criminal proceedings. Justices of the Peace are usually appointed by the Governors of the various states, but are sometimes elected.

A Justice of the Peace may personally arrest an offender in a case of felony or breach of the peace committed in his presence or may command others to do so, and in order to prevent the riotous consequences of a tumultuous assembly may command others to arrest when the affray has been committed in his presence.

The Constitution of the United States directs that no warrant shall issue but upon probable cause supported by oath or affirmation. So, if the magistrate is not present when a crime is committed, before he can take a step to secure the arrest of the offender an oath or affirmation must be made by some person that the offense has been committed by the person charged or that there is probable cause to believe he committed it. The justice then issues a warrant for the arrest of the alleged offender who is brought before him and, after hearing, is discharged, held to bail to answer the complaint, or for want of bail, committed to prison. Justices under local statute laws have jurisdiction in many minor civil cases and in suits for fines and penalties, with a right of appeal annexed thereto unless the amount claimed is very small.

A Justice of the Peace is also permitted to marry people in some states.

JUSTIFIABLE HOMICIDE The killing of a human creature without fault or blame, even in the minutest degree; as when it is required by the absolute command of the law, or permitted for the advancement of public justice, or the prevention of some atrocious crime. In these instances, the slayer is to be totally acquitted and discharged, with commendation rather than blame.

JUSTIFICATION A valid defense to an action; a proof made by sureties that they are responsible in the amount of the bond which they have executed.

JUVENILE COURT Special courts having jurisdiction over delinquent and neglected children.

K

KIDNAPPING The forcible abduction or stealing away of a person, either for money or for some other unlawful purpose. *Every* case of kidnapping is also a case of false imprisonment.

KITE CHECKS To execute and deliver a check in payment of a debt at a time when the drawer has insufficient money in the bank, but with the intention of making a deposit to cover the shortage before the check is presented for payment.

KLEPTOMANIA An irresistible impulse to steal.

L

LACHES Slackness, negligence or remissness. Neglect to make a claim within a reasonable time.

LANDLORD The owner of property to whom a tenant pays rent.

LANDLORD AND TENANT A landlord is one who owns property; the tenant is his lessee. The relation of landlord and tenant may arise through express contract called a lease or by necessary implication as when there is ownership of land on the one hand, and an occupation of it by permission on the other. This occupancy will raise a presumption that the occupant intends to compensate the owner for the use of the premises, which, however, may be rebutted by proof of a contrary intention. Actual payment of rent is an acknowledgment of the existence of the relation of landlord and tenant.

If a term of lease has expired and a tenant holds over, the landlord may, if he chooses consider him a tenant, and he is presumed to be such unless the landlord proceed to eject him promptly. If the landlord receives rent from him this is an acknowledgment of a further tenancy and a renewal for the year of the old contract of lease.

A mere participation in the profits of land or working it upon shares where the owner is not excluded from possession, does not make one a lessee, for there may be an agreement to pay one for the work he does by a portion of the crop or profits. This is no lease. In order to constitute a lease or create the relationship of landlord and tenant there must be an agreement on the part of the tenant to pay for the use of the land either in money or in part of the crops that he may raise or other valuable consideration. One is not a tenant if he agrees to purchase land, moves on it, and the purchase afterwards falls through, and he cannot be charged with rent and converted into a tenant without his consent.

The rights and obligations of the parties begin from the date of the lease if there is one, if no other time for its commencement is mentioned therein. If the lease is not dated it begins from the delivery of the papers. If there is no writing it takes effect upon the date the tenant enters into possession. The right of possession with all the rights and obligations incident thereto remain in a landlord until the tenant enters and takes possession. Before such entry, injuries incident to the possession fall on the owner. After entry they are on the tenant and he may recover damages therefor. After entry the interest of the landlord is termed his reversionary interest and even after the entry of the tenant he will be entitled to damages therefor, that is, he will be entitled to damages for injury that will affect him after the termination of the lease, such as breaking windows, cutting timber or damming up a stream whereby the timber will be spoiled. If one interferes with his tenant's use of the property so far as to cause him loss of rent he may recover damages therefor.

The landlord may go upon the premises peaceably to learn whether waste or injury has been committed, first giving notice of his intention. He may also do so to demand rent, make necessary repairs or remove obstructions and may make use of all ways appurtenant to the premises. If he is to receive a part of the produce by way of rent he may not go upon the land and take it until delivered to him by the tenant or until reserved and set apart for his use.

If, during the tenancy, a stranger is injured by the ruinous state of the premises or by the tenant's negligent use of the property as where he negligently permits snow to fall on a passer-by, or if the tenant creates a nuisance on them, the landlord is not responsible unless he had undertaken to keep the premises in repair or unless he should renew the lease with a nuisance then upon it.

There is in every lease an implied guaranty that the tenant shall not be deprived of his possession of the whole or any material part of the premises by one having a title paramount to that of the landlord. Also, the landlord must not himself disturb or render his occupation uncomfortable by the erection of a nuisance on or near his premises, or otherwise oblige him to quit the possession, but if the tenant is molested by a third person or is ousted by one having no title the landlord is not responsible.

In the absence of express agreement to the contrary the landlord must pay all taxes, ground rent and interest on mortgages and judgments to which the property is subjected, and if the tenant is compelled to make any payment which the landlord should have made, as for example, to prevent seizure or sale of his (the tenant's) goods on the premises for taxes, he may demand the same from the landlord or deduct it from the rent.

If a tenant covenants to pay rent as stated in his lease but no place of payment is mentioned, he must seek out the lessor on the day the rent falls due and tender him the money. It is not sufficient that he was on the premises on the day when the rent came due ready to pay, and that the latter does not come to receive it.

Unless otherwise stipulated the landlord is not required to make repairs, and the tenant having once taken possession is liable for rent though the house is uninhabitable, since he is bound to judge before entering, whether or not the house suits him. An agreement to keep the premises in repair is construed to mean in as good repair as when leased; yet a covenant to keep in good repair will require him to keep a roof so that the building will be habitable though it was out of repair at the time of the lease. If a building is destroyed by fire during the term, the landlord will not be required to rebuild and may still collect the rent. The landlord in such cases loses the house and building and the tenant the use of it. Even if the landlord recovers insurance money the case is not altered and the tenant cannot compel him to use the money in rebuilding. It is even said that though the landlord may have covenanted to repair the tenant cannot leave the premises and escape payment of rent because repairs are not made unless there is an express agreement to that effect, the agreement to repair and the agreement to pay rent being, it seems, independent of each other and the subject of separate suits in case of non-fulfillment of either.

The tenant is entitled to all the privileges and easements appurtenant to the property and, unless an express provision is made with relation thereto, he may have such wood as is sufficient and necessary for his fuel, fences and other agricultural operations and after the termination of his tenancy may take away such annual products as may have resulted from his care and labor. He may sue the landlord or any other person causing him injury by disturbing his possession or illegally trespassing upon the premises.

The tenant is liable for neglect to repair highways, fences or walls where the duty of such repair is imposed upon the occupant. He is liable for injury resulting from the mismanagement or negligence of his employees or from a nuisance maintained by him on the premises or for an obstruction of the highway adjacent to them, and in general must so manage the property as not to injure others. If, for example, in repairing the building he does not properly provide against accidents to persons passing he will be liable for the injury. While repairing a roof the landlord must exercise reasonable care to protect the tenant within and his property and he cannot shift the responsibility upon a contractor who does the work. As to obstructions, the law allows the occupant to create only such partial and temporary obstruction of a street as may be necessary for business purposes, as in receiving and delivering goods and the like.

The landlord is bound to inform his tenant, before contracting with him, of latent defects which would make the premises dangerous or unhealthful if he knows of them, or if with proper diligence he should know of them, and will be liable for damages resulting to the tenant who was unaware of them, or who failed to discover them upon examining the premises.

If the amount of rent is not fixed by the lease or there is no express verbal agreement, the amount the premises are fairly worth may be collected from the time the tenant had the beneficial enjoyment of the premises. If there is an express agreement to pay during the term, no injury by fire or otherwise and nothing short of an eviction will excuse him from payment. If there is an eviction or if he is deprived of possession of the premises or any part therof by a third person under title superior to that of his landlord, or if the landlord annoys his tenant or erects or causes the erection of a nuisance on or near the premises such as to render hi occupation so uncomfortable as to justify his removal, he is discharged from the obligation to pay rent.

The tenant must return the property to the landlord at the end of the term unimpaired by any wilful or negligent conduct on his part. If a building is leased for specific purposes but used for other purposes but more dangerous with respect to fire, and a fire results, the tenant will be liable for the loss. He is bound to make fair repairs, such as keeping fences in order and replacing doors and windows that are broken during his term. If he has leased the house furnished, he must exercise due care in preserving the furniture and leave it clean and in good order, but he is not bound to rebuild premises which have by fire or accident become ruined, or to provide against wear and tear, or to put a new roof on a building, or to make what would be termed general or substantial repairs, or generally, to do painting, whitewashing or papering. As to farming leases, the duty of repairs above-mentioned would seem to apply to the dwelling house, the repairing of out-buildings and other erections depending upon what is the common custom in the neighborhood. The tenant is also bound to cultivate the farm in a husbandman-like manner, to keep the fences in repair and preserve timber and ornamental trees.

When the landlord sells his property, the rent subsequently accumulating is payable to the vendee or buyer, and if he sells part or different parts of it, the rent must be apportioned among the owners of the several portions. The tenant's consent to an apportionment made by the landlord is necessary unless the proportion of rent chargeable upon each portion of the land has been settled by legal proceedings. If a tenant, however, subleases a portion of his land he is still liable to the landlord for the whole. If the landlord dies and the land descends to several heirs the tenant must pay each rent thereafter accruing, proportioned to the quantity of his interest in the property. The widow, if there is one, receives an amount equivalent to her dower interest, in most places one-third for life.

The tenant's rights will not be altered by sale of the property by the landlord nor will the tenant be relieved of his responsibility by transferring his lease without the landlord's consent. In the one case the purchaser becomes the landlord with the same rights and remedies against the tenant that the original landlord had, and in the other the purchaser of the lease assumes all the liabilities and is entitled to the same protection as the original lessee, without, however, the original lessee being discharged from his obligation.

If the tenancy is for life it will, of course, terminate upon the death of the person upon whose life the lease depends. If it is for a given number of years, it will expire in the last year of the tenancy, at the last moment of the anniversary of the day from which the tenant was to hold, and in such case no notice to quit will be necessary unless there are statutory requirements to the contrary. A tenancy from year to year or at will can only be terminated by a notice to quit in writing which must be explicit and require the tenant to remove from the premises, and must be served upon the tenant and not upon a sub-tenant, and the notice must be in form to the person leasing and not to his agent. If only one tenant in common (owner) of the land gives such notice it is valid only to the extent of his share. Statute laws usually regulate the length of the notice. At common law it was six calendar months, ending with the period of the year at which the tenancy began. The time is the same in most of the states. In others three months' notice only is required.

The lease will be forfeited only in case of breach of some express stipulation contained in the contract, as for the commission of waste, non-payment of rent and the like. A forfeiture may be waived by subsequent acceptance of rent or distraining for the rent or by giving notice to quit in the usual way or by any act acknowledging the continuance of the tenancy, and the courts will afford relief against forfeiture in all cases where it happens accidentally, and the injury is capable of compensation or where the damages are a mere matter of computation.

If a tenant purchases the property there will be a merger of the tenancy in the greater estate which he has purchased, thus dissolving the tenancy, but the purchase must be for the tenant's own self and for his own proper use. For if the land simply vests in him for the use of another, as trustee, the tenancy will continue.

A lease may be terminated by surrender with the consent of the landlord, by the entire destruction of the thing leased, or if it is taken for public uses. The landlord may consider the lease at an end if the tenant converts the house into a house of ill fame or if he disclaims to hold under the landlord, refusing to pay him rent and asserting that he himself or some other person is the owner. When the tenancy has terminated, the right of possession reverts to the landlord. He may again take possession of the premises if he can do so without violence or a breach of the peace. He must not, however, resort to forcible entry, but in a case of resistance should resort to proper legal process to obtain possession by a suit at law or a proceeding before a magistrate.

On obtaining peaceable possession of the premises in the absence of the tenant who is in default in the payment of rent, and upon whom was served a proper notice to quit, the landlord may defend his possession thus acquired with such reasonable force as is necessary.

The tenant after quitting the premises may usually remove fixtures erected by himself for his own purposes.

The ordinary common law remedy to recover possession is an action of ejectment, and in this suit the tenant will not be allowed to set up against his landlord a title acquired by himself during his tenancy hostile to that which he acknowledged in accepting the premises under the landlord. This procedure is so slow that, almost universally, statute laws have been passed enabling the landlord to obtain possession by a more summary and rapid procedure before a magistrate.

LEASE OF A DWELLING HOUSE

Indenture made this 1 day of June, 19___, between John Doe, hereinafter called the lessor, which expression shall include his heirs and assigns, where the context so requires or admits, and Richard Roe, hereinafter called the lessee, which expression shall include the executors, administrators, and assigns, where the context so requires or admits. The said lessor doth hereby demise and lease unto the said lessee a certain dwelling house situate in the city of Louisville, Kentucky, and numbered 4000 N. Western Parkway. To hold the premises hereby demised unto said lessee from the day of the date hereof for the term of 3 years, the said lessee paying therefor the rent of $3,600.00 for each and every year, and in the same proportion for any part of a year, by equal quarterly payments on the first days of September, December, March, and June in every year, the first of such payments to be made on the 1 day of September next. And the said lessee doth covenant with the lessor:

1. That he will, during the continuance of the term hereby granted, pay said rent hereinbefore reserved at the times at which the same is made payable;

2. That he will also from time to time during said term, pay all taxes, charges, and water rates which may be assessed upon the demised premises, or on the owner or occupier, in respect thereof, and that he will not suffer nor commit any waste of the premises;

3. That he will, during the said term, keep the said premises in good and tenantable repair, externally and internally, reasonable wear and tear excepted;

4. That he will make no alterations or additions to or upon said premises without the consent of the said lessor being first obtained in writing;

5. That he will not assign this lease nor underlet the said premises, or any part thereof, without such previous consent in writing (but such consent shall not be unreasonably or arbitrarily withheld to an assignment or underletting of said premises to a respectable and a responsible person);

6. That the lessor or his agents may, at reasonable times, enter upon said premises to examine the condition of the same;

7. That he will at the termination of said tenancy, quietly yield up the said premises, with the fixtures which are now or at any time during said term shall be thereon, in as good and tenantable conditions, in all respects, reasonable wear and use and damage by fire and other unavoidable casualties excepted, as the same now are.

Provided always, and these presents are upon the condition, that if said rent, or any part thereof, shall at any time be in arrear or unpaid, or if the lessee shall at any time fail or neglect to perform or observe any of the covenants, conditions, or agreements herein contained and on his part to be performed and observed, or if the lessee shall become bankrupt or insolvent or shall compound with his creditors, then and in any such case it shall be lawful for the lessor or any person or persons duly authorized by him in that behalf, without any formal notice or demand, to enter into and upon said demised premises, or any part thereof, in the name of the whole, and the said premises peaceably to hold and enjoy thenceforth as if these presents had not been made, without any prejudice to any right of action or remedy of the lessor in respect of any antecedent breach of any of the covenants by the lessee hereinbefore contained.

Provided also, that in case said buildings and premises, or any part thereof, shall at any time be destroyed or damaged by fire or other unavoidable casualty, so that the same shall be unfit for occupation or use, then the rent hereby reserved, or a fair and just proportion thereof, according to the nature and extent of the damage sustained, shall be suspended and cease to be payable until said premises shall be rebuilt or made fit for occupation and use by the said lessor, or these presents shall thereby be determined and ended, at the election of the said lessor.

In Testimony Whereof we have set our signatures.

_____
                                        LESSOR

_____
                                        LESSEE

_____
WITNESS

LEASE OF A HOUSE, WITH USE OF FURNITURE, PLATE, LINEN, ETC.

Agreement made this 1 day of June, 19____, between John Doe hereinafter called the landlord, of the one part, and Richard Roe hereinafter called the tenant, of the other part. The landlord agrees to let and the tenant agrees to take the house situate and being No. 4667 Park Heights Ave., in the City of Baltimore, State of Maryland, with the outbuildings, stable, garden, and appurtenances thereto belonging, together with the use of the fixtures, furniture, plate, linen, utensils and effects particularly mentioned in the schedule hereunder written; and also with the right to such produce of the garden as the tenant shall require for the use of himself and his household and establishment; and also with such attendance as is hereinafter mentioned, for the term of six calendar months commencing from the 1 day of June next, at the rent of $600.00 for the said term, payable in advance, upon the execution of this agreement. The landlord agrees to pay all rates, taxes and assessments, except gas and water rates, and to make at his own cost all repairs of the premises (except as hereinafter mentioned) which may be necessary during the term, upon being requested by the tenant so to do, and to leave or provide his servants, who shall reside in the house and attend upon the tenant, and also a gardener, and to pay the wages of such indoor servants and gardener. The tenant agrees to pay the said rent in manner aforesaid, and to leave the premises, including the said fixtures, furniture, plate, linen, utensils and effects, in as good state and condition in all respects as the same now are, reasonable wear and tear excepted, and to replace such of the same respectively as shall be broken, damaged, or missing, with other articles of the same pattern and equal value; and to permit the said indoor servants to reside in the house, and to provide them with proper and sufficient board and nourishment; and to bear all expenses of washing and mending all table or house linen which he shall use; and not to assign or underlet the premises, or any part thereof, without the previous consent of the landlord. Provided that if there shall be any breach by the tenant of the conditions herein contained, the landlord may re-enter upon any part of the premises in the name of the whole, and determine the tenancy without prejudice to his other remedies.

_____

LANDLORD

_____

TENANT

_____

WITNESS

LEASE OF CITY PROPERTY—NEW YORK CITY LEASE

This indenture, made this 1 day of June, in the year one thousand nine hundred and _____, between John Doe, hereinafter called the lessor, party of the first part, and Richard Roe, hereinafter called the lessee, party of the second part:

Witnesseth: that the lessor has agreed to let and hereby does let and demise unto the lessee, and the lessee does hereby take and hire from the lessor, the Vacant Store, located at
          , to be used as drugstore for the term of 5 years, to commence on the 1 day of June, 19____, and equal monthly installments of $300.00 each in advance on the 1 day of each month until said expiration of the term, but the said term shall be subject to the limitations hereinafter mentioned in paragraphs numbered tenth and eleventh.

The above letting is upon the following conditions and covenants, all and every one of which the lessee does covenant and agrees to and with the lessors to keep and perform:

1. To pay the rent at the times and in the manner herein provided.

2. To pay and discharge all debts of every kind, which, during the term hereby granted, may be imposed upon or grow out of or become a lien upon the said premises, or any part thereof, within thirty days after the same shall be payable.

3. To promptly comply with and execute, at the lessee's own cost and expense, all laws, rules, orders, ordinances and regulations of the city of New York or any of its boroughs, and of any and all of its departments and bureaus, and of the county and state authorities, and of the Board of Fire Underwriters, which shall impose any duty upon the lessors or the lessee with respect to the premises hereby demised or the use thereof.

4. To make and pay for all necessary repairs, including repairs to the roof and the exterior of said premises and to the sidewalks in front of the same, of whatsoever nature required to keep the premises in good order and condition during said term and, at the expiration of said term, to deliver up and surrender the said premises in as good state and condition as they were at the commencement of the said term, damages by fire not occasioned by the negligence of the lessee or the lessee's agents, and damages occasioned by the direct, sudden and violent action of the elements excepted.

5. To keep the sidewalk in front of said premises free from rubbish and encumbrances and to remove ice and snow therefrom with all diligence.

6. To permit the lessors and their agents to enter upon the premises or any part thereof, at all reasonable hours, for the purpose of examining the same or making such repairs or alterations as may be necessary for the safety

or preservation thereof, and no claim or action for damages or set-off of rent by reason or on account of such entry, repairs or alterations, shall be made, had or allowed.

7. To permit the lessors or their agents to enter upon and show the premises to persons wishing to hire or purchase the same at all reasonable hours, and, during the three months next preceding the expiration of the term, to permit the usual notice "To Let" and, at any time, the notice of "For Sale" to be placed upon the doors or walls of said premises, and remain thereon without hindrance or molestation.

8. To protect the lessors and save them harmless from any and all liability for any damage to any occupant of the said premises or to any other person, during the said term, occasioned by or resulting from the breakage, leakage or obstruction of the water, gas or soil pipes or of the roof or rain ducts, or other leakage or overflow in or about the said premises, or from any carelessness, negligence, or improper conduct on the part of the lessee or the lessee's agents, on, in or about the said premises or the sidewalk in front of the same, and the lessors shall not be liable for any damage, loss or injury to the person, property or effects of the lessee or any other person, suffered on, in or about the same by reason of any present, future, latent or other defects in the form, character or condition of said premises or any part or portion thereof, and the said rent shall not be diminished or withheld by reason or on account of any such loss or damages.

9. No alteration, addition or improvements shall be made in or to the premises without the consent of the lessors in writing, and all additions and improvements made by the lessee shall belong to the lessors.

10. If, during the term of this lease the demised premises shall be destroyed by fire, the elements, or any other cause, or if they shall be so injured that they cannot be repaired with reasonable diligence within 6 months, then this lease shall cease and become null and void from the date of such damage or destruction and the lessee shall immediately surrender the premises to the lessors and shall pay rent only to the time of such surrender, and the foregoing provision of this paragraph shall be a limitation of this lease, but, if the premises shall be repairable within 6 months as aforesaid, then the lessors may repair the same with all reasonable speed, and the rent shall cease until such repairs shall be completed, provided, however, that this lease shall continue of full force and effect, unless the lessors shall neglect to commence such repairs within seven days after the lessee shall notify them of such damage, except as to the payment of rent, and provided, further, that in case any portion of the said premises shall, during the period of such repairs be fit for the purpose for which these premises are demised, then the rent shall be equitably apportioned and paid for the part so fit for occupancy. It is expressly agreed that the provisions of section 197 of the Real Property Law of the State of New York shall not apply to the estate hereby granted or to the premises hereby demised.

11. That the lessee will not assign this indenture or the estate or term hereby granted, or any part thereof, or let or underlet the said premises, or any part thereof, without the lessors' written consent thereto, or use the said premises, or any part thereof, for any purpose deemed extra-hazardous on account of fire, or contrary to law or good morals or to the city ordinances and regulations. It is expressly understood and agreed that the stipulations contained in this paragraph and in the paragraphs numbered 3 and 6 hereof, respectively, shall be limitations of this lease; and, in case of a violation of

any one or more of such stipulations, this lease shall become null and void and the estate and term hereby granted shall cease and determine, but without prejudice of any right of action on the part of the lessors for damages for any such violations.

12. That, if the lessee Richard Roe shall neglect or fail to pay any tax, assessment, water rent or meter charges, or to make any of the repairs hereinbefore mentioned in paragraph 4, or, if any liability for damages or otherwise shall be imposed upon the lessors by reason of the failure of the lessee Richard Roe to observe or perform any convenant or condition herein contained, or, if by like reason the lessors shall be put to any other charges or expense, or any charge or lien shall be imposed on said premises, the lessors shall have the right and privilege, at their option, to pay such tax, assessment, water rent or meter charges, or pay for such repairs as they may make pursuant to the provisions contained in paragraph numbered 6 hereof, or to discharge such liability, charge or lien, or any portion thereof, with any interest or penalties thereon, and the amount of such tax, assessment, water rent or meter charges, and the amount paid for such repairs, and the amount paid by the lessors in discharging such liability, charge or lien, and in defraying such charges and expense shall, after notice thereof to the lessee Richard Roe, become rent, and the installment of rent next payable under the provisions of this lease shall be augmented by the amount so paid as aforesaid, and, upon default of the lessee Richard Roe in the payment of any installment or installments of rent as thus augmented, in addition to all other appropriate remedies, summary proceedings for the removal of the lessee from the possession of the said premises for the nonpayment of the rent as thus augmented may be instituted and prosecuted by the lessors in the same manner as would be lawful in case of the nonpayment of the rent herein otherwise reserved.

13. If default be made in the observance or performance of any of the covenants or conditions of this lease, it shall be lawful for the lessors to re-enter and resume possession of said premises, and the same to have again, repossess and enjoy, or to dispossess and remove all persons and their goods and chattels therefrom without liability in law or equity for any damage caused by such removal. The lessee does hereby expressly waive the service of any notice in writing of intention to re-enter, as provided for in the third section of an act entitled "An Act to Abolish Distress for Rent," passed May 13, 1846. In case of such re-entry, or, if the premises become vacant, or the lessee is dispossessed by summary proceedings, the lessee Richard Roe shall be liable for the amount, which the rent hereby reserved would equal for the remainder of the term hereby granted, in the same manner as he would otherwise be liable for said rent, provided, however, that the lessors may relet the premises or any part thereof for the remainder of the term for the account of the lessee, Richard Roe, and the lessee does expressly covenant and agree to pay and make good to the lessors any deficiency in the amount of rent and also the expense of the lessors in re-entering and reletting.

14. That failure of the lessor to insist upon the strict performance of the terms, covenants, agreements and conditions herein contained, or any of them, shall not constitute or be construed as a waiver or relinquishment of the lessor's right to thereafter enforce any such term, covenant, agreement or condition, but the same shall continue in full force and effect.

The lessee herewith deposits with the lessors the sum of $100.00, the receipt whereof is hereby acknowledged, the same to be held by the lessors as security for the full and faithful performance and observance by the lessee of all the terms, covenants and conditions herein contained, and to be returned to the lessee as, when and provided that the lessee shall have fully performed and observed all of the said terms, covenants and conditions on his part to be performed and observed; and it is expressly understood and agreed that the sum so deposited is not an advance payment of or an account of the rent herein reserved, or any part of installment thereof, or a measure of the lessors' damages, and in no event shall the lessee be entitled to return or particular application of the said sum or any part thereof, until the full end of the term hereby granted, and until a reasonable time and opportunity shall have been had thereafter to inspect the said premises for the purpose of determining whether the terms, covenants and conditions hereof have been fully performed and observed; and it is further agreed that the issuance of a warrant in summary proceedings shall not effect a cancellation of this lease so as to make sooner recoverable the said sum or any part thereof.

All of the aforesaid agreements, covenants and conditions should apply to and be binding upon the parties hereto, their heirs, executors, administrators, successors, and assigns.

In witness whereof, we have set down our signatures.

_____
LESSOR

_____
LESSEE

_____
WITNESS

In the Presence of John Doe.

In consideration of the letting of the premises above mentioned to the above-named Lessee, and the sum of One Dollar ($1.00) to him paid by the said Lessors, the undersigned, do hereby covenant and agree to and with the said lessors, their legal representatives and assigns, that if default shall at any time be made by the said lessee in the payment of the rent or the performance of the covenants above expressed on his part to be paid and performed, that he will well and truly pay the said rent, or any arrears thereof, that may remain due unto the said lessors, and also all damages that may arise in consequence of the nonperformance of said covenants, or either or any of them, without requiring notice of any such default from the said lessors.

Witness my hand and seal.

(Seal) _____
GUARANTOR

In the Presence of John Doe.

AGREEMENT FOR A BUILDING LEASE
FOR NINETY-NINE YEARS

An agreement made the 1 day of May, 19____, between John Doe, who and his heirs and assigns, unless the contrary appears, are hereinafter called the lessee, of the other part; whereby it is agreed as follows:

1. When and so soon as the lessee shall have erected, built, and finished the buildings mentioned in the fifth clause of this agreement, the lessor

will grant to the lessee a lease of all that piece or parcel of land situate, 410 Bond St., Baltimore, Maryland, and the real estate and buildings to be erected thereon, with the appurtenances, which premises are delineated in the plan annexed to this agreement, from the 2 day of May, 19___, for the term of ninety-nine years, at the yearly rent of $10,000.00 for the first year of the said term, and the yearly rent of $12,500.00 during the residue thereof, payable quarterly on the 2 day of August, November, February, and May, free and clear of all and every rate, tax, charge, duty, assessment, or imposition whatsoever, to which the landlord, tenant, or premises is or are or hereafter shall or may be liable; the first quarterly payment of the said yearly rent of $3125.00 to be made on the 2 day of May, 19___.

2. (Include here terms, conditions, covenants and provisos of intended lease.)

3. The lessee will accept such lease on the terms and conditions aforesaid, and execute a counterpart thereof when required, and pay the charges of and incidental to the preparation and execution of the same, as well as the charges of and incidental to these presents, and a duplicate hereof.

4. Until such lease shall be granted, the lessee will pay the rents agreed to be thereby reserved, and all such rates, taxes and assessments as hereinbefore mentioned, and will, as far as circumstances will admit, observe and perform the covenants and conditions to be contained in the said lease, as if the same had been actually granted, and the lessor shall have all such remedies for recovering rent, and for breach of any covenant, as if the said lease had actually been granted.

5. The lessee will, on or before the 15 day of July next, at his own costs and charges, pull down and remove the buildings now standing and being on the said piece of ground, and on the site thereof, in a good, sound, substantial and workmanlike manner and with fit and proper materials of all kinds, to be approved by the architect or surveyor of the lessor, and under the direction and inspection of such architect or surveyor and to his satisfaction, erect, build and complete, and in a workmanlike manner finish, a good and substantial brick building fit for use as a Motion Picture Theater, and in all things conformable and agreeable to the specification thereof hereunder written; and will lay out and expend thereon the sum of $50,000.00 and upwards; and also will bear, pay, and discharge the said architect's or surveyor's fees or five per cent on the expenditure, for superintending and directing the same.

6. The lessor or his architect, surveyor, or agent, may at all reasonable times during the continuance of this agreement, enter upon the said premises to view the state and progress of the work and building operations hereby agreed to or authorized to be executed and carried out.

7. The lessee shall be entitled to take for his own absolute use and benefit all materials of the said buildings so to be pulled down and removed as aforesaid.

8. The lessee shall not assign, or sublet, or otherwise part with, the benefit of this agreement, except with the consent in writing of the lessor first had and obtained.

9. In case the lessee shall not erect, build, complete, and cover in, and in all respects finish and make fit for use, such buildings as aforesaid to the satisfaction of the lessor's architect or surveyor on or before the said 2 day of May, 19___, or if the said yearly rent of $12,500.00 shall be in arrears for the space of 30 days after the same shall have become due, or in case of

breach of any of the stipulations herein contained, or if the lessee shall not proceed with the works with proper diligence, then and in any such case it shall be lawful for the lessor, if he shall think fit, to re-enter and take possession of the premises hereby agreed to be demised, and of all buildings, erections, plant and materials which may be thereon, without making to the lessee any allowance or compensation in respect thereof.

10. This agreement shall not, nor shall anything herein contained or to be done in pursuance hereof, except the granting of a lease as aforesaid, operate as an actual or present demise of the premises, or any part thereof, or to create any leasehold interest therein or tenancy thereof; but the lessee shall only have a right to enter upon the premises for the purposes of performing this agreement. Any rents or yearly sums hereby agreed to be paid by the lessee, which shall be in arrear, shall be recoverable by the lessor as if the same were rent in arrear, and the lessee were the tenant of the premises.

In Witness whereof we have set here our signatures.

_____
LESSOR

_____
LESSEE

AGREEMENT TO LET FURNISHED APARTMENTS

Agreement made the 15 day of June, 19___, between John Doe, hereinafter called the lessor, of the one part, and Tim Brown, hereinafter called the lessee, of the other part.

The said lessor agrees to let, and the said lessee to take, the 5 rooms on the 2nd floor of the dwelling-house situated at 3000 Denison St., in the county of Calvert, Md; and also the furniture, articles and effects now being in the said rooms respectively; and also the other articles and things specified in the schedule hereunder written, for the term of 1 year from the 15 day of June, 19___, at the yearly rent of $2,000.00, payable quarterly. And the said lessee hereby agrees to keep and preserve the said furniture and effects, so far as reasonable wear will permit, in a proper state and condition, and supply and replace any articles that may be destroyed, broken, or lost, by articles of a like kind and of equal value; and on the expiration or sooner determination of the said term to deliver up to the said lessor the said rooms, furniture and effects, or such articles as shall be so substituted in the place of any of the said articles as shall have been so destroyed or broken as aforesaid. Witness the hands of the said parties.

_____
LESSOR

_____
LESSEE

LEASE OF APARTMENT—MONTH TO MONTH TENANCY

This agreement, made and entered into this 10 day of May, 19___, between John Doe, party of the first part, hereinafter called lessee. (It is mutually agreed by the parties hereto, where either is mentioned herein, that same refers to their heirs, executors, administrators, successors or assigns, who are bound as fully and completely by the covenants herein as the parties hereto.)

Witnesseth: That the said lessee has this day rented and leased from said lessor the following described unfurnished apartment: 3 Rooms, Kitchen and Bath, located at No. 10 Vine Street, in the City of Akron, Ohio, for the term of 1 year, commencing on the 1 day of June, 19____, and ending on the 1 day of June, 19____, for which the lessee agrees to pay the lessor, at his office, promptly on the first day of each rental month, in advance, a monthly rental of $75.00; and on failure of lessee to pay same when due, all further rent under this contract shall immediately become due and payable, and the said lessor has the right, at his option, to declare this lease void, cancel the same, re-enter and take possession of the premises. Lessor, at his option, upon a breach of this contract, may card for rent and sublet the premises at the best price obtainable by reasonable effort, under private negotiations, and charge the balance, if any, between said price of subletting and the contract price to lessee and hold him therefor. Such subletting on the part of the lessor will not in any sense be a breach of the contract on the part of the lessor, but will be merely as agent for the lessee and to minimize the damage. Said lessor is not required, however, to let same for any other purpose than that specified herein. These rights of the lessor are cumulative and not restrictive of any other rights under the law, and failure on the part of lessor to avail himself of these privileges at any particular time shall not constitute a waiver of these rights.

It is further mutually agreed as follows:

1. Lessee hereby waives and renounces for himself and family any and all homestead and exemption rights he or they may have under or by virtue of the laws of this state, or the United States as against any liability that may accrue under this contract. Lessee agrees to pay all costs and 15 per cent attorney's fees on any part of said rental that may be collected by suit or by attorney after same has become due.

2. Lessee is to repair, at his own expense, any damage to water or steam pipes caused by freezing or any neglect on his part, also to be responsible for all damages to the property of lessor's other tenants in said building, if there be any, or to the adjoining buildings, caused by the overflow or breakage of waterworks in said premises, during the term of this lease. Lessee agrees not to sublet said premises, or any part thereof, without the written consent of said lessor, and will deliver said premises at the expiration of this lease in as good order and repair as when first received, natural wear and tear excepted.

3. Lessee hereby releases said lessor from any and all damages to both person and property during the term of this contract.

4. Should the premises be destroyed or so damaged by fire as to become untenantable, this lease shall cease from the date of the fire.

5. Lessee is to make no changes of any nature in the above-named premises without first obtaining written consent from said lessor or his agent; and the lessor or his agents shall have the right to enter said premises at reasonable hours, to examine the same, make such repairs, additions or alterations as may be deemed necessary for the safety, comfort and preservation of said building, and to enter upon said premises at any time to repair or improve lessor's adjoining property, if any.

6. Lessee agrees not to permit any act which would vitiate or increase the fire insurance policy upon said property; to pay all electric light, heat, water, gas and power bills accruing against said property during the term of this contract, and to comply with all rules, orders, ordinances and regula-

tions as attached hereto and of the city government of the city of Akron, in any and all of its departments.

7. In the event bankruptcy or state insolvency proceedings should be filed against lessee, his heirs or assigns, in any federal or state court, it shall give the right to said lessor, his heirs or assigns, at their option, to immediately declare this contract null and void, and to at once resume possession of the property. No receiver, trustee, or other judicial officer shall ever have any right, title or interest in or to the above-described property by virtue of this contract.

8. Lessor has the privilege of carding the above-described premises for rent or for sale at any time within thirty days previous to the expiration of this lease, and during the said time to exhibit said premises during reasonable hours.

In Witness Whereof, we have hereunto set our hands, this the day and year above written.

_____
LESSOR

_____
LESSEE

LEASE OF APARTMENT FOR A YEAR

Indenture made the 1 day of June, 19____, by and between John Doe, of _____, hereinafter called the lessor, which expression shall include his heirs, and assigns and Richard Roe, of _____, hereinafter called the lessee, which expression shall include his executors, administrators, and assigns. The lessor doth hereby demise and let unto the lessee all those unfurnished rooms or apartments consisting of 5 rooms on the 2nd floor of the dwelling house numbered 5 in Pine Street, in said city of Baltimore, Maryland, together with the free use of the front entrance, the hall, staircase, and passageways leading to said rooms, the water closet and bathrooms, and part of the cellar for the storage of fuel. To hold the same from the 1 day of July next, for the term of 1 year, determinable, nevertheless, as hereinafter mentioned, yielding and paying therefor the annual rent of $2,000.00, which is to include all taxes and water rates (and furnace heat).

The lessor agrees that he will at all times keep the front entrance, hall, staircase, and passageways leading to said rooms, and also the water closet and bathroom, clean, dry, and free from noise and annoyance.

It is mutually agreed that the said lessee may quit the said rooms and apartments at any time on giving to the said lessor 4 weeks' notice of his intention so to do, and on paying a proportionate part of the said rent up to the time of quitting the same, and also that the said lessee shall be at liberty to terminate the said tenancy, and to quit the said rooms and apartments, on any breach of either of the agreements herein contained on the part of the lessor to be performed.

_____
LESSOR

_____
LESSEE

ASSIGNMENT OF A LEASE BY ENDORSEMENT

This agreement, made the 1 day of June, 19____, between the within named John Doe, of _____, hereinafter called the vendor, of the one part, and Richard Roe, of _____ _____, hereinafter called the purchaser, of the other part, witnesseth, that in consideration of One dollar ($1.00) to the said vendor paid by the said purchaser, and of the covenants of the said purchaser hereinafter contained, the said vendor doth hereby assign unto the said purchaser, his executors, administrators and assigns, all that tenement demised to the said vendor by the within-written lease, with all rights, easements and appurtenances as within mentioned; and all the estate, right, title and interest of the said vendor in and to the said premises.

To have and to hold the said premises unto the said purchaser, his executors, administrators and assigns, for the residue of the term granted by the within-written lease, at the rent thereby reserved, and subject to the covenants by the lessee and conditions therein contained, and thenceforth to be performed and observed by the said purchaser; and the said purchaser doth hereby for himself, his heirs, executors and administrators, covenant with the said vendor, his executors and administrators, that he and they will henceforth pay the rent reserved, and perform the covenants on the part of the lessee contained in said lease, and will keep the said vendor, his executors and administrators, indemnified against all actions, claims and liability for the nonpayment of said rent, or breach of the said covenants, or any of them.

ASSIGNOR

ASSIGNEE

Note: If desired add acknowledgments to the following forms for the purpose of recording. For forms of acknowledgments see also ACKNOWLEDGMENT.

LEASE FOR A TERM OF YEARS

This indenture, made the _____ day of _____, in the year of our Lord one thousand nine hundred and _____, between A.B., of _____, of the first part, and C.D., of _____, of the second part, witnesseth: That the said A.B., for and in consideration of the yearly rent and covenants hereinafter mentioned and reserved, on the part and behalf of the said C.D., his executors, administrators and assigns, to be paid, kept, and performed, hath demised, granted and leased, and by these presents doth demise, grant, and lease, unto the said C.D., his executors, administrators, and assigns, all that messuage and lot of ground, situate, lying and being in the aforesaid, bounded northward, etc., (here describe the premises) together with all and singular, buildings and appurtenances thereunto belonging. To have and to hold the said messuage and lot of ground, and all and singular the premises hereby demised, with the appurtenances, unto the said C.D., his executors, administrators, and assigns, from the _____ day of _____ next ensuing the date hereof, for and during the term of _____ years thence next ended; yielding and paying for the same unto the said A.B., his executors, administrators, and assigns, the yearly rent or sum of _____ dollars, in four equal quarterly payments (or as the case may be) of _____ dollars each the first of which to be made on the _____ day of _____ next.

And the said C.D., for himself, his heirs, executors, and administrators, doth covenant, promise, and agree to and with the said A.B., his heirs, executors, administrators, and assigns, by these presents that he, the said C.D., his heirs, executors, and administrators, shall and will well and truly pay or cause to be paid unto the said A.B., his heirs, executors, administrators, or assigns, the said yearly rent of _____ dollars, hereby reserved, on the several days and times hereinbefore mentioned and appointed for the payment thereof, according to the true intent and meaning of these presents. And the said A.B., for himself, his heirs, executors, and administrators, doth covenant, promise, and agree to and with the said C.D., his executors, administrators, and assigns, (paying the rent and performing the covenants aforesaid), shall and may peaceably and quietly have, hold, use, occupy, possess and enjoy the said demised premises, with the appurtenances, during the term aforesaid, without the lawful let, suit, trouble, eviction, molestation, or interruption of the said A.B., his heirs or assigns, or any other person or persons whatsoever.

Witness the hands and seals of the said parties the day and year first above written.

A.B.　(Seal.)

C.D.　(Seal.)

Signed, sealed and delivered in presence of
E.F.
G.H.

TENANT TO LANDLORD OF DESIRE TO PURCHASE THE PREMISES UNDER OPTION

In pursuance of the power contained in a lease dated the 1 day of June, 19____, and made between yourself of the one part, and myself of the other part, I desire and agree to purchase the premises comprised in the said indenture at the sum of $5,000.00; and I request you, on or before the expiration of 60 days from the date hereof, to deliver to me a good and sufficient deed of coveyance of said premises in accordance with the provision in said indenture.

_____

TENANT

TENANT TAKING OPTION FOR ANOTHER TERM

City of Baltimore, State of Maryland

1 day of June, 19____

To John Doe:

By a certain lease executed on the 1 day of May, 19____, between yourself of the one part and myself of the other part, you demised to me for a term of 3 years from the date thereof the premises which I now occupy, with the proviso that I should have the right and option to lease said premises for a like term on like conditions. In the exercise of the power reserved in said lease I hereby notify you of my intention to lease said premises for another term.

_____

TENANT

NOTICE BY TENANT OF INTENTION TO QUIT

I hereby give you notice that I shall quit and deliver up to you, on the 1 day of June next, the possession of all that dwelling house, with the garden and appurtenances thereto belonging, situate at 10 Small St., now held by me of you.

Witness my hand this 1 day of May, 19___.

_____

TENANT

TENANT TO LANDLORD TO TERMINATE A LEASE CONTAINING AN OPTION FOR ANOTHER TERM

City of Baltimore, State of Maryland

1 day of April, 19___

To John Doe:

By that certain lease made between yourself of the one part and myself of the other part on the 1 day of May, 19___, the premises now occupied by me as your tenant were demised for a term of 3 years from the 1 day of May, 19___, with the provision that I should have the right and option to lease the said premises for a like term on the same conditions, and to give you notice if it should be my desire not to do so. In pursuance thereof, I hereby notify you that it is my intention to terminate said lease at the expiration thereof, on the 1 day of May, 19___, when I shall quit and deliver up to you the possession of the buildings and lands therein comprised.

_____

TENANT

NOTICE TO TENANT TO MAKE REPAIRS

In pursuance of the stipulation contained in the lease made by me to you, dated the 1 day of June, 19___, whereby it was agreed that you should keep in good repair the premises described in said lease, which you now hold as my tenant (or which you lately held as my tenant), I hereby give you notice, and require you within 30 days from the date hereof, to put said premises in good repair, and particularly that you make in a workmanlike manner the several repairs mentioned in the schedule hereunder written (or mentioned in the specification by my architect hereunder written).

_____

LANDLORD

LANDLORD TO TENANT TO MAKE REPAIRS

I do hereby give you notice, and require you to put in good and tenant-able repair the dwelling house and premises situate at 5 Peal St., which you now hold under and by virtue of a certain indenture of lease executed by me to you, bearing date the 1 day of June, 19___, pursuant to your covenant in such indenture of lease contained, and particularly that you fix and repair all broken windows on said premises.

_____
LANDLORD

LANDLORD TO TENANT TO QUIT FOR NON-PAYMENT OF RENT

I hereby notify you to quit and deliver up, in 10 days from this date, the premises now held by you as my tenant at No. 14 Wolfe Street.

_____
LANDLORD

LANDLORD TO TENANT FROM YEAR TO YEAR TO QUIT

I hereby give you notice to quit, and deliver up to me on the 1 day of June next, the possession of all that dwelling house, with the garden and appurtenances thereto belonging, situate at 10 Vine St., in the county of Calvert, which you now hold under me as tenant from year to year.

_____
LANDLORD OR LESSOR

LICENSE TO SUBLET A PART OF LEASED PREMISES

I, the undersigned, being the lessor named in a lease made between myself, of the one part, and Richard Roe, of _____ _____, the other part, do hereby consent that the said lessee may underlease a portion of the premises comprised in said lease, namely, one bedroom of said apartment, unto John Doe, of _____, for the whole remaining term of said lease, provided that this consent shall not authorize any further underletting, or parting wholly or partially with the possession of said premises, or any part thereof, or prejudice or affect any of the covenants, conditions, or provisions in the said lease contained except to the extent hereinbefore expressed.

Witness my hand the 1 day of July, 19___.

_____
LESSOR

LICENSE TO SUBLET

I, the undersigned, hereby consent that John Doe, lessee in a certain lease made by me to him, dated the 1 day of June, 19___, for the term of 5 years, may underlease the premises demised to Richard Roe, for the term of 2 years. Provided that this license shall be restricted to the particular underlease hereby authorized, and the covenant in said lease made by me against assigning or underletting shall remain in full force and effect.

Dated the 10 day of July, 19___.

_____
LESSOR

LARCENY The wrongful and fraudulent taking and carrying away of the personal goods of another with the felonious intent to make them the property of the taker without the owner's consent. The distinction between grand and petit larceny has been abolished in most places. In some places, however, the penalty is different depending upon whether the larceny is of goods valued at more or less than a given sum.

The taking of goods must be against the consent of the owner and the property of the owner in the goods may be general or absolute, or it may be special, that is, it may be in his hands as bailee or for the exercise of some particular function or right or duty in connection therewith. There will be no larceny if consent to the taking was given, though the contrary is true if the consent is obtained by fraud. Neither will there be larceny if the taking is under claim of right, that is, if the party honestly believes the property belongs to him or that he has a right to take it even though he does not actually have such right.

It is not larceny if one comes rightfully into possession of an article and appropriates it to his own use. To meet such cases, statute laws have been quite commonly passed making larceny by bailee or trustee, and certain embezzlements, criminal. Mere custody has been construed not to be possession, the dominion over a property being of a very limited character. In cases where custody only of the property has been parted with by the owner there may be, it seems, such a taking and carrying away by the custodian as will constitute larceny.

The taking must be in the county where the criminal is to be charged, but by construction of law there is a fresh taking in every county into which the thief carries the stolen goods. He may be tried wherever caught with the stolen property in his possession, if it is within the state where the theft took place. To constitute a taking the property must be actually removed, but a slight removal only is necessary if it is actually taken into possession.

No larceny can be committed of things affixed to the soil, but if actually severed by the owner, a third person or the thief himself as a separate transaction, it then becomes a subject of larceny. The article must have some value even though it is slight.

Possession of the fruits of the crime soon after its commission is evidence of guilt if unexplained either by direct evidence or by attending circumstances or by showing the character and habits of life of the possessor or otherwise. The longer the time elapsing before discovery of the stolen article, the weaker this presumption, particularly if the goods are of such character as frequently change hands.

Where conviction depends alone upon evidence of the possession of the stolen goods, the possession proven should be exclusive. For example, if the goods should be found in a house in which other persons reside capable of committing the larceny this would be insufficient to prove guilty possession unless coupled with other proof of suspicious circumstances against the defendant. The presumption of guilt arising from possession is much greater if the possession consists of fruits of a series of thefts, or if it consists of the multiplicity of miscellaneous articles, or if it is of a kind of value inconsistent with the means and station of the party accused, or where the party has suddenly and otherwise inexplicably acquired means or has an unusual amount of money to spend.

This rule of presumption of guilt from possession of stolen property, however, must be exercised with caution and should never be applied when there is reasonable ground to conclude that the witness may be mistaken, or where from any cause the identity of the stolen article with that found in the possession of the accused is not clearly and satisfactorily established, because of the danger of convicting innocent persons. Usually, however, there are corroborative or explanatory circumstances to be proven in support of this presumption of guilt arising from possession. This may arise either in the conduct of the party or otherwise, as where he has secreted the property or falsely denied possession of it or cannot in a credible manner give consistent accounts thereof, or where he has attempted to dispose of it at an unreasonably low price, or where instruments of crime are found in his possession. These and many other circumstances will aid the presumption of guilt.

LAST CLEAR CHANCE In negligence, a doctrine allowing a plaintiff to win if despite his own negligence the defendant had finally a clear chance to avoid an accident.

LAST WILL This term is most commonly used where lands and tenements are devised, and "testament" where it concerns chattels. Both terms, however, are now generally employed in drawing a will either of lands or chattels, as descriptive of the instrument—("my last will and testament")—the general word of description being "will."

LATENT DEFECT A defect in materials not discernible by examination. Used in contradistinction to patent defect which is a discernible defect.

LAW A system of regulating conduct by means of sanctions imposed and enforced by the state. Sanctions are the very essence of law, and by sanctions I mean the pains and penalties laid down and the threats made by the state, to the effect that if the law is violated certain consequences will follow.

In criminal law, for example, the pains and penalties may be in the form of fine and imprisonment. In civil law a sanction may take the form of a restraining order or injunction, allowing or forbidding a company to do some certain thing.

The judicial system is merely an arm of the state and enforces the laws promulgated by the state. The laws of the state—whether on a local or federal level—are normally obeyed voluntarily. But the armed forces of the state or federal government may be and often have been used—as in the case of riots and sit-ins in colleges and universities—to compel compliance.

Law differs from morality, even though they often coincide. Many laws, for example, have nothing to do with morality. It is not a question of right or wrong that the law requires two or three witnesses to a will, rather than one, but a matter of practicality, so that if one witness dies there will still be a survivor to testify to the mental competence of the one making the will. Nor is it a matter of ethics that the law says that the driver of a motor vehicle shall keep to the right of the road instead of to the left.

On the other hand, an act may be immoral in the eyes of some but still legal. For many centuries slavery was thought immoral by many, but was sanctioned not only by Christianity itself but by the Supreme Court of the United States, until a constitutional amendment called a halt. So with gambling. Many consider gambling immoral, but it is perfectly legal in Nevada and elsewhere. So-called sexual promiscuity is considered immoral by many, but is not necessarily illegal. Even penalities against adultery—which formerly was almost universally considered immoral—are rarely, if ever, enforced.

Finally, law, like morality itself, tends to change with time and circumstance, fulfilling new needs and conditions.

LAW MERCHANT The general body of usages in matters relative to commerce. Otherwise termed commercial law.

LAWYERS' REFERRAL A pool of attorneys who serve in rotation and provide a sort of potluck of legal assistance. The service is a means whereby any person who needs a lawyer and can afford to pay for one but does not have one and is too unsophisticated to find one on his own, may be referred to one through the local bar association. Typically, the applicant pays a registration fee of one dollar for the referral and pays the counsel a fixed fee of five dollars or so for the initial consultation, which may last up to thirty minutes. The attorney makes a nominal charge for any additional services. Periodic reports are required of the attorneys.

When a dispute arises between attorney and client, they agree to arbitration by the Lawyers' Referral Committee. Lawyers' Referral is a sort of half-way house between free legal aid and private legal counsel. The legal fees charged for divorce, for example, are apt to be less than normal, since clients who use Lawyers' Referral usually come from low-income groups. Many clients are directed to Lawyers' Referral by a Legal Aid Society if their incomes suggest they can afford to pay some fee.

Lawyers' Referral Service can usually be located in the yellow pages of the telephone directory or by contacting the local bar association.

LEADING CASE A case often referred to by the courts and by counsel as having finally settled and determined a point of law.

LEADING QUESTIONS Those questions which suggest to the witness the answer desired, those which assume a fact to be proved which is not proved, or which, embodying a material fact, admit of an answer by a simple negative or affirmative.

LEASE A lease is a species of contract for the possession and profits of land tenements either for life or for a certain term of years or during the pleasure of the parties. Its duration must be for a shorter period than the duration of the estate which the lessor has in the land, otherwise there is in general no limitation as to the time a lease may continue. If after the expiration of the term the tenant continues to hold possession, the landlord making no effort to remove him, this gives rise to a tenancy at will continuing until there is payment of rent or until the parties do some other act recognizing the existence of the tenancy which will then be construed to be a tenancy from year to year, and indeed tenancies at will are commonly construed to be tenancies from year to year, which are terminable by the landlord at the end of the year.

Not only things corporeal, as lands and houses, but also incorporeal rights connected, such as ways, fisheries, franchises, estovers (the right to use whatever timber there may be on the premises to promote good husbandry) and annuities may be leased. There may also be contracts for the use of goods and chattels or other personal property, but these are not called leases. Under the statute of frauds, passed in the reign of Charles II, leases for more than three years must be in writing, and this statute has been re-enacted quite generally in the United States, in some cases, however, the period for which a lease may be made being reduced to one year.

No particular form of words is required to create a lease, so long as the intent is clear, and a mere permissive holding is in itself sufficient to raise a presumption of a verbal lease. In general it is desirable that a written lease be under seal, though in most places this is not necessary. Leases are but a species of contract.

A lease cannot be operative so long as the land is held adversely to the lessor, that is, the lessee cannot by virtue of his lease demand possession from the adverse holder, but the lease will inure to the benefit of the lessee if the lessor comes into possession of the land before the lease expires.

The date of the lease fixes its commencement, if no other time is specified; and if there is no date or there is an impossible one, the time of the lease will be from the delivery of the agreement. The inserting of a middle name of a party is immaterial and the lease will be good if the name of the party is not his real name but one by which he is well known. The consideration for the lease may be rent in money, crops, or other valuable thing, payable in gross or periodically, or may be simply natural affection arising from close bonds of relationship. An agreement to render personal service will be a sufficient consideration.

If a dwelling house is leased it will be implied that the garden is included, and a lease of a farm will include the houses appurtenant and lands appertaining to the farm. From the lessor's standpoint a lease should provide for a forfeiture of the rights thereunder and a right to re-enter in case of refusal or neglect on the part of the tenant to pay rent, commit waste, repair, insure or the like. In case of forfeiture, however, for non-payment of rent or where the damages resulting to the landlord are a mere matter of computation, the tenant will be relieved and not required to remove by a payment of the proper amount with interest and costs any time during the progress of proceedings to effect a re-entry.

A lease will be terminated by a taking of the property under the right of eminent domain or if there is a total destruction of the thing leased or if the house is turned into a house of ill fame, or if the title of both lessor and lessee become vested in one person in his own right, but not where the one party holds one title for himself and also as trustee for another.

LEGACY A disposition of personal property by will.

LEGAL AID A free, community-sponsored service for those who need legal advice or assistance from an attorney. To be eligible, a client must prove that his income and assets are so negligible that he cannot afford to pay any fee. Most Legal Aid Societies are supported by contributions from the city or the state. Legal Aid will not handle criminal and divorce cases. In a criminal case the accused, if he cannot afford private counsel, may request the court to appoint counsel for him. Under recent United States Supreme Court decisions, the accused is entitled to have counsel present at every step of the proceedings.

For the name and address of your local Legal Aid Bureau, consult the yellow pages of the telephone directory under "Attorneys" or consult your local bar association.

LEGAL TENDER Such currency as is sufficient under the law to effect payment of a debt or obligation is called legal tender. In the United States, Congress alone is qualified to legislate upon this subject.

LEGATEE The person to whom a legacy is given; sometimes used in the sense of devisee.

LESSEE He to whom a lease is made for life, or years or at will.

LESSOR He who lets land for a term of life, or years or at will.

LETTER OF ATTORNEY A power of attorney; a formal document authorizing some act which shall have a binding effect upon the person who grants the authority. It is usually under seal, and while the want of a seal might not invalidate the instrument as a power of attorney, it is not true that every paper conferring authority upon another is a letter of attorney.

LETTER OF CREDIT A letter of credit is a letter containing a request that the party to whom it is addressed pay the bearer or person named therein money, sell him commodities on credit, or give him something of value, with the intention that the addressee later seek payment from the writer of the letter. It is used by a buyer to secure goods without the necessity of having cash in hand.

The letter may be directed to the writer's friends or correspondents or to some particular one of them. When the letter is presented

LETTER OF CREDIT

The _____ National Bank, of _____,
Circular Letter of Credit.

No._____.   **$ 1000.**

Baltimore, Md. U.S.A., 10 day of June__, 19__.

Gentlemen: we beg to introduce to you and commend to your courtesies Samuel G. Kling, a specimen of whose signature appears in the accompanying list of correspondents.

Kindly provide Samuel G. Kling with such funds as may be required up to an aggregate amount of U.S. One thousand dollars ($1000.00) dollars (or the equivalent of same at current market rates for checks on New York) against _____ drafts drawn at sight on the _____ Bank of England, Ltd., London, the _____ Trust Company of New York, Paris, France.

We engage that such drafts negotiated by you before the _____ day of _____ will be duly honored.

The amount of each payment must be indorsed on this letter and each draft must bear the clause, "Drawn under letter of credit No. _____" of the _____ National Bank of _____, dated _____ day of _____, 19___.

This letter must be attached to the last draft drawn.

We remain, dear sirs,

Yours faithfully,

_____
VICE-PRESIDENT

_____
CASHIER

To Messieurs: To bankers mentioned in the accompanying list of correspondents. (To be accompanied by book containing letter of introduction; signature of beneficiary; directions for using; and list of correspondents. This book is to be kept separate from the letter of credit.)

---

to the person to whom it is addressed he either agrees to comply or refuses. If he refuses, the letter should be returned to the writer unless it is addressed to a merchant who is a debtor of the writer, in which case the person holding it should have it protested.

If the holder of the letter has paid the writer for it or has secured payment therefor to be made, the letter is similar to a bill of exchange. If given merely as an accommodation, it amounts to a guaranty of payment of any advances made to the holder, or for any draft accepted or bill discounted for him by the party to whom the letter is addressed.

LETTERS OF ADMINISTRATION

The instrument by which an administrator or administratrix is authorized, by the surrogate or other proper officer, to have the charge or administration of the goods and chattels of a party who has died intestate, or has left a will without appointing an executor.

LETTERS TESTAMENTARY

An instrument granted by a surrogate, or

ther proper officer, to an executor, after probate of a will, authorizing him to act as executor.

EVITICAL DEGREES The Biblical ist of persons forbidden to marry because of their blood kinship, set orth in *Leviticus* 18.

EVY The seizure of property by a sheriff, marshal or other court officer under an execution or attachment.

EVY (TAXES) The word as applied to taxation means to impose or assess or to charge and collect a sum of money against a person or property for public purposes.

LEX DOMICILII The law of the domicile.

LEX FORI The law of the country or state where the suit or legal proceeding is conducted. Frequently suits are brought in one state or country affecting or relating to persons or property in another or to contracts made in another. It is in this connection that the term *lex fori* or law of the forum applies.

Though the law where the contract was made usually controls in ascertaining the rights of the parties, the form of the remedy or suit, and the mode of proceeding and execution of judgment when obtained, are regulated solely and exclusively by the laws of the place where suit is brought. This law will determine who are the proper parties to a suit.

Generally, all persons whether foreigners or not may sue if not under legal disability to act for themselves, such as minors, etc., and foreign corporations may sue, and if they have property within the state or country, they may be sued.

Proofs of the existence of a claim and questions relating to the competence of witnesses, as well as to the course of procedure, are determined by the law of the forum and even though an arrest may not be made in bringing suit in the place where the contract was made, yet if the law permit this in the place where suit is brought the arrest will be legal.

Under the Constitution of the United States the insolvency laws of the various states which discharge a debtor from the obligation of his debts can be allowed that effect only as against the citizens of the state, and cannot defeat a claim of a citizen of another state bringing suit in another state if he has not presented his claim in the insolvency proceedings in the insolvent's own state, provided there is nothing in the contract requiring performance thereof in the state where the discharge is obtained.

The statute of limitations of the state or country where suit is brought is the one that will be applied in the suit, whether the suit is brought by a citizen or a stranger, and even if the suit is brought upon a judgment obtained in another state. The law of the forum will control as to the right of set-off, as to liens, and as to priorities of claims generally, and as to the admissibility and effect of evidence.

LEX LOCI The law of the place where the contract was made. As a general rule contracts concerning matters other than real estate are made with reference to the law of the place where made, which is presumed to be the intended place of the performance of the thing contracted for, unless by the contract the place of performance is fixed elsewhere.

If the place of performance is shown to be different from the place of making the contract, the law of the former will prevail. As a general rule then, the law where a contract is to be performed (whether that place is fixed by the terms of the contract or by implication) enters into the contract and determines the questions relating to its validity and to the rights, duties and obligations of the parties under it, as well as to the use, construction and meaning of the language used in the contract.

If a contract is to be performed partly in one state and partly in another it will be affected by the laws of both. In case of negotiable paper, every endorsement is a new contract and is governed by the law of the place where made. The law of the place where the note or bill is to be paid, however, will control as between the drawer and any other party to the note, the drawer having contracted with reference to the place of performance or payment. The place of acceptance of a draft or bill supplies the law as to the acceptor unless some other place of payment is designated.

Where the law of the place of contract or performance is different from that of the law where suit is brought it is the duty of the person invoking the former to show the fact. The capacity or incapacity of the parties to contract on account of marriage, minority or the like will be controlled by the law of the place where the contract is made, and penal disqualifications to sue in one state or country will not be enforced in another.

A contract legal by the law where it is made is legal everywhere unless injurious to public rights or morals or in opposition to public policy, or unless it is in violation of a positive law of the place of suit.

The law of the place of contract governs as to the formalities requisite to its execution and a lien or privilege created in one place with respect to personal estate will generally be enforced wherever the property is found, though not necessarily in preference to claims arising under the law of the place where found.

If one is discharged from the performance of a contract under the law of the place where it is made this will operate as a discharge everywhere. If a contract is made partly in one country and parly in another, the contract will be of the place where the assent of the parties first concurs and becomes complete.

LEX REI SITAE The law of the place where the thing is situated. Any title or interest in land or real estate can only be acquired or lost in accordance with the law of the place where situated. This law governs as to the capacity of the parties to any transfer of real estate whether by will or otherwise. It applies with respect to rights, arising from the relation of husband and wife, parent and child, or guardian and ward and with respect to rights and powers of executors and administrators concerning real and personal estate.

LIBEL Any malicious defamation expressed in printing or writing and intended to blacken either the memory of one who is dead or the reputation of one who is living and xpose him to public hatred, contempt or ridicule is a libel. The person guilty may be proceeded against by indictment or may be sued for damages.

Slander when spoken is not a subject of indictment. It is if it is written or printed.

The exhibition of a picture imitating that which in print would be libelous is a libel. So also is fixing a gallows at a man's door, burning him in effigy or exhibiting him in any ignominious manner. It is a libel to publish a ludicrous story in a newspaper, if it tends to ridicule him, even though he had told the same story himself.

The sale of each copy of a book or paper containing the libel is a distinct publication and a separate offense. The publication must be malicious and evidence of the malice may be either expressed or implied, and where a man publishes a writing which on its face is libelous the law presumes a malicious intent and it is unnecessary to prove other circumstances showing malice. Though he does not know of the publication of a libel in his paper, the managing editor is nevertheless responsible. Criticism of a book is not libelous so long as it does not impugn the character of the author, or contain misstatements as to the facts set forth in the book. Alleging falsely that one is "slippery," for example, is libelous. Communications to merchants impugning the credit of another merchant by alleging that he does not pay his debts, and deterring others from dealing with him, are libelous, if not true. Statements made in affidavits and in similar legal proceedings, though injurious are nevertheless not libelous.

LIBELANT One who libels; one who proceeds by libel, or files a libel; the complaining party in an admiralty suit.

LIBER A book; a volume; one of the units of a published work; a book in which public records are made.

LIBERTY The word "liberty" is generally defined with reference to the Constitution of the United States. In its broad sense, the word means, "The right of every person not only to be free from servitude, imprisonment, or restraint, but the right of every person to use his faculties in all lawful ways, to pursue and work where he will, to earn his living in any lawful calling, and to pursue any lawful trade or profession, to worship God according to the dictates of his own conscience," and to write and speak his opinion limited only by the law of libel and slander.

LICENSE (GOVERNMENTAL REGULATION) A license is a privilege granted by a state or city upon the payment of a fee, which confers authority upon the licensee to do some act or series of acts, which otherwise would be illegal. A license is not a contract and may be revoked for cause. It is a method of governmental regulation exercised under the police power. Examples: license to keep dogs in the city; to sell commodities in the street.

LICENSE (PRIVILEGE) A license is a mere personal privilege given by the owner to another to do designated acts upon the land of the owner. It is revocable at will, creates no estate in the land, and such licensee is not in possession.

"It is a mere excuse for what otherwise would be a trespass."

LICENSEE A person who has been given permission to enter upon the land of another for a specific purpose.

LIEN A charge on property usually for the payment of some debt or obligation.

LIFE ESTATE An estate held for the life of the party holding it, or of some other person; a freehold estate, not of inheritance.

LIMITATION A period of time within which certain acts are to be performed in order to render them legally valid. Formerly suits might be brought at any time. Experience has shown, however, that for the quieting of titles and rights and the prevention of injustice it is best that the time within which suits may be brought should be limited. Such limits are now in fact imposed by statute with respect to suits in courts of law everywhere and the rules established in the courts of law are usually adopted in courts of equity. Indeed, courts of equity will sometimes refuse to grant relief within a less time than the statutory period where the transaction has become obscure by lapse of time, and consequent loss of evidence, though a lapse of time less than that provided by the statute of limitations will not be held a bar to a right without sufficient reasons.

In proper cases, as where there is fraud undiscovered until the statute has become a bar, or where it is the fault of the defendant that suit was not instituted sooner, courts of equity, in order to do justice, will entertain suits even after the statutory period.

The period within which suit must be brought in a court of law or before a magistrate, as the case may be, begins to run from the time the plaintiff's right of action or right to sue accrues or begins. In the case of a contract it runs from the breach of the contract and not from the time that damages result from the breach which may be afterwards. Thus a notary employed by a bank neglected to give reasonable notice of non-payment of a note and the bank was held responsible for the failure. The bank sued the notary more than six years (the limitation period) after his default but within six years of the time when the bank paid the damages. It was held that the bank's right of action was barred by the statute of limitation. One contracted to deliver goods on demand. He was unable to do so but managed to prolong the negotiations for settlement until the statutory period after the demand had expired. He could not be held responsible. The directors of the bank liable by statute for mismanagement are charged only after six years (if this is the statute period of limitation) after the insolvency of the bank is made known.

Limitation with respect to a note payable at a given date begins to run from the time fixed for payment. If payable on demand it begins to run from its date and, if it has no date, from delivery, and likewise, if the note is payable "at any time within six years" or if borrowed money is to be aid "when called on." If the note is payable in a certain number of days after demand, sight or notice, the demand itself should be made in such cases within the statutory period of limitation. If grace is allowed, the statute runs from the last day of grace. Where one is entitled to recover back money paid by mistake, the statute runs from time of payment, and money is payable by installment it runs against each installment as it becomes due.

Where a contract is to take effect upon some condition to be performed or the happening of a future contingency or event, the statute runs from the time of performance of the condition or the happening of the contingency or event. If services are continuous in character as where an attorney conducts a suit or a mechanic performs work, the statute runs from the completion thereof. Where one indemnifies another against loss the statute will run from the time the loss occurs or the party is compelled to pay, for it is at that time his right to sue the indemnifier begins.

In cases of negligence, carelessness and unskillfulness the statute runs from the commission of the negligent, careless or unskillful act. In cases of nuisance, as between individuals, the statute begins to run from the time the nuisance is established. Suit cannot be maintained for the recovery of personal property, where possession has been held adversely (that is, under claim of right or title to it), for more than the statutory period, which in most places is six years.

The decisions are at variance as to whether the day when the statute begins to run is to be included or excluded in ascertaining when the statutory period ends. Generally, however, when the computation is from an act done or an event happening, the day when it is done or happens is included, but when the computation is from a given day simply the day of the date is excluded, yet in all cases courts will give effect to the apparent intent of the parties and will be governed by circumstances and the reason of the thing. A fraction of a day is regarded as a whole one in the matter of limitation.

There are cases in which and circumstances under which statutes of limitation do not apply. Where there is no one in existence to exercise the right to sue the statute does not begin to run until such a person is raised up. Thus if a note against one matures after his death and before the administrator is appointed the statute will not begin to run until the appointment, but if it had begun to run before the death it will continue to do so even before an appointment. Where the law or a legal procedure interposes and prevents the suit, the running of the statute will be suspended for the time being, thus, if there be an injunction granted or an assignment of an insolvent's effects preventing suit, the statute will be suspended as between the estate and the creditors but not as between the debtor and his creditor.

Infants or minors, married women in some places, persons non compos mentis and those imprisoned and beyond seas are under disability to sue, and limitation does not run against them during their disability. The disability, however, must be continuous. If it ceases and the statute once begins to run or if it began to run before the disability existed no intervention of another and subsequent disability can stop it. In general the term "beyond the seas" means out of the jurisdiction of the state or country, but in some states as in Pennsylvania and Missouri the term is held to mean beyond the limits of the United States. In case of a debtor beyond seas, in order that the statute may be set in motion in his favor by a return, the return must be open, public and under such circumstances as will give his creditor or the claimant against him who exercises ordinary diligence an opportunity to bring suit.

Usually if suit is brought and the suit fails through accident of some kind for which the plaintiff is not responsible and if he uses due diligence he will be allowed to bring another suit within a reasonable time even though the statutory period has meanwhile elapsed. But a dismissal of the suit is generally fatal to any further action if the statutory period has passed.

Questions of limitation are decided by the law of the place where suit is brought and not by that of the place where the contract is made or the wrong is done. Therefore one may have a right to sue in one jurisdiction and not in another.

Statutes of limitation, it must be noted, do not apply as against the state or the public generally, unless expressly so stated by the statute itself. They do apply as against counties, towns and municipal bodies not possessed of the attributes of sovereignty. If the state, however, become party to private enterprise or a stockholder in a bank, it is subject as such to limitation laws. Where a defendant is permitted by law to set off a claim of his own, growing out of the subject matter of the suit, this may be done even though, if he were to bring a separate suit therefor, he would fail by reason of the bar of a statute of limitation.

Statutes of limitation do not in general apply to cases of trust exclusively within the jurisdiction of courts of equity where the question arises between the trustee and the *cestui que trust*, that is, between the trustee and the person for whose benefit the trust exists. Of this character are the trusts of executors, administrators, guardians, assignees of insolvents and the like. If, however, the trustee denies that he is such or denies the right of the *cestui que trust* and this fact comes to the knowledge of the *cestui que trust*, the statute will begin to run against the latter from the time the fact becomes known.

With respect to a claim against an agent for a breach of duty the statute will begin to run from the time of the breach, and in some cases before a breach can be committed it is necessary for the principal to make a demand upon him, as where he is entrusted with money to purchase property or where property is given to him to sell, if he neglect to make the purchase or sell the property there must be a demand for the money or property before the statute will begin to run. If, however, the agent's conduct is such as amounts to a declaration that he will not perform the duty or if he has disabled himself from performing it, no demand is necessary.

The rendering of an untrue account by a collection or other agent would warrant an action without a demand, and limitation would begin to run at once without a demand. In general, where it is the clear duty of one to perform an act at a particular time and he fails to do so at the time the right to sue immediately exists and limitation begins to run.

If fraud is practiced upon the plaintiff so as to prevent his knowledge of the fact that his right to sue has accrued until after the expiration of the time limited by the statute, this will have the effect of extending the time so that he will be allowed the time fixed by the statute, counting from the discovery of the fraud. However in such a case there must be clear proof of fraudulent concealment and also no negligence on the part of the claimant in discovering the fraud.

Running accounts between merchant and merchant or other persons if they contain upon either side any item upon which the right of action accrued within the statutory period, will not be barred with respect to other items beyond the statutory period. Such an account, however, must be one of reciprocity of dealing between the parties and they must be such as to raise a fair implication that the items on one side are to be set off so far as they go against the items on the other side of the account. If the items are all on one side as is frequently the case between a storekeeper and his customer or where the goods are charged and payments only are credited there is no mutuality, and items beyond the statutory period are barred. If a balance be struck and agreed upon between the parties the statute at once applies to the balance as a distinct demand unless it be the first item in a new and further mutual account when the general rule as to mutual accounts will apply to it as well as to the remaining part of the account.

A new promise to pay an indebtedness made at any time within the statutory period (which is usually six years) before suit is brought or an acknowledgment of the indebtedness within such period, under such circumstances as to be equivalent to a new promise to pay, will take the case out of the operation of the statute even though the original cause of action would in itself be barred. The new promise forms a new cause of action. If it is to pay the principal of a debt only, this will not except interest from the operation of the statute. An agreement to refer a case to arbitrators will not prevent one from taking advantage of the statute.

Nor can the benefit of limitation laws be waived. That is, an agreement incorporated in the contract, note or other instrument not to take advantage of the statute will not be binding, for the object of the law would then be in practice defeated, nor will a devise in a will of property to pay debts exempt debts from the bar of the statute which have already become barred at the testator's death, nor in general will any statement of debts made officially and in pursuance of legal requirement or made with any other purpose than to recognize it as an existing debt with a view to paying it, exempt it from the operation of a statute of limitation. A signed schedule of one's liabilities made for his own use will not be interpreted as a new promise to pay, nor will the existence of an undelivered mortgage to secure an outlawed debt, for a mortgage is not effective until delivered.

The new promise to pay or the acknowledgment of the existence of the debt equivalent to such a promise must be clear. Where one said the account is due and he supposed it had been paid but did not know of it being ever paid, this is no new promise, and the remark: "I am too unwell to settle now; when I am better, I will settle your account," was held insufficient. It was not an unequivocal promise to pay and was indefinite and uncertain. If the debtor even admits the existence of the debt but asserts his purpose to take advantage of the statute, this is no new promise, or if he says that he will pay if he owes but denies that he owes, or if he does in fact owe and denies his liability, so also if he merely states his inability to pay, or if he admits that there was a claim but alleges that it was paid, or if he offers to pay a part in order to settle the dispute.

A mere admission that the account was right has even been held to be insufficient to prevent the bar of the statute, and in general if the supposed new promise is subject to conditions or qualifications or in any way is limited or contingent, the party seeking to avoid the bar of the statute must show that the condition has been performed or that the contingency has happened. If the new promise is to pay when able, the plaintiff must prove the ability. If there is a promise to pay in specific articles, the plaintiff must show that he offered to accept them. It must clearly appear that the new promise was made with reference to the particular demand in suit, though a general admission or promise to pay will be sufficient unless the defendant shows that there were other demands between the parties.

Part payment is evidence of a new promise to pay the balance, though it may be rebutted by other evidence of a contrary intention. It would seem that to revive the unpaid portion, the new payment must be stated to be a payment on account of a sum admitted to be due, involving an implied promise or accompanied by an express promise to pay the remainder. Payment of interest has the same effect as payment of part of the principal, and giving a note for part of the debt or for accrued interest is payment. If one holds two notes against another, one out of date and the other not, and a general payment is made to him, the debtor not specifying to which note it shall be applied, the creditor may apply it to the note out of date if he desires and revive the note, but if both notes are out of date he cannot apportion it between them and revive both notes. A payment made to an agent will have the same effect as if made to the principal himself. An acknowledgment or new promise by one joint promisor cannot take the case out of the statute as to the other joint promisors. An agent, however, may revive the claim in behalf of his principal if acting within the scope of his authority.

The most common period within which suits must be brought to recover real estate is within twenty years after the wrongful adverse possession thereof by another begins, though the statutes vary in different states somewhat as to this. Adverse possession for the statutory period gives title against the true owner, but this adverse possession must be open, uninterrupted and with intent to claim against the true owner. The possession must be an actual occupation so open that the true owner ought to know it and must be presumed to know it, and in such manner and under such circumstances as to amount to an invasion of his rights. The fencing of land or erecting a house on it is an unequivocal act of adverse possession, such also is cultivation of the soil, digging stones or making any permanent improvements, or cutting trees and making lumber therefrom. But there is no adverse possession where one simply enters upon a lot and marks the boundaries by chipping the trees or by getting rails and other timber once or twice from timber lands, or ranging cattle upon the property, or overflowing the land by stopping a stream or surveying or even conveying a piece of land, unless there is also open occupation. A grave-stone standing, marking a burial place will constitute sufficient adverse possession to maintain title without enclosure of the lot.

The adverse occupation in order to give title must be continuous for the whole statutory period. Where one trespasser occupies the land a part of the time and leaves and another takes his place without any conveyance of the rights or pretended rights of the former in the land to the latter, this will not be a continuous possession, but there will be a continuous possession by several successive occupiers where the supposed rights of one are conveyed to the other, and the possession of a lessee of one wrongfully in possession will be construed as the possession of the lessor. The occupation of the one claiming title by possession for the statutory period must not be permissive, that is, by permission of or in subordination to the rightful owner, but it must be by claiming to be the owner. One in possession by permission will so continue and will not become an adverse claimant until he has given the owner out of possession a clear and unequivocal notice of his claim to hold adversely.

To claim by adverse possession the land must have some definite boundaries showing how far the claim extends. A sufficient enclosure or fencing will fix the limits, but it must be an actual, visible and substantial enclosure. An enclosure on three sides without the limit being fixed upon the fourth side is not sufficient to enable a trespasser to obtain title by adverse possession as against the real owner. An unsubstantial brush fence is not sufficient nor is one formed by lapping of falling trees. If the claim is made by virtue of possession only, without any color or pretense of title, the enclosure will limit the extent of the claim, and this enclosure or marking of the boundaries must be fixed and not movable from place to place. The extension of the enclosure within the limit by statute will not give title to the part included in the extension. Where, however, the claim in the land rests upon color of title as well as possession, the possession will be regarded as co-extensive with the land as described in the deed or other instrument under color of which title is claimed, unless indeed, the acts or declarations of the occupant restrict the claim within narrower boundaries.

Therefore, with some relaxation of the rule with respect to wild, remote and uncultivated lands, if title be gained by possession during the statutory period the possession must be adverse, open or notorious and not clandestine and secret, and must be exclusive, uninterrupted, definite as to boundaries and fixed as to its locality.

One joint tenant owner or tenant in common cannot gain title by adverse possession against a co-tenant unless the latter is actually excluded or expelled, for the possession of one is construed as the possession of all and inures to the benefit of all. To effect an exclusion or ouster of the co-tenant, force is not necessary but there must be an unequivocal denial of his right and this denial may be expressed or it may be by acts of a character unmistakably importing such denial. However, if one tenant in common attempts to convey the whole interest in the land, the grantee taking possession will hold adversely to the others, and if he continue to hold adversely for the statutory period he will have title as against the other.

A lessee does not hold adversely against his lessor so long as he acknowledges himself as lessee and payment of rent is conclusive evidence that the lessor is the owner and that the lessee's possession is not adverse, and a holding over the expiration of the lease does not change the character of the possession. If a trustee holds real estate, he holds not for himself but for another called *cestui que trust*, and the possession is not adverse against the latter unless the supposed trustee expressly denies and repudiates the right of the *cestui que trust*, in which case limitation will begin to run from the time of denial or repudiation.

If the rightful owner is under legal disability to sue or look after his own interest when the right to the property accrues to him, the limitation will not run against him until the removal of the disability. However, this applies only to disability existing at the time the right accrues, for if the statute once begins to run, no subsequent disability will stop it, and the disability of one joint tenant or tenant in common or co-partner will not inure to the benefit of the others. Below are the various times in which suits must be begun.

LIMITED PARTNERSHIP A partnership consisting of one or more general partners, jointly and severally responsible as ordinary partners, by whom the business is conducted, and one or more special partners, contributing in cash payments a specific sum as capital to the common stock, and who are not liable for the debts of the partnership beyond the fund so contributed.

LINEAL DESCENT The descent of one person from another; as a son from a father, in the right or direct line.

LIQUIDATED DAMAGES A fixed sum of money expressly and specifically agreed upon between the parties to a contract, to be paid in the event of the non-performance of the contract by either.

LIS PENDENS A pending suit; the actual pendency of a suit, or other judicial proceeding. In equity, a pending suit. A notice of *lis pendens* is one of the proceedings in a foreclosure suit.

LISTING CONTRACT A so-called contract whereby an owner of real property employs a broker to procure a purchaser without giving the broker exclusive right to sell. Under such an agreement, it is generally held that the employment may be terminated by the owner at will, and that a sale of the property by the owner terminates the employment.

LOST ARTICLES AND PAPERS When deeds, will, agreements, and other instruments of writing have been lost, the party desiring to prove their contents must first prove that he has made diligent search and in good faith exhausted all sources of information regarding them, and accessible to him, before secondary evidence can be used, that is, before it can be proved by a copy of the original or by a memorandum made of its contents from the instrument itself or by the recollection of witnesses.

Even a will proved to be lost may be admitted to probate upon secondary evidence, but the fact of loss must be shown by the clearest evidence, for the presumption would be that the testator had destroyed it unless the loss were clearly shown. Recovery may be had even on a negotiable note upon proof of loss thereof, but the claimant must indemnify the debtor against a second payment to another holder who may have purchased it for value not knowing of loss by the previous holder.

LOWEST BIDDER The words "lowest bidder" for public works does not mean the mathematical and grammatical "lowest," but the best, most practical and responsible "lowest bidder."

LUNACY Mental unsoundness to the point of irresponsibility. Insanity in some of its forms at least, relieves one from criminal responsibility and disqualifies one from the performance of certain civil acts. An insane person is unable to make a contract. Difficulty, however, often arises in many cases in the application of the principle. Frequently, in criminal cases, it has been considered sufficient for a court to instruct the jury to consider whether or not the prisoner was sane or insane, or was of sound memory or discretion. The decision may turn upon the question as to whether or not the prisoner in the commission of a homicide acted from an irresistible and uncontrollable impulse. It has been held that one is responsible in a criminal case if he knows right from wrong, also that the true test of insanity as annulling responsibility for a crime is delusion. The question of knowledge of right and wrong, however, may refer solely to the act for which the party is being tried, for one may be sane with respect to one subject and insane as to another.

It seems that insanity as an excuse for crime, or rather as nullifying criminal responsibility, must be more clearly made out than insanity as nullifying a contract.

M

MAGISTRATES A class of inferior judicial officers such as Justices of the Peace and Police Justices. They have the power to issue warrants for the arrest of a person charged with a crime. Magistrates are usually appointed by the governor.

MAGNA CHARTA or CARTA The celebrated charter of English liberties granted by King John at Runnymede on June 15, 1215, and confirmed, with some alterations, by Henry III. It established the supremacy of law over the rights of kings.

MAINOUR A stolen article when found in the thief's possession.

MALA FIDES Bad faith.

MALA IN SE Acts that are bad in themselves and are void of any legal consequences. A contract to do immoral acts is illegal and void because it is *mala in se*. Such acts are in contradistinction to acts *mala prohibita*, which means illegal because prohibited by statute.

MALFEASANCE The performance of a wrongful and unlawful act.

MALICE Doing a wrongful act intentionally, without just cause or excuse is all that is necessary to constitute malice. Malice is necessary to the commission of some criminal offenses. Malevolence and unkindness of heart and enmity towards an individual are not essential. It is rather the intent from which flows any unlawful and injurious act committed without legal justification.

If one sets poison for another and a third party takes it and dies, there will be by legal construction a murder of the third person with malice aforethought. Malice is implied frequently from the facts proven or the act committed. It is implied in every case of intentional homicide and, the killing being proven, it devolves upon the defendant to show circumstances to overcome this implication, such as excusable accident, justification and the like.

MALICE AFORETHOUGHT or MALICE PREPENSE Malice previously and deliberately entertained. This is an essential in constituting the crime of murder.

MALICIOUS MISCHIEF The wanton or reckless destruction of property or the wilful perpetration of injury to the person. There are many statute laws making injury to particular kinds of property criminal. To convict of malicious mischief, wantonness or wicked revenge must be shown.

MALICIOUS PROSECUTION The wanton prosecution by regular process in a criminal proceeding or even in a civil suit without probable cause and where the facts do not warrant it. A suit for damages may be brought against the prosecutor or even against a mere informer when the proceedings are malicious. Grand jurors, however, furnishing information to their fellow jurors on which a prosecution is founded, cannot be held liable. A civil action for malicious prosecution will not lie against a lawyer who brings suit for a client when regularly employed. In all cases, to recover it must be shown that the prosecution or suit was instituted with malice and without probable cause and in a regular proceeding in the ordinary course of justice. If the proceedings are irregular the prosecutor is a trespasser only. Before suit may be brought the malicious prosecution or action must have resulted in an acquittal or final judgment in favor of an accused.

MALPRACTICE The rule making dentists, physicians and surgeons liable in damages for lack of reasonable and ordinary care, skill and diligence resulting in injury to a patient. This is equally applicable to professional nurses or midwives. When a physician or surgeon treats a case, he undertakes to bring to that treatment what is termed reasonable or ordinary care, skill and diligence, and if injury results to his patient by reason of want of such care, skill or diligence he is liable for damages, though he is not an insurer of results unless he expressly and absolutely contracts therefor.

To render him liable, however, two conditions must exist: there must be lack of ordinary care, skill or diligence and it must appear that the injury resulted therefrom. It must appear also that his default is the proximate, not the remote, cause of the injury, and mere ignorance of the case will not render him liable if his treatment is correct. The medical man is not required to possess or exercise the skill which some other specially skillful physician or surgeon might have exercised. It is sufficient if he show that his treatment was in accordance with the usual and ordinary treatment practiced by competent physicians or surgeons in such cases.

A physician stating to one who applies to him for professional aid that his method of treatment will cure the ailment, he, at the time not having a belief either that it would or would not, is liable for injuries resulting from the treatment. Though one lacks ordinary skill, yet if he informs the patient thereof, and the patient nevertheless employs him he cannot complain of consequent evil results. Refusing the assistance of other medical men will neither increase nor diminish a physician's or surgeon's obligation.

One rendering services gratuitously is liable for injury resulting from gross negligence only. A county physician whose practice is limited to a sparsely settled district will not be held to the same degree of skill in surgical cases as one residing in a city where he is supposed to have had much larger experience and practice in surgery.

A physician or surgeon is not liable for any error of judgment unless so gross as to be inconsistent with reasonable care, skill and diligence. Cases are often obscure in their character, and it is sometimes impossible to know with certainty the nature, cause or attributes of physical disorders, and no one can be held to have absolute knowledge with regard to many cases which he is called upon to treat. Having once undertaken to treat or care for a patient, the physician is obliged to continue to do so until he is discharged, or until at least a reasonable time is given to procure other attendance, or until the patient has so far recovered that the services of a physician or surgeon are no longer needed or useful.

The law does not recognize "schools" in the practice of medicine, and will merely require the practitioner to exercise the ordinary and usual skill in administering the treatment commonly approved by the school to which he belongs. The patient is bound to follow instructions of his physician and if he does not or if the injuries arise through negligence on his part, he cannot recover, nor can he recover even though the physician or surgeon was negligent or unskilled in his treatment if his own negligence contributed to or assisted in bringing about the injury.

One treating physical or mental ailments by the practice known as Christian Science is not within the prohibitions and liable to the penalties imposed upon one practicing medicine, because it is felt that the Christian Science practitioner is engaged in a purely spiritual activity and does not physically diagnose disease, manipulate patients, prescribe material remedies.

The burden of proving malpractice is upon the plaintiff. It is said where a professional man is on trial before a jury of laymen the court is bound by duty to protect him against prejudices likely to arise in such case. If malpractice is once established by the evidence, the jury, in fixing damages, may consider the pain and suffering and inconvenience resulting therefrom, the loss of earning power occasioned to the plaintiff and whether it is temporary or permanent and the expenses incurred by reason of the negligent or improper treatment. Their aim should be so far as is possible to fix an actual money value upon the injury inflicted.

The implied contract of the physician or surgeon is either with the patient himself or the person bound under the law to furnish him or her with necessaries, such as the husband of a married woman, father of a child, guardian of a ward and the like. Where the services are rendered to one person at the special instance and request of a third party and upon the credit of the third party there may be an implied contract on his part to pay even though there is no express promise to do so.

It has been held that the physician himself is the proper judge as to the necessity of frequent visits, and the presumption is that all visits made are necessary, though this presumption may be overcome by competent evidence to the contrary. It has even been said that a physician charging for his services may consider the patient's ability to pay and is not bound to charge all alike. He may also, as bearing upon the value of his services, prove his professional standing to be high. If there is a fixed price in a neighborhood for attendance in particular kinds of cases, which the physician is known to have adhered to, this price will control where there is no express contract fixing a different one. Where the law requires the physician to be licensed and imposes a penalty for practicing without a license, he cannot recover for services rendered or medicines furnished unless licensed. If the treatment rendered by a physician was the treatment which was clearly improper, or if reasonable or ordinary skill, care and diligence were not exercised, this will be a good defense in a suit to recover for services.

In a suit by a physician for his services it has been decided that the defendant cannot as a defense prove general low professional character or standing of the physician.

MALUM IN SE Evil in and of itself. An offense or act is *malum in se* which is naturally evil as adjudged by the senses of a civilized community. Acts *malum in se* are usually criminal acts but not necessarily so.

MALUM PROHIBITUM An act which is wrong because it is made so by statute.

MANDAMUS A writ issued from a court directed to any person, corporation or inferior court requiring him or it to do some particular thing therein specified pertaining to his or its office or duty. It issues when the party requesting it has no other remedy to enforce a right to secure compulsion of the performance of that which the applicant has a right to insist upon being done, but the right must be clear and perfect.

A mandamus will issue to compel the performance of a specified act where the act is ministerial in its character, that is, where a duty is imposed upon one to do a certain act without its being left to him to judge whether it shall be done or not, and in such case he may be commanded to do the act in a particular way, that is, the way in which it is his duty to do it.

Where the party against whom the writ issues has discretionary power or acts in a judicial capacity, a writ of mandamus cannot do more than direct him to proceed with the case in accordance with that discretion, the manner entirely to his judgment. The office of sheriff is an example of a ministerial office and he is bound to obey the judicial commands of the court, and if he does not, a mandamus may issue against him. A mandamus will not issue to compel one to do an act where he not only has discretion as to the manner of doing it, but as to the need for doing it.

A mandamus will issue to compel a corporation or public officer to pay money awarded against it or him in pursuance of a statutory proceeding where no other specific method of enforcement is provided. It is the appropriate remedy to compel corporations to produce and allow an inspection of their books and records for the benefit of a stockholder where a controversy exists in which such inspection is material to his interest. It is resorted to for restoring persons to corporate offices of which they are unjustly deprived where the right to the office has been determined by legal proceeding. The fact that the party at fault might be indicted for non-performance of a duty is no conclusive reason against the issuance of a mandamus to compel performance.

A mandamus is issued only where there is no other adequate remedy and is not always demandable as a matter of right, but frequently is awarded in the discretion of the court. Before issuing, a demand should be made upon the party for performance of the required act and the intention to follow up the demand with an application for a mandamus in case of refusal should be stated to him, and the refusal to perform should be absolute and unqualified, but such refusal may be implied either from silence or from conduct. The imposition of costs in a mandamus case is in the discretion of the court but usually they are imposed upon the losing party. Disputes about fact on applications for mandamus are usually determined by the court.

MANSLAUGHTER The unlawful killing of another without malice, either express or implied. Though the act occasioning it is unlawful or likely to be attended with bodily mischief, yet it differs from murder in that malice, which is the very essence of murder, is lacking. It differs from murder also in the fact that there can be no accessories before the fact, there having been no time for premeditation.

Manslaughter is involuntary where effected without an intention to inflict the injury and voluntary where such intention does exist.

Manslaughter may occur as a consequence of provocation, or in mutual combat, or in the prosecution of an unlawful or wanton act, or of a lawful act improperly performed or performed without lawful authority. Provocation, in order to reduce murder to manslaughter, must have been reasonable and recent, for no words or slight provocation will be sufficient, and if the party has had time to cool, malice will be inferred.

In case of mutual combat where one party is killed, it is usually manslaughter only, but not necessarily so, for the killing may have been premeditated and the combat brought on for the purpose of killing. Death from dueling is murder. Killing an officer by resisting him while acting under lawful authority, is murder, but if the officer is acting under a void or illegal authority or out of his jurisdiction, the killing is manslaughter or excusable homicide according to the circumstances of the case. If one, while doing an act of mere wantonness, kills another, this is manslaughter, so also is the performance of an act done negligently even though it is otherwise lawful. Death ensuing from gross negligence of a medical or surgical practitioner is manslaughter. So is carelessness in administering medicine producing death.

Manslaughter is in some places raised to murder where the killing, though unintentional, is done in the course of committing another offense of a heinous character such as burglary, arson, etc.

MARGIN A deposit by a buyer in stocks with a seller or a stockbroker, as security to cover fluctuations in the market in reference to stocks which the buyer has purchased, but for which he has not paid.

Commodities are also traded in on margin.

MARRIAGE AND MARRIED WOMEN Marriage is the state of being legally wedded. All persons are able to contract marriages unless under the required legal age or unless under other disability. At common law the age of consent to marriage in males is fourteen years and in females twelve. A person under a marriageable age can, upon arriving at such age, either avoid or confirm the marriage, but it cannot be confirmed as to both until both have reached the legal age. If either of the parties is under seven years old at the time of marriage it will be absolutely void and cannot be confirmed. Marriage is void if either party is insane or non compos mentis or has a husband or wife living. It is also void if the parties are within the prohibited degrees of consanguinity or affinity.

A woman induced to become married to a man who is already married may recover damages, where she relied upon his repeated statements that he was single, even though she had been informed that he was married. One so intoxicated as not to know what he is doing cannot enter into a valid contract to marry, and a marriage procured by fraud by one of the parties may be voided by the other irrespective of any divorce laws. A marriage may be set aside by the injured party if accomplished under compulsion or duress. If one of the parties was mistaken in the person of the other, it is no marriage, and if consent is obtained by fraud the marriage will be valid only until set aside by a legal procedure, though one may waive the fraud and affirm the marriage in which case it will be binding.

The forms and requisites to accomplish the contract of marriage must be in accordance with the law of the place of marriage. In the absence of statutory provisions, no particular form of words or ceremony is necessary. Mutual assent to the relation of husband and wife or any words importing a present assent and agreement that they are married are sufficient, but assent to a future marriage is not enough to constitute a marriage. The consent may be given in the presence of a magistrate or any other person as a witness, or it may be shown from the subsequent acknowledgment of the parties or from general reputation as to their being married persons resulting from their conduct.

Statutes have been passed in most states to guard against the abuse of the marriage ceremony such as those requiring license or publication of the marriage or consent of parents or guardians, and penalties are imposed for non-compliance therewith. Non-compliance with such provisions does not render a marriage void unless the statute expressly states so. Nearly everywhere under statute laws, marriage of the parents legitimates their children begotten out of wedlock.

Marriage is a good and sufficient consideration for the transfer of property or for an agreement for the transfer of property to or for the use of the party entering into the relation. It is, indeed, regarded as one of the strongest considerations. Such a contract, however, must be in writing. Letters from parents or persons standing in the place of parents making promises of this kind, if specific and explicit, are binding upon them.

If money or a note is given to one by a third party to induce a marriage by giving him or her an appearance of wealth, it will be binding in the event the marriage takes place though there was a secret agreement to restore the same, since the enforcement of the secret agreement would operate as a fraud upon the person thus induced to marry. Creditors concealing or denying debts due them from a man about to marry will be bound by their concealment or denial, and anyone entering into any similar private agreement may expect to lose by his fraud.

Contracts in restraint of marriage are void, such as a promise not to marry a woman, or to marry no one but her, or an agreement not to marry again or a wager by a party that he will not marry within six years. Contracts to pay money for procuring or bringing about a marriage are void on the ground that they are against public policy and morality.

If a man and woman live together, acknowledge each other as man and wife, are received as such by their families, and are generally reputed to be married persons among people who know them, these facts furnish evidence of the actual existence of the marriage relation, without direct proof of a marriage ceremony. This is not true if the marriage is polygamous, incestuous, or between parties too nearly related to marry by the laws of the civilized world and not where it is contrary to the positive law at other places than where contracted.

Formerly, the legal entity of a married woman was mostly absorbed by that of her husband. He was entitled to her personal property entirely upon reducing it to possession and had a very extensive control over her person. The last three-quarters of a century have witnessed a revolution with respect to the legal status of married women, so that now a woman's legal rights are pretty similar to those of her husband.

The marriage requirements in the various states and territories are as follows:

MARRIAGE REQUIREMENTS BY STATE

State	With consent Men	With consent Women	Without consent Men	Without consent Women	Blood Test Required	Blood Test Other state accepted	Wait for License	Wait after License
Alabama (b)	17	14	21	18	Yes	Yes	None	None
Alaska	18	16	21	18	Yes	....	3 days	None
Arizona	18	16	21	18	Yes	Yes	(g)	None
Arkansas	18	16	21	18	Yes	No	3 days	None
California	18	16	21	18	Yes	Yes	None	None
Colorado	16	16	21	18	Yes	....	None	None
Connecticut	16	16	21	21	Yes	Yes	4 days	None
Delaware	18	16	21	18	Yes	No	None	96 hours (a)
Dist. of Columbia	18	16	21	18	Yes	Yes	4 days	None
Florida	18	16	21	21	Yes	Yes	3 days	None
Georgia	18	16	19	18	Yes	Yes	None (b)	None
Hawaii	18	16	20	20	Yes	No	3 days	None
Idaho	18	16	21	18	Yes	Yes	None (i)	None
Illinois (a)	18	16	21	18	Yes	Yes	None	None
Indiana	18	16	21	18	Yes	No	3 days	None
Iowa	18	16	21	18	Yes	No	3 days	None
Kansas	18	18	21	18	Yes	Yes	3 days	None
Kentucky	18	16	18	18	Yes	No	3 days	None
Louisiana (a)	18	16	21	21	Yes	No	None	72 hours
Maine	16	16	21	18	Yes	Yes	5 days	None
Maryland	18	16	21	18	None	None	48 hours	None
Massachusetts	18	16	21	18	Yes	Yes	3 days	None
Michigan	18	16	18	18	Yes	No	3 days	None
Minnesota	18	16	21	18	None	....	5 days	None
Mississippi (b)	17	15	21	18	Yes	....	3 days	None
Missouri	15	15	21	18	Yes	....	3 days	None
Montana	18	16	21	18	Yes	Yes	5 days	None
Nebraska	18	16	21	21	Yes	Yes	None	None
Nevada	18	16	21	18	None	None	None	None
New Hampshire(a)	14(e)	13(e)	20	18	Yes	....	5 days	None
New Jersey (a)	18	16	21	18	Yes	Yes	72 hours	None
New Mexico	18	16	21	18	Yes	No	3 days	None
New York	16	14	21	18	Yes	No	None	24 hours (h)
North Carolina	16	16	18	18	Yes	Yes	None	None
North Dakota (a)	18	15	21	18	Yes	No	None	None
Ohio (a)	18	16	21	21	Yes	No	5 days	None
Oklahoma	18	15	21	18	Yes	No	None (i)	None
Oregon	18(e)	15(e)	21	18	Yes	No	7 days	None
Pennsylvania	16	16	21	21	Yes	No	3 days	None
Rhode Island(a)(b)	18	16	21	21	Yes	No	None	None
South Carolina	16	14	18	18	None	None	24 hours	None
South Dakota	18	16	21	18	Yes	No	None	None
Tennessee (b)	16	16	21	21	Yes	Yes	3 days	None
Texas	16	14	21	18	Yes	Yes	(b)	None
Utah	16	14	21	18	Yes	Yes	None	None
Vermont (a)	18	14 (e)	21	18	Yes	....	None	5 days
Virginia	18	16	21	21	Yes	Yes	None	None
Washington	17	17	21	18	(d)	....	3 days	None
West Virginia	18	16	21	21	Yes	No	3 days	None
Wisconsin	18	16	21	18	Yes	Yes	5 days	None
Wyoming	18	16	21	21	Yes	Yes	None	None
Puerto Rico	18	16	21	21	(f)	None	None	None
Virgin Islands	16	14	21	18	None	None	8 days	None

(a) Special laws applicable to non-residents. (b) Special laws applicable to those under 21 years; Alabama—bond required if male is under 21, female under 18. (c) 24 hours if one or both parties resident of state; 96 hours if both parties are non-residents. (d) None, but male must file affidavit. (e) Parental consent plus court's consent required. (f) None, but a medical certificate is required. (g) Wait for license from time blood test is taken; Arizona 48 hours. (h) Marriage may not be solemnized within three days from date of blood test. (i) If either under 21: Idaho—3 days; Oklahoma—72 hours.

MARRIAGE SETTLEMENT A settlement made by a husband out of his estate, before or after marriage, for the benefit of his wife, or for his wife and children.

MARSHALING ASSETS A principle in equity for a fair distribution of a debtor's assets among his creditors. For example, when a creditor of A, by reason of prior right, has two funds X and Y belonging to A out of which he may satisfy his debt, but B, also a creditor of A, has a right as to X fund, the first creditor will be compelled to exhaust Y fund before he will be permitted to participate in X fund.

MARTIAL LAW A system of law concerned with the government of hostile, captured territory during war or of domestic territory at times of civil insurrection. It is arbitrary in nature, and is controlled merely by the command of the chief officer.

MASTER IN CHANCERY An important officer of courts of equity, who acts as assistant to the chancellor or judge, and whose principal duty consists in inquiring into various matters referred to him for the purpose of reporting them to the court.

MATERIAL ALTERATION Any alteration of a written instrument that affects the identity of the parties or changes the legal obligations and rights of the parties is material.

MATTER OF DEED A fact which may be proved by exhibition of a deed which contains it.

MATTER OF FACT That which is known by the senses or is to be found by a jury on the evidence of what has been perceived.

MATTER OF LAW That which is concluded by the application of principles of law to established facts.

MATTER OF OPINION A matter of fact which is not ordinarily apparent to the senses but can be known by special knowledge, and hence can be testified to by persons qualified as experts.

MATTER OF RECORD That which can be proved by being contained in an authenticated court record.

MAXIMS Those ancient rules, axioms or postulates of the common law which are general or universal in their application. The authority of these maxims rests entirely upon general reception and usage, and the only method of proving that this or that maxim is a rule of common law is by showing that it has always been the custom to observe it.

MAYHEM The criminal offense of unlawfully and violently depriving another of the use of such of his members as may render him less able in fighting to defend himself. The cutting or disabling or weakening a man's hand or finger or striking out his eye or foretooth or depriving him of those parts, the loss of which reduce his courage, are held to be mayhems. Cutting off an ear or nose or the like are not mayhems.

MECHANIC'S LIEN A means whereby mechanics and others may obtain payment for labor and materials in constructing any building. In general, it may be said, that mechanic's liens give preference to persons supplying materials or labor or both in the construction of buildings, and, in some places in erecting bridges, fences, wharves, etc. All mechanic's liens against the same building share pro rata in the proceeds of the property in case it is sold at a judicial sale for an amount insufficient to pay the entire claims. The lien usually attaches to the building and to adjoining land necessary to its use. To retain the lien in most places a statement of the claim must be filed in a prescribed public office within a given time.

MECHANICS Artisans or handicraftsmen. Where mechanics or artisans are employed to make up materials or to finish, alter or repair a specific thing, the contract existing is for the benefit of both the owner and the mechanic and the latter is required to exercise such ordinary care of the article or material as a man of ordinary capacity and caution might be reasonably expected to take of it if it were his own. What constitutes ordinary care varies with the circumstances and the nature of the thing in charge. The mechanic must exercise reasonable time if none is specified.

If work requires great or particular skill, but is committed to one known not to possess it, the owner cannot recover for results arising from the lack of it from him. The workman may maintain a suit to recover the article from one wrongfully taking it from him, and if the property perishes in his hands, without his fault, he is entitled to be paid for the work already expended upon it.

If the mechanic does not obey instructions and in consequence the work is useless, he is not entitled to be paid; also, if his work is left imperfect and unfinished through his own fault. If he deviates from his instructions, putting more work on it than required, he cannot recover for the additional work unless it was expressly or impliedly assented to by the owner. If assent is given to alterations or additions, either expressly or by silence, where the owner knows that they are being made, payment must be made at the same rates as in the case of the origianal work contracted for, unless there is a special agreement as to the price for the additions. The workman has a lien upon the article to which the work is applied for his pay, and may hold it until payment is made, but may not sell it unless so authorized by a statute law.

MEDICAL EVIDENCE Testimony given by physicians and surgeons as experts within the scope of their professional study and experience.

In obtaining the evidence or opinions of physicians or any other class of witnesses as experts, care must be taken not to put them in the position of usurping the functions of the jury. They must not be required to give an opinion in favor of the plaintiff or defendants based upon the evidence adduced in the case. It is not for them to determine which witnesses testify truthfully and which falsely and which are credible and which are not, or what part of the testimony applies to the particular case under consideration, or what weight should be given to the testimony of the several witnesses. For this reason medical witnesses who do not have personal knowledge of the facts of the case are asked hypothetical questions; that is, they are asked to give their opinions as to causes and results which would accompany facts and conditions enumerated to them, assuming them to be true, leaving it to the jury entirely to determine under instructions from the court whether or not the enumerated conditions have been proven. The facts detailed to the expert witness should correspond with testimony or evidence adduced in the case, and the witness should be asked what his opinion would be as to the particular subject matter inquired about—whether the treatment was such as the case demanded, proper or improper, skillful or unskillful—if the facts so detailed in the hypothetical question are true. It is then for the jury to determine how far the facts in the case accord with the hypothetical question, and how far the opinion of the witness applies to the case under investigation. It is proper to obtain from expert witnesses their reasons for their opinions.

Physicians and surgeons are permitted as witnesses to give opinions as to the nature, cause and effect of disease and injuries and wounds and of their consequences. In case of whether they are fatal or lasting wounds, by what instruments they are caused. They may also testify as to the effect of a given treatment, or whether it was proper under given circumstances or in accordance with ordinary care, skill and diligence, and to mental soundness or unsoundness and the like, as well as to the nature and effect of different poisons, etc. It seems too that they may testify relating to diseases among animals as well as people. The knowledge from which they testify may be derived from either study or experience.

Before being allowed to testify to the jury as an expert it must be shown that the physician or surgeon is qualified to testify as such; that in fact he is an expert. This may be shown either by the testimony of the witness himself addressed to the court as to the extent of his study and experience, and graduation in a regular medical school, or it may be shown by the testimony of others. Whether or not he is shown to be sufficiently qualified is a matter for the court alone to determine. Graduation in a reputable medical institution granting the degree of doctor of medicine and a legal license to practice medicine and surgery are in general prima facie sufficient to enable one to testify as a medical expert. Yet it seems he should have the ordinary ability of members of his profession, also that a specialist only should testify regarding matters concerning which the knowledge of the ordinary practitioner is necessarily limited. Medical books may not be offered as evidence to prove what is therein stated. The persons who wrote them were not under oath when they wrote and they cannot be cross-examined. In some places, however, counsel may read from medical books by way of argument and cross-examination.

Confidential communications to physicians or surgeons are not at common law privileged, that is, a medical man who is a witness may not refuse to testify regarding such communications because communicated in secret or because they would prove detrimental to his patient. In many of the states, however, information committed in confidence to a physician necessary to enable him to prescribe for his patient, or by a surgeon in order to do an act for a patient, may not, if detrimental to the patient, be disclosed on the witness stand.

MENS REA A guilty mind. Said of one who has a criminal intent.

MERGER The absorption of one corporation by another, including all of its assets. Its individual existence is subsequently discontinued.

MESNE Any conveyance or transfer of property which was executed previously to the last one.

MESNE PROFITS Intermediate profits or profits accruing between two points of time.

METES AND BOUNDS The boundary lines of lands, with their terminating points or angles; terminal lines, with their distinctive objects; end lines and side lines.

MINOR One who is less than twenty-one years of age. He or she reaches majority the first instant of the day preceding the twenty-first anniversary of his or her birth. At common law there is no distinction between the sexes as to arriving at full age though by statute in some of the United States it is different.

Before arriving at full age, however, there are some acts that minors may legally do. A male at fourteen may consent to marriage and at that age may disagree to and annul a marriage contract made before that time. He may choose a guardian and at common law may make a will of his personal estate if it is shown that he had attained proper discretion, and may act as executor at seventeen. At common law, which of course prevails except where altered by statute (not, however, in Louisiana), a female at seven may be betrothed or given in marriage, at nine is entitled to dower, at twelve may consent or disagree to marriage and at seventeen may act as executrix.

A minor, or infant, as he is commonly called in legal language, is not bound by contracts he may make unless they are to supply him with necessaries or unless he is empowered to do so by some legislative provision as in enlisting in the military service. On becoming of age he may set aside contracts that he has made, but this must be done within a reasonable time and it does not apply to contracts for necessaries. The repudiation can only be by himself and may not be by any other person for him. The person he contracts with if he is an adult or capable of contracting is bound by the contract if the minor chooses to insist upon it. Nevertheless, where a contract has been performed and the minor upon arriving at the age still has the thing contracted for, and no undue influence has been exercised over him, he can not retain both the thing and the price of it or retain the thing and recover back the price if paid for. He can only take the price or the thing, not both, if both are still in existence, or at least he must return such portion as he still has if he would get back what he has parted with. If, while a minor, he has been paid wholly or in part for a thing he has contracted to sell but has not delivered, and if he refuses to deliver after arriving at majority he must pay back the money, if he still has the same money or has not used it during his minority. If he has used up or consumed during minority the money or thing he has obtained, the party dealing with him must nevertheless suffer the loss, and must return what he has obtained from the minor under the contract.

Such, it is believed, are the rules most generally prevailing on this subject, though the law varies somewhat in different states. The law extends protection to minors because of their supposed lack of discretion to protect themselves properly, but, so far as it can, consistently with this aim, it requires them to be honest. The law will not shield minors from perpetrating fraud or doing injury to others. They are therefore responsible for their torts such as negligence, slander, trespass, damage to the person or property of others and the like. However, if the injury arises out of contract they are not responsible, and a minor is not liable for falsely stating his age in order to obtain credit in purchasing goods.

No child under seven years old can be guilty of felony or punished for capital offense. Between seven and fourteen years of age it must be shown that he possesses sufficient descretion to understand the wrong involved in the act committed before he can be convicted, but after fourteen, as to such crimes, he stands in the same position as an adult.

A minor is entitled to maintenance and support from his or her father. On the other hand the father is entitled to the earnings of the minor. To relieve the child from absolute want, necessaries may be furnished to it and the father held liable even where he does not order them. Ordinarily, however, the parents must be the judges of the child's necessities. But little evidence is required to show the assent of the father to the purchase of ordinary necessaries. Thus if he sees the child with a new suit on and knows where it was supplied and does not object, this is sufficient to show assent.

If the child is expelled from home, or caused to leave by the wrongful or cruel acts of the parents, third parties may supply reasonable necessaries to it and recover from the parent. Where the parents are divorced or separated the father is liable for the maintenance and education of his minor children even if he permits the mother to take them.

The father is liable for his minor child's support and education even if the child has independent means of his own, though if he is without adequate means, the proper court will allow a sufficient part of the minor's estate to be used for the child's advantage. The mother would not be so bound, unless where under the law she has the reciprocal right to his earnings.

A husband who makes the child of his wife by a former husband one of his family, it would appear, is entitled to his custody and his earnings, and is bound to support him. Though the father is entitled to collect wages from the employer of his minor child, yet he may relinquish to the child his own right to the wages and to demand them from either the employer or the child. This relinquishment may be inferred from circumstances, as where the father leaves the son to transact his own affairs.

While the child is in the control and care of a father able to support him, the former is not liable for necessaries though he expressly promises to pay for them.

MINUTES The record of a court or the written transactions of the members or board of directors of a corporation. Under the certificate of the clerk of a court or the secretary of a corporation, the minutes are the official evidence of court or corporate action

MISCARRIAGE The expulsion of the ovum or embryo from the uterus within the first six weeks after conception. Between that time, and before the expiration of the sixth month, when the child may possibly live, it is termed abortion. When the delivery takes place soon after the sixth month it is called premature labor. But the criminal act of destroying the foetus at any time before birth is termed, in law, procuring miscarriage.

MISCEGENATION Marriage between persons of different races, especially between a white person and a Negro.

MISDEMEANOR A name given to criminal offenses inferior to felony, such as perjury, assault and battery, libel, conspiracies and numerous others. Misdemeanors are punishable by indictment or by particular prescribed proceedings and include a great variety of statutory offenses over which magistrates are given summary jurisdiction.

MISFEASANCE The negligent performance of an act in itself lawful.

MISPRISION Silently observing the commission of a felony without endeavoring to apprehend the offender. It is the duty of every citizen having knowledge of treason or felony to inform a magistrate of the fact. Misprision of treason is the concealment of treason by being merely passive. Active assistance of the traitor makes one guilty as a principal.

MISREPRESENTATION To represent incorrectly any material part of the consideration of an executory contract, that is, one in which some act remains to be done. The misrepresentation will void or cancel the contract, and if the misrepresentation is both false and fraudulent the party making it will be held responsible to the other for damages. To constitute fraud, a misrepresentation must be contrary to fact and either the party making it must know it to be such or he must falsely assert that he knows when he does not, and his assertion must have given rise to or resulted in the contracting by the other party. If the misrepresentation results from mistake only, this will not amount to fraud.

MISTAKE As a general rule, both at law and in equity, mistakes of law only do not excuse a wrongful action or afford a ground of relief from the consequences of acts done because of such mistakes. But if the act done, or the contract made, is under mistake or in ignorance of a material fact it may be either voided or relief may be obtained in equity. The fact, however, must be a material one and it must be an efficient cause of the doing of the act or the making of the contract.

The rule applies especially where there has been a studied suppression of facts on one side, and to cases of mutual ignorance or mistake. An award of arbitrators made from mistake of law or fact on their part, if apparent on the face of the award, may be set aside. In equity, a word which the parties intended to use in an instrument may be substituted for one actually used by clerical error.

MISTRIAL An erroneous trial on account of some defect in the persons ·trying, as if the jury came from the wrong county, or because there was no issue formed, or as if no plea was entered.

MITIGATION OF DAMAGES A term relating only to exemplary damages and their reduction by extenuating circumstances, such as provocation or malice. The theory of such mitigation is based on the regard of the law for the frailty of human passions, since it looks with some indulgence upon violations of good order which are committed in a moment of irritation and excitement.

MOIETY One-half.

MONEY The circulating medium or standard by which the value of other things is measured and which is commonly given in exchange for such things is money. It includes coins and circulating notes issued by government authority and, by common consent, even bank notes.

The parties to a contract cannot be deprived of the right to contract for payment in gold coin of the United States by a statute which provides that payment of a debt may be made in any kind of lawful money. It has been decided that a bill or note with a piece torn from the upper left-hand corner, an inch and a half long and an inch and a quarter wide, need not be accepted in payment, though otherwise it would be legal tender money.

MONOPOLY In its broadest meaning, the word signifies the sole power of dealing in an article or doing a specified thing, either generally or in a particular place.

MOOT CASE A judgment in advance of a presumed controversy, the decision of which has no legal effect upon any existing controversy.

MORAL TURPITUDE Conduct contrary to justice, honesty or good morals.

MORGANATIC MARRIAGE A marriage between a man of superior rank and a woman of inferior rank, in which it is stipulated that the latter and her children shall not enjoy the rank or inherit the possessions of her husband.

MORTALITY TABLE A life table. It is used largely in ascertaining the value of life estates, and is accepted by courts as evidence in fixing such value. It is used largely to determine pecuniary loss in case of a death caused by negligence.

AVERAGE FUTURE LIFETIME IN UNITED STATES

Source: U.S. Dept. of Health, Education and Welfare,
National Center for Health Statistics, 1966 Data

| Age interval | Number living† | Total | Average remaining lifetime‡ | | | |
| | | | White | | Nonwhite | |
			Male	Female	Male	Female
0-1	100,000	70.1	67.6	74.7	60.7	67.4
1-5	97,639	70.8	68.2	75.1	62.4	68.8
5-10	97,276	67.1	64.4	71.3	58.8	65.2
10-15	97,063	62.2	59.6	66.4	54.0	60.4
15-20	96,863	57.3	54.7	61.5	49.2	55.5
20-25	96,368	52.6	50.1	56.7	44.6	50.7
25-30	95,727	48.0	45.5	51.8	40.3	46.0
30-35	95,072	43.3	40.8	47.0	36.0	41.4
35-40	94,258	38.6	36.2	42.2	31.9	37.0
40-45	93,118	34.1	31.6	37.5	28.0	32.8
45-50	91,390	29.7	27.2	32.9	24.2	28.8
50-55	88,753	25.5	23.1	28.5	20.8	25.0
55-60	84,779	21.5	19.3	24.2	17.6	21.3
60-65	79,029	17.9	15.9	20.2	14.9	18.1
65-70	71,298	14.6	12.9	16.3	12.4	15.2
70-75	60,781	11.6	10.3	12.8	11.0	13.4
75-80	48,078	9.0	8.0	9.6	9.8	11.2
80-85	34,040	6.7	6.1	6.9	8.4	9.2
85 and over.........	19,855	4.7	4.4	4.7	6.7	7.0

†Of 100,000 born alive, number living at beginning of age interval.
‡Average number of years of life remainng at beginning of age interval.

YEARS OF LIFE EXPECTED AT BIRTH*

Year	Total	Male	Female	Year	Total	Male	Female
1967†....	70.5	67.0	74.2	1935.....	61.7	59.9	63.9
1966.....	70.1	66.7	73.8	1930.....	59.7	58.1	61.6
1965.....	70.2	66.8	73.7	1925.....	59.0	57.6	60.6
1960.....	69.7	66.6	73.1	1920.....	54.1	53.6	54.6
1955.....	69.5	66.6	72.7	1915.....	54.5	52.5	56.8
1950.....	68.2	65.6	71.1	1910.....	50.0	48.4	51.8
1945.....	65.9	63.6	67.9	1905.....	48.7	47.3	50.2
1940.....	62.9	60.8	65.2	1900.....	47.3	46.3	48.3

*Based on Death-Registration States 1900-1925, and United States 1930-1966. †Provisional.

MORTGAGE A conveyance of an estate or property by way of pledge for the security of a debt which becomes void on payment of the debt. All kinds of property, real or personal, capable of an absolute sale may be the subject of a mortgage. This includes rights in remainder and reversion, franchises, and choses in action.

It is said a mere possibility of expectancy, that is, something which has not vested but may possibly vest at a future time provided certain things happen, cannot be mortgaged. This is true in law. But where an assignment of any such expectancy has been made to secure a debt, immediately upon its vesting, the assignment will in equity take hold of it and become operative.

Even a bill of sale of personal property or a collateral assignment of a debt or note or legacy or bequest or distributive share of an estate to secure payment of a debt is in the nature of a mortgage though not commonly called such. The term is usually applied to mortgages upon real estate and in some states to chattel mortgages upon movable personal property also.

A mortgage may be recorded and thereby become a lien against the real or personal property, as the case may be, of the mortgagor, giving the holder priority over mortgage and judgments and other liens subsequently recorded or entered. Acknowledgments in proper form before a proper officer must precede recording.

A mortgage of real estate is in form a conveyance thereof with a clause of defeasance, that is, a clause providing that, if the mortgagor pay to the mortgagee debt, interest, etc., owing to him at a given time, the mortgage shall become void. This defeasance, however, may be by separate instrument and even a deed without a defeasance will be treated in equity as a mortgage if it is proven that the conveyance was made for purposes of security merely, equity thus in reality superseding the law.

In law the defeasance must be of as high a nature as the conveyance, that is, the conveyance being by deed under seal, the defeasance should be also. A verbal defeasance will therefore be void at law as against a conveyance which must be in writing, though good in equity. Equity, indeed, for the most part, controls mortgages. Technically speaking, one having conveyed his right away is in law practically a tenant, subject to the right of the mortgagee to enter immediately unless a contract is made to contrary. In equity, the mortgage is held as a mere security for the debt and is only a chattel interest and is not considered real estate at all. The mortgagor is regarded as the real owner until proper proceedings are had to put the mortgagee in possession upon default of payment or to effect a sale of the property in order to give the mortgagee his money.

Even though the time of payment of the mortgage may have arrived and according to the terms of the mortgage it would appear as if the right of the mortgagor in land was at an end, he will still have what is termed his equity of redemption, that is, he may yet pay the amount of the debt, interest and costs and retain the property. This equity of redemption continues to exist until it has been defeated or extinguished by proper proceedings on the part of the mortgagee under some statute specially enacted for the purpose or in a court of equity. Of these proceedings the mortgagee will have due notice and an opportunity to pay and one purchasing the property from the mortgagor will have the like right as will also the mortgagor's heirs, devises, executors and administrators in case of his death. The equity of redemption may likewise be exercised by subsequent encumbrancers or judgment creditors or by tenants for years or by a doweress or tenant by curtesy, or by one having an easement in the property, for such persons have rights to be protected as well as the mortgagor.

Foreclosure of a mortgage may result from occupation by the mortgagee for twenty years or whatever period is equal to the length of time within which suit must be brought to recover possession of land against an adverse holder, as well as in the ways above indicated. An assignment of a mortgage must be in writing and delivered to the assignee, and not by delivery of the mortgage only.

Provision is made by statute for the recording of mortgages. They are binding as between the parties to the mortgage themselves and their privies without recording. As to third persons, such as subsequent encumbrancers or purchasers of the property, they are not binding unless recorded or unless the third parties have knowledge of the existence thereof prior to the attachment of their own interests. Thus, if the third party lends money to the mortgagor without knowing of the mortgage, the mortgage not being recorded, and himself takes a mortgage or a judgment as security and has it recorded or entered, thereby making it a lien against the real estate, such lien will have priority over unrecorded mortgages. The notice to the third party of the unrecorded mortgage must be of a tangible character. A mere neighborhood rumor is insufficient.

MORTGAGE FORM

Note—The following form, it is believed, will supply all the information required to draft a mortgage for use anywhere in the United States or Canada. For forms of acknowledgments to be appended to the mortgages see Acknowledgments. For forms of chattel mortgages see Chattel Mortgage.

This indenture, made the _____ day of _____, A.D., 19____, between _____ of the first part, and _____ of the second part: Whereas, the said _____ in and by his certain obligation of writing obligatory under his hand and seal duly executed, and bearing even date herewith, stands bound unto the said party of the second part, in the sum of _____ dollars conditioned for the payment of _____ dollars _____ year after the date thereof with interest at the rate of _____ per centum per annum from said date _____ without any fraud or further delay, as in and by them said recited obligation and condition thereof, relation to the same being had, may more fully and at large appear.

Now this indenture, witnesseth, that the said party of the first part, as well for and in consideration of the aforesaid debt or sum of _____ dollars and for the better securing the payment thereof, unto the said party of the second part, his executors, administrators and assigns, in discharge of the said obligation above recited, as for and in consideration of the further sum of one dollar in specie, well and truly paid to the said party of the first part, by the said party of the second part, at and before the ensealing and delivery hereof, the receipt of which one dollar is hereby acknowledged has granted, bargained, sold, released and confirmed, and by these presents does grant, bargain, sell, release and confirm unto the said party of the second part, his heirs and assigns, all the premises. (Describe the premises.)

Together with all and singular, the buildings, improvements, woods, ways, rights, liberties, privileges, hereditaments and appurtenances, to the same belonging, or in anywise appertaining and the reversion and reversions, remainder and remainders, rents, issues and profits thereof: To have and to hold the said hereditaments and premises above granted, or intended so to be, with the appurtenances, unto the said party of the second part, his heirs and assigns forever.

Provided, however, and it is expressly agreed, that if at any time default shall be made in the payment of any installment of principal or interest for the space of _____ days after the same becomes due by the terms hereof, then and in such case, the whole principal debt and interest aforesaid, shall, at the option of the said party of the second part, his executors, administrators or assigns, become due and payable immediately; and the said party of the second part may at once proceed to collect the same by suit upon said obligation, or *scire facias* hereon, any law, usage or custom, or anything herein contained to the contrary notwithstanding, and in such suit, or upon such *scire facias*, judgment shall be recovered for the said principal sum, and all interest then due, together with _____ per cent on the whole amount thereof as attorney's commission.

Provided always, nevertheless, that if the said _____ heirs, executors, administrators or assigns, do and shall well and truly pay or cause to be paid unto the said party of the second part, his executors, administrators or assigns, the aforesaid debt or sum of _____ on the day and time hereinbefore mentioned and appointed for the payment thereof, together with lawful interest for the same, in like money, in the way and manner hereinbefore specified therefor, without any fraud or further delay, and without any deduction, defalcation or abatement to be made, for or in respect of any taxes, charges or assessments whatsoever, that then and from thenceforth, as well this present indenture, and the estate hereby granted, as the said obligation above recited, shall cease, determine and become absolutely null and void, to all intents and purposes, anything hereinbefore contained to the contrary thereof in anywise notwithstanding.

Witness our hands and seals.

_____(Seal)
_____(Seal)
_____(Seal)

Test:
_____

MORTGAGEE One to whom a mortgage is made, the lender.

MORTGAGOR One who makes a mortgage, the borrower.

MOST-FAVORED-NATION CLAUSE A provision in treaties that the citizens of the contracting parties shall receive the most favorable treatment given by either of the parties to citizens of non-contracting parties.

MOTHER, DUTIES OF THE It is generally the mother's duty, if a widow, to support her child until he becomes of age or is able to maintain himself, and even after he becomes of age. If he is a charge upon the public, she may in most places be compelled to support him if she has sufficient means. But if the child has sufficient property for his own maintenance she is not obliged to support him even during his minority but will be allowed sufficient income out of his estate and if necessary out of the principal, to maintain him, and during the life of the father she will not be required to support him even if she has separate estate and the father has none. The widowed mother's right to the service and earnings of her minor child seems to be somewhat indefinite and uncertain. At least, it is not so certain as the right of the father, varying somewhat with the different jurisdictions.

MOTION A formal application made to a court asking for incidental relief during the progress of a lawsuit.

MOTIVE The cause or reason that induced a person to commit a crime.

MULCT A pecuniary fine, penalty, or punishment for the commission of a crime or a tort.

MULTIPLE WILLS Copies of the same will, each executed as if it were an original.

MUNICIPAL   CORPORATIONS Cities and boroughs, and quasi-municipal corporations, such as counties, townships, and school districts which exist for the purpose of promoting and caring for local public needs and for protection and convenience. Their powers are limited to those delegated to them by the legislative authority, either by express words or necessary implications. The methods prescribed by the same authority for exercising those powers must be strictly followed. Contracts made by a municipal corporation in excess of its powers cannot be enforced against it, and parties dealing with it should for their own protection inform themselves as to the extent of those powers, and whether or not they have been exercised in such manner as to be legal and binding. Indebtedness incurred beyond the limit prescribed by law cannot be collected.

All municipal corporations are liable for damages resulting from negligence, as, for example, in permitting dangerous places to remain in highways longer than necessary. This liability extends to acts of officers and employees done in the course of their duties or employment. Quite extensive powers are usually granted municipal corporations in the matter of general police regulation, that is, power to enact ordinances affecting the good order, peace, health, protection, comfort, convenience and morals of the community. The right of eminent domain, the right to impose local taxes and license taxes, the right to purchase or lease real estate necessary to corporate purposes, to establish public works, as for illumination, sewerage and water supply, to open, pave or repair highways, to borrow money to a given amount and issue bonds therefor, are among the many rights commonly vested in municipal corporations.

Though a municipal corporation may have contracted with another party, as a railroad company, to keep a street in safe condition, yet this will not relieve the municipality from liability to the person injured for damages resulting from their unsafe condition.

MUNICIPAL LAW As opposed to international law, the law of a particular community, state or nation.

MURDER The unlawful killing of one person by another with malice aforethought, either express or implied. To be guilty of murder one must be possessed of a sound mind, that is, there must be will and legal discretion. The killing need not be by direct violence. Setting poison for another, resulting in his death, is murder. It is sufficient if the act done apparently endangers life and eventually proves fatal. And there must be malice aforethought, which especially distinguishes murder from other kinds of homicide.

Murder is usually divided into two degrees. All murder which is perpetrated by means of poison or by lying in wait or by any other kind of wilful, deliberate and premeditated killing or which is committed in the perpetration of or attempt to perpetrate any arson, rape, robbery or burglary, is murder of the first degree. All other kinds of murder are murders in the second degree.

MUTINY Mutiny is a criminal offense and consists in the unlawful resistance of a superior officer by the raising of commotions and disturbances on board a ship, whether a merchant or war vessel, against the authority of its commander, or in the army in opposition to the authority of the officer.

MUTUAL AND RECIPROCAL WILLS Separate instruments executed by individual testators and containing reciprocal provisions for the disposition of their individual property in accordance with an agreement between them.

MUTUALITY That essential of every contract to make it binding upon both parties at the same time. It is a rule of law that there must be mutuality in a contract; that is, it must be binding upon both parties at the same time, if it is to be deemed valid and enforceable as to either.

MYSTIC TESTAMENT In Louisiana law, a will specially executed, signed and sealed in an envelope.

N

NAME That by which a person thing is called.

The surname is the last or family me. Only one Christian name is cognized in law; if a person has o Christian names they are in ntemplation of law but one com unded name. A middle initial in ted as an abbreviation of part of e Christian name is not part of her the Christian name or sur me.

In a warrant of arrest the real me of the party to be arrested ist be inserted if known, and if known, some description must given with the reason for the ission. Mistakes in name or scription of legatees in wills may corrected whenever it can be arly shown by the will itself at was intended. The only in nce in which parol evidence is missible to show the intention of testator as to a legatee imper ctly described is that of a strict uivocation, that is, where it ap ars from extraneous or outside idence that two or more persons swer the same description in the ll. An incorrect spelling of a name will not matter in law pro vided the pronunciation or sound is not changed or materially changed.

Where one in making a contract under seal uses an incorrect name he will not afterwards be per mitted to say that it is not his name. If one in the body of a deed or instrument under seal describes himself as James and signs it John he cannot, on being sued by the latter name, escape by alleging that his name is James. If one sign such an instrument as "Smith & Jones" (being his own and his partner's names) without lawful authority from the partner, either express or implied, he cannot deny that his name is "Smith & Jones." In gen eral a corporation must contract, sue and be sued by its corporate name, but a slight alteration in stat ing the name is unimportant if there is no possibility of mistaking the identity of the corporation.

NATURAL AFFECTION Affection existing between near relatives and sufficient for good consideration, as opposed to valuable consideration.

ATURALIZATION The process of becoming a citizen. Article 1, Section of the Constitution of the United States, vests in Congress the power to ablish a uniform rule of naturalization.

The naturalization laws apply to both men and women. They become izens of the United States in the same way and under the same cedure.

Generally, an applicant for naturalization must have been "lawfully ad tted for permanent residence." Whenever that or similar term is used it ans the status of having lawfully accorded the privilege of residing rmanently in the United States as an immigrant in accordance with the

361

immigration laws, such status not having been changed. One admitted the United States as a visitor for business or pleasure, for example, m remain only for a fixed time. Such a person does not meet the requir ment of this paragraph. Neither, of course, does one who gained ent into the United States in violation of law, as by falsely denying convictic of a crime involving moral turpitude, by entering without inspection, stowing away on a ship, or by becoming a member of a ship's crew an deserting.

The bar to the naturalization of persons of certain races has been r moved, and now persons of any race may become citizens of the Unit States.

The law requires that aliens living in the United States be registered. registered alien is given evidence of his registration which generally known or referred to as an alien registration receipt card. Any alien wl has not complied with the registration requirement should notify the nea est Immigration and Naturalization office at once. The number of tl alien registration receipt card must be shown on all application forms.

A person admitted to the United States as an immigrant on or after Ju 1, 1928, but before August 27, 1950, was issued an "immigrant identific tion card"; that is, a small green card bearing his photograph, descriptio and certain other information. Some applicants may have received a cert icate of registry or lawful entry in connection with legalization of residen or a resident alien's border-crossing identification card. These a presented by the applicant when he appears to file his petition for natur ization and are given by him to an officer of the Immigration and Natur ization Service when he is admitted to citizenship.

Under legislation effective December 24, 1952, it is no longer necessa to file a declaration of intention, or as commonly known, a first pape prior to filing a petition for naturalization (formerly the second pape However, a declaration of intention may be filed by an alien, who, f example, may require it for purpose of employment but is not ready f naturalization because he has not completed the period of residence r quired by law.

1. An applicant for a declaration of intention must be over 18 years age.

2. He may make and file a declaration of intention at any time if he residing in the United States pursuant to lawful admission for permane residence. He cannot file a petition for naturalization until he has lived the United States for a specified number of years, but there is no su requirement with respect to the declaration of intention.

3. The making and filing of a declaration of intention may take place any naturalization court regardless of the applicant's place of residence the United States. (He must file his petition for naturalization in a natur ization court in the district in which he lives.)

4. He is not required to read, write, and speak English when he appl

his declaration of intention; if necessary, he may sign that paper in any guage or by mark. But he cannot become a citizen until he can read, te, and speak words in ordinary usuage in the English language, unless is physically unable to do so or unless on December 24, 1952, he was r 50 years of age and had been living in the United States for periods aling at least 20 years.

An applicant must use Naturalization Form N-300 when he applies for declaration of intention. If he cannot get a copy of that form from a rk of the court, a teacher, or a social agency in the place where he s, he can get it from any Immigration and Naturalization office. There o charge for this form. After he has filled it out according to directions must take it, or mail it, to the office of the Immigration and Naturaliza-Service together with three photographs of himself.

n filling in item (1) on page 1 of the Form N-300, the applicant must sure to spell his name exactly as it was spelled in his home country, as he used it in coming to the United States. If he does not do so, it y be difficult to prove that he was legally admitted for permanent idence and is entitled to obtain a declaration of intention

The three photographs which the applicant must submit with his appli-ion to file a declaration of intention (Form N-300) must be identical otographs, 2 by 2 inches in size, unmounted, printed on thin paper, e a light background, and clearly show, without hat, a full front view the features (with head bare, unless the person is wearing a headdress required by a religious order of which he is a member). In the photo-phs the distance from the top of the head to point of chin must be ut 1¼ inches. They must have been taken within 30 days of the date y are furnished. The applicant must write his name in the margin of h photograph, but must be careful not to write it so as to hide the face the photograph. If he is unable to write he may make his mark on the rgin of the photograph and have someone else write in his name. The ections in this paragraph also apply to photographs needed in connec-n with other naturalization applications

After the Government has found the record of the applicant's lawful manent admission, and his application is approved, he is notified to ear before the clerk of the naturalization court to make and file the laration of intention. The applicant executes his declaration on Form 315 before that official, and in so doing, the information he gave in his rm N-300 is used. It is, therefore, very important that the information correct. The applicant must sign the declaration of intention with his ne or his mark before the clerk of the court and swear that the state-nts in it are true. If it is later found that an applicant has given wrong ormation on any important point he may have serious trouble.

The applicant pays $5.00 to the clerk of court for his declaration of ention.

Under legislation effective December 24, 1952, an applicant's first step toward naturalization is the filing of a petition for naturalization. No loer is he required to make a declaration of intention, but may do so if he wishes.

1. (a) The applicant must be at least 18 years of age.

(b) If a child under 18 years of age has not become a citizen throu his parents, and one of the parents is a citizen, that parent may file petition in the child's behalf.

2. Generally, an applicant must be residing in this country after hav been lawfully admitted for permanent residence.

3. A person who applies for naturalization on his own petition m understand English and be able to read, write, and speak words in ordin usage in the English language unless he is physically unable to do Persons who, on December 24, 1952, were over 50 years of age and been living in the United States for 20 years are also exempt from requirement

4. Generally, an applicant is required to have resided continuously the United States for 5 years and, for the last 6 months of that period, have resided in the State where he petitions for naturalization. For h bands and wives of citizens of the United States the required residence years, including residence for the last 6 months of that period in the St in which the petition is filed, provided that during the said 3 years, applicant has been living in marital union with the spouse who has bee United States citizen during all such period.

Continuous residence does not mean that the applicant may not ha been outside of the United States for short periods during the requi residence. However, he must have been physically present in the Uni States for at least half of his required residence, which is 2½ years, or months for applicants requiring 5 years' residence, and 1½ years, or months, for the persons married to citizens described in the preced paragraph.

These short periods of absence from the United States may be as mu as 6 months, and under certain circumstances, for any period less tha year, if the applicant can prove that he did not abandon his residence the United States. However, an absence of 1 year or more within required period breaks the required residence and prevents the applic from obtaining naturalization until the expiration of a period of 5 years 3 years, whichever is required in his case), during which he has not be absent from the United States for a full year or more.

Under certain conditions permission may be obtained from the migration and Naturalization Service to be absent for a year or m without breaking the required residence. The application for such appr al generally must be made in advance of the absence.

5. The applicant must be a person of good moral character. For purposes of the Immigration and Nationality Act [sec. 101 (f), Public L 414, 82d Cong., 66 Stat. 172], a person is not a person of good mo

racter who, during the period for which good moral character is re-
red to be established, is, or was (1) a habitual drunkard; (2) one who
ing such period has committed adultery; (3) a member of one or more
he classes of persons, whether excludable or not, described in speci-
paragraphs of section 212 (a) of the Immigration and Nationality Act
ting to polygamists, sexually immoral persons, and certain violators of
ninal laws; (4) one whose income is derived principally from illegal
ibling activities; (5) one who has been convicted of two or more gam-
ig offenses committed during such period; (6) one who has given false
imony for the purpose of gaining any benefits under the Immigration
Nationality Act; (7) one who during such period has been confined, as
isult of conviction, to a penal institution for an aggregate period of one
idred and eighty days or more, regardless of the offense, or offenses,
which he has been convicted. The fact that any person is not within
of the foregoing classes does not preclude a finding that for other
sons such person is or was not of good moral character.

. The applicant must be "attached to the principles of the Constitu-
a of the United States and well disposed to the good order and happi-
s of the United States." Each applicant will be required to demon-
ite a knowledge and understanding of the fundamentals of the history,
l of the principles and form of government of the United States.

he Federal Government supplies textbooks on citizenship to help ap-
ants for naturalization in preparing for citizenship. In many places the
ilic schools conduct citizenship classes. These textbooks are furnished
e for the use of applicants for naturalization who are attending such
ises or who are studying under the supervision of the public schools. A
of these books may be obtained by writing to the nearest Immigration
l Naturalization office. Persons who are not attending the public
ools may buy the books at a very small cost from the Superintendent
)ocuments, Government Printing Office, Washington, D.C. 21325.

. Generally, application to file a petition for naturalization must be
de in the court district in which the applicant lives.

. In most cases, application must be made on Form N-400. The form
is not cost anything. If the applicant cannot get the form from a clerk
:ourt, a public school teacher, or a social agency in the place where he
is he can get it from the nearest Immigration and Naturalization office.

. The applicant must take or mail the application, after it has been
:d out, to the nearest Immigration and Naturalization office named in
application. With it he must submit three unsigned photographs of
iself. He will be required to sign them when he appears for examina-
i, and the signature must be in the English language unless he is exempt
m this requirement.

n completing Form N-400 the applicant must be careful to spell his
ne exactly as it was spelled in his home country and as he used it in
ning to the United States. If he does not do so, it may be difficult to

find the record of his admission to this country, and, therefore, difficult prove that he was legally admitted for permanent residence and is titled to proceed to naturalization.

4. The applicant must also submit with his application a fingerpri card on which his fingerprints have been recorded. These cards, w necessary instructions, may be obtained from any office of the Immig tion and Naturalization Service.

5. The applicant will be notified by the Immigration and Naturaliza office to which he sent his application, when and where he is to app for his examination.

6. Every applicant to file a petition for naturalization must bring t witnesses to his examination. In some courts, he must also bring witnesses with him to the final or court hearing.

The witnesses must be citizens of the United States and, if naturaliz bring with them proof of their citizenship. They must be persons of g moral character. They must know the applicant well and should h seen him frequently, ordinarily at least once a month. They are requi to testify to his good moral character, his attachment to the principles the Constitution of the United States, his residence in the United Sta including the length of time he has been physically present in this co try, and other qualifications. These witnesses should know the applic for at least the 6 months immediately before filing of the petition if applicant is required to prove 6 months' residence in the State where petition is filed. If the witnesses who sign the petition have not known applicant for the entire period of the required United States reside (generally 5 years, and for wives or husbands of citizens, 3 years), applicant will be asked for the names and addresses of additional citi witnesses who knew him for the remainder of the required time. Th witnesses do not have to go with the applicant to his examination. Th make a sworn statement before a naturalization examiner or other G ernment official in the place where they live, telling about his reside there and his conduct while living there.

7. The naturalization examiner questions each of the witnesses to m. sure the applicant meets the requirements of the naturalization laws.

8. The examiner then helps him file a petition for naturalization. At time the applicant pays $10.00 to the clerk of the court. This sum pays the filing of the petition and also for the certificate of naturalization and when such a certificate is issued to the applicant.

9. If the examiner believes the applicant is not qualified for citizensl he suggests that the petition not be filed.

Final Court Hearing

1. After the Immigration and Naturalization Service has completed investigation, the applicant is notified to appear in the naturalization co for a final hearing on his petition. As a rule, no final hearing may be h within 30 days after the filing of the petition.

In some courts, the witnesses also must go with the applicant to the
hearing, but in most courts they are needed only for the first hearing.
applicant will be notified whether he is to bring witnesses to the final
ring.

Most judges do not ask questions of the applicants at this court
ring; a Naturalization examiner has already done so, and the judge
lly follows the recommendation of the Immigration and Naturalization
vice in regard to an applicant.

. The Service may recommend that a petition for naturalization be
ted, denied, or "continued" (that is, put off until a later date).

. If the Service recommends that the petition be denied, notice of this
mmendation is sent to the applicant before the case is put on the
rt calendar for final hearing. The applicant is notified at the same time
he may ask to be examined by the judge in court if he feels that the
mmendation is not just.

. When the court grants a petition for naturalization, the applicant
s an oath of renunciation and allegiance—that is, he renounces alle-
ce to the foreign state of which he is a subject or citizen and promises
ear allegiance to the United States of America.

. When a large number of applicants are admitted to citizenship at a
rt session, they must not expect to get their certificates at once. Usu-
the clerk of the court sends their certificates to them by registered
some time later.

Sickness or Other Disability of Applicants

ometimes an applicant for naturalization is prevented by sickness or
er physical disability from appearing in the courthouse to make and
the necessary papers, or to appear for the final hearing on his petition.
ler certain conditions, it is possible for such an applicant to become a
en without appearing in the court building. Further information as to
procedure in such cases may be obtained from the nearest Immigra-
and Naturalization office.

person whose declaration of intention or naturalization certificate has
n lost, mutilated, or destroyed may apply for a copy of it. A special
n, N-565, is used when applying for such a duplicate. The applicant
t enclose a fee of $5.00 with this application. No currency should be
. The fee may be paid by check or money order payable to the
asurer of the United States and should be sent with the application to
Immigration and Naturalization office shown in the application.

n the cases of some foreign-born persons in the United States there is
record showing admission for permanent residence, or at least no rec-
can be found. Such persons may have been brought here during
dhood and never have known just when or how they came; or they
 have come here as visitors or as seamen and decided to stay; or they
 have entered unlawfully.

nce no record of their lawful admission for permanent residence can be found, they cannot become citizens of the United States until suc record has been made. An alien not ineligible to citizenship who prove he came to the United States before July 1, 1924, has been h ever since, has shown himself to be of good moral character, and is subject to deportation, may legalize his stay by having created for hi record of admission for permanent residence. Form N-105 is used in m ing application to create such a record. This form, together with infor tion about the procedure to be followed, may be obtained from the n est Immigration and Naturalization office. The cost of filing this appl tion is $25.00. The applicant must enclose a money order or check that amount and two photographs with the Form N-105 when he take or mails it to the Immigration and Naturalization office shown in application. After such a record of admission for permanent residence been made, he can apply for citizenship.

Persons who came to the United States illegally on or after July 1, 19 cannot obtain a record of admission for permanent residence, and t may be deportable. It is possible for the Immigration and Naturaliza Service to help certain classes of these persons. Information and adv should be sought from the nearest office of the Service or from a so service agency.

NAVIGABLE Capable of being passed over by boats or ships. Technically speaking only the sea and rivers which flow and re-flow with the tide, the bed or soil of which are the property of the crown or state, are navigable. In the United States this technical meaning is in some places applied in designating and defining tidewaters, the bed or soil of which belongs to the state, but in some states this technical use of the word has been entirely discarded, and the large freshwater rivers are considered navigable not only as being subject to public use as highways but as having their bed or soil vested in the state. Even though, in some cases, the soil of the bed of the river which is navigable in the popular sense of the term belongs to the riparian owner, it will still be a public highway for navigation and open to the general use of the public. All rivers which are of suf-ficient capacity to float the pr ucts of the mines, the forests the tillage of the country thro which they flow to market, which are capable of floating v sels, boats or logs, are subject the free and unobstructed nav tion of the public, except wh there is usage or legislation to contrary. The state, as trustee the people, may make such imp vements at tidewater as to it r seem fit for the public benefit.

NE BAILA PAS He did not liver. A plea whereby the def dant claims that he never receiv goods allegedly delivered.

NE EXEAT Let him not go. writ prohibiting a defendant f leaving the jurisdiction.

NECESSARIES Everything, incl ing many of the convenien that is requisite to support life. ▶

a relative term and must be applied according to the circumstances and conditions in life of the parties concerned. Things would be considered necessaries in connection with persons of large means and wealth which would not be necessaries with respect to persons of limited or very small means. What kinds and classes of things a minor may make a valid contract for as necessaries, if a dispute arise, is for the court to determine and to instruct a jury about. As to whether any particular things purchased come within such classes is for the jury to determine, including whether or not the quantity contracted for is excessive or beyond the limits of necessity.

With proper restrictions minors may contract for necessaries where not supplied to them otherwise, but cannot be held for more than a fair price for them and will not be liable for borrowed money even though expended for necessaries. If the minor has wife and children, debts contracted for necessaries for them will have the same standing as if contracted for himself. A wife may make contracts for necessaries and her husband will be responsible for them, his assent being presumed, and he will be liable for actual necessaries even if he gives notice not to trust her. If she deserts him or elopes, he is not chargeable for necessaries ordered by her, and if the husband and wife live apart, this fact alone, if known by the party selling to her, is sufficient to put him upon notice as to whether or not she had so deserted him or eloped, or whether they were separated by necessity or from the fault of the husband

NEGLIGENCE The failure to exer-

cise that degree of care which an ordinarily careful and prudent person exercises under the same or similar circumstances. In general, one causing an injury or loss to another by his negligence is responsible for resulting damages. If, however, the injury is caused even in part by the negligence of the party complaining, or if there is negligence by both parties, and if there is contributory negligence, even the smallest, on the part of the plaintiff, there can be no recovery of damages. But where the injuring party was aware of the danger the other party was in and did not use ordinary care to ward it off the contributory negligence of the opposite party will not excuse. Where the injury would necessarily have occurred whether the injured party was negligent or not there is no such contributory negligence as will defeat a claim for damages.

Examples of negligence are almost infinite. If one drives an automobile on the wrong side of the road, thus committing an injury to another, it is negligence. If the proper officers of a municipal corporation fail to keep the highways in safe condition or to provide proper protection in the form of guard rails or the like at dangerous places, the municipal corporation will be held liable for damages resulting to persons who themselves are exercising due care. If the negligence of two parties concurs in producing an injury, where it would not have occurred through the negligence of one alone, both will be liable to the party injured. Employers are bound to arrange their machines and appliances so as to afford all proper protection to employees.

An injury arising exclusively from natural causes which could not be prevented by human skill, care and foresight, is said, in law, to be due to the act of God, and no one can be held responsible therefor, unless he specially contracted or guaranteed against such accidents or unless he negligently brought the thing injured within the operation of such natural causes. One will not be exempt from liability for damage by lightning who negligently leads a wire over the house of another, attaching it to a flagpole without the owner's consent. Persons are not excused from negligence or from committing torts because insane, if injury result to others.

If the law imposes a duty on an officer and he neglects to perform it, he may be indicted for the neglect, and, in some cases, will forfeit his office. If a legal duty is imposed upon one and death results from omission to discharge it, the party thus omitting his duty is guilty of homicide, but it must appear that the death was the direct and immediate, that is, not the secondary, result of the personal neglect or default of the party charged.

NEGOTIABLE Transferable or assignable, transferable by endorsement; that which may be negotiated or transferred from one to another, so as to pass a right of action. A term constantly applied to bills of exchange, promissory notes and checks, which are made negotiable by being made payable to order or to bearer.

NEGOTIABLE INSTRUMENT A written promise or request for the payment of a certain sum of money to order or bearer. It includes bills of exchange, promissory notes, checks, trade acceptances, certain bonds and letters of credit. To be negotiable, an instrument must be in writing and signed, must contain an unconditional promise or order to pay a certain sum of money on demand or at a fixed and determinable future time. It must be payable to order or to bearer; where it is made out to the drawee, he must be named or otherwise indicated with reasonable certainty. The negotiability of the instrument is not affected by the fact that it is not dated or that it bears a seal or that it fails to mention that any value was given.

NET ASSETS The property or effects remaining after all its obligations have been paid of a firm, corporation, institution, or estate.

NET CASH As between buyer and seller, the term means the buyer shall pay to the seller a price which shall include all expenses.

NET EARNINGS A sum remaining from the operation of a business, trade, profession, institution, trust, fund, estate, etc., after the deduction of all necessary charges and expenses.

NEW PROMISE A new agreement which recognizes and revives the obligations under a lapsed contract.

NEW TRIAL A frequent means of averting a miscarriage of justice. A new trial is granted for a number of causes, among which are mistakes or omissions of officers in summoning or drawing jurors when the irregularity deprives the party complaining of a substantial right;

where either officer summoning the jury or one of the jurors is related (if not too remotely) to a party to the trial, or is interested in the event of the suit or where there is any unfairness or trickery in the selection of a jury. Irregularity, however, may be waived by a party having knowledge thereof.

Conscientious scruples on the part of a juror against finding a verdict of guilty, or mental or bodily disease unfitting him for the performance of his duties, or the fact that he is a foreigner, have been held to be grounds for new trials. So, too, is misconduct in connection with the trial by one party prejudicial to the other, examination of witnesses by a jury after retiring to deliberate, or a communication by one juror to his fellows of private information influencing their finding. Betting by jurors on the result, sleeping during the trial, taking refreshment at the charge of the successful party, talking to strangers about the trial, determining the verdict by resort to chance and other misconduct of the jury are other grounds for setting aside the verdict.

An error of the judge in admitting illegal evidence which has been objected to, unless it is wholly immaterial, or in improperly rejecting evidence tending to aid the jury in determining a material fact, and indeed any error of law by the judge in the progress of the trial material to the matter in dispute and which may have affected the verdict, furnish grounds for a new trial. If an unforeseen accident has prevented the attendance of a material witness or if the party himself by unexpected compulsion is detained, or if it is shown there was false testimony which probably secured the verdict but which the injured party could not contradict or expose until after the trial, or if evidence is discovered after the trial which is material and will probably produce a different result and the non-production of which at the trial was not through lack of diligence in the party in discovering it, a new trial will be granted. But in case of newly discovered evidence it must not be merely cumulative or corroborative of what was already proven nor must it be merely to impeach witnesses at the former trial. Courts sometimes grant new trials where it is clear that greatly excessive damages have been awarded or where the verdict is clearly against the law or is palpably against the evidence or the weight of the evidence.

In criminal cases where a person has been acquitted in due course of law and the acquittal has not been procured by his own fraud or evil practice, a new trial will not be permitted, nor will it in case of conviction fairly and regularly obtained except with the consent of the accused, but new trials are frequently granted for cause upon application of the party convicted.

NEWLY DISCOVERED EVIDENCE Proof of new facts previously undiscoverable, but of sufficient importance to affect the decision, obtained after a verdict has been rendered.

NEXT FRIEND One who brings an action on behalf of an infant or other incompetent, an office now filled by a guardian ad litem.

NEXT OF KIN Those most nearly related to the deceased by blood.

NIHIL DICIT He says nothing. A phrase denoting that a judgment may be entered by default.

NIHIL HABET He has nothing. A term used in a sheriff's return to indicate that he has been unable to serve a writ.

NISI PRIUS A term used to denote the system of trial of issues of fact, in civil cases, before a jury, as distinguished from the argument of issues and questions of law before the court in bench.

NISI PRIUS COURTS Those in which cases are tried either before a jury or by the court acting as a jury; they are sharply distinguished from appellate courts which hear cases on appeal from nisi prius courts.

NO ARRIVAL, NO SALE A sale of goods "to arrive" or "on arrival," per or ex a certain ship, has been construed to be a sale subject to a double condition precedent, namely, that the ship arrives in port and that when she arrives the goods are on board, and if either of these conditions fails, the contract becomes void.

NOLLE PROSEQUI A declaration that a plaintiff will no longer press his cause; more commonly, in criminal law, a declaration that the state will no longer prosecute. If a jury is impaneled a *nolle prosequi* cannot be entered without the consent of the defendant. Usually the prosecuting officer may enter it at his discretion, but in some states leave of court must be obtained. It may be entered as to one defendant and not another. It does not operate as an acquittal, for the party may be again indicted. In a civil suit a *nolle prosequi* does not ordinarily prevent another suit for the same cause of action.

NOLO CONTENDERE A defense plea in a criminal action which admits the facts of the indictment as does a plea of guilty, but which is not an admission of guilt to be used in other causes.

NOMINAL DAMAGES A trifling sum awarded in a case where a breach of duty or an infraction of the plaintiff's rights has been shown, but where no serious loss or injury has been sustained.

NONAGE Under age; under majority; infancy.

NON COMPOS MENTIS Mentally incompetent.

NONFEASANCE The total omission or failure of an agent to enter upon the performance of some distinct duty or undertaking which he has agreed with his principal to do. It is not every omission or failure to perform a duty that will constitute a nonfeasance, but only an omission to perform such distinct duties as he owes to his principal, as distinguished from those which he owes to third persons or to the public in general as a member of society.

NONJOINDER The failure to make necessary persons parties to a lawsuit.

NON OBSTANTE VEREDICTO A judgment *non obstante veredicto* is a judgment entered, by order of the court, for the plaintiff in an action at law, notwithstanding a verdict in favor of the defendant.

NON-PAR VALUE STOCK Stock of a corporation having no face or par value.

NON SUI JURIS Not of legal age, or legal capacity.

NONSUIT The dismissal of an action by the plaintiff's failure to prove a case or by his neglect to prosecute after the issue has been joined. An involuntary nonsuit takes place where the plaintiff fails to appear when his case is called for trial or where he has given no evidence on which the jury could find a verdict in his favor. Neither kind of nonsuit prevents another action for the same cause.

NOTARY PUBLIC One whose duties generally are to protest bills of exchange, authenticate and certify copies of documents and take acknowledgments of deeds and other instruments, administer oaths, etc. The acts of a notary are respected by the custom of merchants and the law of nations. Their protest of a bill of exchange is received as evidence in the courts of all civilized countries. Except in cases of protest of bills the signature of a notary to an instrument going to a foreign country should be authenticated by the consul or representative of that country. In this country they do not administer oaths unless authorized by statute, except in cases where the oath is to be used out of the state or in the courts of the United States. Notaries are liable for damages arising from the negligent or imperfect discharge of their duties

NOTE *See* CONFESSED JUDGMENT NOTE AND PROMISSORY NOTE.

NOTICE Actual notice exists where knowledge is brought home to the party to be affected by it; constructive notice where the party by any circumstances whatever is put upon inquiry; or where certain acts have been done which the party interested is legally presumed to have knowledge of on the ground of public policy, as in case of a recorded deed or mortgage or the entry and indexing of a judgment or an advertisement in a newspaper authorized by law as a means of giving notice. Such notice is usually as binding upon the party affected as actual notice, actual notice being in many cases impracticable. Constructive notice exists of public acts of government and of suit pending.

Notice to an agent is, in general, notice to the principal. In some cases notice is necessary before bringing a suit, as in case of an endorser of a note who cannot be held liable unless he is promptly notified of a failure of the drawer to pay at maturity. Whenever the defendant's liability to perform an act depends upon another occurrence, which is best known to the plaintiff and of which the defendant is not legally bound to take notice the plaintiff must prove that due notice was in fact given. Except where expressly designated by law notice may be written or oral, but written notice is generally preferable as making it easier and more exact.

NOTICE OF DISHONOR A notice given to a drawer or endorser of a bill of exchange that it has not been accepted, or to an endorser of a negotiable note or accepted bill that it has not been paid, the notice being given by a subsequent party on the note or bill or by the holder thereof. It must contain a description of the note or bill sufficient to leave no reasonable doubt in the mind of the endorser which note is meant. The fact of non-payment or dishonor must be clearly and explicitly set forth.

A waiver of notice or of demand and notice by a party to the note will be binding upon him, but a waiver of notice of dishonor will not operate as a waiver of demand. Where an endorser makes a general assignment for the benefit of creditors, notice to the assignee will be sufficient. The decisions, however, are somewhat contradictory on this point and the safe course would be to notify both assignor and assignee.

The notice is generally in writing but may be oral. It may be sent by mail, at least where the party to be notified does not live in the same town, or it may be left in the care of a suitable person representing the party to be notified. It should be sent to the place where it will most probably find the person to be notified most promptly. Either the party's domicil or his place of business will do. Notice to partners may be left at the place of business of the firm or with any one of the partners. Every person is entitled to an immediate notice who is liable upon dishonor of the note or bill, but the holder need give notice only to the parties and to the endorser or endorsers whom he intends to hold liable. The notice may be given by the holder's agents, or by an endorsee who holds it for collection only, by a notary public or by an administrator or executor of a deceased person.

Omission to give notice will be excused where impossible, but great diligence to give it is requisite. An endorser receiving a notice if he would hold prior endorsers liable to him must in turn give them notice, and in doing so must exercise the same diligence and promptness as is required in giving him notice. The holder or an endorser already fixed by notice may give notice to any or all others and this will inure to the benefit of all.

Unless otherwise regulated by statute, notes falling due on Sundays and legal holidays are considered as falling due the next succeeding day, except where days of grace are allowed, when it is considered as coming due the day before the last day of grace.

If the holder, even after notice given, makes a binding agreement, that is, one for consideration or by writing under seal, with the acceptor of a bill of exchange or maker of a promissory note to delay collection or payment, the endorser will be relieved.

If a note is payable in installments prompt notice should be given of non-payment of each installment as it comes due, but failure to give notice as to any installment will not bar the right to give proper notice as to subsequent installments, and thereby to hold the party to the payment of the same.

If the holder fails to give legal notice to the endorser, but if the endorser afterwards promises to pay the holder, he will still be bound. A notice that demand was made on some other day than the day the note or bill came due or is to come due, is insufficient, even if the demand was in fact made on the right day, unless the circumstances connected with the notice or the service are such as to reveal to the party that there is a mistake and to put upon him the duty to investigate and ascertain the truth.

NOTICE TO QUIT The notice from a landlord to his tenant to quit the premises leased and give possession of the same to him at the end of the term of lease. The notice to quit should describe the premises with sufficient particularity to identify them with certainty and should mention a day certain for the delivery, and generally when the lease is for a year, or years, or from year to year, the day mentioned should be the same day of the year on which the lease commenced. If there is doubt as to the time when the lease will expire it is proper to mention a particular day and add thereto "or at the expiration of the current year of your tenancy."

The notice should be dated, signed by the landlord himself or a duly authorized agent in his name and addressed to the tenant. It should not refer to part of the premises only and it should be certain and decisive. If ambiguous or optional it will be invalid. Though not absolutely necessary it should nevertheless be in writing, and there should be two copies made and both examined, compared and attested by witnesses so that they may know that they are precisely alike, and to make the proof of service more certain it is best that the witnesses be present when the one copy is handed to the tenant, the other copy being retained and marked by the witnesses so that they can afterwards identify it.

The notice must be given to the tenant and served by the landlord or his agent duly authorized, but in the latter case it is sufficient if the agent's authority be afterwards recognized, and the notice must be given to the tenant of the party giving the notice whether part or all of the premises is sublet or assigned or not, unless the lessor has recognized the subtenant as his tenant. If there are two or more general lessees the notice should be addressed to all, but if served only upon one it will be a good notice though it would be better practice to serve a copy upon each if possible.

At common law a notice must be served at least six months before the end of the term, but this has been for the most part changed by statute and three months' notice is now required in many places. If the tenant on delivery of the notice assents to the terms of it, he will thereby waive any irregularity as to the period of expiration of the lease.

If the landlord accepts or distrains or sues for rent accruing after the time for quitting under the notice has expired, it will operate as a waiver of the notice, and a recognition of a renewal of the tenancy, unless there are facts or circumstances connected with such acceptance showing a contrary intent, such as an express declaration at the time that the notice is not intended to be waived and if the money is not received and paid as rent the notice will remain in force.

NOTING PROTECT The act of making a memorandum on a bill or note at the time of, and embracing, the principal facts attending its dishonor. The object is to have a record from which the instrument of protest may be written, so that a notary need not rely on his memory for the fact.

NOVATION The substitution of one obligation for another. When debtor A is substituted for debtor B, and by agreement with the creditor C, debtor B is discharged, a novation has occurred.

NUDUM PACTUM A naked promise, a promise for which there is no consideration.

NUISANCE That which annoys or disturbs an individual in the possession of his property. Nuisances may endanger life or health, offend the senses or violate common decency. A public nuisance is one which affects an indefinite number of persons; a private nuisance is one violating the rights of a single individual; nuisances may be punished criminally or be the ground for a civil action.

A private nuisance is anything done to the hurt or annoyance of the lands, tenements or hereditaments of another, and a public or common nuisance is such an inconvenience or troublesome offense as annoys the community in general and not merely some particular person. In a case of a private nuisance there may be a suit for damages by the person injured or he may abate it, or there may be an injunction to prevent it. A person suffering from special damages, in case of a public nuisance, may sue for damages, and the person injured in such case may abate the nuisance if no riot is committed. One committing a public nuisance may be indicted.

If a thing is calculated to interfere with the comfortable enjoyment of a man's house it is a nuisance. Offensive trades are nuisances if they make the enjoyment of life and property uncomfortable. A neighborhood has a right to pure and fresh air, and rendering the air offensive and noxious is a public nuisance as are also acts of public indecency, such as bathing in a river in sight of neighboring house, or acts tending to a breach of the peace or disturbing the neighborhood or keeping a disorderly house, gaming house, or bawdy house, keeping of a dangerous animal knowing it to be such, and suffering him to go at large, or exposing a person or animal having a contagious disease in public, thus endangering the health of the citizens.

Whether a thing is a nuisance or not depends somewhat upon its locality. A trade or business may be a nuisance in a thickly populated town but would not be so if isolated. One beginning an offensive trade in a neighborhood where the same trade is carried on by others will not erect a nuisance unless the offensiveness is materially increased. What was not originally a public nuisance may become such by the erection of dwellings in the neighborhood of the same. A nuisance may arise from a noise and other causes as well as from offensive odors and unhealthful emissions.

Whether a nuisance is public or private is determined by a jury. Private nuisances may be either to things corporeal, as where one erects a house or other thing so as to throw rain water upon another's land or obstruct his ancient rights, or they may be to personal rights, as by keeping hogs or animals so as to annoy one's neighbor and render the air unwholesome, or they may obstruct a right of way by laying logs across it or the like, or obstruct a spring or interfere with a franchise, such as a ferry or railroad.

NULLA BONA No goods. An officer's return of a writ signifying that he had made a strict and diligent search and was unable to find any property liable to seizure.

NUNC PRO TUNC A latin phrase meaning now for then. It means that a thing is done at one time which ought to have been done at another. A *nunc pro tunc* entry is one made now of something which was actually done previously, to have effect as of the former date. Its purpose is to supply an omission in the record, but which was omitted through mistake.

NUNCUPATIVE WILL *See* WILL.

O

OATH A solemn declaration of intention to tell the truth. The method of administering an oath may be varied to conform to the religious belief of the party so as to make it binding upon his conscience. Most commonly it is on the gospel by the taking of the book in hand and kissing it after the words have been addressed to the party taking the oath, though the kissing has in some places been abolished. Not unfrequently, oaths are administered by the uplifted hand, the party or witness holding up his right hand while the proper officer repeats to him the necessary words. Another form of attestation, called an affirmation, is commonly used by persons who have conscientious scruples against taking an oath.

A Jew is sworn on the Pentateuch, or Old Testament, with his head covered, a Mohammedan on the Koran, a Gentoo by touching the foot of a Brahman, a Brahman by touching the hand of another Brahman, a Chinese by breaking a china saucer. The persons authorized to administer oaths are commonly designated by statute; frequently, also, is the form and time of administering the same.

Oaths and affirmations are administered as follows or substantially so:

ON THE BIBLE. You do swear that the evidence which you shall give in the matter now being heard shall be the truth, the whole truth and nothing but the truth so help you God.

BY THE UPLIFTED HAND. You do swear by Almighty God, the searcher of all hearts, that the evidence you shall give in the matter now being heard shall be the truth, the whole truth and nothing but the truth, and that as you shall answer to God at the great day.

AFFIRMATION. You do solemnly, sincerely and truly declare and affirm that in the evidence which you shall give in the matter now being heard, you will tell the truth, the whole truth and nothing but the truth, and so you affirm.

OBITER DICTUM An opinion of a judge delivered or expressed by the way, and not on the point in question before him.

OBJECTION The formal remonstrance made by counsel to something which has been said or done, in order to obtain the court's ruling thereon; and when the court has ruled, the alleged error is preserved by the objector's exception to the ruling, which exception is noted in the record.

OBLIGEE The party to whom another is bound; the party to whom a bond is given.

OBLIGOR A party who binds himself, as by a bond; the party by whom a bond is given.

OBSCENITY Such indecency as is calculated to promote the violation of the law and the general corruption of morals. It is indictable. The exhibition of an obscene picture is indictable at common law even though not charged to have been exhibited in public, if exhibited to persons for money.

OBSTRUCTING PROCESS Attempting to prevent or actually preventing the execution of lawful process. It is considered a high offense, more particularly so where the obstruction is of an arrest upon criminal process, in which case the person opposing the arrest thereby becomes a party to the crime, that is, an accessory in felony or a principal in high treason. To constitute such obstruction the officer must be prevented by actual or threatened violence on the part of one having capacity to employ it.

OFFER A proposal. One may revoke a simple offer at any time before it is accepted, and in order that it may become binding it must be accepted as made and not with variations or conditions unless the variations or conditions are agreed to by the party offering. An offer, so long as it is unrevoked, may be accepted within the time designated in the offer and if no time is designated, then within a reasonable time under the circumstances. An offer indefinite as to time of acceptance cannot remain open forever, and what is a reasonable time will usually be a question for a jury to determine. If, however, some consideration is given or promise is made by the other party to secure continuance of an offer to a given time (commonly called securing an option), the offer will remain open to the expiration of the time agreed upon. When the withdrawal of an offer is made it will be effective only when it reaches the other party, and if the party accepts before the withdrawal reaches him the bargain is completed. If the acceptance is by mail it will be effective from the time of mailing it, and the contract will have been made, though the withdrawal be previously sent but not yet received.

OFFICE A position of trust or authority in government. All officers may be deposed for misbehavior in office. An office is not a contract with the government or the appointing or electing power, and, in the absence of constitutional prohibition, the term of an officer may be abbreviated or extended by the legislature, or the emoluments of the office may be increased or diminished during the term. Not unfrequently, however, there are constitutional provisions preventing the increase or diminishing of emoluments of state officers during the term and similar legislative prohibitions with respect to local offices.

OFFICERS OF CORPORATIONS, DUTIES OF Corporation officers have authority, in general, to perform such duties as customarily devolve upon them as well as those which are expressly allotted to them by the by-laws or by statute. Acts done by them within the scope of their usual and customary duties are presumed to have been legally done, and are binding upon the corporation in the absence of some express prohibition in the by-laws or elsewhere.

The president's authority to act as chief executive officer may be shown by a general acquiescence on the part of the corporation or directors in his acts as such, even where authority has not been expressly granted. The public in dealing with him is entitled to assume that he has authority to act for the corporation except in matters of more than usual concern, if the business transacted is in the regular course of the corporation's business. He must not, however, undertake to sell or mortgage real estate or to sell personal property or dispose of the general assets of the company in bulk without express authority. One lending money to the corporation should see either that authority has been expressly granted to him or some other proper officer to borrow and to execute a proper instrument, or that such officer has been in the custom of borrowing and executing such instruments.

Officers of themselves have no right ordinarily to relinquish or assume debts, or purchase or mortgage real estate, but the president, unless expressly prohibited, may appear in a suit against the corporation, conduct litigation against it and employ counsel to defend it. A treasurer or other officer borrowing without authority from the company to do so, though he signs an obligation as treasurer, will render himself and not the company liable to the lender if his action is not ratified by it.

The treasurer has the right to control the depositing and safekeeping of funds of the association even as against the orders of the directors, but his authority does not extend to paying the debts or compromising claims without permission of the directors, unless it appears that his performance of such functions has been acquiesced to by the corporation. He must keep corporate funds separate from all others. Neither he nor any other officer has authority by virtue of his office to confess judgment against the corporation.

In elections of officers those receiving a majority of the legal votes cast will be elected. Those entitled to vote are the owners of the stock as they appear by inspection of the books of the corporation, not those who may have purchased stock which has not been transferred on the books. The corporation cannot buy stock and use it in voting at elections either directly or indirectly through the intervention of a nominal stockholder taking the stock for the corporation. The by-laws should provide for time and place of election of officers, also for some kind of notice of such election to the stockholders. If they do not, notice must nevertheless be given to them.

It is common to provide that elections be conducted by judges or inspectors, and if such provision exists either by statute or in the charter or in the by-laws, it should be strictly followed, and in any case it is necessary that in elections the stockholders have a fair opportunity to give expression to their preferences. In some states cumulative voting is allowed, that is, a stockholder may in elections of directors cast a number of votes ascertained by multiplying the number of shares he holds by the number of directors to be elected, depositing all for one person or distributing them as he pleases. This can, however, be made to apply to corporations chartered before the adoption of the law permitting such voting.

In case of a failure to elect new officers, the old officers hold over until their successors are elected and qualified unless this is expressly prohibited.

The stockholders only can authorize an increase of capital stock. Where the seal is to be used, as in case of deeds, mortgages and bonds, the officers using it should be authorized to do so by the board for the particular case, or by some form of general authority. When so affixed, however, it is presumed to have been done by proper authority until the contrary is shown.

Where a committee is authorized to act, the scope of its authority should be specifically stated in the resolution appointing it, and the proceedings of the committee in transacting the business should be similiar to those of the board itself. Authority granted to an officer or to a committee impliedly includes the power to enlist any necessary assistance in the transaction of the business, such as the employment of attorneys or other persons. One who is director of two companies has no right to act in relation to transactions between them, if authority to do so is not especially granted by the stockholders. Directors may even hold their meetings out of the state, but it is doubtful if this would be extended so far as to permit the organization of a corporation in one state for the purpose of evading the law of the state where the business is really to be conducted and the capital of the company is located. Officers cannot be removed except for just cause, and then only after proper investigation and opportunity to be heard.

Officers generally are bound to the exercise of ordinary care and diligence in the performance of their duties whether paid or not. If paid, the degree of care and diligence required of them is increased, and they are liable personally for loss arising from failure to perform their duties with the requisite care and diligence, and one doing an act on behalf of a corporation forbidden by law is liable personally therefor. Officers of a corporation as well as the corporation itself may be held responsible for maintenance of a public nuisance even though that nuisance consists of the business of the corporation itself.

Where the directors of a financial institution pay out large amounts of money to creditors on obligations in which they themselves are interested when the institution is heavily insolvent, thus giving them a preference over other creditors, the transaction will be construed as a fraud upon other creditors, and the money may be recovered from the officers so making or directing payment. Lack of knowledge of the insolvency of the association on their part will not be an excuse. The law imputes knowledge of the condition of the association to them.

Bonds given by officers to the corporation for faithful performance of their duties, etc., should be accepted by the corporation in order to make it binding upon the sureties in the bond, but this acceptance need not necessarily appear in the minutes. Any evidence that the board accepted it is sufficient. No bond, however, for the performance of illegal acts is valid. The liabilities of the sureties extend only to the strict terms of the bond, and not to duties imposed upon the officer not expressed in the bond, or not contemplated when the bond was executed. Any change made by the corporation with respect to the status of the officer or the employee, which would in any way increase the officer's liability or responsibility, will release the sureties on his bond.

If the officer holds over beyond his term, sureties will not be responsible for acts committed after the expiration of the term, unless it is otherwise expressed in the bond. A corporation taking a bond of one of its officers known by it to be untrustworthy is bound to inform the sureties of his untrustworthiness, as, for example, that the officer has already proven a defaulter. If the corporation has discovered that its officer is a defaulter and does not discharge him, the sureties will not be liable for subsequent defalcations.

OPINION OF THE COURT A statement by which the court sets forth the factual and legal reasons for its decision.

OPTION A continuing offer or contract by which the owner agrees with the prospective purchaser that the latter shall have the right to buy certain property at a fixed price within a certain time. Options are usually given for a cash consideration. If the option is refused by the prospective buyer or purchaser, the cash consideration is forfeited. If the option is accepted, the cash consideration may be utilized as part of the purchase price of the goods, wares, merchandise or real estate. Options should be in writing.

OPTION TO BUY REAL ESTATE

In consideration of the sum of One hundred dollars ($100.00), receipt of which is hereby acknowledged, I hereby agree to give Thomas Brown the option to buy the following described real estate in the City of Baltimore, State of Maryland, to wit: 3000 Denison Street.

Said Thomas Brown shall have the right to close this option at any time within 30 days from date, and I agree to execute to him or any person named by him, a good warranty deed to said real estate, and to furnish therefor an abstract of title showing said title to be perfect, upon demand therefor. Upon execution of said deed and abstract, I shall be paid the sum of Five thousand dollars ($5,000.00) as full payment of the purchase price of said real estate. I further agree neither to sell nor encumber said real estate during said term, and should I do so I hereby agree to pay the sum of Five hundred dollars ($500.00) to said Thomas Brown as liquidated damages. Likewise, should I fail, neglect or refuse to make said deed, or to furnish said abstract as above provided, I hereby agree to pay to him as liquidated damages the sum of Five hundred dollars ($500.00). I waive all claims for damages for failure to close this option.

Dated August 10, 19____.

(Seal) /s/   John Doe

JOHN DOE

NOTICE OF ELECTION TO EXERCISE OPTION

You are hereby notified that I elect to exercise my option to purchase 3000 Denison Street, Baltimore, Md., upon the terms and conditions specified in the agreement dated August 10, 19____.

/s/   Thomas Brown

ORDER OF A COURT A formal direction requiring that a certain act be performed or restrained.

ORDINANCE An ordinance is, generally speaking, the legislative act of a municipality. A city council is a legislative body and passes ordinances that are the laws of the city.

ORDINARY CARE That care that a prudent man would take under the circumstances of the particular case.

ORGANIC LAW The base of the system of law of a state or nation, whether or not it is in writing. It may be a single codification, scattered documents, or a single constitution.

OSTENSIBLE AUTHORITY Such authority as a principal, either intentionally or by want of ordinary care, causes or allows a third person to believe the agent to possess. If a principal, by his acts, had led others to believe that he has conferred authority upon his agent, he cannot assert, as against third persons who have relied thereon, in good faith, that he did not intend such power.

OSTENSIBLE PARTNERS Members of a partnership whose names are made known and appear to the world as partners, and who in reality are such.

OVERDRAFT The withdrawal from a bank by a depositor of money in excess of the amount he has on deposit there.

OVERDRAW A depositor overdraws his account at a bank when he obtains on his check or checks from the bank more money than he deposited in the account.

OVERPLUS That which remains; a balance left over.

OVERT ACT Overt means open. Overt act is any motion, gesture, conduct, or demonstration that evidences a present design to do a particular act that will lead to a desired result.

OWNER'S RISK A term employed by common carriers in bills of lading and shipping receipts to signify that the carrier does not assume responsibility for the safety of the goods.

OYER To hear. To demand oyer or to crave oyer was a demand as of right to hear an instrument read. The modern practice is usually to demand the privilege of inspecting the document or to demand a copy of it.

P

PAR VALUE The words mean face value. The par value of stocks and bonds on the date of issuance is the principal. At a later date, the par value is the principal plus interest.

PARDON To absolve from the penalty of a crime. The power of granting pardons in the United States is vested in the President with respect to violations of the United States laws, and in the governors of the several states with respect to offenses against the laws of the state, though in some states the concurrence of some other body is required. It applies to all cases of conviction except impeachments. Not uncommonly, the case with reasons for granting a pardon are presented along with evidence and argument before a pardoning board, which makes a favorable or unfavorable recommendation to the executive, who usually acts in accordance with such recommendation.

A pardon protects the criminal from the offense pardoned but from no other. It has been held that a pardon of assault and battery which afterwards became murder by the dying of the person beaten will not operate as a pardon of murder. For the most part the pardon restores the person to all his rights. It does not, however, restore his civic capacity nor will it affect the status which other persons have rightfully acquired by reason of the commission of the crime or the imprisonment; for example, if a wife has obtained a divorce as a result of the commission of the crime or of the imprisonment of her husband, the status will not be changed by the pardon.

PARENTS Father and mother. Resemblance to a parent furnishes at least some evidence of paternity and in most places it is permissible to exhibit the child and the alleged parent to the jury to assist in determining the question, particularly if the child has passed mere babyhood with its known immaturity of features. Blood tests to determine paternity are also often used.

PAROL That which is given, or done by word of mouth.

PAROL CONTRACT A written contract not under seal; a simple or verbal contract.

PAROL GIFT A voluntary transfer of property without consideration. The gift may be either personal property, land or real estate. Where one declares that he gives a tract of land specifically desribed and identified so that it may be clear what land is meant and included, and the donee upon faith of the declaration enters into possession and improves it, this will give him title by what is termed parol gift, for it would be inequitable that he should spend his money upon the faith of the gift and that it should be afterwards taken from him. Such a gift, however, cannot take effect as against the rights of third parties, such as creditors of the donor, whose rights already existed at the time the gift was made.

PAROL PROMISE A simple contract; a verbal promise.

PAROLE A conditional release from prison. The condition being that if the prisoner fulfills the requirements of his parole, he will be given an absolute discharge; if he fails to fulfill the terms of the parole, he may be returned to prison to serve out the unexpired term.

PARTICEPS CRIMINIS A party to the crime. The term, which commonly means an act that may be visited by an indictment or other criminal prosecution, applies to other transactions contrary to good morals, whether they are immoral per se, or prohibited by statute under penalty, or by a simple prohibition, or as militating against the policy of a statute, or fraud, or other corrupt contract.

PARTICULARS A written statement (usually termed a bill of particulars) of the items of a plaintiff's demand, or defendant's set-off, in an action at law.

PARTITION Where lands belong to two or more co-heirs or co-owners, each of them is entitled to have a partition or division of the land. The partition may be voluntary and by mutual agreement which may be effected by mutual conveyances or releases to each person of the share which he takes under the agreement, executed by the other owners. Where the parties cannot agree, application may be made to a proper court by anyone interested to effect a partition or division of the property, or to enable one or more to take the property at a valuation, he or they paying the others an equitable amount of money in place of their shares. Another method is to secure a sale of the property and a distribution of the proceeds. Such proceedings are usually regulated by the statutes of the various states.

PARTNERSHIP An association of two or more persons to carry on, as co-owners, a business for profit. The essential feature of a partnership contract is the agreement to share profits in the business or undertaking in connection with which the combination exists. Consequent upon the sharing of profits is the sharing of losses, unless it is otherwise agreed, for there may be a partnership without all the partners sharing the losses.

Usually there is a community of interest in the capital employed and a community of power in the management and business, but neither of these is essential to a partnership for one partner may contribute skill or labor alone, and the business may be managed by one to the exclusion of the others. In fact there may be little or no capital for there may be a partnership between persons acting merely as managers or disposers of the goods of others, and there may be a partnership in a single transaction as well as in a continuous series of transactions. One who receives compensation for his services in the form of a share of the profits in a particular department or branch of the business is not a partner. This is also true where one in good faith lends money to the firm upon an agreement to receive a share of the profits in lieu of interest.

If one holds himself out to be a partner or knowingly permits it to be done by others, though he may not actually be a partner, as between himself and members of the firm, he will be a partner as to third persons and be liable as such even though he does not so intend it, and will be bound by the contracts made by his supposed partners. This is to prevent the fraud to which creditors and parties dealing with the firm would be subject if the rule were otherwise. It also serves to prevent false credit being given to a partnership on the faith of the supposed partner's responsibility, for every partner is personally liable for the entire debts of the partnership after exhaustion of the partnership assets. So binding is this rule that in order to hold a nominal or pretended partner it is not necessary that the creditor at the time of the contract be aware of the composition of the partnership. There is no particular method thus constituting one's self a partner as to outside parties. The use of his name over a shop door or in printed notices or bills or advertisements or the doing of various acts indicating partnership and sufficient to induce others to believe him to be a partner will effect the result. If, however there is a stipulation among the partners that a person appearing to be a partner shall be liable to no loss he will not be so liable to one having absolute knowledge of the stipulation.

The presumption is that there is a partnership where there is a sharing of profits. This presumption, however, may be overcome by showing that one receives a share of percentage of profits merely as employee, agent, factor, broker or otherwise by way of compensation for labor, trouble or services, of for rent of factory or for some other privilege, for there is a distinction between an agreement to share profits as such, and an agreement to share and pay out profits not as profits but in payment for something.

Officers and crews of sailing vessels who are paid by a portion of the produce of the voyage are not partners, nor is a captain who takes a vessel under an agreement to share profits or to pay certain charges and receive a portion of the earnings, and those making shipment or freighting goods for part of the profits are generally not considered partners with the owners.

Dormant partners are liable to third parties when discovered, as well as others. Sharing in profits, they must also share in burdens. Any other rule would furnish a means whereby one might obtain what would be in effect usurious interest on money invested by him.

The formation of a partnership may be in writing or verbally or from tacit understanding evidenced by mere acts but it must be voluntary and no stranger can be introduced into the firm without the consent of the whole firm. Therefore, unless it is otherwise expressed in the contract of partnership, executors and representatives of a deceased partner will not take his place in the partnership, and even such an express provision only has the effect of giving such executors or representatives an option to become partners or not. Under the statute of frauds an agreement of partnership to commence more than a year subsequent should be in writing. An agreement of partnership for buying and selling land should be written.

There may also be a partnership with a partner or a sub-partnership, but the sub-partner will not have relations with the main partnership. He participates in the profits of the particular partner with whom he contracts and his responsibility or liability for the debts of the general partnership are co-extensive with those of the particular partner with whom he contracts. If he causes damage to the partnership by his default the party taking him into partnership will be liable to the other partners.

A partnership may exist in any business or transaction which is not a mere personal office. There may be a partnership to trade in land, or to own and make use of a ship, though mere joint ownership of a ship will not constitute the owners partners.

Partners ordinarily are liable personally for partnership debts after exhaustion of partnership assets, yet statutes in all or nearly all the states authorize the formation of limited partnerships, limiting the liability of the individual partners,—usually to the extent of the capital subscribed by them individually.

Certain requirements in such cases are made as to the character and method of execution of articles of association and as to recording the same in the proper public office open to public inspection and usually notice of the character of the partnership must be given by posting a notice in the chief place of business or using the word "limited" as a part of the name of the concern and the like.

The term"joint stock company" is sometimes applied to ordinary partnership containing a large number of members and in some instances, possibly, to limited partnerships. Partnerships with limited liabilities are much in the nature of corporations and are sometimes called quasi-corporations and the general rules of law relating to them are similar to those relating to corporations.

Any person of legal capacity to enter into a contract may become a partner. A minor may become a partner or make any other trading contract which will possibly turn out to his benefit, but persons dealing with him or entering into partnership relations with him run the risk of his avoiding and repudiating the contract if it proves disadvantageous to him. If arriving at age he agrees to carry on the partnership or receive profits from it, this will amount to a confirmation, and will make him liable on the contracts of the firm made during minority. A married woman can enter into partnership as well as conduct business for herself.

In all partnerships in trade each individual partner is an agent for the other and his act or contract binds all with reference to matters in the usual course of partnership business or necessary thereto, whether the partners are ostensible, dormant, actual or nominal. He may effect insurance, receive or receipt for money for the firm, compromise with its debtors or creditors, release debts due to it, borrow money, purchase goods and may even sell the whole personal effects of the firm at a single sale.

A partner may pledge or mortgage the partnership goods unless otherwise provided by statute, as security to prior debts or debts thereafter to be contracted on account of the firm. He may assign the property for the benefit of one creditor or several or all the creditors of the firm, but, of course, each assignment must be for the benefit of all and not of one or several where the statute laws in force so provide. It should be added that authorities differ as to his power to make a general assignment alone for the benefit of creditors. The power of a single partner, however, to dispose of the partnership property does not extend to real estate.

A partner may draw, accept and endorse bills, notes and checks in the name and for the use of the firm and if so executed it is presumably for partnership purposes. But if a partnership is carried on in the name of a single person, in order to hold the partnership liable it must be shown that it was given in connection with the partnership business.

Though one is held out as a partner, yet if he is not a partner, one who gave the firm credit not knowing that he was so held out, cannot hold him responsible. Where there was a change in the composition of a firm, the new firm undertaking to pay the debts of the old out of the business, it was held that creditors of both the new and the old firm have preferences against partnership assets over the creditors of the individual members of the new firm.

One partner will be bound by the fraud of his co-partner in contracts relating to partnership affairs made with third persons innocent of the fraud, but not where there is collusion between the third party and the contracting partner. If the partner, in pursuit of the partnership business and with partnership belongings, injures a person or his property, the other partners will be liable. For a wilful tort, however, committed by one partner, another is in general not liable. All the partners will be responsible for a wrongful conversion by one of them of the property of an outsider to the use of the firm.

Generally the act or admission of one partner in legal proceedings is binding on the firm. Notice to one is notice to all.

One partner cannot bind the firm in guaranteeing the debt of another, or as surety, or as a party to an accommodation bill or note, unless there is a special authority given for that purpose, or one implied from the common course of business, or from a previous habit of dealing known and consented to by the other partners, or unless the transaction is subsequently adopted or ratified by the firm. If one takes the instrument knowing the partnership is a party thereto as guarantor, surety or accommodation endorser, it devolves upon him to show circumstances establishing the liability of the members of the firm other than the one signing.

One partner without authority express or implied from circumstances cannot bind the firm by a contract to convey real estate or by conveyance thereof or by the execution of any instrument which the law requires to be in the form of a deed (that is, an instrument of writing under seal), but this does not apply to an instrument which may legally be under seal or not at the option of the parties. One partner cannot bind his co-partners by a voluntary confession of judgment against the firm. The act of a partner in a matter wholly unconnected with the partnership business binds himself only.

Partnership assets are first liable for the debts of the firm, and this will include real estate used by the partnership and purchased with partnership funds, and such real estate will not be subject to dower or to inheritance until the partnership liabilities have been met. Each individual partner is likewise liable for all the debts of the partnership, and his property may be sold by a creditor of the firm after exhaustion of the partnership assets.

In an ordinary partnership no arrangement between the partners themselves, however valid and binding between them, limiting their several liabilities can limit or prevent their liability to persons dealing with the firm. Where, however, a creditor has express notice of a private arrangement between the partners by which either the power of one to bind the firm, or his liability on partnership contracts is qualified or defeated, such creditor will be bound by the arrangement. And where one contracting with one partner has express notice from the others before the contract is closed that they will not consider themselves responsible, they will not be liable, for the authority from one partner to another to contract and act as his agent is implied only, and the right to control and direct that agency, if expressly exercised and declared, in each partner. If the dissenting partner, however, afterwards assents and ratifies the transaction or receives benefit from it, he will be bound by it. When the majority acts it must be fairly constituted and proceed in entire good faith.

Each partner has a specific lien on partnership stock for the payment of debts made by him to third persons, and for the amount of his own share of the partnership stock and for all moneys advanced by him and the moneys abstracted by the partners beyond their shares. Such lien also attaches to partnership real estate, and any stock extracted by a partner having the lien to an extent sufficient to make him equal with other partners. Such prior claims of partners must be satisfied before a creditor of the individual partner can realize on his share of the partnership assets, or in other words, the partner's share as against his individual creditors will be diminished to the extent of the liens of his co-partners.

The exact firm name should be employed by each partner in signing papers, otherwise there is danger of the one signing becoming personally liable to the firm, no partner having implied authority other than by the firm name. If, however, the firm has no fixed name one signing in the name of himself and associates will bind the partnership, but it should appear for whom he signs. An adopted partnership name may be the name of a single person and that person not even interested in the business, but if adopted its use in the partnership business will bind all the partners. If the name of one partner is used as the firm name and he does business also on his own private account, a contract signed by him will be presumed being by him individually until it is shown to be on behalf of the firm.

It is said that a partner can be neither debtor nor creditor of the firm of which he is a member, though he may be a debtor or creditor of a co-partner, and a firm may not sue or be sued by one of its members for this would result in the suing of himself. Partnerships sue and are sued in the names of all partners. Similarly one firm cannot sue another where the same individual is a partner in each, though, as to this, statute laws have in some instances been enacted enabling suits to be brought in such cases. The above must not be construed to mean that suits in equity cannot be brought for an accounting between partners, or for the purpose of correcting wrongs committed by partners against other partners in the conduct of the affairs of the concern.

A firm name may operate as a trade-mark and if so its use by others will be illegal where they pass off themselves or their goods for the original firm or its goods, and if done intentionally it will be illegal even though the imitators really have the same name as the original firm.

A partner has no right as between the partners to pay his individual debt by setting off against it a debt due from his creditor to the firm. But if he does this and the credit is made accordingly on the books of the firm, the partnership cannot afterwards recover it.

A partnership will be dissolved by the termination of the period for which it was formed if this is for a definite period (unless there has been an express or tacit agreement to continue it), or at any time by mutual consent of the parties and if no fixed time is limited for its continuance any partner may dissolve it at any time. The death of a partner terminates the partnership unless there is an express stipulation for the continuance thereof to the personal representatives of one dying. Upon the death of a partner, the surviving partners have a right to realize upon the assets of the firm, pay the debts and distribute the balance among the living partners and the representatives of the one deceased.

Bankruptcy of a partner will terminate the partnership; so will the assignment of the partnership effects for the benefit of creditors or sale of the share of a partner under execution. The civil death of one of the partners effects the same result. Dissolution may take place also by the extinction of the subject matter of the partnership or the completion of the business undertaking to which the partnership pertains; also by the assignment of one partner's interest to a co-partner or a third person.

Members of a mining partnership holding the larger interest or portion of the property have power to do what is necessary and proper for carrying on the business and controlling the work, in case of disagreement, for the benefit of all concerned, but, of course, the business must be carried on in good faith. A partnership in boring for oil is of this nature. With respect to such a partnership it may be said that if a member dies or becomes bankrupt, or sells to a stranger or to an associate, these incidents do not effect a dissolution as in ordinary partnerships, owing to the disastrous consequences that would result in such cases from following the usual rule.

A partnership for a term may be dissolved before the expiration of the term by a decree of a court of equity founded on a wilful fraud or gross misconduct of one of the partners, or upon his gross carelessness or waste, or on his exclusion of other partners from a just share of the management, or upon the existence of violent and lasting dissensions between the partners which prevent the business from being conducted upon the stipulated terms or destroy the mutual confidence amongst the partners. But a partner cannot intentionally create such conditions for the purposes of securing a dissolution and thus effect the result desired by himself. A dissolution by decree may be obtained if the business is in a hopeless state, and the property is liable to be wasted and lost.

The confirmed insanity or other infirmity of a partner may be cause for a decree of dissolution both to protect the lunatic and to relieve the co-partners, but neither insanity nor some other infirmity will of themselves dissolve the partnership without some action taken, and to secure a decree, the lunacy or malady must be clearly established. A temporary illness is not sufficient. A partnership dissolved by death of a partner is dissolved as to the whole firm.

As to third persons, partnerships will not be dissolved without notice to them that the partnership no longer exists, and this notice must be actual and brought home to persons who have been in the habit of dealing with the firm, but as to persons who did not have such previous dealings, notice fairly given in the public newspapers is sufficient. Notice is necessary to terminate the agency of each partner and consequently his power to bind the firm. It is not necessary to give notice of the withdrawal of a dormant partner from the firm to any creditors who do not know of his being a partner. Though notice is not given, the estate of a deceased partner will not be bound by contracts made after the death, nor is notice necessary where dissolution is compelled by operation of law as in the case of bankruptcy of a member of the firm.

A disolution terminates all transactions between the partners and between them and third parties except for the purpose of winding up the concern and carrying out contracts already made. The firm continues to exist so far as is necessary to wind up the business and complete contracts and to convert the assets for payment of debts and distribution amongst the partners. Where there is a disagreement or dispute amongst the partners a receiver may be appointed by a court of equity to wind up the affairs and make proper disposition of the proceeds. If all the partners agree, however, and debts are all paid and satisfied, the dissolution and distribution of the assets may be made in a way satisfactory to them.

SIMPLE PARTNERSHIP AGREEMENT

This agreement made this 4th day of August, 19___ by and between John Doe of the one part and of Harry Smith of the other part, witnesseth as follows: that the said parties hereby agree to become partners in the business of "wholesale groceries," under the firm name of Doe, Smith and Company, for the term of five years from the date hereof, upon the terms and conditions hereinafter stated, to wit:

1. That the business shall be carried on at number 487 N. Bond Street in the City of Baltimore, State of Maryland, or at any other place that may hereafter be mutually agreed upon for that purpose.

2. That proper books of account shall be kept, and therein shall be duly entered, from time to time, all dealings, transactions, matters and things whatsoever in or relating to the said business; and each party shall have full and free access thereto at all times, but shall not remove the same from the premises.

3. That the capital requisite for carrying on the said business shall be advanced by the said partners in equal parts, and the said capital, and all such stock, implements and utensils in trade, purchased out of the partnership funds, as well as the gains and profits of the said business, shall belong to the said parties in equal parts.

4. That each party shall be at full liberty to draw three hundred dollars monthly for his own private use, on account, but not in excess of his presumptive share of the profits, so long as the said business shall be found profitable, and the capital advanced as aforesaid shall remain unfinished.

5. That neither party shall become bail or surety for any other person; nor lend, spend, give or make away with any part of the partnership property; or draw or accept any bill, note, or other security in the name of the same firm, except in due course of the said partnership business.

6. That an account of the stock, implements and utensils belonging to said business, and of the book debts and capital shall be taken and a statement of the affairs of the said partnership shall be made yearly, to be computed from the date hereof, when the sums drawn by each party during the preceding year shall be charged to his share of the profits of the said business; but if, at the end of any one year of the said partnership, it shall be found to be unprofitable, the said partnership shall thereupon be dissolved, unless it shall be occasioned by some unavoidable loss or accidental circumstance.

7. That each party shall sign duplicate copies of each of such statement of affairs, and shall retain one of them for his own use; and another copy thereof shall be written in one of the partnership books, and likewise signed by each of them; such accounts shall not again be opened, unless some manifest error shall be discovered in either of them, within three months thereafter, and then so far only as respects the correcting of such error; and every such statement of affairs shall, in all other respects, be conclusive evidence between and binding on said parties.

8. That at the termination or expiration of the said partnership, by death or otherwise, a valuation and similar account of the stock, effects and capital, and good will, if any, of the said firm, shall be taken, stated, copied and signed in like manner and become equally conclusive; and the balance of such account then found to exist shall belong to the said parties in equal moieties and be realized and divided accordingly, and thereupon they shall execute mutual releases.

9. That all disputes and differences, if any, which shall arise between the said parties, shall be referred to and decided by two indifferent, competent persons in or well acquainted with the wholesale grocery business, one to be chosen by either party, or by an umpire to be chosen by the referees in the usual course in such or similar cases; and their or his decision shall, in all respects, be final and conclusive on both the said parties, and shall be given in writing within 15 days next after such submission or within such further time, not exceeding 30 days as they or he shall require.

10. That either party may terminate the partnership hereby created on breach of this agreement by the other of them, on giving unto the other of them six calendar months' notice thereof in writing.

Witness our hands and seal this fourth day of August, 19____.

(Seal) John Doe _____
                                    JOHN DOE

(Seal) Harry Smith _____
                                    HARRY SMITH

Richard Roe _____
WITNESS

PARTY WALL A wall erected on the line between two adjoining properties, belonging to different persons, for the use of both estates. In general, by statute such walls must be built equally on both properties at the general expense of the owners; but, if only one owner wishes to use it, he builds it at his own expense, the other paying half of its value when in the future he makes use of it. Each owner has a right to put his joists in it and use it for the support of his roof and house.

When the party wall has been built and the adjoining owner wishes to have a deeper foundation under it, he may undermine the wall, using due care and diligence to prevent injury to his neighbor, and if he does this he is not liable for injury that may arise. If one, in tearing down his building takes down the party wall with it he must erect another within a reasonable time and with the least possible inconvenience to his neighbor. If the wall requires repairs the other owner must contribute to the expense which, however, may not exceed his portion of the cost of the old wall, or of a new wall similar to the old one. If the wall is taken down negligently so as to injure the neighboring houses damages may be recovered.

One does not have a right to put windows in a party wall. The adjoining owner has a right to have the wall built solid.

PASSBOOK A book in which a bank enters the deposits made by a depositor, and which is retained by the depositor.

PATENT A patent is a grant by the government to an individual for the exclusive right to manufacture, use or sell his invention for a limited period. The Federal Law provides that "any person who has invented or discovered any new and useful art, machine, manufacture, or composition of matter, or any new and useful improvement thereof, not known or used by others in this country and not patented or described in any printed publication in this or any other foreign country, before his invention or discovery thereof, and not in public use or on sale for more than two years prior to his application, unless the same is proved to have been abandoned, may, upon payment of the fees required by the law, and other due proceeding had, obtain a patent thereof."

In an invention or discovery, two things are essential before a patent be granted: novelty and utility or usefulness.

To obtain a patent, the inventor or discoverer must make written application to the Commissioner of Patents in Washington, D.C., and file what is known as "specifications," or written description of the invention or discovery, "and of the manner and process of making, constructing, compounding, and using it, in such full, clear, concise, and exacts terms as to enable any person skilled in the art or science to which it appertains, or with which it is most nearly connected, to make, construct, compound, and use the same." It is further provided that "in case of a machine, he shall explain the principle thereof, and the best mode in which he has contemplated applying that principle, so as to distinguish it from other inventions, and shall particularly point out and distinctly claim the part, improvement, or combination which he claims as his invention or discovery."

This "specification" and claim must be signed by the inventor and witnessed by two persons. The applicant must also furnish a drawing, specimen or model to illustrate his claim; finally, he must make oath that he believes himself to be the original and first inventor or discoverer of the art, machine, manufacture, composition or improvement for which he seeks a patent; that he does not know and does not believe that the same was ever before known or used; he must also state of what country he is a citizen. All this information, together with the necessary fees, is filed with the Patent Office in Washington, D.C., usually through an attorney. A patent is then granted if it appears that the claimant is entitled to one.

Patents are issued in the name of the United States of America, under the seal of the Patent Office, signed by the Secretary of the Interior and countersigned by the Commissioner of Patents.

Patents are granted for seventeen years to the patentee, i.e., the person who applies for the patent, giving him the exclusive right to make, use and sell the invention or discovery throughout the United States and its territories.

If the inventor dies before the patent is issued but after application is made, the right to apply for and obtain the patent passes to the heirs of the patentee.

A patent may also be assigned or transferred by the inventor to a third party. Not only the patent, but any legal interest in it may be assigned or transferred to a third person, provided the assignment is made in writing. As a precaution and protection, such assignment should be recorded in the Patent Office within three months from its date.

When two persons file an application for a patent for the same invention, and both inventions are pending in the Patent Office at the same time, the Commissioner of Patents may compel the two interested persons to appear before him and offer evidence as to who was really the first inventor.

Injunction is a proper remedy to prevent the violation of any right secured by patent. In connection with the suit for an injunction the complainant will be entitled to recover, in addition to the profits to be accounted for by the defendant, damages which the complainant has sustained. The court will assess the same or cause them to be assessed under its direction and may increase them in its discretion in like manner, as in the case of a verdict of a jury as above mentioned, but there can be no recovery of profits or damages for any infringement committed more than six years before the filing of the bill of complaint or the issuing of a writ in a suit or action.

Patents are also granted for certain distinct and new varieties of plants. Patents for 3½, 7, or 14 years may be requested by the inventor for new, original and ornamental designs for articles of manufacture. The filing fee is $30.00 with $1.00 additional for each claim in excess of $20.00. If the inventor desires a fee for 3½ years, the fee is $10.00; if for 7 years, the fee is $15.00; for 14 years the fee is $30.00. Information about patents can be obtained from the Patent Office, Department of Commerce, Washington, D.C.

ASSIGNMENT OF INTEREST IN PATENT

Note: To protect himself, the person to whom the patent is assigned should have it recorded in the Patent Office within three months from the date of the agreement.

Whereas I, John Doe, of New York City, did obtain letters patent of the United States for an improvement in the mechanism of a washing machine, which letters patent are numbered _____, and bear date the 15th day of September, 19___, and whereas I am now the sole owner of said patent and of all rights under the same, and whereas Thomas Brown of New York City is desirous of acquiring the entire interest in the same, now therefore to all whom it may concern, be it known that for and in consideration of the sum of ten thousand dollars to me in hand paid, the receipt of which is hereby acknowledged, I, the said John Doe, inventor, have sold, assigned and transferred, and by these presents do sell, assign and transfer unto the said Thomas Brown, purchaser, the whole right, title, and interest in and to the said improvement in the washing machine, and in and to the letters patent therefor aforesaid; the same to be held and enjoyed by the said Thomas Brown for his own use and behoof, and for the use and behoof of his legal representatives, to the full end of the term for which said letters patent are or may be granted, as fully and entirely as the same would have been held and enjoyed by me had this assignment and sale not been made.

In testimony whereof I have hereunto set my hand and seal this 10th day of November, 19___, in the presence of the two witnesses whose signatures appear below.

/s/   John Doe
_____
JOHN DOE

/s/   Richard Roe
_____
WITNESS

/s/   Louis Gold
_____
WITNESS

PATENT AMBIGUITY An uncertainty in a written instrument that is obvious upon reading.

PATERNITY See PARENTS.

PAYMENT Recompense. Payment must be made by money unless there is an agreement to accept something else, and the payee may insist upon having legal tender money. The creditor may waive this right, however, and anything he accepts in satisfaction will be considered payment. If one agrees to pay a debt in stock, but fails to do so at the time agreed upon, upon demand being made, the indebtedness then becomes due in money. Though Bank of England notes are legal tender in England, bank notes are not legal tender in the United States. Yet by common usage they are regarded as cash and effect payment when accepted.

PAWN The act of pledging property as security for a loan.

Giving a check is not considered payment, that is, does not cancel the debt until paid or collected, and the holder may treat the check as a nullity if he derives no benefit from it, provided he has not been guilty of negligence in holding it until the bank on which it is drawn has failed or until in other manner loss is caused to the drawer thereof.

Payment in forged bills or counterfeit coin is generally a nullity unless it is agreed that specific money be accepted when the goods are sold or the debt is contracted, but the false money must be returned promptly or within a reasonable time. Payment to a bank by its own note which is received as cash and passed to one's credit is good payment. If a bill of exchange or promissory note is accepted as payment it will be good as such, but it will not effect payment, unless it is shown that such was the intent of the parties, until the money is collected thereon. Giving one's own note for the amount of a debt he owes, in general, does not nullify the debt for which it is given. That is, it is not payment unless it be so expressed. In the sale of goods if the note of a third person is accepted for the price it is a good payment. It is otherwise, however, if the note is that of one of the partners in payment of a partnership debt. Generally, too, it may be said that if at the time of sale it was agreed that payment was to be made in notes, a note given accordingly will effect payment and discharge the original debt, but if the note was received as a mere accommodation to the purchaser there will be no payment, and the creditor may retain the note until due and sue upon it or may sue immediately upon the original indebtedness after it becomes due.

Payment may be made through a third party. Where betting is not illegal, money deposited with a stakeholder may be paid to the winner. If illegal, the depositor may reclaim the money at any time before it is paid over, or give the stakeholder notice not to pay and hold him responsible if he does. If one owes another and gives the money to a third person to pay to the other, the right to the money becomes vested in the creditor and the debtor cannot recover it back from the third party. If both the debtor and creditor agree with the third party that the last named shall do the paying instead of the debtor, this is payment as to the debtor and releases him, and the third party takes his place as debtor.

A legacy may operate as payment of a debt if such is the intention of the testator. If the creditor authorizes the debtor to send money in payment by letter and he does so this would operate as a payment. If the money is lost the loss will be the creditor's but the debtor must exercise care in sending it.

A receipt is only prima facie evidence of payment and it is permissible to show that it was given by mistake, and that notwithstanding the receipt the money was not paid. The receipt for the last year's or quarter's rent is prima facie evidence of the payment of all rents previously due, and in fact the receipt for any periodical payment is prima facie evidence of the payment of all periodical payments or installments previously coming due.

Possession of an accepted bill of exchange by the acceptor, or a note by the drawer, is prima facie evidence of the payment thereof. Irrespective of the bar of the various statutes of limitation, a debt will be presumed to have been paid after twenty years, even if in the form of a judgment or mortgage or if evidenced by an instrument under seal. This presumption, however, may usually be rebutted by evidence that the debt has not in fact been paid. The lapse of time shifts the burden of proof as to payment from the debtor to the creditor. A jury may even infer payment from a shorter lapse of time if there be circumstances favoring the presumption.

An agent may make payment for his principal and an attorney-at-law may discharge the debt against his client. Payment may be made to an authorized agent of the creditor, but generally if made to the agent it must be in money in order to bind the principal, but if he takes goods without authority, even slight, subsequent acts of acquiescence will be deemed a ratification. If the payment is made in the ordinary course of business to an agent without notice requiring the payment to be made to himself, this is binding upon the principal, and payment to any third person whether agent or not by direction of the principal will bind him. Payment to a broker or factor who sells for a principal not named is good. Payment to an attorney is as effectual as payment to his client, and an attorney of record may even discharge and satisfy a judgment for his client, but an agent appointed by the attorney to collect may not.

If a sheriff collects money on execution he may pay it to an attorney for his client, but not if the power of attorney to act as such has been revoked and the sheriff has notice. Payment to one partner extinguishes the debt either before or after dissolution of the partnership. Payment to the creditor's wife will not discharge the debt unless she is his agent. The mere fact that one is an auctioneer to sell real estate does not authorize him to receive a receipt for the purchase money. Payment to one of several joint creditors or to one of several executors is sufficient.

Payment should be made at the exact time agreed upon. If this is not done interest will be allowed thereafter by way of damages. If payment is to be on a future date nothing can be previously demanded, and if there is a condition precedent to the liability, the condition must be performed before payment can be exacted. The debtor cannot require the creditor to receive payment before the debt is due. Payments must be made at the place agreed upon unless changed by the consent of both parties. If no place of payment is mentioned the debtor must seek out the creditor to pay him. The creditor may require payment of his whole claim at one time, unless there is a stipulation for payment in parts, and may refuse part payment.

If a payment is erroneously made under a mistake of fact it may be recovered back, but a mistake as to one's legal liability under an admitted state of facts furnishes no grounds for recovering back money paid voluntarily under a claim that it was owing. This latter rule does not hold good, however, in some states where the law is more liberal to the mistaken party. In this connection it may be said that laws of another country or state are matters of fact rather than law. Hence a payment made under mistake as to what is the law in another state or country could be recovered back. If one ignorantly pays a public officer fees which he is not entitled to, and the officer does not inform him of the fact, the money may be recovered back. If payment is made by letter, in general it may be said that the debtor is discharged, though the money does not reach the creditor.

If one owes another on two distinct accounts, he may direct any payment that he makes to be applied to whichever account he desires. If the debtor thus makes no appropriation of the payment to a particular debt, the creditor may then apply it as he desires. If one of the two debts is barred by limitation (out of date), the creditor may apply it to the debt so barred unless the debtor has applied it to the other debt, but his doing so will not have the effect of reviving and putting new life into the unpaid balance of the debt which was barred. If the debtor in making the payment enters it upon his book, as against a particular debt and communicates the fact to the creditor, this will be an appropriation, but if he does this without informing the creditor or without the creditor knowing it, it will not operate as an appropriation by the debtor, and the creditor has the privilege to apply the payment as he likes.

If the debtor owes one amount personally and another amount as an executor, or in any other representative capacity the creditor will not have an election but must apply the payment to the personal account unless otherwise directed or permitted. Where either the debtor or creditor has made an appropriation of the money to a particular debt, the law will apply it in accordance with justice and equity and this will usually be to the most precarious debt, unless there is some reason to the contrary. Where, however, one debt is a mortgage and the other a simple account, the mortgage will be first paid on the ground that it appears more for the interest of the debtor to have this debt discharged. If the sum paid will exactly satisfy one of the debts, it will be applied to that one on the presumption that such was the intention.

If one debt is absolute and the other contingent, as where the creditor is a surety or an endorser for the debtor on a note not yet paid, the payment will be applied to the absolute debt unless the debtor directs otherwise. If a partnership is indebted to one, and a partner who is also indebted to the same person makes a payment from partnership funds, without designating the debt to which it shall be applied, it must be applied to the partnership debt.

PAYMENT INTO COURT Money paid into court by direction or leave of court upon application of the party owing or holding it where the person entitled will not accept it, or his whereabouts is unknown, or where different parties are claiming it or where there is no one qualified to receive it. When so paid the party paying escapes further responsibility with respect thereto, and divests himself of all right to withdraw the money except by leave of court.

Sometimes where suit is brought for a given amount the defendant admits that a smaller amount is due. Such smaller amount with all costs accrued may be tendered by the defendant to the plaintiff and, if not accepted by him, may be paid into the court, the object being to escape payment of any further costs in case the plaintiff fails to recover more than the amount tendered. By such payment into court the defendant admits conclusively all that the plaintiff will be obliged to prove in order to recover the amount so paid. He admits that the amount is due in the manner alleged in the plaintiff's declaration or statement.

PECUNIARY LEGACY A legacy of a sum of money; a gift of a sum of money by will. Otherwise called a general legacy.

PENAL BOND A bond given by an accused, or by another person in his behalf, for the payment of money if the accused fails to appear in court on a certain day.

PENAL STATUTE A statute enacting or imposing a penalty or punishment on the commission of a certain offense.

PENDENTE LITE Pending the suit; during the actual progress of a suit; during litigation.

PER CURIAM A decision by the full court in which no opinion is given.

PER SE The expression means by or through itself; simply, as such; in its own relations.

PER STIRPES An expression used in connection with the descent or distribution of a decedent's estate, where, the parent being dead, his children stand in his place and take equally his share.

PEREMPTORY CHALLENGE A species of challenge which a prisoner is allowed to have against a certain number or jurors without showing any cause.

PERFORMANCE The carrying out of provisions in a contract. Performance of a contract must be in accordance with the intention of the parties as it appears in the contract. It is apparent that there may be cases in which a literal, accurate performance may not be in accordance with the evident intent of the parties, in which case the evident intent must control. Thus a contract for the conveyance of real estate is not satisfied by a mere formal conveyance. The conveyance must in addition be valid and give a good title, unless the contract expresses and defines the exact method of conveyance, in which case, if the method is actually followed, there will be a sufficient performance though no good title pass. If the contract is to convey by a "good and sufficient deed," the deed must not merely be right in form, but it must transfer a good title.

If a contract is severable, or may be fairly divided into parts, and there may be performance of one of the parts, recovery may be had for such part performance. But if the contract is entire and indivisible, there must be, in general, complete performance before there may be recovery. Thus if there is a contract of sale and delivery of a large number of a given article at an agreed price for each, and a part only is delivered, recovery may be had for those delivered with a proper deduction for any loss the party may have sustained by reason of a failure to complete the contract.

Where, however, in process of removal by a contractor a building was consumed by fire through no fault of his, the contractor is entitled to recover the value of the work already done, although he had contracted to do the entire job for a specified price.

Usually, if there is a time limit within which a contract shall be completed and it is not completed until some days after, an action may be sustained for the price, but the party may require a deduction for any injury he sustained by the delay. But if the parties state in unequivocal language that there shall be no payment unless fulfillment is accomplished within the time designated, then in case of failure to comply no recovery can be had. In such cases time is said to be of the essence of the contract, though even then if the party receives and accepts the article after the time of delivery, it can hardly be said that he would not be bound to pay a reasonable amount for it though it is less than the contract price and though due allowance is made to him for loss sustained by tardy delivery.

Where no time for the performance of the contract is specified a reasonable time is intended, and what is a reasonable time will depend upon the circumstances of the case. Where a place of delivery is designated but no time, usually the delivery must be made upon demand. When a given length of time is allowed for performance, in computing this the date when the contract was made must usually be excluded, unless it appear that the language of the contract imports a different intent. The expression "between two days" excludes both. Where the time of performance under a contract happens to be on Sunday, it may be done on Monday. If one has undertaken to do a thing by a given time, and by some act distinctly incapacitates himself from doing it at that time, the injured party may sue at once and not await the fulfillment of the time.

Although where one fails to perform his part on the contract, or disables himself from doing so, the other may treat the contract as rescinded if he himself has not been in default, yet he cannot rescind the contract in its entirety if a distinct part which is severable from the entire contract has been performed, for it would be unfair that he should profit from a partial performance without any corresponding performance or payment what-ever on his part.

Where one has contracted to do a thing he must either do it according to the contract before he can recover anything by reason of the contract, or he must show inability to perform by reason of some act or failure on the part of the other contracting party, accompanied by a tender of performance by himself. It is not sufficient for him to show a mere readiness to discharge his part of the agreement, but he must show that he did all he could under the circumstances. If either non-performance is caused or if performance is prevented by the act or fault of the other party, this will relieve the party whose duty it was to perform.

Where a contract provides that a thing shall be done on notice given, the provision as to notice should be carefully complied with. Where a thing is to be done by one on performance of an act by another, the other must give notice to the first party that the act has been performed.

Where a natural intervention or a so-called act of God prevents performance this will relieve a party of responsibility, but if the prevention is only in part he will be relieved only to that extent. If one is bound to perform a future act and before the time for doing it declares an intention not to do it, this will not constitute a breach of contract unless he puts himself in such position that it will be impossible to perform it when the time arrives.

PERJURY Swearing wilfully, absolutely and falsely, under oath, in a matter material to the issue. In general, perjury may be committed in case of an affirmation as well. Subornation of perjury is the offense of procuring another to make such false oath as would constitute perjury in the principal.

To constitute perjury the oath must be taken and the falsehood asserted with deliberation and with consciousness of the nature of the statement made, for if made through inadvertence, surprise or mistake of the import of the question, there is no corrupt motive. If one swears wilfully and deliberately to a matter which he rashly believes, but which is false, and which he has no probable cause for believing, he is guilty of perjury. Even if one intending to deceive, asserts what may happen to be true, without a knowledge of the fact, the accidental truth of his evidence will not excuse him.

Before one can be convicted of perjury it must appear that the oath or affirmation was administered by one having competent authority to do so in the particular case, and an oath before a private person or before an officer having no jurisdiction is no crime. The proceeding must be before him who is in some way entrusted with the administration of justice, and the testimony must be in respect to a matter regularly before him. The assertion must be absolute. If, however, one swears merely he believes that to be true which he knows to be false it will be perjury; and it is immaterial whether the testimony is given voluntarily or in answer to a question.

Another necessary element in perjury is that the oath must be material to the issue. If the facts sworn to are foreign to the matter in question there can be no perjury; yet even questions on cross-examination asked for the proper purpose of testing the credit of the witness, as for example whether he has before been convicted of felony, are considered material.

PERPETUATING TESTIMONY A witness's testimony reduced to writing under oath so that it may be used in a later trial. This procedure is employed when a witness is aged, infirm, or about to leave the state.

PERPETUITY The rule to prevent the trying of estates and property, so as to make them incapable of being conveyed for any great length of time. This is the well-known rule against perpetuities. A limitation of property making it inalienable for a longer period than a life or lives in being and twenty-one years beyond, and, in case of a posthumous child, about nine months more allowing for the period of gestation.

PERSON The term includes men, women and children, citizens and aliens, legitimates and bastards. A corporation is included within the term "person." It is an artificial person, but whether it should or not be so included depends on the connection in which the word is used.

PERSONAL ASSETS Personal property in the hands of an executor or administrator, chargeable with the debts or legacies of the testator or intestate and applicable to that purpose.

PERSONAL PROPERTY Things movable or separate from real estate. It includes choses in action such as bonds and other obligations and debts, also most things of a perishable character or of possible brief duration. A crop growing in the ground is commonly considered personal property, and contrary to the rule with respect to land, it may be sold without any instrument in writing. Yet in a sale of the land, if not reserved, it will go with it.

Stock in corporations is personal property even though the possessions of the corporation are real estate. Though trees in general are part of the real estate, this is not true of nurseries which are much like crops in this respect. Bricks in a kiln are personal property, so also are buildings where erected on another's land with the agreement with the landowner that they shall not belong to him or that they shall not be part of his land. Mortgages and leases of land are personal property; so are rents, copyrights and patents.

Title to personal property may be acquired in different ways as by original acquisition by occupancy, capture in war, or finding a lost thing by accession, by intellectual labor, as in case of copyrights and patents, by transfer, by forfeiture, by judicial sale, by will or through intestate laws or by gift.

PERSONAL REPRESENTATIVES These are executors or administrators of a deceased person. In wills, where such intent appears these words are sometimes construed to mean next of kin.

PETIT or PETTY JURY Small jury; the ordinary jury of twelve men, as distinguished from grand jury, consisting of a larger number.

PHYSICIANS AND SURGEONS *See* MALPRACTICE.

PICKET A workman, member of a trade union on strike, posted in front of a struck place of employment for the purpose of publicizing that the workmen are on strike.

PLACE OF BUSINESS The place where a person continues to conduct his calling, trade, business or profession for the purpose of a livelihood, gain, and profit.

PLAGIARISM Palming off another's ideas or writings as one's own.

PLAINTIFF One who complains or brings suit.

PLAINTIFF IN ERROR The unsuccessful party to the action who prosecutes a writ of error in a higher court.

PLEA An answer or allegation of fact which a defendant, in an action at law, opposes to the plaintiff's declaration.

PLEA IN ABATEMENT A plea which goes to abate the plaintiff's action, that is, to suspend or put it off for the present.

PLEAD TO THE MERITS A phrase denoting pleas which answer the cause of action by direct challenge and on which a trial can be held, rather than those which avoid the asserted liability by such indirect defenses as statutes of limitations.

PLEADINGS The individual allegations of the respective parties to an action at common law, proceeding from them alternately, in the order and under the distinctive names following: the plaintiff's declaration, the defendant's plea, the plaintiff's replication, the defendant's rejoinder, the plaintiff's surrejoinder, the defendant's rebutter, the plaintiff's surrebutter, after which they have no distinctive names.

In equity; the formal written allegation or statements of the respective parties in a suit, to maintain or defeat it. These are: the plaintiff's bill, the defendant's answer and the plaintiff's replication or reply.

PLEDGE A pledge is the delivering of personal property as security for a debt or engagement. To constitute a pledge, possession of the property to be pledged must be delivered to the pledgee or to a third person upon a contract to hold the same for the purposes agreed upon. There is a distinction between a pledge and a mortgage. In the former the legal title remains in the pledgor. In a mortgage it passes to the mortgagee and the mortgagee need not have possession. In a pledge, what is termed constructive possession by the pledgee is frequently sufficient. By constructive possession is meant that which exists in contemplation of law without actual occupation. Thus possession of goods at sea or in a warehouse may pass by way of pledge, by transfer of the evidence of title, or by symbolic delivery as by transfer of a warehouse receipt.

Where one has been directed to deliver securities as a pledge and dies before delivery, the authority to deliver them is at an end, and there is no pledge.

When a pledge is sold, only so much of the proceeds as will pay the debt for which the goods are pledged can be retained by the pledgee.

Stocks and equitable interests may be pledged, if by proper transfer the property is placed within the power and control of the pledgee. Stocks are usually pledged by delivery of the certificate of the stock with an assignment thereof in blank or otherwise without an actual transfer on the books of the company. Any tangible property may be pledged, such as goods and chattels, negotiable paper, choses in action, patent rights, bonds, manuscripts, insurance policies, and it seems that even a pledge to secure an obligation not yet existing at the time the pledge is made, will become good and binding when the obligation is created. The policy of the law forbids the pledging of the pay, emoluments, pensions, and bounties of officers, soldiers and sailors. Notes discounted by a bank may be pledged by it.

The pledgee is bound to take ordinary care of his pawn, and if he has exercised such care, and it is lost, stolen, or injured, he may still recover his debt. If the thing is stolen, however, the presumption is that ordinary care was not used, and it devolves upon the pledgee to show that the theft could not have been prevented by ordinary care on his part.

The pledgee has a special property in the pledge and is entitled to exclusive possession of it during the time and for the objects for which it is pledged. If a wrong-doer takes it the pledgee may bring suit to recover it. The pledgor may also bring suit against the wrong-doer, but after either the pledgor or pledgee has obtained judgment, the other cannot proceed with the suit. The pledgee may even sue the pledgor, if he takes possession before paying his debt, for the value of his special property in the thing, or he may recover the thing itself from him.

If the pawnor fails to pay the debt when due, the pledgee or pawnee may sell the pledge but a demand of payment must be made before sale and the sale may be at the expiration of a reasonable time after demand, if no time is fixed in the contract of pledge. Personal notice must be given to the pledgor of an intent to redeem together with the time and place and manner of the intended sale. If the pledge is divisible only enough to pay, the debt should be sold, and the sale should be at public auction unless the contract between the parties permits a private sale. If the pledgee buys the pledge at the sale, the pledgor may, if he desires, avoid the sale. If the thing sells for more than enough to pay the debt the surplus must be turned over to the pledgor, and by accepting such surplus the pledgor ratifies any purchase that may have been made by the pledgee. Necessary expenses such as costs of sale, etc., incurred by the pledgee, will be taken out of the proceeds of the sale, and if the proceeds are insufficient to pay the debt and expenses, the unpaid part of the debt will continue to be a claim against the pledgor.

A pledge cannot be held for any other debt than that which it was given to secure, except by agreement of the parties. A pledgor may transfer his right in the property to a third person, who, upon tendering the amount of the debt to the pawnee, will be entitled to the pawn. The same is the case with the creditor of the pledgor who purchases his interest in the pawn at a judicial sale. A factor cannot ordinarily pledge his principal's goods, and if he does, the principal may recover them from the pledgee. Statute laws, however, in some instances give factors such authority.

One pledgee may hold a pledge for himself and one or more other pledgees, and it will be good as to all. If the property on being sold does not yield sufficient to pay all, the one having the first pledge will be first entitled to the proceeds, and if there is no priority in time between the pledgees they will share the proceeds. If the pledgee holding possession for himself and others loses the pledge by his negligence he will be liable to his co-pledgees.

POLICE POWERS This is the right to legislate for the general welfare, to prescribe regulations for the order, peace, protection, comfort, health, and convenience of the community at large, even though individual rights are apparently interfered with. The interests or desires of the individual must bend to the evident good of the community at large. The power is a very broad and searching one. It does not, however, extend to the taking of private property for public use without compensation. Unhealthful or adulterated foods, intoxicating liquors, lotteries, bawdy-houses, public places or houses of public entertainment, gaming, fire, common carriers, such as railway companies, public utilites, etc., in which the general public in contradistinction to individuals are concerned, are all subjects of what is termed police regulation.

PORNOGRAPHY The simple, dictionary definition of pornography is "obscene literature or art." When we look up the dictionary meaning of "obscene" we find that it means "offensive to modesty or decency; indecent; lewd; as in obscene pictures." Pornography isn't merely limited to "dirty" pictures and books. To the prurient minded, pornography may and often does cover a wide spectrum of books, "French" and even Hollywood films, stag parties, burlesque shows, lewd photographs, "cheesecake" magazines, classic or modern art, and serious literature with some amount of erotic content. To the impure, all things are impure and these people, unfortunately, often take it upon themselves to be the judges of what is or is not pornographic.

The aim of pornographic writing is usually to stimulate or titillate sexual desire. The aim of a serious work of literature which has some erotic content is not its aphrodisiac appeal, which is incidental, but to describe life realistically. The distinction is both fundamental and valid. To the lascivious, the *Song of Songs* is frankly pornographic. So is *Lady Chatterley's Lover*, *Playboy* Magazine, and anything else that fits in with their own highly personal views of what is and what is not obscene.

In defining pornography, the United States Supreme Court set down the following guideline: "Whether to the average person, applying contemporary standards, [the] dominant theme of [the] material taken as a whole appeals to the prurient interest." The test is whether the book as a whole, not an isolated passage, is obscene and thus appeals to the prurient interest of the average person. This is true not only of books, photographs, and paintings, but also of motion pictures. In short, for material to be judged obscene, the work must be "utterly without redeeming social importance." "A thing is obscene if, considered as a whole, its predominant appeal is to prurient interest ... *and* if it goes substantially beyond customary limits of candor in description or representation."

The Supreme Court defined the community not as an isolated backwoods village but national in scope, so that "contemporary community standards" is really a "national standard of decency." Otherwise, said the Court, there might be the "intolerable consequence of denying some sections of the country access to material, there deemed acceptable, which in others might be considered offensive to prevailing standards of decency." Thus a jury in sophisticated San Francisco might come to a completely different conclusion about a film or a piece of literature than a community off the mainstream of American culture and civilization.

POST-DATED CHECK One which is complete in all respects but dated in the future. It is not payable until that later date is reached.

POSTHUMOUS After death; a term used to describe a child born after the death of the father or (by means of a Caesarian operation) after the death of the mother. A posthumous child has the same legal status or standing as one born before the father's or mother's, death.

POST-MORTEM After death. Commonly applied to examinations of a dead body by a coroner.

POWER OF ATTORNEY An instrument in writing authorizing a person to act as the agent or attorney-in-fact for the person granting it is called a power or letter of attorney. It may be general, authorizing the agent to act generally in behalf of the principal, or special, limiting his authority to particular acts. It may be by parol, that is not under seal, or it may be under seal. The attorney cannot execute a sealed instrument so as to bind his principal unless the power to him be under seal.

Powers of attorney will not be construed to mean more than they clearly import, that is, they will be strictly construed, and if general terms are used in connection with a particular subject matter such terms will be construed to refer to that particular matter only. A power of attorney authorizing the execution of a recordable instrument should itself be recorded, and to be recorded it must of course be acknowledged or be accompanied with other legal requisite to recording.

PRECEDENT A previous decision relied upon as authority. The doctrine of *stare dicisis,* commonly called the doctrine of precedents, has been firmly established in the law. It means that we should adhere to decide cases on settled principles, and not disturb matters

GENERAL POWER OF ATTORNEY

Know All Men by These Presents:

I, John Doe, residing in the City of Louisville, Ky., by these presents hereby make, constitute and appoint Thomas Brown, also of Louisville, Ky., my true and lawful attorney in fact for and in my name, place and stead, to (here insert the power intended to be conferred which should be stated in clear and precise language, as for example, to purchase a 19___ Buick Sedan to cost not more than nine hundred dollars).

I hereby grant and give unto my said attorney in fact full authority and power to do and perform any and all other acts necessary or incident to the performance and execution of the powers herein expressly granted, with power to do and perform all acts authorized hereby, as fully to all intents and purposes as the grantor might or could do if personally present, with full power of substitution.

In testimony whereof I have set my hand and seal this fourth day of February, 19___.

/s/   John Doe
GRANTOR

/s/   Richard Roe
WITNESS

/s/   John Smith
WITNESS

---

which have been established by judicial determination.

PREFERENCE The act of a debtor in paying or securing one or more of his creditors in a way more favorable to them than to other creditors or to the exclusion of such other creditors. In the absence of statute, a preference is perfectly good, but to be legal it must be bona fide, and not a mere subterfuge of the debtor to secure a future benefit to himself or to prevent the application of his property to his debts.

PREFERRED STOCK Stock which entitles its owners to dividends out of the net profits before or in preference to the holders of the common stock.

PREMIUM The consideration paid by the insured to the insurance company in return for which the company agrees to reimburse him for the loss agreed upon in the policy.

PREPONDERANCE Preponderance of the evidence means that evidence which in the judgment of the jurors is entitled to the greatest weight, which appears to be more credible, has greater force, and overcomes not only the opposing presumptions, but also the opposing evidence.

PRESCRIPTION A method of acquiring, by immemorial or long continued enjoyment, title to incorporeal hereditaments, that is, to things which are inheritable, but not tangible or visible, such as ways, franchises, easements of light, air, etc. In short, they are the rights growing out of real or personal property but not the property or substance of the thing itself. Grants of incorporeal hereditaments are presumed upon proof of enjoyment of the same for a period of years (most commonly twenty years), equal to that fixed by statute as the period within which suit may be brought to recover land against one holding adverse possession.

PRESENTMENT A bill of exchange or note which must be presented for payment on the day it falls due, or the endorser is no longer liable. Failure to present a check with reasonable promptness and consequent inability to collect will not only relieve an endorser of the check of his liability, but will also extinguish the debt for which he delivered the check. The same is true of an endorser on a negotiable promissory note where the holder fails to make demand for payment at maturity.

Even if the maker of the note or acceptor of the bill has died, demand must be made by his executor or administrator or, if there is none, at his house. Where there are several makers of a promissory note, demand should be made on all in order to hold the endorser, unless the note is drawn by partners in connection with a partnership transaction. The endorser, if discharged by a failure to make the required demand, may waive his advantage by promising to pay or by part payment after (not before) the failure.

Demand need not be made of one who has absconded, or has no usual place of residence or regular place of business and cannot be found with reasonable effort.

Where the instrument is made payable at a bank or other particular place, demand must be made there. If this is at a place of business the demand should be in business hours; if elsewhere, at a reasonable hour, to hold the endorser. If payable at different places it may be presented at any one of them. If the payor has moved elsewhere within the state and the note is not payable at the particular place the holder, if he knows where he lives, must endeavor to make demand there, or if he has moved out of the state, at his former residence. Where days of grace are allowed the demand must be made on the last day of grace, but notes payable on demand are not entitled to grace.

The statement of a grand jury that a crime has been committed, arising from its own knowledge or investigation, as distinguished from an indictment, which is made at the instance of an official.

PRESUMPTION A statement, sometimes of fact, sometimes of law, and sometimes mixed, which can be considered as true without further proof. There are some presumptions called conclusive presumptions of law which cannot be rebutted or overcome by evidence. Of this class are estoppels, solemn and formal admissions, and even unsolemn admissions which others have acted upon who would be injured if the party were permitted to maintain rights contrary to the admission. As between the parties to a suit the sheriff's return (or report to court as to what he has done with respect to a writ or command issued to him from court) is presumed to be correct, though if the return is in fact false, the sheriff will be liable for resulting damages. Other conclusive presumptions are that an infant under seven years of age is incapable of committing a felony, that all persons subject to a law duly enacted or established through general or immemorial custom are acquainted with it. Amongst them are included the presumption that one is innocent until guilt is proven; that the possessor of property is the owner; that one possessing the fruits of crime is guilty of crime; that things done in the course of trade have been done in accordance with the custom in that trade or business; that official acts have been properly performed; that a personal relation or state of things such as life, or partnership, insanity, or the like, once shown to exist, continues to exist; that the holder of a bill of exchange or promissory note endorsed in blank is its owner.

PRETRIAL PROCEDURE Established in many courts to speed up the disposition of cases by encouraging and assisting settlements before trial.

PRIMA FACIE At first sight; a prima facie case is established when the evidence is sufficiently strong for an opponent to be called on to answer it.

PRIMA FACIE EVIDENCE Evidence sufficiently strong to be accepted unless either rebutted or contradicted.

PRINCIPAL One who delegates another to act for him. Everyone of full age not under legal disability is capable of being a principal. Idiots and lunatics are not. A minor's power to appoint an agent is limited to such acts as will be beneficial to him, and he may repudiate such acts of an agent as will be to his prejudice. His appointment of agents may be said to be co-extensive with his power to contract.

Principals are entitled to recover from their agents actual loss or damage occasioned by their negligence, or omission to perform their duties, or by exceeding their authority, or by their positive misconduct. The principal may require his agent to account at all times in relation to the business of the agency and to keep him informed of its progress. The principal is bound by any fraud, misrepresentation or concealment of the agent as if committed by himself, and if the person dealing with the agent dealt with him as owner, believing him to be a principal, he will be entitled to set off any claim he may have against the agent even if suit is brought by the principal against him.

If a principal gives notice to a debtor not to pay an agent, and he does so, the debt may be again recovered from the debtor, unless the agent has some superior right in the fund or debt, and was himself entitled to a part of it. If money has been paid by an agent through mistake of fact or illegally extorted from him in the course of his employment, or if it has been fraudulently applied by the agent for an unlawful purpose, the principal may recover it back, and if goods are entrusted to the agent for a specific purpose and he disposes of them for another purpose or in an unauthorized manner, the title will not in general pass and the principal may reclaim them.

The principal must reimburse the agent for all advancements, expenses and disbursements lawfully incurred about the agency and pay him interest wherever interest may fairly be presumed to have been stipulated for or to be due, and must indemnify the agent when he has, without fault of his own, sustained damages in following the directions of his principal. Thus if the principal supplies him with goods of a third party and he sells them under direction from the principal and the third party recovers damages against him, the principal will be liable to the agent. The principal is not liable to a criminal prosecution for the misdeeds of his agent unless he authorized them or co-operated with him, though he is liable in civil suit to third persons for the misfeasance, negligence or omission of the agent in the regular course and scope of the agency, even if he does not authorize or know of the same or even forbade it. The principal's responsibility is the same with respect to sub-agents retained by his direction, express or implied.

In criminal law principals are of two kinds, principals in the first degree who are actual perpetrators of the offense, and those in the second degree who are present aiding and abetting its commission.

A principal in the first degree is usually but not necessarily present at the committing of the offense, as in the case of one who lays poison for another or where one incites a child or other irresponsible person to perpetrate a crime, or a person of discretion ignorantly and innocently to commit a criminal offense. If the person is aware of the consequences of the act he is principal in the first degree, and the employer, if present when the act is committed, is a principal in the second degree, and if absent, an accessory before the fact.

A principal in the second degree is one who is present aiding and abetting. He need not be an actual witness of the transaction if, with the intention of giving assistance, he is near enough to afford it if occasion arises. He is then constructively present. Yet he must participate in the act. His mere presence, not consenting to the felonious purpose, and not endeavoring to prevent it or to apprehend the felon, will not make him a principal in the second degree. A distinction between the two degrees is not of great importance for if one is charged in an indictment with being a principal in either degree he may usually be convicted if it is proven that he was a principal of the other kind.

PRISONER A person in custody, arrested, or in prison. Prisoners awaiting trial are considered innocent, and are entitled to be treated with as little severity as possible. They are entitled to discharge on bail, except in capital cases when the proof is strong. Where imprisoned after sentence they must be treated according to the requirements of the law. Since abolition of imprisonment for debt there are few cases of imprisonment in civil cases but where there is such imprisonment in suits based on torts, the prisoner may generally be discharged on bail, or if he has no means, under insolvent laws.

PRIVATE CORPORATION A corporation founded by a private individual, or the stock of which is owned by private persons, such as a hospital or college, a bank, an insurance, turnpike or railroad company.

PRIVATE NUISANCE Anything done to the hurt or annoyance of the lands, tenements or hereditaments of another.

PRIVIES Persons connected together or having mutual interests in the same action or thing by some relation other than actual contract between them.

PRIVILEGE FROM ARREST A privilege from arrest on civil process, is enjoyed either permanently, as by ambassadors, public ministers, and their servants, etc., or temporarily, as by members of Congress and of state legislatures, during their attendance at the session of their respective houses, and in going to and returning from the same.

PRIVILEGED COMMUNICATIONS Statements which would ordinarily be slanderous or libelous that are not so by virtue of their being in a privileged state. One is not liable, either civilly or criminally, in respect to matters published or stated by him as a member of a legislative body in the course of his legislative duty, or similarly in the course of his duty in any judicial proceeding. This privilege extends to party, counsel, witnesses, jurors and jury in a judicial proceeding and to all who, in the discharge of public duty and the honest pursuit of private right, are compelled to take part in the administration of justice or in legislation.

A fair report of any judicial proceeding or inquiry is also privileged, nor is this privilege confined exclusively to legal and legislative proceeding. Communications of so-called slanderous facts made between persons having an interest in the subject matter thereof or in the pursuit of prosecution of their moral and social duties not of a gossiping character or intended to be prejudicial to the individual, and made not out of malice or wantonness or carelessness of the reputation of others, but rather with some beneficial object in view, are not slanderous.

PRIVITY Mutual and successive relationship to the same interest. Offeror and offeree, assignor and assignee, grantor and grantee are in privity. Privity of estate means that one takes title from another. In contract law, privity denotes parties in mutual legal relationship to each other by virtue of being promisees and promisors. At early common law, third-party beneficiaries and assignees were said to be not in "privity."

PRIZE COURTS Courts to which prizes taken in time of war are brought for adjudication and condemnation, and the sentence of which is necessary to invest a capture with the character of prize. In the United States, the district courts act as the prize courts of the country.

PROBATE The act or process of proving a will by a court having competent jurisdiction.

PROBATION A method by which a convicted offender is given a suspended sentence and released on supervision. Probation differs from parole in that the latter involves imprisonment and the former does not. Probation is usually given to those found guilty of minor or first offenses. If one on probation violates the rules of his probation he may be committed to prison to serve the original, suspended sentence.

PROCESS In a general sense, the entire proceedings in any action or prosecution, real or personal, civil or criminal, from the beginning to the end.

PROCTOR One who manages the business of another, on the mandate or commission of his principal; an attorney.

PROFITS Excess of returns over expenditures from a transaction or business. A division of gross returns, though it may include a division of profits, is nevertheless not a division of profits as such. Hence it has been held that a pure, simple agreement to share gross returns does not constitute a partnership, for the essential element in a partnership is an agreement to share profits as such. A participation in commissions has been held to be such a participation in profits as to make the parties sharing the commissions partners, and commissions received are not unfrequently accounted as profits.

An authority in a will to raise money out of rents or profits of an estate for payment of debts and legacies or for other purposes within a definite period, which cannot be raised out of such rents and profits, amounts to an authority to sell. A devise of rents and profits of land is equivalent to a devise of the land itself, and will carry the legal as well as beneficial interest therein. A direction by a testator that a certain person shall receive for his support the net profits of the land is a devise of the land itself for such period as the profits are devised. One acting in a trust capacity, as a trustee, executor or guardian, may be required to account for and pay to the person whose money he has used, all profits made by him whether by investing the moneys in trade or otherwise.

The profits which would flow directly and immediately from the fulfillment of a contract may be reckoned as part of the damages for non-fulfillment. But this is not true of profits that might simply be expected to grow out of the contract indirectly or from independent future bargains that might be made relating to it, nor profits speculative in character depending upon the future state of the market. Such matters are considered too remote and uncertain to be relied upon as a proper basis of damages. The purchaser of an article or a piece of property is entitled to the profits from the time it was to be delivered or transferred, whether he takes possession or not, if the failure to deliver was from no fault of his own.

PROMISE OF MARRIAGE A promise to marry may be inferred from and proven by showing the conduct of the party and general circumstances which usually attend a marriage engagement, such as visiting, understanding among friends and relations, and preparations for marriage. If the offer is by letter by one at a distance, it will be presumed to continue for a reasonable time for the other party's consideration and if accepted within a reasonable time and before it is revoked the contract is completed. If made, however, and both parties do not treat the contract as continuing it will be considered to be abandoned by mutual consent.

If one of the parties is a minor or otherwise incapable of being bound by a promise of marriage and the other is under no disability to contract, the latter will be liable for damages for a breach even though the former is not.

The following are considered good defenses against a suit for damages; if either party has been convicted of an infamous crime or has sustained a bad character generally, and the other was ignorant of it at the time of the engagement; if the woman has committed fornication without knowledge by the man at the time of engagement; if false representations are made by the woman or by her friends in collusion with her as to her circumstances and situation in life and the amount of her fortune and marriage portion. However, the fact that the person suing may, at the time of the engagement, be already engaged to another, will not be a defense, unless the prior engagement was fraudulently concealed.

A man having a wife living and making a promise of marriage to another woman will be liable for breach of promise even though performance of the contract on his part was impossible, provided the woman did not know of the marriage at the time. If the situation and position of either of the parties with regard to fitness for the marriage relation are permanently and materially altered for the worse after the engagement, whether with or without the fault of such party, this will release the other.

In many states breach of promise suits have been abolished.

PROMISSORY NOTE Any written promise to pay a certian sum of money at a future time, unconditionally, is a promissory note. It usually contains a promise to pay at a certain time a sum of money to a certain person, therein named, or to his order, for value received. No particular form of promise is necessary. The promise to deliver the money, or to be accountable for it, or that payee shall have it, is sufficient. If there is any contingency about the payment it will not be a promissory note, nor will it if payable out of a particular fund, though this will not prevent the obligation from being binding.

In accepting a note it is well to see that it is without erasures or alterations, is dated, specifies the amount of money to be paid, names the person to whom it is to be paid, is made payable "to the order of" the payee or includes the words "or order" after the name of payee if it is intended to make the note negotiable, states a place where payment is to be made, that it is "for value received" and is signed by the maker or his duly authorized representative.

Though a promissory note of an individual under seal is not negotiable, a corporate seal of a corporation on its commercial paper, otherwise negotiable in form, will not destroy its negotiability. To be negotiable a promissory note must be certain as to the sum to be paid and the time of payment; provision in a note payable in installments

PROMISSORY NOTE

Negotiable Note

Philadelphia, _____, 19___

$100.00

Ninety days after date I promise to pay to the order of John Doe one hundred dollars, without defalcation for value received.

Richard Roe

---

that in case any installment is not paid when due the whole of the note may be considered as due, will not destroy its negotiability for there is a time certain at which at all events it must be paid.

Adding the word "trustee," "agent," "executor," etc., to the name of the payee in a note does not destroy its negotiability.

The promissory note when endorsed, although different in form, is similar to a bill of exchange. The endorsing payee of a note stands in the position of the drawer of a bill of exchange, the maker in that of the acceptor and the endorsee in that of the drawee in the bill. Most rules applicable to bills of exchange equally affect promissory notes. A promissory note payable to order passes or is transferred by endorsement. If there is an endorsement in blank already on it or if it be payable to bearer, it will pass by delivery without endorsement or further endorsement, and the holder may bring suit on it in his own name. The holder may elect to sue any endorser or he may sue the drawer, and any endorser paying the holder will have recourse to the drawer or any prior endorser unless a contrary agreement between the parties is shown.

PROMOTERS The persons who bring about the incorporation and organization of a corporation. These officials must be fair to other stockholders, and where their compensation is not set forth in the subscription paper, or unless the stockholders are otherwise informed of the compensation to be paid the promoters at the time of subscribing, their compensation can be fixed only by a vote of the stockholders subsequently obtained. It is fraud on future stockholders for the promoters to organize and secretly vote a block of stock to themselves for their services and afterwards to attempt to obtain subscriptions of other stockholders without informing them of the facts.

PROOF Evidence presented at a trial which is believed by the judge or jury. Proof is established by evidence but there may be evidence which does not amount to proof. The burden of proving the existence or non-existence of a given fact lies upon him who alleges it.

PROPERTY Property in goods and chattels may be either absolute or it may be qualified. For example, one has property in wild animals when reduced to his possession and subject to his power, but as soon as the possession is lost his property is gone, unless the animal has acquired the habit of returning upon going away or has become tame. A bailee has a qualified or special property in goods and chattels committed to him, the owner having the absolute property. The property may be either corporeal, that is, visible or tangible, or it may be incorporeal, consisting of legal rights such as choses in action.

PROPINQUITY Closeness; the relationship which exists among members of a family or their descendants.

PROSECUTOR One who institutes and carries on a criminal suit. Anyone may be a prosecutor against another whom he knows or has reason to believe is guilty of a criminal offense whether he is the one directly injured by the offense or not, but no one is bound to prosecute except for a few of the grossest offenses, as treason.

PROSPECTUS An introductory proposal for a contract in which the representations may or may not form the basis of the contract actually made; it may contain promises which are to be treated as a sort of floating obligation to take effect when appropriated by persons to whom they are addressed, and amount to a contract when assented to by any person who invests his money on the faith of them.

PRO TANTO For so much; to such an extent.

PROTEST A solemn declaration against an act about to be done or already done. A formal statement in writing by a public notary, under seal, that a certain bill of exchange or promissory note (describ-

ing it) was, on a certain day, presented for payment or acceptance, and that such payment or acceptance was refused.

PROTOCOL The first draft or rough minutes of an instrument or transaction, the original copy of a dispatch, treaty or other document.

PROXIMATE CAUSE That cause of an injury which, in natural and continuous sequence, unbroken by any efficient intervening cause, produces the injury, and without which the injury would not have occurred.

PROXY One delegated to represent another person at a meeting or public body; it is also the instrument containing the appointment of such a person.

PUBLICATION The act or process of making anything public. Libel or slander must be published or given forth in order that it may become effective so that a right of action may exist. A libel may be published by picturing or painting another in an ignominious manner, or by making the sign of a gallows or other reproachful or ignominious sign upon one's door or before his house. It may be published by maliciously repeating or singing it in the presence of others, or by delivering it or a copy of it to another. If the libel is contained in a letter addressed to another this will not be a publication to support a civil suit for damages, but it will support an indictment for the criminal offense of libel. If the letter, however, was forwarded to the plaintiff during his absence and with intent that it should be obtained and read by his family or employees and it is read by them this will be sufficient to support a civil suit. If not read it is no publication.

The sale of a copy of a newspaper, even to one who was sent by the person libeled to procure a copy, is sufficient publication to sustain an action for damages. A sealed letter or other communication delivered to the plaintiff's wife is publication. If the libel is in a newspaper, proof that copies were distributed is evidence of publication.

In criminal cases it must be shown that the publication was made within the county where the trial was had, or if printed out of the county, that it was circulated and read within the county. If a libel is written in one county and mailed to a person in another, this is evidence of publication in the latter county, and if written in one county with intent to publish in another, and it is so published, this will charge the party in the county where it was written.

Uttering slanderous words in the presence of the person slandered only, is not publication, whether spoken in a public place or not. They must have been spoken so as to have been heard by a third person and in the presence of someone who understood them whether spoken or written. If they were in a foreign language which the person hearing did not understand the plaintiff is not prejudiced.

The publisher of a libel, that is, one who by himself or his agent makes a thing publicly known, is responsible as if he were the author of it, and it is immaterial whether he has knowledge of its contents or not, and it is no justification to him that the name of the author accompanies the libel. He may be indicted if the publication is written or printed, and if made by his direction or consent; but if he is merely the owner of the publishing newspaper he will not be criminally responsible if the publication was made by his employees or agents without his consent or knowledge, though he would be liable in a civil suit for damages.

The publication must be malicious to be libelous, but malice will be presumed if the matter is libelous. It will not be libel, however, to read, in the presence of others, libelous matter, without beforehand knowing it to be such. Allegations made in legal proceedings are not considered either libelous or slanderous.

PUNITIVE DAMAGES Damages given by way of punishment; exemplary or vindictive damages.

PURCHASE The word applies to the buying of real estate and goods and chattels. In legal phrase it means every method of acquiring estate and property, except that by which an heir becomes substituted in the ownership of the property on the death of his parent or ancestor. Title by purchase may be acquired by deed, will, prescription, possession or occupancy, by escheat or through execution.

PURCHASE MONEY A term used often in real estate dealings. In case of conveyance of real estate the seller has a lien upon the property for the unpaid purchase money. This lien exists, however, only between the parties to the sale and those having notice that the purchase money has not been paid. Third parties who, not knowing of the non-payment, lend money to the purchaser upon mortgage or judgment duly recorded or entered, will be preferred. As against such, however, one holding a purchase money mortgage* or judgment note will have time if he acts with all possible diligence in getting his judgment or mortgage entered for record, and if it is so entered, it will have priority over other mortgages and judgments whether entered before or after.

PURCHASE MONEY MORTGAGE A mortgage given to secure the unpaid balance of the purchase price on the conveyance of land.

PUTATIVE Reputed; supposed; commonly esteemed.

PUTATIVE FATHER The alleged or reputed father of an illegitimate child.

Q

QUALIFIED ACCEPTANCE A conditional or modified acceptance. In order to create a contract an acceptance must accept the offer substantially as made; hence a qualified acceptance is no acceptance at all, is treated by the courts as a rejection of the offer made and is in effect an offer by the offeree, which the offeror may, if he chooses, accept and thus create a contract.

QUANTUM MERUIT If one is employed without a price being agreed upon for services, he is entitled to receive what he deserves or merits, and this the law considers to be what is commonly paid in the particular locality for services of like character. This sum is called the *quantum meruit*.

QUANTUM VALEBAT This term applies where goods are sold without specifying the price. The price to be recovered in such case is that at which goods are commonly sold in the neighborhood or locality. This is what the purchaser presumably undertakes pay.

QUASH To overthrow, annul or make void. Proceedings clearly irregular and void will be quashed by courts both in civil and criminal cases. An array of jurors, for example, will be quashed if the jurors have been selected by persons not authorized by law. In criminal cases where there is an indictment or charge made for an offense not indictable, or if the charge is one over which the court has no jurisdiction, or if it is so worded that it does not set forth with sufficient clearness what the alleged offense is, or if the offense is so set forth that it does not clearly appear that it is an indictable offense within the meaning of the law, or if there is some other substantial defect in the indictment, it may be quashed. Or, in the discretion of the courts, the quashing may be refused, in which case the defendant if convicted may have the legality of the indictment tested upon a motion in arrest of judgment. The application for quashing should be made before the defendant enters his plea of not guilty or other pleas, or before the forfeiture of his recognizance for not appearing in the court at the required time.

QUASI-CONTRACT An implied contract; an improper contract; a contract in which the obligation was founded on the consent of the parties, not actually expressed, but implied or presumed by law.

QUASI-CORPORATIONS *See* MUNICIPAL CORPORATIONS, PARTNERSHIP.

QUASI-JUDICIAL The acts of an officer which are executive or administrative in their character and which call for the exercise of that officer's judgment and discretion. They are not ministerial acts and his authority to perform such acts is quasi-judicial.

QUI FACIT PER ALIUM FACIT PER SE He who acts by or for himself. The doctrine of the liability of a master for the wrongful acts of his servant rests upon this maxim and the maxim "respondeat superior" and the universal test of the master's liability is whether there was authority express or implied for doing the act.

QUID PRO QUO Something for something; an equivalent or consideration.

QUITCLAIM DEED A form of deed in the nature of a release containing both words of grant and of release. It presupposes a previous conveyance or subsisting estate and possession in the grantee. The operative words are "remise," "release" and "forever quitclaim." It is usually given to quiet title, and to clear the property of outstanding claims or of possible claims or rights thereto or therein.

QUO WARRANTO By what war-

QUITCLAIM DEED

Know all men by these presents, that I, J. J., of the borough of _____, in the county of _____, and state of _____, for and in consideration of the sum of _____ dollars, to me in hand paid, or secured to be paid, by W. B., of _____, and state aforesaid, the receipt whereof is hereby acknowledged, have remised, released, and quitclaimed, and by these presents do _____ remise, release, and quitclaim, unto the said W. B., and to his heirs and assigns, forever, all that, &c., (here describe the premises). Together with all and singular the hereditaments and appurtenances thereunto belonging or in anywise appertaining, and the reversions, remainders, rents, issues and profits thereof; and all the estate, right, title, interest, claim, or demand whatsoever of me, the said J. J., either in law or equity, of, in, and to the above-bargained premises. To have and to hold the same to the said W. B., and to his heirs and assigns, forever.

In witness whereof, I have hereunto set my hand and seal, this _____ day of _____, A.D., 19____.

_____(Seal.)

Signed, sealed and delivered in the presence of

_____

_____

rant. A writ testing the franchise of a corporation or the right of a usurper to claim a public office by requiring proof of valid status.

A proceeding by the government to recover an office or franchise from a person or corporation in possession of it, either where the right thereto never existed, or where it has been forfeited by neglect or abuse. Where a writ of *quo warranto* has been issued the burden is upon the defendant to show that he has a right to the franchise or office in question, and judgment will be rendered against him if he does not. A franchise is regarded as a trust vested in a person or corporation by the state, and if the trust is violated with respect to any of the conditions, it will work a forfeiture of the franchise or charter.

Corporate powers must be construed strictly and must be exercised in the manner and by the agents prescribed by law and the charter, and those powers must not be exceeded. If a corporation does an act inconsistent with the nature or purposes of its franchise, so as to injure the public, this will work a forfeiture of its charter. But if it exercises a power which it has no right to exercise or which is a mere perversion of its powers or rights, there will be a forfeiture whether there is an injury to the public or not. The usurpation of an office by an individual, or of a franchise, must be of a public nature in order that there be a remedy by a writ of *quo warranto*.

In this country, upon dissolution of a corporation, its franchises revert to the state. Under a statute passed in the reign of Queen Anne in force in the United States, information in the nature of *quo warranto* may by leave of court be applied to a dispute between parties about the right to a corporate office or franchise, and the person instituting the proceedings is called the relator, though the suit must be in the name of the government or state. The suit may be instituted even after the expiration of the term of office.

QUORUM The number of members whose presence is required before a meeting can legally take action. It is usually a majority of the entire body.

R

RAILROADS, THE OBLIGATIONS OF A charter conferring a franchise upon a private company or natural person is irrevocable unless so stated or unless granted upon condition, and is only subject to general legislative control like other persons and things. A franchise, like land, may be taken and be used under the right of eminent domain, due compensation being paid therefor. Railway companies are granted the right of eminent domain. They may enter onto lands for the purpose of making preliminary surveys without becoming trespassers and without compensation.

Through the right of eminent domain the company commonly only acquires the right of way or use of the land taken, the title or fee still remaining in the owner, and the company can take nothing from the soil or from under the soil except for the purpose of construction of the railway. The damages for taking possession of and using the property will be such sum as, being added to the value of the remaining land, after construction of the road, will make it as valuable as the whole would have been if none had been taken. Even where there is a public highway, the fee or title of which is in a private individual, and a railroad is constructed on the highway, the owner of the land will be entitled to be fairly compensated for the additional servitude thus imposed upon his land if he suffers damages or injury to his property.

As a general rule the duty is imposed upon a railroad of furnishing at least one passenger train a day not carrying freight, if the revenues of the road, and not of the particular part or branch of it, warrant it.

The road must be constructed within the limits prescribed in the charter. The right of deviation secured by the charter or by-law is lost when the road is once laid. The company is not liable for injury to animals straying onto its track unless it has been neglectful in building fences where it is by law required to build them, or in the management of its trains.

The company is not liable for the act of a contractor or sub-contractor or his agent, except when doing strictly what is contemplated in the contract. It is liable for the acts of its agents and sub-agents within the range of their employment, but not for their wilful acts clearly beyond the range of their employment or authority or unless subsequently adopted by the company. If there is doubt as to whether the act is within the range of employment or not, it will be resolved against the company.

Railroads, in general, are liable for injury accruing to the person or property of another through any want of reasonable care or prudence on their own part or on the part of agents and employees, but not where the party injured is himself in any measure guilty of negligence. One having no right to the use of a railroad track and who is a mere trespasser on it cannot recover for injury occasioned by him by a train, unless the train men actually observed his imminent danger in time to arrest the progress of the train, even though it were running at an unlawful rate of speed. The engineer ordinarily has the right to assume that the trespasser will get out of the way. It is negligence on the part of a railroad company to let passengers out of a train at a time when another train is about to pass along over an adjoining track which the passengers may be reasonably expected to cross. Whether the passenger may have used due care in crossing is for the jury to decide.

Railway bonds with coupons attached, payable to bearer, pass by delivery like bills of exchange. Exclusive rights granted to corporations will not be construed beyond the plain meaning of the grant, and will be liberally construed in favor of the public.

RAISING A CHECK A class of forgery where the signatures on the check are all genuine, but the amount of the check has been increased by the forger's alteration.

RANSOM A sum paid to redeem a person from captivity, imprisonment or punishment; or to redeem property from seizure.

RAPE The carnal knowledge of a woman forcibly and against her will. There can be no rape between husband and wife. A boy under fourteen is supposed to be incapable of committing it, but may be guilty as an abettor or principal in the second degree, as may also a man or a woman. The offense is complete if the woman's consent is not freely and voluntarily given, and her subsequent consent is insufficient as is her consent obtained by force, threats or administering stupefying drugs or liquors.

By statute, consent of the female will not avail as a defense if she is under a given age varying in different places from ten to eighteen years.

RATE OF EXCHANGE The actual price at which a bill, drawn in one country upon another country, can be bought or obtained in the former country, at any given time.

RATIFICATION An agreement to adopt an act or contract performed or made by another for oneself. It may be express, when stated in direct terms of assent, or implied from acts or conduct showing assent. Thus, if one buys goods for another without authority and the latter, knowing the fact, receives them and applies them to his own use, this is a ratification of the

purchase without an express declaration to that effect. By ratifying the contract, one adopts what is detrimental in it as well as that which is beneficial. A ratification to be binding, however, should be made upon full knowledge of all the material circumstances. Such ratification is retrospective and binds the principal from the date of the contract and not merely from the time of ratification, the ratification being equivalent to an original authority. Another effect of it is to relieve an agent from all liability on the contract where otherwise he would have been personally liable.

Though a minor is in general not liable on his contract, he may ratify it after coming of age by an actual or express declaration. If he does, he will be bound. His ratification must be voluntary, deliberate and intelligent, and he must know at the time that without such ratification he would not be bound. His confirmation of the contract may also be implied from his acts after coming of age, as by enjoying or claiming or accepting a benefit thereunder, when he might have wholly rescinded it. A minor partner will be liable for the contracts of the firm so far as they were known to him if, after becoming of age, he transacts business of the firm, receiving profits and benefits or the possibility of profits therefrom. Possession and use of the property after coming of age, or a refusal to redeliver it or an assertion of ownership, will frequently operate as a ratification and raise an implied promise to pay for the property. It would require less to operate as a ratification of the purchase of personal property than of a conveyance of real estate.

Mere silence or acquiescing for a considerable time will be esteemed a ratification. A minor is not liable for suit for breach of promise of marriage, though suit may be brought on his or her behalf against one who is of age for the same cause.

If a minor takes possession of property, notwithstanding his disability to contract, he must meet the liabilities incident thereto. If he leases real estate he must pay the rent unless he disclaims his contract of lease and ceases to be a tenant before the rent comes due. Where property vests in a minor no act is necessary on his part to continue ownership after arriving at age. The interest being vested continues until deserted by express repudiation on his part. A minor acquiring shares of stock in a corporation must pay a call or assessment on it when due, if he retains the stock.

REAL ACTION An action for the recovery of real property.

REAL ESTATE Real estate includes land and in general whatever is erected or growing upon it, with whatever is beneath or above to the center of the earth and to the sky itself. This includes houses and things erected permanently upon the land or growing on it, but not chattels or movable objects such as stock on a farm, furniture in a house, etc.

Even houses, however, and growing trees may assume the character of personal property where agreements exist for their severance, or where, in the case of a house, it is erected by one not the owner of the land with the intent and agreement that it shall be removed. If a nurseryman plants trees to grow them for the market upon land leased, they will be personal estate. So growing crops, planted by the owner of the land, are part of the real estate. However, the owner may sell them and thus constructively sever them from the real estate and convert them into personal property. An owner of land, in fee, may convey by deed the trees growing on it to another, to be cut at his pleasure, in which case the property in the trees becomes real estate. He may likewise convey a title in fee in a dwelling house exclusive of the soil but including the right to let it stand upon the land, and this right in the dwelling house will be real estate. In such a case there is no constructive severance either of the trees or of the house, the right to remain where they are continuing. In like manner there may be a conveyance of a single room or apartment in a house as real estate.

Certain articles which would ordinarily be personal property are under proper circumstances regarded as real estate, such as a key to a lock fastened to a door, millstones in a mill and irons under proper circumstances even though taken out of the mill for purposes of repair, also windows, blinds, though temporarily removed from the house, and fragments of a house destroyed by a storm.

In the case of corporations in which the interest of an individual is represented by stock, the status of real estate is somewhat peculiar. The real estate with respect to the corporation as a whole is real estate, but with respect to the individual member of the corporation or tockholder it is personal property. Stock in a corporation, no matter what the character of the property it owns, is regarded as personal property unless otherwise expressly declared by law or the charter creating the corporation.

Mortgages, though in form conditional conveyances of real estate, accompanied as they are with the equity of redemption or right to pay them off and redeem the land, are regarded for most practical purposes as personal property. In computing or appraising assets they are always counted as personalty. Where real estate has been wrongfully converted into money or where money is held which should be converted into real estate, in equity it is frequently regarded as real estate for purposes of inheritability and the like.

REAL ESTATE BROKER One who engages in the purchase and sale of real estate as a business and occupation, and so holds himself out to the public in that character and capacity.

REASONABLE CARE The care that prudent persons would exercise under the same circumstances.

REBUTTABLE PRESUMPTION A legal presumption that may be disproved by evidence.

REBUTTAL That proof presented at a trial by the plaintiff intended to overcome the evidence introduced by the defendant.

RECEIPT A written acknowledgment that money or a thing of value has been received. Since a receipt is a mere acknowledgment of payment, it may be subject to explanation or contradiction. A receipt may be used as evidence against one just as any other declaration or admission. A simple receipt not under seal is presumptive evidence only and may be rebutted or explained by other evidence of mistake in giving it, or of non-payment or of the circumstances under which it was given. A receipt expressed to be in full, or in full of all accounts, or of all demands, is of a much more conclusive character because it furnishes evidence of mutual compromise and settlement of the claim of the parties. Such a receipt will often operate to extinguish a claim although the creditor may be able to show he did not receive all that was due him. Where parties after consideration mutually agree upon a balance between them, even if there is an honest dispute about the account, they will be bound by it, and a receipt in full, given with a knowledge of the circumstances or with apparent intent to settle in full, will be evidence of full satisfaction. Nevertheless, even such receipt may be overcome by proof of fraud or misrepresentation, or ignorance of fact, or such mistake as enters into and vitiates the compromise, showing that in fact, no intended and valid compromise was made, or by evidence of the taking of an unconscionable advantage.

As to receipts in deeds for purchase money, generally the seller and persons claiming under him are estopped (precluded) from denying that the consideration therein mentioned was given or passed, insofar as any attempt to defeat the conveyance is concerned. In a suit for the recovery of the purchase money, or in an action to recover a debt which was in fact paid by the conveyance, or in an action for a breach of a covenant in the deed, the grantor may show that the consideration, in addition to that mentioned in the deed, was to be paid; also where the deed was attacked for fraud or is impeached by creditors as being without consideration and fraudulent against them and therefore void, or where it is the purpose to show the conveyance to be otherwise illegal, the receipt may be explained or contradicted.

Receipts under seal, however, where they are not merely a part of a sealed instrument designed to have some other effect than that of a mere receipt, are conclusive to the same extent as other specialties or instruments under seal, and are impeachable only for fraud or mistake of a material fact. A receipt embodying a contract is not open to the explanation or contradiction permitted in the case of a simple receipt. For example, where one gives a receipt for money and in the same instrument follows this by a statement that it is in payment for certain goods to be delivered, the instrument becomes a written contract not ordinarily open to explanation by verbal evidence.

A bill of lading which is a receipt for goods delivered to a carrier for shipment is an exception to this rule, for such a receipt may be explained by parol, and it may be shown by verbal testimony that the things actually received were not as receipted for. This is due to the impracticability of examining and counting articles offered for shipment in every instance. The part of the contract in a bill of lading, however, which consists of an undertaking to transport the goods cannot be varied by parol evidence.

Where goods have been attached or levied on execution, the officer attaching, under the practice in some places, frequently delivers them to a third person and takes a receipt for them on agreement to redeliver them to the officer upon demand. The receiptor in such case cannot afterward deny that the attachment was made or that it was insufficient or illegal.

The receiptor, also, cannot deny that the property was that of the debtor except in mitigation of damages where he is sued for non-delivery.

Where a negotiable instrument or check is given for an indebtedness it is presumed to have been accepted on the condition that it shall not work a discharge of the demand until paid. If a receipt in such case is given which is silent as to the fact that it was a check or negotiable instrument which was actually received, the effect of the receipt may be overcome by proof that the payment admitted was in fact by an instrument, which was not good or which has not been paid, in which case the original indebtedness will still exist. The extinguishment of the original indebtedness by delivery of the check or new obligation, and giving a receipt for the amount thereof, is not to be presumed unless it is shown that such was the intent of the parties.

RECEIVER An officer appointed by a court of chancery or equity, to take possession of the property of a defendant, or of property which is the subject of litigation, and to hold the same and apply the profits, or dispose of the property itself, under the direction of the court.

Where a receiver has been appointed for a concern in the state where it has its home, an ancillary receiver may be appointed by a proper court in another state where it has property to be taken in charge and administered, or claims to be collected. The latter receiver will be simply aid of the former.

RECEIVING STOLEN GOODS One who has received stolen goods knowing them to have been stolen is criminally responsible. An aider or abettor in the stealing cannot be regarded as a receiver for he is a party to the theft itself. If the goods are found in the house of a man who is not the thief prima facie, he is a receiver, though if found in the room of a boarder in the house, this would not be true. The actual manual possession or touch of the goods by the defendant is not necessary to constitute him a receiver. If they are in possession of his agent or of one over whom he has control so that they will be forthcoming on his order, this is sufficient.

The defendant, if guilty, must know the goods to have been stolen or it must appear that the circumstances under which he obtained them were such that a person of ordinary understanding and prudence must have been satisfied that they were stolen. This would

be the case if he should receive watches, jewelry, large quantities of money, bundles of clothes of various kinds and the like from boys or persons destitute or without means of acquiring them, or if brought to him at untimely hours, or if offered far below their value, or if evident falsehood is resorted to by the thief to account for possession of them.

RECIDIVIST A person who reverts to criminal activity.

RECOGNIZANCE An obligation entered into before a court or officer, duly authorized to receive the same, with condition to do some act or pay some money therein specified as required by law. It is kept as a matter of record. In some cases it is signed and executed by the parties; in other cases it is entered into by appearing before the proper authority and making acknowledgment of the obligation, which is noted on the record without being signed by the party or parties bound.

In some cases the recognizance is entered into by the party to the suit only, in others by bail. A surrender by the bail of the party for whose benefit the recognizance is given merely to secure his appearance will work a discharge of the bail from his obligation; so will the death of the defendant before the time for his appearance; so will the loss of custody or control of the person bailed through an act of government or through law, as by requiring him to engage in the military service; and also long delay in proceeding against the bail.

RECORD The word as here used is limited to records kept by public officers under authority and intended to serve as evidence of something written, said or done. Acts of Congress or of a legislature are the highest kind of records. Certain instruments of writing such as deeds, mortgages, releases, etc., when properly executed and acknowledged, are common subjects of record.

When any instrument is authorized by law to be recorded, the record furnishes constructive notice which is equivalent in its force and effect to actual notice, to all subsequent purchasers of any estate or rights in the same property. In order to have this effect, however, all the requisites to authorize its recording must be complied with. Thus the recording of a deed or mortgage, without being duly proved or acknowledged, or if the acknowledgment is invalid by reason of some defect, will furnish no legal notice to anybody of the existence of the instrument.

RECOUPMENT The defendant's right to claim damages in reduction of the plaintiff's demand in the same action because he did not comply with all of his obligations under the same contract.

When one is sued on a contract the defendant may set up a counterclaim by way of reduction arising out of the same contract resulting from a violation of the contract by the person suing. It differs from a set-off in that the latter consists in the setting up of one claim or one account, in a course of dealing against another, while recoupment is in the nature of deduction or extinguishment of a claim by reason of matters growing out of the same contract or transaction on which the claim is made.

If the defendant's claim for damages in recoupment exceed the plaintiff's claim, he cannot obtain the benefit of more than the amount of the plaintiff's claim by way of recoupment. If he desires to recover more he should bring a separate suit and not set up the defense in the suit against himself by way of recoupment. The recoupment may result from a tort, but it must be a tort which is a violation of the contract in suit and not one distinct and separated from it. However, in setting up a tort by way of recoupment only actual damages resulting are allowable. No punitive damages, which may be allowed in ordinary suits for torts by way of punishment of the offender where malice is shown, will be permitted by way of recoupment.

The defendant may avail himself of the recoupment or bring an independent suit for his damage, at his option. If he has begun a suit and if it is still only pending, he may nevertheless set up his claim against the other parties to the suit by way of recoupment if he desires; but he cannot avail himself of both methods and must elect to take one course or the other. The recoupment must in all cases be only for damages occurring prior to the bringing of suit against which recoupment is invoked. Where real estate is conveyed by deed containing covenants as to the title, and suit is thereafter brought to recover the purchase money, and the purchaser still has possession and has not been evicted by one having a superior title, the fact that a superior title exists cannot be set up by way of recoupment against the claim for purchase money before eviction of the purchaser. However, it may be after eviction, for though the title is defective there is no failure of consideration until damage has actually been suffered. Where, however, there is failure of consideration as to the quantity and quality of the land intended to be conveyed there may be a recoupment irrespective of eviction.

RECRIMINATION A counter-accusation; an accusation made by an accused party against the accuser.

REDEMPTION The buying back of one's property after it has been sold. The right to redeem property sold under an order or decree of court is purely a privilege conferred by, and does not exist independently of, statute.

REDRESS Remedy; indemnity; reparation.

RE-ENTRY The right to re-enter for non-payment of rent or for breach of some covenant in the lease, forfeiting the estate of the tenant. Conveyances reserving ground, rents and leases for a term of years usually contain this reservation. Without such reservation in the lease, though he may sue for the rent or for damage, he would have no right to re-enter until the end of the term, unless the conveyance or lease states that it was upon condition that certain things be or be not done, in which case the right to re-enter would exist if the condition were violated.

Before a landlord proceeds to re-enter for non-payment of rent he must make a specific demand of payment and be refused, unless such demand has been dispensed with by the express agreement of the parties.

Demand necessarily must be for the payment of the precise sum and it must be made upon the date when it becomes payable under the lease, and if days of grace are allowed it must be made on the last day of grace. It must also be made at a given time before sunset while there is light enough to see to count the money, and it must be at the place appointed for payment, if any, and if no particular place is specified, then at the most public place on the land, which, if there is a dwelling house, is the front door. If the release provides that re-entry shall be made in case no sufficient distress (that is personal property which can be seized for rent) is found on the premises, the landlord must search the premises, to see that no such distress can be found. Such are the strict requirements of the common law in the matter of demand, but in most places these strict rules have been altered by statute.

Though proceedings for re-entry have been begun, the tenant may pay the rent in arrears and all costs and charges in the proceedings and retain possession. In some places, even after possession has been recovered by the landlord, the tenant may be reinstated upon paying all arrearages and costs in certain cases. The courts will not, however, relieve against a forfeiture wilfully incurred by a tenant who has transferred his lease, or neglects to repair or insure as agreed upon, or exercises a forbidden trade, or cultivates the land in a manner prohibited by the lease.

REFEREE An officer of the court appointed for the purpose of taking testimony.

REFEREE IN BANKRUPTCY One who assists the court in bankruptcy cases by relieving the judge of matters of detail or routine and by taking charge of all administrative matters as well as the passage of preliminary consideration of questions requiring judicial decision.

REJECTED A claim of a creditor is said to have been rejected, when, after having been presented in due form to the proper officer for allowance or approval as a valid claim, it has been disallowed by that officer in the manner provided at law.

REJOINDER A defendant's answer of fact to a plaintiff's replication or reply.

RELEASE This term is commonly applied to a formal acquittance under seal of all claims and demands with respect to a particular subject matter, or it may be in general and in respect to all subject matters. Releases are often procured by transit companies, railroads, insurance companies, etc., as a discharge for liability for accidents. When so formally executed a release is of a very binding character, and can be overcome only by showing force, fraud, accident or mistake of fact in connection with its execution. Where an account between parties has been settled and a mutual release passed, one of the parties will not be allowed to reopen it because he was mistaken as to the amount of his account. Such releases are most frequently given executors, administrators, trustees and the like, upon making distribution of the funds in their hands to the parties entitled thereto. Commonly, such releases are authorized by law to be recorded upon due acknowledgment before a magistrate or notary public or other proper officer.

The term release is also applied to an instrument wherein one gives up some interest or right which one has in land to some other person having possession of the same or some estate therein. In this sense a release in this country is practically a quitclaim deed.

REMAINDER The enjoyment of either real or personal property by one may be preceded by its enjoyment by another person for a given period, or until a given event hap-

---

GENERAL RELEASE

Know All Men by These Presents:

That I, John Doe, do hereby remise, release and forever discharge Richard Roe, his heirs, executors and administrators and from all and all manner of actions, and causes of action, suits, debts, dues, accounts, bonds, covenants, contracts, agreements, judgments, claims and demands whatsoever in law or equity, which against the said Richard Roe I ever had, now have, or which my heirs, executors, administrators or assigns, or any of them, hereafter can, shall, or may have, for or by reason of an automobile accident which occurred on the 3300 block Pulaski Highway, Baltimore, Maryland on or about May 1, 1965 in which I was injured.

In Witness Whereof, I have hereunto set my hand and seal the 1 day of May, 1965.

JOHN DOE

Note: Never sign such a release without first consulting a lawyer.

pens, or a given condition is performed. The prior estate is properly called the particular estate, and the succeeding one the remainder or estate in remainder. The term is more commonly applied in connection with real estate. There are two kinds of remainders. One is a vested remainder where a present interest passes and actually vests in the party though the enjoyment is not to take place until a future period. The other is called a contingent remainder, which is to take place on an event or condition which may never happen or be performed, or which may not happen or be performed until after the preceding particular estate is ended. The distinction is important because the former is a present subsisting property owned by the party though not to be enjoyed until later, and is subject to the general incidents of ownership.

Where the party having the particular or present estate is wasting the property or unwarrantably injuring it, the remainderman may prevent such waste or injury, either by compelling the person in possession to give proper security, or by removing the causes or preventing the acts resulting in the injury.

REMAINDERMAN One who is entitled to a remainder.

REMAND To send back a cause from the appellate court to the lower court in order that the lower court may comply with the instructions of the appellate court. Also to return a prisoner to jail.

RENEGOTIATION A clause in some contracts which allows both the buyer and seller the opportunity to further negotiate the terms and conditions of a contract, usually arranged for in an emergency. This actually is a new term which came into general use as a result of World War II. Illustrative of this type of contract would be an order for a million Army uniforms where a condition precedent is at work, to be begun immediately and the entire job to be completed within 90 days. The purpose behind such renegotiation contracts is to allow a greater flexibility since the cost, wages and materials may have changed since the contract was executed. Renegotiation may also apply to preclude cases of fraud where, because of an emergency or critical situation, the government is unable to go into the details of the contract to determine whether or not it is being charged a fair price. When a contract is renegotiated, both parties have an opportunity to change or modify the provision of the contract previously agreed upon. Similar provisions are frequently inserted in contracts where the government is not a party.

RENT Rents may be in the form of money, provisions or crops issuing out of lands and tenements in return for their use. Usually, if the premises become untenantable without fault of either party, the rent continues, but if the landlord ousts the tenant from any considerable portion of the premises or erects a nuisance near them so as to oblige the tenant to remove or if possession of the land should be recovered by a third person by a title superior to that of the landlord, the obligation to pay rent will cease.

If the landlord conveys property

or a part of it, the purchaser will be entitled to the rent thereafter accruing. Every occupant of the property is chargeable with the rent whether a tenant or whether he holds under the tenant. The original tenant cannot avoid his liability by transferring his lease to another, but the one to whom he transfers is liable only so long as he remains in possession, and will be discharged by transferring his lease to still another party. If the contract is silent as to the time or times of payment, it will be payable at periods in accord with the custom of the locality where the property is.

REPAIRS Restoring to good use that which has been broken or worn. Where there is no express agreement between landlord and tenant the tenant is required to make repairs, such as of windows and doors that may have been broken by him, necessary to prevent the dilapidation of the premises. He is not, however, required to put a new roof on the old, worn-out house or to repair against natural and unavoidable decay even though he may have contracted to keep the house in repair and leave it in as good a condition as when the lease was made. Nor does such an agreement require him to rebuild a house if destroyed by a public enemy. In case of accidental fire, neither the tenant nor the landlord is bound to rebuild unless there is an express agreement to that effect.

REPLEADER To plead again; to plead over again.

REPLEVIN A suit at law (action of replevin) whereby goods or chattels that have been unlawfully taken from one may be recovered. Not only ordinary articles of movable personal property may be recovered but such things as records of a corporation, local official records, trees cut down or cut into boards, or even money if it can be found and identified as the same money which was taken.

Even a special property in an article such as that of a factor is sufficient to enable one to recover it by replevin. Goods cannot in general be so recovered if they are in the custody of the law, as when they are attached or seized in execution by a sheriff or other officer.

If one wrongfully takes goods or retains them in his possession, the owner is entitled not only to the goods but to damages or compensation for the wrong done him in depriving him of them, or in compelling him to recover them by process of law. If the plaintiff has caused the goods to be seized in an action of replevin and it is determined that they belong to the defendant, the defendant is entitled to have the goods and likewise damages for the taking. Either party establishing his right to the goods may recover damages for any deterioration which the goods may have suffered while wrongfully in the hands of the other party.

REPLEVY To get back goods on a writ of replevin.

REPRIEVE The temporary suspension of a death sentence.

REPUTATION The opinion or regard in which one is generally held. The general opinion among persons who know a man regarding his character and condition are generally considered evidence of what that character and condition re. Similar evidence is admissible to show one's pedigree. The common understanding as to customs and as to matters of public notoriety are evidence of this existence. When such evidence relates to the exercise of a right or privilege of a public character, it should be preceded by proof of the actual enjoyment or exercise of the right or privilege within the period of living memory.

One charged with a criminal offense may prove, by witnesses acquainted with his general reputation in the neighborhood where he is well known, that such reputation is good with respect to the subject matter of the charge against him. This testimony must relate to the reputation of the individual and not to the witness' opinion as to the individual's actual character. When the defendant has thus attempted to establish a good reputation, but not until then, other witnesses may be produced to show a contrary reputation. The reputation of any witness for veracity may be similarly attacked.

In civil cases questions of general reputation in the neighborhood cannot be proven and are not the subject of evidence, except where the reputation is really the question or one of the questions at issue between the parties, as in a suit for libel or slander, where the amount of damages or injury to the individual depends largely upon what his previous reputation has been with respect to the libelous or scandalous matter charged against him.

RES A Latin word that means "thing."

RES IPSA LOQUITUR The thing speaks for itself. A presumption of

negligence on the part of the defendant in accident cases. Such presumption may be rebutted.

RES JUDICATA The determination that something in controversy or dispute has been finally settled by a court of law and that the case having been *res judicata* cannot be retried or re-opened again.

RESCISSION When both parties to a contract agree to return to the same position as before the creation of the agreement, with a return to each of the considerations given and received, the contract has been rescinded, and rescission has occurred.

RESCISSION OF CONTRACTS The revocation of contracts and agreements. Contracts may be abrogated or annulled by mutual consent of the parties, which may be either expressed or inferred from acts or which may occur by the act of one party where the other has failed to perform his contract in its entirety but not where the failure has been partial only. The contract may, however, be rescinded for fraud even though partially executed.

If the purchaser wishes to rescind the purchase, where goods are not as warranted, the safe course is to return the goods or make all reasonable effort to do so. To delay in this respect or do anything that might fairly be construed as evidence that he accepts the goods after knowing of the deficiency, operates as an admission that there was no deficiency, or as a waiver of the right to rescind.

Courts of equity will rescind and cancel agreements, deeds and other instruments where the transaction is illegal or fraudulent, or where carried on in ignorance or mistake of facts material to their operation. A proceeding in a court of equity to annul is sometimes desirable to prevent instruments from being injuriously used against the one seeking relief, or to prevent the rights of innocent third parties attaching on the faith of the improper agreement or instrument to the detriment of the party seeking relief. The court will decree that a deed or other solemn instrument be delivered up and cancelled not only when avoidable on account of fraud but also when it is absolutely void, unless its invalidity appears so obviously that it could be defeated at any time by a defense in a suit at law.

Ignorance or mistake of fact in the making of an instrument will authorize a rescission in any court of equity if it relates to material facts, but it seems the mistake must be mutual. Where the mistake or ignorance is as to a matter of law merely and not of fact, such relief will not be granted. Instruments may be rescinded and cancelled when obtained from persons who were at the time under duress or legal incapacity to execute them, or where they are obtained by persons who stand in a confidential relation to others and who take advantage of that relation. Gross inadequacy of consideration, fraudulent representation and concealment, hardship and unfairness and undue influence, are frequently grounds for rescission of contracts.

RESIDUARY CLAUSE That clause in a will by which a testator disposes of such part of his estate as remains undisposed of by previous devises or bequests.

RESIDUARY ESTATE That which an estate has left after debts and expenses of administration, legacies and devises have been paid and satisfied.

RESIDUARY LEGATEE The person to whom a testator bequeaths the residue of his personal estate, after the payment of such other legacies as are specifically mentioned in the will.

RESPONDEAT SUPERIOR The principle in law which transfers liability to a principal for the negligent acts of his agent.

RESPONSIBLE BIDDER The word "responsible," as used by most statutes concerning public works in the phrase "lowest responsible bidder," means that such bidder has the requisite skill, judgment, and integrity necessary to perform the contract involved, and has the financial resources and ability to carry the task to completion.

REST The term used in a trial when each side has completed its submission of the evidence.

RESTITUTION, WRIT OF A paper which restores to a party all that which he has been deprived of by court order.

RESTRAINING ORDER An order issued by a court of equity in aid of a suit to hold matters in abeyance until parties may be heard. A temporary injunction is a restraining order.

RESTRICTIVE ENDORSEMENT Used in negotiating a negotiable instrument to a person for a specific task such as "for collection."

RETAIL INSTALLMENT SALES AGREEMENT In substance, such agreements provide for the sale and method of payment of personal property and the purchaser should read such an agreement with great care. Most such agreements usually provide that in case of default of any single payment, the seller has the right to recover the property through proper legal procedure. The buyer has the right to anticipate payments and is entitled to a pro rata refund of carrying charges. The purchaser should make certain that he is given an exact copy of the agreement he is asked to sign before affixing his signature and he should also insist that all blanks be properly filled in. Finally, the buyer should discount the verbal promises of the seller since they are not binding and cannot be offered in evidence to vary or alter the terms of the written agreement.

RETAIL INSTALLMENT SALES AGREEMENT Acct. No._____
UNDER MARYLAND ACTS OF 1941, CHAPTER 851
(CONDITIONAL SALES CONTRACT)

AGREEMENT, made this _____ day of _____ 19____,
between _____
whose place of residence is _____,
and whose post-office address is _____
Maryland, herein called "Seller," and _____
_____ whose place of residence is _____
_____, and whose post-office address is _____
_____ Maryland, herein called "Buyer."

WITNESSETH that Seller hereby sells to Buyer, and the latter buys from the former, the merchandise hereinafter set forth at the price and on the terms hereinafter specified.

DESCRIPTION OF GOODS PURCHASED

_____
_____
_____
_____
_____

The additional terms of this contract are:—
1. The cash price of the merchandise sold is . . . . $_____
2. The charge for _____ is $_____
   (Indicate delivery, installation, repair and other service
   items for which additional charge is made)
3. The total cash price is . . . . $_____
   (The sum of Items 1 and 2)
4. The amount of buyer's down
   payment is, in cash . . . .$_____
   and in merchandise as follows:
               valued at $_____ $_____
   (The down payment shall be forfeited entirely if the
   Buyer refuses to accept delivery of the merchandise
   sold to the Buyer under this contract; the Buyer being
   entitled to delivery of such merchandise before making
   further payments)

5. The unpaid balance of the cash price is .... $_____
(Item 3 less Item 4)

6. The premium on the policy, if any, insuring this merchandise
against loss by fire, etc. is .... $_____
(The amount of this insurance, if any, is the same amount as to the
total cash price owing by the Buyer, it expires on the date upon
which the final installment is payable, as hereinafter indicated, and
is payable jointly to the Buyer and the Seller)

7. Notary fees and recording charges are .... $_____

8. The principal balance owed is .... $_____
(The sum of Items 5, 6 and 7)

9. The finance charge is .... $_____

10. The time balance owing by Buyer to Seller is .... $_____
(The sum of Items 8 and 9)

It is agreed that this balance shall be payable by Buyer to Seller in
_____ consecutive installments of $_____ each and finally
$_____. These installments shall be payable on the _____ day of
every week/month after the date upon which this contract is signed by the
Buyer. It is agreed that Seller, or its assigns, may also collect from the Buyer
a delinquency and collection charge for default in the payment of this contract or any installment thereof, where such default has continued for a
period of ten days; such charge equalling five per cent of the amount of the
installments in default or the sum of five dollars, whichever is the lesser. In
addition to such delinquency and collection charge, the Buyer shall be obligated to pay the attorney's fees, not exceeding fifteen per cent of the
amount due and payable under this contract, where this contract is referred
to an attorney, not a salaried employee of the holder of this contract, for
collection, plus the court costs.

Title and ownership of said merchandise is to remain in Seller, or its
assigns, until all of the payments herein required to be made by Buyer have
been made, whereupon full ownership shall pass to Buyer. Should Buyer fail
to make any of said payments at the time when due, as herein set forth, or
to comply with any of the other agreements herein set forth, Buyer agrees to
return said merchandise to Seller, or its assigns, who may repossess said
merchandise if not returned.

The Buyer agrees to take good care of said merchandise and to be
responsible for its loss by theft, fire or other casualty, and to keep the same
at _____, Maryland. The Buyer further agrees
that he will not change the place of keeping said merchandise without first
securing the assent of the Seller, in writing.

No other collateral security has been taken by Seller from Buyer for the
performance of Buyer's obligations.

No statement or representation shall be binding on the Seller unless it
be in writing and signed by the Seller or the Seller's authorized agent.

The Seller reserves the right to cancel this contract before said merchandise has been delivered to the Buyer; whereupon any deposit or down
payment made on account of it shall be returned to the Buyer.

Subsequent purchases may be added to this contract by mutual agreement, upon terms acceptable to the Buyer and the Seller.

The term "Seller" and the term "Buyer," as used throughout this contract, include the plural number when more than one.

NOTICE TO BUYER

1. You are entitled to a copy of this agreement at the time you sign it.
2. Under the State Law regulating installment sales, you have certain rights, among others:
   (1) to pay off the full amount due in advance and obtain a partial rebate of the finance charge;
   (2) to redeem the property if repossessed for a default;
   (3) to require, under certain conditions, a resale of the property if repossessed.

_____, 19____   _____
DATE OF SIGNING BY BUYER

                                            _____
                                                BUYER'S SIGNATURE

                                            _____
_____, 19____ By_____
    DATE OF SIGNING BY SELLER   **SELLER'S SIGNATURE**

Buyer hereby acknowledges delivery to Buyer this _____ day of _____, 19____, of a copy of this agreement, signed by Seller.

Witness:

_____   _____

                                            _____
                                                BUYER'S SIGNATURE

LANDLORD'S WAIVER

The undersigned landlord of the premises known as _____ _____ in _____, Maryland, hereby waives, renounces, relinquishes and releases any or all rights of distraint such landlord may now or hereafter have, in respect of the merchandise sold to the Buyer under the foregoing contract, until the title to such merchandise becomes vested in the Buyer; this being a condition precedent to the execution of such contract and the delivery of such merchandise by the Seller.

                                            By_____
                                                LANDLORD'S SIGNATURE

RECEIPT FOR PAYMENT

Where buyer signs installment sale agreement, but before receiving a copy thereof signed by seller,

or

Receipt for payment made before either buyer or seller signs installment sale agreement.

BALTIMORE, MD.,_____19____

Received of_____ the sum of $_____
                    BUYER

being a payment or deposit made by the Buyer on account of the purchase of goods this day selected by the Buyer and proposed to be itemized and incorporated in a prospective conditional or installment sale agreement.

If the Buyer has signed such agreement, but has not received an exact copy of it signed by the Seller within 15 days after the date of the Buyer's signature, then such agreement shall be void without any action by the

Buyer, and the Seller shall immediately refund to the Buyer all payments and deposits theretofore made; or

Until the Buyer signs such agreement and receives a copy of it signed by the Seller, the Buyer has an unconditional right to cancel such agreement and to receive the immediate refund of all payments and deposits made on account of, or in contemplation of it. A request for such refund shall operate to cancel such agreement.

This receipt is non-negotiable and non-transferable.

RETAINER A down payment on an attorney's fee paid by a client soliciting his services. A retainer binds the attorney not to take a fee from anyone having a conflicting interest from the party employing him. A retainer is merely a partial payment on the final fee to be agreed upon between an attorney and client.

RETURN-DAY When writs or orders are issued from a court to a sheriff or from a magistrate to a constable a date, the return-day is fixed therein, or by the law, for returning the same with a report as to what the officer has done respecting the command therein contained. If he does not make the return accordingly, a rule or order may be obtained for him to do so, and if he disobeys this he may be attached or arrested for contempt.

RETURN OF A WRIT A sheriff's return of a writ is an official statement written on the back of a summons or other paper that he has performed his duties in compliance with the law or a statement as to why he has not complied with the law.

REVERSION The return of land or property to the estate of the original holder, after the death of the person or persons to whom it

has been temporarily willed or granted.

REVERSIONARY INTEREST A right to the future enjoyment of property, at present in the possession or occupation of another.

REVERSIONER A person having the reversion of an estate; a person entitled to a reversion.

RIGHT OF REDEMPTION The right to free property from a claim or lien by payment of what is due with interest, etc.

RIGHT OF WAY *See* WAY, RIGHT OF.

RIOT A tumultuous disturbance of the peace by three or more people assembling together of their own authority with intent to assist each other against any who oppose them in the execution of some enterprise of a private nature. The enterprise must be executed in a violent and turbulent manner, to the terror of the people. It is immaterial whether the act intended itself was lawful or unlawful.

The gathering together must be with an unlawful intent, for if people are together for a lawful purpose and afterwards engage in a quarrel or fight, the offense is an affray and not a riot. If being lawfully assembled they form into parties with promises of mutual assistance, either express or implied, the offense will be a riot, for there will be an unlawful assembling within the meaning of the law, and in this manner a lawful assembly may be converted into an unlawful one. One joining the rioters after the riot has actually commenced will be equally guilty as if he had joined them while assembling.

To establish this offense actual violence and force must be shown or such circumstances as have an apparent tendency to force and violence, and are calculated to strike terror into the public mind. It must be shown that the accused either actually participated in the disturbance or was present encouraging or giving countenance, support or acquiescence to the act. It is not requisite to the offense that personal violence be actually committed. It is sufficient that the acts of the persons engaged are to the terror of the people, as by a show of arms, threatening speeches or turbulent gestures.

RIPARIAN Belonging to or relating to the bank of a river.

RIPARIAN OWNERS Where a stream constitutes the boundary between property owners, the owners in such cases known as riparian owners, the property of the respective owners will extend to the middle of the stream, unless the courses which constitute the bounding lines of the property are expressly stated to be elsewhere. In some streams that are navigable, even where the tide does not ebb and flow, the soil of the bed of the river belongs to the riparian owners, subject to the right of navigation in the public.

RISK IN INSURANCE The specific event covered by the policy which may cause loss or damage to the property insured.

ROBBERY The felonious and forcible taking from the person of another of goods or money to any value against his will by violence, or by putting him in fear. The violence necessary to this crime, however, is not confined to an actual assault of the person by beating and knocking him down or forcibly wresting the thing from him. Whatever goes to intimidate by apprehension of personal violence or by fear of life, with a view to compelling the delivery of property, is sufficient. The "taking from the person" need not be in its strictly literal sense, for the taking may be from the person's presence, when it is done with violence and against his consent.

The violence and putting in fear need not concur, and if a man is knocked down and robbed while unconscious the offense is still robbery. If one is put in fear by threats and then robbed, no other violence is necessary to constitute the crime, though the violence or putting in fear may be at the time of the act or immediately preceding.

It has been held that when an article is snatched merely by a sudden pull, even though a momentary force be exerted, this is not such violence as to constitute a robbery, though if there is any struggle or disruption the offense is robbery. If the property is taken under a bona fide claim of right and not with a view to wrongfully taking another's property there is no robbery.

ROYALTY An amount paid to an author, patentee, etc., for the right to use, manufacture or sell the book, composition or patented article.

RULE TO SHOW CAUSE A court order commanding a person to appear in court and to show some reason why a certain act should not be done.

S

SAFETY DEPOSIT BOX One rented from a bank or trust company for the purpose of storing papers or other valuables. Such banks and trust companies are not insurers of the contents of such boxes. Thus, where the contents of safe deposit boxes are rifled by a burglar or robbed at gun point, the bank would probably not be liable unless it could be shown that there was gross negligence on its part. Money and securities in a safe deposit box may be attached if the process is legal and regular, and the bank or trust company will be exempt from all responsibility if it acts under such a court order.

SALE A sale is an agreement by which one of two contracting parties conveys a thing and passes a title to it in exchange for a certain price to another who on his part either pays the price or agrees to pay it. Strictly speaking, it differs from a barter or exchange in that the consideration is money instead of goods or property. When a sale depends for its validity upon the fulfillment of some condition it is said to be a conditional sale.

A forced sale is one without the owner's consent by an officer of the law, under the mandate or direction of a competent tribunal. Its effect is to transfer the supposed owner's rights without a guaranty that he had title to the same.

Persons acting as trustee, executor, guardian, assignee and the like, may not purchase the property that their trusts relate to. The purchase, however, is voidable only at the instance of a party in interest and not absolutely void, and purchases by attorneys and others holding confidential or trust relations with the seller will be carefully scrutinized by the courts.

If the thing sold has at the time of the sale ceased to exist, though this is not known by the parties, there will be no sale, and the contract will be void for lack of consideration. If a mistake has been made as to the article sold, or if it is an article of one description while the parties believe it to be another, there is no sale. If a loss by fire occurs on the premises while a contract for sale thereof exists, the loss falls on the vendor.

The sale must refer to something specific. Thus there cannot be a consummated sale nor the passing of title to one hundred bushels of wheat, for example, while in a heap. To consummate the sale the wheat must be measured or set apart. Until then there is but an agreement to sell, and a mere agreement to sell, to become operative in the future, does not convey a legal title or ownership in the property, though in general it will give one a right to sue for damages upon failure to carry out the bargain. If there is an agreement to pay a certain price for an article, and in the same agreement it is stipulated that the price be paid back, this constitutes a gift and no sale.

To effect a sale a price must be agreed upon or the circumstances must be such that a price can be arrived at. If the price to be fixed is left to a third person this will be sufficient. If goods are sold for "what they are worth" this is also sufficient, since what they are worth can be ascertained. If goods are sold and delivered without anything being mentioned about the price there is an implied agreement to pay what they are worth, which will be ascertained by evidence as to what goods are commonly sold for in the neighborhood or locality where sold. Though one may not have entered into a contract to purchase, yet, if afterwards he makes use of goods left at his house for sale, by that act he confirms the sale and must pay for them.

As a general rule, when a bargain is made for the purchase of specific goods set apart or not commingled with other like goods, and to which nothing remains to be done, the property or title as between the purchaser and seller passes immediately to the buyer who thenceforth assumes the risk, even though he cannot take them away without paying the price.

When a contract for the sale of real estate is made, however, the legal estate in the land will not pass until delivery of a lawful deed or conveyance, and the only remedy at law for non-fulfillment of the contract is an action to recover damages for a breach of the contract. The purchaser, however, though he does not have a legal title is said to have an equitable title, and may, where he cannot be compensated or properly recompensed in a suit for damages, secure a decree of specific performance in a court of equity compelling delivery of a deed in accordance with the contract. This is true where the purchaser has taken possession of the property made with expenditures and improvements on them. Specific performance of a contract to convey land cannot, however, be enforced so as to divest the dower right of a wife who has not joined in a contract of sale.

In general, a guarantee of title does not accompany a sale of real estate unless there is a covenant or warranty to that effect.

Unless there is an agreement to purchase on credit the purchaser is not entitled to the goods without tendering the price. If there is a failure to deliver in accordance with the contract, the damages will consist of what the injured party may have lost by non-delivery. This would be represented usually by any advance in price over the purchase price, or by the difference between the purchase price and what the purchaser could have gotten for the goods at any time before suit is brought, though perhaps this would not apply to accidental and momentary inflations in the price.

If one contracts to purchase and pay for goods and fails or refuses to take them in accordance with the contract, the vendor still retaining the goods in his possession may either treat them as his own or as the vendee's. In the former case he will be entitled to damages represented by the difference between the purchase price agreed upon and their market value in his hands, or he may treat them as the vendee's and sell them with due precaution and proper effort to obtain an advantageous price, or he may hold the goods subject to the vendee's call or order, and recover the whole of the purchase price. If payment is to be made at a future day, no suit can be brought for the price until after that day. If, however, it was agreed that a note be given, immediately payable at a future day, and this is not given accordingly, suit may be brought at once.

If one purchases goods with a warranty as to their quality, quantity or kind and it turns out that they fall short of this, the purchaser is entitled to compensation to the extent of such shortage or deficiency. The purchaser of an article, if it is not according to contract and he does not want to accept it, should give prompt notice of non-acceptance to the person supplying it, otherwise he will be considered as having waived the defect or shortcoming. He should either return it or notify the other party that it is held subject to his order. If the specifications in the manufacture of an article are departed from with the knowledge and consent of the purchaser he cannot hold the manufacturer responsible for its not working properly.

No sale will be binding if based upon gross misrepresentation or fraud or intentional concealment of an important defect in or objection to the thing sold, but mere inadequacy of the price to be paid is not sufficient to avoid a sale. If there is a material misdescription of the property to be sold, this will avoid the sale even though the seller offers to make an allowance or deduction to set off the mistake.

Puffing at sales, that is, secret bidding by persons not intending to buy, by arrangement with the vendor, is discountenanced as unfair to bona fide bidders, and if there is to be such bidding with a view to preventing a sacrifice of the property or to securing a price at which the vendor is willing to sell, the fact should be publicly announced.

Where one conceals his insolvent condition, and purchases with no reasonable expectation or intention of paying, the transaction is so far fraudulent that the vendor is entitled to reclaim the goods even from a voluntary assignee. One selling goods for a fraudulent purchaser under such circumstances as to visit him with the knowledge of the fraudulent character of the purchase, can be held liable as well as the party who actually committed the fraud.

Unless there is an understanding to the contrary, purchase is presumed to be accompanied by payment at the time, and one making a purchase but leaving without paying, cannot hold the vendor to his agreement. If part payment is made this furnishes evidence that there is an agreement for the future payment as to the balance, and the effect is to make the bargain binding as would anything else showing an intent or agreement between the parties that payment should not be made at the time of purchase. If a thing is sold for cash or if sold on credit, the vendor reserving the right to hold possession until payment is made, the vendee can only reacquire a right to possession by payment. If the contract is such that title to the property passes without the right of possession and the thing is destroyed through no fault of the vendor, the purchaser must bear the loss.

A mutual agreement to sell and purchase is no sale, and effects no transfer of title to the property. In itself it will not enable the intended purchaser to claim the property, though the one agreeing to sell will be liable for such damages as might accrue to the other from failure to fulfill his agreement.

A vendor retaining the thing sold until time for delivery is liable for injury occurring for want of ordinary care, or for want of good faith in caring for it. If the vendor follows the instructions of the purchaser as to shipment, loss in transportation will fall upon the purchaser. It is the duty of the shipper to notify the purchaser of the shipment so that he may insure the goods or take other necessary measures to protect them. If the vendor fails to deliver at the time agreed upon, injury to the goods thereafter occurring will fall upon himself even though he is diligent in caring for it. But if the purchaser neglects or refuses to accept it at the time agreed upon the vendor is not responsible for loss unless it occurs through his gross negligence.

If the purchaser becomes insolvent before the time of delivery, the vendor may refuse to deliver until security is given for payment. Where there is no agreement as to place of delivery the presumption is that the buyer must take the goods where they are, unless the sale is to pay an antecedent debt, in which case the owner is required to deliver them at such place, indicated by the purchaser, as shall be reasonable under the circumstances.

In a sale at auction, a misstatement fraudulently made and capable of effecting the sale, will render it void; so will conditions that place the purchaser under disadvantages he could not readily apprehend without legal knowledge or advice.

The rule of *caveat emptor* (let the purchaser beware or look out for himself), which imposes upon the purchaser the responsibility of judging for himself as to the character and value of the thing purchased, does not apply where the seller induces him to believe that he buys with a warranty that the article is of a certain character or quality or prevents him from making a proper examination and inquiry, for this would be in the nature of a fraud. Nor will it apply where there is an express guaranty or warranty as to quality, quantity or soundness. Any words importing an undertaking on the part of the owner that the thing is what is represented to be will amount to a warranty. Mere silence on the part of the vendor, however, will not ordinarily render the contract void; neither will mere persuasion. If, however, the vendor makes the sale under such circumstances that he alone has knowledge of the character of the thing sold, so that the purchaser must depend upon his judgment and honesty, the validity of the sale will depend upon the correctness of his representations regarding it.

Where goods are sold by sample there is an implied warranty that the goods furnished will correspond with the sample, and if they do the purchaser will be bound notwithstanding a defect in the sample which he did not observe but which he had opportunity to observe. If a thing is sold for a given purpose, the purchaser not having the opportunity to examine it beforehand, there is an implied warranty that it is fit for that purpose. Where real estate is leased, however, there is no implied warranty that it is fit for occupation or cultivation or for any particular purpose for which it is taken. The lessee must himself judge whether or not the property suits him.

Where goods have been sold accompanied by a warranty, if they are not as warranted, the purchaser may recover a proper amount by way of damages if he retains the goods and has paid for them. If he returns the goods and rescinds the sale, as he may do, he may sue for the price if he has paid it. If the vendor then refuses to receive the goods, the purchaser may sell them for what they are reasonably worth within a reasonable time, and if proper effort is made to secure a fair price, he may recover all above the price received even if this be less than the value.

BILL OF SALE OF RESTAURANT

This agreement witnesseth that John Doe, party of the first part, has this day sold, and does hereby sell and transfer to Thomas Brown, party of the second part, the following described personal property located at 1010 W. Baltimore Street, Baltimore, Maryland, to wit: (here itemize completely the personal property sold) and all fixtures and appurtenances belonging to and forming a part of what is known as Nick's Restaurant, located at the above address, including the good will of the first party thereto, for and in consideration of the sum of five thousand and five hundred dollars, payable as follows: two thousand dollars cash, the receipt of which is hereby acknowledged, and the balance to be evidenced by a promissory note of even date herewith in the sum of three thousand dollars, secured by a mortgage on said personal property. Said note payable one hundred dollars per month until the full amount of said note is paid, with interest at the rate of six per cent after maturity.

Immediate possession to be given said second party.

It is hereby understood and agreed that the said first party hereby conveys all his right, title and interest in and to the groceries and provisions, and the said second party is to assume the payment of any indebtedness thereon if there be any indebtedness thereon remaining unpaid on said goods taken and no more. The said first party warrants the title to the fixtures.

Witness my hand this 3rd day of April, 19____.

/s/   John Doe
VENDOR

/s/   Robert Smith
WITNESS

Accepted this 3rd day of April, 19____.

/s/   Thomas Brown
BUYER

CONDITIONAL SALES AGREEMENT

This agreement, made this first day of November, 19____, between William Taft, of Baltimore, Md., called the vendor, and Thomas Gay, called the vendee or buyer, witnesseth:

Whereas the vendor has this day delivered to and hereby agrees to sell to the vendee, for the sum of three hundred dollars, upon the conditions hereinafter set forth, the following personal property (describe exactly the personal property to be sold):

The vendee agreeing to and does receive said property, and to pay the vendor therefor, at his place of business said amount as follows, to wit:

The sum of one hundred dollars upon the execution hereof and the sum of twenty-five dollars on the first day of each and every week hereafter until the whole sum first above mentioned, or any judgment obtained therefor, is fully paid, when title to said property shall vest in the vendee; but until then title shall remain in the vendor.

It is further agreed that in the event of failure by the vendee to pay any installment, as it becomes due, or in case the vendee removes the property from his present residence or place of business, without the written consent of the vendor, or in case the property is destroyed in any manner, the whole of the said sum shall immediately become due, and the vendor may take possession of such property with or without legal process and sell the same according to law, in which case it is expressly understood and agreed the vendor may retain all installments previously paid as and for compensation for the use of said property by the vendee, and the vendee will pay any deficiency arising on account thereof together with the expense of retaking and sale thereof.

No verbal contract or agreement contrary to any of the terms conditioned in the foregoing contract has been made.

/s/   William Taft
VENDOR

/s/   John Doe
WITNESS

/s/   Thomas Gay
VENDEE

CONTRACT FOR THE SALE OF A GROWING CROP OF FRUIT

This agreement made this 2nd day of August, 19___, between John Doe, vendor, and Thomas Brown, purchaser, witnesseth:

It is agreed that the vendor will sell and the purchaser will buy all that crop of apples growing on the trees of the vendor's orchard, situate in Worcester County, Maryland, for the sum of fifteen hundred dollars, of which five hundred dollars shall be paid before any part of the crop is gathered, and the purchaser shall not be at liberty, without the consent of the vendor, to remove from the premises any part of the crop not paid for until the purchase price thereof is paid.

The fruit shall be gathered when sufficiently mature for gathering, and the purchaser and his workmen shall have, for the purpose of gathering and taking the fruit, full liberty to enter upon the said orchard and trees with ladders and other necessary appliances.

/s/   Thomas Brown
PURCHASER

/s/   John Doe
VENDOR

/s/   Robert Smith
WITNESS

FORMS OF BILLS OF SALE

NOTE: *If the bill of sale is to be recorded add a proper acknowledgment for forms of which see* ACKNOWLEDGMENT.

Short Form

Know all men by these presents, that I, John Doe of _____ in consideration of two hundred dollars, to me paid by Richard Roe, of the following goods and chattels, to wit: one gray horse, one wagon, and three cows.

Witness my hand and seal, this fourth day of _____, A.D. 19___.

Signed, sealed and delivered in presence of

E. F.
G. N.

(If the horse is to be warranted the following may be inserted.)

And I do hereby warrant the said horse to be sound in every respect, to be free from vice, well broken, kind and gentle in single and in double harness, and under saddle; and I do covenant for myself, my heirs, executors and administrators, with the said Richard Roe, to warrant and defend the sale of the said horse unto the said Richard Roe, his executors, administrators, and assigns, from and against all and every person or persons, whomsoever lawfully claiming, or to claim the same.

Another General Form

Know all men by these presents, that _____ of _____ in the county of _____ and state of _____ part _____ of the first part, for and in consideration of the sum of

_____ dollars, to _____ in hand paid by _____ of _____, part _____ of the second part, the receipt of which is hereby acknowledged, do _____ hereby grant, bargain and sell unto the said part _____ of the second part, _____ heirs and assigns, the following goods and chattels, to wit: (state what and describe it).

To have and to hold, all and singular, the said _____ unto the said part _____ of the second part, _____ heirs and assigns forever. And the said part _____ of the first part, for _____ heirs, executors and administrators, do _____ hereby covenant to and with the said part _____ of the second part, and _____ assigns, that _____ lawfully possessed of the same goods and chattels as of _____ own property, that the same are free from all encumbrances, and that _____ will warrant and defend the same to the said part _____ of the second part, and _____ assigns, against the lawful claims and demands of all persons.

In witness whereof, the said part _____ of the first part ha_____ hereunto set _____ hand _____ and seal _____ this _____ day of _____ A.D., 19____.

Signed, sealed and delivered in presence of

_____(SEAL)

_____(SEAL)

AGREEMENT FOR SALE OF LEASE, FIXTURES, AND GOOD WILL OF BUSINESS

Agreement entered into this 1 day of January, 19____, between John Doe, hereinafter called the vendor, for himself, his heirs, executors and administrators, of the one part, and Richard Roe, hereinafter called the purchaser, for himself, his heirs, executors and administrators, of the other part.

1. The said vendor doth hereby agree with the said purchaser to sell and assign unto him, the said purchaser, all the workshop, warehouses, buildings and premises, situate, 2110 Fayette Street, whereon the said vendor has for several years past carried on the trade or business of Furniture Manufacturer, and which he now holds for the residue of a term of 5 years, under an indenture of lease dated the 1 day of January, 19____, made between Sam Brown as lessor, of the one part and the said vendor as lessee, of the other part; as also all the fixtures, engines, machinery, utensils, tools and implements used or employed in carrying on the said trade or business, together with the said business and the good will of the same.

2. In consideration whereof, the said purchaser doth hereby agree with the said vendor to purchase the residue of the said term in the said premises, as also the said fixtures, engines, machinery, utensils, tools and implements used or employed in carrying on the said trade or business in or upon the said premises, together with the said business, and the good will thereof, upon the terms and conditions hereafter mentioned.

3. It is mutually declared and agreed by and between the said vendor and purchaser that if the attorney of the said purchaser shall approve of the title of the said vendor the said vendor will, on the 15 day of February next, at the cost of the said purchaser, by proper deed of assignment, assign the said lease, workshop, warehouses, buildings, and premises, with all usual and proper covenants, unto the said purchaser, his executors, administrators, and assigns, for all the residue of the said term of 5 years; and also all the

fixtures, engines, machinery, utensils, tools and implements employed in carrying on the said trade or business in or upon the said premises; and which said deed of assignment, in addition to the usual and ordinary covenants, shall also contain a covenant on the part of the said vendor that he will from time to time and at all times hereafter, recommend the said purchaser to all the customers of him the said vendor, and use his utmost endeavors to induce them to deal with the said purchaser; and that the said vendor shall not, at any time hereafter, either directly or indirectly, alone or in partnership with any other person or persons whomsoever, carry on the trade or business of a Furniture Manufacturer at Fayette Street, or any other place or places within the distance of twenty miles thereof.

4. Immediately upon the execution of the said deed of assignment, the said purchaser shall pay unto the said vendor the sum of $20,000.00 as for the purchase of the residue of the said term in the said workshop, warehouses, buildings, and premises, and for the purchase of the said trade or business, and the good will thereof. Also, within the space of 3 months, a valuation shall be made and taken of the said fixtures, engines, machinery, utensils, tools and implements, by two indifferent persons, one to be chosen by the said vendor, and the other to be chosen by the said purchaser, who, previously to their entering on their reference, shall choose an umpire between them, whose decision, in case the said referees shall not agree, shall be binding on both parties; and in case either of the said parties shall refuse to name a referee within seven days after request by the other party, then the referee named by the other party may proceed alone, and his award shall be conclusive on both parties.

5. The said purchaser shall pay or secure unto the said vendor the amount of such valuation by four equal installments, at three, six, nine and twelve calendar months. Further, the said vendor shall remain in the possession of all and singular the said premises which are hereby agreed to be assigned, with full and free liberty to have, hold, use and enjoy the same in the same manner as heretofore, up to the 1 day of February next; and shall pay and discharge all rents, rates, taxes and other outgoings up to that period, on which day the possession of all the said premises shall be delivered to the said purchaser.

In witness whereof we have set down our signatures.

———————————————
PURCHASER

———————————————
VENDOR

———————————————
WITNESS

SALE BY DESCRIPTION Refers to a transaction in which the merchandise is described in detail and the bulk must conform to that description.

SALE BY SAMPLE Occurs when the buyer is shown a sample of the merchandise he is buying. When the merchandise is delivered, the bulk must conform in quality to the sample.

SALE OR RETURN An agreement that goods are delivered with an option to purchase or return the merchandise.

SALVAGE Compensation allowed those who have helped save a ship's cargo or the ship itself from impending danger or disaster. A salvage loss is the difference between the amount of salvage, that is, that which has been saved after deducting the charges, and the original value of the property insured.

SATISFACTION PIECE The document which states that a recorded mortgage has been satisfied.

SCHEDULE IN BANKRUPTCY An inventory filed by the bankrupt in bankruptcy proceedings, containing a list of all his property and his credits.

SCIENTER Knowledge by a defrauding party of the falsity of a representation. In a tort action of deceit, knowledge that a representation is false must be proved.

SCINTILLA OF EVIDENCE A very slight amount of evidence which aids in the proof of an allegation. If there is a "scintilla of evidence," the court generally presents the case to the jury.

SCIRE FACIAS A writ used both to obtain a judgment where none has previously existed or to obtain execution or continuation of a judgment previously entered.

SEAL At common law, a seal is an impression on wax, wafer, or some other tenacious material, but in modern practice the letters "l.s." (*locus sigilli*) or the word seal enclosed in a scroll, either written or printed, and acknowledged in the body of the instrument to be a seal, are often used as substitutes.

If an instrument concludes with the words "witness our hands and seals" and is signed by two persons with only one seal the jury may infer from the face of the paper that the person who signed last adopted the seal of the first, and that therefore the instrument is under seal as to both of them.

Seals other than scroll seals are now commonly made with metal instruments making an impression or indentation in the document itself. The public seal of a foreign state proves itself. Its genuineness need not be proven by extraneous evidence, and public acts. Decrees and judgments exemplified under such seals are accepted as true and genuine, provided the foreign state is acknowledged by the government of the country within which the seal is presented. The judicial seal of a notary public must not be a scroll. The seal of a superior court need not be proven in lower courts in the same jurisdiction. This is generally not true of seals of foreign courts, except admiralty or maritime courts.

SEARCH The act of seeking. The Constitution of the United States protects the people from unreasonable searches and seizures, and a search of a man's house, premises or person for the purpose of discovering proof of his guilt in relation to some crime or misdemeanor of which he is accused, can only be made by an officer on a warrant called a search-warrant issued from a justice of the peace or other lawfully authorized officer. Before a warrant will be issued, probable cause for doing so must be shown by the party applying for it, supported by oath or affirmation, particularly describing the place to be searched and the person or thing to be seized. The warrant directs the officer to bring the goods stolen, if found, together with the body of the person occupying the house or premises, before the justice or officer granting the warrant.

The person applying for the warrant should not only allege probable cause for suspecting the goods to be in the house or place named, but also his reasons for the suspicion. The warrant must designate the place to be searched. Damages for trespass cannot be recovered from a party who has procured a search-warrant to search for stolen goods if the warrant is duly issued and regularly executed.

There is a right recognized among nations existing in a belligerent to examine and inspect the papers of a neutral vessel at sea. This does not extend to a ship of war, being confined entirely to the searching of merchant vessels. The object is to prevent the carrying of contraband to the enemy of the searching party.

SECOND MORTGAGE The second lien on property.

SECURITY Security may be bonds, stocks, and other property placed by a debtor with a creditor, with power to sell if the debt is not paid. The plural of the term, "securities," is used broadly to mean tangible choses in action such as promissory notes, bonds, stocks, and other vendible obligations.

SECURITY FOR COSTS A security which a defendant in an action may require of a plaintiff who does not reside within the jurisdiction of the court, for the payment of such costs as may be awarded to the defendant.

SEDITION An offense against the government of a country, not capital and not amounting to treason, consisting of attempts made by meeting, or by speeches or publications, to disturb the tranquillity of the state, or to excite discontent against the government.

SEDUCTION The offense of inducing a woman to consent to unlawful intercourse.

SEISIN In a legal sense, the word means possession of premises with the intention of asserting a claim to a freehold estate therein; it is practically the same thing as ownership. Seisin in law exists where there is a right of immediate possession. A mere tenant or lessee is not seized of the real estate which he has leased. He claims no freehold interest, and possession by himself is at the same time possession by the landlord through him. Seisin once established is presumed to continue until the contrary is shown, and as a general thing the making and delivery of a deed passes the seisin of land without any formal entry.

SELF-DEFENSE This term applies both to the defense of one's person and his property. One may defend himself even to the commission of homicide where necessary to prevent any forcible and atrocious crime, which, if completed, would amount to a felony. He may repel force by force in defense of his personal property or habitation against anyone who manifests, intends, or attempts by violence or surprise to commit a forcible felony such as murder, robbery, arson, burglary and the like. In such cases he is not required to retreat, but may resist his adversary until he secures himself from all danger.

One may defend himself although no felony is threatened or attempted, as where another attempts to commit an assault and battery upon him or attempts or offers to strike him when sufficiently near so that there is danger, and in such case the one assailed need not wait until he is struck but may strike first.

If there is a combat or quarrel both parties may or may not be aggressors. If they are and one is killed it will be manslaughter, unless the person who gave the lethal blow had refused further contest and had retreated so far as he could with safety, and the killing was from necessity and to avoid his own destruction. One may defend himself from animals and kill them during the attack, but, in general, not afterwards.

SELLER'S LIEN A lien which the vendor of goods has at common law for the whole or the unpaid portion of the purchase price of the goods, where he has parted with title but not with possession. It is in the nature of a pledge raised or created by law upon the happening of the insolvency of the buyer, to secure the unpaid purchase money to the seller.

SEPARATE MAINTENANCE An allowance paid to a wife who is separated from her husband. It is often paid pending the outcome of a divorce, after which it may be superseded by alimony.

SEPARATION Contracts of a man and wife to live apart. These do not affect the marriage, and they may at any time become reconciled and annul the contract and live together. A divorce from bed and board simply is a species of separation.

SEPARATION AGREEMENT, ALLOWING THE WIFE AN ANNUITY DURING THEIR JOINT LIVES

Note: To be binding, this agreement must relate to a separation that has already taken place, or is to take place immediately. If it relates to a separation to take place some time in the future, the agreement is void as against public policy.

This agreement made this 31st day of July, 19___, by and between John Doe, husband, party of the first part, and Jane Doe, wife, party of the second part, witnesseth:

Whereas unhappy differences have arisen between the said husband and wife, by reason of which they have agreed to live separate and apart from each other for the future, and to enter into the following agreement contained herein, as follows:

1. It shall be lawful for the said wife at all times hereafter, to live separate and apart from the said husband, and free from his marital control and authority, as if she were sole and unmarried, and to reside from time to time at such place as she may deem proper, without any interference whatever on the part of the said husband.

2. Neither of them, the said husband and wife, shall molest the other of them, nor compel, nor endeavor to compel, the other of them to cohabit or dwell with him or her by any legal proceeding for restitution of conjugal rights, or otherwise howsoever.

3. Neither of them, the said husband and wife, shall take any proceedings against the other of them to obtain a divorce or judicial separation in respect of any misconduct which has heretofore taken place, or is alleged to have taken place, on the part of the other of them.

4. The husband shall, during the joint lives of himself and the said wife, pay to her, the said wife, the sum of $5,000.00 per annum as her separate estate, but so that she shall not have power to anticipate the same, in quarterly payments on the quarter days, the first payment to be made August 15, 19____.

5. All the wearing apparel and personal ornaments of the said wife, and all movable personal property belonging to the said wife, now in her possession, shall belong to the said wife as her separate estate, independently of the said husband. All the property of the said wife, both real and personal, now held by her, or which shall hereafter come to her, shall be and remain her sole and separate property, free from all rights of the said husband, with full power to her to convey, assign, or deal with her said property.

6. On the death of the said wife in the lifetime of the said husband, all her separate estate, whether real or personal, which she shall not have disposed of in her lifetime or by will, shall, subject to her debts and engagements, go and belong to the persons or person who would have become entitled thereto if the said husband had died in the lifetime of the said wife.

7. If the said wife shall die in the lifetime of the said husband, he shall permit her will to be proved, or administration upon her personal estate and effects to be taken out by the persons or person who would have been entitled to do so had the said husband died in her lifetime.

8. The said wife shall have the sole custody and control of Mary and Tom, infant children, and of their education and bringing up, until they respectively attain the age of 16 years, without any interference whatsoever on the part of the husband.

9. The said husband further agrees to pay unto the wife for the support and maintenance of the aforementioned children of the parties the additional sum of $2,000.00 per annum, to be paid in quarterly installments, the first installment to be payable August 15, 19____, until each child reaches the age of 21 years, or remains unmarried.

10. The said husband and wife shall respectively, at all convenient and reasonable times, have access to and communication with the children or child for the time being living with or under the control of the other of them.

11. The said wife, her heirs, executors and administrators, shall at all times hereafter keep indemnified the said husband, his heirs, executors and administrators, from all debts and liabilities, heretofore or hereafter to be contracted or incurred by the said wife, and from all actions, proceedings, claims, and demands, costs, damages, and expenses whatsoever in respect of such debts and liabilities, or any of them.

12. In case the said husband shall be obliged to pay any sum or sums of money for or on account of any debt or liability heretofore or hereafter contracted or incurred by the said wife, or in case the said wife shall at any time take any proceedings against him, the said husband, for restitution of conjugal rights or otherwise for compelling him to cohabit with her, or shall

at any time directly or indirectly molest the said husband, then and in any such case the said annuity of $5,000.00 shall cease to be payable.

13. In case the said husband shall at any time or times hereafter be called upon to pay or discharge, and shall actually pay or discharge, any debt or liability heretofore or hereafter contracted or incurred by the said wife, then and in every such case it shall be lawful for the said husband, at his option, instead of availing himself of the rights secured to him by the preceding paragraph, to deduct and retain out of the said annuity the amount which he shall have so paid, together with all costs and expenses.

14. Each of them, the said husband and wife, or their respective heirs, executors or administrators, shall at any time execute and do all such assurances and things as the other of them, his or her heirs, executors, administrators or assigns shall reasonably require for the purpose of giving full effect to these presents, and the covenants, agreements and provisions herein contained.

15. Provided always, and it is hereby agreed, that if the said husband and wife shall be reconciled and return to cohabitation, or if their marriage shall be dissolved, then and in such case all the covenants and provisions herein contained shall be void, but without prejudice to any act of the parties hereto in respect of any antecedent breach of any of the covenants or provisions herein contained.

Witness our hands and seals this 31st day of July, 19___.

(Seal) /s/ John Doe
HUSBAND

(Seal) /s/ Jane Doe
WIFE

/s/ Tom Brown
WITNESS

SEQUESTRATION The proceeding by which property belonging to a judgment debtor, or to a husband ordered to pay alimony, is taken and sold to satisfy his obligation.

SERVED OR SERVICE The delivery of a writ issued out of a court to a proper officer, usually the sheriff, by which a court secures jurisdiction over the defendant.

SERVICE OF PROCESS The term used for properly delivering a summons, subpoena or citation upon a person in a legal proceeding.

SET-OFF A counter-claim or demand; a cross-demand; a demand set up against another demand, for the purpose of reducing its amount, or of extinguishing it altogether.

SETTLEMENT Where two or more persons having dealings together agree upon a balance due from one to the other, this is a settlement. Settlements and compromises are highly favored by the law.

Settlements of property in trustees on the prospect of marriage (mostly for the benefit of the husband and wife for the joint lives and then for the benefit of the survivor of them for life, and afterwards for the benefit of the children), were formerly quite common. They are enforceable in equity if fair and valid, as are also settlements made after marriage in pursuance of an agreement entered into prior to marriage, but settlement of the husband's property upon the wife and children without consideration after marriage will not be valid against creditors if at the time of making, the debts were already in existence or if he were about to begin a hazardous undertaking.

SEVERABLE CONTRACT A contract which is not entire or indivisible. If the consideration is single, the contract is entire; but if it is expressly or by necessary implication apportioned, the contract is severable. The question is ordinarily determined by inquiring whether the contract embraces one or more subject matters, whether the obligation is due at the same time to the same person, and whether the consideration is entire or apportioned.

SHARE OF STOCK A proportional part of the rights in the management and assets of a corporation. It is a chose in action. The certificate is the evidence of the share.

SHERIFF The chief executive and administrative officer of a county chosen by popular election. He or his deputies, whom he appoints, serve processes, summon juries, execute judgments, hold judicial sales, etc. He is also the chief peace officer within his jurisdiction.

It is the sheriff's duty to preserve the peace within his bailiwick or county. He may arrest and commit to prison persons breaking or attempting to break the peace. To keep the peace he may arrest, imprison, break doors, etc. He may arrest without warrant on reasonable grounds of suspicion that felony has been committed, and with the power follows the duty to do so. He must pursue all traitors, murderers, felons and rioters. He must keep the county jail and defend it against rioters, and may command the inhabitants of the county or the *posse comitatus* to assist him, and every person over fifteen is bound to obey such summons. He must execute within his county all process issued from courts of justice unless he is a party to the proceeding in which case the coroner acts. He may take bail where it is his duty. He must summon jurors and is the one to carry into effect the final judgments of sentences of the court relating to prisoners in his custody.

A sheriff has no power or authority out of his county except in special cases. He may appoint an under-sheriff and as many special and general deputies as the public interests may require, who may discharge all the ordinary ministerial duties of the office, but none that are of a judicial or quasi-judicial character. Acts of deputies or of an under-sheriff are done in the name of the sheriff, who is responsible for such acts.

The sheriff also appoints a jailer, sometimes with the approval of the court, who is held responsible for the escape of the prisoner, and for this he will be excused by nothing but an act of the public enemy or something beyond the control of man. He must not be wantonly or unnecessarily cruel to criminals. Where a prisoner against his will was confined by a jailer in a room with one having smallpox and caught the disease and died, the jailer was held guilty of murder. If the jailer is attacked he may defend himself. He may properly discipline the prisoner.

A deputy cannot delegate another to perform his duty though he may have another assistant, provided he remains present. In executing criminal process he may, after demanding admittance, break open the outer door of a house, but in case of civil process he cannot forcibly enter a dwelling house, but he may forcibly enter a warehouse, store, or barn or break an inner door of a dwelling house, if he has peaceably entered. Service of process and writs may not be made on Sunday except in cases of treason, felony or breach of the peace, and it has even been said that the sheriff may not on that day retake a prisoner who has escaped from custody.

SILENCE Abstaining from speech. This alone cannot be considered as consent to a contract, but where the circumstances are such that the person is bound in good faith to explain himself, then silence gives consent. No assent will be inferred unless the party knows his rights and what he is doing, nor unless his silence is voluntary.

If one is accused of a crime or charged with a fact and does not deny it, this, in general, furnishes evidence of the truth. But this does not apply to the silence of a prisoner while on examination before a magistrate charged by another prisoner with having joined him in the commission of an offense.

SIMULATION A word synonymous with "collusion" which means a fraudulent arrangement between two or more persons to give false or deceptive appearance to a transaction.

SINE DIE Adjournment without appointment of a day to appear again.

SINE QUA NON Without which it is not; an indispensable requisite.

SITUS Location; local position; the place where a person or thing is, is his situs. Intangible property has no actual situs, but it may have a legal situs, and for the purpose of taxation its legal situs is at the place where it is owned and not at the place where it is owed.

SLANDER Words spoken or written which are injurious to the character of another. Most commonly, however, slander is applied to spoken words. When written or printed slander is meant, the term "libel" is used. Persons guilty of verbal slander are liable in a civil suit only, while for libel both criminal and civil suits may be brought.

Verbal slander is of two kinds: First, that which is of such a character as to render the guilty party liable in a civil suit without proof of actual or special damages accruing therefrom; secondly, that which cannot be sustained except by proof of actual consequential damages. Slander of the first class must be such that if the party slandered were found guilty, he might be indicted and punished by the criminal courts, or, in case of one exercising a professional trade or business, that he lacks integrity or capacity either mental or pecuniary to conduct such a business or profession.

Thus no proof of actual special damages will be required for slanderously calling one a traitor, thief, perjurer, murderer, or imputing to him the commission of any crime involving moral turpitude and which is punishable by the law. Calling a man a leper, or imputing that he has venereal disease, are in themselves slanderous, but charging another with having a contagious disease is not actionable because the party will thereby not be rendered unfit for society. Accusing an attorney or artist or physician of inability or inattention or want of integrity in his occupation or a clergyman of being a drunkard or an officer of inability or bad morals, impeaching his fitness for his duties, are slanders without proof of special damages on the ground that the party is necessarily thereby disgraced or injured in his profession or trade or exposed to the hazard of losing his office.

Slanders other than as above described require proof of actual or special damages before recovery can be had or the action sustained, the law in such cases permitting no inference of damage, and the special or particular damages sued for must be particularly set forth and specified. Even where slanderous words are actionable in themselves recovery may be had in addition for special damages alleged and proved.

To be slanderous the charge must be in general false, and the falsity of the accusation is implied until the contrary is shown. If, however, an employer falsely represents his employee when asked for a statement as to his character, there is no such presumption that his allegations were false and they must be proved false by the employee claiming damages. The slander must be published, that is, communicated to someone else before it is actionable. The party slandered must be the plaintiff in the suit, hence a mother cannot maintain suit for her daughter having been called a bastard however much her feelings may be injured. Whether the slander is oral or written it is no defense that it is merely a repetition of what another has previously put forth or that the name of the other party was disclosed, or that the party accused of the slander believed the statements to be true, or that it was not his design to extend the circulation or credit.

The uttering or setting forth of slanderous words is justifiable in some cases. It is considered so where there is proper legal occasion, as where one is compelled to testify in a suit. In other cases it is excusable if without express malice. It is justifiable for an attorney to use scandalous words in support of his client's cause if pertinent thereto, and members of Congress and other legislative assemblies cannot be called to account for anything said in debate.

SOCIAL SECURITY The basic idea of social security is a simple one: During working years, employees, their employers and self-employed people pay social security contributions which are pooled in special trust funds. When earnings stop or are reduced because the worker retires, dies, or becomes disabled, monthly cash benefits are paid to replace part of the earnings the family has lost.

Part of the contributions made go into a separate hospital insurance trust fund so that when workers and their dependents reach 65 they will have help in paying their hospital bills. Voluntary medical insurance, also available to people 65 or over, helps to pay doctors' bills and other medical expenses. This program is financed out of premiums shared half-and-half by the older people who sign up and by the Federal Government. Nine out of ten working people in the United States are now building protection for themselves and their families under the social security program.

To get monthly cash payments for yourself and your family, or for your survivors to get payments in case of your death, you must first have credit for a certain amount of work under social security. This credit may have been earned at any time after 1936.

Most employees get credit for one-quarter year of work if they are paid $50 or more in covered wages in a three-month calendar quarter. Four quarters are counted for any full year in which a person has $400 or more in self-employment income. A worker who receives farm wages gets credit for one-quarter year of work for each $100 of covered wages he has in a year up to $400.

You can be either fully or currently insured, depending on the total amount of credit you have for work under social security and the amount you have in the last three years. The table given later shows which kinds of cash benefits may be paid if you are fully insured and which kinds may be paid if you are currently insured.

If you stop working under social security before you have earned enough credit to be insured, no cash benefits will be payable to you. The earnings already credited to you will remain on your social security record; if you later return to covered work, regardless of your age, all your covered earnings will be considered.

Just how much credit you must have to be fully insured depends upon the year you reach 65 if you are a man, or 62 if you are a woman, or upon the date of your death or disability.

The amount of credit you will need is measured in quarter-year units of work called quarters of coverage; but for convenience the following table is given in years. The people in your social security office will be glad to give you further details if you have questions.

You are fully insured if you have credit for at least as many years as shown on the appropriate line of the following chart. (See page 456.)

If you become disabled or die before reaching 65 (62 for a woman), you are fully insured if you have credit for one-quarter year of work for each year after 1950 and up to the year of your disability or death. In counting the number of years after 1950, omit years before you were 22.

No one is fully insured with credit for less than 1½ years of work and no one needs more than ten years of work to be fully insured. Having a fully insured status, however, means only that certain kinds of cash bene-

WORK REQUIRED TO BE FULLY INSURED

If you reach 65 (62 if a woman) or die or become disabled	You will be fully insured if you have credit for this much work
In 1965	3½ years
1967	4
1969	4½
1971	5
1975	6
1979	7
1983	8
1987	9
1991 or later	10

fits may be payable—it does not determine the amount. The amount will depend on your average earnings.

You will be currently insured if you have social security credit for at least 1½ years of work within the three years before you die or become entitled to retirement benefits.

The amount of your monthly retirement or disability benefit is based on your average earnings under social security over a period of years. The amount of the monthly payments to your dependents or to your survivors in case of your death also depends on the amount of your average earnings.

The exact amount of your benefit cannot be figured until there is an application for benefits. This is because all of your earnings up to the time of the application may be considered in figuring your benefit. The Social Security Administration will, of course, figure your exact benefit at that time.

You can estimate the amount of the worker's benefit, however, by following the steps given below:

1. Count the number of years to be used in figuring your average earnings as follows:
   - If you were born before 1930, start with 1956;
   - If you were born after 1929, start with the year you reached 27.

   Count your starting year and each year up until (but not including):
   - The year you reach 65, if you are a man;
   - The year you reach 62, if you are a woman;
   - The year the worker becomes disabled or dies, for disability or death benefits.

   (Note: At least 5 years of earnings must be used to figure retirement benefits and at least 2 years to figure disability or survivor benefits.)

2. List the amount of the worker's earnings for all years beginning with 1951. (Include earnings in the year of death or the year disability began.) Do not count *more than* $3,600 for each year 1951 through 1954; $4,200 for each year 1955 through 1958; $4,800 for each year 1959 through 1965; $6,600 for 1966 and 1967; and $7,800 for 1968 and after.

3. Cross off your list the years of lowest earnings until the number remaining is the same as your answer to step 1. (It may be necessary to leave years in which you had no earnings on your list.)

4. Add up the earnings for the years left on your list, and divide by the number of years you used (your answer to step 1).

The result is your average yearly earnings covered by social security over this period.

Look in the table given later and estimate your benefit from the examples shown there.

If you work after you start getting benefits and your added earnings will result in higher benefits, your benefit will be automatically refigured after the additional earnings are credited to your record.

Special payments of $40 a month ($60 for a couple) can be made under the social security program to certain people 72 and over who are not eligible for social security benefits. These payments are intended to assure some regular income for older people who had little or no opportunity to earn social security protection during their working years.

People who reach 72 in 1968 or later need credit for some work under social security to be eligible for special payments. Those who reach 72 in 1968 need credit for a three-quarter year of work under social security. The amount of work credit needed increases gradually each year for people reaching 72 after 1968, until it is the same as that required for retirement benefits. (This will be in 1970 for men and 1972 for women.)

The special payments are not made for any month for which the person receives payments under a federally aided public assistance program. The special payments are reduced by the amount of any other governmental pension, retirement benefit, or annuity. Payments to people who have credit for less than three-quarters of a year of work covered by social security are made from general revenues, not from social security trust funds.

If you become disabled before 65, you and certain members of your family may be eligible for benefits. Do not wait too long after you are disabled to apply for benefits; if you wait more than a year, you may lose benefits. Payments may begin with the seventh full month of disability. If you are found eligible for disability insurance benefits, you will remain eligible as long as you are disabled. When you reach 65, your benefit will be changed to retirement payments at the same rate.

A person is considered disabled only if he has a severe physical or mental condition which—

- Prevents him from working, and
- Is expected to last (or has lasted) for at least twelve months or is expected to result in death.

A person with a severe medical condition could be eligible even if he manages to do a little work.

If you become disabled before you are 24, you need credit for 1½ years of work in the three years before you become disabled. If you become disabled between 24 and 31, you need social security credits for half the time after you are 21 and before you become disabled. To get disability benefits if you become disabled at 31 or later, you must be fully insured and have credit for five years of work in the ten years just before you become disabled.

The amount of your monthly disability payment is generally the same as the retirement benefit you would get if you were 65. Figure your average earnings as if you reached 65 (62 for a woman) at the time you become disabled. If you are a disabled widow, surviving divorced wife, or dependent widower, the amount of your benefit is figured from what your spouse would have received. (See below.)

EXAMPLES OF MONTHLY CASH PAYMENTS

Average yearly earnings after 1950*	$899 or less	$1800	$3000	$4200	$5400	$6600	$7800
Retired worker—65 or older Disabled worker—under 65	55.00	88.40	115.00	140.40	165.00	189.90	218.00
Wife 65 or older	27.50	44.20	57.50	70.20	82.50	95.00	105.00
Retired worker at 62	44.00	70.80	92.00	112.40	132.00	152.00	174.40
Wife at 62, no child	20.70	33.20	43.20	52.70	61.90	71.30	78.80
Widow at 62 or older	55.00	73.00	94.90	115.90	136.20	156.70	179.90
Widow at 60, no child	47.70	63.30	82.30	100.50	118.10	135.90	156.00
Disabled widow at 50, no child	33.40	44.30	57.60	70.30	82.70	95.10	109.20
Wife under 65 and one child	27.50	44.20	87.40	140.40	165.00	190.00	214.00
Widow under 62 and one child	82.50	132.60	172.60	210.60	247.60	285.00	327.00
Widow under 62 and two children	82.50	132.60	202.40	280.80	354.40	395.60	434.40
One child of retired or disabled worker	27.50	44.20	57.50	70.20	82.50	95.00	109.00
One surviving child	55.00	66.30	86.30	105.30	123.80	142.50	163.50
Maximum family payment	82.50	132.60	202.40	280.80	354.40	395.60	434.40

*Generally, average earnings are figured over the period from 1950 until the worker reaches retirement age, becomes disabled, or dies. Up to 5 years of low earnings can be excluded. The maximum earnings creditable for social security are $3,600 for 1951-1954; $4,200 for 1955-1958; $4,800 for 1959-1965; and $6,600 for 1966-1967. The maximum creditable in 1968 and after is $7,800, but average earnings cannot reach this amount until later. Because of this, the benefits shown in the last two columns on the right generally will not be payable until later. When a person is entitled to more than one benefit, the amount actually payable is limited to the larger of the benefits.

Everyone who applies for social security disability benefits is referred for possible services to his state rehabilitation agency. These services help many people to return to productive employment. Social security often helps pay the cost of services provided to applicants by rehabilitation agencies. For more information about the disability benefits for blind people and disabled widows, disabled surviving divorced wives, and disabled dependent widowers, get in touch with your social security office.

Monthly payments can be made to certain dependents:
- When the worker gets retirement or disability benefits;
- When the worker dies.

These dependents are—
- Unmarried children under 18, or between 18 and 22 if they are full-time students;
- Unmarried children 18 or over who were severely disabled before they reached 18 and who continue to be disabled;
- A wife or widow, regardless of her age, if she is caring for a child under 18 or disabled and the child gets payments based on the worker's record;
- A wife 62 or widow 60 or older, even if there are no children entitled to payments;
- A widow 50 or older (or dependent widower 50 or older) who becomes disabled not later than seven years after the death of the worker or, in the case of a widow, not later than seven years after the end of her entitlement to benefits as a widow with a child in her care;
- A dependent husband or widower 62 or over;
- Dependent parents 62 or over after a worker dies.

In addition to monthly benefits, a lump-sum payment may be made after the worker's death.

Children are considered dependent on both their mothers and their fathers, and they may become eligible for benefits when either parent becomes entitled to retirement or disability benefits or dies.

Payments may also be made under certain conditions to a divorced wife at 62, or a surviving divorced wife at 60 (or a disabled surviving divorced wife 50 or older). To qualify for benefits, a divorced wife must have been married to the worker for twenty years and also meet certain support requirements. Benefits also can be paid a dependent surviving divorced wife at any age if she is caring for her deceased former husband's child under 18 or disabled who is entitled to benefits. For more information about this provision, get in touch with your social security office.

Monthly payments to the wife or dependent husband of a person entitled to retirement or disability payments generally cannot be made until the marriage has been in effect at least one year unless the couple are parents of a child. Payments can be made to the widow, stepchild, or dependent widower of a deceased worker if the marriage lasted nine months or longer; or in the case of death in line of duty in the uniformed services, and in the case of accidental death if the marriage lasted for three months, under special circumstances.

Cash benefits to your dependents, and to your survivors in case of your death, are figured from the amount of your retirement or disability benefit.

Permanently reduced benefits are received by:

- Workers and their wives who choose to start receiving retirement benefits while they are between 62 and 65;
- Widows who choose to start receiving benefits between 60 and 62; and
- Disabled widows and disabled dependent widowers 50 or older who receive benefits before they reach 62.

The amount of the reduction depends on the number of months they receive benefits before they reach 65 (62 for widows and disabled dependent widowers). On the average, people who choose to get benefits early will collect about the same value in total benefits over the years, but in smaller installments to take account of the longer period during which they will be paid.

If a person could be entitled to monthly benefits based on the social security records of two or more workers, he will receive no more than the largest of the benefits.

The lump-sum payment at a worker's death is ordinarily three times the amount of his monthly retirement benefit at 65, or $255, whichever is the less.

Social security benefits you receive are not subject to federal income tax.

Before payments can start, an application must be filed. When you are nearing 65 or if you become disabled, get in touch with your social security office.

It is important for you to inquire at your social security office two or three months before you reach 65, not only for the possibility of retirement benefits, but also for Medicare benefits, which are available whether or not you retire. If you wait until the month you reach 65 to apply for the medical insurance part of Medicare, you will lose at least one month of protection. It is always to your advantage to apply before you reach 65, even if you do not plan to retire. If you have high earnings which would increase the amount of your benefit in the year you are 65 or later, your benefit amount will be refigured. You will always be sure of receiving benefits at the highest possible rate.

When a person who has worked under the social security law dies, some member of his family should get in touch with the social security office.

If you cannot come to the social security office—perhaps because you

TYPES OF CASH BENEFITS

This table shows the principal types of payments and the insured status needed for each.

Retirement

Monthly payment to—	If you are—
* You as a retired worker and your wife and child	Fully insured.
Your dependent husband 62 or over	Fully insured.

Survivors

Monthly payment to your—	If at death you are—
* Widow 60 or over or disabled widow 50-59	Fully insured.
* Widow (regardless of age) if caring for your child who is under 18 or disabled and is entitled to benefits	Either fully or currently insured.
Dependent child	Either fully or currently insured.
Dependent widower 62 or over and disabled dependent widower 50–61	Fully insured.
Dependent parent at 62	Fully insured.
Lump-sum death payment	Either fully or currently insured.

Disability

Monthly payments to—	If you are—
You and your dependents if you are disabled	Fully insured and if you meet requirements explained on page 458.

*Under certain conditions, payments can also be made to your divorced wife or surviving divorced wife.

are housebound or hospitalized—write or telephone. A social security representative can arrange to visit you.

Long delay in filing an application can cause loss of some benefits, since back payments for monthly cash benefits can be made for no more than twelve months.

An application for a lump-sum death payment must usually be made within two years of the worker's death.

When you apply for social security benefits, take your own social security card or a record of your number; and if your claim is based on the earnings of another person, his card or a record of the number. You will need proof of your age. If you have a birth certificate or a baptismal certificate made at or shortly after your birth, take it with you when you apply. If you are applying for wife's or widow's benefits, take your marriage certificate; if your children are eligible, take their birth certificates. Take your Form W-2 Wage and Tax Statement, for the previous year; if you are self-employed, a copy of your last federal income tax return.

Proof that the applicant was being supported by the insured person is required before benefits can be paid to a parent after the death of a working son or daughter, or to a husband or widower whose working wife has retired, become disabled, or died. Generally, this proof must be furnished within two years after the worker dies, or, in the case of husband's benefits, within two years after his wife applies for cash benefits.

Do not delay applying because you do not have all of these proofs. When you apply, the people in your social security office can tell you about other proofs that may be used.

If you apply for retirement or survivor payments and supply all of the necessary information and then four to six weeks go by after the time you thought your benefits should start and you do not hear about your claim, get in touch with your social security office. There are special procedures for speeding payments in these cases and your social security office will be glad to do everything possible to prevent delays in your payments.

Under the law and regulations, social security records are confidential. Information from your record may not be disclosed without proper authorization.

When you apply for retirement or survivor's insurance benefits, your social security office will explain how any future earnings you may have will affect your payments and when and how to report your later earnings to the Social Security Administration. If you earn $1,680 or less in a year, you get all the benefits.

If you earn more than $1,680 in a year while you are under 72, the general rule is that $1 in benefits to you (and your family) will be withheld for each $2 you earn from $1,680 to $2,880. In addition $1 in benefits will be withheld for each $1 of earnings over $2,880.

Exception to the general rule: Regardless of total earnings in a year, benefits are payable for any month in which you neither earn wages of more than $140 nor perform substantial services in self-employment.

The decision as to whether you are performing substantial services in self-employment depends on the time you devote to your business, the kind of services you perform, how your services compare with those you performed in past years, and other circumstances of your particular case.

Benefits are also payable for all months in which you are 72 or older, regardless of the amount of your earnings in months after you reach 72.

Your earnings as a retired worker may affect your own and your dependents' right to benefits. If you get payments as a dependent or survivor, your earnings will affect only your benefit and not those of other members of the family.

Earnings which must be counted—

Earnings from work of any kind must be counted, whether or not the work is covered by social security. (There is one exception: tips amounting to less than $20 a month with any one employer are not counted.) Total wages (not just take-home pay) and all net earnings from self-employment must be added together in figuring your earnings for the year.

However, income from savings, investments, pensions, insurance, or royalties you receive after 65 because of copyrights or patents you obtained before 65, do not affect your benefits and should not be counted in your earnings for this purpose.

Earnings after you reach 72 will not cause any deductions from your benefits for months in which you are 72 or over. However, earnings for the entire year in which you reach 72 count in figuring what benefits are due you for months before you are 72.

For more information about how working after you apply for benefits will affect your retirement or survivor's payments, inquire at your social security office.

Special rules affect the payment of benefits to people outside the United States. If you intend to go outside the United States for thirty days or more while you are receiving benefits, ask your social security office for Leaflet No. SSA-609.

If you are not a citizen or national of the United States, your absence from this country may affect your right to benefits. The people in your social security office will be glad to explain these provisions to you.

When monthly payments are started, they continue until they must be stopped for one of the reasons given below. If any of these occurs, it must always be promptly reported to the Social Security Administration.

Marriage—Benefits for a child, an aged dependent parent, a disabled dependent widower, a divorced wife, a disabled widow, or widow receiving mother's benefits generally stop when the beneficiary marries a person who is not also getting social security dependent's or survivor's benefits.

There is an exception for the widow who remarries after reaching age 60. If she could have qualified for benefits on her deceased husband's record, she may still get benefits on that record. She would qualify for one-half of her deceased husband's retirement benefit, or (at 62) for the amount of the wife's benefit on her later husband's record, whichever is larger. A similar provision applies to widowers who remarry after 62.

Divorce—Payments to a wife or a dependent husband generally end if a divorce is granted. However, if a wife 62 or older and her husband are divorced, benefits to the wife may continue if the marriage lasted at least twenty continuous years before the divorce. (If a wife under 65 and her husband are divorced after twenty continuous years of marriage, she may receive benefits at 62 or later providing certain conditions are met. For more information, get in touch with any social security office.)

No child "in her care"—Payment to a wife under 62 or to a widow or surviving divorced wife under 60 will generally stop when she no longer has in her care a child under 18 or disabled. A widow or surviving divorced wife who is 50 or over and is severely disabled should get in touch with her social security office for information about any benefits that may be payable.

Child reaches 18—When a child reaches age 18, his payments stop unless he is—

- Disabled (if so, he and his mother may be eligible for benefits for as long as he is disabled), or
- A full-time, unmarried student (if so, he may be eligible for benefits until he reaches 22).

Adoption—When a child is adopted, his payments end unless he is adopted by his step-parent, grandparent, aunt, uncle, brother, or sister after the death of the person on whose record he is receiving benefits.

Death—When any person receiving monthly benefits dies, his or her payments end.

Disability benefits—When the benefits payable to a person stop because he is no longer disabled, the benefits payable to his dependents also stop.

If payments end because of any of these reasons, the last check due is the one for the month before the event.

Nearly all people 65 and over are eligible for health insurance protection under Medicare, including some people who do not have enough credit for work covered by social security to qualify for monthly cash benefits. There are two parts to Medicare: hospital insurance and for those who choose, medical insurance.

If you are 65 or over and are entitled to social security or railroad retirement benefits, you are automatically eligible for hospital insurance; if you are not entitled to either of these benefits, you should ask about hospital insurance and medical insurance at your social security office.

Nearly everyone who reached 65 before 1968 is eligible for hospital insurance, including people not eligible for cash social security benefits. If you reached 65 in 1968 or later and are not eligible for cash benefits, you will need some work credit to qualify for hospital insurance benefits. The amount of credit needed depends on your age. Eventually the amount of work required for hospital insurance will be the same as for social security cash benefits.

After you establish your eligibility, you receive a health insurance card, which shows that you have hospital insurance, medical insurance, or both. Hospital insurance will pay the cost of covered services for the following hospital and follow-up care:

- Up to 90 days of hospital care in a participating hospital during a "benefit period."* For the first sixty days of care, your hospital insurance will pay for all covered services except for the first $40.† For the 61st through the 90th day, hospital insurance pays for all covered services, except for $10 a day.

---

*A "benefit period" (or spell of illness) starts on the first day you receive covered services as a bed patient in a hospital or extended care facility. It does not end until for sixty consecutive days you have not been a bed patient in any hospital or skilled nursing home.

†Once you have taken care of the first $40 of hospital expenses in each benefit period, you do not have to pay it again, even if you have to go back into a hospital more than once in that same benefit period.

You also have a sixty-day "lifetime reserve" which can be used after you have exhausted your ninety days of hospital care in a "benefit period." "Lifetime reserve" days are not replaced after you use them. Hospital insurance pays all but $20 a day of your covered expenses during the reserve days.

- Up to 100 days of care in a participating extended care facility (a skilled nursing home or special part of a hospital which meets the requirements of the law) during each "benefit period." Your hospital insurance will pay for all covered services for the first twenty days of care and all but $5 daily for the next eighty days. You will be covered for extended care facility services only if you have been in the hospital for at least three days in a row and you enter the facility within fourteen days after you leave the hospital.

- Up to 100 home health visits by nurses or other health workers from a participating home health agency (but not doctors) in the 365 days following your release from a hospital (after at least a three-day stay) or from an extended care facility.

The medical insurance part of Medicare is voluntary and no one is covered automatically. You will receive this protection only if you sign up for it within a specified period. You will have protection at the earliest possible time if you enroll during the three-month period just before the month you reach 65. You may also enroll the month you reach 65 and during the three following months, but your protection will not start until one to three months after you enroll.

If you do not enroll during your first enrollment period, you will have another opportunity during the first three months of each year, provided this period begins within three years after you had your first chance to enroll. However, if you wait to enroll, you may have to pay a higher premium for the same protection; and your coverage will not begin until three to six months after you enroll.

Medical insurance is financed with monthly premiums paid by people 65 or over who have signed up for this insurance. The government matches these premiums dollar for dollar. Starting with April 1968, the medical insurance premium is $4 per month. Once you enroll for medical insurance, you do not have to do anything to keep your protection. It continues from year to year without any action.

If you wish to drop your medical insurance, you may give notice to do so at any time. Your medical insurance protection will stop at the end of the calendar quarter following the quarter you give notice.

Generally, your medical insurance will pay 80 percent of the reasonable charges for the following services after the first $50 in each calendar year:

- Physicians' and surgeons' services, no matter where you receive the services—in the doctor's office, in a clinic, in a hospital, or at home.

- Laboratory and radiology services of physicians when you are a bed patient in a hospital. The full reasonable charge (100 percent) will be paid, instead of 80 percent.

- Home health services even if you have not been in a hospital—up to 100 visits during a calendar year.
- A number of other medical and health services, such as diagnostic tests, surgical dressings and splints, and rental or purchase of medical equipment.
- Outpatient physical therapy services—whether or not you are home-bound—furnished under supervision of a participating hospital, extended care facility, home health agency, approved clinic, rehabilitation agency, or public health agency.
- All outpatient services of a participating hospital, including diagnostic tests or treatment.
- Certain services by podiatrists (but not routine foot care or treatment of flat feet or partial dislocations).

Federal retirement, survivors, and disability benefits, and hospital insurance benefits are paid for by contributions based on earnings covered under social security.

If you are employed, you and your employer share the responsibility of paying contributions. If you are self-employed, you pay contributions for retirement, survivor's, and disability insurance at a slightly lower rate than the combined rate for an employee and his employer. However, the hospital insurance contribution rate is the same for the employer, the employee, and the self-employed person. As long as you have earnings that are covered by the law, you continue to pay contributions regardless of your age and even if you are receiving social security benefits.

If you are employed, your contribution is deducted from your wages each payday. Your employer sends it, with an equal amount as his own share of the contribution, to the Internal Revenue Service.

If you are self-employed and your net earnings are $400 or more in a year, you must report your earnings and pay your self-employment contribution each year when you file your individual income tax return. This is true even if you owe no income tax.

Your wages and self-employment income are entered on your individual record by the Social Security Administration. This record of your earnings will be used to determine your eligibility for benefits and the amount of cash benefits you will receive.

The maximum amount of earnings that can count for social security and on which you pay social security contributions is shown in the following table:

Year	Amount
1937-50	$3,000
1951-54	3,600
1955-58	4,200
1959-65	4,800
1966-67	6,600
1968 and after	7,800

Earnings over the maximums may have been reported to your social security record and may appear on your earnings statement, but cannot be used to figure your benefit rate.

When you work for more than one employer in a year and pay social security contributions on wages over $7,800, you may claim a refund of the excess contributions on your income tax return for that year. If you work for only one employer and he deducts too much in contributions, you should apply to the employer for a refund. A refund is made only when more than the required amount of contributions has been paid. Questions about contributions or refunds should be directed to the Internal Revenue Service.

The following table shows the schedule of contribution rates now in the law:

CONTRIBUTION RATE SCHEDULE FOR EMPLOYEES AND EMPLOYERS (EACH)

	PERCENT OF COVERED EARNINGS		
Years	For Retirement, Survivor's, and Disability Insurance	For Hospital Insurance	TOTAL
1968	3.8	0.6	4.4
1969-70	4.2	.6	4.8
1971-72	4.6	.6	5.2
1973-75	5.0	.65	5.65
1976-79	5.0	.7	5.7
1980-86	5.0	.8	5.8
1987 and after	5.0	.9	5.9

CONTRIBUTION RATE SCHEDULE FOR SELF-EMPLOYED PEOPLE

	PERCENT OF COVERED EARNINGS		
Years	For Retirement, Survivor's, and Disability Insurance	For Hospital Insurance	TOTAL
1968	5.8	0.6	6.4
1969-70	6.3	.6	6.9
1971-72	6.9	.6	7.5
1973-75	7.0	.65	7.65
1976-79	7.0	.7	7.7
1980-86	7.0	.8	7.8
1987 and after	7.0	.9	7.9

Social security contributions for retirement, survivor's, and disability insurance go into the Federal Old-Age and Survivors Insurance Trust Fund and the Federal Disability Insurance Trust Fund. They are used to pay the benefits and administrative expenses of these programs and may be used for no other purpose.

There are two other trust funds—a Federal Hospital Insurance Trust Fund into which hospital insurance contributions are placed, and out of which hospital insurance benefits and administrative expenses are paid; and a Federal Supplementary Medical Insurance Trust Fund, into which the enrollees' premiums, along with the government's matching contributions, are placed, and out of which the benefits and administrative costs of the medical insurance program are paid.

Funds not required for current benefit payments and expenses are invested in interest-bearing U.S. Government securities.

Certain costs, however, are financed from general funds of the U.S. Treasury, including the cost of hospital insurance benefits for people who are uninsured for cash social security benefits; the government's share of the cost for supplementary medical insurance; and cash payments for certain uninsured people 72 and over.

Almost every kind of employment and self-employment is covered by social security. Some occupations, however, are covered only if certain conditions are met.

You receive social security credit as a farm operator or rancher if your net earnings from self-employment are $400 or more in a year. You must report your net earnings from self-employment as a part of your income tax return.

If your gross earnings from farming in a year are between $600 and $2,400, you may report two-thirds of your gross earnings, instead of your net earnings, for social security purposes. If your gross earnings from farming are more than $2,400 and your net earnings are less than $1,600, you may report $1,600 for social security purposes.

If you rent your farm land to someone else, you receive social security credits for your rental income if you "materially participate" in the actual production of farm commodities or the management of production.

Earnings from services as a clergyman are automatically covered unless the clergyman files an application to have it excluded, stating that he is conscientiously opposed, or opposed by reason of religious principles, to receiving social security benefits based on services as a clergyman. A clergyman who qualifies to be excluded from coverage may complete Form 4361 and file it with the Internal Revenue Service. This form may be secured at any social security office or at any Internal Revenue Service office. Once this form is filed it cannot be withdrawn. A clergyman reports his income and makes his tax contributions as if he were self-employed, even though he may be working as an employee. Members of religious orders who have taken a vow of poverty are not covered by social security. For more information about social security coverage for clergymen, ask for a copy of Leaflet No. 9 at your social security office.

Work done by a parent as an employee of his son or daughter in the course of the son's or daughter's trade or business is covered by the law. Domestic work in the household of a son or daughter is not covered unless special conditions are met.

Work for a parent by a daughter or son (also a stepchild, adopted, or foster child) under 21 is not covered. Also not covered is any work performed by a wife for her husband or by a husband for his wife.

A domestic worker's cash wages (including transportation expenses if paid in cash) for work in a private household are covered by the law if they amount to $50 or more from one employer in a calendar quarter. If you employ a household worker who will come under the law and you are not receiving the forms for making the earnings reports, ask your social security office or your Internal Revenue Service office for a copy of Leaflet No. 21. This leaflet explains how to get the forms and make the reports.

Cash tips amounting to $20 or more in a month with one employer are covered by social security. You must give your employer a written report of the amount of your tips within 10 days after the month in which you receive them. Your employer will collect your contributions due on these tips from other wages he owes you or from funds you turn over to him for that purpose. Otherwise, your contribution must be paid by you to the Internal Revenue Service.

If your report is late or incomplete, you will be liable for your social security contribution on tips not reported, and you may also be subject to a penalty in an amount equal to one-half of that contribution. Your employer includes your tips reported to him along with your other wages in his social security wage reports and on Form W-2, but he does not have to match your social security contribution on the tips. If you receive tips, you can get further information at your social security office.

Employees of non-profit organizations operated exclusively for religious, charitable, scientific, literary, educational, or humane purposes, or for testing for public safety, may be covered by the social security law if—

- The organization waives its exemption from the payment of social security contributions by filing a certificate (Form SS-15) with the Internal Revenue Service, and
- Those employees who wish to be covered indicate their desire to participate by signing the Form SS-15a that goes with the certificate.

Employees who sign the form and employees who are hired or rehired after the calendar quarter in which the waiver certificate is filed are covered. If any employee of a non-profit organization earns wages of less than $50 in a quarter, his wages for that quarter are not covered.

State and local government employees may be covered by social security under voluntary agreements between the individual state and the Federal Government.

When you work for a farmer, a ranch operator, or a farm labor crew leader, you earn social security credits:

- If the employer pays you $150 or more in cash during the year for farm work, or
- If you do farm work for the employer on 20 or more days during a year for cash wages figured on a time basis (rather than on a piece-rate basis).

For more information about farm labor crews and the conditions under which the farmer or the crew leader is the employer, get Leaflet No. 15 from your social security office.

Household workers employed on a farm or ranch operated for profit are covered under the same rules as other farm employees.

Most employees of the Federal Government not covered by their own staff retirement system are covered by social security.

For Active Military Duty in 1957 or Later—

Active duty or active duty for training you perform as a member of the uniformed services of the United States after 1956 counts toward social security protection for you and your family. Your basic pay is credited to your social security record. Credits, in addition to military basic pay, generally amounting to $100 for each month of active duty after 1967 count toward social security. No additional deductions will be made from your pay for these credits.

Social security credits of $160 a month are given to most veterans who served after September 15, 1940 and before 1957. When credits are given, they count the same as wages in civilian employment. These credits are not actually listed on your record, but if they would affect your benefit, the people in the social security office will ask for proof of your military service when an application is filed on your record.

Earnings from railroad work are reported to the Railroad Retirement Board and not to the Social Security Administration. Your social security record will not include any work you may have done for a railroad. Benefits based on work for a railroad are ordinarily paid by the Railroad Retirement Board. However, if you have less than 120 months (10 years) of railroad service when you retire or become disabled, your earnings for railroad work after 1936 are considered in figuring your disability or retirement payments under the social security law. A retired worker who has at least 120 months of railroad service and who has also done enough work under social security to qualify for social security benefits may receive retirement benefits under both railroad retirement and social security.

Survivors of a worker can be entitled under one system only, either railroad retirement or social security, even though the worker may have been entitled during his lifetime under both. Regardless of which program will pay the benefits, records of the deceased worker's railroad earnings after 1936 and his earnings under social security will be combined to determine payments to survivors. Railroad workers or their survivors can get further information from the nearest social security or railroad retirement office, or they may write to the Railroad Retirement Board, 844 Rush Street, Chicago, Illinois 60611.

United States citizens employed by American employers in foreign countries or aboard vessels or aircraft of foreign registry are covered by social security. Seamen and airmen employed on American vessels or aircraft are usually covered regardless of citizenship. United States citizens working abroad for a foreign subsidiary of an American corporation may be covered if the parent firm makes an agreement with the Secretary of the Treasury to see that social security contributions are paid for all these citizens employed abroad by the foreign subsidiary.

Agricultural work performed by foreign workers admitted to the United States on a temporary basis to do agricultural work is not covered. Work performed by foreign nationals temporarily in the United States to study, teach, conduct research, etc. under a foreign exchange program is not covered under social security if it is performed to carry out the purpose for which they were admitted to the country.

You must have a social security number if your work is covered by the social security law or if you receive certain kinds of taxable income. Your social security number is also used for income tax purposes. Show your card to each of your employers when you start to work. Upon request, show it to anyone who pays you income that must be reported. You can get a social security card at any social security office. The number on your card is used to keep a record of your earnings and of any benefits to which you and your dependents become entitled.

You need only one social security number during your lifetime. Notify your social security office if you ever get more than one number. If you change your name, or if you lose your social security card, go to a social security office to get a card showing your new name or a duplicate of the card you lost.

Each employer is required to give you receipts for the social security contributions he deducts from your pay. He does this at the end of each year and also when you stop working for him. These receipts, such as Form W-2, will help you check on your social security record. They show the amount of your wages that counts for social security. For most kinds of work, your wages paid in forms other than cash—for instance, the value of meals or living quarters—must be included. For domestic work in a private household or for farm work, only cash wages count. You should keep a record of the amount of self-employment income you have reported. You should check your record from time to time to make sure your earnings have been correctly reported. This is especially important if you have frequently changed jobs. Simply ask your social security office for a postcard form to use in requesting a copy of your record, complete, sign and mail it.

If your records of your earnings do not agree with the amounts shown on the statement you get from the Social Security Administration, get in touch with your social security office promptly. If you write, give your social security number, the periods of work in question, your pay in each period, and your employer's name and address. If the earnings in question were from self-employment, include the date your tax return was filed and the address of the Internal Revenue Service office to which the return was sent.

If you feel that a decision made on your claim is not correct, you may ask the Social Security Administration to reconsider it. If, after this reconsideration, you are not satisfied the decision is correct, you may ask for a hearing by a hearing examiner of the Bureau of Hearings and Appeals. And if you are not satisfied that the decision of the hearing examiner is correct, you may request a review by the Appeals Council. The Social Security Administration makes no charge for any of these appeals. You may, however, choose to be represented by a person of your own choice, and he may charge you a fee. The amount of such a fee is limited and must be approved by the Social Security Administration. Someone in your social security office will explain how you may appeal and will help you get your claim reconsidered, or request a hearing. If you are still not satisfied, you may take your case to the federal courts.

The Social Security Administration has over 750 offices conveniently located throughout the country. These offices have representatives who regularly visit neighboring communities. For the address of your nearest social security office, look in the telephone directory under Social Security Administration, or ask at the post office.

SODOMY The crime against nature. The carnal copulation by human beings with each other against the order of nature, or with a beast.

SOLE OWNERSHIP In insurance contracts, ownership is "sole," when no other person has an interest in the insured property.

SOUNDNESS Free from permanent injury or defects, healthy. It is sometimes interesting to know what is meant by the term "soundness" where an animal is sold accompanied by a guaranty that it is sound. At the time of its sale if an animal has disease, or the seeds of disease, actually diminishing its natural usefulness and making it less capable of work, and which in its ordinary progress will diminish its usefulness, or if the animal has from disease or accident undergone some alteration of structure which diminishes its usefulness or will in its ordinary effect do so, such animal is unsound.

A temporary injury not disabling the animal from present service is not unsoundness, and it does not matter whether the defect is curable or incurable if it is unfit for present use. A defective formation which has not produced lameness but simply may do so, as in the case of curby hocks, is said not to be unsoundness. A nerved horse or one having bone spavin or navicular disease is unsound, so is one having thick-wind or ossification of the cartilages. Usually soundness or unsoundness is a question to be determined by a jury.

SPECIAL APPEARANCE The appearance in court of a person through his attorney for a limited purpose only. A court does not get jurisdiction over a person by special appearance.

SPECIAL DAMAGES Damages not necessarily resulting from an injury complained of; damages which must be specially stated, and are not implied by law.

SPECIAL DEMURRER A demurrer to a pleading on the ground of some defect of form, which is specially set forth.

SPECIAL VERDICT A special verdict is one in which the jury finds the facts only, leaving it to the court to apply the law and draw the conclusion as to the proper disposition of the case.

SPECIALTY The word "specialty" in commercial law means a promise under seal to pay money—a bond. In early law there were two kinds of "specialties." "Common law specialties" were formal instruments under seal—bonds and covenants; "mercantile specialties" included bills and notes, insurance policies, and other unsealed commercial papers.

SPECIFIC LEGACY A legacy or gift, by will, of a specified thing.

SPECIFIC PERFORMANCE The performance of a contract to its exact terms. Courts of equity will direct the specific performance of contracts as a general rule whenever courts of law cannot supply an adequate remedy, that is, where mere damages are inadequate and an insufficient compensation. It is immaterial whether the subject of the agreement is real or personal estate. Where courts of law, however, can furnish an adequate remedy they must be resorted to.

Before a court of equity will interfere and decree a specific performance of a contract it must appear that the contract was founded upon a valuable consideration either in the form of benefit bestowed upon, or disadvantage sustained by, the party in whose favor relief is sought. And this consideration, it seems, must be proved even though the contract is under seal, and though in a suit at law a seal imports consideration and consideration therefore need not be proven. A specific performance will not be decreed if a contract not based upon a strictly valuable consideration as distinguished from a good consideration, such as an agreement to convey to a wife or child in consideration of the moral duty and affection existing towards them.

Specific performance of course will not be decreed where the contract is to do something that one is unable to do or which is contrary to law or equity. It will not be decreed unless the enforcement is necessary or is really important to the plaintiff and not oppressive to the defendant. Where damages recovered at law would answer his purpose as well as the possession of the thing contracted for, the party must sue in an action at law, not in equity, for specific performance.

Mere inadequacy of consideration to be given for a thing will not prevent a decree in equity for the delivery and conveyance thereof, but if the inadequacy is so great as to induce a conclusion that fraud or imposition has been practiced, a court of equity will refuse to aid in the enforcement.

As to contracts required by law to be in writing under the statute of frauds, if they are not in writing, no decree of specific performance will be made. But if they are in writing it is immaterial in what form the instrument may be. It should be noted, however, that part performance of a contract not in writing will sometimes in equity take the case out of operation of the statute of frauds. It will do so where it would be a fraud upon the opposite party if the agreement under the circumstances should not be carried out in its entirety. An example of this is where one takes possession of land under a verbal contract for conveyance to himself and makes improvement and expenditures on it. A mere part payment of the purchase money or the entire payment without improvements would not take the case out of the statute of frauds, and specific performance in such case would not be decreed, but the party would have an adequate remedy in a suit for repayment of the purchase money and for damages.

Even though a contract cannot be performed in its entirety either by reason of an unexpected failure in the title to part of the estate, or of inaccuracy in the terms or the description of the property in the contract, or by reason of diminution in value on account of a charge against the same, yet if there are other circumstances entitling one to a decree of specific performance the decree will be made coupled with a direction as to just compensation for the defects, whenever this can be done with justice between the parties.

SQUATTER One who settles on another's land without title. One who settles on public land without title or authority.

STAR CHAMBER The name of a celebrated court in England known especially for its secret sessions and cruel and arbitrary punishments and proceedings. It was abolished in the reign of Charles I.

STARE DECISIS The policy of courts to stand by previous judicial decisions.

STATUS QUO The situation in which he was.

STATUTE OF LIMITATIONS A statute fixing and limiting certain periods of time, beyond which rights of action cannot be enforced.

STAY To stop a judicial proceeding by court order; to hold a court order in abeyance.

STAY OF EXECUTION A temporary period during which the execution of the judgment of the court is delayed.

STAY OF PROCEEDINGS A temporary delay in the proceedings of an action, usually ordered by the court to compel one of the parties to comply with its requirements.

STERILITY The inability to procreate or have children. If incurable at the time of marriage and it arises from impotency, it is ground for divorce.

STIPULATION Any agreement between opposing counsel concerning the conduct of a case, such as an agreement to allow additional time to plead or to admit certain facts.

STOCK Shares issued by a corporate enterprise. Stock held by individuals in a corporation, even though the corporation property is altogether or in part real estate, is personal property. Certificates of stock are usually issued by the corporation as evidence of ownership of the stock. When the stock is sold and the certificate delivered to another, this certificate is surrendered and cancelled, and a new one is issued to the purchaser.

A sale of stock is commonly effected simply by delivering the certificate accompanied by an assignment on the back thereof containing a power of attorney to transfer it on the books of the company. This assignment is sometimes made in blank, the purchaser having the right to fill up the blank, and have the stock duly transferred in the books of the company. This last is necessary in order that the transferee may be recognized by the company as one of its stockholders, the transfer by delivery of the certificate amounting to no more than a mere equitable assignment until the actual transfer on the books of the company.

STOCK DIVIDEND The issue by a corporation of new shares of its own stock to its shareholders as dividends.

STOCKHOLDER One who is a proprietor or holder of shares in a corporate enterprise. Stockholders who have not paid the full par value of their stock may be required to pay the unpaid balance to satisfy the claims of creditors of the corporation, though as between the corporation itself and the subscriber to its stock it would appear that an agreement that the entire par value should not be paid is valid. And it would appear that this agreement would also be binding upon the creditor who becomes such after the agreement is known to him. Where, however, either property or services are given to the association in payment for stock if it appears that any fraud or overreaching were done in fixing its value, the stockholder will be allowed credit for the actual value only.

The liability of a stockholder with respect to creditors already existing cannot be escaped by surrender and cancellation of his stock, but the rule is different if the surrender and cancellation occurred before the indebtedness was incurred, and if it was done in contemplation of indebtedness about to be incurred. The rights of creditors being once fixed cannot be interfered with by a reduction of the capital or of the subscriptions to the capital stock. As against debts owing for labor there are statutory provisions in most places increasing the liability of stockholders to a fixed amount above the par value of the stock subscribed by them.

Subscribers to capital stock are liable to the corporation for the amount subscribed so long as the conditions contained in the subscription paper are complied with, and even the corporation may not relieve the subscriber to the prejudice of the rights of its creditors.

Usually the law requires the payment of a given percentage of capital stock into the treasury before the issuing of a charter. With this exception payment for stock may be made in money, property, services, or otherwise as may be agreed upon, if the valuation is fair and fraud has not been imposed upon the stockholders or upon others than stockholders. Unless the right is specially granted by law, one corporation may not subscribe to the stock of another.

The preliminary expenses of organization are chargeable against the organizers as well as against the corporation. If there is no legal organization or if the act authorizing the organization is unconstitutional, stockholders are liable as partners. So also are they personally liable for fraudulent acts and representations in connection with corporate affairs operating injuriously to others, or in case they transact an illegal business under cover of the corporation.

Unpaid portions of stock subscriptions must be paid as called for by the association unless the time of payment otherwise is fixed, even though there may be, for the time being, a temporary suspension or abandonment of corporate operations, but it is otherwise where a permanent abandonment is contemplated.

To render a subscription binding where it is to a given total sum or fund, the whole amount must be subscribed, and in making up that amount, unless permitted by the terms of the subscription, subscription with conditions not in common to all must not be included; nor must subscriptions that are invalid by reason of the incompetency of the parties to make the same, or subscriptions taken in bad faith from insolvents from whom payment cannot be enforced, simply to complete the necessary amount. Debts due a stockholder from the corporation may usually be set off against his stock subscription, but not against any amount above the par value of the stock for which he would be liable for labor done for the corporation as above indicated.

A sale and transfer of stock in general relieves the transferor of further payments, and imposes the liability therefor upon the purchaser. Though one purchase stock paid for by the former owner by overvalued services or property and though such overvaluation was in the nature of a fraud, yet, if he was unaware of it he will not be held to further payment on the stock.

In case of an increase of capital stock beyond that originally authorized, the owners of the old stock are ordinarily entitled to subscribe to the new at par to an amount proportional to their holdings of the old. This does not apply to further issues of the stock previously authorized where a part only had been already issued.

STOPPAGE IN TRANSITU This occurs in the shipment of goods from one party to another. The term implies a stoppage of the goods while in transit. This may be done for various reasons. The shipper may stop the goods while on their way to the purchaser and resume possession of them if not paid for and if he finds the purchaser is insolvent. For most purposes, however, the possession of the carrier is considered to be that of the buyer. By insolvency in this connection is meant not merely excess of liability over assets, but making an assignment for creditors, going into bankruptcy, or some overt act amounting to stoppage of payment. The vendor or a general or special agent acting for him may exercise the right. Manual seizure of the goods is unnecessary. It is sufficient if claim upon the carrier is made by the seller or his agent during the passage of the goods and before delivery, and the goods must be either wholly or partially unpaid for.

To defeat the right of such stoppage the goods must have come into the hands of the vendee, or some person acting for him actually or constructively, as by reaching the place of destination, or by being deposited for the vendee in a public store-house or by delivery to him of a part for the whole. When such right of stoppage has been exercised the parties are in the same position with respect to the goods as they were before they were sold.

To exercise the right of stoppage in transitu it appears that the insolvency must occur after the sale. Where the title to the goods has been legally transferred by the consignee by an endorsement of a bill of lading or otherwise, it is said that the right of stoppage in transitu will be extinguished if the transfer is in good faith and for a valuable consideration. If the bill of lading is transferred and endorsed in favor of another to secure the purchaser's debt the right of stoppage in transitu will exist, subject, however, to the right of the person so secured.

STRIKING A JURY The mode of constituting a special jury which has been ordered by the court for the trial of some particular cause, each party striking out a certain number of names from a list of jurors so as to reduce it to the number of persons prescribed by law, who are to be summoned and returned as jurors by the sheriff.

STRUCK JURY A special jury. So called because constituted by striking out a certain number of names from a prepared list.

SUBORN In criminal law, to persuade a person to commit perjury.

SUBORNATION OF PERJURY Persuading another to commit perjury. The offense is not consummated unless a false oath is actually taken. No abortive attempt to solicit one to take a false oath will complete the crime of subornation of perjury. It is a misdemeanor at common law to solicit one to commit perjury even though the solicitation is unsuccessful.

SUBPOENA or SUB POENA A writ commanding the attendance or appearance of a witness or party in court, or before a judicial officer, under a penalty. Upon proof of service of the subpoena on the witness, he may, if he does not ap-

pear, be arrested for contempt. If it is desired that the witness bring with him books, papers, etc., in his hands tending to elucidate the matter at issue, a clause must be inserted in the subpoena requiring him to bring them with him and produce them in court. A subpoena with such a clause is called a *subpoena duces tecum*.

SUBROGATION The substitution of one person for another with respect to a claim, a right, or the like. It is common in insurance cases in which a company, having paid A for damages, becomes the owner of A's claim against B.

If one creditor has preference over another by reason of priority of liens and securities, the latter may pay off the claims of the former and be subrogated or substituted to these rights. This is allowed so that he may better secure his own debt. If one purchases land for a given price and, before conveyance to him, pays off those holding encumbrances against the land, he will be subrogated with respect to the debt to the rights of the creditor against the debtor. If the debt is prosecuted to judgment he may proceed on the judgment as the creditor or plaintiff could have done.

If several are jointly and equally bound and indebted on an obligation and one of them pays it he will be subrogated to the rights of the creditor with respect to the portion or portions of the debt which the others should have paid. If one or more of the others are insolvent those who are solvent must equally share the loss. The rights as between co-securities are similar. They will all, so far as possible, be put on an equal footing, and if the principal in the case of a suretyship pay any one co-surety the proportion of the debt he was compelled to pay for the principal debtor, this must inure to the equal benefit of all the sureties paying in like manner.

In connection with the above it should be noted that where one pays the debt of another without any legal constraint or compulsion or necessity to protect his own interest, that is, as a mere volunteer, the law does not put him in the place of the creditor whom he pays as against the debtor. He is not subrogated.

Most cases of subrogation arise out of suretyship and it is a settled rule that where a party, only secondarily liable on an obligation, is compelled to discharge it he has a right in a court of equity to stand in the place of the creditor and to be subrogated to all his rights against the party primarily liable. He will also be entitled to the full benefit of all collateral securities both of a legal and equitable nature which the creditor has taken from the primary debtor or principal as an additional pledge for his debt. If a surety on a debt secured by a mortgage pays the debt he is entitled to the mortgage and the holder should assign it to him. The creditor, however, must have his claim paid in full and the surety claiming subrogation must have paid it. The subrogation extends only to the amount paid even though the creditor may have accepted less than the full amount of the obligation in settlement. If the creditor accepted a note from the surety in payment and settlement of his claim, this entitled the surety to subrogation.

In all cases of subrogation it should be noted that the party entitled to the right must be liable for the debt or must be otherwise interested in the subject matter with respect to which the subrogation takes place. No mere volunteer or party not legally liable to pay is entitled to or can enforce subrogation upon payment of the claim by himself.

Sureties in a judgment, if they pay it, are entitled to be subrogated and to stand in the position of the plaintiff against the principal debtor, and even an entry of satisfaction on the judgment does not destroy this right if the entry was not made at the instance of the surety. The same right exists in a surety on a bond and a surety of a surety has the right. An accommodation endorser who is obliged to pay a note is subrogated to the rights of the creditor with respect to collateral which he held from the principal as security for the payment of the note and a company insuring real estate will, upon payment of the insurance, be subrogated to the rights of the party insured against third persons who may be responsible for the loss.

If one has a lien on two funds and he satisfies himself out of one against which another holds a later lien so as to extinguish that fund, the junior lien holder will be subrogated to the rights of the prior lien against the other fund. This right of subrogation is something which may be assigned or transferred, and the creditor of the person entitled to the subrogation may avail himself of it either by means of an assignment or by the use of proper legal process.

SUBSCRIBING WITNESS An attesting witness. He must himself sign his name to the instrument, the execution of which he witnesses, and this must be done at the time of its execution, and at the request or with the assent of the party executing the instrument. He should actually see the signing by the party executing the instrument or the party signing should admit the signature to be his.

SUBSCRIPTIONS A written contract by which one engages to take and pay for capital stock of a corporation. If the subscription is made upon condition (as for example that a given amount shall be subscribed), the condition must be

complied with before it will be binding. If the subscription is to a fund of a given amount, it will not be binding until the full amount is subscribed for.

The subscription should be in the form of an agreement on the part of the subscribers to pay to each other or some particular person or committee for some particular purpose, and that the particular thing will be done or the particular purpose carried out.

SUBSTANTIAL   PERFORMANCE The complete performance of all the essential elements of a contract. The only permissible omissions or deviations are those which are trivial, inadvertent, and inconsequential. Such performance will not justify repudiation. Compensation for defects may be substituted for actual performance.

SUBTENANT An undertenant; one who leases premises from a tenant.

SUFFERANCE Negative permission by not forbidding; passive consent; a license implied from the omission or neglect to enforce an adverse right.

SUI GENERIS Of its own kind; peculiar to itself.

SUI JURIS Having capacity to manage one's own affairs.

SUICIDE Self-murder. It is criminal if the party is sane at the time. An attempt to commit suicide is even a misdemeanor. In cases of doubt as to whether one has committed suicide or not, the law presumes that he did not. This presumption may of course be overcome by evidence to the contrary. One is guilty of murder who, being actively or constructively present, encourages another to commit suicide and he does so.

SUMMARY PROCEEDINGS Those in which the ancient established course is disregarded, especially in the matter of trial by jury, the trial or hearing being usually had before a magistrate or judge without a jury. Such a proceeding, except in cases of contempt, can only be had where expressly authorized by legislative authority.

SUMMATION The closing statement to the jury made by each side in a lawsuit.

SUMMONS A writ issued by a court to the sheriff directing him to notify the defendant that the plaintiff claims to have a cause of action against the defendant and that he is required to answer. If the defendant does not answer, judgment will be taken by default.

SUNDAY The Christian Sabbath. In most states contracts made on Sunday are void under statutory regulations. Elsewhere the fact that they are made on Sunday will not affect their binding character. One is not bound to work on Sundays in order to perform his contract unless he expressly agreed to do so and can do so without a breach of the law. If the last day for the performance of an act happens on Sunday, in general it must be done the day preceding. Such is the case with notes and bills of exchange which fall due on Sunday, in the absence of statutory law to the contrary.

In general, it may be said that contracts made in violation of legislative acts prohibiting work and making of contracts on Sunday, except in connection with matters of necessity and mercy, are illegal and not binding. This is true unless the contract is actually executed or performed by the one party, thus rendering it against good conscience that the other party should repudiate it, having received its benefit. If a contract is begun on Sunday but not completed till afterwards, or if it merely grew out of a transaction which took place on Sunday, it is not thereby void. It has been decided that a note signed on Sunday if delivered on another day is binding. The note is not effective or operative until delivered, and the contract therefore is not made or consummated on Sunday but at the time of delivery.

One will not be relieved from liability for damages for negligently discharging a revolver and injuring the other, merely because the injury occurred on Sunday and both parties were at the time violating the law by hunting on that day.

SUPPORT *See* DESERTION.

SUPRA Above; above mentioned; in addition to.

SURETY One who engages to be responsible for the debt or default of another.

SURETYSHIP A contract which gives security, or a ground or basis of certainty or security. Under the English statute of frauds (in force in America, if not in its original form, then with minor statutory changes), contracts of guaranty and suretyship must be in writing, and signed in order to be binding.

It should be noted, however, that every promise to pay the debt of another is not a guaranty of suretyship. If such promise arises out of some new and original consideration or benefit or harm moving between the new promisor and the creditor, it is not such a contract as must be in writing under the statute of frauds. For example, if one is the holder of a promissory note drawn and endorsed by others and delivers it as payment for the purchase of a horse by himself, and, without endorsing it, verbally guarantees payment to the seller of the horse, this will be binding because the guaranty is made upon the new and distinct consideration existing only between the purchaser and seller. The new promise is made solely for the benefit of the purchaser of the horse and not the benefit of the maker of the note or any part thereto.

It should be noted also that where a credit is given to one person only, though the goods or consideration pass to another by his direction, this is not guaranty or suretyship but an original promise of a principal debtor, the person to whom the credit is given only being bound. Thus if one says, "deliver goods to A and I will pay you," there is no obligation on the part of A to pay the seller, and the person giving the order will be the only and original promisor; but if he says, "I will see that you are paid," or "I will promise you that you are paid," or "if he does not pay I will," this is an undertaking for another and is within the statute of frauds, and such a contract, to be valid, must be in writing.

In a contract of suretyship there are always at least three interested parties: the principal debtor, the surety and the creditor. The contract of suretyship is an undertaking to answer for the debt, default or miscarriage of the principal by which the surety becomes bound in the same manner as and equally with the original or principal creditor. Here it differs from a guaranty which is only a collateral undertaking to pay in the event that the debtor does not pay. So far as the creditor is concerned, in a contract of suretyship he may regard the surety as the principal debtor just as much as the one who actually is the principal.

When the contract of suretyship or guaranty is made simultaneously with the contract with the principal (and a promissory note or other obligation is a contract), the consideration existing between the principal debtor and the creditor will be a sufficient consideration to support the guaranty or suretyship and make it binding. Giving additional credit where a debt already exists has been held to be a sufficient consideration to render binding a guaranty of both the old and the new debt, and in others not. An extension of time for a definite period to the debtor upon consideration that a third party will guaranty the debt will make it binding upon the guarantor. In fact, any benefit granted to the debtor or disadvantage suffered by the creditor will, if a definite and certain character, support and make binding a resulting simultaneous guaranty of the third party.

The contract of suretyship may be absolute or it may be made so as to be binding only upon given conditions, but in order that there may be a surety there must also be a principal, and a bond executed by a surety is not valid until executed by the principal. If a surety signs upon condition that others sign also, he is not liable until they do so, provided the obligee or creditor knows of the conditions, and a surety is not bound if the signatures of his co-sureties previously obtained or to be obtained are forged even if his signing has not been conditional upon their doing so. A mere offer to guaranty is not effective until the guarantor has notice of the acceptance, and the acceptance may be shown by acts as well as by words.

The liability of a surety cannot exceed that of the principal, and the contract of suretyship will be strictly construed in favor of the surety. He can never be held responsible beyond the clear and absolute terms and meaning of his undertaking, and presumptions and equities are never allowed to enlarge or in any degree to change his legal obligation. Where, however, one is surety for another who is legally incapable of making a binding contract, as in the case of a minor, the surety will nevertheless be bound.

If one is surety on an official bond given to secure the faithful discharge of the duties of the office, it is the rule that the bond applies only to the particular term of office for which it was given and need not be expressed in the bond. If the character of the office or employment in connection with which the bond is given ceases or changes, the surety will be released as to the subsequent acts; similarly where the principal on the bond, or the party to whom the bond is given, dies even though the business is carried on by executors. If one is surety for two or for either of two persons on such a bond, the obligation ceases to be binding with the death of one, and a contract of guaranty or suretyship will be terminated by the death of one of several obligees in the bond or contract except with respect to matters transpiring before the death.

A surety for a lessee is not liable for rent after the term of lease if the lessee holds over. In bonds of officers, public or otherwise, the surety's liability is limited to the acts of the principal in his official capacity, nor will the surety be liable for a breach of new duties attached to the office of the principal subsequent to the execution of the bond. A bond for faithful performance of duties renders the surety liable for ordinary skill and diligence as well as for integrity.

A guaranty may be continuous or it may be exhausted by one act depending upon the intent of the parties. A guaranty to pay for any goods up to $1,000.00 is continuous, so also is a guaranty of any debts not exceeding a given sum, or that payment shall be made for any given kind of merchandise not exceeding a given quantity.

Where an executor was indebted to the decedent, the sureties on his bond became liable for the amount of the executor's debt to the estate, even though he was insolvent, and the collection of the debt could not have been effected against him otherwise.

Though a creditor has a fund or other security from which he may collect his debt, he is not obliged to exhaust this before resorting to the surety. Though a surety may claim an assignment of the debt from the creditor upon paying it, he cannot require an assignment of part where he has paid part. Upon payment of the debt he is entitled to receive from the creditor such collateral security therefor as the latter may hold. The creditor is not in general required to give notice to the surety of the default of the principal debtor, particularly where the engagement is absolute and for a definite amount.

The principal debtor, owing the same creditor different debts, may apply a payment to whatever debt he chooses, and the surety has no power to direct the application. If the debtor makes no such election the creditor has choice of its application. If a note is once paid, the surety cannot again be held liable if the note is put in circulation again. A release of the principal debtor discharges the surety; so does any material alteration in the contract between the creditor and the principal without the surety's consent, or any extension of time to the principal made without the surety's assent whether the change be prejudicial to the surety or not. A mere forbearance to press the debtor, however, without an agreement not to do so, will not release the surety.

The extension of time to release the surety must be binding upon the creditor, and it will not be unless there is some consideration for the agreement to extend, and a part payment by the principal is no such consideration though payment of interest before due is. If the time is extended without the surety's assent and the surety afterwards gives his assent, he will not be bound unless there is some new consideration for the assent.

The surety will also be discharged if the creditor releases any security he holds against the principal debtor, whether received at the time the contract is made or after, but if the security covers only part of the debt the surrender will only release the surety to that extent. Even if the creditor takes other security as good or bad as that surrendered in place of it, the surety will be discharged. If the creditor compounds or settles with one surety this will not release his co-surety, except insofar as it relieves him of liability for the portion which would properly fall upon the surety settled with.

A surety has a right to institute a proceeding in equity to compel payment of the debt by the principal after it is due. This is to protect himself against future insolvency of the principal or contingencies. The surety paying the debt may recover from the principal, and the indebtedness from the principal to the surety will be considered as dating back from the time when the suretyship began. A surety, however, who pays a claim which is out of date, that is, barred by limitation, cannot recover against the principal.

If the surety has in his hands funds or securities of the principal, he may apply them to the discharge of the debt, but if there are several sureties they must all share the benefit of such funds or securities. The surety is not obliged to make use of the security which he holds. He may look to the principal to reimburse him, and though he has paid off the creditor by note and the note has not been paid, he may still demand reimbursement from the principal.

If the surety incurs and pays costs in contesting the claim of the creditor in good faith, he may recover this from the principal as well as the debt, but he cannot recover costs where he is indemnified for his liability if he defends against the creditor's suit contrary to the express wishes of the principal, and after being notified by him that there was no defense.

A surety paying too much by mistake cannot recover the excess nor can he recover usurious interest paid to obtain an extension of time for payment of the debt. A creditor is not ordinarily bound to make use of active diligence against a principal debtor on the mere request of a surety. The surety who pays the debt in full is entitled to be put in the position of the creditor and to have all his rights against the principal with respect to securities he may hold and otherwise, and he may have an assignment of the debt or be subrogated.

Co-sureties are bound to contribute equally towards the payment of the debt unless their liability is separate and successive in which case one would be liable to another for the entire debt if the other paid it. The creditor, however, may collect the whole amount from one surety alone, the others being bound to contribute their portions to the one, and all of those paying being entitled to reimbursement from the principal. The right to compel contribution among sureties extends to the costs and expenses of defending a suit if such defense was warranted, and in the matter of contribution one surety is entitled to no advantage over another through a reduction in the amount paid to the creditor or by reason of his having in his possession any securities obtained from the principal. It is not necessary that the sureties be bound by the same instrument.

It should be noted that where one becomes surety at the request of another surety, he cannot be called upon to contribute by that person, and if a surety is fully indemnified by his principal by collateral placed in his hands he must exhaust the collateral before calling upon a co-surety for contribution. If one surety is insolvent there must be equal contribution among the others, and if one co-surety is absent from the jurisdiction of the court, the surety who has paid may require contribution from those within the jurisdiction without regard to the one who is absent.

The contract of suretyship like other personal contracts is controlled by the law of the place of performance which is the place where such contract is made unless a contrary intent is expressed. In the case of an endorsement on a note the contract is to pay at the place of endorsement if not paid by the maker at the place designated in the note. In case of a bond given to secure faithful performance of the duties of a public officer, the sureties are bound as if the contract had been made at the seat of the government to which the bond is given.

SURRENDER The abandonment of leased premises by a tenant. If a landlord accepts the abandonment as a termination of the lease, a surrender has occurred.

SURROGATE A synonym for a judge of probate, register, judge of the Orphan's Court, etc., who has to do with administrations of estates, guardians, etc.

T

TAFT-HARTLEY ACT OF 1947 Under this legislation, employees may join or refrain from joining any union, without restraint or intimidation. Under the Act, the closed shop, in which only union members are employed, is banned. However, an employee must join the union when such arrangement is supported by a majority vote of the workers.

Certain unfair labor practices are banned under the Taft-Hartley Act:

1. Coercion by unions or employers in the selection of bargaining representatives.

2. Discrimination against non-union employees.

3. Union refusal to bargain.

4. Illegal strikes and boycotts.

5. Discriminatory or excessive initiation fees for joining a union.

6. "Featherbedding," or forcing an employer to pay for services that are not performed or not to be performed.

Benefits provided under the Taft-Hartley Act include:

1. Free speech is guaranteed to employers in expressing their views of labor problems to their employees, so long as they contain no threat of reprisal or force or promise of benefit.

2. Unions must file reports on money taken in, and give an accounting thereof.

3. Communists cannot hold union office.

4. Compulsory check-offs are abolished. Employers are not compelled to deduct union dues from the wages of employees and turn them over to the unions; each worker now has the right to decide for himself whether he will permit a check-off on his wages.

5. Threatened strikes which may create national emergencies are subject to study by a board of inquiry appointed by the President of the United States. The board's report, which is made public, is coupled with the President's authority to procure an injunction against the strike, followed by a sixty-day period for collective bargaining and, if necessary, a further fifteen-day period for a secret ballot under the auspices of the National Labor Relations Board.

6. When there is a danger of a work stoppage toward the expiration of a collective bargaining contract, the Taft-Hartley Act provides for a "cooling off" period of sixty days prior to such work stoppage. When such a situation exists, neither party to the dispute may terminate or modify it without:

a. First serving written notice on the other party sixty days prior to the expiration of the contract of the proposed termination or modification.

b. Offering to meet and confer with the other party for the purpose of negotiating a new or modified contract.

c. Notifying the Federal Mediation and Conciliation Service and corresponding state agencies of the existence of the dispute.

d. Continuing, without work stoppage, under all the terms and conditions of the existing contract for at least sixty days after serving the written notice.

TAIL Limitation; abridgement; limited; curtailed, as a fee or estate in fee, to a certain order of succession, or to certain heirs.

TALESMAN One called to serve as a juror from among the bystanders in a court.

TALISMAN A juror summoned to fill up a panel for the trial of a particular case. Such person is not bound to serve the term.

TANGIBLE Tangible is a word used to describe property that is physical in character and capable of being moved. A debt is intangible, but a promissory note evidencing such debt is tangible.

TARIFF A schedule or tabulated list of rates.

TAX Money paid to the government in return for its services and protection.

TAX SALE A sale of property for the purpose of paying accrued or back taxes. Tax sales are subject to statutory laws, and the particular law under which the sale is held as to time, place and notice of sale, demand of tax, pursuing collateral remedies, assessments, etc., must be strictly pursued and carried out before a valid sale can be effected. If part of the land sold is liable to sale and the residue not, the entire sale is void. If several parcels of land belonging to the same person are separately assessed, each part is liable for its own specific tax but not more. If a new county is formed the proper officer in the old county may sell land lying in the newly created county for taxes, unless there are other statutory regulations. The production of a tax deed does not in itself furnish evidence of title, but it must be accompanied by evidence of all the steps required by law to be taken in order to effect the sale.

TELEGRAPH COMPANIES, DUTIES OF A telegraph company is bound to receive properly written messages tendered to it along with the regular rates for transmission. A delivery to the wife of the one to whom a telegram is addressed, when he is absent from town, may or may not be a sufficient delivery according to circumstances, depending upon whether or not she is his agent, and whether or not the man himself can be found. Damages resulting from mistakes in transmission are collectible from the company, which is required to exercise a reasonable degree of care and skill in transmission. A provision in the contract on which the message is written, restricting the liability of the company or relieving it from the exercise of due care and skill, is probably void as being against public policy.

A telegraph company is liable for damages arising directly and naturally from negligence or lack of promptness in its transmission.

TENANCY IN COMMON The holding of an estate in lands by several persons, by several and distinct titles, but by unity of possession.

TENANT One who has temporary possession and use of that which is in reality the property of another; as a tenant for life or years.

TENANT BY OR AT SUFFERANCE One who comes into the possession of land by lawful title, but holds over by wrong title, after the determination of his interest.

TENANT BY THE CURTESY One who, on the death of his wife seized of an estate of inheritance, after having by her issue born alive and capable of inheriting her estate, holds the lands and tenements for the term of his life. After the birth of the issue and before the death of the wife, he is called tenant by the curtesy initiate; after the death of the wife, tenant by the curtesy consummate.

TENANT FOR LIFE One who holds lands or tenements for the term of his own life.

TENANT FOR YEARS One who holds lands or tenements under a lease or demise from another, for the term of a certain number of years agreed upon; a lessee for years.

TENANT FROM YEAR TO YEAR One who holds lands or tenements under a lease from year to year.

TENANT IN FEE SIMPLE or TENANT IN FEE One who has lands, tenements or hereditaments, to hold to him and his heirs forever, generally absolutely and simply.

TENDER To offer money in satisfaction of a debt or obligation by producing the same and expressing to the creditor a willingness to pay.

A tender of money must be made by the debtor or someone authorized by him or someone whose act he subsequently ratifies, and it must be to the creditor or another properly authorized person having capacity to receive it, and in such money as is made legal tender by law. A tender in bank notes, though not a legal tender if objected to, will nevertheless be good; so will a check. The full amount due must be tendered, yet one may owe two or more distinct debts to the same person and an effective tender may be made with respect to one of the debts alone. Asking change will not vitiate the tender unless objection is made on that account.

The tender must be unqualified, and the amount must be stated in making the offer. If a time has been agreed upon for the tender, the agreement must be observed as to this, but if made subsequently before the suit is brought, this fact may be given in evidence in mitigation of damages. The tender must be made at a convenient and suitable hour and place agreed upon, or, in the absence of such agreement, wherever the person authorized to receive payment may be found. The money must be actually produced and offered unless the circumstances of the refusal to accept it amounts to a waiver thereof. In any case, it should be in the debtor's possession ready for delivery. If the creditor is absent from the appointed place at the appointed time of payment, the presence of the debtor with the money ready for delivery is sufficient.

A tender of payment of a given amount operates as an admission that that amount is due, and makes the party liable for it thereafter. The purpose of a tender is frequently to prevent the opposite party from recovering costs in a suit for more than the amount tendered provided he shall recover no more.

Tender of specific articles must also be made to a proper person by a proper person at the proper time and in accordance with the contract, or in the absence of specific agreement as to such matters, in accordance with the situation of the parties and circumstances of the case and the customs of the particular trade. If an article in a store is sold, tender of it should be made on demand at the store or where the goods are at the time of the sale. If a creditor is to be paid by articles which are portable such as cattle, they should be tendered at his place of abode or place of dealing in cattle, unless a specific agreement as to place of delivery be made. The articles to be delivered in order to make a tender must be set apart and distinguished from others so as to admit of identification, and it has been said that the tender must be in daylight and the articles must remain at the place of tender or delivery to the last hour of the day.

A tender will put a stop to accruing damages and interest. It admits the plaintiff's right to the amount tendered and the benefit of a tender may be lost by a subsequent demand and refusal of the amount admitted to be due, but it will not be lost by demand of more than the sum tendered.

TENDER OF PERFORMANCE The offer by one of the parties to perform his obligations under a contract.

TENEMENT Any thing that· may be held, provided it is of a permanent nature, whether it is of a substantial or of an unsubstantial kind.

TENOR The tenor of an instrument is an exact copy of the instrument. Under the rule that an indictment for forgery must set out in the instrument according to its "tenor," the word imports an exact copy—that the instrument is set forth in the very words and figures.

TENURE In its technical sense, the word means the manner whereby lands or tenements are held, or the service that the tenant owes his lord. In the latter case there can be no tenure without some service, because the servi e makes the tenure. The word is also used as signifying the estate in land. The most common tenure by which lands are held in the United States is "fee simple."

TERM A limitation of time; the duration of an estate. A limited and fixed period of time during which courts are held, sit, or are open for the hearing and trial of causes.

TESTAMENT A disposition of personal property, to take effect after the death of the person making it.

TESTAMENTARY Pertaining to a will or testament.

TESTAMENTARY CAUSES Causes or matters relating to the probate of wills, the granting of administrations, and the suing for legacies.

TESTATOR One who writes or dies leaving a will.

TESTATRIX A female testator.

TESTIMONIUM CLAUSE That clause of an instrument with which it concludes: "In witness whereof, the parties to these presents have hereunto set their hands and seals."

TESTIMONY In some contexts the word bears the same import as the word "evidence," but in most connections it has a much narrower meaning. Testimony is the words heard from the witnesses in court, and evidence is what the jury considers it worth.

THEFT The fraudulent taking of personal property belonging to another without his consent, with intent to deprive the owner of its value and to appropriate to the use or benefit of the thief.

THREAT A declaration by one person that he intends to work injury to the person, property or rights of another. Threats may be made either verbally or in writing. Sending threatening letters for the purpose of extorting money is a misdemeanor at common law. The threat, with respect to the general nature of the evil threatened, must be such as is calculated to overcome a firm and prudent man. One making threats of bodily injury so as to put another in fear may be held to bail for good behavior.

TIMBER Wood suitable for use in building, either in the tree or dressed and cut, as lumber. If land is owned in common by two, one cannot grant or sell the timber without the consent of the other. And the purchaser of the timber cannot sell and give good title to a purchaser from him, and the purchaser for him, if he should buy, would be liable to the co-tenant for the amount of his interest in the logs.

TIME, HOW TO COMPUTE In computing the time from one day to another either the first or the last day may be excluded. Time from and after a given day excludes that day. Where a party was allowed until a given date to file a certain instrument it would be in time if filed on that date. If the last day prescribed for doing a thing falls on Sunday it should be done on the Saturday previous, if it is illegal to do it on Sunday, unless there are statutory provisions to the contrary.

TITLE This term is most commonly applied to real estate, though it properly refers to personal property also. Title or just possession of real estate may be acquired either by descent to heirs at the death of an ancestor, or by purchase, which includes title by deed, will and every other means except descent. It is almost a universal rule that a seller must himself have title in that which is the subject of transfer.

There are exceptions to this however. Property in lawful coin of the United States will pass by a transfer of possession, and property in a negotiable instrument endorsed in blank is transferable by the person holding it so as to give a good title to a person honestly acquiring it, even though there was no title in the former holder of the coin or instrument.

TONNAGE In marine insurance, registered tonnage means the vessel's carrying capacity as stated in the ship's papers at the date of the policy, and not the tonnage fixed by the law of the government under which the vessel is registered.

TORT A private or civil wrong or injury independent of contract. The injury may be to real or personal property or to one's person or reputation. It may be direct or indirect and may be from an act of commission or omission.

There are some wrongs which in their nature may be considered either torts or breaches of contract. They partake of the nature of both. In such cases the injured party may sue for a breach of the contract or for the tort as he may prefer. As an example, the case of timber wrongfully taken by one not the owner and converted into money may be cited. This is plainly a tort, yet the injured party if he chooses may waive the tort, assuming that there was a contract on the part of the party taking it, pay for it (the law indeed implies such a contract), and sue on that contract for the value of the timber. In most cases of fraud there is both a tort and violation of the contract.

Parties jointly committing torts are severally and separately liable without contribution from each other. Herein a tort differs from a contract, for in case of a contract the joint contractors would be liable as between themselves to suffer the loss equally. Persons under legal disability to contract are nonetheless liable for their torts.

Imprisonment has been abolished in connection with claims based on contract, but not with respect to actions and judgments for torts, though even in such cases very extensive relief is now granted under insolvent laws for most torts. Both a criminal and a civil suit may frequently be brought, the former for the public wrong and the latter for the wrong done to a private party. The two suits, however, would be entirely separate and distinct, and the private action would be for a special injury to the individual aside from the injury to the public generally, all crimes being considered in the light of injuries to the public and not to the private individual.

Even if a party is rightfully in possession of property but does something about it to its injury, in excess of and contrary to his authority, and inconsistent with the rights of the owner, he will commit a tort. Acts lawful and innocent in themselves may become torts when done without just regard for the rights of others, or at an improper time or place or in an improper manner. Instances of torts are assault and battery, false imprisonment, slander, libel, malicious prosecution, injuries to person or property arising from negligence or wilful intention such as automobile accidents, trespass, private nuisances, injuries to ways, water courses, etc., etc. Possession of property alone without ownership is sufficient to maintain an action for tort if it is wrongfully injured. A wrongful possessor even may sue any party other than the owner for an injury to the property.

To justify a suit there must be a loss, as well as a wrong, though in some cases if the wrong is committed, the law conclusively presumes that a loss or injury has occurred. Thus, in certain kinds of slander and libel, special or particular damage need not be proven. The special damages to furnish ground for a suit must be immediate and direct in its character; that is to say, remote and consequential results which cannot be directly traced to the wrong committed are not the subjects of suit for special or particular damages, since their cause is too speculative and they may have arisen wholly or in part from other causes than the wrong committed. Nor can damages be recovered for what may happen as a result of the wrong, but only for necessary and probable consequences. The right to damages ceases where mere speculation begins.

TORT-FEASOR A person who commits a tort; a wrongdoer.

TORTIOUS Partaking of the nature of a tort; wrongful; injurious.

TOTAL DISABILITY In a contract of insurance, these words do not mean, "absolute helplessness." Their meaning is relative, depending on the circumstances of each case, the occupation, and capabilities of the insured.

TRADE FIXTURES Personal property placed upon or annexed to leased land by a tenant for the purpose of carrying on a trade or business during the term of the lease. Such property is generally to be removed at the end of the term,

providing it can be so removed without destruction or injury to the premises. Trade fixtures include show cases, shelving, racks, machinery, and the like.

TRADE-MARK A symbol, emblem or mark which a tradesman or manufacturer puts upon wraps or attaches in some way to goods he manufactures or has caused to manufacture. It may be in the form of letters, words, vignettes or ornamental design. A name by use may become property, and one will be protected in the use of it though not registered as a trade-mark where others attempt to appropriate it for fraudulent and deceptive purposes; but this property is limited to the name and not the size, color or form of the letters used in making up the name. A common name of an article in combination with a place may become a trade-mark. But no property can be acquired in words, marks or devices which set forth merely the nature, kind and quality of articles.

One will not be protected as to his trade-mark if the article it applies to is put forth under false representations, as where it contains a falsehood as to its ingredients. Foreigners are entitled to the same protection with respect to trade-marks as citizens. One adopting a trade-mark of another with colorable changes or alterations with intent to deceive customers, even though there are striking differences, will be prevented from using it. Where the difference is such that injury is not probable from the use of an adopted trade-mark, an injunction will not be allowed. Though wholesalers may know the difference between true and false articles, yet if retailers will be deceived by a simulated trade-mark, an injunction and damages may be recovered.

An injunction has been granted even where there was a dissolution of a partnership, and one of the partners continued business under the old partnership name. Where fraud is committed in the use of trade-marks it may be stopped, as where a label for one grade of goods is put on a lower grade or upon an inferior article and where genuine wrappers are surreptitiously obtained and put on other goods. One may lose his right to a trade-mark by discontinuing to use it, by not stopping the use of it by others, or by adopting a new one.

The United States, by statute, gives protection to owners of trade-marks used in commerce with foreign nations, or among the several states, or with Indian tribes, if the owner is domiciled in the United States or resides or is located in any country affording similar privileges to its citizens. Registration of a trade-mark is effected: First, by filing in the Patent Office an application in writing addressed to the Commissioner of Patents, Washington, D.C., signed by the applicant, stating his name, domicile, location, and citizenship; the class of merchandise and the particular description of goods comprised in such class to which the trade-mark i appropriated; a statement of the way in which the same is applied and attached to goods, and the length of time during which the trade-mark has been used; a description of the trade-mark itself shall be included, if desired by the applicant or required by the Commissioner, provided such description is of a character to meet the approval of the Commissioner. With this statement there must be filed a drawing of the trade-mark, signed by the applicant, or his attorney, and such number of specimens of the trade-mark as may be required by the Commissioner of Patents.

Secondly, registration is effected by sending $100.00 with the application. Application must be accompanied by declaration under oath setting forth certain facts. Certificates of registration issued in pursuance of application are good for 20 years, and may, from time to time, be renewed within six months before the expiration of a 20-year period. If previously registered in a foreign country it will not be effective after ceasing to be in force in the foreign country, and in no case will it be in force over 20 years unless renewed. An assignment of a trade-mark should be recorded in patent office within three months from its date.

For further information as to trade-marks communicate with the Commissioner of Patents, Washington, D.C.

PETITION AND STATEMENT FOR AN INDIVIDUAL APPLYING FOR A TRADE-MARK, INCLUDING OATH OF INDIVIDUAL MAKING APPLICATION

To the Commissioner of Patents:

John Doe, a citizen of the United States of America, residing at New York City in the State of New York, and doing business at 122 Fifth Avenue, has adopted and used the trade-mark shown in the accompanying drawing for canned fruits and vegetables in Class _____, food and ingredients of foods, and presents herewith _____ specimens or facsimiles showing the trade-mark as actually used by applicant upon the goods, and requests that the same be registered in the United States Patent Office in accordance with the Act of _____ day of _____, 19___, as amended. The trade-mark has been continuously used and applied to said goods in applicant's business since January 4, 19___. The trade-mark is applied or affixed to the goods, or to the package containing the same, by placing thereon a printed label on which the trade-mark is shown.

/s/   John Doe
APPLICANT'S FULL SIGNATURE

State of New York

City of New York

John Doe, being duly sworn, deposes and says that he is the applicant named in the foregoing statement, that he believes the foregoing statement is true; that he believes himself to be the owner of the trade-mark sought to be registered; that no other person, firm, corporation or association, to the best of his knowledge and belief, has the right to use said trade-mark in the United States, either in the identical form or in any such near resemblance thereto as might be calculated to deceive; that said trade-mark is used by the United States and foreign nations or Indian Tribes; that the description and drawing presented truly represent the trade-mark sought to be registered; that the specimens (or facsimiles) show the trade-mark as actually used upon the goods.

/s/ John Doe
FULL SIGNATURE OF APPLICANT

TRADE UNION A combination of workmen usually (but not necessarily) of the same trade, organized for the purpose of securing by united action the most favorable working conditions for its members.

TRANSCRIPT A copy of a writing.

TREASON The Constitution of the United States defines treason as levying war against the United States or adhering to her enemies or giving them aid or comfort. It is punishable with death. Confession in open court or the testimony of two witnesses to the same overt act, that is, an act manifesting an intention to commit treason, is necessary for conviction. One giving assistance to a traitor becomes a principal in the offense, and the concealment of treason by being passive is criminal.

TREASURE TROVE Money or coin, gold, silver plate or bullion found hidden in the earth or other private place, the owner being unknown.

TREASURY STOCK Stock of a corporation that has been issued by the corporation for value, but that is later returned to the corporation by way of gift or purchase or otherwise. It may be returned to the trustees of a corporation for the purpose of sale.

TREES AND THE LAW Trees are real estate when growing but are personal property when cut down. This does not apply in its full sense to trees growing in a nursery, which are about in the same position as growing crops. If the roots of a tree extend into the land of an adjoining owner or the branches spread over the same, insofar as they extend beyond the line, the adjoining owner may cut them off. If the roots grow into the adjoining land, the adjoining owner may hold the tree in common with the owner of the land where it is planted, but if the roots do not penetrate the land of the adjoining owner and the branches overhang only, the tree belongs wholly to the owner of the land where the roots grow, and if the tree grows directly on the boundary line it is the property of both owners.

TRESPASS An unlawful act committed with violence, actual or implied, to the personal property or rights of another. This name is also given to a particular form of action brought for injury to one's person, property or reputation. If a trespasser forcibly breaks a door or gate for an illegal purpose it is lawful to oppose force with force, and if one unlawfully enters upon the land of another he may be expelled immediately with no greater force or violence than is necessary without a previous request.

The owner's license to pass upon the land of another will frequently be presumed, and in such case will be in force until actually revoked by the owner. The proprietor of goods and chattels may enter upon the property of another upon which they are placed and remove them if they are there without his fault, as where a tree is blown down into the adjoining lands or fruit has fallen from a branch of a tree belonging entirely to the party upon whose soil it grew.

It is not trespass for a landlord to go upon the leased property to distrain or demand rent, or to see whether waste has been committed or repairs made, and he may go into the house for either purpose if

the outer door is open, and if he himself is bound to repair he has the right to enter for that purpose. Similarly if he has reserved any rights or privileges in the premises himself he may enter for the purpose of obtaining the advantage of them. A man may throw down or abate a public nuisance without committing a trespass; a private nuisance may be abated by the party aggrieved even before an injury takes place, and if so, its occurrence is inevitable.

TROVER An action which lies to recover the value of a personal chattel, or goods, wrongfully converted by another to his own use.

TRUE BILL When an indictment has been presented to a grand jury and is found to warrant a prosecution, it is endorsed as a true bill.

TRUST AND TRUSTEES A right of property, real or personal, held by one party called the trustee for the benefit of another called the *cestui que trust* or beneficiary. Trusts are active where the trustees have some duty to perform, or passive, where there is no duty to be performed by the trustee in order to carry out the trusts, in which case the control of the property passes to the beneficiary. Trusts are also express, those created in express terms in a deed or other instrument, and implied or those which are assumed to have been intended from the nature of a transaction or which are superinduced upon the transaction by operation of law independent of the mere intention of the parties.

Among the trusts which are implied are resulting trusts. If the legal estate in land is taken in the name of one person while the consideration is given or paid by another, a resulting or presumptive trust arises from the transaction and the person named in the conveyance will be a trustee for the party from whom the consideration proceeds unless there is a close relationship between the parties or from other cause it appears that a gift or loan is intended; and irrespective of the relationship of the parties if it appears that the intention was that the party advancing the money should have the property and it nevertheless conveyed to another, the other will hold it as trustee. The fact that a conveyance is voluntary, that is, without consideration, may raise a resulting trust, especially when accompanied by other circumstances indicative of such an intention.

Where a disposition of property is made by deed or by will to a person as trustee, and no beneficiary is named or the trust is ineffectually declared, or does not extend to the whole interest given to the trustee, or fails either wholly or in part, the interest so undisposed of will be held by the trustee not for his own benefit but for a resulting trust for the donor himself or his heir at law or next of kin according to the nature of the estate, for a resulting trust may apply to personal property as well as real estate.

All trusts as to real estate must be in writing, but a trust relating to personal property may be proven by verbal evidence. If a trustee dies, resigns, or fails or refuses to execute or accept the trust, or no trustee is named to execute it, the proper court will appoint a trustee to attend to the execution of the same.

Merely naming a person a trustee does not make him one. There must be an acceptance of the trust express or implied on his part, but if he does not wish to be held responsible as trustee he should refuse to act before performing or meddling with the duties of a trustee, for this will be construed as an implied acceptance. Having once accepted he can only become discharged from a performance of the duties by the provision of the instrument appointing him, if it contains such provisions, or by the consent of all parties interested or by the order of a competent court.

All executors, administrators, guardians, and assignees are in a measure trustees, and like other trustees are not allowed to speculate with the trust property or to retain profits made through the use thereof. If they become purchasers at the sale of the trust property, unless it is by special permit of the court, parties in interest may cause the sale to be set aside, or may require the trustee to be charged with the full value of the property if he has purchased for less than full value.

If one of several trustees dies, the survivor or survivors will have full power to act and the trust property will become vested in them, but as a general rule those acting cannot bind the trust separately but must act jointly, nor can they delegate their powers to those others unless expressly authorized to do so. Executors, administrators and assignees, however, may act separately as to most matters and bind the estates of which they have charge. They also have considerable authority to deputize others to act for them. As a general thing, one trustee is not responsible for the act of another done without his knowledge, but will be held liable for losses which he has enabled a co-trustee to cause though there was no active participation in the act on his part.

The trustee must not exercise his legal power to the prejudice of the beneficiary, and he may not speculate with trust property. The trustee will be responsible to the beneficiary for any breach of the trust arising either from negligence or bad faith, and his liability will extend to an amount which with good management he might have received on account of the trust including interest on sums he needlessly allowed to remain where they would earn no interest. He must not only protect the trust property from unnecessary waste and diminution, but must be active to secure its reasonable productiveness and increase. He must not use trust property for his own purposes or about his own business, and if he does, he is not entitled to any of the increase resulting therefrom. He must not purchase that which as trustee he sells. As a general rule, trustees, public or private agents, and public officers who contract in excess of their authority become liable personally.

TRUSTEE A person entrusted with the management and control of another's property and estate. A person occupying a fiduciary, or confidential, position; as, for example, an executor or a guardian.

TRUSTEE IN BANKRUPTCY An agent of the court authorized to liquidate the assets of the bankrupt, protect them, and to bring them to the court for final distribution for the benefit of the bankrupt and all the creditors.

U

ULTRA VIRES Literally the words mean "beyond power." The acts of a corporation are *ultra vires* when they are beyond the power or capacity of the corporation as granted by the state in its charter.

UNDERWRITER An insurer; so called from his underwriting or subscribing the policy. A term constantly applied to insurers, whether corporations or individuals. In the United States, where insurances are generally made by incorporated companies, the underwriting or subscription usually consists of the signature of the president or vice-president of the company and the sum insured, with the attestation of the secretary.

UNDUE INFLUENCE The improper or wrongful persuasion of a person to do something which without such persuasion he would

not do; it usually consists of taking unfair advantage of another's mental, emotional or physical weakness.

UNEMPLOYMENT COMPENSATION Such insurance which provides for payment to unemployed workers. It is managed jointly by the states and the national government. Before an employee is eligible he must generally wait one week before collecting his unemployment insurance; some other prerequisites are that the worker must be able to work, must not have quit without good cause or have been discharged for misconduct; he must not be involved in a labor dispute and he must be willing to take a job in his field at prevailing wage rates. An employee is not eligible for such payments if he leaves his job for marriage, pregnancy or further education. A worker is also ineligible for unemployment compensation if he receives vacation or dismissal pay, workmen's compensation or veterans' allowances.

To be eligible the unemployed worker must go to his local state unemployment office and register his claim for benefits and he must register for work. If he is offered a suitable job in his field at more or less the same rate he received while employed and he refuses such job opportunity, he is ineligible for unemployment payment. However, an otherwise eligible employee who moves out of the state may still collect his unemployment compensation if he notifies his new state unemployment

office, which will serve as an agent for the other state.

UNFAIR COMPETITION The imitation by design of the goods of another for the purpose of palming them off on the public, thus misleading the public by inducing it to buy goods made by the imitator. It includes misrepresentation and deceit; thus, such conduct is fraudulent not only as to competitors but as to the public.

UNILATERAL CONTRACT A contract in which the party to whom an engagement is made, makes no express agreement on his part.

UNINCORPORATED ASSOCIATIONS Organizations and associations not given corporate form and legality. Associations though unincorporated are recognized by the law as having a status and an existence. Such an association and its members have rights that may be enforced, and can incur legal liabilities. Yet that status, those rights and those liabilities are not so well and so satisfactorily defined or certain as in the case of a corporation, the legal entity, unity and compactness of which are complete. It is usually more satisfactory to deal either with a partnership or a corporation than with an association, such as an unincorporated literary society, social club, church or charitable or beneficial association.

Contracts entered into by such associations are usually effected through some individual or committee, and whether they have authority to act or not depends for the most part upon the law or agency, for it is in the capacity of agent of the association that they contract, if at all. They can do nothing to bind the members. They can do only what they are authorized to do by the articles of the association or by-laws of the organization duly adopted, or by a majority vote of the organization duly and regularly passed. They cannot go beyond the expressed limits of their authority. They cannot deal on credit or borrow money or give notes or the like, without express authority, and persons dealing with them, if they expect to hold the association and its members generally liable, should know beforehand that they can prove the existence of this authority.

Unless the articles of association or by-laws of the organization provide otherwise, all the members are bound by a vote of the majority in regular meeting or at a special meeting, duly called, with due notice of the time and place thereof given to each member. This notice should also contain information as to the business to be acted upon. The will of the majority, however, will not control in connection with a proposed change in the fundamental principles or purposes of the association and no one can be compelled by any vote to be drawn into a project entirely foreign to his original purpose and intent when he joined the organization. However, with regard to ordinary matters, the very fact that one becomes a member raises an implied contract on his part to abide by the will of the majority.

Membership in such an association is regarded as a right, or as legal property in the possession of which one is entitled to legal protection. A member may not be expelled for insufficient reasons, or without fair opportunity of being heard and offering a defense. A member may be expelled for any offense set forth in the by-laws after proper proceedings, that is, if the by-law itself is reasonable, for no association can undertake to expel members without cause or without a reasonable cause, or from improper motives. He may be expelled if he has been convicted in the regular way by a jury for an offense of so infamous a nature as to render him unfit for the society of honest men, such as perjury, forgery and the like; and where he has clearly violated his duties to the corporation. The acts of his associates will be usually sustained, however, if done in good faith. Persons illegally expelled may institute legal proceedings to restore their rights.

Members of an unincorporated association may make themselves liable on an obligation incurred without authority by subsequently ratifying or acquiescing in the act done. Subscriptions by the membership may be enforced if the conditions of the subscriptions are complied with.

The property of an unincorporated association is held by the members in common. Each owns an undivided part of it, and unless the right of disposition has been surrendered by the members to the majority or to somebody elected by the association, in pursuance of the articles of association or by-laws adopted before the acquisition of the property, awkward questions are likely to arise; for no portion of the members would have a right to control the disposition of the interest of the remaining portion of the property, and this fact might result in an expensive proceeding in equity. Commonly, however, property is purchased in the name of the trustees elected by the association, and control over the same is regulated by the by-laws.

UNLAWFUL ASSEMBLY Three or more persons who assemble together to do an unlawful act with force and violence and who part without doing it or making any motion towards it. If they move forward towards its execution, it becomes a rout, and if they actually execute their design it amounts to a riot. The unlawful assembling is itself criminal.

UNSOUND MIND A mind incapable of reasoning. Courts of law and of equity will protect those of unsound mind against their own folly. They will not distinguish, however, between mere degrees of intelligence or intervene in case of mere imprudence, lack of judgment or liability to mistake which does not amount to unsoundness of intellect.

USURY An excess over the legal rate charged the borrower for the use of money. In order that the law against usury may operate, it is necessary that there be a loan. The bona fide sale of a note, bond or other security at a greater discount than would amount to legal interest is not a loan, and the sale is not void for usury even though the seller of the note endorses it and becomes responsible for the payment thereof; but if the note or other security is made and sold simply for the purpose of escaping the law against usury, the transaction will be considered a loan and only the amount paid for the note with legal interest can be collected. However disguised, if the contract is in fact a loan, it will be usurious if more than legal interest is obtained. If one draws a note in favor of himself and endorses it and obtains money thereon, it will be a loan.

A contract in its inception not usurious will not be invalidated in general by a subsequent usurious transaction in connection therewith, but if originally usurious and a new contract is substituted for it, the new contract will in general be considered usurious. If the return of the principal under the contract is to depend upon a contingency there can be no usury, but if the contingency extends to interest, the law against usury applies. It is not usury to take the highest legal rate of interest in advance on a negotiable note.

The effect of usury upon contracts varies somewhat in different states. In some places it voids the entire contract. In other states it renders the interest only uncollectible, for the most part it is void only with respect to the excess of interest.

UTTER As applied to counterfeiting, to utter and publish is to declare or assert, directly or indirectly, by words or actions, that the money or note is good. Thus to offer it in payment is an uttering or publishing. To utter and publish a document is to offer directly or indirectly, by words or actions, such document as good and valid. There need be no acceptance by the offeree to constitute an uttering.

V

VACANCY As applied to a fire insurance policy, the words "vacancy," "vacant," or "unoccupied" mean, "that if the house insured should cease to be used as a place of human habitation or for living purposes, it will then be vacant or unoccupied." The period of time is unimportant. Vacant property increases the risk of the insurer, hence violates the policy.

VAGRANT One who wanders from place to place having no lawful or visible means of support, does not work though able to do so. The crime which is a misdemeanor is known as vagrancy.

VALID Effective; operative; not void; subsisting; sufficient in law.

VALUABLE CONSIDERATION A consideration which the law esteems an equivalent for a grant, such as money, marriage or the like.

VALUED POLICY As used in fire insurance, a valued policy is one in which the sum to be paid in case of loss is fixed by the terms of the policy. No reference can be made to the real value of the property that is lost.

VENDEE The person to whom a thing is sold; a buyer or purchaser.

VENDOR A seller; the person who sells a thing.

VENDOR'S LIEN An equitable lien allowed the vendor of the land upon the land sold, for the purchase money.

VENIRE To come into court; a writ used to summon a jury. The word is used sometimes to mean jury.

VENUE The word originally was employed to indicate the county from which the jurors were to come who were to try a case, but in modern times it refers to the county in which a case is to be tried.

VERDICT The finding of a jury in favor of one or the other party to an action at law, with such damages (in case of a finding for the plaintiff) as it considers him entitled to. The answer of a jury made upon any cause, civil or criminal, committed by the court to its examination.

VERSUS Against.

VEST To give an immediate fixed right of present or future enjoyment.

VESTED LEGACY A legacy, the right to which vests permanently in the legatee, though the legacy is not payable until a future time.

VESTED REMAINDER A fixed interest in lands or tenements to take effect in possession, after a particular estate is spent.

VESTED RIGHT Such a complete, well-consummated right that it cannot be divested without the consent of the person to whom it belongs; one that is fixed or established and no longer open to controversy.

VIS MAJOR The force of nature, sometimes called "act of God," which excuses persons from liability. If the ordinary exertion of human skill and prudence cannot avoid the effect of the force of nature, then an obligor may be excused under the doctrine of impossibility of performance.

VISA An endorsement on a passport by proper authorities permitting the person who bears it to enter a particular country.

VOID Of no force or effect, absolutely null; that which cannot be confirmed, or made effectual.

VOIDABLE Not absolutely void

or void in itself; that which may be avoided or confirmed.

VOIRE DIRE A preliminary oath administered to a witness, to discover whether he has such an interest in the cause, in which he has offered to testify, as would disqualify him.

VOLUNTARY ASSIGNMENT An assignment in trust made by a debtor for the benefit of his creditors.

VOLUNTARY CONVEYANCE The transfer of an estate without any adequate valuable consideration. Such a conveyance is good as between the immediate parties but not as to third parties if their rights and interests would be defeated. (See also FRAUD.) One cannot give his property away, or practically give his property away, as against creditors who are entitled to be paid out of it. While void as to creditors already existing, such a transfer will, however, be good as to creditors who become such after the conveyance, at least if the conveyance is not made in contemplation of entering upon some hazardous enterprise involving probable loss.

A voluntary conveyance by a father to son will not necessarily be fraudulent, though the father is in debt if the conveyance is merely a reasonable provision for the son and he still retains the principal part of his property.

All gifts of goods and chattels as well as lands, by writing or otherwise, made with intent to delay, hinder or defraud creditors are void as against the person prejudiced thereby. A voluntary conveyance is also void as against a subsequent purchaser of the same property who has neither actual notice of the voluntary conveyance nor constructive notice resulting from the recording of the same.

VOLUNTARY MANSLAUGHTER Manslaughter committed voluntarily in a sudden heat of passion; as if, in a sudden quarrel, two persons fight, and one of them kills the other.

VOTE A ballot cast for or against something or someone by someone qualified under either a charter, by-law, or constitution.

VOUCHER A written instrument which attests, warrants, maintains and bears witness.

W

WAGES The compensation agreed upon by one person to be paid to another who is employed by him for some specific purpose.

WAIVE To throw away; to relinquish voluntarily, as a right which one may enforce, if he chooses.

WAIVER The intentional relinquishment of a known right. It is a voluntary act, and implies an election by the party to dispense with something of value, or to forgo some advantage which he might at his option have demanded and insisted on.

WAREHOUSE Mainly used for the storage of goods in bulk or in large quantities; a place used in connection with a wholesale business for the purpose of storing goods.

WAREHOUSEMAN One who receives goods and merchandise for storage in his warehouse for pay. He must use ordinary care in preserving the goods, and neglect to do so will render him liable for injury to them. His responsibility commences immediately upon their being in his charge or custody for the purpose of being housed when his crane is applied to raise them into the warehouse. He may hold the goods until his charges are paid, or he may deliver part and retain the remainder to secure his compensation.

WARRANT An order authorizing a payment of money by another person to a third person. As a verb, the word means to defend; to guarantee; to enter into an obligation of warranty.

WARRANT OF ARREST A legal process issued by competent authority, usually directed to regular officers of the law, but occasionally issued to private persons named in it, directing the arrest of a person or persons upon grounds stated therein.

WARRANTY A promise that a fact is true. In the sale of personal property a warranty is a statement of fact concerning the quality or character of goods sold made by the seller to induce the sale and relied on by the buyer. A breach or violation of a warranty gives rise to a suit for damages. In insurance a warranty is a statement by the insured that a fact is literally true and that on such statement of fact the validity of the contract depends. A breach of warranty in an insurance contract by the assured may cause the policy to be cancelled by the company.

WASH SALES A stock exchange term designating sales which are merely bets upon the market, in which it is understood between the parties that neither is bound to deliver or accept delivery.

WASTE A spoiling and destruction of an estate either in houses, woods or lands by demolishing not the temporary profits, but the very substance of the thing, to the injury of him who has the present interest, or him who has the remainder or reversion. It may be voluntary, as by actual and designed demolition, or permissive, arising from negligence and want of care. The law of waste has frequent application in connection with life estates, where the life tenant injures the property to the injury of him who is to hold the property at the termination of the life estate, that is the remainderman.

Voluntary waste is committed whenever a tenant uses fields, orchards, gardens, meadows and the like contrary to the usual course of husbandry, or so as to exhaust the soil by negligent or improper tillage. It is waste to convert arable land into woodland, to cut down the fruit trees though planted by the tenant himself, or even to plow up strawberry beds which the tenant had bought of a former tenant when he took possession. Mines of metal or coal, pits of gravel, lime, clay, stone and the like if already opened may be worked by the one at the time holding the land, but if he opens new mines or pits, this will be waste as against the interests of the remainderman.

Any carrying away of the soil is waste. Pulling down houses, removing wainscoting, floors, windows and other things affixed to the freehold though erected by the lessee himself will be waste unless they are mere fixtures. Waste may be also committed by changing the form of houses or parts of them or pulling down a house and erecting a new one, or converting two rooms into one and the like. The extent to which wood and timber may be cut without waste depends upon circumstances. It is commonly a question of fact for a jury to determine.

The tenant may cut trees for the repair of the house, fences, stiles, gates and the like on the premises, and for making aand repairing all instruments of husbandry, and unless contrary to the terms of his lease he may cut timber for firewood if there is enough dead or false timber for such purpose but this does not apply to ornamental trees or those planted for shelter or to exclude objects from sight. Where timber is scarce the law of waste with respect to it is more stringent than where it is abundant, and a clearing up of land for tillage in a new country where trees abound, instead of being an injury is a benefit to the remainderman so long as there is sufficient timber left, and the land cleared bears a proper relative proportion to the whole tract.

The mere fact that property has become severed from the land by a tempest or a trespasser will not entitle the tenant thereto. In general, a tenant is answerable for waste though committed by a stranger. He is the custodian of the property and is responsible for proper care thereof, but is not liable if the damage is caused by lightning or storm. He is not responsible for accidental fire, that is, one which cannot be traced to any wilful cause or which is not due to neglect or carelessness. If a fire occurs on one's premises through the negligence of himself or his servants which is productive of injury to his neighbor he is liable to the neighbor.

Waste may occur by omitting to keep buildings in tenantable repair or allowing the timbers to become rotten by neglecting to cover the house, or permitting the walls to fall into decay for want of plastering, or the foundation to be injured by neglecting to turn off a stream of water and the like. In general, however, permissive waste with respect to buildings applies only to such tenants or occupiers of the property as are bound to repair, such as life tenants. It does not apply to a lessee for years or from year to year with respect to natural decay or ordinary wear and tear unless the lease specially obliges him to repair as against such decay and wear and tear.

Damages may be recovered for voluntary waste by a reversioner or remainderman, and the prevention of future waste may be effected either by a bill in equity or under procedure provided by statute, and a compensation for past waste may be obtained in the same proceeding. The one having a reversionary interest in the land need not wait until waste has actually been committed but as soon as he learns that the one in possession is about to commit an act which would operate as a permanent injury to the estate or his interest therein, or if he threatens to show an intention to commit waste, an injunction may at once be obtained to prevent his doing so.

WATERED STOCK Stock issued by a corporation as fully paid up, when in fact it is not fully paid up.

WAY, RIGHT OF A right of way is the privilege which an individual or a particular description of individual, such as the inhabitants of a village or the owners and occupiers of a farm, have to pass over another's land.

The right may become established by immemorial usage or by an uninterrupted enjoyment required by law to obtain title by adverse possession, mostly twenty years. It is perhaps most commonly acquired by grant or deed. The right will occur sometimes by necessity; thus where one purchases land accessible only over the land of the vendor, or sells, reserving land accessible only over the land of the vendee, there is an implication that a right of way is granted in one case, and reserved in the other. The necessity, however, to give one this right must be absolute and not merely a convenience, and when the necessity ceases the right of way ceases with it.

Sometimes the right is expressly reserved in the deed by one granting the land. Where a way must be established for necessity, the one over whose land it is to go has the right to locate it, if he does so with due regard to the interests of the party who is to use it, but

being once fixed it cannot be altered.

The right of way is usually limited of course to a definite space or width of ground to be passed over. Sometimes the right is purely personal and cannot be transferred to another. Sometimes it is annexed to an estate and will pass to the heir or to a vendee along with the property to which it is annexed. Most commonly it is of the latter class, and when so, is said to be appurtenant to the real estate. If appurtenant to the land it is appurtenant to all and every part of it, and if the land is divided and conveyed in separate parcels the right passes to each of the grantees. Twenty years' occupation of land adverse to the right of way and inconsistent therewith bars or extinguishes the right, but this time is varied by statute in some places. Where a private way or passage is used as such and is also used by the public at the same time, no prescriptive right or right by long usage will rise in favor of the public and the way may be closed by the owner. The right to pass on foot will not prevent the erection of a structure overhead which will not interfere with that right.

WIDOW A deceased husband's wife who has not remarried.

WIFE'S EQUITY The equitabl

right or claim of a married woman to a reasonable and adequate provision, by way of settlements or otherwise, out of her choses in action, or out of any property of hers which is under the jurisdiction of the court of chancery, for the support of herself and her children.

WILL A will is the disposition of one's property to take effect after one's death.

At common law, wills could be made by females at twelve and by males at fourteen. Statute laws now, however, quite commonly require the party to be twenty-one years old. The disability of a married woman to make a will unless by consent of her husband is now removed by statute.

In case of blindness there should be express and satisfactory proof, in addition to what is required in other cases, that the testator understood the contents of the will. The same is true of deaf and dumb persons who are unable to write. Idiots, of course, are incapable of making wills, as are lunatics except during such lucid intervals as allow the exercise of memory and judgment sufficient to enable one to have a comprehension of what he is doing.

If one is subject to partial insanity his will will not be valid if it is made the offspring or result thereof. If one is in a state of delirium, depriving him of his reason, he cannot make a will while in such a state. If the testator, however, has sufficient memory and mental capacity remaining to enable him to collect the elements of the transaction, that is, the amount and kinds of property he has and the number of his children and other persons entitled to his bounty, and to hold them in mind sufficiently to form an understanding judgment in regard to them, he may execute a valid will. The place of signing is immaterial unless by statute it is required to be at a particular place, as at the end. Therefore, where a will was apparently complete and in the handwriting of the testator and began, "I, John Smith, etc.," this was held to be a sufficient signing. It would have been insufficient, however, if it had appeared from the will itself that the testator had not completed it.

The testator should produce the will to the witnesses to be witnessed by them, and acknowledge his own signature in their presence. It is said, however, that the production of the instrument by him for the purpose of being attested by the witness if it bear his signature will be a sufficient acknowledgment of the signature, and that the will is his. Witnesses may attest by mark and the testator may sign by mark.

Wills may be revoked commonly by burning, cancelling, tearing or obliterating or otherwise destroying the same. If the maker tears off or defaces his signature at the end of the will it will be presumed to have been done with the intention of revoking it, also where lines were over his name. Throwing it on the fire with intent to burn it is a revocation, even though someone snatches it away when it is but slightly burned and preserves it without the maker's knowledge.

A mere intention to burn or destroy is not sufficient. There must be an actual burning or tearing to some extent, and if the testator is arrested in his purpose of revocation before he regards it as complete there will be no revocation, though the will is torn to some extent. Partial revocations made in anticipation of making a new will and intended to be conditional upon that are not regarded as complete until the new will is executed. This does not apply to the defacing of a will by accident or without intention to revoke, or under a misapprehension that a later will is good. A revocation of a will is presumably a revocation of codicils, but it is proper to show that such was not the testator's intention. The same capacity is required to revoke a will as is necessary to make one.

Making a new will purporting to be a last will, which contains no reference to another paper and which disposes of all the testator's property and is so executed as to be valid and operative, will revoke all former wills, even though it contains no express words of revocation. The execution of a second will without a clause of revocation will not revoke a former one, except insofar as they cannot stand together. A will, if the words so allow, will be construed so as to dispose of the whole estate. The appointment of an executor is a circumstance indicating that the will is the only will of the testator and that any prior wills are revoked.

Where a former will is still in existence and a later one is revoked, whether the earlier one is thereby reinstated seems to be a question of intention to be decided by all the facts and circumstances of the case. If not contrary to a statute the republication of a prior will ordinarily amounts to a revocation of all later wills or codicils. Marriage alone, or the birth of a child alone, is insufficient to operate as a revocation, but almost universally, provision is made by statute for the widow or after-born child irrespective of the will. Not uncommonly the after-born child takes the same share as he would have taken had there been no will.

More than one instrument may be proved and admitted to probate, as wills, where their contents are not wholly inconsistent with each other, the whole constituting the last will and testament of the deceased. The probate may be contested on any ground tending to impeach its validity, as that it was not executed in due form of law and according to the required statutory solemnity, or that it was procured by force, misrepresentation or undue influence over a weak mind, or that the testator was incompetent by reason of idiocy, insanity, delirium or otherwise.

The probate of a will has no effect outside of the state in which it is granted. Properly certified copies of the will after probate within the state or county where the decedent had his domicil may be filed with the proper officer in other states or counties, and letters there may be filed by the executor or by an administrator with the will annexed, with authority to act with respect to any estate within that jurisdiction. Proof of the execution of the will by the attesting witnesses is indispensable if the contestors insist upon it, if these witnesses can be obtained; but if dead, out of the state or disqualified, their handwritings may be proved.

<u>Wills over thirty years old</u> and appearing to be regular and perfect coming from the proper custody are said to prove themselves. Those lost, destroyed or mislaid at the time of the testator's death may be admitted to probate upon proper proof of the <u>loss</u> and of the execution.

In general, a will speaks from the death of the testator as it becomes operative only at that time, but if necessary from the language of the will, it will be interpreted with reference to the time and conditions of things when the will is made.

A gift in a will is void if not so defined as to be ascertained with reasonable certainty, or if the recipient is not designated so that he can be identified.

The rule that a will cannot be varied or controlled by evidence outside of the will itself is quite strict, and insofar as such evidence is admissible, the purpose of it must be to place the court in the position of the testator in order, as far as practicable, to enable it to more fully understand the sense in which he probably used the language found in his will. Letters and oral declarations of the testator are not admissible to show his intention or to supply any word or defect in the will, though such declarations are admissible to show his state of mind or testamentary capacity.

If a wrong name is inserted in a will by mistake of the writer of it, and if the place where the name should be is left blank, parol evidence is not admissible to carry into effect the testator's purpose, but it is said a partial blank may be supplied in this way, and in a case where a residuary legatee was described by a wrong Christian name, evidence was received to show who was intended. A latent ambiguity may be explained or removed by parol evidence.

Where two portions of a will are contradictory and incapable of standing together, the one last set forth will control as being the latest declaration of the testator's intention. If, however, they can be construed to stand together or so as to give two persons a joint estate in a thing, this will be done.

<u>To execute a valid will two witnesses are required</u> in Alabama, Alaska, Arizona, Arkansas, California, Colorado, Delaware, District of Columbia, Florida, Hawaii, Idaho, Illinois, Indiana, Iowa, Kansas, Kentucky, Maryland, <u>Michigan</u>, Minnesota, Mississippi, Missouri, Montana, Nebraska, Nevada, New Jersey, New Mexico, New York, North Carolina, North Dakota, Ohio, Oklahoma, Oregon, Pennsylvania, Rhode Island, South Dakota, Tennessee, Texas, Utah, Virgin Islands (two or more witnesses), Virginia, Washington, West Virginia, Wisconsin and Wyoming.

<u>Three</u> witnesses are necessary in Connecticut, Georgia, Louisiana, Maine, Massachusetts, New Hampshire, Puerto Rico, South Carolina and Vermont.

A nuncupative or <u>oral will</u> is one made during the last illness of the deceased, in the presence of witnesses, respecting the disposition of his personal property after death. Soldiers in actual service and mariners at sea may verbally dispose of their wages and personal property to any amount, provided they are in actual fear or peril of death, or in expectation of immediate death from an injury received that day. Most states recognize some form of oral will.

Following are the statutes of the various states concerning nuncupative or oral wills:

Alabama A verbal or oral will is valid only when personal property bequeathed does not exceed $500.00. Such a will must be made during the last illness of the deceased, at his dwelling or where he resided ten days or more, except when the testator is taken ill away from home and dies before his return. It must be shown that the deceased called upon persons present, or some of them, to bear witness that the statement is his will. Oral wills made by soldiers and sailors in actual service or mariners at sea are also valid in Alabama.

Alaska An oral will is permitted if the deceased's words, or substance thereof, are reduced to writing within thirty days after they are spoken and the writing probated after fourteen days and within six months after such words are spoken. Any mariner at sea or any soldier in military service may dispose verbally of his wages or other personal property.

Arizona A verbal will is allowed if made in the last sickness of the deceased, where property does not exceed $50.00 in value. Three competent witnesses must testify that the testator called on some person to take notice and bear testimony that such is his will, and that the testimony, or its substance, was reduced to writing within six days after the making of such will. Where this is done, the amount that may be disposed of is without limit.

Arkansas An oral will must be made at the time of the last illness of the deceased in the presence of at least two witnesses. The amount is limited to $500.00. Such a will must be proved not less than twenty days nor more than six months from the date thereof; it must be reduced to writing and signed by the witnesses within fifteen days after the will is made.

California Amount limited to $1,000.00. An oral will must be proved by two witnesses present at the time it was made, one of whom was asked by the testator, at the time, to bear witness that such was his will. In addition, the deceased must have been, at the time, in actual military service in the field or doing duty while at sea. Finally, the deceased must have been in actual contemplation, fear or peril of death, or in expectation of immediate death from an injury received that same day. The verbal statement of the deceased must be reduced to writing within thirty days after the making.

Colorado Verbal wills not recognized.

Connecticut Oral wills are invalid.

Delaware An oral will is valid if confined to personal property not exceeding $200.00 in value. It must have been pronounced in the last illness of the deceased before two witnesses, be reduced to writing within three days, attested by the signatures of the witnesses, provided the testator dies before the expiration of the said three days or subsequently becomes incapable of making a will.

District of Columbia An oral will is invalid, except in the case of soldiers and sailors in actual military service who may dispose of wages and personal property by word of mouth. Such a will must be proved by two witnesses and reduced to writing within ten days after its making.

Florida It must be proved by three witnesses present at the time of making. The oral will must have been made during the deceased's last sickness and be reduced to writing within six days from making. Personal property only may be disposed of in this way.

Georgia It must be made during the last illness of the deceased at the place where he resided for at least ten days preceding the declaration, except in case of sudden illness and death away from home. Three witnesses are necessary to prove such a will.

Hawaii Verbal wills not recognized.

Idaho It must be reduced to writing within thirty days after making. The will must be probated not less than fourteen days after the testator's death.

Illinois Verbal wills not recognized.

Indiana It must be made in the testator's last illness, be witnessed by at least two people and reduced to writing within fifteen days after the words are spoken. Valid only to extent of $100.00 worth of personal property.

Iowa Personal property up to $300.00 may be disposed of by a verbal will if witnessed by two competent persons. Those in actual military or naval service may dispose of all their personal estate orally.

Kansas To be valid, the verbal will must be reduced to writing and witnessed by two disinterested persons within ten days after words are spoken. It must be proved that the testator called upon some person or persons present when words were spoken who bore witness that the words were his last will.

Kentucky Only a soldier in actual service or a mariner at sea may dispose of personal effects verbally, provided it is done ten days before death, in the presence of two competent witnesses and reduced to writing within sixty days after the words are spoken.

Louisiana An oral will must be witnessed in the presence of a Notary Public by three persons residing in the place where the will is executed, or by five persons not residing in the place.

Maine The oral will is allowed when made in the last illness of the testator, at his home or at the place where he resided ten days before making it. Maximum amount which may be disposed of in this way is $100.00. The will must be proved by three witnesses present at the time of making, who were requested by the testator to bear witness that such was his will. If the words are not reduced to writing within six days after being spoken, they must be proved in court within six months. A soldier in actual service or a mariner at sea may verbally dispose of his personal estate.

Maryland A verbal will is valid only as to soldiers in actual service or mariners at sea who may dispose of their wages, movable and personal property.

Massachusetts Same rule as in Maryland.

Michigan The maximum amount is $300.00. The will must be proved by two competent witnesses; this applies to soldiers in actual military service and mariners on shipboard.

Minnesota Verbal will may be probated within six months after the words are spoken if reduced to writing within thirty days and evidenced by two credible and disinterested witnesses. Such a verbal will is valid only as to the personal estate and testator must have been a soldier in actual service or a mariner at sea.

Mississippi It is valid only when made during the testator's last illness. The maximum amount is $100.00, unless it is proved by two witnesses that the testator called them to bear witness to his will. Such a will cannot be proved after six months unless reduced to writing within six days of speaking. There is a soldier and sailor provision.

Missouri The maximum amount to be disposed may not exceed $200.00 it must be proved by two witnesses and that the testator, in his las sickness, at his home, called some person to witness the will. Proof of such will must be given within six months after words are spoken or substance of words reduced to writing within thirty days. Wills of soldiers and sailors are governed by the common law.

Montana An oral will is valid when proved by two witnesses present at the making thereof, one of whom, at least, was asked by the testator to bear witness that such was his will. The maximum value is set at $1,000.00; the testator at the time must have been in actual military or marine service and the will must have been made in the expectation of immediate death from injury received that day; the will must be proved within six months and not less than fourteen days after the death of the testator.

Nebraska The maximum amount is $150.00. The will must be proved by three witnesses present at the making and it must be proved that the testator called them to witness his oral will; the will must be made during testator's last illness at home or while taken sick away from home. Unless reduced to writing within six days after oral declaration, the will is not allowed. These rules are not applicable to soldiers in service and mariners on ships.

Nevada The maximum value is $1,000.00; must be proved by two witnesses present at making thereof; must be made during last illness and proved not less than fourteen days nor more than three months after words are spoken.

New Hampshire The maximum value is $100.00; the will must be declared in presence of three witnesses or be made during testator's last illness, at his usual dwelling place or away from same if taken ill while away from home and died before his return, or unless a memorandum of the oral will was reduced to writing within six days.

New Jersey An oral will bequeathing personal property exceeding $80.00 is invalid unless it is proved by the oaths of at least three witnesses present at the making thereof and unless the testator requested the persons present to bear witness to his verbal will or words to that effect. The will must be made during the testator's last illness, in his house or where he was a resident for ten days or more, except where the deceased was surprised or taken sick while away from his home and died before returning to his dwelling place.

New Mexico Verbal wills not recognized.

New York Only soldiers in service and mariners at sea may bequeath personal property by oral will; such a will must be made within the hearing of two persons and its execution proved by at least two witnesses.

North Carolina An oral will must be proved by at least two witnesses present at time verbal will was made. The will must have been made during the testator's last sickness and in his own residence, or where he had previously resided.

North Dakota The maximum amount is $1,000.00; must be proved by two witnesses who were present at making; the deceased must have been in actual military service in the field or doing duty on shipboard at sea; in either case, he must be in peril or fear of immediate death from injury received the same day that the will was made.

Ohio The oral will must be made in the last sickness of the testator; it must be reduced to writing and witnessed by two competent witnesses within ten days after the verbal declaration.

Oklahoma The maximum amount is $1,000.00; must be proved by two witnesses who were present at the making thereof; one of whom was asked by the testator at the time to act as a witness. In addition, the testator must have been in actual military service in the field or doing duty on shipboard at sea and must have been in actual contemplation, peril or fear of death, or in expectation of immediate death from an injury received that same day.

Oregon Oral wills apply only to soldiers in service and sailors at sea.

Pennsylvania An oral will is valid only if made during testator's last illness, in his own home or one in which he resided for at least ten days before making it, or where he is taken sick while away from home and dies before returning. If property bequeathed is over $100.00 in value, the oral will must be proved by two witnesses present at the time of the making thereof, and that the testator requested persons present to witness his will; words spoken must be reduced to writing within six days after they are spoken, but no proof of the words spoken can be received after six months from the speaking thereof unless they are reduced to writing.

Puerto Rico Verbal wills are recognized only in case of epidemics when the testator may make his will orally before three witnesses who must be over sixteen years of age. In such cases a will becomes void on the expiration of two months after the peril or epidemic ceases or three months after the death of the testator unless the matter is brought before the proper court to have the will declared a public instrument.

Rhode Island Verbal wills are not recognized.

South Carolina An oral will disposing of personal property in excess of $50.00 is invalid unless proved by the oaths of three or more witnesses to the will. The will must be made in the testator's last illness and in his house or place where he died; proof of such will cannot be made after six months from the time the words were spoken unless reduced to writing within six days after the making of such will and then not after one year.

South Dakota The maximum amount is $1,000.00; must be proved by two witnesses present at time words were spoken.

Tennessee Verbal wills are now valid.

Texas An oral will is valid if made during the last illness of the deceased; must be made at his home, unless he was taken sick away from home and dies before returning; no oral will allowed when personal property bequeathed exceeds $30.00 in value unless proved by three credible witnesses; must be proved within fourteen days from testator's death and not after six months from the date of speaking, unless committed to writing within six days therefrom.

Utah Where the estate is not in excess of $1,000.00, an oral will may be admitted to probate at any time after deceased has been dead ten days and within six months after the words are spoken; words must be reduced to writing within thirty days after they are spoken.

Vermont An oral will may not pass personal possessions exceeding $200.00 in value; memorandum in writing must be made by a person present at the time of the making of said will within six days from making of the oral will.

Virgin Islands A verbal will may be made by a mariner at sea or a soldier in actual military service to dispose of wages or personal property. Proof must be offered within six months after the testamentary words have been spoken unless the words or their substance is reduced to writing. No probate is granted until fourteen days after death.

Virginia Only soldiers in military service and mariners at sea may dispose of personal property by oral will.

Washington An oral will is allowed if personal estate does not exceed $200.00; it must be made during testator's last illness and must be proved by two witnesses who were requested by the testator to witness his will; must be reduced to writing.

West Virginia Only soldiers and sailors in actual service may dispose of personal property by verbal will.

Wisconsin A verbal will disposing of an estate in excess of $150.00 in value is of no effect unless proved by the oath of three witnesses present when the will was made who were requested by the testator to witness it; it must be made during the last illness of testator in his home or dwelling or where he resided for ten days prior to the making of the will, except when he was taken sick while absent from his home and died before returning.

Wyoming Verbal wills are not recognized.

A holographic will is one written *entirely* by the hand of the testator. It may be written in pencil or ink, or partly in both. It may take the form of a letter or a notation or a note. It must be entirely written, signed and dated by the testator. Not all states recognize such wills, nor are witnesses required in all jurisdictions allowing holographic wills. Holographic wills are recognized as legal in the following jurisdictions:

Alaska: no witnesses.

Arizona: no witnesses.

Arkansas: three disinterested witnesses.

California: no witnesses.

Idaho: no witnesses.

Kentucky: no witnesses.

Louisiana: no witnesses.

Mississippi: no witnesses.

Montana: no witnesses.

Nevada: no witnesses.

New York: holographic wills by soldiers or sailors while in actual military service, or by a mariner while at sea, are valid during the war. Such wills are unenforceable and invalid upon the expiration of one year following discharge from military service, provided testator still retains capacity to execute a valid will. Where, after his discharge from service, a testator still lacks such capacity, the holographic will is valid and enforceable until the expiration of one year from the time capacity is regained.

North Carolina: must appear that the will was found among the valuable papers of the testator. Testator's handwriting must be proved by three witnesses.

North Dakota: no witnesses.

Oklahoma: no witnesses.

Pennsylvania: no witnesses.

Puerto Rico: no witnesses.

South Dakota: no witnesses.

Tennessee: substantially the same provisions are in force as in North
   Carolina.

Texas: no witnesses.

Utah: no witnesses.

Virginia: no witnesses.

West Virginia: no witnesses.

Wyoming: no witnesses.

WILL

I, John Doe, a resident of the city of Baltimore, state of Maryland, and
residing therein at 5 South Street, being over the age of twenty-one (21)
years and of sound and disposing mind and memory, and not acting under
duress, menace, fraud or undue influence of any person whomsoever, do
make, publish and declare this my last will and testament, in the manner
following to wit:

1. I direct that all my debts, including my funeral expenses, expense of
my last illness and the expenses of the administration of my estate, be paid
by my executor, hereinafter named, out of the first moneys coming into its
hands and available therefor.

2. I hereby declare that I am married; that my wife's name is Jane
Doe; and that I have but two (2) children, a son, Thomas, and a daughter,
Mary.

3. I give, devise and bequeath all of the rest and residue of my property, after the payment of the debts and expenses provided for in paragraph
1 hereof, whether such property be real, personal or mixed, or whatsoever kind or character and wheresoever situated, to my wife.

4. I hereby nominate and appoint Bank of Maryland the executor of
this, my last will and testament.

Lastly, I hereby revoke all former wills and codicils to wills heretofore
by me made.

In Witness Whereof, I have hereunto set my hand and seal this 1 day of
October, 19___.

(Seal)

_____
JOHN DOE

The foregoing instrument, consisting of one (1) page besides this, was, at
the date hereof, by said John Doe, signed, sealed and published as and
declared to be his last will and testament, in the presence of us, who at his
request and in his presence and in the presence of each other, have signed
our names as witnesses hereto.

_____
WITNESS

Residing at 101 St. Alban's Way,

_____
WITNESS

Residing at 84 Fulton Street,

AGREEMENT TO SETTLE ESTATE OUT OF COURT

This agreement entered into by and between Jane Doe, Thomas Doe, and Robert Doe, witnesseth:

That whereas Henry Doe, late of Miami County, Florida, departed this life on the 1 day of May, 19____, intestate, and the owner of real and personal property in Miami County, State of Florida. He left as his sole and only heirs Jane Doe, his widow, and Thomas Doe and Robert Doe, his grandchildren, all over twenty-one (21) years of age.

Now, therefore, the said heirs desiring to settle the said estate out of court and avoid administration on the same, hereby make the following family settlement of said estate as follows, to wit:

The said Thomas Doe and Robert Doe hereby transfer and convey to Jane Doe, widow of deceased, all their right, title and interest in and all the personal property belonging to said estate of every kind whatsoever including money and choses in action.

The said Jane Doe, widow, hereby agrees in consideration of said personal property to convey to Thomas Doe and Robert Doe, heirs, by quitclaim deed, all her right, title and interest in and to the following described real estate in Miami County, Florida, to wit:

House, Including All Its Contents, located at 4004 Boakman Avenue in said County and State.

It is understood that this agreement is evidence of the full family settlement as between said parties, and the parties hereto agree to abide by this agreement, and hereby waive all our rights under the law.

The said Jane Doe, widow, hereby agrees to pay all undertakers' and physicians' claims, and other claims, if any.

In Witness Whereof, we have hereunto set our hands and seals this 10 day of October, 19____.

(Seal)_____
                    JANE DOE

(Seal)_____
                    THOMAS DOE

(Seal)_____
                    ROBERT DOE

State of   ,
County of   ,   } SS.

Before me, John Brown, a notary public in and for said county and state aforesaid, personally appeared Jane Doe, Thomas Doe, and Robert Doe, who acknowledged the execution of the annexed and foregoing agreement to be their voluntary act and deed.

_____
                    NOTARY PUBLIC

My commission expires 10 day of Jan., 19____.

WITHDRAWING A JUROR The withdrawing of one of the twelve jurors impaneled to try a cause. The withdrawing of a juror is always by the agreement of the parties and is frequently done at the recommendation of the judge when it is doubtful whether the action will lie; and in such case each party pays his own costs.

WITHOUT PREJUDICE When an offer or admission is so made, it is a declaration that no rights are surrendered other than those specifically the subject of the action; when a suit is dismissed in this manner, it means that a new suit may be made on the same cause of action.

WITHOUT RECOURSE A clause used in the endorsement of negotiable instruments, by which the endorser intends to exempt himself from liability to other parties.

WITNESS One who has a personal knowledge of anything or any event. Witnesses are exempt from arrest while going to, or in attendance upon, court under compulsion of a subpoena, and while returning home.

WORKING CAPITAL The amount of cash necessary for the convenient and safe transaction of present business.

WORKMEN'S COMPENSATION A series of acts passed by practically every state in the country which provides for compensation to employees who sustain accidental injury arising out of and in the course of certain extra-hazardous employments, irrespective whether the employee was at fault or not. Most Workmen's Compensation Acts preclude the employee from recovering only in cases of drunkenness and wilful self-infliction of injury.

Under Workmen's Compensation Acts, the employee is entitled to be paid a proportion of his regular salary for the time he is unable to work because of his injury. If the claimant or employee suffers or sustains permanent disability as a result of his accident, he is entitled to additional compensation for such permanent disability. Workmen's Compensation Acts also provide for compensation for certain occupational diseases acquired while engaged in certain prescribed employments.

Immediately upon receiving such injury or acquiring an occupational disease, the employee or claimant, as he is called, should immediately notify his employer and request that he be given medical or hospital assistance. Under such Workmen's Compensation Acts the employer has a right to have the employee treated by a physician of the employer's choice; but if the employer fails to offer such hospital or medical assistance, the employee or claimant has a right to engage a physician or surgeon of his own choice and if he is successful in his claim for compensation, he will also be allowed reimbursement for whatever medical, surgical, or hospital expense to which he has been put.

In all cases where the employee or claimant has sustained an accidental injury arising out of and in the course of his employment, he should immediately engage the services of an attorney who will promptly file the necessary papers so that his claim will not be barred by limitations or because it was filed too late.

No claimant or employee should attempt to settle his claim without first engaging the services of a lawyer. To do so may mean that the claimant may jeopardize his legal rights or receive inadequate compensation for his injuries. Following are the provisions of the various Workmen's Compensation laws throughout the country as to when notice must be given the employer. If such notice is not given to the employer, the claimant may find that his application for compensation is barred.

WRIT A judicial instrument by which a court commands some act to be done by the person to whom it is directed.

WRIT OF ERROR A writ to correct an error.

WRITING Written instruments.